Black Nationalism in the United States

Black Nationalism in the United States

From Malcolm X to Barack Obama

James Lance Taylor

LYNNE
RIENNER
PUBLISHERS

BOULDER
LONDON

Published in the United States of America in 2011 by
Lynne Rienner Publishers, Inc.
1800 30th Street, Boulder, Colorado 80301
www.rienner.com

and in the United Kingdom by
Lynne Rienner Publishers, Inc.
3 Henrietta Street, Covent Garden, London WC2E 8LU

Library of Congress Cataloging-in-Publication Data
Taylor, James Lance.
  Black nationalism in the United States : from Malcolm X to Barack Obama /
by James Lance Taylor.
      p. cm.
  Includes bibliographical references and index.
  ISBN 978-1-58826-778-8 (hardcover : alk. paper)
  1. Black nationalism—United States. 2. Black power—United States.
3. African Americans—Politics and government. 4. African American political
activists. 5. African Americans—Intellectual life. 6. African American
leadership. 7. United States—Politics and government. I. Title.
  E185.615.T387 2011
  320.54'60973—dc22

                                                        2010026518

British Cataloguing in Publication Data
A Cataloguing in Publication record for this book
is available from the British Library.

Printed and bound in the United States of America

The paper used in this publication meets the requirements
of the American National Standard for Permanence of
Paper for Printed Library Materials Z39.48-1992.

5 4 3 2 1

For Yasmin, Zion, Massai, and Tsion

I also dedicate this book:

To my maternal grandfather, Louis Perrett (1905–1969).
I have never forgotten him, and I have missed him all my life.

To his daughter, my mother, Carrie Taylor,
the most important intellectual influence in my life. With her love and
dedication to children, she has raised and anchored four generations
of her family. She gave me her strength and determination.

To "oottie" for being determined to never give up.

Contents

Acknowledgments

There are a number of people whose support and patience have made this book's completion possible. I especially would like to thank Robert C. Smith, who never seemed to tire of me asking him questions, sometimes multiple times a day. At different stages he read parts of the manuscript and a draft of the full manuscript. While all of its shortcomings are mine, the book is a compilation of what I took from his responses to the many questions I put to him. I am also grateful for the encouragement and support given by friends, colleagues, and family who are not named here.

Errol Henderson's encyclopedic knowledge of key political figures, writings, and other research material helped me throughout the project. I would also like to thank Katherine Tate for her groundbreaking research and for granting me access and permission to use the 1996 National Black Election Study data sets and Sekou Franklin and Joe McCormick for providing me with critical details. In trying to understand both the political context of Chicago and Barack Obama's place in it, I have benefited significantly from conversations with Tim Black, Horace Campbell, and Robert Starks. Michael B. Preston has also played a very important role as an academic mentor and as a scholarly influence. I am very grateful to colleagues and friends from the National Conference of Black Political Scientists (NCOBPS) for allowing me to serve in its leadership and as its president. The quality of scholarship, analysis, critiques, and mentoring that NCOBPS provides colleagues, students, and the engaged and intellectual communities is indispensable.

At the University of San Francisco (USF), I would like to thank former dean (now provost) Jennifer Turpin for her patience and support of my research program. Through the James Irvine Foundation and later the Dean's Office at the College of Arts and Sciences, she provided funding for writing retreats for faculty in general and faculty of color in particular in beautiful Napa Valley and other Northern California sites. I am thankful for my Department of Politics colleagues at USF, especially former chair Robert Elias, who was instrumental in the earliest stages of this work. I am deeply thankful to my colleague Pamela Balls Organista for "sister-mothering" my research agenda and professional career. I am indebted to colleagues in the African Studies and African American Studies programs at USF. My colleague and friend Ronald Sundstrom has influenced my thinking and writing, and I cherish the discussions we have had along the way, especially when we differ in opinion. I would also like to thank the editors at Lynne Rienner Publishers for never giving up on what at times seemed to be an interminable project. Lynne Rienner was especially helpful in the final stages. They believed in this project from the beginning, and I am thankful for their efforts in helping me to complete the work.

Introduction

This book is about black nationalism. In African American politics, ideology matters as a vital site that organizes strategic approaches, policy concerns and formulations, leadership styles, institutional commitments, and class or group preferences. *Black Nationalism in the United States* attempts to articulate how and why individuals who were born during or near the 1960s employed the persona of Malcolm X and his ideological orientation to speak to their times and circumstance in racial politics. Although this is not another book about Barack Obama, it is about his generation cohort, whether identified as the metaphoric Joshua Generation, or as the hip-hop generation(s) and the encounter with black nationalism in the decades following the civil rights and Black Power eras. What I hope it provides for readers is an understanding of the religious dimension of black nationalism as a political orientation and the ways in which individuals in the late twentieth century engaged what remained of it as an imagined means to address pressing issues affecting African American communities.

Scholars and intellectuals have contributed several generations of research and thought to the subject of black nationalism. Literary historians, in particular, tend to dominate research and conceptualize the tradition almost exclusively in terms of land or geographic racial separation. Other research, often driven by scholars who emerge from analytical standpoints that focus on the most salient contradictions in black nationalist thought and tradition, routinely highlight the shortcomings of key figures such as Martin Delany, Marcus Garvey, Malcolm X, Black Power militants, and, later, the likes of Minister Louis Farrakhan and many affiliated organizations. Political science research on black nationalism in the post–civil rights and Black Power eras

1

tends to rely mainly on opinion research that delineates measures of communal, racial separatist, and emigrationist tendencies in African American political thought. The political history of black nationalism tends to be reduced in its importance in many of these studies. A recent tendency to view black nationalist tradition as being essentially mimetic of white nationalism, similarly narrow in its religious imperialism toward Africa, and essentialist, chauvinistic, and masculinist tendencies toward others in the United States, has emerged from the earlier historical analyses.

Black Nationalism in the United States offers an alternative reading of black nationalist discourse from David Walker to Malcolm X and from Malcolm X to Black Power and the hip-hop generations. I analyze the arc of black nationalist discourse across some 180 years between David Walker's *Appeal* and Jeremiah Wright's jeremiad against war imperialism that imposed on (and arguably made possible) the election of Barack Obama. I posit that David Walker's *Appeal* and his organizing among Boston's black abolitionist community foregrounded an organic US form of black nationalist discourse that would emerge most coherently in the middle twentieth century in the public ministry of Malcolm X. The book thus presents a transhistorical treatment of black rage, or "revolutionary anger" in the research of Wilson J. Moses, as a formulation of "stay at home" black nationalism that is distinct from the emigrationist strand. If it fails to make a persuasive case, it is not because there is no evidence of its persistence in African American political thought and history—from David Walker's certain *Appeal* to Malcolm X's "jihad of words," to Louis Farrakhan's practicum and performance (1983–1995), to Barack Obama suggesting in *Dreams from My Father*, *more* black rage, *not less*, is warranted to curtail the Reagan revolution's social and policy impacts on black people in the United States. The book asks readers to consider the historical backdrop to black nationalist discourse in the United States from its religious foundations in early-nineteenth-century protest fulcrums to the hip-hop generations' attempts to activate it to articulate the social and political circumstances that confronted them in the late twentieth century. It ultimately asks readers to consider how the widely criticized quest to raise Malcolm X from death as a symbol of opposition to the Reagan revolution, during which they were politically socialized, served as a jeremiad of the hip-hop generations to speak to their sense of besiegement in society and in public policy.

I argue that this "longing for Malcolm" contributed to Louis Farrakhan's (and Khallid Muhammad's) prominence in African American politics in the late twentieth century. The hip-hop generation embraced an ascendant parochial form of black nationalism recast as that which Malcolm X proffered—even though the religiosity of the Nation of Islam and Farrakhan was largely put in abeyance in deference to his jeremiadic "truth-telling" performances in the Reagan era. The black jeremiad political sermon device was previously written and spoken by the likes of David Walker against Thomas Jefferson, Frederick

Douglass against Abraham Lincoln, William Monroe Trotter against Woodrow Wilson, Martin Luther King Jr. against Lyndon Johnson, and Jesse Jackson against Ronald Reagan. Malcolm X and Louis Farrakhan spoke in the black jeremiad tradition, and they were also held up as jeremiads against these times, the Reagan revolution, and conservative reactionism.

In order to give context to hip-hop's shortsighted attempt at leadership recruitment, the book delves further into a reading of historical, intellectual, movement, and electoral politics facets of the black freedom struggle as they pertain to and bridge a coherent understanding of the period that shaped their political socialization—from Jesse Jackson's campaigns to the Million Man March/Day of Absence (MMM/DOA). If Jackson's campaigns and Farrakhan's alliances were impositions in black politics, especially with the latter, the hip-hop generation was equally rendering a "no confidence" statement to those living, mainstream elites who emerged in the Democratic Party and remaining civil rights organizations such as the NAACP, by attempting to recruit nonelectoral, nonintegrationist elites into their politics.

Still later, when Trinity United Church of Christ pastor Jeremiah Wright Jr.'s criticism of the Bush administration's aggression against Iraq was streamed in media outlets throughout the United States in the 2008 presidential primaries and general election, the defeat of his longtime church member Barack Obama seemed a foregone conclusion. The looping of the words "no, no, not God-bless America, God-damn America" led to widespread condemnation of Wright as "un-American," "Obama's crazy pastor," and racist. Not since the *Los Angeles Herald Examiner* attributed comments to Malcolm X— claiming a 1962 Paris airplane crash was Allah's justice in retaliation for the murder of a Los Angeles member of the Nation of Islam—had Americans been so shocked over the words of a black American religious and political leader, calling down the judgment of God on the United States. But at closer view, Wright's articulation of black liberation theology discourse was within the mainstream of many African Americans' feelings toward the US government during the Reagan revolution. Concern over the source of the HIV/AIDS crisis, the War on Drugs and crack cocaine, and neoliberalist abandonment of national responsibility for the group character of African Americans' experience in the United States was held by either majorities or pluralities just a decade earlier. The jeremiadic nationalist tradition that Wright represents, and that Obama and other members of Trinity United Church of Christ embraced for decades, has deep roots in African American religious discourse. That it has been perennial is the premise of *Black Nationalism in the United States*. Like his peers, Barack Obama embraced many of its black solidarity tenets. But Barack Obama subsequently distanced himself from the man and the ideological and spiritual traditions that grounded his own encounter with everyday black people in Chicago for two decades. It was the act of managing the Jeremiah Wright controversy that convinced many potential primary and general election voters that Barack Obama represented something new in US politics. This book, *Black Nationalism in the United States*, makes the case that Wright's ministry was embedded in the most "American" form of oppositional political rhetoric and speech: the jeremiad political sermon. That it nearly prevented the election of the first individual of African ancestry to the US presidency was merely a historical accident that brought the two phenomena together, but its precedents, as noted above, were many.

The campaigns of Barack Obama were resonant with many themes in black politics. With the emergence of Michelle and Barack Obama, analysts rushed to scuttle the traditional leadership and ideological modalities that directed previous epochs of African American politics; indeed, there is now much questioning concerning whether we have reached the end of black politics. In terms of governing the United States, what Barack Obama's emergence means is an ongoing development, and it is not my interest here. But his election cannot be isolated from the movement efforts in black politics, to position the black freedom struggle in a way that maximized the bargaining position of black voters since the passage of the 1965 Voting Rights Act, including the 1971 Northlake, Illinois, black strategy meetings, the 1972 National Black Political Convention, and the campaigns of Jesse Jackson.[1] The fact that disavowing Wright and Nation of Islam leader Louis Farrakhan became the single most important litmus looming over the Obama campaign is testament to the persistence of black prophetic discourse despite the ascendancy of materialist and state-friendly religion in contemporary African American churches.[2] What we witnessed was a coming together of core elements of African American politics. There was the matter of black women having to weigh their stakes in the extraordinary plausibility of a woman "first" and a black "first" nomination. There was the matter of civil rights–era elites confronting an emergent hip-hop cohort (which included, in my estimation, the Obamas no less than it included Michael Jordan and Chuck D, age-wise). There was the matter of loyal black Democrats (in the Clinton camp) pushing against an upstart black presidential candidacy (as was the case with Shirley Chisholm in 1972 and Jesse Jackson in 1984). There was the matter of black religious discourse intruding on unprecedented electoral political achievement. And then there was the ideological matter of black nationalism imposing on mainstream integrationist political ambition, approaching Obama's call for a *more disruptive form of black nationalism* than that which Farrakhan promoted. Disappointed with Farrakhan's mangling of a patently salient period of black nationalist assertion in black politics, Obama returned from the 1995 MMM/DOA with a resolve to effect policy changes in Chicago and Illinois.

It is important to note here that I do not attempt a structured historical or political analysis of black feminism except where it or womanist perspectives inform or debunk aspects of traditional masculinist black political thought discursively throughout the book. It is worth noting that in all of the feminist discourse about black nationalism, we have yet to see a full-length study of black women nationalists that treats them as subjects (not objects of men's activities) with agency.[3] The multiple and intersectional effects of race, gender/sexuality, and poverty/class are integral to the serious study of African American political ideologies. Important African American women who held race, gender, and class political critiques, such as Maria Stewart of Boston and Harriet Tubman, have from the very beginning informed black politics and inundated the black liberation struggle. This takes into account Sojourner Truth among the abolitionists, Ida B. Wells's and Mary Church Terrell's valiant antilynching campaigns through to Fannie Lou Hamer's; Gloria Richardson's, Septima Clarke's, and Ella Baker's antimasculinist and commitments in the modern civil rights movement; and those younger women activists/artists, such as Elaine Brown, Lorraine Hansberry, Nikki Giovanni, Ntozake Shange, Alice Walker, and Kathleen Cleaver in the Black Power era. As ideology, black feminism and womanism have always included a strong race-consciousness at the center of their intersectional analyses of gender, race, and poverty socioeconomic status. And at least with regard to majority feminist interests, this race-consciousness was patently nationalistic, particularly concerning interracial social and political relations—and especially in the realms of black male to white female relationships and marriage.[4]

I also do not include black conservatism as an integral political tradition in African American social and political thought, first because this form of conservatism emerged as an extrinsic development among a minute cadre of intellectuals and political elites in the 1980s and 1990s in tandem with syncretistic Goldwater-Nixon-Reagan (West Coast) racial and political conservatism as it became dominant in the Republican Party.[5] This is not to suggest that political conservatism is novel among African Americans as much as it is to mark the trajectory of white establishment and foundation sponsorship of the cadre of African American elites and intellectuals who developed somewhere between Lyndon Johnson's attempt to promote Samuel Reilly Pierce in the political sphere as an alternative to Martin Luther King Jr. and recent conservative black Republicanism.[6] Second, where African Americans have tended to yield relatively high levels of support for socially conservative positions on abortion rights, death penalty, same-sex marriage (and gay rights generally), they have not embraced an operational political conservatism or mobilized en masse in opposition to these and related issue areas.[7] As stated in his *Autobiography*, Malcolm X expressed the general feeling among many African Americans that conservatism in US politics (regardless of partisanship) means "let's keep the niggers in their place." In politics, black conservatives have acted patently hostile toward the issue areas and policy matters that most African Americans support, and some, such as Shelby Steele, have expressed racial resentment toward African Americans in a manner that confounds the black nationalist academic concepts, racial solidarity, and "linked fate."[8] Scholar Ronald Walters notes that "contemporary Black conservatives manifest views that are seemingly consistent with those of whites who espouse an orthodox conservatism either directly or indirectly connected to race."[9] Thus, black conservatives are perceived as largely hostile antiblack *racial* conservatives whose social criticisms and policy preferences have been at odds with preponderant African American support for state intervention. The political biography of freeborn Negro writer William Hannibal Thomas (1843–1935), author of the infamous antiblack diatribe *The American Negro: What He Was, What He Is, and What He May Become* (1901), is an early-twentieth-century example of ideologically driven black self-loathing that characterizes the long line of black "Negrophobic" thought that comports with contemporary black racial conservatism.[10] Of the six broad categories that are the subject of Michael Dawson's *Black Visions*, he contends, "the most marginal tendency during most historical periods has been black conservatism."[11] In the end, black conservatism is parasitic to the extent that it can attach itself to nationalism, integrationism, feminism, and Black Power.[12]

The foregoing analysis is outlined in three broad sections listed respectively as Foundations (Part 1), Formulations (Part 2), and Transformations (Part 3). Each section consists of three chapters. The chapters of Part 1 outline the book's framework and theoretical grounding. Chapter 1 introduces readers to the concept of black political development as a theoretical framework that focuses on Reconstruction-era elected officials and the towering alternative presence of Booker T. Washington and his Tuskegee machine that significantly undermined them. Because black political development also has to do with how leaders emerge among constituent groups, I focus as well on the most definitive example of grassroots recruitment of Harold Washington to the mayoral elections in Chicago, and the independent challenge to Daley machine and national Democrats. Washington's election germinated as a manifestation of black rage in the city, and it prompted the modern phase of black politics. Further, the notion of elite recruitment is inherent in the hip-hop generation's activation of Malcolm X and Louis Farrakhan, as noted, to speak to their times at the height of the Reagan conservative revolution. Black religious leaders, with the major exception of Jesse Jackson, were left out of the series of Voting Rights Act–initiated meetings held throughout the 1970s and early 1980s before his campaigns. Chapter 2 outlines the monadic role of black religion in formulating a paralleling cultural fulcrum that provides for the counterpublic narrative against Eurocentric readings of black political discourse. Chapter 3 outlines the relationships between African American religion and the major political and ideological orientations—black nationalist, and black liberal and radical integrationism—that have constituted the basis of black politics since the early nineteenth century, according to Harold Cruse and other scholars.

The chapters of Part 2 provide an analysis of the ways in which African American religious elites in the nineteenth century actually implemented black nationalist discourse. It seeks to intervene in a persistent debate in the literature concerning black nationalism and its origins. Chapter 4 analyzes a religiosity-nationalism nexus and traces it in religiopolitical elites of the nineteenth and twentieth centuries as a way of explaining the perennial importance of black nationalism in the African American freedom struggle and the specific variant of black nationalism, which I argue is traceable in the black freedom struggle from abolitionism through the modern civil rights era as a historical point of departure to speak to ongoing scholarly discourse concerning the qualities, characteristics, and origins of black nationalism.

Chapter 5 preferences black religion in black nationalist discourses in answer to a tendency in several works to compartmentalize black nationalism as a discontinuous, episodic phenomenon that simply reacts to and mimics white nationalism, where its essential identity is thought derived from its Anglo cultural heritage but otherwise ought not be historicized because such could only be accomplished through ahistorical readings. What started with Wilson Moses's sympathetic historicity of black nationalism, with its resurgence in the 1960s, morphed into a kind of you-are-not-the-father paternity; this ultimately lends itself to the lie that black nationalism—as a *black* political formulation—does not exist: It was—in all of its classical and modern manifestations from Delany to Garvey—white nationalism in blackface. I take issue with the conventional understanding of black nationalism as necessarily entailing the acquisition of land. Where Chapter 5 focuses on Martin Delany and his role as a father of black nationalism, Chapter 6 focuses on the orientation that is represented by David Walker and his *Appeal*. On several scores, Chapter 6 attempts to intervene in scholarly discourse concerning Malcolm X and David Walker, arguing that ideological parallels are striking enough to assert that either both individuals should be considered "nationalist" or that Malcolm X (and Louis Farrakhan and the Nation of Islam) should cease being regarded as such, because the doctrine of racial separation they advocated in the Nation of Islam can only be interpreted as *rhetorical*—a jeremiad. In my view, it is the nonterritorial, dissident psychic orientations promoted by the likes of Walker, Maria Stewart (even Delany in *Blake*), Richard Wright, and Malcolm X that set off their revolutionary anger as a coherent strain of black nationalist thought that was born of the claims and demands of the American Revolution no more than the Haitian Revolution.

The chapters of Part 3 focus on key black nationalist projects that emerged with Black Power and the brief but transformational hegemony it underwent in the late 1960s and early 1970s. It places Malcolm X at the center of black politics, particularly in terms of the hip-hop generation's encounter with his persona and with Louis Farrakhan's co-optation of their effort. Chapter 7 attempts, discursively, to address the several "deaths" of black nationalism since the civil rights and Black Power eras of African American politics on the way to discussing the attempts at black nationalism on the part of the hip-hop generation in Chapter 8. It is not an attempt to cover the subject exhaustively. Nowhere in this book, for instance, are there lyrical, narrative, or cultural production samplings of hip-hop as a phenomenon. Most treatments of the politics of the hip-hop generation tend to focus on its cultural politics, its subterranean veil of "thug and gangsta" antiestablishmentality, misogynistic elements, and corporatization; this book is a concrete political analysis of its actual political inclinations and activities epitomized in the MMM/DOA event. The chapters here focus on events in black politics, from Black Power and the Million Man March to the election of Barack Obama. Following a treatment of the hip-hop generation's recruitment of Malcolm X and Louis Farrakhan to articulate their repudiation of the conservative ascent in the early Reagan era, Chapter 9 returns to the beginning, focusing on Chicago's role as the site of incubation for modern black politics, from Harold Washington to the election of Barack Obama.

Notes

1. Concerning Northlake, please see James Richardson, *Willie Brown: A Biography* (Berkeley: University of California Press, 1996), pp. 193–195. Also see Robert C. Smith, *We Have No Leaders: African Americans in the Post–Civil Rights Era* (Albany: State University of New York Press, 1996), pp. 41–43.

2. Michael Leo Owens, *God and Government in the Ghetto: The Politics of Church-State Collaboration in Black America* (Chicago: University of Chicago Press, 2007).

3. Ula Yvette Taylor Garvey, *Garvey and Garveyism* (New York: Macmillan, 1970).

4. See esp. Michele Wallace, *Black Macho and the Myth of the Superwoman* (New York: Verso, 1990). It is also noteworthy that implicit in the occasional black nationalist Booker T. Washington's 1895 metaphoric "five fingers" (separatist) and "united as the fist" (interracial cooperation) rhetorical devices were the clear message and prohibition that interracial marriage, love, and intercourse fell under the former category. For Washington's contemporaries, this must have been a welcome perspective in light of Frederick Douglass's marriage to a white woman (his second marriage) and heavyweight champion Jack Johnson's open courting of white women and hostility to the "white slave" Mann Act.

5. Ronald Walters, *White Nationalism, Black Interests: Conservative Public Policy and the Black Community* (Detroit: Wayne State University Press, 2003), pp. 223–224.

6. Robert Smith, *We Have No Leaders.*

7. Ronald Walters, *White Nationalism.*

8. Michael Dawson, *Black Visions: The Roots of Contemporary African-American Political Ideologies* (Chicago: University of Chicago Press), 2001.

9. Ronald Walters, *White Nationalism*, p. 233.

10. John David Smith, *Black Judas: A Story of Racial Self-Hatred in America, William Hannibal Thomas and the American Negro* (Chicago: Ivan R. Dee, 2000). Black conservatives have been associated with the accommodationist philosophy of

Booker T. Washington, but contemporary black conservatives have more in common with Strom Thurmond, Barry Goldwater, and Ronald Reagan than, say, the pragmatic accommodationism of Booker T. Washington.

11. Michael Dawson, *Black Visions*, p. 19. The six are radical egalitarianism, black nationalism, disillusioned liberalism, black feminism, black socialism, and black conservatism.

12. Harold Cruse, *The Crisis of the Negro Intellectual* (New York: Quill, [1967] 1984), p. 564.

PART 1
Foundations

1

Black Political Development in the United States

The Christian religion has failed you. Your leaders, of that religion, have failed you. Now the government of America has failed you. You have no justice coming from no one.
— Nation of Islam Leader Elijah Muhammad
at Uline Arena in Washington, DC, 1959

In a white racist society, it is both necessary and essential that the oppressed minority fully develop new *values, new approaches, new assumptions and new institutions to* assert *its interests and* protect *its interests. It is from that perspective, then, that* regardless *of temporary confusion, ideological differences, etc., blacks, once a level of awareness is reached, are* forced *to attempt to institutionalize that awareness and such institutionalization is clearly a political process in that it directly challenges the dominant society to change.*
— Reginald E. Gilliam, *Black Political Development*, 1975

Although the focus here is black nationalism, particularly the black jeremiad form, it is important at the outset to provide a framework for understanding its relevance to the pendular shifts between available leadership modalities. Because I am interested in how the hip-hop generation recruited Malcolm X and (vicariously) Louis Farrakhan, in this chapter I take up the matter of elite recruitment and conceptualize the relationship between leaders and constituent groups. This is reflected particularly as local nationalist groups and individuals in Chicago recruited Harold Washington to run for mayor of the city, prompting the modern phase of black politics. This phase resonated with an emergent political consciousness among hip-hop age sets on one end and the subsequent election of their peer, Barack Obama, to the US presidency on the other. As I discuss in the first and final chapter of this book, it was the recruitment of Harold Washington that signaled local and national disenchantment with the major political parties among many African Americans, that drew

Barack Obama there as an organizer. Elite recruitment is less about personalities and more an articulation of potential constituencies' resolve to have a say in the political process, whether Harold Washington (and other black elected officials) or so-called organic elites like Malcolm X, Jesse Jackson, and Louis Farrakhan. The book then delves into further theorizing about the black jeremiad and its relationship to black nationalist thought and traditions.

Karen Orren and Stephen Skowronek insist scholars observe and articulate development "through their dedication to analyzing American politics through intensive research in American history." They think of political development in terms of the dynamic relationship between past and present, "by what bridges or processes; about how time comes to exert an independent influence on political change, apart from the notion that time 'passes'; about how these things illuminate the nature of American politics, including whether, and in what sense, it may be said to '*develop*.'"[1] The authors' definition of political development focuses essentially on "governing authority" that betrays "the exercise of control over persons or things that is designated and enforceable by the state."[2] The focus of the definition tends to be on national institutions and the competing forces engaged in a process of capturing the American state.[3] The scholarly issue of American political development (APD) attends to race politics as one of many interrogative categories of the present-past; church-state relations and federal land management are others.[4] At critical junctures, "racial politics" epitomizes APD; as the authors note, "no other single act in American history changed so many lives so profoundly as did the Thirteenth Amendment. . . . *The termination of the master-slave relationship was political development of the first magnitude*."[5] The conflict in "authority relations" among Congress, the courts, and the executive branches to emerge in the form of Reconstruction constituted yet another pertinent demonstration of a "developmental episode." With it, "authority to protect those persons who had been freed was expressly given to Congress in the Thirteenth Amendment, the first amendment adopted since the generation of the Framers." Reconstruction has come to be understood as both a tremendous deconstruction of existing social, political, and economic relations and at the same time a "developmental misfire," which promised more than it achieved for the newly freed person in the burgeoning democracy. Its incompleteness—despite the various Civil Rights Acts (1866 and 1875) and passage of the Fifteenth Amendment—precipitated the modern civil rights movement. At its heart, APD "coincided with the 'movement culture' of the last third of the twentieth century, with popular mobilizations, one upon another, that challenged long-established social relations and called for a new inventory of America's political resources. Associated with these were insurgencies within the major political parties, first from the left and then from the right, that undercut the received wisdom of liberal consensus and thrust legitimacy of American state institutions to the center of political controversy."[6] Orren and

Skowronek are careful to explain that "the analytic template we have lighted upon may well recommend itself for use in *other national settings*. The *A* in APD would, in this sense, refer to *one* among *many* laboratories for research on the historical construction of politics and its significance."[7] Black political development (BPD), however counter to traditional American political history, does not warrant its own narrative in this perspective; to Orren and Skowronek APD and BPD are redundant. And this may well be true, but the few scholars who have taken black political development head-on seem to have less of a top-down bias than one focused on formal authority. What African American elites generally engaged in, while serving in elected office during Reconstruction and during the modern civil rights project, was less a capture of state apparatuses and more reform from long-standing discrimination in the North and South. In this regard, black political development's most significant contribution is its panoplies of strategic options based on the internal deliberations of constituents and broadly constructed representative leadership fulcrums. In black political development the processes by which elites are recruited or "questions of accountability and the actual processes of leadership selection" are central.[8] Lester Salmon concurs that "elite recruitment patterns are particularly good indicators of development and change." To miss this is to miss the premise of the book. For Reginald Gilliam and many others, "Mass black interests and problems *have not* and cannot be effectively served without independent black political articulation and that they can be served best and *most effectively with* independent black political articulation. . . . Given the unique status of United States blacks, political independence from white-controlled parties allows a *fuller* range of options, potential, equitable alliances and coalitions than does subservience to and being 'in the bag of' one camp or the other."[9] As an analytical category, black political development has been applied to institutional and electoral political involvement on the part of African American elites, although it is clear that movement activities carried out by large numbers of ordinary commonfolk nonelites have been the capital with which elites have emerged, coalesced, and brokered with their white establishment sponsors, locally and in national politics.[10] This framework is rooted in domestic "political modernization" discourse in which protest strategies were conceived as nascent, undeveloped politics and coalition and electoral politics are viewed as a maturation of black politics. The optimism of the short Reconstruction era in the late nineteenth century represents at least a precedent to the matter of leadership representation. Nonelected, but widely recognized, individual leaders such as Booker T. Washington at the "national" level of black politics and preachers and teachers at local levels contested with newly elected Reconstruction leaders such as Hiram Revels, Blanche K. Bruce, and John R. Lynch, among others, as the legitimate or representative voices of ordinary African Americans usually in clientage relationships with representatives of the dominant group.[11] The cooperative and competitive interaction between elected officials (such as Bruce) and nonelected individuals (such as Booker Washington);[12] the early emergence of preachers in state legislatures such as Mississippi;[13] the salience of a dominant ideology among elites (emigration, abolition, accommodation, assimilation, liberalism, nationalism, integration); and the interplay in the careers of Reconstruction-era elected officials such as Holland Thompson constitute how I understand political development.[14] This framework is pertinent to understanding how and why black Americans selected from or rejected available leadership personalities, ideologies, and forms. Gilliam explains:

> Perhaps more than most comparable groups, blacks can be said to have been and to be, of necessity . . . a "political" people. Black politics then, is not solely the electoral process but the *total* process of articulating black needs and of eliciting white response. An analysis of black politics is an examination of the many devices, responses and ideologies involved in addressing the unique black condition . . . *we speak now of the specifics on nonelectoral leadership, the black ideological spectrum and the roles of the church and community organizations as substitutes for electoral politics.*[15]

This book provides a framework for understanding the imposition of Malcolm X and Louis Farrakhan in late-twentieth-century black politics, especially among those younger individuals whose political socialization came up against the limits of formal politics epitomized in black Democratic responses to the juxtaposition under President Ronald Reagan. Black political development as a theoretical formulation accounts for the inchoate, disorganized, bottom-up features of black politics, which is where nationalism and religious life have long provided a way of interpreting the material realities of black people in the United States. The cycles of recruitment patterns of black leaders, those who emerge from more or less conventional modes of leadership; their ideological orientations; and institutional mechanisms are of critical importance to understanding African American political history. The ideological orientations (and their alternatives) preoccupied the earliest leadership classes among African Americans. Homesteading, emigration, political equality, voting, education, and institution-building focused the energies of Reconstruction-era leaders who created the 1879 National Conference of Colored Men led by John R. Lynch.[16] There were also individuals such as the African Methodist Episcopal (A.M.E.) bishop Henry McNeal Turner, who transitioned from elected leader to nationalist protest leader in the face of the Reconstruction disappointment. And no single individual epitomizes the conflation of factors that contribute to an analysis of political development (personal, institutional, ideological, and charismatic) as did Adam Clayton Powell Jr., the preacher politician.[17]

Adolph Reed Jr. does not *expressly* define the concept of black political development in his analysis of it.[18] His treatment focuses less on the accoutrements of what black political development is and more on its function epiphenomenally. His assessment of formal and informal networks in post-segregation-era black politics explains what development in African American political history looks like, and for him the yield has been found woefully wanting. Indeed the major weaknesses in the programs, agendas, organizing, leadership representations, and largely failed praxes of the civil rights era are traceable to the immediate post-Reconstruction era, where Booker T. Washington emerges to usurp the leadership prerogatives of the elected leaders of the period who had been maligned by leading intellectuals from Columbia University. Obsessed with "uplift" ideology (wherein African American bourgeois elites trade and barter on the miseries of their poorer kin), African American leaders set the tone for what would become the single most demobilizing feature of African American politics: the personality notion of "the leader" among them. Reed notes, "Not only did the segregationist regime hinder normal mechanisms of accountability, but, to the extent that a strategic vision stressing the elite's custodial and tutorial mission became dominant in black politics, concern with accountability to a popular constituency was easily made a nonissue."[19] The elites who emerged in this milieu tended to engage in "racial agenda setting" that betrayed a "class-based ideological orientation and language of politics that became hegemonic within black discourse as a direct result of disfranchisement at the turn of the twentieth century."[20] Following the consolidation of nodes of racial authenticity, "what remains is a clear view that the dominant politics of generic racial advancement—though it has won genuinely popular victories and has had many beneficial consequences, especially during the antisegregation period—has always rested on a nonparticipatory, undemocratic foundation of elite custodianship and brokerage."[21] The course of African American political realities did not make informal leadership modalities inevitable. Uplift ideology, to him (and others such as Kevin Gaines and Joy James),

> became hegemonic in black politics not because of inevitable historical forces or popular racial consensus but because its adherents' social position enabled them to establish that outlook's interpretive and strategic imperatives as the boundaries of legitimacy under prevailing political conditions . . . as the premises and practices of uplift ideology came to monopolize the effective substance of publicly visible black political discourse and action, they came to be seen as the only way of conceiving of black American politics.[22]

The Racial Vision of Black Political Elites

Claims of authenticity, organic leadership, the "black community," and the "black perspective" all flow from the uninterrogated notion that there is a corporate racial "we" among African Americans that is "the least common denominator" among them. Black politics has been an elite-directed politics. The intellectual *study* of black politics throughout the twentieth century was as complicit as was its failed praxes. Altogether, where there are protest elites they are too given to bourgeois class interests; where there are elected elites such as Maynard Jackson they are too easily inclined to manipulate racial cues and generic racial oppression in their own interests; where there are protest-oriented elites seeking formal democratic means to being held accountable to a given constituency, such as Jesse Jackson, it is surrender to defeatism. At least this is how it seems. Reed notes, for instance, that "the problem with the main lines of scholarly inquiry into black politics . . . is that their partisanship has been unself-consciously fastened onto the racial vision of the black petit-bourgeoisie—a singular class vision projected as the organic and transparent sensibility of the group as a whole."[23] While calling for the "return to the path that black political development was on before the distortions of the Jim Crow era," Professor Reed argues for a revival of "liberal democratic popular politics" as a metanarrative to displace the hegemonic "corporate racial interest inherited from uplift ideology."[24] Like left-critical discourse throughout the twentieth century, the "yield" of black politics is inherently pathological essentially because it prioritized race-over-class (or race-*as*-class) classifications and sought to manufacture a popularly based political mobilization on the salient rubric of racial solidarity rather than working-class labor activism. This is also because in the end it gives way to conservative machinations in black politics from the accommodationism of Washington; the emergence of the rightward Democratic Leadership Council (DLC) due to, between, and after the Jesse Jackson presidential campaigns;[25] or Farrakhan's numerology on the national mall at the 1995 Million Man March/Day of Absence (MMM/DOA). All of these, more or less, were underwritten by "the mystification of an organic black community."

There is little evidence that all or even most of the "leadership" classes among African Americans were cynical, self-interested persons who did not seek to alleviate the material conditions of rank-and-file blacks any less than, say, Danny O'Connell (1775–1847) sought to speak to the concerns of the nineteenth-century Irish who shared with blacks "a common culture of the lowly."[26] Paul Robeson's public life and personal and ideological commitments perhaps best frustrate uplift mystifications. Robeson escapes the trappings of the "leader" label in part because his call to Soviet internationalism placed him outside the mainstream of the liberal integrationist camp of the NAACP-styled leadership class of James Weldon Johnson or Walter White. Yet his condemnation of US imperialism, capitalism, and antiblack racial policies earned him widespread, if muted, respect among elites and ordinary Negroes. The communist leader William L. Patterson referred to him as an advocate for the "people's spokesman ['the leader' idea]. A great people's artist has become a world leader in the battle for human rights and democracy."[27] Likening himself to Frederick Douglass—who foregrounded Booker T. Washington in "*the* black leader" mode with abolitionists, Abraham Lincoln, and white feminists *for half a century*[28]—during house arrest, Robeson wrote the delegates of the 1950 World Conference on Peace in Warsaw. He insisted, "I remain in the United States as Douglass returned to it, and in his words, 'for the sake of my brethren.' I remain to suffer with them, to toil with them, to endure insult with them, to undergo outrage with them, to lift up my voice in their behalf, to speak and work in their vindication and struggle in their ranks for that emancipation which shall yet be achieved by the power of truth and of principle for that oppressed people." Operating in this tradition would seem to locate Robeson in the self-serving species of uplift elitism, but absent some Freudian psychoanalytic or Durkheimian altruistic suicide motive, Robeson's repression was grounded in identifying with the folk culture of ordinary Negroes as much as in his communistic inclinations. He anticipated Huey Newton's explicitly Durkheimian notion of "revolutionary suicide," where one's commitments to commonfolk concerns leads to a predictable "self-murder," by hostile forces in law and society. Melissa Harris-Lacewell insists, rather than passively submit to elite agendas, the pedestrian common sense of rank-and-file individuals "structures African American political thought while still leaving space for variation in political approaches"; it does not yield to "only one set of ideological conclusions."[29] Ronald Walters and Robert C. Smith illuminate further the direction of relationships between leaders and community. They forcefully contend "that Black leadership emanates from the Black community in the sense that the individuals who present themselves for leadership have their origin in that community and its culture and that they should reflect the needs and aspirations of that community."[30] Finally, they assert that this community is just as self-evident as "the American community" and is the source of black leadership in the United States. To them the black community is a "historically constructed community of shared history and memory; with distinctive cultural, political, and economic interests and with a geographic or spatial anchor in the nation's urban centers and the heavily populated black belt countries of the rural South."[31]

Uplift ideology, especially of the bourgeois sort, itself becomes an ideological reification, given a power and elasticity—across time, epochs, conflicted ideological orientations, contentious political conventions, elite fragmentation, class interests (including gender), and regional and other particularities. The attention that uplift ideology is given in the literature usually and deliberately mutes the reciprocity that often exists between leaders and those who prefer them and formally and informally accept them to articulate their broad group interests. Acceptability within a group is measurable by a number of variables related to leadership preferences, from attitudinal opinion research to "plebiscites," organizational affiliations, institutional support, and voting. Attempts to define black political leadership have focused primarily on idiosyncratic styles, intrapsychic motivations, and their relationship to institutions, ideological orientations, interests, and coalitions.[32] Hanes Walton Jr. insists there is generally a lack of agreement concerning black political leadership.[33] But he offers two key components. First, "inside any black community there are a variety of black leaders: educational, religious, social, fraternal, professional, and artistic all seeking to address their own narrow concerns and those of the larger black community."[34] Second, black leadership is reflective of structural conditions. These conditions influence the nature, styles, and methods used by black political leaders. Understanding black leadership as a function or effect of the varied political interests of African Americans empowers the very constituents who are often lost when leadership is conceptualized as cause—for instance, in uplift-ideology tropes. At the dawn of the modern civil rights movement, E. Franklin Frazier argued that "the position of the Negro leader on the race problem is being determined more by the outlook and ideology of the group which he represents than by the fact that he is radical or conservative."[35] The formulation of leadership as a by-product of its ideological, situational, and relational contexts provides the definition of black leadership employed in this book. Functional leaders adapt to the diversity of needs that may develop among the constituent black community. It is generally accepted that the major function of political leadership in the black community is to determine what actions are required under various conditions if it is to achieve its objectives, and also to have different group members take part in these group actions. Leadership consists of actions by group members that aid in defining and setting group goals, move the group toward goal attainment, improve the quality of the interactions among the members, build cohesiveness, make resources available to the group, and encourage consciousness among members toward realizing group objectives. Finally, the nature of functional leadership considers that the styles and traits of leaders are dictated by the moment or political context and may consequently be different from context to context.

Political scientist Robert C. Smith summarizes the inability of African American elites for two centuries to forge a strategic and operational consensus due largely to the vast ideological diversification that exists among the leadership classes. Scholars have steadfastly insisted that African American political history is replete with competing ideological conflict that problematized the consolidation of an elite-driven consensus. The fact that the nationalists and integrationists (of different stripes) were of the bourgeois stratum is put in relief by the undeniable detail that *at no point* did a majority of African Americans, especially of commonfolk origins, embrace either orientation or the cues of elites seeking to influence them. Students of uplift theology tend to understate the reciprocity between leaders and contituent groups or communities. Smith notes that "history confirms in the convention process of the 1830s, 1930s and 1970s one simple proposition: The black community is too ideologically diverse to operate for long in a single, all-inclusive organization capable of representing the interests of the race in its relationships to whites or the larger external political order."[36]

Adam Green's study of Chicago between 1940 and 1955[37] observed "hybrid affinities of class feeling among African Americans, more than their clear differentiation along lines of material condition and social position."[38] The founding of *Ebony* and *JET* magazines reflected the mobilization of a redefined *national* race consciousness driven by elites, such as John H. Johnson and his colleagues in post–World War II Chicago, who urged in 1948 that "race is not the issue." Instead, it was the determined, strained effort of Mamie Till Bradley, mother of the slain teenager killed during widespread reactionary pogroms in Mississippi in 1955, who mobilized local and national sentiment among blacks by permitting Chicago *Defender* and *JET* photographers, respectively, to take pictures of the casket and tortured corpse, images that were seen in black communities throughout the United States. For Green, the terrorism, denial, mock court "trials" of the murderers, and courage of a widowed single black woman powerfully demonstrated "evidence of the capacity of Black Chicago's cultural infrastructure to offer new ideas of African-American community [and a] modern occasion of black national feeling, confirming Chicago's pivotal role in articulating those notions of racial community."[39] When abandoned by the NAACP's national establishment in less than four months after her son's murder, Mamie Till Bradley pressed forward its meaning that the horror was not hers alone, and to date it has never been widely recognized by whites.

The internal deliberations among African American interests, which William J. Grimshaw relates below, characterized the city of Chicago's increasingly expanding economically and politically heterogeneous black populations in the so-called black belt wards. Three sections of his work detail respectively the original poorer black belt wards (which are the 2nd and 3rd, followed by 12th, 14th, and 16th); those south of these (the 6th, 8th, 17th, 21st, and 34th) were the emergent militant and hostile antimachine middle-class districts that expanded significantly after successful legal challenges to housing discrimination and restrictive covenants (*Shelley v. Kramer* [1948]); far removed from these were the West Side's so-called plantation wards (the 24th, 27th, 28th, and 29th), which emerged in the 1960s and were run ruthlessly by white machine syndicate bosses. Each segment had its own development over the six decades between the 1930s and 1980s. Despite black wards being less heterogeneous along class lines than the city's working-class white ethnic blocs, Grimshaw found

the unique social composition of the black wards explained their unique political behavior. With the vast majority of blacks confined within a black belt, the overwhelmingly poor black wards contained a novel middle-class element, and the countervailing political activity of the middle class provided voters in the black wards with a political choice rarely found in the more class-homogenous poor white wards. The political strength of the middle class was reinforced by the church, the black community's historic institution of racial advancement and political protest.[40]

Collaboration Against the Machine: The Black Church as Proxy Political Arena

Along with a good deal of class heterogeneity and the special role of a "hidden middle class" faction among the poor, Grimshaw found a shared "racial interest" (which trumped class interests) born of the experiences with racistly calculated mayoral campaigns and administrations of the city's Irish Catholic machine: Martin Kennelly, then Richard J. Daley (amid civil rights activism), and then Jane Byrne. Others have described the 1980s Chicago movement as one that originated in the tangible grievances of African Americans in the areas of public health, housing, education, political representation, business and job opportunities, unemployment and welfare, and private housing that gave way to a "broad Black community unity, supported by white and Latino progressives and neighborhood activists."[41]

"Black political development" is a theoretical approach for understanding the intersectional utility of conventional and unconventional politics and the manner in which they have undermined a coherent systems–challenging strategy aimed at improving the material conditions of poor and working-class African Americans and communities. This was on display during Jeremiah Wright's imposition into the campaigns of Barack Obama. The persistence of protest-oriented leadership modalities in a "postprotest" political milieu provides an important backdrop to understanding the rejectionist strain among young people of the post–Black Power era who largely found conventional politics and establishment elites and institutions wanting as solutions to the multifaceted crises that they sought to confront. Among other scholars, Patricia Hill Collins provides an important outline of the religiosity of Black Power and its relationship to the post–civil rights hip-hop generation's cultural and political ambitions, which culminated more than a decade of flirtation with Farrakhan black nationalism and academic Afrocentrism.[42]

In *The Jesse Jackson Phenomenon*, Professor Reed views the political involvement of the church as "antiparticipatory, antidemocratic, conservative quasisecular"; it is a politically "quietist" institution, and he opposes the "organic" leadership class (e.g., Martin Luther King Jr., Jesse Jackson, and Louis Farrakhan) that it has produced.[43] Yet Grimshaw notes the vital role that the black Protestant churches played in opposing the Irish Catholic machine and supporting the Harold Washington campaigns. Although support was not unanimous among the city's churches and ministers, community activists were quick to confront those who supported either Byrne or Daley.[44] For Patricia

Hill Collins, the religious influence is sometimes overlooked by students of black politics because "the very standards of judgment within the academy eschew faith-based approaches to understanding the world and instead value scientific epistemologies as the currency of acceptability."[45] Prior to, during, and after segregation, and despite differentiation, the black church is where black politics were carried out. Mainly within the separatist and separate sphere of the National Baptist Convention, USA, which contained more than 60 percent of all black church members in the United States at the turn of the twentieth century, African American women and men experienced the black church as a center of civic purpose.[46] Evelyn Brooks Higginbotham's treatment of the Women's Convention movement among black Baptists over the four decades prior to the Great Depression highlights the particular ways in which, despite a myopic tendency to focus on male ministers,

> African Americans, looking now to themselves to educate the masses of their people, care for the needy, facilitate economic development, and address political concerns, tapped their greatest strength from the tradition of their churches. From the early days of slavery, the black church had constituted the backbone of the black community. . . . It functioned not only as a house of worship, but as an agency of social control, forum for discussion and debate, promoter of education and economic cooperation. And arena for the development and assertion of leadership.[47]

She argues convincingly, "for African Americans, long excluded from political institutions and denied presence, even relevance, in the dominant society's myths about its heritage and national community, the church itself became the domain for the expression, celebration, and pursuit of a black collective will and identity."[48]

E. Franklin Frazier's assessment of the church's role in African American life emphasized its proto-political qualities, especially as Jim Crow flourished throughout the country and disfranchised African Americans. For Frazier, one of the positive political features of the "Negro church" was its function as a proxy political arena, especially in denominations where people voted to select leaders and officers. He notes, "The Negro church was not only an arena of political life for the leaders of Negroes, but it had political meaning for the masses." Indeed the church constituted a "nation within a nation." Reginald Gilliam focuses on the role of the church in the political career of Adam Clayton Powell Jr. The African American church served as the main institutional source of organized black politics. In Powell's struggles against the Tammany Hall machine, the church "*has* contributed in a more autonomous way to black politics than has 'traditional machine' styled black politics . . . Powell became a national, state and local black political figure with a base being a Harlem constituency and organizational structure that was rooted in a black church."[49] Moreover, "from his black power base, Powell's 'politics' were primarily ac-

tivist and bluntly outspoken as to whites and continually adept in the formation, maintenance, and reformation of consensus and agreement among the
broad internal spectrum within Harlem community . . . In that sense, Powell's
politics was not a 'control' particularly in its early stages, but it clearly was always an aggressive black politics and a productive institutional politics."[50]
More so than Harlem and Powell, Chicago and the winning Harold Washington mayoral campaigns, elections, and administrations brought together a
wider, multidimensional engagement of African Americans across class, machine versus community political loyalties among elites, clashing ideological
orientations, religious denominational lines, the black wards of the city, and
grassroots organizations and institutions; they were driven by actual and perceived racial hostility both locally and in national politics.[51]

The political history of Chicago's African American communities, especially with the emergence of the city's machine apparatus and new black arrivals
between the wars and during the civil rights movement, is instructive. William
Grimshaw chronologically describes three major analytical perspectives—
the economic, the political, and the sociological—that have informed the complex experiences, interests, and elite recruitment processes that brought the
larger African American community to loggerheads with the city's Democratic
machine—in the pre-Daley years, the Daley years (1955–1976), and still later,
during Jane Byrne's administration. He insists that "each of the three theoretical perspectives we have identified is driven by a logic that tends to explain
elite recruitment in distinct terms."[52] The *economic perspective* reflects conventional wisdom concerning the patronage and barter between machine pro-
prietors and ward residents as consumers. The *political perspective* highlights
the elites' competing interests in relation to the organization's need to maintain viability in winning elections and forging coalitions. (The tensions between the organization and the community intensify elites' need for political
survival in one or the other, but rarely both.) The *sociological perspective* focuses on coalition-building in the urban politics literature with the understanding that "cities had to be understood as containing influential political and cultural spheres as well as an economic sphere, which is to say, cities are
governed by multiple interests rather than a unitary interest."[53] Here, a collectivist ethos yields a "collective ethnic-cultural interest" that fueled much of the
opposition to the machine apparatus. Residents in the first black belt wards
(2nd and 3rd) were reluctant to develop strong local Democratic ties in the machine, even as they moved favorably toward the New Deal's ancillary economic overtures.[54] Especially after President Franklin Roosevelt publicly addressed racial discrimination in 1944, African Americans manufactured a
steady and consistent pattern of ambidextrously supporting national Democrats while demonstrating electoral reticence toward the local Chicago machine; they embraced the New Deal and rejected the "raw deal" of the local

party.[55] When the Supreme Court banned restrictive covenants, the poorer wards in Chicago were left by the middle classes beholden to the machine's symbolic patronage administered through loyal surrogates; the poor black wards became the stronghold of Daley's support until "race replaced class as the city's political divide" among the working-class ethnics.[56]

Not a full generation since Booker T. Washington's 1915 death, eventually the poorer wards defied the favors-for-votes logic of the economic model and demonstrated a reluctance to shift to the Democratic machine more than did the middle classes. The emergent middle-class wards were the most independent and fiercely oppositional toward the racism of the local Democrats and remained so through the Daley and Byrne administrations. As the poorer wards grew disillusioned with the machine, "the middle class black wards broke in open revolt, and the white ethnic wards set aside fiscal concerns over the machine's excesses to embrace it on racial grounds." The institutional center of this opposition rested in the black churches of the city. They were expected to facilitate the political interests of the community as well as the religious ones. Critically, "the black church rather than the Republican party was the machine's principal opponent in the black wards."[57]

Black Chicago and the Daley Machine
Before and After Martin Luther King Jr.

Blacks forged a stronger alliance with local Democrats with Daley's 1955 election due to the overtly racist campaign that Kennelly used against him in order to consolidate white ethnic support in white wards. Over the ensuing twenty years, the different sectors of black Chicago (but to a lesser extent in the West Side's transitioning and indifferent plantation wards) would betray a flexibility and racial calculus that frustrated an otherwise ironclad rule of city politics. Between 1955 and 1963, the Daley machine benefitted from strong but unrequited support from African Americans. From the time of his election through Martin Luther King's attempt to nationalize the southern civil rights movement, the Black Power revolt, and the 1968 Democratic Party convention police riot, black Chicagoans were a restive machine constituency. Along with the corrupt claims of officials (such as Edward Hanrahan) involved in the murders of Black Panther activists Mark Clark and Fred Hampton, Daley especially alienated black Chicagoans with his comments urging police to shoot, kill, and maim rioters following the April 4, 1968, horror of King's murder. In order to maintain political domination over African American communities when confronted by the local political struggle, Daley installed his own manageable elites, who were variously challenged by the middle-class wards at the level of alderman after 1963, when his regime shifted to an openly antiblack agenda. With the exception of a few judicial appointments and a cadre of "bosses," including an aged William Dawson, Claude Holman (4th Ward), and Ralph Metcalfe (3rd, who would later become an accidental symbol of black antipathy for the machine's rule), Daley was careful to maintain a cadre of controllable men in the black ward organizations. And he was certain to keep individuals such as these men at odds with one another so they could not challenge his dominance. Daley's earliest sponsorship was of those referred to as "civic notables." This cadre consisted of individuals, including Robert Miller of the 6th Ward, with high community visibility resulting from personal and professional achievements before allying with the machine, but with no significant political clout.[58] Stirred by the civil rights movement, ordinary African Americans did not passively accept the machine's meager spoils or symbolic representation. Rather, *the civic notables were rejected in the communities*, and "they would be the only black elites who eventually buckled and fell under the community pressure." When Daley imposed mostly Black Catholic individuals known as "loyalist elites" (William Shannon in the 17th, Fred Coles in the 21st, John Stroger in the 8th, and Eugene Sawyer, a Protestant protégé of Miller's), to offset the Protestant-driven civil rights movement, the matter of elite recruitment became central to the machine's tactical errors in African American communities. As racial politics supplanted class divisions in the city, many African Americans, especially from the restive middle-class wards, sought to undermine the machine's hold on the community through its offering of leaders. And when Jane Byrne emerged as the first and only woman mayor of Chicago in 1979, she, like others before her, sought to aggravate the racial antipathies of the city's black and ethnic white communities. Most salient, the machine's post-Daley bifurcation, reinforced by elite rivalry, created space for Byrne's eventual challenge to Mayor Michael Bilandic. Byrne's main support initially came from the antimachine black middle-class wards, which she immediately scuttled in deference to her racial appeal to the city's white ethnic communities. Byrne, like the early Daley, benefited from strong support among black voters. She won the Black Belt wards, middle-class wards, and even the machine's plantation wards enough to eke out a victory over Bilandic. Her awkward alliance with Daley machine holdovers, known as the "Young Turks," as well as her blatant agitation of the city's communities through the removal and appointment of elites, was interpreted by black communities as betrayal. She had abandoned her electoral coalition for an uneasy governing coalition that was intentionally hostile to African Americans. According to Grimshaw: "The black political condition actually worsened under Byrne, and so, in turn, did her relationship with the black community . . . during the Byrne mayoralty the city's politics swirled more openly and tumultuously around racial antagonism and conflict than ever before."[59] A stunning set of developments led Grimshaw to describe the following:

The black community rallied in opposition to a gala summer event, ChicagoFest, sponsored by the mayor. In a galaxy of special events favored by Mayor Byrne, ChicagoFest was the crown jewel. Black opposition to the festival initially was launched by the Reverend Jesse Jackson, but soon a broad array of black organizations joined in, which included several new and reinvigorated groups with political orientations that were springing up like mushrooms in response to Byrne's racial assaults. The opposition to ChicagoFest took the form of a black boycott, which proved so successful that the popular festival's revenues were driven down into the loss column.[60]

It was in this atmosphere of disrespect and betrayal, punctuated by the desire to punish the Byrne administration, that Harold Washington emerged; it is also where Chicago's Jesse Jackson and Louis Farrakhan catapulted their near-simultaneous drives to be the informal "national representative" of either of the two major ideological orientations among African Americans: integrationism and nationalism. If earlier King saw Chicago as an opportunity to become the same, by nationalizing the Birmingham movement, Jackson and Farrakhan sought to catapult the momentum of the Chicago movement to national black politics. The 1983 Harold Washington campaign became the impetus and context for the entrance of the Nation of Islam into national black politics. And there simply is no better available modern example than Minister Louis Farrakhan and the Nation of Islam of an elite recruitment process—where elite indifference to local mobilization of grassroots activism attaches to the massive movement of peoples. And the timing could not have been more conducive. By the 1980s, Chicago had supplanted Harlem as the major ideological station of African American intellectual, cultural, and political life. Harlem nearly killed King (in 1958), but black Chicago took from the ashes of King's "defeat" by Daley's machine (in 1966) a renewed sense of political efficacy that would undo the patronage system and overt racism of the machine a full decade after Daley's death in 1976. The Chicago movement inspired blacks in Philadelphia, Boston, and New York in their efforts to be politically incorporated with black-first mayoralties and to shield the communities from the policy and psychological effects of Reagan's "nationalizing" of the *ethnic* hostility witnessed in Chicago and other cities. Local voter registration in Chicago resulted in more than 125,000 newly registered African American voters in the city; 600,000 of the city's 665,000 eligible black residents were registered.[61] It was ordinary people among "the poor [who] led the voter registration drive (especially public housing residents and welfare recipients), and were later joined by the black middle class segments. Harold Washington was drafted in the neighborhoods and the churches, and not in conference rooms in Chicago's financial district."[62]

Dianne Pinderhughes insists that Washington's electoral coalition was a demand-protest alliance of "several associations of organizations which had grown into structures that mobilized and unified the black community for the mayoral campaign." Nationalist organizations such as the Task Force for Black Empowerment, Chicago Black United Communities (CBUC), and VOTE, as well as the religious bodies and some ward organizations, played vital roles in the community's euphoric victory over the machine. This electoral strategy had a strong independent current but aimed ultimately to achieve maximum black mobilization and interracial coalition networks. When Washington was elected to his first term in November 1982, the demographic makeup of the city had become increasingly diverse compared to the previous decade. Various white ethnics constituted 43.6 percent of the total population; blacks constituted 39.5 percent; Chicanos/Latinos—who played a vital role—made up 14 percent. With maximum black mobilization, Pinderhughes suggests, blacks in Chicago "forged an intragroup coalition in the early 1980s that served as a basis for broader, multiracial coalition through which Harold Washington was elected."[63] Chicago's black voting-age populations increased from its mid-century low of 13.4 percent to 37.5 percent by 1980, whereas white ethnic segments steadily declined from an 86.5 percent high in 1950 to 53.5 percent by 1980. Latinos constituted 7.5 percent of the city's voting-age population.[64] These patterns enabled black residents to operate more autonomously—though still within the Democratic Party—which alienated black Chicago when Democratic presidential candidates endorsed Byrne and Richard M. Daley, the former mayor's son, over Washington.[65] Michael Preston adds, "the group most surprised by the results of the primary was the Democratic organization. Its members simply did not believe that Washington was a serious threat until a week before the election. . . . However, by the time of the 1979 mayoral election, black voter attitude and voting turnout had undergone a rather remarkable change." He continues: "Black voter dissatisfaction with machine politics and programs led them not only to become more antimachine but more independent voters as well. *Indeed, in an unusual twist of events, blacks instead of whites became the leaders of the independent political movement in Chicago.*"[66] Abdul Alkalimat and Doug Gills point to a "nationalist oriented community based middle class leadership in advancing the interests of the Black community through militant electoral protest."[67] Along with a burgeoning political organization and independent parallel organizations, the nationalist contingency was a coherent segment that powered the campaign at the neighborhood, ward, and street levels of the black community. Respected community activists, including Timuel Black, Bob Starks, the Reverend Al Sampson, Lou Palmer, and Conrad Worrill, made signal contributions to Harold Washington's election and at times pushed the formal campaign beyond its liberal reformist intentions, often at loggerheads over the tactics, the role of whites, and black integrationist elements.

What is most pertinent about developments in Chicago is the conflation of germinating forces and the broader nationalization of an ordinary people's movement against actual and perceived antiblack forces in formal politics. It was activated saliently within this nationalization process of Chicago's black politics—which Adam Green locates in the creation of *Ebony* and *JET* magazines and crystalized in the Emmett Till murder—around the Harold Washington campaign. Here the mobilization of ordinary people contextualizes the emergence of Jesse Jackson and Louis Farrakhan to vie for national prominence in post–civil rights black politics. Although Jackson's Operation PUSH/Rainbow Coalition and Farrakhan's Nation of Islam Chicago headquarters predated Washington's 1983 campaign, Washington's election seems to have catapulted Jackson's 1984 presidential bid and Farrakhan's prominence among African Americans outside Chicago. It is also the political milieu into which Barack Obama moved as an organizer on the South Side of Chicago, which encompassed the largest black electoral district in the country. With increased electoral opportunities afforded black people after the civil rights movement, black political elites were confronted with new strategic challenges as they ventured to gain political offices in districts that were majority white (Carl Stokes in Cleveland, Tom Bradley in Los Angeles, Harold Washington in Chicago, Wilson Goode in Philadelphia, and David Dinkins in New York). The political climate facing black Americans in the 1970s and 1980s demanded a programmatic front familiar with the internal workings of the political process. Yet scholars have noted that despite marked gains, subsequent developments brought into question the effect of black elected officials in realizing policy objectives and providing material rewards to constituents. The thrust of their success came about as a result of affirmative-action mandates in increasing entry- and middle-level public-sector employment opportunities for constituents. The civil rights and Black Power movements highlighted blacks' ability to effect massive transformations in the political system. Black elected officials' political experience within the electoral system could either serve these ends or discourage them. The mass mobilization that came with the early 1980s was as much an effect of the Democratic Party's indifference and hostility as it was the specter of Ronald Reagan and political conservatism in national politics. Reed rightly characterizes this specter as "the clearly observable intensification of oppression over the 1980s—seen in a worsening of material conditions, a narrowing of life options, increasingly institutionalized marginalization, and an expanding regime of social repression and political terror."[68]

Old-Time Religion and the New Black Politics

One of the great miscalculations of the 1980s and 1990s is that black religiosity should be understood as a sort of nascent stage that gave way to a new phase of postmodern conditions and to the expanded opportunity structure evident most clearly in the increase in the number of black elected officials in the public sector, especially at the municipal level but also in Congress. As early as Reconstruction, black religious and political elites coalesced and contested in the proscribed role of race spokespersons. This pitted the likes of Booker T. Washington against the Reconstruction-era cadre of black elected officials. Of course, the patently religious civil rights movement forged the social space that made the 1965 Voting Rights Act and the post–civil rights "new elite" blacks in office possible. Moreover, black politics is exigent within the "specifics of non-electoral leadership, the black ideological spectrum and the roles of the church and community organizations as substitutes for electoral politics."[69] Each major epoch or regime in the African American freedom struggle has produced competing, and at times overlapping, political elites, organizations, programs, and ideological social and political orientations.[70] The accommodationist, nationalist, and integrationist strains have been the most enduring of these and formed the basis of black politics for the twentieth century.

Grimshaw argues that they engaged in a jeremiad, "often fierce [in] demeanor and the fire and fury of their rhetoric," and employed a belief that people needed to be moved on a visceral level toward registration, mobilization, and voter turnout. If the jeremiad is conventionally understood as an extension of the charismatic personality, then the black empowerment ethos of the Harold Washington coalition's more radical elements demonstrated that the jeremiad could channel from community to the charismatic leader as a way of confronting—speaking to—hostile political and social forces—in this case Jane Byrne's Democratic machine coalition in the city, the national Democrats, and a Republican Party increasingly dominated by Reaganism. Harold Washington was "drafted by Black people, then his candidacy was affirmed by community activists and most political reformers across the city," according to Alkalimat and Gills. They conclude,

> the general assessment of many observers is that the *movement* for Harold Washington led to his victory and was followed by organization. . . . What surprised many was the failure by key black leaders and others, who for months had been discussing the viability of a Black candidate to put more of the campaign "nuts and bolts" into place. . . . Chicago's Black community was fired up by a series of racial incidents involving Mayor Byrne. Further, many of the incidents also involved other sectors of the community, broadening the dissatisfaction. Simultaneously, this built the basis for Black unity against City Hall, and Black-white-Latino unity against City Hall.[71]

This political style of "protest at the polls"[72] also "undeniably helped transform the campaign into a movement."[73] Noticeably absent from this local contingency, in terms of engaging the political process in Chicago, was Nation of Islam leader Louis Farrakhan, who at the behest of Jesse Jackson mobilized the Fruit of Islam and Muslim Girls in Training (MGT) to distribute campaign literature and urged the members of the Nation of Islam to register to vote; he registered for the first time at the age of forty-eight.[74]

Conclusion

Black political development, then, makes it possible to account for the hip-hop generation's decision to resurrect the personae of Malcolm X and Louis Farrakhan (see Chapter 8) to speak to the political environment, which is best characterized as cultural backlash and racial conservatism epitomized in the person and policies of Ronald Reagan. The framework of black political development allows us to place the alternations between formal elected leadership and informal protest leadership in context, for it is clearly as much about leadership as it is about political institutions. In order to place the nationalism of the hip-hop generation into relief and to understand their recruitment of Malcolm X, the next chapter turns to the religious dimensions of African American political ideologies that grounded the black jeremiad nationalism that Malcolm X and Farrakhan employed and represent.

Notes

1. Karen Orren and Stephen Skowronek, *The Search for American Political Development* (New York: Cambridge University Press, 2004), p. 4.
2. Ibid., p. 123.
3. New developments, as in ideas, leaders, wars, or movements, are centered only to the extent to which they contribute to the larger phenomenon of political development; they are of political development. But alone, conflicts, compromises, and political events do not fit what the authors intend. They are concerned with authority—which is more than law, power, or violence, although these are essential to authority. Ibid., pp. 123–126.
4. Ibid., p. 133.
5. Ibid., p. 136. Emphasis added.
6. Ibid., p. 2.
7. Ibid., p. 26.
8. Ibid. See also Adolph Reed Jr., *Stirrings in the Jug: Black Politics in the Post-Segregation Era* (Minneapolis: University of Minnesota Press, 1999), p. 35.
9. Reginald Gilliam, *Black Political Development: An Advocacy Analysis* (Port Washington, NY: Kennikat, 1975), p. 281. Emphases in original.
10. Adolph Reed, *Stirrings in the Jug*; Reginald Gilliam, *Black Political Development*; Lester Salmon, "Leadership and Modernization: The Emerging Black Political Elite in the American South," *Journal of Politics*, no. 35 (1973): 615–646.
11. Howard Rabinowitz (ed.), *Southern Black Leaders of the Reconstruction Era* (Urbana: University of Illinois Press, 1982).
12. Ibid., p. 28.
13. Ibid., p. xiii.
14. Ibid., ch. 10.
15. Reginald Gilliam, *Black Political Development*, p. 4. First emphasis in original; latter emphases added.
16. Ibid., p. 53.
17. Ibid., pp. 121–127.

18. See Adolph Reed, *Stirrings in the Jug*, ch. 1.

19. Ibid., p. 20.

20. Ibid., p. 18.

21. Ibid., p. 49.

22. Ibid., pp. 28–29.

23. Ibid., p. 47.

24. Ibid, pp. 33, 49,

25. See ibid., pp. 148–150.

26. Noel Ignatiev, *How the Irish Became White* (New York: Routledge, 1995), p. 2.

27. William L. Patterson, "Our People Demand Freedom," *Masses and Mainstream* 4, no. 1 (January 1951): 64 (New York: Masses and Mainstream).

28. I make this emphasis because scholars tend to begin the criticism of uplift ideology with Booker T. Washington or, say, the women of the National Council of Negro Women while passing on an extensive treatment of Douglass as its progenitor. Note, for instance, how Douglass is given only passing reference in Adolph Reed Jr.'s "'What Are the Drums Saying Booker?': The Curious Role of the Black Public Intellectual," in Reed's book, *Class Notes: Posing as Politics and Other Thoughts on the American Scene* (New York: The New Press, 2000), pp. 77–90.

29. Melissa Victoria Harris-Lacewell, *Barbershops, Bibles, and BET: Everyday Talk and Black Political Thought* (Princeton: Princeton University Press, 2004), p. 25.

30. Ronald Walters and Robert C. Smith, *African American Leadership* (Albany: State University of New York Press, 1999), p. 61.

31. Ibid., p. 249.

32. Charles P. Henry, *Culture and African American Politics* (Bloomington: Indiana University Press, 1990); Cornel West, *Race Matters* (Boston: Beacon Press, 1993); Eugene V. Wolfenstein, *The Victims of Democracy: Malcolm X and the Black Revolution* (Los Angeles: University of California Press, 1981); Michael Eric Dyson, *Making Malcolm: The Myth and Meaning of Malcolm X* (New York: Oxford University Press, 1995).

33. Hanes Walton Jr., *Invisible Politics: Black Political Behavior* (Albany: State University of New York Press, 1985), pp. 231–238.

34. Ibid., p. 351.

35. E. Franklin Frazier, *The Negro Church in America* (New York: Schocken Books, 1964), pp. 68–81.

36. Robert C. Smith, *We Have No Leaders: African Americans in the Post–Civil Rights Era* (Albany: State University of New York Press, 1996), p. 76.

37. This was a critical year in the city's history and racial politics, during which Richard J. Daley's machine emerged; the ghastly lynching of fourteen-year-old Emmett Till, while visiting relatives in Money, Mississippi, galvanized local black leaders.

38. Adam Green, *Selling the Race: Culture, Community, and Black Chicago, 1940–1955* (Chicago: University of Chicago Press, 2007), p. 108.

39. See especially chapter 5 in ibid., p. 10. This study traces the importation of uplift ideology to Chicago through the likes of Claude Barnett, a student of Booker Washington's Tuskegee philosophy, founder of the floundering American Negro Press, and leading figure (in a most ambitious effort at the time) attempting to organize the 1940 American Negro Exposition. Further, it outlines the emergence of *Ebony* and *JET* magazines under the leadership of John H. Johnson and the Johnson Publication Company in formulating a form of national (not nationalist) racial affinity around a mobilization of a kind of black glitterati success ethic.

40. William J. Grimshaw, *Bitter Fruit: Black Politics and the Chicago Machine, 1931–1991* (Chicago: University of Chicago Press, 1992), p. 68.

41. The "Committee of 500" white and Latino reformists of different stripes participated in the black-led coalition with broad-based potential for reform that appealed to

Latinos and some whites. See Abdul Alkalimat and Doug Gills, *Harold Washington and the Crisis of Black Power in Chicago* (Chicago: Twenty-First Century Books, 1989), pp. 22, 28, and 33.

42. Patricia Hill Collins, *From Black Power to Hip Hop: Racism, Nationalism, and Feminism* (Philadelphia: Temple University Press, 2006), p. 86.

43. Adolph Reed Jr., *The Jesse Jackson Phenomenon* (New Haven: Yale University Press, 1986), p. 57. The means and procedures by which bishops and pastors are selected among ordinary people in religious circles, such as the Church of God in Christ or African Methodist Episcopal denominations, or the ways in which aggrieved congregants at a given religious site may periodically withhold tithes or contributions from church coffers are set aside for a discourse on how those elected individuals might trade on corporate racial mobilizations.

44. Alkalimat and Gills, *Harold Washington*, pp. 58, 66–67.

45. Patricia Hill Collins, *From Black Power to Hip Hop*, pp. 86, 89.

46. Evelyn Brooks Higginbotham, *Righteous Discontent: The Women's Movement in the Black Baptist Church, 1880–1920* (Cambridge: Harvard University Press, 1993), p. 6.

47. Ibid., p. 5.

48. Ibid., p, 9.

49. Reginald Gilliam, *Black Political Development*, p. 121.

50. Ibid., p. 122.

51. For a brief discussion of the relationship between Harlem's and Chicago's African American communities, including cultural and political histories, see Adam Green, *Selling the Race*, pp. 4–5.

52. With a much different emphasis, Alkalimat and Gills, *Harold Washington*, p. 22, similarly see the economic struggles of black Chicagoans as precipitous to the political struggles of African Americans during the Jane Byrne era.

53. William Grimshaw, *Bitter Fruit*, p. 7.

54. Ibid., pp. 1–6.

55. Ibid., p. 49.

56. Ibid., pp. 21, 24.

57. Ibid., p. 64.

58. Ibid., pp. 111–114.

59. Ibid., pp. 147–148.

60. Ibid., p. 162.

61. See Alkalimat and Gills, *Harold Washington*, p. 42. Moreover, the Democratic National Committee endorsed Byrne over Harold Washington—after Vice President Walter Mondale experienced rabid white-mob anger aimed at Washington while attending St. Pascal's Catholic Church on the Northwest Side—amid the specter of Ronald Reagan's reelection. See William Grimshaw, *Bitter Fruit*, p. 180.

62. Alkalimat and Gills, *Harold Washington*, p. 59.

63. Dianne Pinderhughes, "An Examination of Chicago Politics for Evidence of Political Incorporation and Representation," in Rufus Browning, Dale Rogers Marshall, and David H. Tabb (eds.), *Racial Politics in American Cities*, 2nd ed. (New York: Longman, 1997), pp. 119–122.

64. Ibid., p. 122.

65. Lucius J. Barker and Ronald Walters (eds.), *Jesse Jackson's 1984 Presidential Campaign: Challenge and Change in American Politics* (Urbana: University of Illinois Press, 1989), p. 39.

66. Michael B. Preston, Lenneal J. Henderson, and Paul Puryear (eds.), *The New Black Politics: The Search for Political Power*, 2nd ed. (White Plains, NY: Longman, 1987), p. 140. Emphasis in original.

67. Alkalimat and Gills, *Harold Washington*, p. 2.

68. Adolph Reed, *Stirrings in the Jug*, pp. 117–118.

69. Reginald Gilliam, *Black Political Development*, pp. 3–4. Emphasis in original.

70. Concerning ideology, Cruse, in *Crisis of the Negro Intellectual* (New York: Quill, [1967] 1984), lists these as "integrationism, separatism, interracialism, nationalism, Marxist and anti-Marxist radicalism, Communist and anti-Communist radicalism, liberalism (Jewish and Christian), anarchism, nihilism and religionism (the Muslim gambit)" (p. 404). Early emigrationism and colonization were met with abolitionism; quasi-nationalist accommodationism was met with NAACP-integrationism and assimilation; Garveyism had to contend with the Du Bois–James Weldon Johnson–Walter White NAACP; the Nation of Islam's Elijah Muhammad and Malcolm X had to contend with the SCLC of King and the NAACP of Roy Wilkins; the 1980s and 1990s featured Jesse Jackson and Louis Farrakhan as the major contenders. It is important to note that many of these contests were "intraideological." Integrationist organizations such as the NAACP and Southern Christian Leadership Conference (SCLC) were often in conflict over strategy and financial matters. Older organizations such as the NAACP and National Urban League (NUL) were often at odds with the younger protest organizations such as the Student Nonviolent Coordinating Committee (SNCC) and the Congress of Racial Equality (CORE). Moreover, the socialist strain also suffered from conflicts between the camps of A. Philip Randolph and Chandler Owens's United Brotherhood of Sleeping Car Porters and Cyril Briggs and Richard B. Moore's African Black Brotherhood. This is so despite the persistence of an African American radical socialist strain, with adherents among political elites, such as George Washington Woodbey (of San Diego, California), Cyril Briggs, Richard B. Moore, Hubert H. Harrison, A. Philip Randolph, Bayard Rustin, and Angela Davis. It has not been successful in gaining widespread adherence among African Americans. For an interesting discussion concerning the general failures of socialism in the United States, see Seymour Martin Lipset and Gary W. Marks, *It Didn't Happen Here: Why Socialism Failed in the United States* (New York: W. W. Norton, 2000). For a discussion of the failures of communism among African Americans, in particular, see Harold Cruse, *The Crisis of the Negro Intellectual*, and Cornel West, *Prophesy Deliverance!* (Philadelphia: Westminster, 1982); see also Philip Foner, *American Socialism and Black Americans: From the Age of Jackson to World War II* (Wesport, CT: Greenwood, 1977).

71. William Grimshaw, *Bitter Fruit*, p. 59. Emphases in original.

72. Abdul Alkalimat and Doug Gills in Rod Bush (eds.), *The New Black Vote: Politics and Power in Four American Cities* (San Francisco: Synthesis, 1984), p. 63.

73. A rally held at the University of Illinois was one critical event that demonstrated the power of local "organic" activists to stir widespread involvement among African Americans (e.g., nationally recognized black elected officials; impassioned ward residents; segments of the black community that held out support for Byrne, including black women's groups; and students). See Grimshaw, pp. 174–176.

74. This information was ascertained through an informal discussion with Bob Starks, August 2008.

2

A Black Sacred Cosmos and the Making of a Black Counterpublic

These all died in faith, not having received the promises, but having seen them afar off, and were persuaded of them, and embraced them, and confessed that they were strangers and pilgrims on earth. For they that say such things declare plainly that they seek a country. And truly, if they had been mindful of that country from whence they came, they might have had opportunity to have returned. But now they desire a better country.
—Hebrews 11:13–16

Michael Dawson's understanding of ideology is consonant with the operational functions of black religion as "a worldview readily found in the population," he states, "including sets of ideas and values that cohere, that are used publicly to justify political stances, and that shape and are shaped by society. Further, political ideology helps to define who are one's friends and enemies, with whom one would form political coalitions, and, furthermore, contains a causal narrative of society and the state. Cognitively ideology serves as a filter of what one 'sees' and responds to in the social world."[1] And thereby "individuals develop a politicized sense of racial identification which influences both their ideological view of the social world as well as their political behavior."[2] The question of divine rescue and liberation powerfully shaped the ideological and political orientations that African Americans utilized in their social and political struggles to define their relationship to the US political system.

God in Black Politics

Perhaps more so than other major traditions, black nationalism evolved out of a larger theological superstructure of black religion, which anteceded its explicitly "Christianized" qualities that emerged relatively late in the plantation division of

35

labor. In 1701 the British Society for the Propagation of the Gospel in Foreign Parts (SPG) set out to effect mass conversions in the United States among New Englanders, including slaves, free blacks, and Native Americans. The SPG was not abolitionist in its commitments. Like other European missionary projects, the SPG was more concerned with the souls of slaves than they were with their captured bodies; baptism of slaves made them *Christians*, not free persons. Neither this campaign nor the first "Great Awakening" in the 1730s and 1740s had a particular effect on slave conversions. In fact, Winthrop Jordan describes a general atmosphere of indifference toward the conversion of Africans to the Christian religion. This indifference was driven, among many other reasons, by the widespread sentiment among slaveholders that "no matter how much conversion might benefit the Negroes' souls, it could only make them worse slaves." This feeling pervaded the SPG as much as it did other European and colonial religious societies. Contrary to the opinion among many scholars that Christianity militated against the slaves' dissidence, many slaveholders and planters felt that baptism and conversion made them too "proud and saucy."[3] The record of American Protestantism in eighteenth-century Puritanism, eighteenth- and nineteenth-century revivalism, and early-twentieth-century social gospel discourses reveals *a protracted alignment with antiblack racial sentiment* and rationale for the social and political oppression of African Americans.

Missionary societies reassured the owning classes that religious instruction and conversion could actually fortify the hold over slaves and that their enslavement was a civil, not a moral or religious, matter. Thus, with a few important exceptions among the Quakers, notable Puritans, and individual white clerics, Jordan argues that

> the most disastrous failing of the churches in America was embodied in the *kind* of slavery they were at least willing to put up with if not endorse. The slavery which the S.P.G. defended in 1768 was marked by complete deprivation of rights; despite the S.P.G.'s somewhat guarded plea for kind treatment and adequate food and clothing for slaves, neither the S.P.G. nor other proponents of conversion put up much of a fight against the many hideous manifestations of the commercial slavery which deprived Negroes of status as human beings.[4]

Protestant Christianity largely ignored black people during the first two hundred years of their time in America. When Baptist and Methodist missions began proselytizing among Africans in the early to middle nineteenth century, black religionists were confronted with the onslaught of doctrines that reiterated their subaltern status and interpreted biblical texts in line with the perpetuation of African American slavery and quietude. They offered up a preferential option to slaveholding Christianity. Article IV of David Walker's *Appeal*, for instance, makes reference to the widespread teaching in the nineteenth century that blacks were the direct descendants of Cain (murderer of his brother,

Abel), thereby implying that blacks inherited "a dark stain" in consequence of some mythical genetic ties to the former.[5] Indeed the uniquely modern idea of *permanent*, inherited servitude of Negroes among Europeans and whites in the Americas was validated by Leviticus 25:45–46, which permits for children of strangers to be purchasable so that they may "be your possession. And ye shall make them an inheritance for your children . . . ; they shall be your bondmen for ever: but over your brethren the children of Israel, ye shall not rule one another with rigor." Sociologist E. Franklin Frazier reports how mid-eighteenth-century slaves who encountered Christianity were routinely subjected to the litmus that equated slave obedience to God with obedience to slaveholders.[6] In contrast, the New Testament account of a runaway slave, Onesimus, being returned to a condition of slavery by the apostle Paul, coupled with his admonition "slaves, obey your earthly masters with respect and fear, and with sincerity of heart just as you would obey Christ," gave credence to the notion that *God was pro-slavery.*[7] For this reason Paul has held a special place in black political thought. The likes of W.E.B. Du Bois, Howard Thurman, Albert Cleage Jr., and Orlando Patterson have acknowledged Paul's contribution to black people's oppression at least to the extent that his writings could be so plainly viewed as an apologetic or, worse still, propagating for slavery. According to one biographer, Howard Thurman "learned to distrust the words of the Apostle, Paul, except for First Corinthians, thirteen. For when the slave master's preacher came to preach to the slaves, he always chose a text from the Apostle Paul, and his favorite text was 'Slaves obey your masters.'"[8] Cleage felt that "the Epistles of Paul are in direct contradiction to the teachings of the Old Testament. Slave Christianity emphasizes these distortions of the Apostle Paul and denies and repudiates the basic teachings of Jesus Christ and the Black Nation Israel."[9] Patterson argues similarly:

> There are really two religions lurking in the bosom of the Christian church. One is the largely neglected religion that Jesus himself preached. It is, by all accounts, a radical gospel, both spiritually and socially. . . . This religion, though, was largely discarded in one of the *greatest distortions and misappropriations in the history of the world*. In the Christologies that emerged after Jesus' execution, the focus of the young religion shifted completely from his life and message to his death and its sacrificial meaning. Absolutely nothing in the authentic sayings of Jesus suggested anything about his death as a sacrifice. This was all an invention after his death, an invention attributable, above all, to *Paul, who became a virtual second founder*.[10]

Protestant Christianity's second most influential personality contributed much to its resonance with American slavery. Patterson states pointedly, "The Christianity that prevails today is really *the creed of Paul*, a devious and possibly disturbed religious genius who stole and reinvented the creed of the Jew Jesus."[11] It was even common among some leading individuals in the nineteenth century (such as nationalist leader Bishop Henry McNeal Turner and his contemporary Booker T. Washington) to insist that slavery was a God-ordained prerequisite condition planned with the religious imperialist "civilizing" objective of sending American Negroes to convert Africans to Euro-American Christianity. With some individuals accepting and others rejecting these ideas, the slave community in the southern colonies and states fashioned systems of belief that were beholden neither to traditional European Christianity nor to unadulterated African ritual practices. In the North, nominally freed residents of major cities such as Philadelphia, New York, New Bedford, Rhode Island, and Boston were especially committed to forming independent institutions such as the African Methodist Episcopal Church (Philadelphia) and the African Meeting House (Boston). From the outset, the black freedom movement itself emerges out of the determination of key leaders to forge independent institutions. Later I argue that a black political apparatus, whether a formal party or convention of some sort, might be understood as kind of judgment against the established order; a jeremiad against the Democratic and Republican Parties, as the A.M.E. Church, led by Richard Allen and Absalom Jones, was an operational jeremiad against the Methodist Church. Eugene Genovese suggests that "the philosophical problem of religion, its truth and falsehood, represents a domain only partially separate from that of politics. Since religion expresses the antagonisms between the life of the individual and that of society . . . it cannot escape being profoundly political."[12]

Theodicy and Black Liberation

It was the subsequent coupling of slavery's trauma with the tendency in Hebraic-Judeo Christianity to provide for group-specific salvation, deliverance, and liberation from this condition that became the basis of a critical protest narrative among blacks beginning in the nineteenth century and resonating in subsequent generations particularly, as Negroes interpreted Christianity according to their collective experience with race and racism in society. In Cornel West's view:

> Black people became Christians for intellectual, existential, and political reasons. Christianity is . . . a religion especially suited to the oppressed. It looks at the world from the perspective of those below. The African slaves' search for identity could find historical purpose in the exodus of Israel out of slavery and personal meaning in the bold identification of Jesus Christ with the lowly and downtrodden. Christianity also is first and foremost a theodicy, a triumphant account of good over evil. The intellectual life of the African slaves in the United States—like that of all oppressed people—consisted primarily of reckoning with the dominant form of evil in their lives. The Christian emphasis on against-the-evidence hope for triumph over evil struck deep among many of them.[13]

The fact of Christianity's failure to commute the same meaning to most of its European and Colonial American adherents *is the beginning of black protest* even if that protest was facilitated by the revolutionary ethos of the European and North American bourgeoisie. Indeed it was a protest that began as an internal appeal to the moral sense and natural rights themes that pervaded Christian Europe and North America that eventually gave way to various forms of protest against the entire apparatus of the North American social, economic, and political structures. In *Black Religion and Black Radicalism*, Gayraud S. Wilmore very usefully defines black religion "as a complex concatenation of archaic, modern, and continually shifting belief systems, mythologies, and symbols . . . sharing a common core related to Africa and racial oppression."[14] Its "most significant characteristic," he insists, is a "fusion between a highly developed and persuasive feeling about the essentially spiritual nature of historic experience, flowing from the African traditional background, and a radical secularity related both to religious sensibility and to the experiences of slavery and oppression."[15] Du Bois acknowledges the centripetal power of these experiences in *Dusk of Dawn*:

> But one thing is sure and that is the fact that since the fifteenth century these ancestors of mine and their other descendants have a common history; have suffered a common disaster and have one long memory. The actual ties of heritage between the individuals of this group vary with the ancestors that they have in common and many others: Europeans and Semites, perhaps Mongolians, certainly American Indians. But the physical bond is least and the badge of color relatively unimportant save as a badge; the real essence of this kinship is its *social heritage of slavery*; the discrimination and insult; and this heritage binds together not simply the children of Africa, but extends through yellow Asia and into the South Seas. It is this unity that draws me to Africa.[16]

The trauma and ontological dizziness of slavery, even in its most paternal or "benevolent" forms, and the triangular trade forced Africans on all ends of its time and spatial trajectories to give supernal explanation for their hellish circumstances. It would be unthinkable for Africans, even before contact with the West, to conceive of natural disasters, sickness, disease, premature or tragic death, or any abnormality, separate from an understanding of their proximate favor with God, native deities, or the ancestors. Cornel West argues,

> Black strivings are the creative and complex products of the terrifying African encounter with the absurd *in* America—and the absurd *as* America. . . . They constructed structures of meaning and structures of feeling in the face of the fundamental facts of human existence—death, dread, despair, and disappointment. Yet the specificity of black culture—namely, those features that distinguish black culture from other cultures—lies in both the *African* and *American* character of black people's attempts to sustain their mental sanity and spiritual health, social life and political struggle in the midst of a

slaveholding, white supremacist civilization that viewed itself as the most enlightened, free, tolerant, and democratic experiment in human history.[17]

Lawrence Levine suggests that "the preliterate, premodern Africans, with their sacred world view, were so imperfectly acculturated into the secular American society into which they were thrust, were so completely denied access to the ideology and dreams which formed the core of the consciousness of other Americans, that they were forced to fall back upon the only cultural frame of reference that made any sense to them and gave them any feeling of security." In fact, their predicament contributed to the sharing of a "fundamental outlook toward the past, present, and future and common means of cultural expression which could well have constituted the basis of a sense of common identity and worldview capable of withstanding the impact of slavery."[18] C. Eric Lincoln and Lawrence H. Mamiya identify this interchangeably as either "the black sacred cosmos or the religious worldview of African-Americans,"[19] which made sense of the world by giving explanation for, and meaning to, the structure of domestic and global white supremacy. This worldview transcended the doctrinal idiosyncrasies of specific religious groups or organizations. Lincoln and Mamiya further contend that the "direct relationship between the holocaust of slavery and the notion of divine rescue colored the theological perceptions of black laity and the themes of black preaching particularly in those churches closest to the experience." The biblical exodus story and the statement that "Ethiopia shall stretch forth her hands to God" (Psalms 68) led generations of Africans and African Americans to anticipate the eschatological "Coming of the Lord" and to have faith in God's interest in the plight of Africa and black people in diaspora. The ability of the slaves to make the Judeo-Christian texts useful enabled them to create an alternative perspective that combined the best of their folk culture with lingering African components and the religion of the New World. John L. Gwaltney argues that "core black culture is more than ad hoc synchronic adaptive survival. Its values, systems of logic and world view are rooted in a lengthy peasant tradition and clandestine theology."[20]

Where religious hierarchies were replaced or supplemented by ideological ones among Europeans in the interest of supplanting the monarchic absolutism of the state with the democratic impulses of bourgeois revolutions, African Americans and other diasporan blacks employed religion and ideology in various ways in their social movements in order to achieve liberation and freedom, *not as much from Europe's absolutism as from the subsequent democracies*. Much of the African American encounter with religion in the New World was experienced with markedly different priorities than those forged among whites in Christian Europe and North America, and this is especially clear within the "power matrix" where the latter dominated. In due time, the Declaration of Independence was the response of the colonists. As universal as natural rights ideals seemed facially, they were narrowly construed in the courts and in society to exclude blacks from "We, the people" or the "we" who are "created equal."

Haiti: A Revolution Within a Revolution

The rhetoric concerning Great Britain's oppression of the *slaveholding* colonists was widely promoted prior to the outbreak of violence. David Brian Davis notes how, for instance,

> slaves and their supporters wrote increasing numbers of petitions. . . . The contradiction between the principles of the American Revolution and any defense of the dehumanizing institution of slavery became harder to evade, especially when slaves themselves began speaking the language of natural rights. This language had not been available even to the most rebellious slaves from Roman times to mid-eighteenth century Jamaica. But now, from Massachusetts to South Carolina, slaves heard whites shouting indignantly about British threats to liberty and the urgent need for resistance to prevent colonists from becoming "enslaved."

Amid the last great bourgeois revolts, the Haitian Revolution (1791–1803) reiterated the clash between the competing interests of those seeking liberty from God's earthly vicegerents in monarchy and those seeking liberation from the global structure of white supremacy that peaked during the enlightenment in America. Benedict Anderson concurs that the likes of Peruvian leader Tupac Amaru (1740–1781) and Toussaint L'Ouverture in Haiti were typical of the peasant-oriented restiveness that disturbed the bourgeoisie of Spain, France, and (Thomas Jefferson in) the United States.

Prior to the outbreak of violence on the island of Saint-Domingue, black slaves had been deserting their plantations with increasing frequency, especially as contact with the escapist Maroons increased. If one accounts for the many internal conflicts among the various antiblack bourgeois interests, including the petit blanc, the free mulattos (initially), the French, British, and Spanish, and white planter elements, that sought to control the most bountiful of all the colonies prior to the Haitian Revolution, and the influence of the French Revolution (1789), events in Haiti represented a revolution *within* revolutions. The revolutions in America and France clearly informed social and political relations in Saint-Domingue (as Haiti would inform theirs for generations), but when the Haitian Revolution commenced, its inspiration was a Petwo voodoo religious service held at Bois-Caiman on August 14, 1791, not the storming of the Bastille in July two years earlier. Just before the violence in Haiti, its initial leader, Dutty Boukman, held a service where a woman named Ce'cile Fatiman, believed to be possessed by Ogoun, the voodoo warrior spirit, sacrificed a black pig and identified the leaders of the slaves and Maroons who should seek justice from their white oppressors and their supporters.[21] Boukman is believed to have proclaimed in August of 1791, "the god of the white man calls him to commit crimes; our god asks only good works of us. But this god [of ours] who is so good orders revenge! He will direct our hands; he will aid us. Throw away the image of the god of the whites who thirsts for our tears and listen to the voice of liberty that speaks in the hearts of all of us." The oath was largely religiously neutral—the same prayer and oath could have been spoken by a Catholic priest on the French side. It was sealing the oath with the blood of the black pig that led its earliest European witness to call it "African barbarism." Laurent Du Bois insists that "the insurrection required community and leaders, and there is little doubt that, in one way or another, religious practices facilitated the process of its organization. Once the insurrection began, religion helped inspire insurgents, and solidified the power of certain leaders."[22]

"Such a Thing as Black Religion"

In *The Souls of Black Folk*, Du Bois contends that two of the most important *antecedent* entities to emerge among antebellum, Reconstructionist, and post-Reconstructionist black people were, first, an at-large black church—E. Franklin Frazier's "invisible institution"—which preceded the black family structure under chattel slavery; and second, the office of the black preacher, which he regarded as "the most unique personality developed by the Negro on American soil." Charles V. Hamilton also identifies the black preacher—the central personality of the organized church—as the critical "linkage figure" that encouraged black communities through several "traumatic experiences" and "abrupt cultural transformations" that include "the slavery epoch, the post-bellum social environment in the rural South, and the westward and northern migrations to the ghettos."[23] Thus Du Bois suggests that black religion be studied "as a development, through its gradual changes from the heathenism of the Gold Coast to the institutional Negro Church of Chicago."[24] Charles Joyner contends, colonial plantation slaves created "a new culture, predominantly African in origin, but different from any particular American culture." Indeed "to underestimate the Africanity of African-American Christianity is to rob the slaves of their creativity. Africans were creative in Africa; they did not cease to be creative as involuntary settlers in America." He continues: "The African-American Christianity that developed was neither a dark version of the Christianity preached by slaveholders nor a continuation of African religion disguised as Christianity. The story of the emergence of African-American Christianity is a story of an emergent African-American culture as well as of residual African cultures, a story of innovation as well as of tradition, a story of change as well as of community."[25] Moreover, Du Bois describes the "successive steps of the social history" of the black religious life, noting

> that no such institution as the Negro church could rear itself without definite historical foundations. These foundations we can find if we remember that *the social history of the Negro did not begin in America.* He was from a definite societal environment. . . . *The first church was not at first by any means Christian nor definitely organized*; rather it was an adaptation and mingling of heathen rites among the members of each plantation, and roughly designated Voodooism. *Association with the masters, missionary effort and motives of expediency gave these rites an early veneer of Christianity, and after the lapse of many generations the Negro church became Christian.*[26]

For Orlando Patterson, African American religiosity and religious tradition were in some ways vestigial. Studying Jamaica, Patterson located persistent African religious traits such as ancestor worship, funereal rituals, and esoteric medicine rituals at the center of plantation life. He rightly insists that Obeah played a prominent role among Caribbean insurrectionists.[27] With time and spatial disconnections between them, the religious world of African Americans was at times hostile toward the "heathenism" of African and Caribbean religious practices of Vodun (voodoo). The importance of religion in the historical narratives of black Americans collectively and in individual biographies points to a broad antecedent valuation structure that subsumed all facets of life—economic, social, political, cultural—and resonated throughout the diaspora of African and hyphenated African peoples for much of four centuries. It was supraordinate to myriad ideological, organizational, associational, institutional, and individual-level groupings and subsequent subhistories, even though it may have developed differently in, say, Brazil or Haiti than in the United States.[28] Reluctant to analyze the religiosity of the burgeoning black consciousness among the African slaves, Cedric Robinson nonetheless contends that "the transport of African labour to the mines and plantations of the Caribbean and subsequently to what would be known as the Americas meant also the transfer of African ontological and cosmological systems; African codes embodying historical consciousness and social experience; and African ideological and behavioural constructions for the resolution of the inevitable conflict between the actual and normative."[29] Durkheim's classic sociological explanation of religion in *The Elementary Forms of Religious Life* (1915) suggests that religion is a social product that in the aggregate is engendered by a "collective effervescence" that emerges out of the shared experiences of groups and individuals, experiences such as slavery and its social, legal, and political aftermaths and not merely its ultimacy and transcendent contemplations.

Formations in slavery and racial oppression homogenized Africans and consequently created a procrustean black American racial identity that subsumed lost

African ethnicities beginning with the Middle Passage journey and shedding them almost entirely by the American Civil War. Walter Rodney notes:

> The similarity of African survivals in the New World points not to tribal peculiarities but to the essential oneness of African culture. That culture was the shield which frustrated the efforts of Europeans to dehumanize Africans through servitude. The slave may have appeared in a profit and loss account as an "item," a "thing," a piece of "property," but [they] faced [the] new situation as an African, a worker, and a [hu]man. At this level of perception, it is quite irrelevant to enquire from which tribe or region a particular African originated.[30]

For centuries this was omnipresent among blacks, slave and free, educated and illiterate, New Englander and southerner, male and female alike— as was the ideology of white supremacism that was born not in fascism or Nazism but in antecedent Western liberal thought tradition.[31] Stephen Skowronek argues that the amenability of appropriable language, moral claims, and ideas (across time and contexts) accommodated the ways in which modern liberalism vis-à-vis elite southern apologists such as John C. Calhoun and Woodrow Wilson underwrote programmatically illiberal intentions in American racial regimes such as slavery, Reconstruction, Jim Crow segregation, and in pertinent foreign policy areas. Orlando Patterson highlights the extent to which at least the Scotch-Irish segment of southern society meshed its fundamentalist Protestant honor code with a totalitarian fixation on control of black lives, especially *after* abolition, to the point that it "fused Christian and 'racial' supremacist civil religion so that each powerfully supported the other."[32] In fact, "throughout the South, among all classes the preoccupation with the ex-slaves became obsessive. The hatred, fear, loathing, and horror of Afro-Americans attained levels of emotional, political, and religious intensity that are hard to imagine."[33] Among the newly free, black male bodies, in particular (but not exclusively), were at the center of the cannibalistic lynch rituals that were inspired by this largely mainstream version of Euro-American Christianity. To capture the contradiction, Countee Cullen's critically unsuccessful poem "Black Christ" (1929) depicts a young militant black man named Jim—who defended the honor of a (white?) woman who was insulted as "a Black man's whore"—as a potential lynch victim in the carnival of ongoing lynchings for whom Jesus becomes proxy, disguising himself as the intended lynch victim, just moments before Jim nearly becomes the "queer fruit of some outrageous tree."[34]

Sterling Stuckey places Robeson, Du Bois, and historian Carter G. Woodson in the camp of those African American scholars and intellectual leaders who traced certain African cultural influences in the early black American social world. For Stuckey, Robeson especially felt that black Americans were betwixt and between both realities—African and American—but their "emotive, intuitive, and aesthetic" structures were "too radically different" *to be simple conduits of white cultural values,* Victorian or otherwise. Stuckey notes: "Robeson realized what few scholars in the United States knew at the time, that there was such a thing as black religion in the Caribbean and in the United States, religions with their own distinctive characteristics." He continues: "The achievement of Robeson's scholarship on African 'survivals' is all the more evident when one takes into account the extreme backwardness of America's colleges and universities vis-à-vis Africa and its descendants in diaspora."[35] Paul Robeson, of course, was a practitioner of the Sorrow Songs of which Du Bois wrote in *The Souls of Black Folk* and, more readily than Du Bois, was inclined to see the development of black nationalist thinking in relation to the enduring cultural influence of African American religion. Robeson argues, for instance, that African American and West Indian blacks "[worship] the Christian God in [their] own particular way and make him the object of [their] supreme artistic manifestation which is embodied in the Negro spiritual."[36] Woodson maintained, "Negroes themselves accept as a compliment the theory of a complete break with Africa, for above all things they do not care to be known as resembling in any way these 'terrible Africans.'" For Woodson the negative feelings that black Americans in the 1930s felt toward Africa stemmed from a massive "miseducation" that could be overcome only through focusing on the linkages between Africa and African Americans. But also the attempt of the early-nineteenth-century American Colonization Society (ACS) to deport free blacks prompted many individuals and organizations to decline association with Africa or things African. The A.M.E. Church was one institutional exception. Still, Woodson subscribed to the belief that the "spiritual makeup" of African Americans, especially as expressed through the "arts," proved that "nothing is ever destroyed altogether. And what the Negro accomplished in Africa was not lost. His art tended to revive in the slave on the American plantation. It appeared in the tasks, proverbs and riddles of the plantation Negroes. The tribal chants of the African paved the way for the spirituals, the religious expression of the slaves."[37] Black religion has developed in separate and mostly in the unmediated enclaves of black life. It is the *single area* where black Americans felt a sense of moral and cultural *superiority* to Euro-American whites due to their perfidy in failing to materialize the ethical mandates of the religion. Blacks' cultural rendition of the Sorrow Songs, ring shouts, and their very different sense of collective destiny than that envisioned by most Euro-American whites is captured by the slave testimonials in Albert J. Raboteau's *Slave Religion*.[38] The ring shout was a source of great consternation to conservative bourgeois black religionists such as the A.M.E. bishop Daniel Payne and the Euro-American white preachers precisely because it resembled an immediate West African regional influence among *African American* slaves and was subsequently emulated by white revivalists. Raboteau (like E. Franklin Frazier before him) highlights a confrontation between Bishop Payne and a leader of the ring-shout band where the former demands that the "ignorant masses" of slaves cease from acting out the ring shout. Payne notes,

> They did for about fifteen minutes. I then went, and taking their leader by the arm requested him to desist and to sit down and sing in a rational manner. I told him also that it was a heathenish way to worship and disgraceful to themselves, the race, and the Christian name. In that instance they broke away. After the sermon in the afternoon, having another opportunity of speaking alone to this young leader of the singing and clapping ring, he said, "Sinners won't get converted unless there is a ring." Said [Payne] "You might sing till you fell down dead, and you would fail to convert a single sinner, because nothing but the Spirit of God and the word of God can convert the sinner." He replied: "The Spirit of God works upon people in different ways. At camp-meeting there must be a ring here, a ring there, a ring over yonder, or sinners will not get converted." This was his idea, and it is also that of many others. . . . To the most thoughtful . . . I usually succeed in making the "Band" disgusting; but by the ignorant masses . . . it was regarded as the essence of religion.[39]

What Payne sought to make disgusting among the masses of uneducated slaves, for its un-Christian and so-called heathenish character, created even greater discomfort for Euro-American white religious elites whenever the un-Protestant musical and dance styles of slave worshippers influenced whites. John Gwaltney notes,

> The notion that black culture is some kind of backwater or tributary of an American "mainstream" is well established in much popular as well as standard social science literature. To the prudent black American masses, however, *core black culture is* the mainstream. The minority of black Americans who significantly depart from core black customs and values may pass, may become bourgeois in spirit as well as income, or swell the ranks of marginal drug and welfare cultures. But far more often than not, the primary status of a black person is that accorded by the people he or she lives among. It is based upon assessments of that person's fidelity to core black standards. The categories "real thing" and "jackleg" cover the spectra of statuses, professions, occupations and character. There are doctors and doctors, clergymen and clergymen, cooks and cooks, professors and professors, and we know the difference. Exemplary heroes are rare in any culture, but most black people are well within the ordinary, acceptable, drylongso standards of core black culture. Most black people agree, on all levels of consciousness and in their overt actions, on what these specific standards are.[40]

Black Religion as Antecedent and Cultural Ideology

If Africans and African Americans internalized the widespread social and intellectual sentiments concerning their cultural inferiority—the more "cultured" blacks notwithstanding—it was slow in penetrating their religious life. It might explain why, for instance, Du Bois placed the untitled, unauthored musical bars of the Sorrow Songs side by side with the works of Europe's cultural talents at the beginning of all but the last chapter of *The Souls of Black Folk* (1903). Rare is the perspective that contends that the Negro spirituals, tonally, viscerally, and in pathos, had anything to do with Euro-American white cultural production; if they were incubated in race oppression, they were not mimetic in the least. This does not deny the pervasive influence of the puritan social milieu in North America, but it is pertinent that any "white over black" rendering of African American and Euro-American white social relations at the cultural subtext is unsustainable. No subsequent movement, political ideology, or elite cadre of individuals has had so powerful a centripetal socializing effect as the black American slavery epoch and racial oppression in accordance with hegemonic use of law, religion, economics, and violence. This experience provided a way of ordering the world for African Americans historically and spatially. It also ran adjacent (and not subordinate) to the "big idea" of white supremacism that developed out of modern liberal market and Christian missionary ambition—not in its xenophobic or racist frocking but in its totaling quality as an essential way of reading the world and interpreting the contours of social and political relations. It derived from a definite shared experience in which the basis of oppression is perennially the most powerful common denominator. It would be unprecedented among the many and various oppression narratives of the modern era for black Americans to fail to develop a commonsense spiritual orientation in response to their traumatic and collective oppression.

Whereas religion and ideology represented "top-down" phenomena among most Europeans and most Euro-American groups—Catholic and Protestant— before they were limited by the various bourgeois states and societies, blacks sought to employ religious faith, spiritually and socially, as a "bottom-up" means to undo the effects of the very racial hierarchies. Du Bois's *The World and Africa* (1944) and Robinson's *Black Marxism* (1983) maintain these were in part the product of West European aristocratic, intraracialist, and hierarchical thought that extended to modern democracies. Melissa Harris Lacewell largely views the African American employment of ideology as an inversion of its hegemonic, even totalitarian, qualities. She insists that "once we allow that the African American counterpublic is operating beyond the reach of powerful whites, we must allow for the possibility that the ideological work being done in that counterpublic is distinct from the hegemonic work of elite discourse."[41] Michael Dawson contends that "just as ideology can sustain oppressive regimes, ideology can sustain the resistance that is developed out of counterpublics such as the black public spheres of the [nineteenth] and [twentieth] centuries."[42] A major driving force in these oppositional ideological projects—some being more loyal to the social order than others—has been a broadly conceived sense of efficacy steered by religious motivation.

Contextual exigencies that relate to the various material circumstances of people of African descent powerfully shape the character of individual, group,

or national consciousnesses and mood. Nevertheless, the modern constructions of race and racism incubated and, conversely, provided a basis for the
subversion of racial proscription by producing a contrary set of ideas for
African Americans, such as a concern with deliverance, freedom, democratic
idealism, racial realism, and moral agency in the form of a black religious
ethos. To be "ideological" in the African American experience implicated a
broader self-determination ethic that would become more or less salient based
on the mobilization of a particular ideological bias in a given context. Even before there was what George Shepperson identifies as a troika of exchange in
ideas, values, and commerce among black Africans, African Americans, and
West Indians, aspects of the centrality of religious expression by Africans and
their diasporic progeny appear to have extended across the Middle Passage
and remained integral to the development of subsequent strategies, organizations, and ideological programs throughout the struggle for civil, political, and
economic equality rights.[43] Eugene Genovese hypothesizes that the intensity
of nationalist militancy among black slaves in the Americas generally was attributable to the nature of their religious socialization. Black religion—in its
pre–New World, pre-Christian, and non- and anti-Christian forms—fostered a
critical tradition of insurrectionism and cohesion among black slaves in other
sections of the Western Hemisphere that would be suppressed and retarded by
southern Protestantism among African Americans due to its predominantly
pacifistic and otherworldly orientations. Thus "a decisive break with the white
man's church [in the United States], if not wholly with his religion [Christian-
ity], has formed a major part of black Nationalist thinking."[44] The religious
worldview of African Americans has been successfully mobilized around a
long line of ideological orientations, political movements, and competing political elites. Michael Dawson's analysis concerning the relationships between
black political ideologies and black public opinion reiterates the ongoing influence of black nationalism in contemporary "community nationalist" discourses, but black religion provides a more comprehensive trajectory of black
nationalist discourses in general. It is also a major component of "community
nationalism," as it continues to organize important social and political aspects
of African American life. Studies that do highlight the relationship routinely
treat religion as a collateral influence.[45] Dawson concedes that his use of "the
crude instrument of public opinion,"[46] although useful in empirically gauging
aspects of black political thought, is devoid of the historical elasticity that I
contend is provided in fundamental elements of African American life, such as
black religiosity. In his recent work, Dawson treats black political ideologies
as competing sources of influence in the black social and political quest for
justice. And this is certainly the case, but black religion (or religiosity) inter-
links the several major traditions like no other historical force, save perhaps
white supremacism itself. This is especially the case with liberal integra-

tionism and black nationalism, which together formed the contours of black political discourse from the antebellum period to the late twentieth century. It is the focus of the next chapter.

Notes

1. Michael C. Dawson, *Black Visions: The Roots of Contemporary African-American Political Ideologies* (Chicago: University of Chicago Press, 2001), p. 5.

2. Ibid., pp. 11–12.

3. Winthrop Jordan, *White over Black: American Attitudes Toward the Negro 1550–1812* (Chapel Hill: University of North Carolina Press, 1968), pp. 181–183.

4. Ibid., p. 198. Emphasis in original.

5. See David Walker's *Appeal: To The Coloured Citizens of the World, but in particular, and very expressly to those of The United States of America*, with an introduction by James Turner (Baltimore: Black Classic, [1830] 1993), pp. 79–80. This is problematized by the fact that the antediluvian world was subsequently wiped out (including Adam's direct descendants) according to the "Great Flood" myth of Genesis 6. In the postdiluvian "new" world of Noah and his family, blacks ostensibly inherited the so-called Curse of Ham (actually, Canaan), which explained dark skin pigmentation and, subsequently, a cover for racial slavery. It remained *the* perennial doctrine of race in Judaic and Christian circles for much of the nineteenth and twentieth centuries. Indeed, the latter borrowed from the former to such a degree that Jordan cites Talmudic and Midrashic sources before concluding that the Curse of Ham was at least initially "a specifically Jewish rather than a Christian" religious teaching. The Genesis account of this story actually refers to a curse cast upon "Canaan" and his descendants, not Ham. Ham's presumed racial identification as "black" derives from the Hebrew, which can be rendered "hot, heat, or black." For a brief but informative critique of this doctrine, see Winthrop Jordan, *White over Black*, pp. 17–20, 35–37, and 40–43.

6. See E. Franklin Frazier, *The Negro Church*, p. 19: "God will reward me [the slave]; and indeed I have good reason to be content and thankful and I sometimes think more so than if I was free and ever so rich and great; for then I am to serve God in the state in which he placed me. I am to do what my master orders me."

7. See the letters to Philemon and to the Ephesians (ch. 6:5–9). Both citations are from the *New International Version* of the Bible.

8. Richard Boeke, "Black Mystic of San Francisco: A Collection of Photos and Remembrances of Dr. Thurman," *Creation Spirituality Magazine* (March/April 1991): 12–16.

9. Cited in Wilson Jeremiah Moses, *Black Messiahs and Uncle Toms: Social and Literary Manipulations of a Religious Myth* (University Park: Pennsylvania State University Press, 1982), p. 221. Original source is Albert Cleage Jr., *Black Christian Nationalism* (New York: Morrow, 1972), p. 44.

10. Orlando Patterson, *Rituals of Blood: Consequences of Slavery in Two American Centuries* (New York: Basic Civitas, 1998), p. 229. It is the sacrificial component of the Paulinian message that contributed to the thinking of many African American elites, such as Martin Luther King Jr., that the suffering of Jesus for the redemption of all humanity be transposed to black Americans who, like Christ, had to suffer to the point of death to "save the soul of America."

11. Ibid., p. xvi. Emphasis added.

12. Eugene Genovese, *Roll, Jordan, Roll: The World the Slaves Made* (New York: Vintage Books, 1972), p. 162.

13. Cornel West, *Prophesy Deliverance!*, p. 35.

14. Gayraud S. Wilmore, *Black Religion and Black Radicalism: An Interpretation of the Religious History of African Americans*, 3rd ed. (Maryknoll, NY: Orbis Books, 1998), p. 24.

15. Ibid., p. 25.

16. W.E.B. Du Bois, *Dusk of Dawn: An Essay Toward an Autobiography of a Race Concept* (Piscataway, NJ: Transaction, [1940] 1984), p. 117.

17. Cornel West, "Black Strivings in a Twilight Civilization," in Henry Louis Gates Jr. and Cornel West, *The Future of the Race* (New York: Vintage, 1996), p. 79. Emphasis in original.

18. Lawrence Levine, *Black Culture and Black Consciousness: Afro American Folk Thought from Slave to Freedom* (New York: Oxford University Press, 1977), p. 13.

19. C. Eric Lincoln and Lawrence H. Mamiya, *The Black Church in the African American Experience* (Durham, NC: Duke University Press, 1990), p. 2. The main elements of their sketch of the sacred cosmos are mostly appropriate, although not exclusively, to black Christian adaptations. These typically find empathy in the oppression ethos of a suffering Christ who, like the race as a whole, suffered an injustice that was part of the redemptive work of God. This explains the state of nature theologies of early Christian and "black Muslim" nationalists who attributed slavery to some Edenic offense of the race precipitating both fall and redemption schemes or in "Yacub's history." Emphasis is also placed on the importance of human personality, where all people are universally "one in Christ" as equal "Children of God."

20. John L. Gwaltney, *Drylongso: A Self-Portrait of Black America* (New York: The New Press, 1993), p. xxvi.

21. Laurent Du Bois, *Avengers of the New World: The Story of the Haitian Revolution* (Cambridge: Belknap Press of Harvard University Press, 2004), pp. 99–101.

22. Ibid., p. 101.

23. Charles V. Hamilton, *The Black Preacher in America* (New York: Morrow, 1972), pp. 33–35. The literature on black religion as it relates to black politics inevitably focuses on the African American church in general and the black preacher in particular. As a leader of a nearly hegemonic institution tending to the needs of blacks in their struggles for social and political dignity for at least two centuries, the preacher was the natural spokesman for their communities. The significance of "public" preachers, such as Martin Luther King Jr., Malcolm X, Louis Farrakhan, Ben Chavis (Muhammad), and Al Sharpton, may be due to an appropriation of this aspect of black cultural and political tradition.

24. See Phil Zuckerman (ed.), *Du Bois on Religion* (Walnut Creek, CA: Altamira, 2000), p. 45.

25. Charles Joyner, "Believer I Know: The Emergence of African-American Christianity," in Paul E. Johnson (ed.), *African-American Christianity: Essays in History* (Berkeley: University of California Press, 1994), pp. 18–19.

26. Zuckerman, *Du Bois on Religion*, pp. 50–51. Emphases added.

27. Orlando Patterson, *Rituals of Blood*, p. 228. His perspective later prompted Wilson Moses to note that Patterson "would seem to support the view that black religion constitutes a support for the black nationalist spirit." *Black Messiahs and Uncle Toms: Social and Literary Manipulations of a Religious Myth* (University Park: Pennsylvania State University Press, 1982), p. 24.

28. Kim Butler, *Freedoms Given, Freedoms Won: Afro-Brazilians in Post-Abolition São Paulo and Salvador* (New Brunswick, NJ: Rutgers University Press, 1998). For in-

stance, a coherent "black consciousness" developed in Brazil only after the idea of *negritude* conjoined the various mulatto and black populations in the 1930s. This was achieved gradually, after more powerful intervening forces (e.g., religion and African slave importation patterns) supplanted concerns for Brazilian national identity with larger pan-African interests.

29. Cedric J. Robinson, *Black Marxism: The Making of the Black Radical Tradition* (London: Zed, 1983), p. 174.

30. Ibid., p. 345.

31. This also complicates the notion that all Americans are mere ethnics, that black Americans, like Euro-Americans, are an ethnic group whose nationalism reflects ordinary patterns of transported ethnicity. Slavery was an artificial transformation of black life where diasporan blacks operated as the gatherer-laborers in social relations and were uniquely property *itself*; workers, due to racial classification and not social class alone, seldom owned their black bodies. Please see Countee Cullen, *The Black Christ and Other Poems* (New York: Harper and Brothers, 1929), p. 95. The entire poem is printed on pages 67 to 110. It is dedicated "Hopefully to White America."

32. Orlando Patterson, *Rituals of Blood*, p. 208.

33. Ibid., p. 192.

34. Jim's nameless brother, who raises the matter of theodicy concerning God's apparent goodness in light of perennial racial oppression, goes to the heart of Cullen's rendition. Jim's mother, the black matriarch described in the poem as "Job's dark sister," determines to hold to faith against the grotesque vicariousness of post–World War I black life. The protagonist is the older brother of Jim, and he moves from agnostic and atheist thought and feeling to a life of faith as Jim, seemingly and miraculously, has been saved from lynching.

35. Sterling Stuckey, *Going Through the Storm: The Influence of African American Art in History* (New York: Oxford University Press, 1994), p. 199.

36. Ibid., pp. 198–199.

37. Ibid., p. 127.

38. Albert J. Raboteau, *Slave Religion: The "Invisible Institution" in the Antebellum South* (New York: Oxford University Press, 1978).

39. Ibid., pp. 68–69.

40. John Gwaltney, *Drylongso*, p. xxiii. Emphasis in original.

41. Melissa Victoria Harris-Lacewell, *Barbershops*, p. 13.

42. Michael C. Dawson, *Black Visions*, p. 51.

43. George Shepperson, "Notes on American Negro Influences on the Emergence of African Nationalism," *Journal of African History* 1, no. 2 (1960): 299–312.

44. Eugene Genovese, *Roll, Jordan, Roll,* pp. 410–411.

45. It is pertinent that the relational direction of black nationalism and black religion (or religiosity) as variables can be interchangeable where public opinion is properly treated as a dependent variable in its relationship to black political ideology generally. This is to say, one can measure black nationalism by virtue of religiosity (e.g., attendance or membership at congregations with an "Afrocentric" theology, such as Detroit's Shrine of the Black Madonna) or religiosity by virtue of the type of black nationalism one embraces (e.g., Islamic [Nation of Islam] or Christian [First African Methodist Episcopal Church] and the Reverend Cecil Murray of Los Angeles or the Reverend Eugene Rivers III of the Azusa Christian Community in Dorchester, Massachusetts).

46. Michael C. Dawson, *Black Visions*, p. xii.

3

The Religious Content
of Black Political Ideologies

*Let the white world keep its missionaries at home to teach the Golden Rule
to its corporate thieves. Damn the God of Slavery, Exploitation and War.
Peace on Earth.*

— W.E.B. Du Bois, *The World and Africa*

Black religion possesses both ideological and theological properties that are
integral to understanding black politics generally and the political orientations
of many of the African American political elites who have advanced various
ideological programs since the nineteenth century.[1] It has been influential in
shaping the different ideological standpoints (radical, conservative, reformist,
revolutionary, feminist) that African Americans have embraced over centuries.
The interaction among these various ideological orientations tends to be a fair
measure of concrete social relations and political conditions relating specifically to the saliency and continuity of internal black political developments
expressed most commonly—as opposed to formal politics—in forms of black
nationalism.

Black Nationalism and Black Religion

A major practical and theoretical problem concerns how or whether the various
ideological projects have interacted differently with black religion and what conditions tend to elicit their interaction in black political life. Whether African
American religion and black political ideologies should be conceptualized
epiphenomenally is a question that filters a definitional problem, which in turn
emits a problem concerning the lineage of a given perspective.[2] Why, for instance, has Islam traditionally interacted with African American social and political life from a "nationalistic" perspective politically and not the integrationist
perspective? Prior to the establishment of Wallace Deen Muhammad's World

Community of Islam in the 1970s, there was no noticeable Islamic integrationism in the United States. However, strains of Christian black nationalism have interacted with Christian integrationism since the nineteenth century. It raises the question concerning which social teachings or religious instruction contribute to the multiple qualities of Christianity, to the extent that it has facilitated Christian emigrationism, Christian black nationalism, and black liberal integrationism. Given this history, why has the recent integrationist movement in the United States had more in common with Judeo-Christian social justice discourses when compared to the nationalistic movements? What "core elements" of black religion reciprocate or betray the distinctive elements of the major political ideologies in African American social thought and political history? And how have these elements served African Americans in the late twentieth and early twenty-first centuries as they relate to their material relationship to the American polity and to African American political development?

Patricia Hill Collins clarifies that because black nationalism was "honed at the intersection of political ideology and religion, Black nationalism may have a similar utility for African Americans. Historically, Black nationalism's flexibility has allowed African Americans to reshape it in response to the specific political challenges raised by slavery, Jim Crow segregation, industrialization, and urbanization."[3] This explains how C. Eric Lincoln, for example, can insist that "for the black masses, black religion and black nationalism are often one and the same, in effect. . . . As a result, black nationalism sometimes assumes the character of religion."[4] Slavery and other legal forms of black oppression in the United States were precipitous in forging the collective sense of destiny among African Americans that was facilitated by their religious heritages. And it is not suggested by this observation that nationalists are more religious per se than are integrationists or socialists. It is to suggest, however, that in the trajectory of black political mobilizations where nationalism has been salient, so, too, has black religiosity—whether as a source of political efficacy (as in the case of the nineteenth-century black nationalists) or as a source of religious criticism against Christianity (as in the case of David Walker's *Appeal* and the Nation of Islam).

James Cone adds that

> Black nationalism was not primarily a Western, "rational" philosophy, but rather a black philosophy in search of its African roots. It was a cry for self-esteem, for the right to be recognized and accepted as human beings. Its advocates knew that blacks could not survive politically or economically in complete separation from others, especially whites in the United States. . . . Everyone was interdependent. The black masses, therefore, did not follow nationalists because of their call for separation from America. Rather it was because of the nationalists' ability to speak to their "gut level" experience, that is, to express what it *felt* like to be black in white America.[5]

Here Cone identifies the perennial visceral sensibility that has been at the center of black nationalist discourse in the United States. The jeremiad has the capacity to articulate the psychical disposition of black people's sense of justice and unreconciled injury. The genesis of the black radical tradition has roots in African American religion, not in the Western radical traditions and not entirely in the frames of European and white North American Christianity. Thus Eugene Genovese notes, "for blacks, the national [issue] expressed a duality as something both black and American . . . in the dialectical sense of simultaneously being itself and the other, both separately and together, and of developing as a religion within a religion, in a nation within a nation."[6] If indeed it is implausible to suggest that black nationalism is synonymous with traditional religious articulations among African Americans in particular, it is plausible to suggest that their histories are *inseparable*. The cultural rootedness inherent in religion is at the heart of Benedict Anderson's oft-mentioned "imagined" nationalist communities, particularly where he asserts that "nationalism has to be understood by aligning it, not with self-consciously held political ideologies, *but with the larger cultural systems that preceded it, out of which—as well as against which—it came into being.*"[7]

Studying black religion's integrality in African American social life has been of interest to historians and theologians, yet even for social scientists the social and political commitments of individuals such as Martin Luther King Jr., Ella Baker, Fannie Lou Hamer, Bayard Rustin, Malcolm X, Jesse Jackson, Al Sharpton, and Louis Farrakhan would be incomplete and truncated, their political movement activities uninspired, and their ethical commitments unrelated to the moral dimensions of black political life in America without some understanding of the force of religion in black politics. To ignore the details, for instance, that Malcolm X and Louis Farrakhan were major critics of the African American church (as well as of the mainstream secular forces in civil rights such as the NAACP) even as they operated *within* the spheres of black religion (of the Islamic sort), and that this criticism exposes an ideological influence in black religious thought and practice in the post–civil rights period, misses a critical point. Martin Luther King Jr. provided temporary relief from the church's antipathy for organizing politics, and he accomplished reiterating its social justice tradition in civil rights and in his later criticisms of capitalism and war imperialism. King is relevant especially because he and Malcolm X were contemporaries who contested over the best social strategy (integration versus nationalism), offered alternative but similar philosophies of *strategic* violence (for King, white violence was indispensable to his boycott and direct-action approaches; for Malcolm X, the rhetoric of self-defense was key) and contested over religious orientation (Christianity versus Islam).[8]

To the degree that religious traditions have been integral to forging collectivist identities among individuals and groups in societies, then, the African

American ideology-religion nexus is not unprecedented.[9] But its particularity rests on the fact that in the absence of distinct centripetal cultural elements such as a shared indigenous language, ethnic ties, or even a common (national) territorial source, black religion (traditional African, Protestant, and Islamic) has been a primary socializing force in shaping a sense of solidarity among many African Americans.[10] As in their religious constructions of solidarity, African Americans have also utilized nationalism differently from white Europeans and North Americans.[11] The parallels among African American, European, and Euro-American appropriations of nationalism, for instance, are not consonant because African Americans were not major protagonists in the various "European transitions" that led to "modernity." If and when black people were relevant to these transitions, they were so acknowledged as cultureless historical objects rather than subjects. Robert Carr explains:

> New World Black history thus develops in a state-sanctioned and irreversible violence, in Africans forcibly transported and sold as captive labor and incorporated into the bottom of the social structures of European design. Initially the narratives justifying such administrative policy were religious, at a historical moment in which European political economic agendas were generally justified in religious terms. . . . If African-American and West Indian black nationalism start as mass movements, . . . it is because the state and federal government of the United States in the cases of African-Americans and West Indians, as well as England in the case of the latter, make it clear that they have reserved a special pocket of brutality and dehumanization of peoples of color in the New World, that they cannot be of the people/nation represented. Rather, in the West's elite national political imaginaries, people of color are deliberately constituted as potential threats to those whom surviving states represent. This alienation by and from the states is constitutive of the shared history of black citizenship of blackness as a sociopolitical category in the New World.[12]

Black Nationalism and the Mainstream of African American Christianity

The proximity of the emergence of black nationalism historically to the periods in which religion, religiosity, and the separatist/independent black churches were prominent among African Americans anteceded all other ideological expressions and social movements,[13] including the Christian missions, missionary emigrationism, colonization, abolitionism, and the early civil rights, "back to Africa," territorial separatism,[14] "Africa for the Africans," and modern civil rights movements. The black theology movement's endeavor to construct a "theological methodology based on black nationalist affirmation"[15] sought to insert a new type of political spirituality into the most important center of institutional life of African Americans. In 1965—probably as a result of his encounter with Albert Cleage Jr.—Malcolm X conceded, "*the political philosophy of black nationalism is being taught in the Christian church.*"[16] But African American Christianity did not (and does not) respond favorably to the call to black solidarity in the churches. Although black religious traditions provide the interpretive basis for reading black nationalism, their salience has been only epochal and marginal. A related dilemma of black religion as it functions in the lives of African Americans institutionally reveals ideological and strategic problems concerning its traditional ties to liberal integrationism, which, at least until the early Elijah Muhammad/Malcolm X and Martin Luther King discourse, was considered a *radical* force in American politics, particularly as it was linked with the NAACP and other organizations. In this chapter I therefore track the process that Gayraud S. Wilmore's *Black Religion and Black Radicalism* (1978) describes as the "deradicalization of the Black church," occurring between post–Reconstruction and World War I, and the "dechristianization of Black radicalism," beginning in the 1920s with the "New Negro" and Garveyism. During this period, black nationalism, first identified with Christian political elites such as David Walker, Martin R. Delany, Henry Highland Garnet, James T. Holly, and Bishop Henry McNeal Turner in the nineteenth century, is supplanted by twentieth-century Islamic and "cultish" movements such as the Moorish Science Temple of Timothy "Noble" Drew Ali and the Nation of Islam of Elijah Muhammad. This process extended to the 1960s and 1970s Black Power movement and partially explains the later attempt of Louis Farrakhan to organize the Million Man March around religious rather than political themes. The Nation of Islam, particularly during the last decade of Malcolm X's public ministry (1955–1965), crystallized its most biting criticisms of the African American Christian church and its prominent preachers like Martin Luther King Jr., Ralph Abernathy of the Southern Cristian Leadership Conference (SCLC), and, to a lesser extent, Congressman Adam Clayton Powell Jr. of Harlem's legendary Abyssinian Baptist Church. The Nation of Islam and its criticisms were instrumental in prompting at least Albert Cleage Jr. (of the Shrine of the Black Madonna Church in Detroit) to construct a Christian nationalist apologetic in admiration of and defense to the Nation of Islam's critiques. Former NAACP executive secretary Benjamin Chavis was one of its 1960s student adherents in Wilmington, North Carolina. He, Cleage, and Chicago's Jeremiah Wright Jr. all employed black nationalist perspectives within the institutional structure of the white-majority—but progressive—United Church of Christ. In the mainstream of African American Protestant churches, black nationalism has largely been poorly received.

In tandem with the waning civil rights movement, black institutions—from the church to radical student organizations such as the Black Panther Party—suffered the fate of near irrelevancy to black communities for jettisoning the religiously derived nationalist appeals that readily facilitate the perception among individual black people that their fates are linked with African

Americans generally.[17] It was also a point not lost on Nation of Islam leader Minister Louis Farrakhan and (then) NAACP executive secretary Minister Benjamin Chavis in the 1990s.[18] It exposes a dilemma in "practical theology."[19] Peter Paris suggests, for instance, that

> the black churches' tendency to promote a "soft" nationalism (i.e., a temporary experiment in racial self-development) dissipated all inclinations toward work-ing for long-term goals of consolidated economic and political power. . . . In short, their ideal vision of a racially integrated society militated against most long-term strategies necessary for the race's full development. Thus, ironically, the long years of commitment to "racial uplift" on the part of the black churches were destined to nonfulfillment, because their ideal vision contra-dicted the idea of separate racial development.[20]

Scholars interested in the study of the sociological, political, and histori-cal aspects of black religion have chronicled the manner in which it has steered "spiritual energy" into political movements in the United States since at least the nineteenth century.[21] This is also true of the various twentieth-century so-cial movements that were driven by the various nationalist, radical-socialist, and liberal integrationist mobilizations among black people.[22] Michael Daw-son's insistence that "in order to understand black ideologies, it is important for the theory and research communities to understand how political discourse developed in the black community, the degree to which it differed from dis-course in the American polity at large, and equally how it influenced and was influenced by discourses in American society" is instructive.[23] In this chapter, black religion provides an excellent beginning point to this end. Patricia Hill Collins insists for instance, that the

> Black public sphere developed a split between the sacred and the secular as interconnected dimensions of Black community life. The two spheres held a common belief in spirituality. In this sense, the split between the over-whelmingly Christian . . . formal religious traditions in Black church culture and the secular spirituality that has formed the creative foundation of music, dance, and other aspects of African American creative cultural production constitute two sides of the same coin. When combined, a spirituality that can take sacred or secular form constitutes an important dimension of African American ethnicity.[24]

For Collins, a nationalistic academic orientation such as Afrocentrism not only possessed patently religious properties of assigned morality and values, bi-nary insider-outsider markers, functionality, theodicy, and authority; it also constitutes "civil religion." This is equally applicable to Black Power, which most scholars fail to link with its *religious* influences—from Martin Luther King and Malcolm X, on one end, to black liberation theology on another. Collins explains, "one reason that religious expressions of Black nationalism have garnered support is that African Americans have long used religion and faith-based sources of resistance to racism."[25] This observation comports with C. Eric Lincoln's contention that "for African Americans . . . religion is never far from the threshold of consciousness, for whether it is *embraced with fervor* or *rejected with disdain*, it is the focal element of the black experience."[26] In even the most "irreligious" renditions of hip-hop pop culture, for instance, religious symbolism and representations abound.[27] For Collins, this influence is sometimes overlooked because the academy values scientific over faith-based considerations.[28] The linkages between religious and political life among African Americans continue to powerfully shape black politics and intellectual discourse. Black nationalism can be understood as more than ideology or philosophy; it also derives from principles or values of solidarity that do not always find neat articulation in formal or informal politics.

It would be expedient, in writing, simply to outline how religion (or religiosity) has intersected in relation solely to social, cultural, and political developments in black nationalist political histories; after all, that is the focus in this book. Yet it is important, as no single ideological formation has developed in a vacuum, to focus as well on social and political elites and their ideologies among African Americans more broadly. It is also pertinent to elucidate the intersecting processes through which religion, both socially and institutionally, has filtered through the major ideologies employed in the black freedom struggle, as it may attest more to the strategic choices of elites afforded them by the "political moment" in which they function than to some reified difference in the distributive qualities of black religion. Black religious traditions were as accessible to "proto"-nationalist individuals as they were to emigrationists, abolitionists, twentieth-century nationalists (Garveyites), socialist radicals, pan-Africanists, and integrationists. Both black Christian and Islamic radical critiques have formed constellations around a few consistent themes; they are no more the product of "nationalistic" Islam than they have been of "prophetic" or integrationist-prone Christianity, though the manner in which they have operationalized their different interpretive and theoretical frameworks has varied. They include *anthropomorphicity of God* (i.e., God's "racial identity" or identifying with the conflicting racial groups), *the social and political agency of the Black church*, and regard for *affinities and antipathies of community or "brotherhood" with Euro-Americans*. Chapter 6 includes a fourth category, namely attitudes toward *self-defensive or emancipationist violence or nonviolence*.[29] These several categories highlight crucial inclinations that point to distinctive characteristics and linkages between African American political ideologies and African American socioreligious traditions as they emanate from the black sacred cosmos. They also represent perennial discourses, conversations that have been spoken by political leaders and intellectuals with some regularity, that hopefully anchor the analysis.

The Anthropomorphism of God

Religion has validity in politics to the extent that it is serviceable to the social needs and political demands of oppressed people and dominant social groups as they define them within contested politics.[30] The anthropomorphic qualities of God have theological meaning for religionists and theologians in ways that are largely useless to oppressed people unless they can be appropriated to their material life circumstances in the daily encounters with the particularity of their oppression. The temporal nature of God or the question of God's corporeality in the African American political experience has had less to do with theological abstractions concerning the divine "putting on flesh" than with its activities in human history. Regardless of whether God is about ultimacy, is transcendent to history, or participates in history, it is likely that individuals and groups in society and politics will locate God within the social locations of the parties in conflict. In the realm of politics, there is neither time nor space for neutralists: God must either choose sides or suffer being made in the image of people and their politics. The theological debates concerning the nature of the relationship between human culture and politics to deity is a discourse in *power*, and it is therefore as much a political as a theological matter. E. Franklin Frazier urged that "the 'color' of God could only assume importance in a society in which color played a major part in the determination of human capacity, human privilege, and human value. It was not and is not a question of whether God is physically black, but it is a question of whether a man who is black can identify with a white God and can depend on His love and protection."[31] Political scientists, however, tend to leave such matters to theologians, sociologists, anthropologists, and historians despite the obvious concern for "who gets *God* when and how"—to borrow from Harold Laswell's early notion of political power—and despite the perennial importance such notions have held across centuries of African American social and political thought. The belief that a supreme God could have links to un-Christian "heathen" Africa was prohibited by the relatively "new" and "scientific" idea of race and racism. Cornel West summarizes his analyses of this development by noting that "it also highlights the cultural and aesthetic impact of the idea of white supremacy on black people. This inquiry accents the fact that the everyday life of black people is shaped not simply by the exploitative (oligopolistic) capitalist system of production but also by cultural attitudes and sensibilities, including alienating ideals of beauty."[32] The degradation of black people in modern social and political history made a black God inevitable. C. Eric Lincoln suggests its more salient features include the promotion of ethnicity and the forging of group solidarity.[33] The religious worldview that African Americans forged beginning at least in the late eighteenth century employed an image of God that had particular utility in fortifying a self-conscious sense of linked fate among them. Identifying oneself phenotypically with God (or the gods) is an ancient rite of peoples throughout the world.[34] What is most exceptional about this artifact of African American religious thought, nevertheless, is that such a notion was achieved among a people whose fundamental *humanity* had been discredited in fields of law, science, and theology in the modern world.[35] For Dwight Hopkins, "A black God affirms every physical characteristic of what the United States calls black. . . . And on the psychological and emotional level, praying to a white male god has meant, in the context of North America, too many black people willingly giving their complete selves to the very same image of the system and structure of the supremacy of whites over blacks."[36] White supremacist cultural praxes and beliefs rendered the possibilities of black humanity, beauty, and enlightenment empirically problematic at best and otherwise unconscionable. The rationalist and scientific assumptions of Western race-culture saturated modern cultural discourse along crude hierarchic structures that produced idealized notions of beauty. Black was thought to be antithetical to these standards.

In the American context, to consider God's "whiteness," "blackness," "redness," or "maleness" is to raise the larger issue of divine sanction or divine will for domination or liberation in social and political life. The idea or reality of God cannot escape the human tendency, as Karl Marx has noted, "to make religion" that validates politics. The rabid anti-Jewish and anti-Semitic commitments from Martin Luther to Adolf Hitler's German Evangelical Church reveal how the structure of Euro-Western Christianity, as it relates particularly to the plights of black people globally, could contribute to southern white Protestantism the notion that God was on the side of white people in racial and social conflicts. White supremacist religionists who, for instance, participated in slaveholding, the lynch mob, or touted the 1950s slogan "God is a charter member of the White Citizens Council" interpreted the ministry of Jesus of Nazareth as "pro-white" because in canonical texts, anachronistically, he never overtly condemned the institution of slavery or racial separation and because selected readings in the Paulinian writings tolerated it among early Christians (Jesus's ministry to the poor and oppressed in Luke 4:18–19[37] and Matthew 25:31–36[38] notwithstanding). An accompanying corollary to God's whiteness is the devil's blackness. As much as David Walker, Du Bois, Noble Drew Ali,[39] and Malcolm X explored the association of white attitudes and conduct toward blacks with evil incarnation—as race "devils"—a tradition of associating the specter of unmastered blacks with Satan emerged in the South after the Civil War. Indeed one of the common explanations for Confederate defeat highlighted by Orlando Patterson was a racist and religious "fundamentalist emphasis on satanic influences," epitomized in black bodies. Moreover, he notes, "Afro-Americans became to the body politic what Satan was to the individual and collective soul of the South. For both, the same metaphor of a 'black' malignancy to be excised was employed. As is well known, Satan, like sin, is always portrayed as black."[40]

Kelly Douglas argues that the view of the "white Christ" had the deleterious effect of justifying slavery and slaveholding among Christians, enabling African Christians to be slaves and for slaves to be treated cruelly.[41] For Du Bois, God's anthropomorphic character was not a trivial matter, and it took particular shape in "A Litany at Atlanta," which he wrote (while "a bit hysterical") in response to a brutal pogrom there in 1906. Writing on a train headed for Atlanta, where his wife and daughter were at the time, Du Bois wails,

> Have mercy upon us, miserable sinners! And yet, whose is the deeper guilt? Who made these devils? . . . Is not the God of the Fathers dead? . . . Doth not this justice of hell stink in Thy nostrils, O God? How long shall the mounting flood of innocent blood roar in Thine ears and pound in our hearts for vengeance? Pile the pale frenzy of blood-crazed brutes, who do such deeds, high on Thine Altar, Jehovah Jireh, and burn it in hell forever and forever! . . . *Surely, Thou too, art not white, O Lord, a pale, bloodless, heartless thing!*

William R. Jones raises the question "Is God a white racist?" in his interrogation of the early black theology movement known as Black Power.[42] For him, "The crucial determinant of God's favor is . . . what is accomplished for the group in whose midst he appears. The liberation event is more critical, at least from the standpoint of theodicy, than the event of incarnation."[43] Thus Jones is concerned to show that despite the 1960s black theologians' various claims to God's coequal suffering with black people, and God's reputation as liberator of oppressed people (e.g., the biblical Hebrews), history has yet to reveal a single event where God liberates black people *as black people*.[44] All evidence points to antiblack "divine racism."

W.E.B. Du Bois's Jesus

Religion—existentially, institutionally, and at the individual level—is interspersed in the prose, intonation, and thematic structure of W.E.B. Du Bois's third book, *The Souls of Black Folk* (1903),[45] and much of his scholarly work thereafter. It is Du Bois, more than any other intellectual figure between Reconstruction and World War I, who sustains a "Christology" of Jesus as a black man.[46] Wilson Moses insists that a "messianic quality had been present in *Darkwater*, where [Du Bois] had waxed poetic once again, conjuring up visions of black gods and goddesses, portraying the masses of Southern black folk as a mystical body of Christ, bruised and suffering for the sins of America."[47]

Du Bois's manner of using religious metaphors, biblical allegory, and empirical and critical knowledge of church history and sociology warrants a closer reading of religion's place in his texts, as well as a reconsideration of his personal religiousness—particularly his reputation as an "agnostic."[48] With various apparitions, Jesus is presented as Christ-child with a black Madonna and again as a Negro stranger in Texas and Georgia—barely escaping the lynch mobs of white Christians.[49] Editorials from the NAACP's *Crisis* publication and other writings demonstrate Du Bois's awareness of the need to also link the paramount symbols of religious tradition (Christ, Madonna, angels) to the esteem of African Americans between the major wars.[50] In Du Bois's vast familiarity with biblical religion, Christ and Mary are variously presented as having a "mulatto" "olive," even "yellow" complexion. Mary is a black woman with a son named Joshua whose skin was "black velvet" with "curly hair." For Du Bois, the incarnation of God—personified in Jesus of Nazareth—warranted a not so subtle association with black people. He noted, for instance, "Jesus Christ was a laborer and black men are laborers. He was poor and we are poor; He was despised of his fellow men and we are despised; He was persecuted and crucified, and we are mobbed and lynched." Thus, "If Jesus Christ came to America He would associate with Negroes and Italians and working people; He would eat and pray with them; and He would seldom see the interior of the Cathedral of Saint John the Divine."[51] Du Bois often separated Jesus of Nazareth from the religion of his white Protestant followers and locates Jesus on the side of subaltern blacks. Herbert Aptheker notes that "if Du Bois is not the first who writes of a Black God, he is certainly among the earliest to express this view and he repeatedly draws a parallel between lynching as practiced by Americans and crucifixion as practiced by the Romans." Du Bois is pertinent to a version of confrontational black Christianity by virtue of his withering criticisms of the nation's religious establishments, especially in "The Souls of White Folk" (in *Darkwater*), where he criticizes "the utter failure of white religion." He adds, "A nation's religion is its life and as such white Christianity is a miserable failure." This is the Christianity of slavery, racism, profit, and war—in his words, "the religion of J.P. Morgan," not that of Jesus of Nazareth.[52] But the undeniable fact of radical abolitionist John (Osawatomie) Brown militated against a total indictment of all manifestations of Euro-American Christianity for Du Bois: *John Brown's was the most authentic expression of prophetic Christianity.*

More so than even major scholars like Benjamin E. Mays and E. Franklin Frazier, Du Bois was among the "first generation" of black church historians and sociological and proto-theological theoreticians of the religious world of African Americans.[53] Du Bois was not a committed theologian in the mode of Howard Thurman, Joseph Washington, Gayraud Wilmore, Mordecai Johnson, or James Cone. Yet serious study of "black religion" must take the unprecedented analyses evident in Du Bois's major works into account. If the meaning of black theology has to do with God's redemptive and salvific work among blacks in the course of slavery, black codes, Jim Crow, the "white riot," and lynching that permeated the lives of African Americans after Reconstruction, then Du Bois was, theologically, *disappointed.* Du Bois suggests, rhetorically, that God is responsible for the tragic suffering of black people—*that*

God created the racist. His response to the Atlanta riots is replete with such disappointment in the providential responses to blacks' predicament—in which white Christianity was deeply implicated. It was one of several factors that fueled his dubiety. But if the meaning of black theology has to do with God's identification with the struggles of black people (*as black people*) and the racial identity of the Christian deity (Jehovah, Jesus of Nazareth, the Holy Spirit[54]), then Du Bois's work should conceivably be considered its precedent.

James Cone's Black Power–era commitment to the construction of a "theological methodology based on black nationalist affirmation" exposed the conspicuous and earlier retreat in the Christian tradition from the revolutionary space that had been occasionally carved among Christian "insurrectionary" religionists and "proto" and "civilizationist" nationalists during the nineteenth century. The notion that the main deity of the two biblical covenants could take on human personality or human attributes—indeed, incarnation—has a particular resonance that, at various stages, has streamed into the major black religious traditions. Both the Christian and Islamic traditions of *the nationalist* sort have placed the question of God's racial identity at the center of their ideological discourses. It is worth noting that this pattern of signification has not resonated as consistently with liberal or radical integrationist elites. The absence of a similar consonance or continuity among either the liberal or radical integrationist traditions marks the question of God's racial identity as exceptional to the nationalist tradition.

In this context, African American individuals such as David Walker, Maria Stewart, Henry McNeal Turner, Timothy "Noble" Drew Ali, Marcus Garvey, Father Divine, W.E.B. Du Bois, and Albert Cleage Jr., as well as black theologians (and a few preachers) impacted by 1960s black consciousness, constructed idealized notions of God's personification in two particular forms. The first resorted to a simplistic chauvinistic retort that "God is black"; the second more frequently concerned Jesus's matrilineal racial-ethnic identity. Laden in the hetero-masculinist social mores (God as Male/Father, Messiah as Male/Son) of the various periods, proponents attempted to construct reflexive and yet affirmative aesthetic devices, which celebrated putatively "Negroid" hair, complexion, and hues. Nationalist and pan-Africanist intellectual Edward Wilmot Blyden contends:

> No one can deny the great aesthetic and moral advantages which have accrued to the Caucasian race from Christian art, through all its stages of development. . . . But to the Negro all these exquisite representations exhibited only the physical characteristics of a foreign race . . . they had only a depressing influence upon the Negro, who felt he had neither part nor lot, so far as his physical character was concerned, in those splendid representations. . . . It was our lot not long since to hear an illiterate Negro in prayer-meeting in New York entreat the Deity to extend his "lily white hands" and bless the waiting congregations. Another, with no greater amount of culture, preaching

from 1 John iii, 2, "We shall be like him," exclaimed "brethren, imagine a beautiful white man with blue eyes, rosy cheeks, and flaxen hair, and we shall be like him." The conceptions of these worshippers were what they had gathered from plastic and pictorial representations as well as from the characteristics of the dominant race around them. The Mohammedan [Muslim] Negro, who is not familiar with such representations, sees God in the great men of his country.[55]

David Walker's *Appeal* referred to "the God of the Etheopeans" who would raise a black messiah to liberate them; but it was the disappointed Reconstructionist A.M.E. bishop Henry McNeal Turner who wrote that in the United States, "white represents God, and black the devil."[56] Thus, Turner insisted,

We have as much right biblically and otherwise to believe that God is a Negro, as you buckra or white people have to believe that God is a fine looking symmetrical and ornamented white man. For the bulk of you and all the fool Negroes of the country believe that God is a white-skinned, blue-eyed, straight-haired, projecting nosed, compressed lipped and finely robed white gentleman, sitting upon a throne somewhere in the heavens. Every race of people since time began who have attempted to describe their God by words, or by paintings . . . have conveyed the idea that the God who made them and shaped their destinies was symbolized in themselves, and why should not the Negro believe that he resembles God as much as other people? . . . Yet we are no stickler as to God's color anyway, but . . . we certainly protest against God being white *at all*. . . . This is one of the reasons we favor African emigration, or Negro naturalization, wherever we can find a domain, for, as long as we remain among the whites the Negro will believe that the devil is black and that he (the Negro) favors the devil, and that God is white and that he (the Negro) bears no resemblance to Him and the effect of such a sentiment is contemptuous and degrading.[57]

Under the weight of the intercontinental and universal rejection of "blackness" aesthetically and theologically in Christendom, pan-Africanist and nationalist intellectuals promoted the countervailing notion that they, too, were perfectly made in the image of God. C. Eric Lincoln notes that black religion "presupposes a God who identifies in a personal way with black people in a society where such human relationships are uncommon. Some black communities outside the conventional church even refer to a 'black God.' The practicality of having a God who is self-consciously black is, of course, the promotion of group solidarity, intragroup and spiritual." More important, "It is also the implicit denial that God is white, which is to be inferred from all of the cultural presumptions and behavior which identify as 'American.'"[58]

This theme resonated among the Moorish Science Temple of America, founded in Newark, New Jersey, by Timothy "Noble" Drew Ali during World War I.[59] Ali insisted that "Asiatic" religious traditions were less amenable to the racialist doctrines emphasized in Eurocentrist Christianity. Like Edward Blyden before him, and his contemporary Garvey, Drew Ali overstated the case of

Islam's record of race benignity.[60] Believing American blacks to be descendants of the conquering Moors of Morocco, Drew Ali and his followers insisted throughout major urban centers (New York, Detroit, Philadelphia, Pittsburgh, Baltimore, Chicago) and the South that blacks should have a nation of their own, within the definite boundaries of the United States, until they could claim their Moroccan birthright in the future.[61] In fact, he argued that "before you have a God you must have a nationality." As a Muslim, Drew Ali adhered to the tradition's strict prohibition against artistic or symbolic representations of Allah. The characterization of Islam as strictly aniconic oversimplifies the manner in which the tradition has employed visual arts.[62] Islam has "never developed a tradition of religious sculpture. . . . It is more accurate to say that Muslims never attempt to depict [Allah] God visually, do not use representational art in cultic settings at all (i.e., in a mosque), rarely depict Muhammad . . . and sometimes look askance at the depiction of other religiously significant figures."[63] Blyden notes the oft-neglected detail that among early Christians, who were mostly ethnic Jews, it was "believed that painting and sculpture were forbidden by the Scriptures, and that they were therefore wicked arts." Further, "among Mohammedans of Negroland [Africa] it is considered a sin to make even the rudest representation of any living thing on the ground or on the side of a house."[64] However, Drew Ali, who considered himself "the second prophet of Islam," wrote the Temple's sacred text: the "Circle Seven Koran." A major theme in the book is the "African genealogy" of Jesus.[65]

McGuire and Garvey constructed a theology replete with black saints, a black Madonna, and a black Christ. Louis DeCaro summarizes Garvey's overall impact on black American religious and political thought, noting, "Garvey and his followers may have inadvertently cleared the way for Islam among black nationalists in the United States. . . . He had irrevocably planted his black nationalist philosophy in the soil of the black liberation movement of the United States. *And perhaps the boldest stroke of that contribution was the creation of a black religion and a black God.*"[66] The idea of a black God impressed Garvey, but, like Blyden and Drew Ali, he was respectful of the Islamic tradition, which he studied under the tutelage of Duse Mohammed Ali in London in 1912.[67] Though the United Negro Improvement Association (UNIA) was institutionally nondenominational in its religious perspectives, Richard B. Turner reports a "cross fertilization of ideas between UNIA and Black Islamic leaders."[68] This cross-fertilization also reflected the personal religiosity of Garvey. Still, McGuire argued that "God is not a Negro; a spirit is nothing physical. But in one's prayer one must vision someone to listen, and we can think only of someone in human form. I had a picture in my mind of a white God. Now came the picture of a black God."[69] The Garveyite African Orthodox Church (AOC) emphasized Christ's Essenian African roots in order to provide a "new religion" for the black masses in the cities. This period produced the initial wave of northern migration among southern blacks, many of whom had been disenchanted with the racism they experienced on the part of white Christian leaders in the church and civil authorities.[70] The exploits of Father Divine (George Baker Jr.) are also related to this general critique of the Negro church, which predominated in Negro life institutionally from at least the late antebellum period. Divine's ability to provide for the followers of the interracial Father Divine Peace Mission movement during the Great Depression convinced many that he was, indeed, *the* deity. Divine's "Christian eclectic" movement, oddly, rejected racial theories of his "divinity," and his racial identification as a Negro had more to do with identifying with oppressed people than with blacks as a racial group.

The Nation of Islam did not advance an explicit doctrine of God's racial identity except to undermine assumptions of its "whiteness." In its view, the black man (and woman) is the "original man" who is closest to God in phenotype; in fact, the black man is divine and has a divine nature. The more important corollary was to mythologize the white man as a "blue-eyed" devil (born of Yacub's bad science), who oppressed black people through and with his "slave religion"—Christianity.[71] Many of the ideas in Yacub's creation story resounded with many southern émigrés in Detroit who felt the brunt of the racial violence (of both the North and the South) and economic desperation during the Great Depression.[72] This would be a favorite device of Malcolm X's in the late 1950s and early 1960s,[73] but after his split with the Nation of Islam his April 1964 "Ballot or the Bullet" speech expressed a different sentiment:

> I studied this man Billy Graham who preaches white nationalism; that's what he preaches . . . the whole church structure in this country is white nationalism. You go inside the white church, that's what they preach, white nationalism; they got Jesus white, Mary white, God white, that's white nationalism. . . . Don't join a church where white nationalism is preached, now you can go to a Negro church and be exposed to white nationalism. When you are in a Negro church and you see a white Jesus, and a white Mary and white angels, that Negro church is preaching white nationalism.[74]

The concern with the anthropomorphic qualities of God and Christ (i.e., Christology) was also integral to the critical view of the proponents of Black Power and black consciousness. Consistent with pre–World War II nationalist constructions of God, Christ, and Mary, post–Black Power religious intellectuals of the nationalist strain continued to stress the doctrine of a corporeal deity and its pertinence to the collective uplift of ghetto-locked individuals. Albert Cleage Jr. especially attempted to reconfigure the Christian concepts of God, Christ, and the Madonna in a manner that had a theological basis in social reality. Cleage's black Christian nationalism set out to answer many of the charges of Elijah Muhammad and the Nation of Islam concerning the presumptions of the "whiteness" of American Christianity. Albert Cleage's was the first real attempt by Christian black nationalists to "recapture" the nationalist mantle from Muslim black nationalists since the "dechristianization of Black radicalism" that Wilmore traces. Cleage elucidated the distortions elaborated by the Nation of Islam, for which he had great respect; he even agreed with much of its Yacub "the bighead scientist" creation mythology. Cleage was critical of the weak social justice legacy of Christianity toward black Americans that was also being rejected by militant students on US campuses and in organizations such as the Student Nonviolent Coordinating Committee (SNCC). Reflecting the feelings and thoughts of many of his peers, Stokely Carmichael was as critical of Islam's impact on Africans as of Christianity's. He reminded a 1971 gathering of pan-Africanists that Islam is not, and has never been, indigenous to the continent of Africa despite its more tolerant disposition toward aboriginal peoples. Not only does Carmichael insist that "Islam is not an African religion"; "it invaded Africa, originating in the Middle East. The Muslim came with the sword in the most barbaric manner."[75] The publication of Cleage's *Black Messiah* (1968) and *Black Christian Nationalism* (1972) outlined the major tenets of his perspective. According to Cleage, (Jehovah) God and (Jesus) Christ/Messiah were ethnically black, as the pre-Renaissance artistic representations and "shrines" of the black Madonna and Christ-child reflect.[76] With the exception of Marcus Garvey, the great prophets of black Christian nationalism were mostly *non-Christian* black nationalists such as Elijah Muhammad, Malcolm X, Stokely Carmichael, and H. Rap Brown, then of the Black Panther Party.[77] Cleage, like Bishop Turner, was not obsessed with the matter of God's racial composite as a theological doctrine as much as he was concerned with emphasizing the bloodline of Christ (vis-à-vis the Moorish Science Temple and Du Bois)—a "black Messiah" (vis-à-vis David Walker) born of his black mother, Mary. He named his Detroit church the Shrine of the Black Madonna and worked closely with Malcolm X and the members of the National Committee of Black Churchmen, which began to promote a "Black theology of liberation" during the Black Power era. Adherents have sought to clarify an "unprecedented movement of theological restlessness and dissent in the Black community since the mid-sixties." The central commitment of the National Committee of Black Churchmen has been "reconciling the catholic and pietistic message of the Gospel with the needs to speak to the anomic Black condition, from *a* Black perspective." Chapman notes,

> Aware that the nationalist critique of Christianity was widely accepted by many in the African American community, prophetic black clergy leaders responded by subjecting the black church to radical, internal self-critique. Basically, they sought to defend biblical Christianity by confessing that they had failed to practice in their churches. By accepting the legitimacy of some aspects of the nationalist argument, black preachers were essentially asking young African-Americans to give Christianity and the church a second chance. The use of this strategy proved to be an effective defense at a time when many militant young people believed that it was impossible to be fully black and Christian at the same time.[78]

For James Cone, the notion of a racially constructed deity was indispensable to the existential needs and demands of black people. Jesus being identified as a working-class Jew in antiquity who came to "preach good news to the poor . . . to proclaim freedom for the prisoners . . . to release the oppressed,"[79] made it possible for him to be appropriated, in relation to possessing black racial identity, in the contemporary struggles of black people. For Cone a key component to the construction of "black theology" relates to "the story of black people's struggle for liberation in an extreme situation of oppression. Consequently there is no sharp distinction between thought and practice, worship and theology, because black theological reflections about God occurred in the struggle of freedom."[80] Cone insists further that the whole structure of black theology—that is, the understanding of God's work among oppressed black humanity—resided in the "degraded status of Blackness." A theoretically and empirically elusive concept, the element of blackness had, at its core, the quality of being black in a racially heterogeneous social order in which structures of power, hierarchy, and relations could be effectively determined by race. Thus, the appropriateness of emphasizing the "ethnic" strains of deity is important to Cone because "the blackness of God means that God has made the oppressed condition God's own condition."[81] In fact, "there is no place in black theology for *a colorless God* in a society where human beings suffer precisely because of their color. *The black theologian must reject any conception of God which stifles black self-determination by picturing God as a God of all peoples. Either God is identified with the oppressed to the point that their experience becomes God's experience, or God is a God of racism.*"[82] Altogether the line of inquiry and interest in enlisting God in history as a partisan to the nineteenth- and twentieth-century racial discourses became an important device of nationalistic religious political thought.

Liberal Integrationists

Integrationists have been more inclined to a "universalistic" understanding of God, which preempted an explicit racial imagery. In social and political contexts, specifically, integrationism as a tactical and philosophical orientation is arguably traceable to some elements belonging to the Negro Convention movement of the middle to late nineteenth century, the protest wing of Garrisonian abolitionism (which included Frederick Douglass and Sojourner Truth), and Reconstruction-era and World War I–era "neo-Garrisonian" associations, mainly in New England and New York. Integrationist thought concerning the anthropomorphism of God—that is, God's morphological and specific "human identity"—has rejected the idea that God could be race-identifiable or care exclusively for a particular community of people in terms of political matters. God, in this view, is pro nobis ("for the world") and is "no respecter of persons."[83] To this extent the integrationists have largely employed an anthropomorphic view of the deity that, consciously or not, betrays the normative, European, and North American hegemonic prescriptions concerning its character and image and that are traditionally packaged as *universal*—as if this "universalism" didn't possess inevitable and particular default ethnic or racial character. Even today one can witness African American churches that unquestioningly display representative images of God, Christ, and the saints as white, where the reverse is perceived as a *political* act to large segments of African American and white churches across the denominational spectrum. Biblical texts that insist, for instance, that "that which is of the flesh is flesh and that which is of the spirit is spirit" have promoted a dualism in integrationist thought where one can pray to a white God, be saved by a white Jesus, and seek the comfort of white saints and angels without them taking on any *particular* racial or ethnic significance. Emphasis is often placed on selected biblical texts, such as John 4:24, which insists that "God is a Spirit" and therefore removed from the political entanglements of human society.[84] In this light the ubiquitous image of a Euro-American deity, particularly Jesus of Nazareth, is only problematized by race "militants" and "troublemakers" in churches, within theological circles, and from the black community—not by those who are "spiritually minded." Such a perspective is consistent with the "otherworldly" orientation of African American religious thought that scholars such as E. Franklin Frazier, Gayraud Wilmore, and Gary T. Marx have noted.

The covenant arrangement between Yahweh-God and the biblical Hebrews, and the "Jewishness" of Mary and Jesus of Nazareth and his early followers has no racial or ethnic significance because their missions were not overtly "political." The racial-ethnic particularity of these narratives militated against the integrationist vision of an antiracist, interracial social order. However, the "great commission" to his followers was to carry the gospel message of redemption to the *goya* (non-Jews) in "all nations" and "whosoever believes" (Matthew 28:18–29; Mark 16:16–18). The Pentecostal gathering of Jews from "every nation under heaven" (Acts 2:5) and Paul's missionary journeys in rejection of traditional Judaism expanded the focus of the gospel to incorporate non-Jews into a newly forged covenant based on spiritual rather than racial criteria.[85] God's exclusivist interest in and covenant relationship with the biblical Hebrews take on a *spiritual* quality in the Paulinian perspective. With Paul, for instance, ritual practices of Judaism (such as circumcision and observance of Sabbath and other holy days) lose their ethnic specificity in deference to "higher" criteria: "*A man is not a Jew if he is only one outwardly, nor is circumcision merely outward and physical. No, a man is a Jew if he is one inwardly; and circumcision is circumcision of the heart, by the Spirit, not by the written code*" (Romans 2:26–29).

The troubling acceptance of Euro-American representations of the Christian deity should not lead to an a priori assumption that integrationist Christians were accepting of Protestant white supremacism ideologically or in practice. In fact, before the Nation of Islam and its elites emerged to render Christianity a white supremacist religion, *black Christians themselves* critically assailed "white Christianity" as a vulgar, oxymoronic misrepresentation of authentic Christian praxes.[86] Indeed, Winthrop Jordan reiterates the extent to which as early as the eighteenth century the comportment of race and religion had germinated in America, noting, "The English settlers most frequently contrasted themselves with Negroes by the term *Christian*, though they also sometimes described themselves as *English*. . . . By this time 'Christianity' had somehow become intimately and explicitly linked with 'complexion.'" By the end of that century the term "Christian" had evolved into a new term, which was "white"—some three centuries before the Nation of Islam made the notion popular in northern ghettoes.

Mark Chapman contends that the black Christian integrationist response to this corruption was the construction of an anthropomorphic view, which he actually calls a "theological anthropology" that emphasizes the "oneness of humanity" and the "interrelatedness of all life," based on the parentage of God as father of all humanity.[87] God is thus racially nonspecific, at least as it pertains to the question of God's "blackness."[88] For the integrationists, there was little question of God's particular interest in blacks collectively that was independent of God's interest in *all* people, at least until integrationist theological suppositions were challenged by the solidarity movements that emerged between the New Negro and Black Power movements. Kelly Douglas notes, however, that "such an image is not inviting to Black youth who are in need of developing positive self-images" and that "the centrality of White Christs in Black churches can potentially alienate significant segments of the Black community."[89] Nevertheless, the assumed "fatherhood of God," and unquestioningly embracing the Euro-American representation of deity, were, consciously or not, as much the political choices of integrationist religious intellectuals as the notion that God was *not* male or "God *is* black" has been, respectively, for womanist or male black nationalist intellectuals. The interpretation of a race-neutral God as it translated into the uneven power relationships in society rendered moot the ontological or theological *intent* of such notions in the real world.

Black Christian integrationist theologian Howard Thurman properly locates the God-color question within the context of a proletarianization of African Americans' determination to correct "the distortions of the story of the black man in the western world and in the Americas." The era after World War II produced a sense of black Americans' need to clarify their self-understanding as a people. Euro-American cultural norms, social mores, and symbols of beauty were jettisoned along with the old concerns; Du Bois noted it as "seeing oneself through the eyes of others." At the center of the historical distortions that Thurman notes was "the white mythology: that black is ugly, black is evil, black is demonic; therefore black people are ugly, evil, and demonic."

Commonfolk, peasant, and ordinary classes of African Americans began to promote an identity and self-image around the very item of denigration and discourse that contributed most significantly to black oppression by Europeans and Euro-Americans. He argues:

> The fresh word about the past had to take to the streets, giving rise to an informed public mind both within and beyond the black community. It had to be a common knowledge that would generate mass enthusiasm for building a different collective self-image, thus providing stature for the design to stake out territory in the domain previously dominated and controlled by white society. Such a reexamination of the roots of history did not exclude the origins of the common religion, Christianity. This emphasis found its most arresting statement in the Black Manifesto delivered to the churches, and in the concepts of the Black Jesus and the Black Madonna.[90]

Thurman's commitments in A. J. Muste's integrationist Fellowship of Reconciliation and its interracial Church for the Fellowship of All Peoples in San Francisco led him to conclude that these developments were "immediatist" and susceptible to the whims and winds of the various antiblack legal, social, cultural, and nativist elements, on one hand, and co-opting compradors and would-be messiahs of black youth, on the other. The epoch of Black Power and the shifting consciousness of Africans and African Americans powerfully influenced even Martin Luther King's conception of the Christian messiah in racial terms. Prior to Black Power, King answered the query "Why did God make Jesus white, when the majority of people in the world are nonwhite?" by stating,

> The color of Jesus' skin is of little or no consequence. The whiteness or blackness of one's skin is a biological quality which has nothing to do with the intrinsic value of personality. The significance of Jesus lay, not in color, but in his unique God-consciousness and his willingness to surrender his will. He was the Son of God, not because of his external biological make-up, but because of his spiritual commitment. He would have been no more significant if his skin had been black. He is no less significant because his skin is white.[91]

Understanding this to be "God incarnate," King conceded *after* Black Power that the corporeality of deity in the person of Jesus of Nazareth mattered and that "Jesus was not a white man."[92] Although black Christianity has been amenable to both nationalistic and integrationist strategies for social justice, it has been mostly inclined toward the latter's social and political orientation, as demonstrated most profoundly in the modern civil rights movement and efforts of elites in some of the African American churches and organizations. In fact, sociologist Orlando Patterson views the activities of the SCLC as a restoration of the authentic religion of Jesus in the United States, which otherwise floundered in white supremacy. He notes: "In the middle of the twentieth century a religion emerged that, for the first time since the death of Jesus, actually succeeded in creating a faith and a community of believers that came fairly close to the gospel of love, fellowship, commitment, and radical engagement that he preached. This was the revitalized Afro-American Christianity that took shape in the church-directed protest movements culminating in the Southern Christian Leadership Conference led by Martin Luther King Jr."[93] King himself sensed that the zeitgeist of black liberation and general white reaction to it confirmed that "the role of the Negro church today, by and large, is a glorious example in the history of Christendom. For never in Christian history within a Christian country, have Christian churches been on the receiving end of such naked brutality and violence as we are witnessing here in America today. Not since the days of the Christian catacombs has God's house, as a symbol, weathered such attacks as the Negro churches."[94]

Strategically, integrationism is interested in undermining discriminatory laws and policies in society while valorizing Anglo-American cultural values and institutions. Du Bois's double-consciousness thesis addresses black American integrationism particularly in terms of the desire of many people to resolve the citizenship problem of being viewed as noncitizens in their native land. Maligned by nationalists from Blyden to Garveyism and through to Baraka's black arts movement as sellouts of black interests, proponents of liberal integrationism invested in a version of constitutionalism that strongly relied on the ostensibly universalist sentiments of the Declaration of Independence and in the Civil War amendments and their enforcement by federal authorities.[95] In social movement politics, its proponents reiterated that enforceable citizenship rights and civil liberty protections have been earned through the sweat of the brow through centuries of uncompensated and cheap labor in slavery, through peonage sharecropping, and by the spilling of blood from US wars and social and political movements. Melissa Harris-Lacewell thus argues that "since Reconstruction, black political and economic fortunes have been tied to the strength of the federal government, and contemporary Liberal Integrationism continues to focus on government strategies for ensuring black progress."[96] And Edward Curtis IV writes how "for the oppressed, universalism can become a vehicle to articulate a more truly egalitarian social order. In African-American history, for example, leaders like Frederick Douglass and Martin Luther King, Jr., appropriated the universalism of American revolutionary ideals to fight for black liberation." Thus, "their actions show the power of employing an alternate 'signified' or definition of the universal in challenging oppression and exclusion. Sometimes, the source of the 'new' universalism may come from the very tradition that is seen as exclusionary."[97] At least since Abraham Lincoln was viewed as a kind of messianic figure after abolition, black Christian liberal integrationists have traditionally linked federal power with God's anthropomorphic activity on their behalf.

Radical Integrationism

There is also the matter of radical integrationism (i.e., socialism). The commitment of radicalism ultimately was integration into a reconstructed political, economic, and social order that provided for and enabled equality in society. And within it African American workers had neither special place nor special claim—despite their fundamentally proletarian character in the social relations of production of the United States.[98] The question of how African Americans perceived Marxism as atheism goes to the heart of how socialists generally understood the corporeality of God. There is a rich history of Christian socialism in which Jesus's proletarian credentials (as carpenter and leader of fishermen) are touted.[99] *But the proletarian Jesus was as white as the bourgeoisie's Jesus.*

If religion is counterrevolutionary in Marxist tradition, as many suppose, then we cannot expect there to be much consideration of an issue such as the anthropomorphism of God. It is largely a nonissue, which typifies the larger disconnect between religious African Americans and socialism, despite its egalitarian appeals. Historian Herbert Aptheker clarifies how the tensions between Marxism and religion (Christianity and Judaism) were existential, social, and emotive. The problems of how to understand and reconcile the forces of nature and the manner in which classes and class oppression emerge out of humans' alienation in both are the genesis of how Marx understood religious feeling in the world. Religion that oppresses or sanctions oppression is not religion in its essence in Marx's view. Friedrich Engels insists:

> The early Christians had a good deal in common with modern-working movements. Like the latter, Christianity was originally a movement of oppressed people: it first appeared as a religion of slaves and emancipated slaves, of poor people deprived of all rights, of peoples subjugated or dispersed by Rome. Both Christians and the workers' socialism preach forthcoming salvation from bondage and misery; Christianity places this in a life beyond, after death, in heaven, *socialism* places it in this world, in a transformation of society. Both are persecuted and baited, their adherents are despised and made the objects of exclusive laws, the former as enemies of the *human race*, the latter as enemies of the state, enemies of religion, the family, social order. . . . Three hundred years after its appearance Christianity was the recognized state religion in the Roman World Empire and in barely sixty years socialism has won itself a position which makes its victory absolutely certain.[100]

His optimism notwithstanding, Engels saw the first-century religious practice of Jesus of Nazareth as *revolutionary* because it "reverses the previous world order, seeks its disciples among the poor, the miserable, the slaves and the rejected, and despises the rich, the powerful and the privileged."[101] Winthrop Jordan insists that, despite the antiblack consensus that streamed through European and North American Christianity for four centuries, "especially after the Protestant Reformation, enthusiasm for equality in Christ tended to spill over into an alarming enthusiasm for equality in temporal conditions . . . because Christianity had always leveled the souls of men before God, it was potentially corrosive of the world's social hierarchies."[102] As for Du Bois, Jesus was to be separated from his modern followers' religious and political praxes. To Marx, Jesus of Nazareth was "the classical saint of Christianity [who] mortified his body for the salvation of the soul of the masses; the modern, educated saint *mortifies the bodies of the masses* for the salvation of the soul."[103] This, according to Aptheker, made Christianity the natural fit for African American slaves. Left to itself, it had patently revolutionary qualities—thus its co-optation by the modern bourgeoisie. Marx's famous statement from the 1844 paper "Contribution to the Critique of Hegel's Philosophy of Right" reads: "Religious distress is at the same time the expression of real distress and the protest against real distress. Religion is the sigh of the oppressed creature, the heart of a heartless world, just as it is the spirit of spiritless conditions. It is the opium of the people."[104] The widespread presumption of the atheism of Marx's criticism of religion pales against his affirmative understanding of religion as *expression*, *protest*, *sigh*, *heart*, and *spirit* in an erstwhile pathetic reality engendered by resource and material maldistribution. For all of Marx's "irreligious criticism" of religion, he nevertheless emphasized its existential functions *in* society—not in an otherworldly afterlife. Marx's opiate thesis is born of "this" world's realities. The tendency among scholars has been to emphasize the "opiate" critique in Marx at the expense of understanding that this reflex is a psychological and moralistic reaction to "real distress." And whereas Marx criticized religion as part of his general criticism of the bourgeois social world, according to Aptheker, he opposed atheists.

Since its founding, class-based conflict has existed in the United States. Yet a sustainable class consciousness among African Americans has been undermined by a perennial race consciousness and by reinforcing cultural variables—language, religion, ethnicity, race—that socialists have historically trivialized, especially as they function in heterogeneous societies.[105] Cedric Robinson adds, "The dismissal of culture, . . . as an aspect of class consciousness, did not equip the Marxian movement for the political forces which would not only erupt in Europe and the Third World, but within the movement itself."[106] According to Seymour Martin Lipset and Gary W. Marks, "intense and often violent discrimination against African Americans produced a distinct underclass that was regarded as a race apart from white workers, and which, as a result, was excluded from their political projects, including socialism."[107] Alternatively embracing nationalism (or nationalist ideals such as a "black god"), then, was considered anathema and potentially counterrevolutionary. Frank Barkenau suggests, for instance,

> In the political field, nationalism is the fact against which the Marxist theory breaks itself. There is a force which has proved definitely stronger in the modern world than the class struggle which for orthodox Marxists makes

the essence of history. The natural result was that the Marxists constantly tended to underestimate a force which did not easily fit into their ideas, and which at the same time was clearly contrasted with the ideals of the class-struggle. It became almost a mark of an orthodox Marxist to despise every nationalist feeling.[108]

And this was precisely because the proletariat could be confused by its national and international commitments. According to V. I. Lenin, this was the problem with the workers in the industrialized polities in World War I. The workers of the world did unite—*but under their respective flags*! Moreover, as Robinson notes, Marx's and Engels's own German priorities "made them generally unsympathetic to the national liberation movements of peoples (e.g., the Russians and Slavs) which historically threatened what Marx and Engels believed to be the national interests of the German people." Herbert Aptheker surmises, "On religion I would say, Marxism does not err in underestimating its lasting potential; in other areas I think Marxism did err in this direction—I mean in the direction of minimizing its potency and lasting force, I would say this is especially true as regards *nationalism*."[109] When Marxists eventually developed a position on the matter, they did so in deference to individuals, such as Harry Haywood, who understood the nationalist implications of the October Revolution, and also in response to organizational and ideological competition with Garveyism in the 1920s. In the introduction to "the 1928 and 1930 Communist International Resolutions on the Negro Question in the United States," Lowell Young concurs:

> While large numbers of Black people respected Communists for defending Negro rights, Blacks did not join the Party in large numbers for the following reasons: 1) its line on matters relating to religion placed the Party in direct opposition to the Church, the single most influential institution in the Black community; 2) instances of White chauvinism periodically occurred within the Party itself; and 3) the Party had done little organizing in the "Black Belt" South, the area in which the majority of Blacks living in the United States were then concentrated.[110]

Young also cites the influence of Garvey and Garveyism as a challenge to communism among Negroes. Moreover, the impression that left-critical social justice discourses tend toward atheism further exacerbated African American support in their potential as alternatives to and criticisms of capitalism and racism.[111] This issue troubled important black socialist preachers, such as the Reverend George Washington Woodbey,[112] James Theodore Holly (a pro-Haiti emigrationist), the Reverend Reverdy C. Ransom (Niagara movement), Hubert H. Harrison (African Black Brotherhood), and Bayard Rustin (Fellowship of Reconciliation). They felt, according to Philip S. Foner, more or less that "most [blacks] had no experience with any organization other than the church and could think of committing themselves to action only in religious terms. The

Bible . . . could be used effectively to imbue religion with radicalism and convince the black working class of the evils of the capitalist system and the virtues of socialism."[113]

Moving and preaching from Kansas to Nebraska and finally San Diego at the turn of the century, Woodbey was particularly committed to a Marxian fundamentalist view of society in which race, even as it affected African Americans, was a passing influence that would wither away with other forms of proletarian oppression (i.e., labor and class inequality).[114] His view of socialism was based on an anticapitalist social and economic biblical literalist interpretation of the Christian gospel. He subscribed to a version of radicalism that was increasingly influential through works such as "What to Do and How to Do It, or Socialism vs. Capitalism," later works like "What the Socialists Want," and more significant, "Why the Socialists Must Reach the Churches with Their Message."[115] In the latter, Woodbey maintains that

> the Socialists cannot win without reaching the millions of working people who belong to the various churches of the country. The only question is how best to reach them. I have found that there are a large number of our comrades, who seem to think that the way to do it is to attack the Christian religion as such. Or in other words that it is necessary to make atheists, infidels or agnostics of the professed Christian before you can make a Socialist out of him.[116]

Woodbey urged US leaders of the Socialist Party in the early twentieth century to reverse the perception that "too many socialists antagonized church members by linking antireligion with socialism."[117] Like Cornel West many years later, Woodbey vehemently rejected the teaching of other socialists that Christianity and socialism were irreconcilable and insisted that "the only way to successfully reach the church people is to show the church member that the economic teaching of the Bible and of Socialism are the same, and that for that reason he must accept Socialism in order to stand consistently by the teaching of his own religion."[118] Woodbey interpreted the "economics of the Bible" in consonance with socialistic ideas that emphasized a future society in which there would be sufficient provisions "to eat and decent places in which to live, [where] socialism would be fulfilling the fundamental ideas set down in the Bible."[119]

The general attitude of American socialists was to collapse the race issue into a more general criticism of social class inequality, and there was a tendency to dismiss religion altogether. Robin Kelley has suggested, "The songs, rituals, religious practices, and styles of ordinary black working people were in conflict with Communist ideology and practice (many African Americans not only showed irreverence for the Party's interracialism but refused to even consider questioning their religion)."[120] An unrelated but mitigating influence was reflected in the opposition of political elites such as Booker T. Washington, T. H. Fortune, and Marcus Garvey to black unionizing.[121] Despite the persistence of an African American radical-socialist line among political elites (such as Woodbey,

Cyril Briggs, Richard B. Moore, Hubert H. Harrison, Paul Robeson, Richard Wright, Ella Baker, A. Philip Randolph, Bayard Rustin, and Angela Davis), it has been no more successful in gaining widespread adherence among African Americans than among the general population.[122]

Black radicals influenced by the Leninist and Trotskyite camps in the Socialist Party and the Communist Party USA (CPUSA) like Harrison, Du Bois, Harry Haywood, and A. Philip Randolph (who never joined the CPUSA) were more disappointed in the racial character of US radicalism than in its antireligious tendencies and reputation. Disappointment characterized African American elites' experiences with American socialism, which partly explains why they looked more to Moscow than, say, to Oklahoma or New York for understanding the coherence between the suspect status of African Americans and Marxism. Cyril Briggs and Richard B. Moore's African Blood Brotherhood attempted to develop a bridge between the emergent black nationalist movement that was centered in Harlem and Soviet-inspired socialism, but the militant tradition of black nationalism and Marxism never developed harmoniously in the twentieth century. Indeed, the main positions of American radicals routinely led them to oppose Garvey and Garveyite nationalism and even banish those elites who were interested in black nationalism. Between 1920 and 1928, the Communist International formed a position on the self-determination of African Americans and their status as an oppressed and colonized nation within the United States. But the CPUSA developed its positions only at the behest of black radicals. For the balance of the twentieth century, it was African American individuals and organizations among the radicals who theorized that the black proletariat took on intersecting modes of oppression as workers and as blacks. Dawson contends that "the main proponents of a black nation in the United States . . . were revolutionary nationalists, such as the Republic of New Afrika, the African Peoples' Party, and the Nation of Islam and Leninist Communist organizations that were either predominately black or had significant black leadership, such as the CPUSA and many Black Leninist groups of the 1960s and 1970s."[123] Foremost among them was Haywood, who essentially forced the issues of self-determination and nationalism.[124] But Du Bois was less optimistic about Leninism in the CPUSA than those black leaders who embraced it during the early decades of the twentieth century, particularly because of its inability to account for the cultural particularities of groups and to transcend petty racialism.

African Americans preferred racial solidarity to other forms of solidarity essentially because their predicament as vulgarly exploited laborers in slavery and the sharecropping system was inseparable from their social status as an oppressed racial population. Dawson thus suggests that one of nationalism's appeals among African American workers is that it has been "the most racialized of the African American ideologies" at their disposal.[125] Ira Katznelson insists that ethnic white US workers tended to be proletarian on the assembly line but ethnically driven in neighborhood enclaves, where black workers and their families were unwelcome and unwanted. It is also true that with, perhaps, the consensus on expelling the "Garvey problem," African American radicals such as Randolph and Briggs were often too fragmented over tactics, ideology, and analyses to confront the duplicity of American radicals.

Cornel West contends that a priori assumptions of an incompatibility between "prophetic" Christianity and "progressive" Marxism emanate from the vulgarization and distortion of both traditions. Like Aptheker, he contends that "both focus on the plight of the exploited, oppressed, and degraded people of the world, their relative powerlessness and possible empowerment."[126] Wilson Moses contends, as have others, that "the Marxist conception of history is similar to the Christian concept of providence. Both envision a millennium in which the righteous living faithful will triumph over the sybaritic denizens of Babylon."[127] For West, the potential of the religious and ideological nexus is especially evident in the black theology of the "prophetic Christian tradition in the Afro-American experience." Through several stages extending from a critique of slavery, of institutional racism, of "white North American theology," of American "capitalism," and maturing to a critique of global "capitalist civilization," this tradition is most amenable to progressive Marxism. Yet the black experience with socialist and Marxist movements has been problematized for, among other reasons, their hostility toward religion, generally, and ignoring the revolutionary potentials of a racial criticism in the pre–civil rights United States, in particular. Christian socialism did not develop among African Americans to the extent that it did among white Christian socialists. The absence of religious appeals, even symbolic ones like the anthropomorphism of the Christian deity, was symptomatic of the larger problem of subordinating culture (African American religion and racial identity) to social class. There was no attempt to meet blacks where they were culturally in a manner in which Jesus was made in the image of the white ethnic proletariat in US socialist projects in the early twentieth century.

The Social and Political Agency of the Church

The institutionalization of black religion, from its early status as the "invisible institution," to its organizational formations in the "African" church (pre-Revolution), to the "Negro" church (antebellum era to after World War II), and to the "black" church (1960s–1990s), has influenced the predominant scholarly views on black religion. Social scientists have tended to focus on the doctrinal areas that emphasize the "social justice" orientation, a "spiritual otherworldliness" or "opiate" orientation, and a closely related "compensatory" perspective.[128] There is some consensus concerning its importance as "the central organ of the organized life of the American."[129] Sociologist E. Franklin

Frazier viewed the "Negro church" in largely negative terms and in terms of its compensatory tendencies.[130] In this perspective, the preacher-centered church and its emphasis on otherworldly concerns had the effect of undermining the full *integration* of African Americans into larger society. As a central community organization, it alleviated individuals' sense of rejection and reinforced isolation from the conventional society by providing them with alternative social networks, culture, and opportunities to develop individual talent. Frazier's analysis is among the first to suggest an inverse relationship between religiosity among African Americans and social and political integration. This was characteristic of the typical southern church in the antebellum period through World War I and even after. The predominant theological idea that history culminated in an afterlife divine plan of group deliverance (rooted in the biblical exodus theme) mixed well with the deferential aspects of the accommodationist social philosophy of Booker T. Washington that dominated social and political discourse during the late nineteenth and early twentieth centuries (1890s–1915).

In one sense, this ensured that African Americans would remain socially a people apart from the societal mainstream. A major aspect of Washington's famous discussion of separate political and social development between whites and Negroes in response to the collapse of Reconstruction in the post–Civil War period was reflected in a famous metaphor: "In all things that are purely social we can be as separate as the five fingers, yet one as the hand in all things essential to human progress." In another sense it guaranteed that retribution for social, economic, and political injustices on earth (e.g., chattel slavery, the black codes, the crop-lien farming system, racial segregation) would be carried out providentially—without human intervention in the form of political agitation.[131]

Gary T. Marx found that a negative relationship between religion and political behavior among African Americans and that religion's "calming effect" on blacks' political initiative is related to the fact that nonreligious blacks are more "militant" than "otherworldly" minded religious blacks.[132] However, the reformist type of militancy that Marx measures is fundamentally different from the confrontational modes that are associated with black radicalism in the middle to late 1960s.[133] Marx qualifies his findings that "at the time of the interviews, the outlook of the conventional civil rights groups and spokesmen had a great deal in common [and] participation in peaceful nonviolent demonstrations was encouraged. *For the purposes of this study . . . we judge militancy by commonly held standards of civil rights activists at the time the interviews were conducted.*"[134] By his own admission, "The relationship between religion and political radicalism is a confusing one," and "the effect of religion on race protest throughout American history has by no means been exclusively in one direction."[135] Orlando Patterson has argued alternatively: "Black religion in the Americas was not an alternative to protest nor an escape from worldly concerns, but an instrumentality through which chiliastic pre-revolutionary consciousness may have found expression."[136]

The Harlem-based "New Negro" of the 1920s was distinguishable—but not unprecedented—when compared to earlier generations essentially by a collective attitudinal shift that was expressed in artistic, literary, political, and cultural forms. The general disposition that emerged from this period was a militant one, and it was exigent among the various classes of blacks. It reflected changes in the group psychology toward the social domain of white society, toward the old Negro church of the South, and toward themselves, as a people, as they consolidated attitudes of race pride. It promoted group solidarity affirmatively among black individuals for the first time in their history in the New World. This fact led E. U. Essien-Udom to note how its patently black nationalist character "displays the mood of alienation from existing society."[137]

It was this militancy that simultaneously influenced Drew Ali and Garveyism. One of its critical objectives was to repeal the influence of the Negro church and the innocuous accommodationist racial orientations. Among the Harlem writers and poets, the likes of Countee Cullen, Claude McKay, Langston Hughes, and Zora Neale Hurston were either critical of, or altogether rejected, the southern Negro church and its embrace of Eurocentric representations of religion.[138] Historian Kinfe Abraham notes, "Both affirmative and rejectionist militancy became a characteristic Spirit of the New Negro which the Harlem poets exploited in their poetry of dissidence."[139] The overwhelming Caribbean influence in this development was in part related to the shock of their introduction to US white supremacism and Jim Crow segregation, with which African Americans had long been familiar. Yet this influence had negative implications for the Negro church, with which it had no historical connection in the United States.[140] Of the more than 140,000 black immigrants who were admitted to the United States between 1899 and 1937, more than 75 percent were Afro-Caribbeans who arrived between 1910 and 1924. The most "peripatetic of all African people," according to Winston James, they were typically skeptical of Christianity.[141] Indeed, Garvey's United Negro Improvement Association movement was considered more of a religious movement than a political one by E. Franklin Frazier. But from Garvey's own perspective, "[Garveyism] is not a religious movement purely, it is not a social movement, purely. It is not a political movement, purely, but it is a movement that includes all the wants and needs of the Negro. We are as much political as we are religious, we are as much religious as we are social, we are as much social as we are [entrepreneurial]."[142]

During this period Garveyism was attractive as much for its religious appeals as for the social, political, economic, and cultural ones it made to unprecedented numbers of blacks in the New World of blackness. Important segments of more ordinary African Americans in this period also opted to adopt alternative religious orientations, including the Nation of Islam, in the North.

Garveyism resonated with religiosity, and it was an essential aspect of UNIA's attractiveness to the masses-class of first-generation southern émigrés and emigrants in the North.[143] The northern elites, who were largely the descendants of previous generations of free blacks and pre-abolition former slaves, were more inclined to support the NAACP, although at times the political career of individuals such as William Monroe Trotter, E. D. Nixon, and Ella Baker entailed both. Garveyism took on the form of a religious mission for many Garveyites, but among its African American contingency the African Orthodox Church was less desirable than UNIA; most Garveyites did not belong to the AOC. Incidents such as the 1908 white riot in Springfield, Massachusetts; the widely publicized 1906 violence between white townsfolk and black infantrymen in Brownesville, Texas; the debut of D. W. Griffith's abhorrent *Birth of a Nation* (1915); and the thirty-six riots that occurred in cities across the nation between 1895 and 1921 gave Garveyism its great appeal among African Americans. In fact, the "mulatto" founder and leader of the Nation of Islam, W. D. Fard, and his successor, Elijah Muhammad, capitalized on the postwar racial climate in order to promote the notion that Allah identified with the oppression of blacks everywhere. The UNIA of Marcus Garvey emerged in New York City shortly after Ali emerged in Newark. Although Garvey had established the UNIA in Jamaica in 1914, he settled his international headquarters in Harlem in 1916, among the largest community of blacks (nearly 2 million), including recently uprooted African American and Afro-Caribbean communities. Garvey had an interest in seeing reform among the black Christian church, which he viewed as increasingly irrelevant to the struggles of blacks. Garvey argued, for instance, that "the Negro preacher is the curse of his race."[144]

The social justice orientation tends to emphasize the church's positive role in history as a catalyst for the social betterment of African Americans in their political and social circumstances. An important focus is placed on the affirmative leadership (most expressly in the work of Martin Luther King Jr. and his male preacher colleagues), organizational, and social and political roles of the church, particularly during the nineteenth and twentieth centuries. Gayraud Wilmore argues that "the transmutation of spiritual energy into a political movement for freedom has been an inherent characteristic of black religion from the slave period. It played an important part in slave insurrections in the U.S. and in the militancy of a significant sector of the black church down to the present."[145] Wilmore provides a comprehensive treatment of the conflation of the effects of urbanization; industrialization; Marxist and socialist influences; pan-Africanism/Negroism; and a dearth of militant religiopolitical elites among blacks at the turn of the twentieth century, which he coined the "*deradicalization* of the Black church." Wilmore insists this juncture represents the point where blacks in many northern cities "retreated into a folk religiosity that lacked the social protest emphasis of the antebellum black denominations."[146] This observation builds on a construction of leadership found in W.E.B. Du

Bois's controversial chapter in *The Souls of Black Folk* (1903; "Of Mr. Booker T. Washington and Others"), where he projects the accommodationist orientation as a betrayal of the earlier, episodic, but more confrontational discourses of individuals such as militant Christian elites and leaders like "Black Gabriel," Denmark Vesey, Nat Turner, "[David] Walker's wild appeal," Frederick Douglass, and several lesser-known individuals.[147] Wilmore notes,

> Washington's gradualism, while opposed by a few who were not dependent upon his influence for personal advancement, was adopted by most black preachers not only because they lacked the courage to fight back, but because it was consonant with the ethics of white Christianity by which they were increasingly influenced. The picture of the nonviolent, self-effacing, patiently suffering white Jesus held up by the conservative evangelicals and revivalists at the turn of the century became for many black preachers the authoritative image of what it is like to be a Christian. The image provided irrefutable confirmation, supported by Scripture, of the wisdom and expediency of Washington's position.[148]

He would not suffer idealistic religion that traded on the practical for abstract theology. Formidable religious elites such as Alexander Crummell and Henry McNeal Turner insisted that Washington's ideas limited the options for those who could learn of letters and lead, and he discouraged agitation for "social equality" with whites.[149] Wilmore's second phase, "the *dechristianization* of Black radicalism," concedes the centuries-long Christian prerogative over black militancy as being undermined and giving way to religious cultism, Islamic religious nationalism, Garveyism, and a ghetto-based cosmopolitanism between World War I and the Great Depression. This process signaled the beginning of what C. Eric Lincoln saw as the passing of the Negro church and the emergence of the more militant Black Power–era black church of the North, where it found vindication for its engagement in the liberation struggles of later years.

To the extent that pre–civil rights black Christian elites embraced an accommodationist social orientation, *they surrendered the prerogative of black Christianity in black nationalism.* The black "Christian heritage" of black nationalism would remain in abeyance until the arrival of James Cone, Albert Cleage Jr., and the black theology movement during the post–civil rights period. The "dechristianization of black radicalism" emanated partly from the self-consciously intraracial cultural and social commitments of the New Negro that the petit bourgeois Harlem Renaissancers and Garveyites *inherited* in the most comprehensive aggregation of black organizations, institutions, and individuals (West Indian, African, and African American) in the nation's history. There was an obvious class dimension in which the proletarian component of the New Negro, more so than its intellectuals, writers, and spokespersons, was decidedly oriented toward a "consciousness of kind" that jettisoned nearly all association with Anglo-American identity, more than any previous generation of African American people; Harlem was its natural home, and at every level it was saliently black nationalist in that it sought to arrest the exclusionary dilemma through self-determination and the veneration of a black social and political world. For the bourgeois literati, this development represented a general "falling away" of African American intellectuals caught up in the agnostic urban cosmopolitanism of the era that commonfolk African Americans mostly rejected.[150] This excerpt from Langston Hughes's poem "Goodbye Christ" is instructive of this feeling among intellectuals:

> Listen, Christ,
> You did alright in your day, I reckon—
> But that day's gone now.
> They ghosted you up a swell story, too,
> Called it Bible—
> But it's dead now,
> The popes and the preachers've
> Made too much money from it.
> They've sold you to too many
> Kings, generals, robbers, and killers—
> Even to the Tzar and the Cossacks,
> Even to Rockefeller's Church,
> Even to THE SATURDAY EVENING POST.
> You ain't no good no more.
> They've pawned you
> Till you've done wore out.
> Goodbye,
> Christ Jesus Lord God Jehova.[151]

The "dechristianization of Black radicalism" accounts for the transition from the "face" of black nationalism in the United States during the post–World War I era to an Islamic critique of Christianity, civil rights integrationism, and, ironically, the commonfolk culture, ethos, and appetites of the burgeoning black ghetto social world. The process that unfolded was more extensive and fluid than the analyses offered by James Cone when he notes that "despite some nationalist expressions, black Christianity was associated with the integrationist tradition. The Nation of Islam, on the other hand, was outspokenly nationalist—antiwhite and problack."[152] It is important to consider that black nationalism's major proponents cease to be *Christian* elites in the tradition of Walker, Delaney, Garnet, Crummell, and Henry McNeal Turner, or the (Christian and Islamic) syncretism of Edward Wilmot Blyden and Garvey, at least to the likes of Muslim clerics, such as Timothy Drew Ali, W. D. Fard, and Elijah Muhammad, as well as their ministers (Wallace Muhammad, Malcolm X, Louis X-Farrakhan, and Muhammad Ali). This development coincided with the tail end of an era that Rayford Logan called the "nadir" in black political and civil life and "the Betrayal of the Negro" at the end of the nineteenth and the beginning of the twentieth century. It is also the period that Philip S. Foner calls "an unhappy period in Afro-American history."[153] Cone does rightly note that "despite the contrasts between the two religious traditions, they were also closely related by their common past, involving continuous struggle for justice in a white American society that did not recognize blacks as human beings. Both traditions were more *black American* than either African or European, which means that one's search for an understanding should begin in the rural South and urban North and not the continents of Africa or Europe."[154] Wilmore's study, more than any other work on the subject of black radical religious tradition since Du Bois's, provides a historical and ideological analysis of the continuities among black slave, Christian, "cultic," and Islamic religious elites and their relationship to one another in black nationalism, and thus provides an important measure of black nationalism's permutations more broadly.[155]

Affinities and Antipathies for Community or "Brotherhood" with Euro-Americans

Empirical studies confirm that most African Americans reject the tenets of racial separatism. Throughout the post–civil rights period the idea that "African Americans should have nothing to do with whites" has been widely rejected by nearly nine of ten African American adults. Whatever African American individuals may feel toward whites as a collective, there is scant ideological coherence that explains attitudes concerning relations with whites. The major religious orientations with which African Americans associate seem to offer greater explanatory clarity than their ideological orientations. The issue here is how religiosity influences the various ideological orientations in relation to attitudes, primarily toward whites.

New associations were sought in the era of Black Power that jettisoned the traditional liberal integrationist coalition for domestic and internationalist alliances with other relatively powerless minorities. Although the focus here is how religiously derived notions of community or "brotherhood" (in the gendered parlance of mainline churches) shape political relations with respect to belonging, implicit in the discussion is the matter of coalition politics and interracial cooperation within politics. Noted above was the propensity for liberal integrationism to comport with Christian notions of social justice, primarily in abolitionism and in modern civil rights. Perhaps the single greatest irony related to African American political ideologies and black religion is that most pre-Garveyite Christian black nationalists tended to be morbidly pro-white, culturally Victorian, and largely anti-Africa (see Chapter 5). The Eurocentric origins of their educations and church fellowships socialized the likes of Blyden, Crummell, Holly, Delany, and Turner. Prior to Garveyism and Black

Power nationalism, black nationalist elites sought out white benefactors to fund their emigrationist schemes when they were unable to do so themselves.[156] It is counterintuitive to the presumed antipathy that black nationalists are thought to hold toward whites in general. The clearest representation of differences between black nationalists and liberal and radical integrationists concerning "Who is my neighbor?" seems to sharpen with the modern civil rights era, particularly as various political elites sought to navigate the spectrum of movement politics.

If one looks seriously at the development of black nationalism as a formal ideology, there are only a few parallels between the elite-driven Christian emigrationist experiments and the revolutionary and cultural nationalisms of students in the 1960s that Malcolm X powerfully impacted. In the Black Power era, the black Christian integrationists purged white liberal allies from their organizations (e.g., the SNCC) and valorized Africa and the rest of the non-European world. To the contrary: Prior to the emergence of Malcolm X in the streets of Harlem, black nationalists were no more disinclined to associate with whites than were the integrationists. In fact, there is very little difference in how nationalists and traditional integrationists viewed relations with whites in US society (although the former were always more pessimistic about coexisting with whites and intergroup race relations). Black Power, it must be remembered, was the product of integrationist strategies, and the major breach between black student activists and white liberal supporters emerged within these liberal integrationist wings of the civil rights movement. Liberal integrationists have sought to employ "black unity" as a means to meld with the majority populations as much as latterday black nationalists appealed to black unity as a means and an end to political organizing. However, it sometimes seems that liberal integrationists *assume* cooperation from blacks as a given in brokerage politics with whites, whereas nationalists tend to *demand* it; this is epitomized in the work of King compared to Amiri Baraka's actions at the 1972 Gary National Black Political Convention. The former spent less mobilization capital demanding "unity without uniformity" or "closing ranks," and unity was not a theoretical tenet of integrationism to the extent that self-help, self-reliance, and group solidarity have been for nationalists.[157]

There has been some fluidity between militant nationalist demands and the reformist and militant Black Power pluralism of the 1960s and 1970s, which Harold Cruse argues equated "imputing revolutionary interpretations to merely reformist methods."[158] Indeed, claims to black nationalism seem to have been made as an afterthought for many student activists. Many were neophyte black nationalists primarily because Malcolm X identified his shifting political philosophy as such, most famously in his well-known "A Message to the Grassroots" speech in 1963. What were the critical elements that set apart the sense of linked fate that liberal and radical integrationists and nationalists felt toward perceived insider and outsider groups? How did the tenets of religion influence or shape the ascent toward multiracial or intraracial cooperation in politics? What reciprocity or bonds of affection have emanated with some regularity from the black Christian, Islamic, and nonreligious responses to the demands of the struggle for social and political empowerment?

Scholars recognize a strong egalitarian character in mainline Protestant Christianity. Essential teachings of the gospel, wherein the followers of Jesus are urged to love their enemies, pray for those who may misuse them, bless those who curse them, and turn the other cheek if they are stricken with violence— combined with the central message of the gospel—all facilitated a universalistic perspective in regard to others. The emphasis on benevolence for the poor and other socially ostracized groups and individuals, those whom Howard Thurman's book *Jesus and the Disinherited* identifies as "the people who stand with their backs against the wall," is crucial to understanding the democratic, inclusionary quality of Protestant belief.[159] The idea that humanity shares monogenesis is integral to civil rights–era Christian integrationists.[160]

Widespread denominationalism among Protestant churches, which reflects their autonomous organizational structures, facilitated the drawing of boundaries that excluded blacks from their religious communities. Winthrop Jordan adds, "The sectarian character of Protestantism fostered a spirit of tribalism, since sectarianism meant emphasis on distinctiveness from others and virtual, though inadmissible, abandonment of the ideal of Christian universality. . . . The spirit of tribalism in Protestantism was probably in some measure responsible for the exclusion of Negroes from the community."[161] W.E.B. Du Bois emphasizes the detail that where slavery existed among European Christians, many "had come to regard it as wrong that those who partook of the privileges and hopes and aspirations of that religion should oppress each other to the extent of actual enslavement." He continues: "The idea of human brotherhood in the seventeenth century was of a brotherhood of co-religionists. When it came to the dealing of Christian and heathen, however, the century saw nothing wrong in slavery. . . . The slaves were to be brought from heathenism to Christianity, and through slavery the benighted Indian and African were to find their passport to the kingdom of God."[162]

Martin Luther King's interest in activating a "beloved community" was consistent with the social commitments of Christian integrationist elites such as Mays, Thurman, and Rustin. Mays, for instance, applied an antiracist "critique of white-Christianity and developed a theology of race relations based on the community's desire for integration."[163] King's thinking on the interrelatedness of human beings was influenced by Howard Thurman. As noted, Thurman famously pastored the first interracial religious fellowship in San Francisco.[164] King's twin commitments to integration and nonviolence derived from a Christian sense of human relationality. He viewed both elements as "nothing more and nothing less than Christianity in action."[165] Cone makes clear the extent to which King's familial black Baptist roots, exposure to personalism, and liberal Protestantism learned in graduate school shaped his belief in a pluralist society that would be governed by the nation's founding democratic principles and sustained by its Protestant religious heritage. At its core was a faith and social commitment that "all races of men and women were created to live together on this planet as brothers and sisters and as children of God. Therefore, color and physical features were secondary to our universal humanity grounded in God's creation."[166]

For many adherents to Islam, the liberal West represents *dar al-kufr* (the abode of unbeliever). At least since the Christian Crusades, and independent of the Nation of Islam's Yacub–"white devil" mythologies, Muslims have viewed the religious, economic, and political orientation of the West as the work of "the Great Satan." The Nation of Islam's demonization of white supremacist thought, actions, culture, and institutions was, in this sense, *closer* to "orthodox" Islamic belief than analysts give credit for.[167] With the exception of the interracial Amaddiyah movement, Islamic integrationism is a post–civil rights–era development, with Wallace Muhammad's determination to apply traditional Islamic teachings and practices to the Nation of Islam beginning officially in 1975; it admitted its first white member during the summer of that year.[168]

Christianity, by contrast, could be prone to exclusionist orientations, vis-à-vis Henry Garnet's African Civilization Society, the racist American Baptist Association and Ku Klux Klan, or integrationist orientations as seen in abolitionism and the modern civil rights movement. Ironically, King's SCLC was a "blacks only" organization with integrationist commitments. Yet Islam promotes an interracial community based on the Quranic principle of *ummah wahida*, which roughly refers variously to the "one community" of submitters, whether individual, the collective nation of Islamic states, or global communities of faithful Muslims. Blyden insists that "the religion, originating at Mekka, has extended west, across Africa, to the Atlantic, and east to North Western China, north to Constantinople, and south to Mozambique, embracing men of all known races; and embracing them not as occasional and individual converts, but as entire communities—whole nations and tribes—weaving itself into the national life, and giving colour to their political and social as well as ecclesiastical existence."[169] Although only believers are necessarily part of the *ummah*, admission into this community is available to all human beings, including other believers in monotheism, such as Judaism and Christianity.[170] The Quran establishes in 49:13: "O people, we created you from the same male and female, and rendered you distinct peoples and tribes, that you may recognize one another. The best among you in the sight of God is the most righteous." In 30:22 it is noted: "Among His proofs are the creation of the heavens and the earth, and the variations in your languages and your colors," without mention of rank or hierarchy. Richard B. Turner insists that "if Muhammad was able to purge notions of black inferiority from himself and his companions during the first generation of Islam, he was not able to eliminate this evil from the Bedouin tribal people who brought Islam to conquered lands. Often their prejudices overlapped with antiblack prejudices embedded in some of the cultures of the lands that they conquered."[171] Prophet Muhammad noted in a final message to his followers in Mecca: "O ye men! Harken unto my words and take ye them to heart! Know ye that every Moslem is a brother to every Moslem, and that ye are now one brotherhood. It is not legitimate for any of you, therefore, to appropriate unto himself anything that belongs to his brother unless it is willingly given him by that brother."[172] Still later in his final sermon, Muhammad seemed to be confronting an active antiblack racism as he admonished: "No Arab has any priority over a non-Arab and *no white over a black except in righteousness*."[173] It approximates the sense of brotherhood that Malcolm X expressed after his *second trip* to Saudi Arabia in 1963.[174] The power of the revelation that whites could be Muslims and, indeed, were part of the ethnic tapestry of Islam could single-handedly impeach Wallace Muhammad's Yacub mythology—the very doctrine that held the Nation of Islam's other teachings together. For this reason Malcolm X did not reveal his observations for several years before then.

As with white supremacist interpretations of Christianity, the universal faith claims of Islam have been undermined where it encountered Africans. Whether or not the racial slavery of Islam—which extends to present-day Mauritania[175] and Sudan—and Christianity are akin to the legal principle "fruit of the poisonous tree," it is clear that a corruption of the original intentions has occurred in the social praxes of the Muslim tradition with regard to Africans. Chancellor Williams suggests that Islam is no less the "white man's religion" than Christianity.[176] This was lost on Malcolm X in 1960, when he insisted that "the Arabs, as a colored people," ought to identify with the Negro struggle and "should and must make more effort to reach the millions of colored people in America who are related to the Arabs by blood. These millions of colored peoples would be completely in sympathy with the Arab cause!"[177] Ronald Segal insists that, as with Christianity, the general encounter between Arabs and Muslims was through the mass importation of African slaves, which in turn fostered identical feelings of black inferiority found among European Christians.[178] Williams bluntly notes how "blacks in the United States seem to be more mixed up and confused over the search for racial identity than anywhere else. Hence, many are dropping their white western slavemasters' names and adopting, not African, but their Arab and Berber slavemasters' names!" He continues: "The role of 'white' Arabs must not be obscured either by their Islamic religion or by the presence of the Africans and Afro-Arabs among them any more than we should permit white Europeans and white Americans to use Christianity to cover their drive for power and control over the lives of other people."[179] It is not so much Islam with which Williams finds fault, but rather the reality that "the Arabs' white superiority complex is not one whit less than that of Europe and America, although their strategy of 'brotherhood' deceives the naive Blacks."[180] White Arabic domination conceded, in essence, to white European domination. Williams notes that "modern Africans and students of Africa have tended to emphasize the destructive impact of European imperialism in Africa while ignoring the most damaging developments from Arab impact *before* the general European takeover in the last quarter of the nineteenth century, a relatively recent period. . . . For what happened, very simply, was that European imperialism in Africa checked and replaced Arab imperialism."[181] The Quran, like Paulinian writings in the New Testament, deals with slavery. However, in these texts, prohibitions against slavery are enforced concerning Muslims' or potential Muslims' wives only.[182]

The story of Bilal ibn Rahib, the first "muezzin" (*muadhdhin*), or leader of Azan call to prayer, led Blyden to celebrate him and a list of subsequent "distinguished Negroes."[183] Bilal, who was previously a slave, was among a group of mostly Ethiopian followers and companions of Prophet Muhammad. Bilal was one of the earliest converts to Islam, black or Arab.[184] Bilal's racial significance took on added importance in the Nation of Islam *after* the 1975 death of Elijah Muhammad, particularly as Wallace Muhammad set out to calibrate the Nation of Islam's core racial doctrines with the self-conscious universalism of traditional Islam. In one sense, the short narrative of Bilal being understood within the Nation of Islam as the first black convert to Islam impeaches the group's initial teaching concerning the blackness of all Muslims, including Prophet Muhammad.[185] If *dar al-Islam* (the house of Islam) downplays the racial significance of Bilal in the spirit of a universal *ummah*, it potentially truncates the broader appeal to ethnic groups skeptical of its acquiescence to Arab slavery, prejudice, racism, and, in the early twenty-first century, jihadist terrorism. But should knowledge of Bilal in Islam absolve its centuries of antiblack feeling any more than the Christian Ethiopian official, being among the first to convert to Christianity (as described in Acts), should absolve Christianity's subsequent racial history in the world?[186]

If Bilal's blackness represents Islam's early commitment to a beloved community, then it was with more veracity that Elijah Muhammad's Nation of Islam imagined a community that acknowledged the racial "yield" of Islam that Arab Muslims practiced but wouldn't openly preach. It isn't the "nationalism" of black nationalists—Christian or Muslim—per se that best explains their centrifugal political, ideological, and religious proclivities. Mainstream Sunni Islam has been no less "racial" than the Nation of Islam. It is evident that traditional Islam's standpoint with regard to race was imperial, whereas the Nation of Islam's formulations emerged from the standpoint of a subaltern people. Since the September 2001 attacks in the United States, immigrant Muslims, their descendants, and organizations that previously condemned Elijah Muhammad and the Nation of Islam's "racist" version of Islam find themselves a pariah people, subject to routine discrimination, vigilantism, and surveillance. Richard B. Turner insists that the Nation of Islam's tendency to call for racial separation was consistent with the African response to the introduction of Islam to West Africa: "In these locations West African Muslims attempted to define their identities both as Muslims and ethnic people in light of the competition between their allegiance to the religions and cultures of their ethnic origins and beliefs and practices of orthodox Islam from North Africa and the Middle East."[187]

Edward E. Curtis's *Islam in Black America* critiques the Nation of Islam's articulation of its communal boundaries. Curtis views this more broadly as tension concerning whether "a religious tradition is *universally* applicable to the experience of all human beings and the idea, on the other hand, that a religious tradition is applicable to the experience of one *particular* group of human beings."[188] Louis DeCaro is reticent, arguing that "the cultic nature of the Nation of Islam as a religious phenomenon is constant because the religious and spiritual DNA of the movement lacks the genre of orthodoxy in either the Muslim or Christian sense." He insists, "The Nation of Islam never correctly taught its followers about the religion of the Qur'an, and neither has it ever encouraged them to become traditional Muslims."[189] This observation ignores what Curtis views as an absolute universalism that Elijah Muhammad inspired in Malcolm X, Wallace Muhammad, and Louis Farrakhan. The anti-Negro "Asiatic" identity of the Nation of Islam is taken seriously by many of its adherents. Elijah Muhammad's Nation of Islam encouraged its black American converts to embrace fully the Asiatic identity of Allah (in the person of Fard/Farad Muhammad), which was a mix of Pakistani and New Zealand heritage.[190] If the claims to Asiatic identity seem esoteric, they are simultaneously indicative of the Nation of Islam's universal understanding of Islam in racial terms. One need only recall Malcolm X's previously noted "Message to the Grassroots" in order to appreciate how the Nation of Islam held to an antiwhite universalism that defined all nonwhites as part of a black nationalist rubric.[191] Without mentioning Elijah Muhammad once—two weeks before his suspension from the Nation of Islam—Malcolm X explained the Chinese, Kenyan, Cuban, Algerian, and US (Native American and black American) revolutions and rebellions to be part of "the Black revolution," and the American, French, and Russian revolutions to be part of "white nationalist" land-based revolutions. Algernon Austin insists that "the Nation was a black nationalist organization, but religiously it was not. Religiously, the organization locates its members in a multiracial community . . . unlike that of religious black nationalist organizations such as the African Orthodox Church or the Shrine of the Black Madonna [in Detroit]."[192] But the AOC, on the contrary, did base its cultural and religious heritage in Afro-Moroccan and Asiatic themes, and Cleage likewise embraced a transcontinental understanding of black nationalism, which Malcolm X defined in the critical speech that outlined his emergent ideological framework. In the "Ballot or the Bullet" speech, delivered in April 1964, weeks after his final break with the Nation of Islam, Malcolm X argued that religion should be a private matter likely because of that sectarianism that he experienced until his death. But he argued in the interim that "whether you are a Christian, or a Muslim, or a nationalist, we all have the same problem. . . . All of us catch hell from the same enemy. . . . We suffer political oppression, economic exploitation, and social degradation." Consequently, Malcolm X argued that black nationalism was a racial common ground philosophy that would be the kernel for broad action programs within communities: "And what [is] so good about it is you can stay right in the church where you are and still take black nationalism as your philosophy; you can stay in any kind of civic organization you belong to and still take Black nationalism as your philosophy; you can be an atheist and still take Black nationalism as your philosophy; this is the philosophy that eliminates the necessity for division and arguing."

Edward Curtis suggests that there is no universally organic Islam apart from the particularistic experiences of African American Muslims (inside or outside the Nation of Islam); if Islam is inseparable from Arab, Persian, Asian, and African realities, then Islam is integral to the realities of blacks in the United States.[193] Indeed, an undifferentiated Islam, with origins in Southwest Asia, not only ignores the obvious violent racial and clerical divisions among the region's states and people (Sunni and Shiite, Persian and Arab) that have prevented solidarity; such a view would also be indistinguishable from the chauvinism for which the Nation of Islam had been lambasted under Elijah Muhammad. Moreover, Yacub's history was *imported*, likely from Pakistan, among American blacks by W. D. Fard, the Muslim immigrant founder of the Nation of Islam who taught Elijah Muhammad that he was the *mahdi* of Islam.[194]

There is a good deal of ambidexterity with which some scholars have viewed black nationalism's reputed centrifugal orientation regarding coalitions and other grouping boundaries, especially concerning whites. On the one hand, the popular "civilizationist" thesis that Wilson Moses proffers accuses "classical" black nationalists in their "golden age" of being thoroughly mimetic and enamored with Eurocentric ideals, values, and anti-Africanism. For Moses, despite their nationalism, "they were still Anglo-Africans, still Victorians, still *assimilados*, and like most men, they found it difficult to view the world except through their own cultural spectacles."[195] Even pan-Africanism is thought sponsored by white missionary activity.[196] This is certainly one dimension of early black nationalism, but it is based precisely on a one-dimensional reading of black nationalism. On the other hand, post-Garvey black nationalism is held by many scholars to be so antiwhite, racist, xenophobic, morally disingenuous, and provincial that one wonders how these ideological strands can be considered the same phenomenon. One common denominator in all black nationalisms, whether traditional (what Moses calls "classical"), modern (in Black

Power), or contemporary, is that all espoused and advocated different coalition partnerships more or less with other groups, whether white, Native American, Latino-Hispanic, or Marxist, in the United States. Internationally, Afro-Caribbean and African nations, Cuba, Canada, China, Russia, and the Middle East have been enlisted as potential partners in means to the end of improving the material conditions of all people.

A Kinder, Gentler Black Nationalism?

Like Harold Cruse before him, Tommie Shelby insists that post–civil rights–era black nationalism, beginning with Black Power, is likely to suffer from a mobilization quagmire to the extent that its alliances are dependent on reluctant bourgeois elites and middle-class individuals. Moreover, intraracial interest differentiation along multiple lines among segments of the African American collective further complicates solidarity projects. The sort of "pro-black" politics that the Nation of Islam and Black Power militants advocated also stands, in Shelby's view, to undermine interracial cooperation in a political milieu where large segments of whites and increasing numbers of Latinos and Asians converge in politics. Shelby, though supportive of black nationalist discourses, ultimately calls for an unblack black nationalism or, better yet, a black nationalism without "blackness," despite his denial.[197] He notes,

> This does not mean that black solidarity is not worth sustaining and cultivating. Blacks continue to need the protection that solidarity affords, as they can use what unity they do have to demand, encourage, work toward greater racial justice. What they cannot do is expect that black solidarity would or could secure all or even most of the wide-ranging political interests of blacks. . . . Blacks should emphasize the continuing importance of black political unity while also recognizing its limitations and its diminished— though not extinguished—progressive potential since the decline of the Black Power movement.[198]

This version of "pragmatic" black nationalism seems to conflate the strategic choices available to (and taken by) committed individuals and groups with the ideological substance of black solidarity. He insists that black demands for racial justice or, say, policies seeking to reduce gun violence in cities are not synonymous with ontological blackness. Whom black Americans form political alliances with (including themselves) does matter. It determines a kind of secular "brotherhood." This is why Shelby concedes that traditional black nationalists *would not* recognize his philosophical offering as black nationalism at all.[199] His conceptualization of the role of blackness in black politics is likely to disturb traditional black nationalists less than when Shelby conceptualizes the participation of whites in post–civil rights politics. Although adherence to the cultural forms of black nationalism that fulminated in Black Power is discouraged—identified in eight tenets that can equally be attributed to integrationists or even black feminists[200]—whites are encouraged to operationalize a political *blackness*. In chapter 5 of *We Who Are Dark*, in a section entitled "The Blackness of Whites," Shelby attempts to construct a white "blackness" on grounds that individual whites have adopted the multifarious expressions of black culture as their own in the arts, sports, entertainment, and so forth. Pop culture, then, is where whites can encounter blackness, but it is in politics where black people and groups must *not* encounter it. In this formulation there is at least an acknowledgement that there is *reciprocity* in cultural contact between these collectives, which the "civilizationist" thesis of black nationalism seems incapable of recognizing. Otherwise, Shelby seems to offer a cultural politics out of history, where the co-optation of black cultural production is read benignly because individual whites in the arts and literature have preserved black culture. Shelby notes that "black solidarity does require a shared set of values or goals. But this normative commitment need not involve embracing black culture as the basis of collective identity. One does not have to possess a black cultural identity—indeed one does not have to be black at all—to appreciate the value of racial equality, to condemn racism, or to abhor poverty." Although not wholly implausible, this rendition not only treats the exploitative nature of these relations (especially in blues, jazz, Jim Jones's leadership among blacks in the Peoples Temple in San Francisco and Los Angeles, and forms of hip-hop) innocuously; it begs the question why a cross-fertilization of culture (between blacks, whites, Latinos, etc.) is identified as "black" at the outset. Would not "mixed" or "shared" American culture be less obtrusive than a formulation of "black culture" that dissuades blackness among blacks while simultaneously acknowledging and encouraging white participation in cultural "blackness" or its preservation? Why stop at pop culture, which is inherently given to minstrelsy in the American context, from Al Jolsen to Jim Jones to "Thug Life"? Would not segregated black prison and gang cultures or the related "culture of poverty"—in which mostly white stakeholders in law, government, and corporations have vested interests in maintaining structures of confinement and inequality—also fit the bill of preserving aspects of "black culture" in Shelby's construction? It allows for participation in "everything but the burden" of being black in America.[201]

* * *

The intersection of religion, religiosity, and ideology in the African American experience has profoundly influenced modern political movements in ways that reflect the perennial concern of generations of black populations striving for liberation and universal freedom. Nikhil P. Singh notes to this end:

What would an account of American national identity look like if it engaged with the recurrent force of white supremacy, particularly from the perspective of the social struggles that have most vigorously opposed it? For while black intellectuals and social movements for equality have undoubtedly drawn from vocabularies that signify an adherence to universal values in the U.S. political imagination, including Christianity, liberalism, democratic-republicanism, and varieties of Euro-American cosmopolitanism, they have also drawn in universalizing discourses that surpass the sanctioned national and transnational boundaries of U.S. political and intellectual culture, including Islam, international socialism, black nationalism, and varieties of third worldism.[202]

Political elites, ranging from early Christian black nationalist men and women to turn-of-the-twentieth-century adherents to Islamic versions of black nationalism, and also in the modern civil rights and Black Power eras, activated interrelated centripetal and centrifugal orientations that included enlisting deity in political and intellectual discourses; the institutional, social, and political roles of the traditional black church; and imagined boundaries of community. The political and ethical role of violence is equally pertinent to understanding how religion has influenced ideology from David Walker's *Appeal* to Martin Luther King's civil disobedience, from Malcolm X's militant jeremiad (interchangeably called a "jihad of words" given his Islamic religiosity)[203] to the conflagrations preceding and following the demand for Black Power. It is important to delineate how black religious elites formulated black nationalist discourse through literature, organizations, movements, and protest politics. The chapters in Part 2 look at these separately.

Notes

1. I identify black religion as the informal and formally institutionalized system of spiritual and religious attitudes, beliefs, practices, and contemplations, which organizes the social, cultural, and political lives of African Americans and black people of African descent more generally. Black religion, as understood in this book, should not be limited to Christianity, Islam, Yoruba, or even predominantly African American traditions. However, the religious practice or observation of black individuals does not constitute "black religion" per se. For instance, regardless of the number of African Americans or other blacks who belong to the Jewish, Roman Catholic, or Mormon faiths, while they may constitute the religion of that number of individual blacks, they do not add up to "black religion."

2. In an unpublished paper, Robert C. Smith identifies several variants of black nationalism that broadly comport with economic (bourgeois and socialist), cultural, religious (Christian and non-Christian), attitudinal (truth-telling), political (revolutionary and reform), territorial separatist, and pan-Africanist projects. William Van De Burg, in *Modern Black Nationalism: From Marcus Garvey to Louis Farrakhan* (New York: New York University Press, 1997), lists the feelings of being "undervalued and oppressed by 'outsiders,'" and concludes that "all manner of black nationalists, past and present, are located somewhere within the gnarled, sprawling expanse of the national-

ist family tree" (page 4). Various analysts have looked at early centrifugal tendencies and characterized them as "proto-nationalism" and "classical nationalism" (covering two centuries leading up to Marcus Garvey), "modern nationalism" (traceable from Garveyism through the twentieth century), "pluralist-nationalism" as outlined in Kwame Ture (formerly Stokely Carmichael) and Charles V. Hamilton, *Black Power: The Politics of Liberation* (New York: Vintage Books, [1967] 1992), and the "cultural" and "revolutionary" variants (associated, respectively, with Amiri Baraka's black arts movement and Maulana Kerenga's US organization, on one end, and the Black Panther Party and Revolutionary Action Movement [RAM], on the other). Robert A. Brown and Todd C. Shaw isolate what they call "community nationalism" and "separatist nationalism" in "Separate Nations: Two Attitudinal Dimensions of Black Nationalism," *Journal of Politics* 64, no. 1 (202): 22–44.

3. Patricia Hill Collins, *From Black Power to Hip-Hop*, p. 76.

4. C. Eric Lincoln, *Race, Religion, and the Continuing American Dilemma* (New York: Hill and Wang, 1999), p. 92.

5. James Cone, *Martin, and Malcolm, and America: A Dream or a Nightmare* (Maryknoll, NY: Orbis), p. 16.

6. Eugene Genovese, *Roll, Jordan, Roll*, p. 280.

7. Benedict Anderson, *Imagined Communities: Reflections on the Origin and Spread of Nationalism* (New York: Verso, 1983 [2006]), p. 12. Emphases added.

8. See Robert C. Smith, *We Have No Leaders*. King was revanent in the middle to late 1990s among proponents of the 1960s integrationist movement because, to them, the March on Washington and the pre-1965 King represented an alternative view of national discourse on race when compared to the contents and tone offered in Louis Farrakhan's "A More Perfect Union" speech at the 1995 Million Man March.

9. See Carlton J.H. Hayes, *Nationalism: A Religion* (New York: Macmillan, 1960), p. 4.

10. This is clearly not to the same extent among the Afro-Cubans, Afro-Caribbeans, or, say, Afro-Brazilians, but none of these were subjected to the thoroughgoing processes of dehumanization and social dislocation evident in the numerical minority situation of African Americans.

11. This is true despite the historicities of some groups, such as the Scotch, Irish, and Welsh in the United Kingdom; the Poles in Russia; the Hungarians in Austria; and Jews throughout Europe, who are noteworthy exceptions to this claim.

12. Robert Carr, *Black Nationalism in the New World: Reading the African-American and West Indian Experience* (Durham, NC: Duke University Press, 2002), p. 14.

13. Black nationalism antedated nineteenth-century Marxism, Garrisonian moral suasionist abolitionism, and twentieth-century radical and liberal integrationism.

14. See Edwin S. Redkey, *Black Exodus: Black Nationalist and Back-to-Africa Movements, 1890–1910* (New Haven: Yale University Press, 1969). Also see William E. Bittle and Gilbert Geis, *The Longest Way Home: Chief Alfred C. Sam's Back to Africa Movement* (Detroit: Wayne State University, 1964).

15. Mark L. Chapman, *Christianity on Trial: African American Religious Thought Before and After Black Power* (Maryknoll, NY: Orbis, 1996), p. 107.

16. George Breitman, *The Last Year of Malcolm X: The Evolution of a Revolutionary* (New York: Pathfinder, 1967), p. 61. Emphasis added.

17. Michael C. Dawson, *Black Visions*.

18. Well-known religious and media personalities, such as the Los Angeles ministers Dr. Fred K. C. Price, Bishop Charles E. Blake, and, more notably, T. D. Jakes—the media's "Black Billy Graham"—began to acknowledge this influence only after the Million Man March's largely Protestant turnout.

19. This phrase is defined by *Webster's Ninth Collegiate Dictionary* (Springfield, MA: Merriam-Webster, 1990) as "the study of the institutional activities of religion (as preaching, church administration, pastoral care, and liturgics)."

20. Peter Paris, *The Social Teaching of the Black Churches* (New York: Fortress, 1985), p. 45.

21. Gayraud S. Wilmore, *Black Religion and Black Radicalism*, p. 46.

22. Beginning with "Black Gabriel" (1800) through David Walker (1820s–1830); Frederick Douglass and Martin Robison Delany (antebellum era and Reconstruction); Henry McNeal Turner, Booker T. Washington, and W.E.B. Du Bois (post-Reconstruction); Marcus Garvey, A. Philip Randolph, the Reverend George Washington Whitbey, the Reverend Reverdy Ramson, and Hubert H. Harrison (post–World War I); to Malcolm X and Martin Luther King Jr. (1950s–1960s); and Jesse Jackson and Louis Farrakhan (1980s–1990s). For an interpretation of A. Philip Randolph's use of religious themes and the influence of "black church culture" in the Brotherhood of Sleeping Car Porters (BSCP) in the post–World War I and Great Depression eras, see Clarence Taylor, *Black Religious Intellectuals: The Fight for Equality from Jim Crow to the 21st Century* (New York: Routledge, 2002); esp. ch. 4. The author's analysis of isolated letters, songs, speeches, and missives by Randolph, and his association with the few supportive ministers of the BSCP, are not convincing proof that Randolph himself was an adherent of religion. However, the author does demonstrate that religion permeated the BSCP movement's interpretation of its struggle against the Pullman porters.

23. Michael Dawson, *Black Visions*, p. 5.

24. Patricia Hill Collins, *From Black Power to Hip-Hop*, p. 84.

25. Ibid., pp. 86, 90.

26. C. Eric Lincoln, *Race, Religion, and the Continuing American Dilemma*, p. xxiv; originally cited in Patricia Hill Collins, *From Black Power to Hip-Hop*, pp. 79–80.

27. For example, the centrality of death and the afterlife, gaudy "Jesus piece" jewelry, Kanye West's "Jesus Walks," "Rap Activism," and some major lyrical expressions in Tupac Shakur.

28. Patricia Hill Collins, *From Black Power to Hip-Hop*, pp. 86, 89.

29. These categories are not exhaustive; neither are they confirmed markers of one or the other perspectives. For instance, how to educate the rank and file among blacks framed the "best strategy" debates among late-nineteenth and early-twentieth-century intellectuals, such as the Reverend Alexander Crummell, Booker T. Washington, the Reverend Henry McNeal Turner, and W.E.B. Du Bois. The education of the recently manumitted Negro population, as well as its descendants, was at the center of the "talented tenth" thesis of Du Bois, and the critical missionary role that churches played in sponsoring religious and secular education has a history of its own, but this debate did not persist in the political thought of African American elites with the constancy of the issue areas that I enlist here.

30. Dwight N. Hopkins, *Head and Heart: Black Theology—Past, Present, and Future* (New York: Palgrave, 2002).

31. E. Franklin Frazier, *The Negro Church in America*, cited in David Remnick, *The Bridge: The Life and Rise of Barack Obama* (New York: Borzoi/Alfred Knopf, 2010), pp. 172–173.

32. Cornel West, *Prophecy Deliverance!*, p. 65.

33. C. Eric Lincoln, *Race, Religion, and the Continuing American Dilemma*, pp. 239–240. The late Professor Lincoln's contributions to the study of black religion cross several decades of research and analyses (1961, 1973, 1984, 1994, 1999, 1990 with Mamiya) that demonstrate his place among a "second generation" of scholars—the

likes of W.E.B. Du Bois, Benjamin E. Mays, and E. Franklin Frazier make up the first—to cover the subject of black religion. His more noteworthy peers include James Cone, Gayraud S. Wilmore, Vincent Harding, Jacqueline Grant, and Delores Williams. Please see Mark L. Chapman, *Christianity on Trial*, esp. ch. 5, for a discussion of Christianity and sexism.

34. It was hardly original to the predicaments of African Americans. Every culture and people has evolved its own mythology and own pantheon of deified personalities, from Amon-Ra (Egypt) to Zeus/Jupiter (Greece/Rome) to Yahweh and Jesus of Nazareth (Judeo-Christian).

35. David Walker's *Appeal* raises this point in defense of his argument that the African American predicament is historically exceptional. For instance, in Article I, he insists, "Show me a page of history, either sacred or profane, on which a verse can be found, which maintains, that the Egyptians heaped the *insupportable insult* upon the children of Israel, by telling them that they are not of the *human family*." Emphases in original.

36. Dwight Hopkins, *Head and Heart*, p. 99.

37. The text reads, "The Spirit of the Lord is upon me, because he has anointed me to preach good news to the poor. He has sent me to proclaim freedom for the prisoners and recovery of sight for the blind to release the oppressed, to proclaim the year of the Lord's favor."

38. The text reads, "When the Son of Man comes in his glory, and all the angels with him, he will sit on his throne in heavenly glory. All the nations will be gathered before him, and he will separate the people one from another as a shepherd separates the sheep from the goats. He will put the sheep on his right and the goats on his left. Then the King will say to those on his right, 'come, you who are blessed by my Father; take your inheritance, the kingdom prepared for you since the creation of the world. For I was hungry and you gave me something to eat, I was thirsty and you gave me something to drink, I was a stranger and you invited me in, I needed clothes and you clothed me, I was sick and you looked after me, I was in prison and you came to visit me.'"

39. See Michael Muhammad Knight, *The Five Percenters: Islam, Hip Hop, and the Gods of New York* (Oxford, UK: Oneworld, 2007).

40. Orlando Patterson, *Rituals of Blood*, p. 215.

41. Kelly Douglass, *The Black Christ* (Maryknoll, NY: Orbis, 1994), pp. 17–18.

42. See William R. Jones, *Is God a White Racist? A Preamble to Black Theology* (Garden City, NY: Anchor Press/Doubleday, 1973).

43. Ibid., p. 126.

44. In fact, abolition was negated by the Black Codes and the post-Reconstruction perfidy of the unionist Republicans and the atrocities and humiliations of Jim Crow, including the lynching pogroms that characterized the daily realities of several generations of black northerners and southerners. Moreover, the material conditions of large segments of poor, desperate black women and men, ghetto-locked despite the achievements of the civil rights movement, make Jones's critique all the more poignant.

45. It followed *The Suppression of the African Slave Trade to the United States of America: 1638–1870* (1896) and *The Philadelphia Negro* (1899).

46. See the excerpt of Turner's *Voice of Missions* article, "God Is a Negro," in John Bracey Jr. et al. (eds.), *Black Nationalism in America* (New York: Bobbs-Merrill, 1970), pp. 154–155.

47. Wilson Moses, *Black Messiahs and Uncle Toms*, p. 172.

48. Consistent with avowed agnostic contemporaries, such as Thomas Henry Huxley (1825–1895)—who is credited with coining the term "agnosticism"—and Hubert

Harrison (1883–1927), Jesus of Nazareth is *never* the subject of criticism and religious doubt in Du Bois.

49. See Phil Zuckerman (ed.), *Du Bois on Religion* (Walnut Creek, CA: Altamira, 2000).

50. This was demonstrated in separate editorials such as "Jesus Christ in Georgia" (1911), "Jesus Christ in Texas" (in *Darkwater*, 1920), "The White Christ" (1915), "The Gospel According to Mary Brown" (1919), and "The Son of God" (1933). Du Bois's unprecedented sociological study of slave and free Negro religion contributed to his understanding of the social and psychological utility of presenting Christ and the Madonna as racial subjects.

51. Zuckerman, *Du Bois on Religion*, p. 100.

52. See Herbert Aptheker (ed.), *Prayers of Dark People* (Amherst: University of Massachusetts Press, 1980), pp. vii–viii.

53. For a more extensive treatment of these individuals, see Mark Chapman's *Christianity on Trial*. Another contender who might warrant being listed among this first generation of scholars is Benjamin Lewis, who wrote *Light and Truth* (1836). His work emphasized the Ethiopian influence in Egyptian history and the racial identities of major biblical figures, including Adam, Moses, Solomon, Yahweh (God), and Jesus of Nazareth. For a discussion of Benjamin Lewis, see Stanley Crouch and Playthell Benjamin, *Reconsidering* The Souls of Black Folk (Philadelphia: Running Press, 2002).

54. Du Bois makes no attempt to link the Holy Spirit with the racial predicament of African Americans. This is odd inasmuch as he admired Hegel's idealist notion of the "volksgeist" (spirit of the people) of Germany.

55. Edward Wilmot Blyden, *Christianity, Islam, and the Negro Race* (Baltimore: Black Classic, [1888] 1994), pp. 17–18.

56. Cited in Gayraud S. Wilmore, *Black Religion and Black Radicalism*, p. 151.

57. Ibid., p. 152. Original source is Turner's editorial in *The Voice of Missions* (February 1, 1898).

58. C. Eric Lincoln, *The Black Muslims in America*, 3rd ed. (Grand Rapids, MI: William B. Eerdmans and Trenton, NJ: Africa World, [1961] 1994), pp. 239–240.

59. The Moorish Science Temple (MST) was known first as the "Canaan Temple."

60. He thus felt it was important to signify to his followers that they were not "Negroes" but law-abiding citizen Muslims who also followed the teachings of Confucius, Buddha, Zoroaster, and Jesus.

61. See Richard B. Turner, *Islam in the African American Experience* (Bloomington: Indian University Press, 1997). Turner reports that the Moorish Science Temple had fifty temples in twenty-five US cities. Cities included Lansing, Michigan; Cleveland and Youngstown, Ohio; Charleston, West Virginia; Richmond and Petersburg, Virginia; Pine Bluff, Arkansas; and Baltimore, Maryland. The male members of the MST were given the name "Bey," which is related to a Turkish term for a nobleman. For a time, until Ali ordered them to stop, many of his followers took their MST-issued "passports" so seriously that they routinely assaulted whites in the streets of many of the cities.

62. See John Renard, *Responses to 101 Questions on Islam* (New York: Paulist, 1998), p. 85. Renard is a Catholic with a Ph.D. in Islamic Studies from Harvard University.

63. Ibid., p. 86.

64. Blyden, *Christianity, Islam, and the Negro Race*, p. 17.

65. Compare the Gospel According to Matthew (1:1–16) with the Gospel According to Luke (3:23–37). Matthew lists Tamar, Rahab, Ruth, and Bathsheba in the ge-

nealogical line of Jesus, whereas Luke omits them altogether. These women are tied to the "Hamitic" genealogical line of the biblical Canaanites; see Genesis 9 and 10.

66. Claude Andrew Clegg III, *An Original Man: The Life and Times of Elijah Muhammad* (New York: St. Martin's, 1997), pp. 16–17.

67. For a full account of Garveyism and Islam, see esp. Richard B. Turner's *Islam in the African American Experience*; see also Andrew Vincent, *Nationalism and Particularity* (New York: Cambridge University Press, 2002); Arthur Huff Fauset, *Black Gods of the Metropolis: Negro Religious Cults of the Urban North* (New York: Octagon, 1970); and C. Eric Lincoln, *The Black Muslims in America*.

68. The list includes Noble Drew Ali and Mufti Muhammad Sadiq of the Ahmadiyya Islamic movement. Garveyites, however, rejected Drew Ali's Moorish Science Temple in several major cities, including Detroit, the city where the Nation of Islam was established. The Nation of Islam's founders and leaders, including W. D. Fard Muhammad, Elijah Muhammad, Malcolm X, and Louis Farrakhan, had immediate ties to Garveyism.

69. Andrew Vincent, *Nationalism and Particularity*, p. 135.

70. The distribution of UNIA branches outside the United States (268) was significantly dwarfed by those within it (838). See Tony Martin, *Race First: The Ideological and Organizational Struggles of Marcus Garvey and the United Negro Improvement Association* (Westport, CT: Greenwood, 1976).

71. Among other esoteric notions concerning the "Fall" of black peoples, Fard explained that Euro-Americans were "human devils," created 6,600 years earlier by "Yacub, "an evil black teenager with a grossly large head. Yacub would carry out a genetic experiment that would result in devolution from black to white and exponential evil in the world. The white man's "tricknology" would serve a function in society similar to what Marx conceived in the "ideological superstructure."

72. Fard inverted many of the ideas that whites used to disparage Africans and their descendants. They lived in caves, practiced bestiality, ate the animals with which they had relations, were born with tails. He told Muhammad, "All white people were devils, but Jews were Beelzebub, Lord of the Flies."

73. See Fauset, *Black Gods of the Metropolis*.

74. Malcolm X, "Ballot or the Bullet," delivered at Cory Methodist Church, April 3, 1964, Cleveland, Ohio. In George Breitman (ed.), *Malcolm X: Selected Speeches and Statements* (New York: Grove, 1965), p. 40.

75. Cited in Edward E. Curtis IV, *Black Muslim Religion in the Nation of Islam: 1960–1975* (Chapel Hill: University of North Carolina Press, 2006), p. 90.

76. See Albert Cleage Jr., *Black Christian Nationalism* (New York: William Morrow, 1972), p. xviii.

77. James Lance Taylor, "The Reverend Benjamin Chavis Muhammad: From Wilmington to Washington, from Chavis to Muhammad," in Jo Renee Formicola and Hubert Morken (eds.), *Religious Leaders and Faith-Based Politics* (Latham, MD: Rowman and Littlefield, 2001), pp. 119–120.

78. Chapman, *Christianity on Trial*, p. 83.

79. See Luke 4:18–19, *New International Version* of the Bible.

80. James Cone, *God of the Oppressed* (Maryknoll, NY: Orbis, 1997), p. 49.

81. Mark L. Chapman, *Christianity on Trial*, pp. 117–118.

82. Cited in Chapman, p. 118. Original citation in James Cone, *Black Theology and Black Power* (New York: Harper and Row, 1969), p. 68. Emphasis added.

83. For an extended discussion, see Josiah Ulysses Young III, *No Difference in the Fare: Dietrich Bonhoeffer and the Problem of Racism* (Grand Rapids, MI: William B. Eerdmans, 1998).

84. It is reiterated in (I John 4:1–4) that the "Spirit of God" is at variance with the "spirit of the world."

85. Whereas Peter and the remainder of the original apostles understood this to be a mission to *Jews of every nation*, Paul confronted Peter and the others for what today would be considered racially discriminatory conduct against non-Jews (Galatians 2:11–21) in an atmosphere where a group of religious individuals commonly known as "Judaizers" sought to impose the standards of Mosaic Law on Gentile Christians. As it relates to the earlier assessment of Paul's connection to modern slavery (Philemon and Onisemus), it may be insignificant that Paul's letter to the church at Galatia (estimated at roughly between 53 and 58 C.E.) was written anywhere between two and ten years before the letter to Philemon (estimated roughly at between 59 and 63 C.E.); the two situations are unrelated. But it might also reflect Paul's "otherworldly" commitment to maintaining the status quo within the first-century caste/class social order (e.g., slavery), whereas the former situation threatened to permanently divide the young Christian church around theological and ethnic divisions, essentially creating a Jewish fellowship and a Gentile fellowship.

86. The assertion that Christianity is the white man's religion grew partly out of a rejection of white supremacist Christianity and of the integrationist forces among black Christians who meshed the faith with social and public policy. It also grew out of a profound slight or ignorance of the non-European "semi-indigenous" African origins of Christianity (Gayraud S. Wilmore, *Black Religion and Black Radicalism*, pp. 6–13), biblical accounts highlighting its promulgation among Europeans as well as Africans *before* Europeans (Acts 8:26–39) (Romans 8), and the powerful drama of the swarthy Jesus of Nazareth and Black Simon of Cyrene carrying the cross together to Golgotha (Matthew 27:32–33).

87. The Book of Acts of the Apostles (17:26–29) is relied upon for explaining that "from one [person] he made every nation of men, that they should inhabit the whole earth; and he determined the times set for them and the exact places where they should live." A related text (3:28) is found in Paul's "Letter to the Galatians," which notes that "there is neither Jew nor Greek, slave nor free, male nor female, for you are all one in Christ Jesus. If you belong to Christ, then you are Abraham's seed, and heirs according to the promise."

88. In fact, Benjamin E. Mays often trivialized the phenotypic, epidermal differences among the major American racial populations in the interest of betraying the likenesses they shared. Integrationist religious intellectuals emphasized the obvious facts that all people share identical anatomical traits, such as the number of limbs, blood types, and heads, none of which represent the basis of black oppression and poverty. Of course, this view is undermined, for example, by gendered biological differences and the attendant political capital that reflects them, and also by the fact that the notion of the interrelatedness of all life is an ontological, even theological, supposition, when the course before subaltern blacks has been shaped in the realm of politics and society.

89. Kelly Douglas, *The Black Christ*, pp. 4–5.

90. Howard Thurman, *Jesus and the Disinherited* (Boston: Beacon, 1976), p. 289.

91. James Cone, *Malcolm, and Martin, and America*, pp. 230–231.

92. Ibid.

93. Orlando Patterson, *Rituals of Blood*, p. 230.

94. James M. Washington, *A Testament of Hope: The Essential Writings and Speeches of Martin Luther King, Jr.* (San Francisco: HarperSanFrancisco, 1986), pp. 346–347.

95. Edward Curtis IV, *Islam in Black America* (Albany: State University of New York Press, 2002), p. 11.

96. Ibid. Harris-Lacewell attributes this to Hanes Walton Jr.

97. Ibid.

98. American radicals, such as three-time presidential candidate Eugene V. Debs and author Jack London, and labor organizations, such as the American Federation of Labor (AFL), reflected the obtuse manner in which many white workers, the unions, and party elites approached the problem of African Americans during the Great Depression. Of course, there were many notable exceptions, such as the Congress of Industrial Organizations (CIO), the United Mine Workers, and the International Garment Workers Union, along with individuals such as Walter Reuther and Harry Bridges, but such was not the rule. And even in such cases, African American workers were incorporated into the unions out of fear that the opposition would undermine organization through strikebreaking. See Komozi Woodard, *A Nation Within a Nation: Amiri Baraka (LeRoi Jones) and Black Power Politics* (Chapel Hill: University of North Carolina Press, 1999), pp. 26–28.

99. See Robert H. Craig, *Religion and Radical Politics: An Alternative Christian Tradition in the United States* (Philadelphia: Temple University Press, 1992).

100. See Herbert Aptheker (ed.), *Marxism and Christianity: A Symposium* (New York: Humanities Press, 1968), p. 30. Original essay by Engels was entitled "On the History of Early Christianity," in *Die Neue Zeit*.

101. Ibid.; see Engels in "Bauer and Early Christianity" (1882), in Herbert Aptheker (ed.), *Marxism and Christianity*, p. 30.

102. Winthrop Jordan, *White over Black*, p. 192.

103. Ibid., p. 32. Emphasis in original.

104. See Terrance Ball and Richard Dagger, *Political Ideologies and the Democratic Ideal*, 4th ed. (New York: Addison Wesley Educational, 2002). Marx's statement emerged in the debate with the "Right" Hegelians who, true to Hegel's own view, overemphasized the religiosity of *geist*-spirit in unfolding historical dialectics.

105. The diversities include the United States, Canada (Quebec), Australia, Bosnia, Iraq, New Zealand, South Africa, and Northern Ireland.

106. Cedric Robinson, *Black Marxism*, p. 17.

107. Seymour Martin Lipset and Gary W. Marks, *It Didn't Happen Here: Why Socialism Failed in the United States* (New York: W. W. Norton, 2000), p. 130. Indeed, African American workers, male and female, encountered widespread discrimination. The manner in which the socialists bungled the "national" question, particularly as it pertained to the American context, reinforced the notion that neither Marx nor Engels developed adequate theses on nationalism, whether Bolshevik or African American.

108. Cited in Cedric Robinson, *Black Marxism*, pp. 77–78.

109. Herbert Aptheker, *Marxism and Christianity*, p. 33. Emphasis added.

110. See "The 1928 and 1930 Comintern Resolutions on the Black National Question in the United States," with an Introduction by Lowell Young (Washington, DC: Revolutionary Review Press, 1975). This document is available at http://www.marx2mao.com/Other/CR75.html.

111. See Philip S. Foner (ed.), *Black Socialist Preacher: The Teachings of Reverend George Washington Woodbey and His Disciple, Reverend G. W. Slater, Jr.* (San Francisco: Synthesis, 1983).

112. Philip S. Foner, *American Socialism and Black Americans: From the Age of Jackson to World War II* (Westport, CT: Greenwood, 1977). Woodbey was a contemporary of Booker T. Washington and remained isolated from the anti-Washington forces rioting in Boston in 1903, even as he criticized the Tuskegee leader's possession of "all the ability necessary to make a good servant of capitalism by educating other servants for capitalism."

113. Philip Foner, *Black Socialist Preacher*, p. 3.

114. Whereas Woodbey prioritized the religious and socialistic aspects of the struggle, he tended to view the specific racial impediments to class consciousness among the white and African American working classes—as did almost all white socialists of the period—as collateral to real revolution.

115. Philip Foner, *Black Socialist Preacher*, p. 30.

116. Ibid.

117. Ibid., p. 170.

118. Cornel West, *Prophesy Deliverance!*, p. 261.

119. Philip Foner, *Black Socialist Preacher*, p. 168.

120. Robin D.G. Kelley, *Race Rebels: Culture, Politics, and the Black Working Class* (New York: Free Press, 1994), p. 115.

121. Ibid.

122. For an interesting discussion concerning the general failures of socialism in the United States, see Seymour Martin Lipset and Gary W. Marks, *It Didn't Happen Here*; for a discussion of the failures of communism among African Americans, in particular, see Harold Cruse, *The Crisis of the Negro Intellectual*; see also Cornel West, *Prophesy Deliverance!*

123. Michael C. Dawson, *Behind the Mule: Race and Class in African-American Politics* (Princeton: Princeton University Press, 1994), pp. 96–97.

124. Cedric Robinson, *Black Marxism*, pp. 306–307.

125. Michael C. Dawson, *Behind the Mule*, p. 86.

126. Cornel West, *Prophesy Deliverance!*, p. 107.

127. Ibid.

128. See, among others, Wilmore, *Black Religion and Black Radicalism*; Hamilton, *The Black Preacher in America*; Frazier, *The Negro Church*; Marx, *Protest and Prejudice*; Benjamin Mays, *The Negro's God as Reflected in His Literature* (New York: Simon and Schuster, [1938] 1968); Paris, *The Social Teaching*; Lincoln and Mamiya, *The Black Church in the African American Experience*.

129. See Phil Zuckerman, *Du Bois on Religion*, p. 16.

130. The works of sociologist E. Franklin Frazier (*The Negro Church*) and Benjamin Mays (*The Negro's God as Reflected in His Literature*) represent a perspective that is only putatively distinct from the "otherworldly opiate" thesis. For Mays, it places primary emphasis upon the "magical, spectacular, partial, revengeful, and anthropomorphic nature of God. . . . Ideas of God that are used to support an otherworldly view are ideas that adhered to traditional compensatory patterns, those ideas that encourage one to believe that God is in his heaven and all is right with the world, and finally, those that tend to produce negative goodness in the individual based on a fear of the wrath of God here or in the next world" (pp. 14–15). It should be noted that C. Eric Lincoln and Lawrence H. Mamiya develop a dialectical interpretive scheme based on the research of Hart M. Nelsen and Anne Kusener Nelsen, *Black Church in the Sixties* (Lexington: University of Kentucky Press, 1975). Social scientists have employed "assimilationist," "isolation," "compensatory," and "ethnic community-prophetic" social-scientific models in the study of black religion. Lincoln and Mamiya place Frazier's interpretive view in the assimilationist category because of his contention that the black church retards the assimilation of African Americans into the national mainstream. Their view of compensatory models includes studies that emphasize the social functions of the black church as an alternative world to the larger, hostile society for individual black Americans.

131. It is noteworthy that most of these criticisms emerged prior to the emergence of Martin Luther King Jr. and the southern clergy, which directed the civil rights move-

ment's integrationist activism. King and associates targeted discrimination in housing, public accommodations, and voting rights in the South. Personally, King possessed the total spiritual, philosophical, intellectual, oratorical, and organizing skills and charisma to activate the black church's latent political efficacy.

132. Gary T. Marx, *Protest and Prejudice: A Study of Belief in the Black Community*, rev. ed. (New York: Harper TorchBooks, 1967). It is important to note that Marx does not measure other methods of participation that black religionists may deem more effective than militant methods. Overwhelming majorities of the 1,119 respondents to his 1964 study saw little value in riots and violence (as a first resort) and, at the time, viewed Malcolm X and the Nation of Islam with disdain. See pp. 25–32.

133. Gary T. Marx's conceptualization is a categorical misnomer. In fact, the "conventional militancy" that he observed in the summer of 1964 was closer to quasi-conventional political behavior, such as protests, boycotts, demonstrations, and sit-ins. These were the typical strategies of mainstream civil rights organizations, not radical activists, students, and individuals. The year 1965 is critical to understanding this especially because it was the year Malcolm X was killed, of the Los Angeles–Watts upheaval, and of passage of the Voting Rights Act. Marx qualifies his findings that "at the time of the interviews, the outlook of the conventional civil rights groups and spokesmen had a great deal in common [and] participation in peaceful nonviolent demonstrations was encouraged. *For the purposes of this study . . . we judge militancy by commonly held standards of civil rights activists at the time the interviews were conducted*," pp. 40–41. Emphasis added. By his own admission, "The relationship between religion and political radicalism is a confusing one," and "the effect of religion on race protest throughout American history has by no means been exclusively in one direction," pp. 94–96.

134. Ibid., pp. 40–41.

135. Ibid., pp. 94–96.

136. Cited in Wilson J. Moses, *Black Messiahs and Uncle Toms*, p. 24.

137. E. U. Essien-Udom, *Black Nationalism: A Search for an Identity in America* (Chicago: University of Chicago Press, 1962), p. 32.

138. See Kinfe Abraham, *Politics of Nationalism: From Harlem to Soweto* (Trenton, NJ: Africa World, 1991), p. 237.

139. Ibid., p. 81.

140. For an extensive discussion, see Winston James, *Holding Aloft the Banner of Ethiopia* (London: Verso, 1998).

141. Ibid., pp. 71, 76–77.

142. Robert A Hill (ed.), *Marcus Garvey and the Universal Negro Improvement Association Papers*, vol. 3 (Berkeley: University of California Press, 1987), p. 302. UNIA (its motto was "One God, One Aim, One Destiny") established the African Orthodox Church in 1921, just one year after UNIA's second most influential male leader, Bishop George Alexander McGuire, joined the organization.

143. Ironically, most of Garvey's UNIA offices were located in Indiana (which explains his attempt to broker a kind of détente between UNIA and the Ku Klux Klan, which had more members in Indiana than any northern state) and in the South.

144. Cited in Theodore G. Vincent, *Black Power and the Garvey Movement* ([1970] 2006), p. 133. Original source, *Daily Worker*, August 12, 1924.

145. Gayraud S. Wilmore, *Black Religion and Black Radicalism*.

146. Lewis Baldwin, "Revisiting the 'All-Comprehending Black Institution': Historical Reflections on the Public Roles of Black Churches," in R. Drew Smith (ed.), *New Day Begun: African American Churches and Civic Culture in Post–Civil Rights America* (Durham: Duke University Press, 2003).

147. It should be clarified here that Booker T. Washington spent a good deal of political capital lambasting the shiftlessness of most preachers and the ephemeral characteristics of black religion more broadly during the years of his dominance among black political elites.

148. Gayraud S. Wilmore, *Black Religion and Black Radicalism*, pp. 164–166, 168. Citation taken, however, from Lewis Baldwin, "Revisiting the 'All-Comprehending Institution': Historical Reflections on the Public Roles of Black Churches," in R. Drew Smith (ed.), *New Day Begun*, p. 29.

149. Whereas Washington's accommodationist philosophy rejected highbrow religious contemplations and instruction, it underwrote its own epoch of otherworldly religion in deference to the overarching commitment to avoid politics.

150. It was an agnosticism that was reinforced more by the anonymity of the metropolises than by an ideological commitment to the philosophy of Thomas Huxley. W.E.B. Du Bois's ostensible agnosticism, as promoted by David Levering Lewis, *W.E.B. Du Bois, 1919–1963: The Fight for Equality and the American Century* (New York: Henry Holt, 2000), and other writers, is closer to a religious disappointment than to atheistic agnosticism.

151. Published in *Negro Worker* (Nov.–Dec.1932). Reprinted by permission.

152. James Cone, *Martin, and Malcolm, and America*, p. 120.

153. For instance, several thousand lynchings between the post-Reconstruction era and World War I—some 1,100 between 1910 and 1914, with fifty-one in 1913 alone—were announced openly in some mainstream media and reported with horror in African American papers such as the *Pittsburgh Courier, California Voice, Call-Missouri, Chicago-Whip*, and William Monroe Trotter's *Boston Guardian*. White race riots in cities across the nation in the postwar period culminated in the bloody "Red Summer" of 1919. Other noteworthy publications include Du Bois's *Crisis* magazine (1909), the *Chicago Defender* (1905), Randolph and Chandler Owens's *Messenger* (1917), Garvey's *Negro World* (1918), Cyril Briggs's monthly *Crusader* (1918), William Bridges's *Challenge* (1918), and Hubert H. Harrison's *Negro Voice* (1918). For a discussion of the impact that these journalistic outlets had in their functions and struggles as major antilynching proponents, please see Sheila Smith McKoy, *When Whites Riot: Writing Race and Violence in American and South African Cultures* (Madison: University of Wisconsin Press, 2001).

154. James Cone, *Martin, and Malcolm, and America*, p. 121.

155. A third, less pertinent, development concerns a general disentanglement in black religious life that contributed ultimately to a "death" of the black church as the dominant organizational influence in African American life. Drake and Cayton's study of Chicago's black migrant populations in the black Bronzeville neighborhood elucidated the "secular patterns of interest," which imposed upon religious elites an obligation to both lead and participate in "racial movements." St. Clair Drake and Horace R. Cayton, *Black Metropolis: A Study of Negro Life in a Northern City*, vol. 2 (New York: Harper TorchBooks, [1945] 1962), p. 653. By overtly accommodating itself to political matters, the black church in essence expedited its own crisis of institutional relevancy. This approximated Peter Berger's understanding of secularization in which exigent demands are placed on religionists to adapt to the modernizing tendencies in society, which impose "a compelling necessity of participation in modern consciousness." See Peter Berger, *The Heretical Imperative: Contemporary Possibilities of Religious Affirmation* (Garden City, NY: Doubleday/Anchor, 1979), p. 62. Also see Mark L. Chapman, *Christianity on Trial*.

156. See Edward Curtis IV, *Islam in Black America*, p. 24. Curtis notes, for instance, the relationship between Blyden and white agents of the American Civilization Society, such as John B. Pinney, Walter Lowrie, and William Coppinger.

157. Robert C. Smith, *We Have No Leaders*, p. xvii.

158. See Harold Cruse (1967), "Postscript on Black Power—The Dialogue Between Shadow and Substance," in *The Crisis of the Negro Intellectual*, pp. 544–565.

159. Martin Luther King was fond of the "Good Samaritan" parable, which teaches compassion and acceptance of racial and religious adversaries. Moreover, the accounts of Jesus's encounter with a Samaritan woman—who was off limits on multiple grounds, including ethnic, religious, and gendered ones—demonstrated an openness that could be put into service for social and political use.

160. Key texts such as Acts 17:26 (humans were "made of one blood, all nations of men to dwell on all the face of the earth") and Galatians 3:28 ("there is neither Jew nor Greek, there is neither bond nor free, there is neither male nor female; for ye are all one in Christ Jesus") inform the ostensible race ecumenism of mainline Protestant and Catholic traditions.

161. Ibid., p. 205.

162. Phil Zuckerman, *Du Bois on Religion*, p. 70.

163. Mark Chapman, *Christianity on Trial*, p. 8.

164. The ghastly community imagined by Jim Jones, minister of San Francisco's Disciples of Christ—infamous in 1978 for the mass murders and suicides of 913 mostly black San Franciscans in Guyana—was deeply rooted in the city's political establishment and civil rights integrationist philosophy. I hope to develop this connection more extensively in a book-length project. San Francisco filmmaker Stanley Nelson's "Jonestown: The Life and Death of Peoples Temple" (2006–2007) points at least tangentially to this link.

165. James M. Washington, *A Testament of Hope*, p. 86.

166. James Cone, *Martin, Malcolm, and America*, p. 122.

167. See, for instance, Louis A. DeCaro Jr., *Malcolm and the Cross: The Nation of Islam, Malcolm X, and Christianity* (New York: New York University Press, 1998), p. 1.

168. Arthur J. Magida, *Prophet of Rage: A Life of Louis Farrakhan and His Nation* (New York: Basic Books, 1996), p. 118; see also Claude Andrew Clegg III, *An Original Man: The Life and Times of Elijah Muhammad* (New York: St. Martin's, 1997), p. 280.

169. Edward W. Blyden, *Christianity, Islam, and the Negro Race*, pp. 282–283.

170. In Islamic social theory, the *ummah* is formed from the threefold consensus of its members: consensus of the mind, consensus of the heart, and consensus of arms. The *ummah* is formed from the consensus of minds in that all members of the society share the same view of reality. It is formed from the consensus of hearts in that all members share the same values. It is formed from the consensus of arms in that all members exert themselves to actualize or realize their values. Although Islamic social theory holds that all communities are formed in this way, the Quran states clearly that the Islamic *ummah* is the best of all human communities given to humanity by God. The antithesis to the *dar al-Islam* is the *dar al-harb* ("House of Warfare"), or the non-Islamic world. This is the world of nonbelievers and must be struggled against by the faithful until either it is Islamicized or it allows for the free practice of Islam and the free commerce in ideas and values.

171. Richard Brent Turner, *Islam in the African American Experience*, p. 13.

172. Ronald Segal, *Islam's Black Slaves: The Other Black Diaspora* (New York: Farrar, Straus and Giroux, 2001), pp. 18–19.

173. Cited in ibid., p. 46. Emphasis added.

174. The revelation that Malcolm X had encountered white Muslims for the first time in 1963 served the exigent purpose of authenticating his transition to mainstream Islam, which began as early as 1960, just one year after his first trip to Southwest Asia (the Middle East). But Malcolm X witnessed white Muslims as early as 1959. See Rod-

nell P. Collins with A. Peter Bailey, *Seventh Child: A Family Memoir of Malcolm X* (New York: Kensington, 1998), pp. 153, 158–159.

175. Mauritania's black population, known as "black Moors" (*haratin*), have been locked in de facto slavery for decades, dominated by settler white Moors (*bidhan*).

176. Chancellor Williams, *The Destruction of Black Civilization: Great Issues of a Race from 4500 B.C. to 2000 A.D.* (Chicago: Third World, 1987), pp. 22–23.

177. C. Eric Lincoln, *The Black Muslims in America*, p. 169.

178. Ronald Segal, *Islam's Black Slaves*, p. 46.

179. Chancellor Williams, *The Destruction of Black Civilization*, p. 22.

180. Ibid., p. 34.

181. Ibid., p. 47. Emphasis in original.

182. In Quranic texts (such as Surah 2:177), righteousness is accounted to those believers who "free the slaves." Elsewhere, slave Muslim women are accepted as marriageable for those Muslim men who could not afford a free wife. Muslim men who marry in this case are told, "God knows best about your belief, and you are equal to one another, as far as belief is concerned." Indeed, these women are granted freedom through marriage in Surah 4:25. Most famously, Muhammad is noted for insisting, "the man who frees a Muslim slave, God will free from hell, limb for limb"; cited in Ronald Segal, *Islam's Black Slaves*, p. 35. See also Edward Curtis IV, *Black Muslim Religion in the Nation of Islam*, p. 9. Black slaves from East Africa, known as the Zanj, initiated insurrections in 694 A.D. and again between 869 and 871 to rid Islam of its Arabocentrism. Despite their insistence that righteousness superseded race and tribe, these groups "ended up taking on the form of a particularism that was both exclusionary and hierarchical." In the last year, the Zanj uprising resulted in more than 300,000 deaths in Basra. Slave uprisings, which resounded through the Islamic world, embittered most of its adherents toward blacks in general. Segal agrees with the opinion of another scholar who noted, "'the black Africans came to be held in contempt, in spite of the teachings of Islam, and there emerged in Muslim literature many previously unknown themes expressing a negative attitude toward black' Arabocentrism." However, Edward Curtis highlights the manner in which ostensible egalitarian movements among "classical" Islamic adherents such as the Khariji—who inspired the Zanji—and the Shu'ubi were duplicitous. See also I. Hrbek, in *General History of Africa*, M. El Fasi (ed.), *Africa from the Seventh to the Eleventh Century*, Vol. 3 (Portsmouth, NH: Heinemann, 1988), p. 30, cited in Ronald Segal, *Islam's Black Slave*, p. 47.

183. Edward Wilmot Blyden, *Christianity, Islam, and the Negro Race*. See also Edward Curtis IV, *Black Muslim Religion in the Nation of Islam*, pp. 79–81. For example: Umar ibn al-Khattab (Umar or Omar the Great) was the second Caliph, according to Sunni Islam, following Abu Bakr. Ibrahim al-Mahdi (al Mubarak, "the blessed") was a famed singer and musician who ruled Syria and was Caliph in Baghdad in the ninth century; he was also the son of a black woman named Shikla or Shakla, according to J. A. Rogers and John Henrik Clarke, *World's Great Men of Color, Volume I: Asia and Africa, and Historical Figures Before Christ, Including Aesop, Hannibal, Cleopatra, Zenobia, Askia the Great, and Many Others* (New York: Touchstone, [1946] 1996).

184. Edward Curtis IV, *Black Muslim Religion in the Nation of Islam*, p. 82.

185. Ibid.

186. See Acts of the Apostles 8:31–32.

187. Richard Turner, *Islam in the African American Experience*, p. 18.

188. Edward Curtis IV, *Islam in Black America*, p. 1. Emphasis in original.

189. Louis A. DeCaro Jr., *Malcolm and the Cross*, p. 3.

190. Claude Andrew Clegg III, *An Original Man*; Karl Evanzz, *The Judas Factor: The Plot to Kill Malcolm X* (New York: Thunder's Mouth, 1993); and Algernon Austin,

Achieving Blackness: Race, Black Nationalism, and Afrocentrism in the Twentieth Century (New York: New York University Press, 2006).

191. Algernon Austin, *Achieving Blackness*, ch. 2.

192. Ibid., p. 44.

193. The focus of Curtis's book is noted black nationalist elites Edward Wilmot Blyden, Timothy Drew Ali, Elijah Muhammad, Malcolm X, Wallace D. Muhammad, and Louis Farrakhan. Each individual is plotted roughly along a black Islamic particularist-universalist continuum. In brief, Blyden is depicted as one who employed particularist means to universalist ends. Noble Drew Ali is said to have employed universal means (linking American blacks to Moroccan Muslims; linking Christianity, Judaism, and Islam in an Abrahamic universalism) to particularist ends, as he thought only non-whites could be Muslims; Elijah Muhammad is depicted most negatively for his "absolutist particularism" vis-à-vis the Yacub creation myth, which was increasingly interrogated by immigrant and Middle Eastern Muslims around the world, as well as Malcolm X and Wallace Muhammad within the Nation of Islam. Altogether, Elijah Muhammad's racial particularism is subsequently interpreted as the starting point to Malcolm's Islamic universalism and the black particularism of his ministers Wallace Muhammad, Malcolm X, and Louis Farrakhan.

194. See Karl Evanzz, *The Messenger: The Rise and Fall of Elijah Muhammad* (New York: Pantheon, 1999), p. 74.

195. Wilson Jeremiah Moses, *The Golden Age of Black Nationalism, 1850–1925* (New York: Oxford University Press, 1978), p. 213.

196. Ibid., pp. 199–200.

197. Tommie Shelby, *We Who Are Dark: The Philosophical Foundations of Black Solidarity* (Cambridge: Belknap Press of Harvard University Press, 2005), pp. 150–151.

198. Ibid., p. 141.

199. Ibid.

200. These are listed as *distinctiveness* (there is a distinct black culture that is unique to white culture); *collective consciousness* (blacks should rediscover and collectively reclaim their culture, developing a consciousness and a lifestyle that are rooted in this heritage); *conservation* (black culture is an invaluable collective good that blacks should identify with, take pride in, actively reproduce, and creatively develop); *rootedness* (unlike white culture, black culture provides a stable and rich basis for feelings of community and for the construction of positive and healthy individual identities); *emancipatory tool* (black culture is an essential tool of liberation, a necessary weapon to resist white domination, and a vehicle for the expression of nationalist ideals); *public recognition* (the state should refrain from actions that prevent the endogenous reproduction of black culture, and nonblacks, perhaps with encouragement from the state, should cultivate tolerance and respect for black culture); *commercial rights* (blacks must become the primary producers, purveyors, and beneficiaries, financial and otherwise, of their culture); and *interpretive authority* (blacks are [or must become] and should be regarded as the foremost interpreters of the meanings of their cultural ways).

201. Greg Tate, *Everything but the Burden: What White People Are Taking from Black Culture* (New York: Broadway, 2003).

202. Nikhil Pal Singh, *Black Is a Country: Race and the Unfinished Struggle for Democracy* (Cambridge: Harvard University Press, 2004), p. 43.

203. Richard B. Turner, *Islam in the African American Experience*.

PART 2

Formulations

4

A Genealogical Inquiry into
Black Nationalism

The task of an Afro-American religious philosophy is to engage in a gene-alogical inquiry into the cultural and linguistic roots—in addition to the economic, political, and psychological roots—of the idea of white supremacy which has shaped the Afro-American encounter with the modern world.
—Cornel West, *Prophesy Deliverance*, 1982

African Americans developed an antiracist, anti-emigrationist domestic or "stay-at-home" form of black nationalism that has largely been absent in the most important accounts of black nationalism and altogether ignored in others. Elucidating this orientation is the focus of this chapter. Like emigrationism and black Zionism, its most coherent explanatory structure is rooted in the eighteenth- and nineteenth-century controversies concerning the "rights of man" in a nation of enslaving Christianity. Since the 1960s, few scholars have taken seriously the domestic tendency toward nationalism among black Americans in deference to more explicit demands for racial separation in a national polity or wholesale assimilation within the United States. More specifically I focus on this middling orientation in black nationalist history and discourse that touted neither racial separation (geographically) nor wholesale integration, which have been at the extremities of black political thought. Because integrationism has become the preferred, but not inevitable, national orientation of African Americans in relation to the larger society, scholars have rarely emphasized the extent to which integration, prior to the civil rights movement, was as fantastical as the idea of more than 20 million African Americans expatriating elsewhere.[1] The realities confronting African American life today are at least partly artifacts of bourgeois liberal integrationist hegemony established institutionally and as an inevitability, in consequence of the modern civil rights movement.[2]

Scholars have also elucidated the conterminous relationship between early black nationalist emigrationists and American political elites, such as Thomas Jefferson, James Monroe, and later Abraham Lincoln, in their support of expatriating nominally free African Americans back to Africa (Liberia and Sierra Leone), and between the American Colonization Society and Henry Highland Garnet's African Civilization Society. After writing *The Golden Age of Black Nationalism, 1850–1925* (at the outset of contributing three decades of formidable research on the subject), Wilson Moses assessed first-generation literature on religion and political thought and concluded that "scholars as diverse as Du Bois, Frazier, and Genovese [agree] that black religion constitutes *the foundation of the black nation.* This seems reasonable enough, although there has never been any systematic demonstration of ties between black religion and black nationalism."[3] It is worth noting here that Gayraud Wilmore's book *Black Religion and Black Radicalism* has since presented a persuasive case linking black religion and black nationalism systematically. Still, the full body of Moses's works is arguably the most influential historical treatment of the intersecting linkages between black religion and black nationalism in relation to how political elites and religious intellectuals formulated them. There is no shortage of scholars who tend to take Moses's historical analyses as intellectual gospel on the subject of black nationalism, especially because they generate an ironic "man-bites-dog"[4] or "black slave masters" shock effect, particularly concerning the "white origins" of black nationalism.

Much of Moses's theoretical critiques and historicizing of black nationalism derive from his focus on the writings, speeches, and manifestos of a very small group of literate individuals who mostly refrained from highlighting the rural peasant to "lumpen" class character of the black southern slave majority. The conceptual problem of defining black nationalism is among its most challenging ones, but to define it in the narrowest and most strident sense, along the lines of elite-sponsored land-grant demands and emigration, further muddles the discourse. Moses notes, for instance, that "in its strictest form, classical black nationalism must be defined as the effort by African Americans to create a modern nation-state with distinct geographical boundaries."[5] This was exemplified in the nationalisms of many black intellectuals and political elites from the United States and the Caribbean islands in the eighteenth and nineteenth centuries, and not a few in the middle to late twentieth century. Among socialists, Leon Trotsky appreciated the class dimension of black nationalism and the extent to which elites tend to co-opt ordinary people's struggles: "I believe that there are two strata: the intellectuals and the masses. I believe that it is among the intellectuals that you find this opposition to self-determination. Why? Because they keep themselves separated from the masses, always with the desire to take on the Anglo-Saxon culture and of becoming an integral part of the Anglo-Saxon life. The majority are opportunists and reformists," he notes. "That is why they are against any kind of sharp [self-determination] slogan."[6] Dawson insists, in this vein, that "the best way to study changes in black ideologies is not to focus on only a few canonical texts or authors, but to try also to understand how various concepts were used within various black activist and grassroots communities."[7] Frantz Fanon does this in outlining the priorities of the masses-class and the nationalist political parties in colonial Africa.[8] We learn little to nothing of what ordinary African Americans felt about colonization, emigration, or their national plight. Neglect of the ordinary, in studies focusing on pre-Garveyite periods of black nationalism, strikes as the glaring bait-and-switch that has been employed in the works of Theodore Draper, Wilson Moses, and their scholarly and intellectual progeny. With them, the nationalism of activists and spokespersons becomes proxy for discrediting all inclinations toward group solidarity among black Americans. Scholars agree that emigrationism was a formula put forth mostly by highly educated religious elites, such as Alexander Crummell,[9] Martin Delany,[10] Edward Wilmot Blyden,[11] and Bishop Henry McNeal Turner,[12] who were rejected by, and disillusioned with, elite white educational, religious, and political institutions but personally *never* experienced chattel enslavement, as had Nat Turner, Henry Highland Garnet, Frederick Douglass, Booker Washington, or, say, Sojourner Truth. And their audiences were white elites (mainly in government, the American Colonization Society, and abolitionists) and other Negro leaders and intellectuals, not everyday people considered the grassroots among some scholars and activists.

Immediately following World War I, radical black nationalist intellectual and organizer Hubert H. Harrison centered ordinary people in his thinking on racism, capitalism, and imperialism, including a responsive race-unity pitch: Elite "uniters" have failed because "they have generally gone at the problem from the wrong end. They have begun at the top when they should have begun at the bottom. To attempt to unite 'intellectuals' at the top is not the same thing as uniting the Negro masses. For, very often the 'intellectuals' assume the air of superior beings," he notes. "When you consider [that the intellectuals] in thirty years [since the era of Booker Washington's dominance] were unable to reduce the number of lynchings, and that the ordinary uneducated Negroes did this just by picking up their feet and coming away from the South in large numbers, it becomes apparent that these Negro masses sometimes have more effective brains in their feet than the 'intellectuals' have in their heads."[13] There have been a few noteworthy exceptions: David Walker, W.E.B. Du Bois, Hubert H. Harrison, and Malcolm X. Whereas Ronald Walters was aware of the major black nationalist elites who formulated nationalism along biblical lines (e.g., the exodus, Ethiopianism, Zionism), he criticized the very perspective that prioritizes "classical" epochs in black nationalist discourse (represented by Moses's works) without reference to its traditional religious discourse.[14] Nevertheless, he insisted that scholars too often miss on "the land question and its relationship to Black Nationalism," resulting in an ignorance of what he called "African American Nationalism."[15]

In the United States, black nationalism has essentially been an articulation of the desire for self-determination in relation to white structures of power in ideas, law, politics, culture, society, religion, and economy on black people's terms, facilitated most fundamentally in forms of group solidarity. Since its earliest articulation in social and political discourse, black nationalists have steadfastly insisted on *perpetual* as opposed to *utilitarian* racial solidarity as both a means and an end to realizing self-determination in a hostile society and world. John Bracey and his colleagues insist, for instance, that "the concept of racial solidarity is essential to all forms of black nationalism."[16] Black solidarity is considerably more nuanced and complex than simplistic "black unity" pitches; Baraka's "unity without uniformity" and Walters's articulation of "African American Nationalism" in the debates and caucuses centering on the early 1970s political conventions illustrate this.[17] Income, regional residence, physical ability, religiosity, class, and other measures of differentiation, such as gender, sexuality, and professional status, have seemingly always tested basic racial nodes of solidarity. All black nationalisms, as well as integrationisms (liberal and Marxist), have sought to negotiate the social, cultural, and *national* dilemmas of black Americans.

In one sense, integrationists are no less "nationalistic" than black nationalists to the extent that they have sought political incorporation into a definite national polity: the United States of America. Yet the *nationalism* of black integrationist leaders is seldom juxtaposed with black nationalism, because the former is routinely conceptualized a priori as nonracial and rooted in pragmatic considerations, whereas the latter is explicitly racial and rooted in unreality. Since the era of Garveyism, black radical and liberal integrationists such as A. Philip Randolph, Ella Baker, Bayard Rustin, Fannie Lou Hamer, Roy Wilkins, Whitney Young, and Martin Luther King Jr. accepted the reality of being led, governed, and incorporated into a national polity with a Euro-American ruling elite and majority. By its very name, the United States that they founded is exclusionary, overtly racial, and proudly nationalist. With some exception, the legitimacy of the US nation-state, its founding documents and principles, and its racial composition was almost idyllic among liberal integrationists; among these, claims that black Americans constituted a nation within a nation, or a colonial-subject people, were repugnant. Thus support for the US political system and society has been thought universal among black liberal integrationists, whereas support for a "Black Nation of America" is thought a nationalism of extremes.

There are considerable and complex intersections evident in the political activation of African Americans' core ideologies. If Harold Cruse oversimplified the relationship between political elites and ideological orientations with his claim that Frederick Douglass and Martin R. Delany epitomize the integrationist-nationalist binary, then his "pendulum" thesis nonetheless suggests a broad fluidity with which we can understand the overlapping tendencies and extremities in African American political thought.[18] Such variation accounts for how Martin Delany echoed David Walker (and many other early nationalists), who made claims to the United States as "our destination and our home," yet fully saw blacks as a people apart within it.[19] Moreover, before E. D. Nixon was an NAACP leader in Montgomery, Alabama, at midcentury, he embraced Garveyism and Asa Phillip Randolph's labor socialism. The collapse of the liberal integrationist civil rights coalition, Black Power, and Vietnam infused a stronger expression of black consciousness in King.[20] This may partially explain the contested placement of Frederick Douglass by Harold Cruse as the quintessential integrationist, whereas Wilson Moses conceptualizes Douglass as the quintessential "stay-at-home" black nationalist. Otherwise, how is it that two of the most important twentieth-century students of black nationalism see the career of a single preeminent African American leader so differently?

Similarly, Frederick Douglass's former secretary, the actress Henrietta Vinton Davis, became Garvey's second in command in international organizing during UNIA's formative years.[21] This is also true of the public careers of William Monroe Trotter, who worked with Hubert H. Harrison in the World War I–era Liberty League, which sought to network Boston and New York black communities in demanding congressional action against "lynching, disfranchisement, segregation, Jim Crowism and peonage by enforcing the Thirteenth, Fourteenth, and Fifteenth Amendments" from a black nationalist standpoint.[22] Du Bois's many ideological alternations are yet another example. The movement of 1960s black student activists, from traditional integrationism (sponsored by the NAACP and SCLC), to militant integrationism in Black Power (sponsored by SNCC and CORE), to competing wings of black nationalism and Marxism (Russo, Sino, and Cuban), reiterates its fluidity. Is it plausible, then, that there might be "ideological" space where, for instance, one's integrationist sentiments give way to one's nationalist sensitivities and vice versa? Sterling Stuckey insists, for instance, that "not only can one trace black nationalism and integrationism back to previous originators more than a decade before either Douglass or Delany rose to prominence, but it is in error to contend that there was not something of the integrationist in Delany and much of the nationalist in the young Douglass; that the ideologies and programs of these men did not overlap."[23] We thus do not accept uncritically the Manichean journalistic caricature of black leaders, individuals, and collectivities as all one (ideology), all the time.

America for the Africans at Home

Writing about "nationalist imaginings," Benedict Anderson insists:

> I am not claiming that the appearance of nationalism towards the end of the eighteenth century was "produced" by the erosion of religious certainties, or that this erosion does not itself require a complex explanation. Nor am I sug-

gesting that somehow nationalism historically "supersedes" religion. What I am proposing is that nationalism has to be understood by *aligning it*, not with self-consciously held political ideologies, but *with the large cultural systems that preceded it*, out of which—as *against* which—it came into being.[24]

In order to clarify the relationship to the general categories of black nationalism, I argue that if the American jeremiad constitutes the soul of "white nationalism," as seems to be widely accepted, then the activation of an oppositional counter-jeremiad by African Americans ought to be understood as no less nationalistic, despite the absence of claims to land autonomy or racial separation. Here the focus is on two major variants that issue *dispensational* and *dispositional* qualities. Both are expressly religious, and both reiterate its monadic nature in relation to black political ideologies generally. Cornel West argues that an important "task of an Afro-American religious philosophy is to engage in a *genealogical inquiry* into the cultural and linguistic roots—in addition to the economic, political, and psychological roots—of the idea of white supremacy which has shaped the Afro-American encounter with the modern world."[25]

Since Theodore Draper's 1970 Marxist salvo, *The Rediscovery of Black Nationalism*, the subject has been dominated by ideologically driven historical interpretations that have privileged some dimensions and altogether ignored equally salient ones, in the end betraying much of the yield of black nationalism in the most unflattering light. At the outset of his tome, Draper acknowledges that his interest in black nationalism was indebted to 1930s Stalinist policy on the Black Belt South. Searching for "native American antecedents for this or any other kind of Negro nationalism," he notes, "I found that the phenomenon had an ancestry going back at least a century" from the 1950s, when he first broached interest.[26] His insistence that emigrationist black nationalism was, at its outset, "a white man's fantasy," with its proponents and "fathers" being the likes of Thomas Jefferson, Kentucky senator Henry Clay, and Abraham Lincoln, committed racial colonizationists, scandalized the study of and advocacy for black nationalism, independence, and self-determination.[27] Draper plainly states that "from Jefferson to Lincoln, 'colonization' was the white man's favorite solution to the Negro problem. It was no mere case of wishful thinking; it was the basis of the first important Back-to-Africa movement."[28] Considering the pervasive support for expatriation among Anglo-American elites, Draper states that the founding generation and the white churches "did more for black nationalism than the black nationalists were able to do for themselves."[29] What would perplex Draper's treatise is how the "white man's fantasy" would give way to a stayed condemnation of the "white man's religion, Christianity," among Harlem nationalist groups, including the Nation of Islam in the twentieth century.

The idea that group separation was initiated by *racist* European and aristocratic North American elites, and not Africentric black-conscious political elites or groups, from Delany to Garvey, trivializes the fact that "back to Africa" was the first response of every individual and tribe extracted from their homeland via the Middle Passage—as if they needed white sponsorship to articulate a desire to end their living death.[30] It also privileges the ambitions of black petit bourgeois elites in its analysis and leaves the impression that the masses-class of Africans, toiling in servitude, could imagine no better predicament for themselves save the enlightened benevolence (or trickery) of white colonizationists, abolitionists, and the self-interested black petit bourgeois leadership class. He further insists that even twentieth-century renditions that were not sponsored by racist whites, such as the Moorish Science Temple, Garveyism, and the Nation of Islam, emerged in the "guise of an African fantasy."[31] Benedict Anderson answers the charge of utopianism aimed especially at nationalism in general by insisting that as "political communities," precisely *all* are imagined fantasies.[32]

Draper's book disingenuously sets aside how the "white man's fantasy" was preceded by black initiative even before the American Revolution and was prompted by *fears* stirred by Black Gabriel's 1800 nationalistic attempt to take over Richmond, Virginia—where Liberia colonizer James Monroe was then governor—and the thirteen-year slave revolution in Saint-Domingue (Haiti). And still later David Walker's *Appeal* appeared.[33] In the whole of Draper's study, the nationalist sentimentalities of those closest to the experience, slaves like Gabriel, are without standing. Wilson Moses, who builds on Draper's original provocation, nevertheless concedes that the earliest articulation of black nationalism was rooted in slavery, not Anglophilia. He notes, "Black nationalism was an expression of the impulse toward self-determination among Africans transplanted to the New World by the slave trade." And it is "one of the earliest expressions of nationalism; while it originated in unison with the American and French Revolutions, it was not an imitation of North American or European nationalism."[34] Moses makes the discrete point that black nationalist "thinking predates the American Declaration of Independence."[35] It was akin more to black struggles for self-determination in eighteenth-century Brazil, subterranean Maroon struggles in Jamaica and Suriname, and the blacks among the Seminoles ("runaways") in Florida.[36]

Draper's work focuses on various schemes and proposals among black and Anglo-American elites calling for colonization, emigration,[37] "internal statism," and the Black Power–inspired "internal colony," self-determination, and racial separatism agendas.[38] This inevitably leads to the "Delany trap," which tells merely one part of a considerably larger black nationalist narrative. Delany is considered by many scholars to be the father of black nationalism,[39] which is certainly appropriate if one defines black nationalism narrowly and with regard to land and race separation. Charise Cheney insists, to the contrary, "there is no question that emigrationism and the nation-state concept are recurrent and prominent ideas within black nationalist thought; however, *limiting the scope*

*of nationalists to those who advocate these tenets excludes or minimizes the im-
portance of theories and activists who were anti-or nonemigrationist yet clearly
nationalist.*"[40] Draper's Old Left criticisms otherwise set off much of the literature on the subject of black nationalism in the 1970s. Subsequent criticism
emerging from studies of the first generations of black nationalists highlights
tendencies among Christian imperialists whose disdain for so-called benighted
Africa barely exceeded their salivating affinity for Euro-American cultural enlightenment. Nell Painter notes, for instance, that black nationalist leader Martin Delany had the good luck of having "his misadventures after the Civil War
ignored by the black nationalists of the 1960s, and the elitism of his brand of
black nationalism did not attract scrutiny. Without knowledge of Delany in Reconstruction, black nationalists of the 1960s could read their black nationalism, centered on the masses, into Delany."[41] She reemphasizes that

> because the black nationalism of the 1960s and 1970s was egalitarian and
> democratic, inspired by anti-imperialism and emphasizing self-determination
> for ordinary black people in the United States and Africa, many assumed that
> as a black nationalist [Delany] must also have held ordinary black people in
> high regard. Few of his twentieth-century admirers realized that his nine-
> teenth-century black nationalism was an elitist, not a democratic creed. His
> chosen constituency was what he called "intelligent colored men and
> women," and he saw the masses as no more than a mute, docile work force to
> be led by their betters—their black betters, but their betters nonetheless.[42]

The reciprocal linkages between black nationalism and black religion are
admittedly made more explicit by focusing on the leading individuals who have
represented them within movement politics (but usually at the expense of ordinary people and communities).[43] Although Delany's influence peaked in the
mid-1800s, the message to students attempting to activate black nationalist
projects in the colleges and neighborhoods in the Black Power era was that
black nationalism was neither Africentric nor "revolutionary" as they had supposed; indeed, it was presented as essentially Eurocentrist and counterrevolutionary. Painter makes something of this point with the suggestion "beyond his
willingness to consider expatriation to Africa . . . the secret of Delany's leadership lay in his eloquent espousal of *purely American ideals purged of racism
and racial subjugation.*"[44] Although scholars like Draper and, more recently,
Wilson Moses have been consistent and thoroughgoing in emphasizing the
"Anglo" Americanness of African American nationalist elites, it is largely the
compartmentalizing (or ignoring) what is plausibly a resilient feature of African
American religion (and its derivatives in ideologies, organizations, and leadership styles) that undermines unidirectional claims of white European and North
American influences on black life, culture, and social matrices.[45] In accom-
plishing this, there is the tendency to set aside cross-fertilizations and reciproc-

ity in cultural and social influences; black culture and values are receptacles of those among Euro-American whites.

Benedict Anderson speaks to a "Eurocentric provincialism" in the earliest studies of nationalism and an attendant "conceit" that "everything important in the modern world originated in Europe."[46] Unbeknownst to Anderson's early reading of nationalist imaginings—in what he calls one of his book's two "theoretical flaws"—was the inclination to mark non-European (and nonwhite) national independence movements or weaker strivings as mimetic essentially because of the ubiquity of the dominant group's linguistic and cultural normativity. He initially adduced that "there is also no doubt that improving trans-Atlantic communications, and the fact that the various Americas shared languages and cultures with their respective metropoles, meant a relatively rapid and easy transmission of the new economic and political doctrines being produced in Western Europe."[47] The "ancestry" of postcolonial nationalist formations, he insisted, was facilitated by the detail that "a very large number of these (mainly non-European) nations came to have European languages-of-state."[48] This attitude is persistent among students of European and Anglo-American nationalisms. To correct this view, Anderson concedes, "my short-sighted assumption then was that official nationalism in the colonized worlds of Asia and Africa was modeled directly on that of the dynastic states of nine-teenth-century Europe. Subsequent reflection has persuaded me that this view was hasty and superficial and that the immediate genealogy should be traced to the imaginings of the colonial state."[49] Even more blunt, Anderson concedes that "it is an astonishing sign of the depth of Eurocentrism that so many European scholars persist, in the face of all the evidence, in regarding nationalism as a European invention."[50] This tendency to see black nationalism as the mime of Anglo and European modalities is a favorite maneuver of some scholars and intellectuals in contemporary political discourse.

Wahneema Lubiano identifies black nationalism as the "common sense" or "everyday" ideology of African Americans that derives from an experiential understanding of their place in the world. Moreover, it "resists both the U.S. state and its socialized and racialized domination."[51] She does not mention the desire for land. Organizing around principles of black nationalism has served the objectives of individuals and groups in terms of their desire to participate and compete in the social, political, and legal domains ruled by whites. And it has powerfully confronted particularly blatant forms of racism, normative cultural impositions, and discrimination. But for ordinary, nonelite African Americans, their black nationalism is rarely claimed, seldom discussed, unconsciously enacted, and poorly conceived yet banally *lived* existentially. It is a sort of default, at-the-ready affinity toward being black in a society that has historically shunned or sought social control and dominion over such a presence.

It might be useful to think of black nationalism as a politics "of, for, and by" blacks in the United States, the Caribbean, Africa, and beyond with a concern for their cultural, social, economic, and political dignity, integrity, psychological survival, and collective self-determination, which may or may *not* entail specific geographic, migratory, and land-grant concerns. *Nowhere* in Draper's study does he take into account the stay-at-home black nationalism or the identical non-Marxist revolutionary strand of black nationalism, which Moses and McAdoo, respectively, associate correctly with David Walker (see Chapter 6).[52] His work seems to engage in the presentist trap of associating long-standing appeals for freedom, independence, and self-determination by black Americans with modern civil rights *integration* rather than a "third-way" nationalist orientation (treated in several published studies).[53] Indeed, the great omission in Draper's search for indigenous black nationalism was the strain of abolitionist black nationalism epitomized in the life and work of David Walker among the Massachusetts General Colored Association (MGCA) in Boston and his *Appeal*, and among the first African Methodist Episcopal Church of Charleston, South Carolina, which supported the Denmark Vesey plot in 1822.[54]

The perennial nationalist tenet that African Americans constituted a nation within a nation (promoted by the likes of David Walker, Frederick Douglass, Edward Wilmot Blyden, Martin R. Delany, and some Black Power advocates) focused less on the *state* as an authoritarian political unit and more on petit bourgeois elites' efforts, from Martin Delany to Amiri Baraka, to organize the linked fate sentiments that are readily detectable among ordinary blacks.[55] For E. J. Hobsbawm, nationalism

> cannot be understood unless analyzed from below, that is in terms of the assumptions, hopes, needs, longings and interests of ordinary people, which are not *necessarily national and still less nationalist*. . . . The view from below, i.e. the nation as seen not by governments and spokespersons and activists of nationalist (or non-nationalist) movements, but by the ordinary persons who are the objects of their action and propaganda, is exceedingly difficult to discover.[56]

In the various black nationalist projects, whether escapist emigrationist, racial separatist, revolutionary, or cultural, an important common denominator has been the sense of *relatedness* that African American individuals feel toward the black collective generally. Here again, Walters and Smith insist, "to us *it is self-evident* that there is a Black community; a historically constructed community of shared history and memory; with distinctive cultural, political, and economic interests; and with a geographic or spatial anchor in the nation's urban centers and the heavily populated Black belt counties of the rural South."[57] Michael Dawson acknowledges several nationalist strains, with rather fluid and overlapping derivatives identified in terms of the focus on "state power and land." In addition, he points to the belief that black Americans are "'more than just another American ethnic group' but as a separate, op-

pressed people, a nation-within-a-nation, with the right to self-determination."
The third "conception of 'the' black nation defines it as a community with a
defined and unique spiritual and cultural identity."[58] The initial formation, according to Dawson, is epitomized in the work of individuals such as Delany
and Garvey, who promoted "the idea of a separate state as a solution to the
problem of continuing black oppression."[59] More pertinent to this study, Dawson delineates the tendency he labels "A Nation Within a Nation: A Landless
Quest for Self Determination." In this orientation, there is no territorial specificity of where the domiciled black nation resides, how it is defined, or
whether it portends a common destiny, as in land-based nationalist projects. It
is epitomized in the rhetoric and advocacy of Malcolm X, who, in keeping
with the Nation of Islam's trope, emphasized "land as the basis" of every desire
that subaltern blacks possessed in their quest for freedom in modernity. Yet Malcolm X (both in and after his break with the Nation of Islam) never seriously
imagined the black nation as an entity defined with definite boundaries outside
of black Americans' situational realities.[60] Manning Marable notes that one
"element of [Booker] Washington's philosophy that black Africans were undoubtedly attracted to was his racial pride and black nationalist tendencies."[61]
If Booker Washington participated in black nationalism, it is when he urged
black people to "cast down your buckets *where you are*." Yet its cultural logic
is set against—indeed, is hostile to—integration into the social and cultural
systems dominated by whites.[62] Washington's political philosophy, which was
juxtaposed to Bishop Turner, his contemporary, hinged on the principle "'that
a return to Africa for the Negro is out of the question.'"[63] For Michael Dawson, Pastor Eugene Rivers III of Boston's Azusa Christian Community
Church—whose Ten Point Coalition is respected for its street-level efforts in
the 1990s at addressing gang violence in that city's Dorcester and Roxbury
sections—represents this orientation.[64] Acknowledging the "segregated existence" of black Americans, Rivers insists that racial equality is as much the
concern of black nationalists as it has been for liberal integrationist individuals. In Rivers, Dawson acknowledges, he "wants to focus black attention inward, to build strong autonomous institutions, reconstruct the indigenous
black counterpublic, and forge an independent economic, social, cultural, and
political agenda." Rivers "is right to say that his agenda is consistent with a
broad black historical tradition that embraces equality, is *not attached to integrationism, and rejects assimilation. But is it nationalism?*"[65] The lingering
question here seems rhetorical, especially as Rivers fully identifies with a desire for a pragmatic black nationalism.[66] Thus, the negative demand that white
supremacy in society, politics, and government be eradicated is not indicative
of support for integration any more than its opposite—that affirmative support
for interracial "brotherhood" should lead to racial separation.[67]

Confusing, however, is Darren Davis and Ronald Brown's study, which collapses the very distinct ideals corresponding with blacks' view of themselves as

a nation within a nation (noun) and the statement that blacks should form a separate nation (verb) as "redundant" concepts.[68] They note, for instance, "we were not sure what the question 'blacks form a nation within a nation' means. . . . If, as we suspect, respondents see it as blacks should form a separate nation, it is redundant." Yet just as readily, these authors insist that even "if the question is interpreted as black people represent a nation within itself, it still may not belong in the analysis because either rejection or support for it does not translate into support for black nationalism."[69] It is implausible that the concept is *redundant* with another expression of black nationalism, as they suggest, and simultaneously *not be nationalism at all*, as they also suggest, unless they strictly regard nationalism as possessing or desiring a nation-state. Noted above was the range of political elites who touted the slogan of "a nation within a nation" as a way of speaking to the "captive" nature of African Americans as a social group in the United States. How should we understand the national citizenship status of Negroes and freed persons for the decade between the 1857 *Dred Scott v. San(d)ford* decision (denying it) and the 1866 Civil Rights Act (conferring it)? Today we take it for granted, but before, and briefly *after* the US Civil War, two of three branches of the United States government rejected (slave and free) Negro citizenship in the states and nation. For the three-year period between the passage of the Thirteenth Amendment abolishing slavery and the Fourteenth Amendment granting Negro citizenship, blacks possessed all of the attributes of "a nation," without a *state* sovereignty to represent their interests or to determine their destiny. There is hardly a more definitive tenet of black nationalism than this, and no major studies have been confounded of its nationalist implications. It corresponded to a large degree with the "internal colony" thesis of Harold Cruse and the Black Power leadership cadre. It is wholly different from advocacy of separatism that is expatriation.[70]

Porous intersections within African American political thought instruct our understanding of the differences between the "nation within a nation" and "community nationalism" orientations. Here it becomes a matter of levels, not of kind; the former is a matter of "national" concern, whereas the latter is a matter in the urban localities. Black Power advocates of the ostensible cultural and revolutionary forms shared in common a rejection of Euro-American cultural imposition. Algernon Austin insists that Black Power's cultural wing, represented by US organization (versus the white "THEM") and its revolutionary wing, represented by the Black Panther Party, "were simultaneously political and cultural nationalists" seeking black cultural and political autonomy in the United States.[71] Indeed, he insists that both groups were "merely Black Power black nationalists." If this distinction glosses over major programmatic, organizational, philosophical, and personality differences, then it also reminds us that they shared in common no interest in conventionally defined nation-state nationalism, though contemporaries in the New Republic of Afrika did.

If Garvey's slogan "Africa for the Africans at home and abroad"[72] epitomizes the focus of pan-Africanism, the "Black World Nation,"[73] and emigrationist black nationalism, then "America for the Africans at Home" plausibly suits the "stay at home in the United States" sentiment of proto- and quasi-nationalist elites.[74] In fact, Garvey historian Theodore Vincent views such a notion as derivative of "Africa for the Africans" to the extent Garvey's concept "had significance for black Americans in that once Africa had been freed from colonial rule, blacks in the United States could be given aid in their fight for equal rights, much as the Zionists in Garvey's time sought to make Palestine a bulwark for international Jewry."[75] Wilson Moses has rightly noted David Walker's importance in clarifying the "stay at home in the United States" version of black nationalism, which differs—at least in terms of its end goal—from expatriatist strategies, such as "back to Africa," or other emigration. Moses lists Frederick Douglass as belonging to "that tradition of black nationalists who militantly asserted their right to American citizenship. *It was the tradition represented by David Walker*, whose case exemplifies the *distinction* between nationalism and emigrationism."[76] This is the clearest statement of the reality that David Walker was the father of a type of black nationalism that is somehow as obscure—and yet self-evidently important—as Walker himself. With this understanding, Walker notes in his answer to white colonizationists and black emigrationists: "What our brethren could have been thinking about, who have left their native land and home [the United States] and go away to [Liberia] Africa, I am unable to say. *This country is as much ours as it is the whites'*, whether they will admit it or not" (Article IV) (emphasis added). Nevertheless, Walker grew increasingly sympathetic to the emigrationist idea in the third edition of the *Appeal* (September 19, 1830), inserting the sentiment that "if any of us see fit to go away, go to those who have been for many years, and are now our greatest earthly friends and benefactors—the English. If not so, go to our brethren, the Haytians, who, according to their word, are bound to protect and comfort us" (Article IV). Walker still regarded the white-led colonizationist plan as a "trick": rid America of those Negroes capable of leadership in antislavery and it should perpetuate the condition of those people of African descent still in chattel bondage. This was colonization. Citing a letter from the renowned A.M.E. cofounder and bishop Richard Allen of Philadelphia, Walker conveys his attack on colonization: "This land which we have watered with our *tears* and *our blood*, is now *our mother country*, and we are well satisfied to stay where wisdom abounds and the gospel is free" (emphasis in original).[77]

Unlike most of the proponents of nineteenth-century emigrationist-Zionism —which was led mostly by immigrant blacks and has been subjected to withering criticism, especially from African scholars—Walker viewed Africa positively as a source of civilization and technological development, indeed, as *the* source of learning and native land of "that mighty son of Africa, Hannibal" of Carthage (Tunisia), and Toussaint L'Ouverture of the Haitian Revolution (Article II). Walker also affiliated with "African" and all-black institutions in his personal life, promoted "Ethiopianism" in the *Appeal*, and inspired a militant form of abolitionism among black Bostonians. Donald Jacobs explains that it was set off against white moral suasionist Garrisonian abolitionism. Indeed, Africa, Walker thought, would be the source of a black messianic leadership that would not operate like Moses, leading blacks out of the United States in exodus to an African promised land, but rather that "God will indeed . . . deliver you through him from the deplorable and wretched condition under the Christians of America" by virtue of leading slaveholders to repentance— or to their graves.[78] Henry Highland Garnet, who vacillated on emigration (as opposed to elite white–sponsored colonization), employed many of its sentiments, namely a call to slave rebellion and other sentiments anticipated by Walker. Garnet wrote in 1848, "America is my home, my country, and I have no other."[79] Later, he advocated emigration.

This is also consistent with the sentiments of most ordinary blacks seeking to carve an independent niche within US society, one where they could experience substantive justice before the law, racial peace, economic sustenance, and safe and healthy community living. Gary T. Marx demonstrated the weak support that the notion of a separate black nation held during its most salient moment since World War II, with only one in five respondents in favor.[80] Of the ten black nationalist measures compiled in Davis and Brown's study, the idea that "Blacks should have their own nation" scored lowest.[81] The idea has never been popular among ordinary nonelite blacks. Brown and Dawson's *National Black Politics Study* (1993–1994) found that less than 15 percent of African American respondents agreed that "Black people should have their own separate nation," whereas a slight majority agreed that "Black people should form a nation within a nation."[82] Various measures of concepts such as "linked fate," "community nationalism," "black autonomy," and "group destiny" mostly reflect attitudes concerning local and domestic American realities; they are rarely connected to antecedents in the history of black nationalism, because they do not fit neatly in the received categories of what black nationalism is.

Harold Cruse's *Crisis of the Negro Intellectual* takes considerable umbrage with Caribbean and African nationalist intellectuals and activists, as well as American Jews in the Communist Party USA for failing to understand the particularly American exigencies that set black Americans' nationalist orientations in Harlem against the interests and foci of Caribbean, African, and American Jewish nationalisms.[83] As for Garveyism, Cruse moves to exclude it from the mainstream of African American nationalism, arguing, "Garvey had, no doubt, his hardcore members [but] his membership, however, was predominantly West Indian and whatever the number of American Negroes attracted to Garveyism, it was *not* an Afro-American Nationalist movement engaged in an historical confrontation with the realities of the American situation out of which it sprung."[84] Cruse implies here that authentic (nonessentialist) expressions of black nationalism are to be tailored to, and understood in light of, the unique circumstances of a given social and political context. Hubert H. Harrison, the forerunner of Garveyism and UNIA,[85] perplexes Cruse's assertion. This is mainly because he emigrated to the United States as a seventeen-year-old orphan from St. Croix, in the Danish West Indies, and while providing the framework for much of what would become Garveyism, Harrison, unlike most West Indian nationalists, argued that "the American Negro is—after all—an American; and generally a deeper, truer American than nine-tenths of the whites."[86] Certainly since the passing of the civil rights movement, understanding and activation of black nationalism have been largely shed of the matters of sovereignty or secession of any sort. But a question remains whether this is a *new* phenomenon or simply a tapping of values that have precedence in African American political experience.

Plotting political elites within the various orientations have been at the center of much disagreement over who, for instance, is nationalist. One analyst's integrationist-assimilationist or accommodationist is another analyst's emigration-Zionist or separatist-nationalist.[87] In response, Sterling Stuckey contends that these characterizations, "when thought of as mutually exclusive, are not simply inadequate as means of understanding the individual being labeled, but prevent us from understanding major ideologies and movements" among black Americans. Stuckey argues further that these "discrete niches" obfuscate historical reality.[88] Much of the same can be said concerning avoidance of the political history of black nationalism, which has become all too common among nonhistorians who prefer attitudinal instruments of inquiry that are important but not necessarily of any greater explanatory power.[89] The point is that black nationalism may inhere all of the standard measures as partial explanatory items, yet assessing ideas and attitudes apart from a definite context tells us only part of the story.[90]

The nineteenth-century Negro Convention movement became a central network for debate and discourse among African American elites committed to the idea of the collective uplift of black people in the pre–Civil War period. Howard M. Bell's important study suggests that the convention movement included an array of ideological positions, mainly corresponding with emigration, black nationalism, and integrationism. The National Negro Conventions convened annually from 1830 to 1835 and again in 1853.[91] There were also pro-emigrationist meetings called by individuals such as James T. Holly, along with state-level Negro conventions throughout the same period. According to Bill McAdoo's little-known *Pre–Civil War Black Nationalism*, the conventions were neither national—being led mainly by "free" black "middle-class" elites in the North, who constituted less than 5 percent of the total population of 2,328,642 African Americans in the early 1830s—nor exclusively Negro, in that "white liberal managers" and philanthropists, mainly from among the abolitionists, also participated.[92] McAdoo delineates the major trends in black nationalism that were extant between 1830 and 1860 and locates them on a continuum and among elites who epitomized their theoretical foundations. McAdoo offers "three roads" in his brief study, which reflected the major political orientations African American political elites employed toward slavery, abolition, and the national citizenship question (all of which remained unresolved in the middle nineteenth century). The three strains, "reactionary" black nationalism, integrationist "reformism," and "revolutionary" black nationalism, contested for the support of sympathetic whites, in the case of the first two, and for the support of the potentially insurrectionary peasant masses-class, in the latter.

Central to his analysis are the leading nationalist personalities of the early to late nineteenth century. The book attempts to correct against the tendency among scholars to develop one-dimensional perspectives that explain black nationalism as a drive for land, with a commitment to establishing a nation-state-styled political unit either within the United States or abroad, usually, and contradictorily, at the expense of white benefactors (i.e., the ACS) or the US government. McAdoo's study provides an understanding of black nationalism that emphasizes a stay-at-home, domestic commitment to improving the material conditions of African Americans as a collective within the federalist structure of the United States by making special claims and demands against the state and nation for the racial legacies and persistent policy effects on black life. For McAdoo, this is epitomized in David Walker's non-Marxist "revolutionary" strand of black nationalism. Separate social, educative, and communal development of the sort promoted by W.E.B. Du Bois in the 1930s as "voluntary segregation" was as plausibly a desired (and more realistic) outcome as social and legally constructed integration in, or emigration from or within, the United States. McAdoo contends,

> There are a wide variety of philosophical and political tendencies which have traditionally been called *black nationalism*. Nevertheless, a disciplined examination shows that there are ultimately and fundamentally only two brands of *black nationalism*: one is *revolutionary* in essence, while the other is *reactionary*. What appears to be a multiplicity of black nationalist philosophical and political tendencies boils down to a variation (or eclectic combination) of either the revolutionary or reactionary theme. Revolutionary nationalism has always advanced the struggle for black liberation *while reactionary nationalism has always tended to retard and subvert this struggle.*[93]

This makes clear that a chief characteristic of the black nationalist projects in the United States since the nineteenth century is that they have never operated with unanimity; indeed, black nationalism is a multidimensional phenomenon. Some have employed nationalism as means to an end (e.g., in support of abolition during slavery, political pluralism with Black Power, or its related "community control" ideal), whereas others have employed nationalism as an end in itself (support for racial separation, internal statism, domestic "exodusing," or emigration-Zionism). The "revolutionary" variant used the *threat* of violence or actual violence in its opposition to race oppression, and it is nearly universally held that Malcolm X adhered to this orientation during and after his split with the Nation of Islam.[94] Martin Robison Delaney represented mostly a singular version of black nationalism, but at times he also took up a multidimensional ideological orientation.

Notes

1. See Ronald Walters, *White Nationalism, Black Interests: Conservative Public Policy and the Black Community* (Detroit: Wayne State University Press, 2003). He reminds us that prior to the contested discourses that centered the Nation of Islam and Black Power activists against traditional black integrationist thinking and strategizing, the NAACP and its attendant integrationism were audacious, even *radical*, to ordinary and leading Americans, black and white.

2. Adolph Reed (ed.), *Race, Politics and Culture*, pp. 6–7.

3. Wilson Jeremiah Moses, *Black Messiahs and Uncle Toms*, p. 28.

4. Adolph Reed, *Class Notes*, p. 34. These comments were written with regard to the moral problem of ostensible black anti-Semitism (see Chapter 7, this volume).

5. He does add a more vague description of other forms of black nationalism, noting, "In a broader sense, it may indicate a spirit of Pan-African unity and an emotional sense of solidarity with the political and economic struggles of African peoples throughout the world. In a very loose sense, it may refer simply to any feelings of pride in a distinct ethnic heritage." See *Classical Black Nationalism*, p. 20 (introduction).

6. George Breitman, *Leon Trotsky on Black Nationalism and Self Determination*, 2nd ed. (New York: Pathfinder, 1978), p. 60.

7. Michael C. Dawson, *Black Visions*, p. 8.

8. Frantz Fanon, *The Wretched of the Earth* (New York: Grove, 1963).

9. Gayraud Wilmore reports that New York native Crummell was refused entrance to the General Theological Seminary before his eventual focus on emigration to Liberia and Sierra Leone. See *Black Religion and Black Radicalism*, pp. 140–142.

10. Delany may be the exception to the pattern among nationalist elites to resort to the ideology following personal disillusionment, as he was accepted to Harvard Medical School in 1849, but he was born free to free parents in Charleston, West Virginia. See ibid., pp. 136–138.

11. See introductory comments written by Samuel Lewis in the Black Classic Press edition of Blyden's *Christianity, Islam, and the Negro Race*, pp. xiii–xiv; see also Gayraud Wilmore, *Black Religion and Black Radicalism*, pp. 142–143.

12. Turner was born free in South Carolina in 1843. His disappointment with the Georgia state legislature's move to eliminate black legislators is widely known among students of black nationalism.

13. Jeffrey B. Perry (ed.), *A Hubert Harrison Reader* (Middletown, CT: Wesleyan University Press, 2001), p. 403.

14. This may have more to do with his intention of clarifying this orientation in response to Theodore Draper's *The Rediscovery of Black Nationalism* (London: Secker and Warburg, 1969), which ignores nationalism's religious character.

15. Ronald Walters, "African American Nationalism: A Unifying Ideology," in *Black World* (October 1973), pp. 9–27.

16. John Bracey et al., *Black Nationalism in America*, p. xxvi.

17. For a largely ahistorical but pertinent study of black opinion in Chicago (and nationally) that taps the intricacies of racial solidarity, see Paul M. Sniderman and Thomas Piazza, *Black Pride and Black Prejudice* (Princeton: Princeton University Press, 2002), ch. 2.

18. As a point of reference, it is significant to find that the "father of black nationalism," Martin Delany, worked for and with Frederick Douglass, a "father of integration" in his own right, at the *North Star* newspaper from 1847 to 1849 and during the Negro Convention debates in the mid-1800s. Draper's study actually places Delany on an integrationist trajectory after the Civil War. See *The Rediscovery of Black Nationalism*, pp. 38–40.

19. Ibid., pp. 24–25.

20. These discourse intersections should be understood in conjunction with the choices available to African American political elites. If the careers of the likes of David Walker, Frederick Douglass, Martin Delany, Henry Highland Garnet, Henry Turner, W.E.B. Du Bois, Richard B. Moore, E. D. Nixon, Ella Baker, William Monroe Trotter, Martin Luther King Jr., and Huey P. Newton are suggestive, then an individual proponent of one ideological orientation can transition and fluctuate almost seamlessly in and out of any other under a given context.

21. Theodore Vincent, *Black Power*, p. xix.

22. If these demands resonate with integrationism, Marcus Garvey's presence and enthusiastic support for the effort at the New York meeting of the League, and a telegram sent to the similarly situated Jews in the bantustan-like Pale of Settlement of Russia upon the 1917 abolition of confessional and national restrictions, reiterate the League's self-conscious national group concerns—what others articulated as a "nation within a nation." See Jeffrey Perry (ed.), *A Hubert Harrison Reader*, pp. 86–89.

23. Sterling Stuckey (ed.), *The Ideological Origins of Black Nationalism* (Boston: Beacon, 1972), pp. 25–26.

24. Benedict Anderson, *Imagined Communities*, p. 12.

25. Cornel West, *Prophesy Deliverance!*, p. 23. Emphasis added.

26. Theodore Draper, *The Rediscovery of Black Nationalism*, p. ix.

27. Despite his slaveholding and racist beliefs that blacks were inferior to whites "in the endowments both of mind and body" (as expressed in the 1781–1782 *Notes on the State of Virginia*) and his personal campaign to blockade the Haitians in their revolution, Thomas Jefferson is considered the progenitor of the "classical" period of black nationalism, particularly as it relies heavily on the revolutionary generation for its nationalist inspiration.

28. Theodore Draper, *Rediscovery of Black Nationalism*, p. 7.

29. Ibid., pp. 7, 11.

30. It is somewhat ironic, as I will argue more extensively below, that the earliest Puritan settlers came with Jonathan Winthrop aboard the *Arbella* to set up their settlements on the "fantasy" of disassociating from their homeland for a "New Canaan" in the American colonies. They were, figuratively, peoples and "ships passing in the night" that would become the United States of America.

31. Theodore Draper, *The Rediscovery of Black Nationalism*, p. 55.

32. Benedict Anderson, *Imagined Communities*, p. 6.

33. Bill McAdoo, *Pre–Civil War Black Nationalism*, pp. 14–15.

34. Although he never abandons his Anglo-African historicist framework, Moses enlists the series of Maroon rebellions and societies in Suriname and Jamaica, and the

cohort of blacks among the nineteenth-century Seminole émigrés, as precedent—and equally plausible—models of proto-nationalist expressions from which early African American nationalists could draw for inspiration.

35. In 1773, four slaves in Boston petitioned the legislature to allow them time off from laboring so that they could finance their return to Africa. See Wilson J. Moses, *Classical Black Nationalism: From the American Revolution to Marcus Garvey* (New York: New York University Press, 1996), p. 7.

36. Ibid., p. 6.

37. Instead, his work focuses on free black elites in emigrationism, coalescing with the activities of white elites in the United States and Britain in their respective colonization plots, including the establishment of Sierra Leone in 1787 and, later, Liberia and Canada. He ignores the extent to which black elites saw colonization as a racist scheme and, alternatively, emigrationism as a project of blacks.

38. Moreover, Draper and Moses, like most students of black nationalism, tend to ignore the structural matter of *federalism* that factored in the political experiences of almost all the white elites to whom he attributes "back-to-Africa" schemes, ranging from an aged Jefferson, who presciently thanked "Providence" that he would not live to see the fallout of the 1820 Missouri Compromise, and Abraham Lincoln, who presided over the war for secession—Jefferson's worst nightmare. Draper does take on the various proposals of 1960s activists, such as Milton Henry's Republic of New Africa, and Floyd McKissick's insistence that blacks were a de facto nation lacking only in the kind of independence that would enable them to "exert enough influence within the federal system to affect the treatment of their Black brothers in America's urban centers." *The Rediscovery of Black Nationalism*, p. 140. In fairness, Draper is one of the few students who actually raises the federalism issue in asserting that the various separate state formulas "imply that the federal government is expected to aid and abet the disruption and dissolution of the existing American nation." *The Rediscovery of Black Nationalism*, p. 141.

39. Tommie Shelby, *We Who Are Dark*.

40. Charise Cheney, *Brothers Gonna Work It Out*, p. 17. Emphases added.

41. Nell Irvin Painter, "Martin R. Delany: Elitism and Black Nationalism," in Leon Litwack and August Meier (eds.), *Black Leaders of the Nineteenth Century* (Urbana: University of Illinois Press, 1988), p. 150.

42. Ibid., p. 170.

43. This is to suggest that if the 1960s emphases on the masses, grassroots, and the people were fictions of student leaders, then their critics have also underestimated the extent to which their own critical historical studies of black nationalism have preoccupied elites at the expense of potential constituent communities.

44. Nell Painter, "Martin R. Delany: Elitism and Black Nationalism," p. 150. Emphasis added.

45. If the tens of millions of Africans who were transported to the Americas are thought to have lost the social cohesion and social bonds extant in the cultures of Africa, then is it not pertinent that those of Anglo or other European descent should be understood as equally disconnected from European cultural influences and vestiges among Euro-Americans? The black presence in America, even in its most marginal state, has powerfully influenced the social and political cohesion of whites, especially influencing the ideology and structure of white supremacy and white fear that are frequently borne out in public policy. African American cultural expression in various forms has affirmed and informed the national and popular cultures, most clearly in musical expressions of spirituals, jazz, and hip-hop.

46. Benedict Anderson, *Imagined Communities*, p. xiii.

47. Ibid., p. 51. The success of the thirteen colonies' revolt at the end of the 1770s, and the onset of the French Revolution at the end of the 1780s, did not fail to exert a powerful influence.

48. Ibid., p. 113.

49. Ibid., p. 163.

50. Ibid., p. 191; see n. 9.

51. Wahneema Lubiano (ed.), *The House That Race Built* (New York: Vintage Books, 1998), pp. 232–237.

52. Instead, Draper opts to focus briefly on domestic separatism, which he calls black nationalist "internal statism," and concludes: "This bifurcation is not usual in nationalist movements and suggests a combination of needs which neither [emigrationism nor internal statism] could satisfy itself." *The Rediscovery of Black Nationalism*, p. 67. This strand corresponds to what Nell Irvin Painter describes as "exodusting," to "Indian Territory" in the territories of Kansas and Oklahoma. There were various attempts among African Americans to distance themselves from the hostilities of the larger social domain ruled by whites through emigration movements led by the likes of Benjamin "Pap" Singleton. According to Redkey's *Black Exodus*, exodusting was driven by the "push" of ongoing race oppression experienced by the many black southern farmers in the post-Reconstruction era and the collapse of the southern cotton economy due to the boll weevil. Draper also ignores the widespread development of emigrationist societies in the United States during the nineteenth century, as well as political and legal developments such as the *Dred Scott* case and the fugitive slave clause of the 1850 Compromise. His work also focuses exclusively on the nation-state strand of emigrationist black nationalism vis-à-vis Martin Delany's and Garvey's pan-Negroism and the ostensible separatism of the Nation of Islam, with a brief sketch of Du Bois's pan-African project. Although it provides a sketch of "internal statism," it makes no attempt to treat those nationalists who did not privilege land, exodusing, or the nation-state in their commitments. For an extended comment on Draper's work, see Cedric Robinson's *Black Marxism* (pp. 125–127, n. 2). McAdoo's work neglects an equivalent to domestic exodusing, and it is unclear where he might locate it along his continuum of reactionary and revolutionary variants of black nationalism.

53. Bill McAdoo, *Pre–Civil War Black Nationalism*; Algernon Austin, *Achieving Blackness*; Ronald Walters, "African American Nationalism: A Unifying Ideology," in *Black World* (October 1973).

54. Herbert Aptheker, *American Negro Slave Revolts* (New York: International, [1963] 1993).

55. Ibid.

56. E. J. Hobsbawm, *Nations and Nationalism Since 1780* (New York: Cambridge University Press, 1990), p. 11. Emphasis added.

57. Ronald Walters and Robert C. Smith, *African American Leadership* (Albany: State University of New York Press, 1999), p. 249.

58. Michael C. Dawson, *Black Visions*, p. 91.

59. Ibid., p. 95.

60. Ibid., p. 104.

61. Ibid., pp. 403–404.

62. Manning Marable insists that Washington supported nationalist causes, especially of a religious sort, among black South Africans and was influential among nationalists because of "Tuskegee's black nationalist and independent image to young blacks." See Manning Marable, "Booker T. Washington and African Nationalism," *Phylon: The Atlanta University Review of Race and Culture* 35 (December 1974): 398–406.

63. Ibid., p. 399.

64. Pastor Frank Reid III (of Baltimore's Bethel A.M.E. Church) is likewise a plausible adherent of this version of black nationalism.

65. Michael C. Dawson, *Black Visions*, pp. 101–102. Emphasis added.

66. Eugene Rivers III, "Beyond the Nationalism of Fools: Toward an Agenda for Black Intellectuals," *Boston Review* 20 (Summer 1995): 16–18.

67. Dawson also addresses contemporary "community nationalism," which he contends is less averse to liberal integrationism. But he readily acknowledges the persistence of overt racial realities, such as residential isolation of working-class and poorer African Americans. At bottom, in keeping with Malcolm X's post–Nation of Islam formulation, community nationalism is community control of all things that pertain to the literal and figurative black community, including elections, cultural production, and economic life. Brown and Shaw took up a study of "community nationalism" and its "separatist nationalism" analogue and found that the two dimensions receive support from overlapping, but divergent, black subgroups. See Robert A. Brown and Todd C. Shaw, "Separate Nations: Two Attitudinal Dimensions of Black Nationalism," *Journal of Politics* 64, no. 1 (202): 22–44.

68. Darren W. Davis and Ronald E. Brown, "The Antipathy of Black Nationalism: Behavioral and Attitudinal Implications of an African American Ideology," *American Journal of Political Science* 46, no. 2 (April 2002): 244.

69. Ibid.

70. For a lucid outlining of the colonial subordination thesis, please see John Bracey et al., *Black Nationalism in America*, p. lvi; see also Robert Blauner, "Internal Colonialism and Ghetto Revolt," *Social Problems* 16 (Spring 1969): 393–408.

71. Algernon Austin, *Achieving Blackness*, pp. 76–78.

72. Theodore Vincent, *Black Power and the Garvey Movement*, p. 98. It is apparent that this slogan originated with Garvey's mentor, Duse Muhammed, editor of the militant publication *African Times and Orient Review*, with whom he worked in London.

73. This phrase is used by Theodore Vincent in the introduction to *Black Power and the Garvey Movement* (2006), p. xii.

74. These include David Walker, Frederick Douglass, Martin R. Delany (as evinced particularly in *Blake* just before the Civil War and after Reconstruction), as well as Du Bois, Hubert H. Harrison, Malcolm X, mainstream Black Powerites, and academic Afrocentrists.

75. Ibid., p. 6.

76. Wilson Jeremiah Moses, *The Golden Age of Black Nationalism*, p. 38.

77. The article by Richard Allen is listed in the *Appeal* as one published in the November 2, 1827, edition of *Freedom's Journal* (vol. 1, no. 34).

78. Ibid., p. 18.

79. Cited in Moses, *The Golden Age of Black Nationalism*, p. 37.

80. Gary T. Marx, *Protest and Prejudice*, p. 29.

81. Darren Davis and Ronald Brown, "The Antipathy of Black Nationalism," p. 243.

82. Michael C. Dawson, *Black Visions*, p. 327.

83. Harold Cruse, *Crisis of the Negro Intellectual*, pt. 2.

84. Ibid., p. 124. Emphasis in original.

85. As well as introducing Garvey to the nationalist and Caribbean circles of Harlem, Harrison provided intermittent leadership, including editing UNIA's *Negro World* publication. Harrison was bitterly resentful of Garvey's personal pomposity and arrogance toward him.

86. Jeffrey B. Perry, *A Hubert Harrison Reader*, p. 27.

87. John Bracey et al., *Black Nationalism*, p. 222; Harold Cruse, *Crisis of the Negro Intellectual*; Stuckey, *The Ideological Origins of Black Nationalism*, p. 26. For instance, although Michael Dawson delineates transitions among some African American elites, he simultaneously places both Du Bois and Martin Luther King Jr. in separate "radical egalitarian" and "disillusioned liberal" categories; see pp. 17–18.

88. Sterling Stuckey, *The Ideological Origins of Black Nationalism*, pp. 26–27. Stuckey expresses particular consternation over Cruse's suggestion that ideological discourse among African American political elites is traceable to Frederick Douglass and Martin R. Delany. See also Robert Smith, *We Have No Leaders* (1996); Lincoln and Mamiya, *The Black Church in the African American Experience* (1990).

89. Consistent with much of what I argue above in this chapter concerning black nationalism's major theoretical and pragmatic manifestations, survey research seems to confirm the range of "stay-at-home" expressions in black American nationalism at local levels. But what a respondent thinks about shopping exclusively at black-owned stores, or whether African Americans should have nothing to do with whites, or teaching black children an African language, is no more a reliable measure of black nationalist feelings and practices than always cheering for a sports team headed by a black coach or for a black quarterback competing against a white one in the Super Bowl. People are considerably more nationalistic about their sports franchises in the universities and in professional ranks than in their shopping habits.

90. See Hanes Walton Jr.'s *Invisible Politics* and *African American Power and Politics: The Political Context Variable* (New York: Columbia University Press, 1997); also see Adolph Reed Jr.'s *Stirrings in the Jug*. This may be a feature of the datedness and underrepresentation of black samples in survey instruments, which tend to inform current empirical studies of black nationalism.

91. Howard M. Bell, "National Negro Conventions of the Middle 1840s: Moral Suasion v. Political Action," *Journal of Negro History* 22: 247–260.

92. See Bill McAdoo, *Pre–Civil War Black Nationalism*, pp. 8–9. In fact, an important class dimension emerges in McAdoo's study. At its core, the Zionist perspective, epitomized in the commitments of individuals like Martin, developed because the religious elites had little faith in the revolutionary capacities of the commonfolk masses-class of African Americans. Their religion was folk religion, not the religion of the theologically trained petite bourgeoisie. And this perspective reflected, at the individual and community levels, resources in African American social thought in which dissent and resentment of the long history of race oppression in the nation are *as strong as the ties to Africa or other diasporan black peoples are culturally weak*, thereby forging a "subnational" or "micronational" critique of white rule and domination in existing society.

93. McAdoo, *Pre–Civil War Black Nationalism*, p. 1. Emphases in original.

94. John Bracey et al., *Black Nationalism in America*; Bill McAdoo, *Pre–Civil War Black Nationalism*.

5

Martin Robison Delany and the Nationalism of Ends

It was a bitter time in Canaan, so difficult and frightening that even Frederick Douglass estimated that no less than one quarter of the black population of the North appeared open to the possibilities of emigration. Since the publication of the Condition *in 1852, Martin Delany had firmly grasped the intellectual leadership of the black emigrationist movement.*
—Vincent Harding, *There Is a River*, 1981

Bill McAdoo's book on pre–Civil War black nationalism enlists a debate that developed at the State Convention of Ohio in 1854 concerning the US Constitution's relationship to slavery.[1] The convention brought together a cross-section of African American national and regional spokesmen who articulated the perspectives of the nominally free black populations in the North. Representing the Zionist perspective was Ford Douglass (no relation to Frederick Douglass),[2] who argued,

Is not the history of the world, the history of emigration? . . . The coming in and going out of nations, is a natural and necessary result. . . . It is not our "little faith," that makes us anxious to leave this country or that we do not believe in the ultimate triumph of the principles of FREEDOM, but that the life-sustaining resources which slavery is capable of commanding may enable the institution to prolong its existence to an indefinite period. . . . You must remember that slavery is not a foreign element in this government nor is it really antagonistic to the feelings of the American people. On the contrary, it is an element commencing with our medieval existence, receiving the sanction of the early Fathers of the Republic, sustained by their descendants through a period of nearly three centuries. . . . It is just as national as the Constitution which gives it an existence. . . . "I can hate this Government without being disloyal, because it has stricken down my manhood, and treated me as a saleable commodity. . . ." When I remember that from Maine to Georgia, from the Atlantic waves to the Pacific shore, I am an alien and an outcast, unprotected by law, proscribed and persecuted by cruel prejudice, *I am willing to forget the endearing name of home and country, and as an unwilling exile seek on other shores the freedom which has been denied me in the land of my birth.[3]*

Sacred State and Sacred Nation

The US Constitution and polity were thus incapable of meeting the nationality concerns of blacks in the United States. On these and other grounds, blacks must not only *not* participate in politics—a position that Garrison held to the detriment of his relationship with Frederick Douglass and Garret Smith and anticipated this aspect of Booker T. Washington's accommodationism—but they must be inclined toward withdrawing from the nation as a whole if conditions for African Americans did not improve. The emigrationist position had as much to do with a pessimistic view of American social relation, and the nation's capability to reform as with any black American elite-led "scramble for Africa." Whereas most emigrationists were motivated by the "push" of slavery and race prejudice, the Zionist and colonizationists, especially the educated religious elites, were attracted by the "pull" of commerce, land, and religion.

In his important work on the religious life of Malcolm X, Louis DeCaro Jr. highlights the millennialist character of the Nation of Islam and founder W. D. Fard's dependency on "Christian Dispensationalism." For DeCaro, dispensationalism was less pertinent to the Nation of Islam's program of domestic race separatism and more pertinent to its theology of eschatology as it relates to Allah-God's redemptive work in human history. DeCaro is critical of dispensationalists, who advocate premillennial and postmillennial eschatologies and assign various importance to international events, vis-à-vis Israel. They dwell on the Second Coming of Christ with a constant recalibration of "their 'prophetic calendar' with the passing of time."[4] Dispensationalism, then, relates to a linear culmination of events in human affairs, particularly in the affairs of *nations* as they act on a grand stage, impassively aligning with God's foreordained intent concerning Israel's destiny and the destiny of the world. God is with Old Israel (Palestinian Jews) for the benefit of New Israel (Christendom) and the coming of the Christ in New Jerusalem, which shall replace earthly governments.

Although DeCaro highlights the hermeneutical and theological approaches common in Christian dispensationalism in its narrowest sense, he nevertheless provides an understanding of dispensationalism as pertinent to the notion of covenantal history and how individuals within nations at a given moment interpret the declension of conditions from a higher state of religio-political history. And dispensationalism—that is, the fall of great or disobedient nations—was integral to the early European settlers in the errand toward America—the New Canaan to which God, in the mode of exodusing Old Israel, had sent them to be a nation, hewn of the American "wilderness," that would shine as a "city on a hill." Congregationalist puritan leaders conveyed the idea that America was to be a city on a hill, the City of God among men.

A dispensation can be understood as "a general state of ordering things," "a system regulating human affairs," and "formal authorization"[5] that presides over the *civil* or sacred matters of a people as does a constitution or a covenant. In the pertinent biblical exodus story, the Law is given over the sojourning, land-seeking nation of Israel, and it initiates a new dispensation that is set apart from Abraham's and that of the early Hebrew patriarchs or by first-century Christianity. Both the Pentateuch (Torah) and New Testament of the Bible make reference to various dispensations, constitutions, or formal covenantal structures (i.e., the "Patriarchal" dispensation, the "Mosaic" dispensation, and the "Christian" dispensation), which institute the fundamental rules, laws, and acceptable conduct in the nation and even the preferred relationship between the sacred community and the state.[6]

The sacred community actually becomes a political unit self-consciously governed by formal authorities such as a priesthood, prophets, or monarchy in compliance with its customs and sacred texts. Perry Miller is clear on the detail that Jonathan Winthrop's 1630 *Arbella* address, entitled "A Modell of Christian Charity," not only had an economic motive but also refracted the "thesis that God disposed mankind in a hierarchy of social classes, so that 'in all times some must be rich, some poor, some highe and eminent in power and dignitie; others mean and in subjection' . . . to drive out of their heads any notion that in the wilderness the poor and the mean were ever so to improve themselves as to mount above the rich of the eminent in dignity." Winthrop told them that the desired end of the errand was "a political regime, possessing power, which would consider its main function to be the erecting, protecting, and preserving of this form of polity."[7] Failure to fulfill the obligation of the errand would be met with certain destruction, such as disease, war with Indians, crop failures, hurricanes, epidemics, infestations, harsh weather, shipwrecks, and "unsatisfactory children."[8]

Slaveholding and, more so, racism were *not* included in the list of puritan or subsequent "national" sins to which the respective jeremiads spoke; the former would be added gradually, and the latter altogether sparingly.[9] Robert Bellah, however, makes the critical point that "the story of America is a somber one, filled with great achievements and great crimes."[10] Initially, he seems to vindicate the crimes rooted in racial oppression with a self-confident and anachronistic notion: "Yet simultaneous with widespread evidence of corruption has been continuous pressure for higher standards of moral behavior. Eighteenth Century Americans with few notable exceptions tolerated slavery, *we do not*."[11] Still, he is cognizant of the impact of the Anglo-American errand on Native and African peoples, noting, "at the very beginning of American society there was a double crime, the incalculable consequences of which still stalk the land. We must ask what in the dream of white America kept so many for so long, so many even to this day, from seeing any crime at all. For that we need to consider the ambiguities of chosenness."[12]

The idea of America's chosenness among nations emanates from the detail that "Americans are not only a religious people in the sense of widespread adherence to religious belief, but that Americans understand American national identity as a people in *religious terms*."[13] At least through the civil rights movement, African American political history reflects a strong sense of group destiny presented in the biblical narratives of Exodus and Mosaic and Messianic leadership typologies. Their collectivist religious orientation operated against the self-understanding of North Americans of European descent as a people of destiny. Africans came before the *Mayflower* and the *Arbella*, and the "wilderness" had long been inhabited by American natives. Bellah hints at the prospect that the national issue of slavery rendered the Anglo-American errand a stillborn nullity, as they "failed the covenant almost before it had been made, for they had founded their new commonwealth on a great crime—the bondage and genocide of other races."[14]

The Jeremiad: God Blesses, God Punishes the Nation

Some scholarls will likely be reluctant to view a rhetorical and literary device such as the jeremiad as an empirically useful category, but it has functioned as a historical and political instrument in American politics as much as a theological one, particularly as it could be variously used to perpetuate, for instance, the Anglo-Saxon cultural status quo or to oppositionally speak against power, as many African American political elites attempted across several centuries.[15] The jeremiad is derived from the name and "political sermons" of the biblical prophet Jeremiah (627–580 B.C.E.), whose legend emanated from the record of Old Testament narratives in the Book of Jeremiah and Lamentations, concerning biblical Israel's captivity in ancient Babylon. Jeremiah was known commonly as the "weeping prophet," and his errand toward Babylon and captive Israel began with Jehovah-God's promise that "I have this day set thee over the nations and over the kingdoms, to root out, and pull down, and to destroy, and to throw down, to build, to plant."[16] Subsequent generations would measure their own status in fulfilling the American mission by their ability to reform the land to the original vision of "the fathers"—William Bradford, John Winthrop, John Cotton, Richard Mather, John Davenport—who were the first to bemoan the declension in their New World, less than a decade after their arrival. Winthrop, for instance, understood himself to be "the leader of a total society in which church and state, though different, were closely connected and in which Christianity informed the political as well as the religious structure."[17]

At each interval, the jeremiad presided mythically over a self-conscious people with a nationality consciousness and a sense of a providentially conceived national destiny. From the puritans and "revivalists" to the opposing political factions' jeremiads (Jeffersonian, Federalist, Whig, Jacksonian), and to Abraham Lincoln's use of religious symbolism in coming to grips with the Civil War, at intervals the jeremiad *defined* the chosen, their "errand" toward themselves and others, and God's covenant with them. David Howard-Pitney notes, for instance, that "the American Revolution was the great formative event of the civil religion. Every subsequent generation inherited an existent set of primary sacred myths and symbols created by the Founding Fathers."[18]

The jeremiad was also patently nationalistic to the extent that it concerned "the sins of 'the people'—a community, a nation, a civilization, [hu]mankind in general—and warned of God's wrath to follow."[19] Jeremiads speak to the times *within* dispensations and, in turn, mediate and frame the covenantal characteristics of different regimes. When nations or groups fail to heed the established laws or covenant, prophetic individuals call the nations and their leaders to reform and correction. Sacvan Bercovitch points to its optimism.[20] The American jeremiad presided over and socialized the myth of American destiny, Native Americans' genocide notwithstanding. Ideologically, it harbored many of the properties that are traditionally identified with the symbols and symbolisms of nationalism—only more so. Bercovitch suggests, for instance, that

> the ritual of the jeremiad bespeaks an ideological consensus—in moral, religious, economic, social and intellectual matters—unmatched in any other modern culture. And the power of consensus is nowhere more evident than in the symbolic meaning that the jeremiads infused into the term America. Only in the United States has nationalism carried with it the Christian meaning of the sacred. Only America, of all national designations, has assumed the combined force of eschatology and chauvinism. Many other societies have defended the status quo by reference to religious values; many forms of nationalism have laid claim to a world-redeeming promise. . . . But only the American Way, of all modern ideologies, has managed to circumvent the paradoxes inherent in their approaches. Of all symbols of identity, only America has united nationality and universality, civic and spiritual, secular and redemptive history, the country's past and paradise to be, in a single synthetic ideal.[21]

Representing the second generation with the "New England jeremiad," Samuel Danforth, for instance, felt that "the errand here in New England is that of any other saint, or group of saints; the American wilderness was no different essentially from that of Moses or John the Baptist. . . . Sacred history unfolds in a series of stages or *dispensations*, each with its own (increasingly greater) *degree of revelation*."[22] For Danforth, the fathers were "unexcelled in their piety, wisdom and fervor—but the errand they began leads *us* toward a *higher, brighter dispensation*. Precisely because of their greatness, we have a sacred duty to go beyond them."[23] America's national destiny was thus suffused with a sense of civic duty in which the vision of the fathers is conveyed in the political order that prevailed in the land. American jeremiads were suited to the nationalism of the puritans and their progeny and subsequently developed into a white middle-class bias.[24] Not only were the elect "saved by grace"; in America they were saved by *place*.

Sacred history, from Moses through Christ and the Protestant church, was in the process of fulfillment among the citizens of Massachusetts Bay and the polity that they had established. Their inclination was toward a kind of theocratic order, for it preceded the European and North American democratic impulses by more than a century. The jeremiad was thus neither abstract nor ethereal, yet it spoke to the material and spiritual affairs of a people in their land. The Reformation and its aftermath represented the antitype exodus from Old European "bondage" to the New Canaan of America. Pitney suggests further that one of the earlier national jeremiads "glorified the American Revolution as a political Exodus in which Americans had escaped Old-World tyranny and entered the New World of Republican liberty. This nationalistic jeremiad became pervasive national discourse and was ornately embellished in countless Fourth of July orations."[25] According to Robert Bellah's "Civil Religion" thesis, "until the Civil War, the American civil religion focused above all on the event of the Revolution, which was seen as the final act of the Exodus from the old lands across the waters, which began with the Pilgrims, and was covenanted with Jonathan Winthrop. The Declaration of Independence and the Constitution were the sacred scriptures, and George Washington the divinely appointed Moses who led his people out of the hands of tyranny."[26]

Whereas the biblical exodus account loomed significantly among the puritans and New England propagandists, it did not figure as much as the Babylonian captivity, exodus, and diaspora (to which Jeremiah spoke). For Anglo-American practitioners of the American jeremiad, the biblical texts in Jeremiah 31:31–33, Jeremiah 50:5,[27] and 2 Samuel 7:10[28] were more important than the exodus story because they spoke to the puritans' sense of themselves as a chosen but fallen people who would ultimately enjoy God's plan of national salvation.[29] Among others, Jonathan Cotton reiterated the idea that God had reserved the American continent for a new chosen people so that they could enjoy a new heaven on earth. The New England jeremiad of subsequent North American generations focused on bringing the chosen—that is, an errant and decadent America—to repentance so that God could fulfill the divine promise made to their fathers, to them, and their land. The American jeremiad thus entailed a history of decline, a fall from an original, albeit reified, higher state of social reality that was lost due to some great national offense—and through which God would ultimately redeem a divine promise to the chosen. According to Bercovitch, the more recent generation tended to shift the focus of the jeremiad from the spiritual realm of covenant to the more mundane matters of the "cultural commonplace." He notes, "recurrently, their allusions to wilderness, vineyard, Canaan, and Zion blur the distinction between historical, moral, and spiritual levels of meaning. . . . The elect of other lands might expect the blessings of heaven, but meanwhile they had to endure deprivation and ill-treatment." Thus: "The Protestant countries of Europe, inspired by God's latter-day church, might covenant for temporal blessings, but individually their inhabitants could expect no special dispensation of grace. . . . Of all the communities on earth, only the new Protestant Israel" inherited the blessings of national election.[30]

Similar themes were persistent among the nineteenth-century emigrationist Zionists who, at bottom, held to an antiracist separatist ethic that would result in a sort of pan-African black "city on a hill." This was especially so as they linked black Americans' special national status—that of being a nation within a nation—with the errand to Africans and to all Africans in diaspora who could benefit from continental Africa's improved standing among nations.

Emigration and the Errand Against Africa

As a religious variant of black nationalism, dispensationalism comports with the American jeremiadic tradition in several important aspects. First, the American jeremiad, which is defined by Sacvan Bercovitch as "a ritual designed to join social criticism to spiritual renewal, public to private identity, the shifting 'signs of the times' to certain traditional metaphors, themes, and symbols,"[31] crossed several major episodes in US religious and political history. Bercovitch further insists that "rhetoric functions within a culture. It reflects and affects a set of particular psychic, social, and historical needs. This is conspicuously true of the American Jeremiad."[32] The clearest expression of psychological black nationalism here is termed *black rage dispositionalism*—the black jeremiad that ran headlong against the dispensational ethos of the Anglo-American jeremiad (whether practiced by Euro-American or African American elites). For most of its history, the American jeremiad did not speak to or about the black presence in the New Canaan. Generally, this self-understanding operated in clear and patent opposition to African American interests and largely muted the claims that otherwise might be made against the colonial and US governments and civil society in the name of the earth-shattering bourgeois revolutions. According to Bernard Bailyn's *The Ideological Origins of the American Revolution* (1992), New England puritan covenant theology was one of several major sources of eighteenth-century revolutionary ideology to the extent that it influenced the revolutionary generation to think of the events of their times in "theological terms."[33] What began largely as a moral crusade in the eighteenth century gave way to a consonant "tradition of opposition thought" that was "devoured by the colonists."[34] Despite the American jeremiad, through which Euro-American whites saw themselves as New Israel, the chosen who escaped Pharaoh and headed for the promised land of America, it was not resonant with how commonfolk blacks understood whites or their religion.[35]

As noted, regardless of whether black nationalism has been committed to expatriation or to domestic empowerment, a common denominator in most pre–Black Power black nationalism has been its religious properties, which have yielded both *dispensational* and *dispositional* structures. The former is typical of black emigrationists in the nineteenth century, from Delany to Bishop Henry Turner; the latter is typical of those who engaged in jeremiadic discourse, including David Walker, Maria Stewart, Frederick Douglass, individuals in the early Negro Convention movement, and, much later, Malcolm X. This detail is neglected by many students of the subject. The dispensational strain concerns itself with territoriality (i.e., land or a nation) or proximity to the larger social domain ruled by whites. A rejection of American society and citizenship by black emigrationists should be understood, essentially, as a jeremiad against the intolerance of racist US society. It actually reflects, more than the dispositional strain, the "errand" metaphor of Euro-American jeremiads and "civil religion" discourses—the perennial puritanical objective of forming an "ecclesiastical government."[36] The black Zionist "reactionary" form of black nationalism (interchangeably called "Zionism" and "colonization" in McAdoo) actually included African American elites who associated with the ACS; who promoted emigration programs, such as Martin Delany of Charlestown, Virginia (1812–1885); who developed organizations such as Garnet's abortive African Civilization Society; or who worked through independent black churches such as the African Methodist Episcopal Church, the African Methodist Episcopal Zion Church, and the African Baptist Church (later the National Baptist Convention). Encouraged by the duplicitous activities of the early-nineteenth-century racist deportation program of the American Society for Colonizing the Free People of Color in the United States, which was founded by a cadre of prominent Americans from the "elite white power structure,"[37] missionary emigrationist petit bourgeois elites looked down on Africa, sought its resources, and loathed to identify with its inhabitants unless there was opportunity in so doing. Generally, emigrationism was one of several black political responses to colonization, although there was substantial cross-fertilization and overlap among elites, organizations, and ideas. And the pursuit of a black national destiny apart from the United States distinguished Zionists from other emigrationists (domestic or foreign) and the white-sponsored colonization project.[38]

Bill McAdoo clearly prefers the revolutionary strain and harshly criticizes the reactionaries' collusion with white colonization schemes as a perversion of a legitimate and authentic expression of black nationalism. For him, the Zionist perspective harbored three major offenses that made it unacceptable. First, although it looked to the oppressed European populations for its self-understanding, it modeled its *national* ambitions on the bourgeois imperial powers of Europe. A second and related offense was its disregard for continental Africans and Africa in its colonizationist plan. In Delany's words, "Our policy must be . . . *Africa for the African race, and black men to rule them*."[39] The third and most unpardonable offense, due to its emphasis on national withdrawal, signaled the low regard that reactionary black nationalists held for the masses-class of black people as a potentially revolutionary force against slavery *within* the United States, as epitomized in the sporadic but persistent threats of, or actual, insurrections. Ordinary blacks, the slaves, and poor "free" blacks would be forsaken in the interest of establishing exploitable land and labor markets in the interest of the bourgeoisie; they were deemed unfit for emigrationist ambitions.[40]

From Blyden and Bishop Turner to modern, ostensible emigrationist groups such as the Nation of Islam during the pre–World War II period, African American emigrationist elites promoted the idea that slavery was both punishment and cause célèbre for God's redemptive work among black people. Implicit in the principal Ethiopianist text, Psalms 68:32 ("Princes shall come out of Egypt; Ethiopia shall soon stretch her hands unto God"), is the notion of reconciliation, perhaps with an African heyday when Egyptian princes *ruled*, fell out of favor, and would be established in a new state of affairs in which Africans would once again rule black nations. The emigrationism of Edward W. Blyden, Dr. Albert Thorne,[41] Marcus Garvey, and his African contemporary, Chief Alfred C. Sam,[42] were mainly African and Caribbean imports with a goal toward trade, commerce, or the Christianization of Africa. *African American* dispensationalism was apparent in Martin Delany's opportunistic missionary emigrationism, which epitomized the early commitment to geographic relocation that was sustained in the twentieth century by the great nationalist and emigrationist Bishop Henry McNeal Turner of the A.M.E. Church and, later, in Garveyism. In conjunction with Ethiopianist commitments, these individuals, as well as some US-born blacks such as Paul Cuffee (1759–1817), Alexander Crummell, James T. Holly, and others, envisioned a model African nation-state that would reflect the biblical prophecy of Psalms 68. It was largely the proof text of black emigrationist nationalists.

The reactionary trend in black nationalism was indeed epitomized in Martin R. Delany, a leading nationalist physician who wrote in roughly three weeks his opus *The Destiny of the Colored People*, primarily advocating emigration to Latin American territories, Canada, and, later, Liberia, East Africa, and the West Indies (his novel *Blake* being centered in Cuba and Mississippi). Delany was preceded by the likes of Paul Cuffee and succeeded by Edward Wilmot Blyden (1832–1912), in part by Garnet, and most notably by Bishop Henry McNeal Turner after the Reconstruction disappointment.

Martin Delany: Moses of the American Negro Bourgeoisie

As a devout Quaker and primogenitor of the colonizationist-emigrationist idea among African American elites, Paul Cuffee was bound up in the Christianizing-civilizing ethos when he led two voyages with African American families in 1811 and 1815 to the British colony of Sierra Leone. The ACS consulted with Paul Cuffee, but the War of 1812 and Cuffee's death in 1817 prevented him from contributing more to his original interest in the African emigrationist project. Cuffee is best understood as a proto-nationalist because he did not advocate "back to Africa" as much as he sought to improve the position of Africans and African Americans through trade.[43] But Delany is regarded as an early nationalist, especially because he believed that blacks constituted a separate and oppressed national body that should withdraw from the United States. He modeled parts of his reasoning on similarities among African Americans with the experiences of national European groups, including the Irish, Scottish, Welsh, Jews, Poles, and Hungarians.[44] The strength of this trend was the manner in which it privileged the citizenship issue of free African Americans and black slaves as part of the national discourse in racism, which had been heightened in pitch as a result of the 1850 Fugitive Slave Act, which itself threatened nominally free blacks as much as it did runaway slaves.

The fact that emigrationist elites were mostly northerners, whereas throughout slavery the majority of free blacks resided in the South, points to an unrepresentative dimension of the emigrationist leaders.[45] Indeed, it was through the Fugitive Slave Act that slavery was reiterated as a *national* institution. Paul Cuffee, Delany, and other early emigrationists sought to depress the value of southern cotton by developing cheaper markets of trade in Africa, rendering the southern monopoly and thereby slave labor obsolete. Yet Delany was reluctant to attribute slavery to white supremacism. It was, instead, a matter of "policy" that was made convenient by the physiological differences of black laborers.[46] Delany's historical understanding of Africa reveals that he related its development to the supposed biological and climatic durability of African peoples.[47]

Delany's view of Africa was devoid of the condescension that would sometimes characterize his attitude after he visited Liberia in 1859. In an important 1861 report on Liberia, Delany referred to the Liberians as "a noble band of brothers."[48] As with other religiously motivated emigrationists, Delany expressed ambivalence toward things African. Liberia was established by the ACS in 1822, gained independence in 1847, and was also referred to by Delany as a climatically "objectionable" place for African American settlement, "a poor *miserable mockery*—a *burlesque* on a government—a pitiful dependency on the American Colonizationists."[49] Delany's attitude, like those of Alexander Crummell and Bishop Henry McNeal Turner, was often obtuse in terms of a concern for the impact of black emigration on African native populations. Still, Delany's subsequently demeaning views of parts of Africa were not held in a vacuum. For one thing, Delany's criticism of Liberia was directed toward the ACS and its client Americo-Liberian black leadership, which facilitated the ACS's slaveholding interests in the colony. In the mid-1850s, Delany distinguished between emigrationism and colonizationism, rejecting the latter and its "infant nation," Liberia. Moreover, Delany's view did not stand apart from his initial commitment to the plan of emigration on the American continent. Because of this he initially maintained, "Where shall we go? We must not leave this continent; America is our destination and our home." He initially ignores Africa as a potential destination for African American emigration in *The Destiny of the Colored People* and includes it (in the appendix) seemingly only as an afterthought. Emigration in the Americas—not the United States—was a theme that he mentioned earlier in chapter 6 of *The Destiny of the Colored People*, titled "The United States Our Country":

> Our common country is the United States. Here were we born, here raised and educated; here are the scenes of childhood; the pleasant associations of our schooling days; the loved enjoyments of our domestic and fireside relations, and the sacred graves of our departed fathers and mothers, and from here will we not be driven by any policy that may be schemed against us. We are Americans, having a birthright citizenship—natural claims upon the country—claims common to all others of our fellow citizens—natural rights, which may, by virtue of unjust laws, be obstructed, but never can be annulled. Upon these do we place ourselves, as immovably fixed as the decrees of the living God.[50]

Here, "country" seems to double for "nationality" and "continent." Delany encouraged emigration to Central or South America based on his observations that blacks were on the continent as early as the time of Columbus and his feeling that black American children should be taught the "Spanish tongue" and languages—not African languages.[51] To the chagrin of modern activists and scholars who advocate black nationalism philosophically, the reactionary black nationalists' attitudes toward indigenous Africans were imperialistic and counterrevolutionary in the same sense that Europe acted imperially toward Africa, Asia, Latin America, and Australia, and in how Euro-American whites acted toward American natives. And in Delany's view, it was to the imperial powers—England and France—that the black bourgeois leaders of the emigration-colonization scheme "should look for sustenance, and the people of those two nations—as they would have everything to gain from such an adventure and eventual settlement on the EASTERN COAST OF AFRICA—the opening of an immense trade being the consequence."[52] Some scholars see Delany as a "secular" nationalist[53]—after all, he did insist that "the colored races are highly susceptible of religion; it is a constituent principle of their nature, and an excellent trait in their character. But unfortunately for them, they carry it too far." He felt that the religiosity of blacks was used against them by those whom he deemed "wicked white men, whom we know to utter the name of God with curses, instead of praises."[54]

Indeed, Delany sharply criticized white Christian missionaries for changing the names of African converts because the psychological impact contributed to a loss of identity. His novel *Blake or the Huts of America* (1861–1862) depicts, through its protagonist Henrico Blacus (also known as Henry Holland and later as Blake), Delany's disappointment with black people's generally quietistic religious orientation and white Christian duplicity. *Blake* simultaneously problematizes and buttresses McAdoo's placement of Delany one-dimensionally as a reactionary black nationalist. According to Floyd J. Miller, *Blake* was Delany's answer to Harriet Beecher Stowe's stereotypic, long-suffering Uncle Tom Christian personality.[55]

In Henry Blake's absence, his wife, Maggie, is sold from the Stephen Franks plantation in the Red River region of Louisiana to Cuba. Upon his arrival, Henry/Blake is informed by her mother, Mammy Judy, who in turn urges him plaintively to "look to de laud, my chile! Him ony able to bring yen out mo' nah conker." She urges Henry/Blake not to lose his religion, only to hear him reply, "Don't tell me about religion! What's religion to me? My wife is sold away from me by a man who is leading members of the very church which both she and I belong! Put my trust in the Lord! I have done so all my life nearly, and of what use is it to me? My wife is sold from me just the same as if I didn't."[56] Still later, in response to Maggie's father's urging, Henry/Blake notes, "I tell you once and for all, Daddy Joe, that I am not only 'losing' but I have altogether lost my faith in the religion of my oppressors. As they are our religious teachers, my estimate of the thing they give [Christianity] is not greater than it is for those who give it."[57] This reflects Delany's earlier sense, as expressed in an 1849 speech, that "the thunders of God's mighty wrath must sooner or later break forth, with all of the terrible consequences, and scourge this guilty nation for the endless outrages and cruelty committed upon an innocent and unoffending people. I invoke the aid of Jehovah, in this mighty work of chastisement."[58] Nevertheless, Delany, as we observe in nearly all reactionary elements (emigrationist-Zionist-colonizationist), was committed to the propagation of Christianity among Africans as a "civilizing" influence, one that would wean them from their "primitive" habits of "eating with the fingers, sleeping on mats, and wearing light clothing that covered only parts of the body. He enjoined missionaries to train Africans in the use of knives, spoons, and forks."[59]

Delany thought Christianity would promote indigenous Africans to a higher civility that would comport with his economic nationalism and trade ambitions.[60] If Euro-American white jeremiads discounted racism as sin or ignored its impact on American natives and African Americans, Delany's task was not to be carried out by all black Americans—only the bourgeoisie. Although Delany at times included the four million slaves in his descriptions of the "nation within a nation," its elite Confidential Council, which would lead in the emigration project, would consist of "a great representative gathering of the colored people of the United States; not what is termed a National Convention, represented en masse, such as have been, for the last few years, held at various times and places; but a true representation of the intelligence and wisdom of the colored freemen; because it will be futile and an utter failure, to attempt such a project without the highest grade of intelligence."[61] This Confidential Council of free, mostly northern black men would be controlled by Delany; it would meet secretly every three years; and it would work "for the settlement of colored *adventurers* from the United States and elsewhere."[62]

Clearly, religious motivation was an essential feature of black Zionist agendas. It was the raison d'être for the emigrationist project. African historian Tunde Adeleke maintains that Delany "strengthened the case for the *mission civilisatrice*, the underlying rationale for European imperialism."[63] Africa was deemed by some emigrationist elites to be the logical home of African Americans and diasporan black populations. Many of those who advocated Christianizing and civilizing Africa held conflicting notions of Africa's premodern Edenic heyday (e.g., Benin, Timbuktu, Egypt, and Abyssinia), which, according to George Shepperson, sustained a "roseate image of Africa alive among American Blacks" and of its developmental backwardness (at least in sub-Saharan Africa).[64] Slavery was deemed, at least by Crummell and Turner—but also by the Nation of Islam—to be functionally necessary and good for blacks in the Americas where they were enslaved.[65] This zealotry led them to variously hold that slavery was the filter through which African Americans and Afro-Caribbean people realized "civilization" in accordance with the will of the Christian deity, setting them apart from the barbarity of the Africans.

Edward Blyden: Islam for African "Civilization"

Edward Wilmot Blyden (1832–1912), a contemporary associate of the major emigrationists (Crummell, Holly, Delany, Turner), was a native of St. Thomas in the Danish West Indies who emigrated to the United States as a teenager. After being denied admission to Rutgers University, Blyden traveled to Liberia at the behest of the ACS. His influence increased during the last quarter of the nineteenth century, during which he visited the United States an additional eleven times. During a trip there in 1883, for instance, he encouraged black Americans to view with skepticism the colonialist policies in Africa and their attendant images of Africa, suggesting that "no people can interpret Africa but Africans."[66] Typical of most emigrationists, Blyden did believe in the providential design concerning slavery. Psalms 68 fueled Blyden's Ethiopian redemptionist beliefs. But unlike the others, the Presbyterian minister's Christian pan-African ideology was informed by the great respect that he held for the teachings of Islam. Islam, with its "benign" participation in African slavery, as Blyden saw it, could provide the basis for a black cultural nationalism in West Africa. According to Richard B. Turner, Blyden felt that "Islam's lack of racial prejudice and doctrine of brotherhood made it a more appropriate religion for people of African descent than Christianity."[67] Blyden reiterated the Islam-over-Christianity trope throughout his career.

His positive assessment of Islam developed during his travels after the Civil War to Liberia, where he observed the "high culture" markers of African Muslims. Blyden did not think positively of traditional African religion.[68] In fact, he thought that European imperialism would raise Africa from its dependence on the local religious systems and that both Christianity and Islam had civilizing potentials for Africa. Blyden was soft on Islam and critical of Christianity's impact on Africa, but he also held to the belief that slavery was providentially sanctioned for the uplift—the Victorianization and Anglicization—of Africans. Although there is some debate as to whether Blyden understood himself to be a Christian and Muslim, many Africans referred to him affectionately as *Tibabu More*, that is, the "Christian Muslim."[69] Ironically, Blyden is seldom, if ever, mentioned in the Nation of Islam's pantheon of individuals who were instrumental in "submitting" to Allah-God and propagating Islam among black people in the United States.

Perceptively, pioneering black journalist T. Thomas Fortune (of the *New York Age*) regarded this perspective as utter "religious nonsense." And, indeed, there was an important class dimension to emigrationism that some scholars ignore. It is instructive that neither Delany, Crummell, Blyden, nor Turner had ever *spent a day* as slave chattel, and only the latter had any extended and direct contact with southern slavery (in South Carolina prior to the Civil War). And whereas Crummell and Turner accepted the idea that slavery, despite its cruelties, would have a positive effect on black Americans in the long run as a tool for the acculturation of Western values, appetites, and styles, Turner nevertheless saw *African Americans* as the lowest of all people: "American Negroes were made up of the most inferior portion of the African tribes, and that no 'big blood,' first class Africans had been sold to Europeans during the slave trade, only small blood, second classes."[70] They were the "tail-end of the African races." These were not the sentiments of the plantation slave majority in America or of indigenous and tribal Africans who were living in the trenches of racism, slavery, and colonialism. Rather, they were those of an imperiled, educated class of disappointed African American elites with a yearning for capital as much as any religious ambition toward Africa.

Crummell, a childhood friend of Henry Highland Garnet's and a onetime influence on Du Bois, who dedicated a chapter in *The Souls of Black Folk* (1903) to Crummell, developed into a major influence in emigrationism and pan-Africanism. Crummell espoused a pan-African version of Christianity, one in which "he appealed for transatlantic black solidarity built on historical and cultural ties and sustained by strong Christian values."[71] Crummell imbued all of the elements of his Victorian acculturation, which was fostered between his ordination to the Anglican ministry at twenty-five, his repeated and frustrated attempts to secure a church in the United States, and his graduation from Cambridge University nearly a decade later. He was *the* towering black intellectual of his generation but felt, like so many European thinkers, that West Africa "had no history." Emigration was in the interest of the thousands of "better Negroes," and it was utter "madness," in the words of Bishop Turner—who embraced black nationalism at *forty-nine* years old—to contemplate the inclusion of the masses-class of free persons, for, he maintained, "two-thirds of the American Negroes would be of no help to anyone anywhere."[72] Emigration was not to be undertaken by the majority of the 9 million African Americans (confirmed in the 1900 US Census). Between 1892 and 1898, Turner went to Africa four times under the aegis of the A.M.E. Church. He went to South Africa in the final year and praised the Boers for their superior religion against the heathenism of the Zulus and trivialized the racism that would represent the very foundation of the mid-twentieth-century apartheid regime.

Regarding pan-Africans' jeremiadic errand or mission to (and *against*) Africa, John T. McCartney notes that "the pan-Negro Nationalists were in fundamental agreement that blacks had a Christian right to their own nation and that African-Americans, as a key segment of blacks in diaspora, had a duty to lead in the attempt to realize this goal."[73] Wilmore suggests even more pointedly that there was a general air of condescension toward "non-Christian non-westernized Blacks."[74] He insists also that "the emergence of Black nationalism in America and *Africa cannot be understood apart from an appreciation of the zeal of believers to christianize the land of their ancestors* and to open up an administrative and communications network connection between churches for the promotion of Christian missions in both Africa and the Caribbean."[75] Focusing specifically on Delany, Crummell, and Bishop Turner, Adeleke provides a critical analysis of these individuals and highlights their imperialistic tendencies. To him, these individuals more or less perpetrated an assault on the African peoples in the blind reach for the "three cardinal" *C*'s: "commerce," "Christianity," and "colonization."[76] The emigrationist elites combined a strong racial consciousness, pan-Africanism, and black nationalism with a missionary zeal to convince their black bourgeois contemporaries to compete with European capitalists for the African field. Africa was not for Africans at home—as Garvey would later have it in his version of "Africa for the Africans, at home and abroad"—but exclusively for those abroad, who would give it their acquired religion and expropriate from it by means of their acquired market ambitions and morality.[77] It is a contradiction that proponents of black nationalism have attempted to reconcile with the tradition's affirmative commitments to black people. Wilson Moses describes this cohort:

The major proponents of classical black nationalism in the nineteenth century invariably believed that the hand of God directed their movement. Their religious beliefs led to a black nationalist conception of history in which Divine Providence would guide the national destiny to an early fulfillment, once the work was taken up. With God at the center of their ideological conceptions of black history, it was not surprising that they had utopian visions of the society they hoped to establish. . . . With its religious optimism, black nationalism met the need for psychological resistance to the slavery, colonialism, and racism imposed by Europeans and white Americans. . . . Ironically, the cultural ideals of nineteenth-century black nationalists usually resembled those of upper-class Europeans and white Americans, rather than those of the native African or African American masses.[78]

Missionary Pan-Africanism: Jesus for Africa and the Africans

This is the great irony of nineteenth-century reactionary black nationalists. Not that as Christians, they were not expected to proselytize their faith, but the irony is that as essentially "race men," they would coalesce against the interest of their kindred at home and cousins abroad with white supremacists in the ACS or imperialists in Europe, even in the name of their religion. Milfred C. Fierce's study of pan-Africanist ideology privileges the essentially missionary interests of African, West Indian, and African American elites committed to the promulgation of the Christian gospel.[79] In tandem with post–Civil War evangelistic fervor and an atmosphere of recalcitrant post-Reconstruction segregation laws, convict leasing, black codes, the defeat of the Blair Bill (1890) and the Lodge Bill (1891),[80] white riots, and lynchings, African American elites capitalized on assumptions that they were best suited to carry out the religious missionary mandates to bring moral, economic, and civil development to Africa.[81] Indigenous Africans, it was thought, despite their ethnic and linguistic complexities, would be more receptive of black missionaries than of Euro-American white ones.[82] This sentiment is traceable in nearly every major colonizationist-emigrationist elite and even in individuals such as Booker T. Washington, who made missionary work the theme of the Tuskegee-sponsored pan-African conference held there in 1912.

The noted theme of "Africa for the Africans" that streamed through most colonizationist plans had an implicit and explicit twin theme among the emigrationists: "Jesus, for Africa and the Africans." Fierce maintains that African American missionaries were pioneers who "contributed significantly to paving the way for an introduction to one aspect of the Pan-African idea—the awakening in African-Americans of an interest in Africa."[83] He attributes this thinking to the "theory of Providential Design," in which "there was a providential relationship between the emancipation of Blacks in America and their missionary role in Africa. In other words, God is now providing an opportunity for Black Americans to vindicate their emancipation and permanently etch their name in Christian history by evangelizing among the 'heathen' of Africa and retrieving the continent for Christ."[84]

Tunde Adeleke sharply criticizes emigrationism.[85] He unfortunately collapses all black nationalisms into the emigrationist column and draws inferences from his treatment of the elites to all black Americans, including the masses-class that these elites apparently held in low regard. Black nationalism is more than the literature and works of a few elites; it cannot be read in its breadth as a mere biography of individuals. Fierce also accentuates the negatives and downplays the influence that they had on subsequent and potentially revolutionary developments in parts of Africa. He ignores the detail that within the emigrationist project, even though wracked with the contradiction of mimicking European and North American white aspirations and attitudes toward Africans (and ordinary black Americans), African American emigrationist elites, especially Bishop Turner, contributed significantly to radical racial consciousness among the Bantus in South Africa, for instance, unnerving many European governments. Rather than being one-dimensional agents of Europe, African American elites, George Shepperson contends, were feared for their ability to motivate revolutionary action among Africans.[86] Motivated by the messianic Ethiopianism that had been perennial in American black nationalism, many of the A.M.E.-affiliated South African churches sought to strengthen the relationship with Bishop Turner and other African American Christians, especially in the late nineteenth century. Shepperson contends that the many African students who were provided educational access to historically black colleges and universities through church missions significantly influenced radicalism on the continent of Africa.[87] It is also pertinent that aside from the well-known elites, there were many cadres of lesser-known individuals, such as John B. Russwurm (cofounder of the first black newspaper, *Freedom's Journal*), Lott Cary, and Daniel Coker, who "envisioned Black nations emerging in Africa that would symbolize Black progress and exemplify Black nationalism"[88] without Protestant Christocentrism.[89]

The Christian Zionist errand in Africa went largely unrequited. For Bellah, the Anglo-American covenant marginalized African Americans, and they didn't "really emerge as part of the imaginative understanding of white Americans *until at least the time of W.E.B. Du Bois, if not Richard Wright or Malcolm X.*"[90] As a result, Bellah insists, "blacks have suffered more than any other group in American history from the projection of every rejected impulse in the unconscious white mind. They have been subjected to an unparalleled history of extreme coercion and violence which did not end with emancipation but has taken ever new forms to the present day."[91] Of necessity, African American voices would need to articulate jeremiads in their own terms, and they did so consistently from the early nineteenth century through the late twentieth century.

The second strain of black nationalism accounts for psychological and attitudinal qualities extant in what scholars identify as a black nationalist variant of the American jeremiad. Its chief function was to bring into question the very ethical constitution of Euro-American jeremiads: violence or the threat of it is a defining characteristic. In this vein, Eddie Glaude addresses the contentious process by which African Americans come into jeremiadic discourse with Anglo or Euro-American messianism that ranged from "hard" white supremacism to a "soft" Jeffersonian natural rights ethos. He asks: "To what extent did [African Americans] draw on the prevailing vocabularies of the American nation to imagine their own in the face of widespread oppression? If they drew on those vocabularies, what did they take and what did they discard?"[92] The black jeremiad counterdiscourse is the focus of the next chapter.

Notes

1. The use of terms such as "Zionism," "reactionary," and "revolutionary" is problematic in several important ways. The religious aspect of the Zionist position, although patently labeled with religious phraseology as such by McAdoo, is altogether ignored in his work; that is to say that the religious dimension of emigrationism is neglected as it is in the treatment of the revolutionary variant that I discuss below. Zionism has its roots in the Hebrew Exodus mythology concerning Yahweh-God's covenantal promise to deliver the Hebrew people from 400 years of Egyptian servitude to Canaan, "the land flowing with milk and honey." Jerusalem, or the City of David, would be established at the center of the national life of Israel as a symbol of God's theocratic rule in the new land. Whereas Theodor Herzl's *The Jewish State* culminated his interest in establishing the biblical account of the exodus and Yahweh's covenant agreement with the patriarchs for modern European Zionist discourse, African Americans have also put this narrative to use in accounting for African American slavery and the hope of redemption in it. The term "reactionary" is not only vague; it is plausible that all political formations among African Americans—liberal, conservative, radical, or feminist—could be so considered. And "revolutionary" has been the adjective applied to several generations of black nationalism, from the Marxist African Blood Brotherhood (ABB) of Cyril Briggs and Richard B. Moore to the Black Panther Party and Stokely Carmichael.

2. Douglass was no relation to Frederick Douglass. His position here is actually taken against Frederick Douglass and J. McCune Smith for their opposition to colonization schemes. His speech was given three years prior to Justice Taney's opinion in *Dred Scott v. Sanford* and one year before the publication of Delany's *Destiny of the Colored People* (1852).

3. Cited in McAdoo, *Pre–Civil War Black Nationalism*, pp. 31–32. Emphasis added.

4. Louis A. DeCaro, *Malcolm and the Cross: The Nation of Islam, Malcolm X, and Christianity* (New York: New York University Press, 1998), pp. 16–17.

5. See Dean E. Robinson, *Black Nationalism in American Politics and Thought* (New York: Cambridge University Press, 2001).

6. See *Merriam-Webster's Ninth New Collegiate Dictionary* (Springfield, MA: Merriam-Webster, 1990). Dispensation is defined as "a general state of ordering things," "a system regulating human affairs," and "formal authorization." A fundamental difference is that in integrationism the dispositional values of assimilationism are identical with the dispensational end of assimilating into the larger, albeit pluralist, social order as equal citizens. Among black nationalists, however, there has been a ten-

dency to articulate both strains as means *or* ends in themselves for black liberation. Although these orientations are not mutually exclusive in nationalist thought, it remains possible for an individual to act and think militantly toward and about the extant social order without being seduced by a utopian ideal state of existence beyond current realities. The distinction is critical for delineating the modalities in nationalist thought, particularly in the United States.

7. The first related to God's covenant with Abraham and the Twelve Tribes of Israel represented in the sons of Jacob. It is explained to Moses by YHWH-God in the Exodus story, which also explains the second dispensation. There, YHWH-God informs Moses that "I appeared to Abraham, Isaac, and unto Jacob, by the name of God Almighty (El Shaddai), but by the name JEHOVAH was I not known to them. And I have also established my covenant with them, to give them the land of Canaan, the land of their pilgrimage, wherein they are strangers. And I have also heard the groaning of children of Israel, whom the Egyptians keep in bondage, and I have remembered my covenant" (Exodus 6:3–5). The third refers to the governance of Christ in the Kingdom of God—the church. Paul promotes the idea that he had a (Christian) dispensation that was distinguishable from the Mosaic dispensation essentially because the former, in concert with John's argument that "the law was given by Moses but grace and truth came by Jesus Christ" (John 1:17), was functioning—as was all Christian belief—in a "dispensation of the gospel" (1 Corinthians 9:17). This was synonymous with the "dispensation of the fullness of time" wherein Christ gathers together "in one all things in Christ, both which are in heaven, and which are on earth" (Ephesians 1:10). It also parallels "the dispensation of grace" (Ephesians 3:2). The Greek term *archos* in Hebrews 3:2–4 elucidates its meaning with reference to Moses and Jesus of Nazareth as servants over their respective houses, which the author of the Book of Hebrews uses metaphorically to describe the extent to which each individual presided over a particular people, such as the land-seeking Hebrew "nation" and the Christian "Kingdom of God." Louis DeCaro Jr., in *Malcolm X and the Cross*, traces the origins of Christian dispensationalism to a nineteenth-century leader of the Plymouth Brethren Movement in England named John Nelson Darby and, in the United States, to a former Confederate soldier and lawyer named Cyrus Ingerson Scofield. See pages 16–17 and 241 (n. 13) and 241–242 (n. 14).

8. Perry Miller, *Errand into the Wilderness* (Cambridge: Belknap Press of Harvard University Press, 1956b), pp. 4–5.

9. Ibid., pp. 6–8. Specifically, Miller enlists (1) the "great and visible decay of godliness"; (2) pride such as congregational dissension, insubordination, fancy dress; (3) heresy among the Quakers and Anabaptists; (4) swearing and sleeping during sermons; (5) disregard of the Sabbath; (6) collapse of fatherly dominance of the family; (7) lawsuits and lawyers on the rise in society; (8) extramarital sex, imbibing alcohol in the taverns with loose women, and prostitution; (9) lying for profit in the marketplace; (10) greed in the marketplace; (11) the refusal of the people to reform; and (12) the absence of any civic spirit among the people.

10. Robert Bellah, *The Broken Covenant: American Civil Religion in Time of Trial*, 2nd ed. (Chicago: University of Chicago Press, [1975] 1992), p. 42. It is also worth including Jon F. Sensbach's book *A Separate Canaan: The Making of an Afri-Moravian World in North Carolina, 1763–1840* (Chapel Hill: University of North Carolina Press, 1998), which assesses the encounter between African imports, by way of the West Indies, and German adherents to the Moravian faith, based primarily in Pennsylvania prior to the American Revolution. Among white Moravian brethren, slavery represented no moral crisis. Not only was the black presence among them miniscule; it could be incorporated into the faith and closed society even in bondage. Moravians emigrated

to America in pursuit of religious freedom, but "as was often the case in the European conquest of the Americas, an attempt to establish a luminous example of a new godly order came partly at the expense of others." See *A Separate Canaan*, p. 53.

11. Ibid., p. xxii.

12. Ibid., p. xviii. This apologetic whitewashes the constancy with which racism emerged out of the slavery epoch and evolved unabated throughout subsequent generations, not the least of which is the one in which Bellah was writing.

13. Ibid., p. 37.

14. Patricia Hill Collins, *From Black Power to Hip-Hop*, p. 78. Emphasis in original.

15. Ibid., p. 62.

16. Jeremiah 1:10.

17. Robert Bellah, *The Broken Covenant*, p. 17.

18. David Howard Pitney, *The Afro-American Jeremiad: Appeals for Justice in America* (Philadelphia: Temple University Press, 1990), p. 8.

19. Ibid., p. 7.

20. 2 Chronicles 7:14, for instance, calls the nation to repentance and restoration.

21. Sacvan Bercovitch, *The American Jeremiad* (Madison: University of Wisconsin Press, 1978), p. 176.

22. Ibid., p. 13. Emphasis in original.

23. Ibid., p. 24. Emphasis in original.

24. Theological dissent to the commingling of the sacred with the secular was prevalent among Roger Williams (founder of the American Baptists) and the Congregationalists —but not sufficiently to undermine the prevailing notion of national election.

25. David Pitney, *The Afro-American Jeremiad*, p. 11.

26. Robert Bellah, *The Broken Covenant*, p. 28.

27. The first text reads: "Behold the days come, says the Lord, that I will make a new covenant with the house of Israel, and with the house of Judah. Not according to the covenant which I made with with their fathers, when I took them by the hand to bring them out of the land of Egypt, the which my covenant they brake, although I was a husband unto them, says the Lord. But this shall be the covenant that I will make with the house of Israel. After those days, says the Lord, I will put my Law in their inward parts, and write it in their hearts, and will be their God, and they shall be my people." The second text reads: "They shall ask the way to Zion, with their faces thitherward, saying, Come, and let us cleave to the Lord in a perpetual covenant that shall not be forgotten."

28. The text reads "I will appoint a place for my people Israel, and will plant it, that they may dwell in a place of their own and move no more" (1 Chronicles 17:9).

29. Robert Bellah, *The Broken Covenant*; see esp. ch. 2.

30. Sacvan Bercovitch, *The American Jeremiad*, pp. 46–47.

31. Ibid., p. xi.

32. Ibid.

33. Bernard Bailyn, *The Theological Origins of the American Revolution* (Cambridge: Belknap Press of Harvard University Press, [1967] 1992), p. 32.

34. Ibid., p. 43.

35. And as if to reiterate the subterranean character of the separate worlds of African Americans and whites in the nation, the non-Christian, illiberal, proto-Islamic Nation of Islam had existed for nearly three decades in cities like Detroit, Chicago, Washington, D.C., Philadelphia, and Harlem before Mike Wallace and Louis E. Lomax introduced the movement to the country and Malcolm X's unrelenting "jihad of words" in 1957. See Richard B. Turner, *Islam in the African American Experience*, esp. pp. 184–189.

36. Perry Miller, *Errand into the Wilderness*, p. 5.

37. These individuals, who had themselves been influenced by the black shipman Paul Cuffee, included James Madison, James Monroe, Francis Scott Key, Andrew Jackson, Henry Clay, and Supreme Court Justice Bushrod Washington (George Washington's nephew).

38. But McAdoo's delineation of which individuals are reactionary and which are revolutionary is undermined, for instance, by Delany's *Blake; Or, The Huts of America*, which called for violent slave insurrection by the book's protagonist, who was an erstwhile integrationist-turned-revolutionary émigré to Cuba. Moreover, there was a jeremiadic rejectionist dimension even in emigration projects. See Floyd J. Miller (ed.), *Blake, or The Huts of America: A Novel by Martin R. Delany* (Boston: Beacon, 1970).

39. Eric J. Sindquist, *To Wake the Nations: Race in the Making of American Literature* (Cambridge: Belknap Press of Harvard University Press, 1993), p. 188. Emphasis in original.

40. These several ironies are evident in the emigrationist project of the nineteenth century, and the emigrationistic nationalists, by all accounts of the 1960s radical discourses, would fit neatly into the categories of Uncle Tom, in that their Christian essentialist commitments, however well meaning, retarded the social and political development of those African Americans whom the 1960s radicals would later lionize: the masses-class.

41. See George Shepperson, "Notes on American Negro Influences on the Emergence of African Nationalism," *Journal of African History* 1, no. 2 (1960): 300. Thorne was a Barbadian forerunner of Garvey, who between 1897 and 1920 tried to lead a movement for black colonization.

42. See Edwin Redkey, *Black Exodus*, p. 293.

43. Assessing his personal letters, Wilson Moses contends that Cuffee, and his contemporary and fellow seaman James Forten, promoted an economic nationalism with regard to trade with Africa from which he stood to gain personally. Whereas Cuffee employed the black Manifest Destiny idea, Forten ignored the biblical figuration of blacks as a "chosen people," pp. 48–52.

44. See his appendix, the only place where he refers to blacks as constituting "a nation within a nation."

45. For example, in 1790, southern blacks constituted 58 percent of free blacks; in 1860, 51 percent of the nearly half-million free blacks lived in the South. McAdoo, *Pre–Civil War Black Nationalism*, p. 5.

46. He asserts, "Nor was it, as is frequently very erroneously asserted, by colored as well as white persons, that it was on account of hatred of his color, that the African was selected as the subject of oppression in this country. This is sheer nonsense; being based on policy and nothing else," p. 21.

47. See Martin Delany, *Destiny of the Colored*, p. 53. He notes, "from the earliest period of the history of nations, the African race had been known as an industrious people, cultivators of soil. The grain fields of Ethiopia and Egypt were the themes of the poet, and their garners, the subject of the historian. Like the present America, all the world went to Africa, to get a supply of commodities. Their massive piles of masonry, their skillful architecture, the subterranean vaults, their deep and mysterious wells, their extensive artificial channels, their mighty sculptured solid rocks, and provinces of stone quarries; gave indisputable evidence, of the hardihood of that race of people. Nor was Africa then, without the evidence of industry, as history will testify. All travelers who had penetrated towards the interior of the continent, have been surprised at the seeming state of civilization and evidences of industry among the inhabitants of the vast country."

48. See his *Official Report of the Niger Valley Exploring Party* (New York: T. Hamilton, 1861), p. 24, cited originally in George Shepperson, "Notes on American Negro Influences on the Emergence of African Nationalism," pp. 301–302. The party consisted of just one other person, Robert Campbell, who was a young Jamaican teacher at the Institute for Colored Youth in Philadelphia. See Martin R. Delany, *Blake*, p. xv.

49. Martin R. Delany, *The Destiny of the Colored People*, p. 169. Emphases in original.

50. Ibid. See also chapter 7, "Claims of Colored Men as Citizens of the United States," pp. 48–66.

51. Ibid. See chapter 21, esp. p. 178.

52. Ibid., p. 212. Emphasis in original.

53. See George Shepperson, "Notes on American Negro Influences on the Emergence of African Nationalism," p. 302. The author distinguishes from the religious emigrationists with a note that "Delany's emphasis was political."

54. See Delany, *The Destiny of the Colored People*, p. 39.

55. See the introduction to Martin R. Delany, *Blake*, Floyd J. Miller, ed.

56. Ibid., p. 16.

57. Ibid., p. 21.

58. Cited by Vincent Harding, *There Is a River: The Black Struggle for Freedom in America* (San Diego: Harcourt Brace, 1981), p. 152.

59. See Tunde Adeleke, *UnAfrican Americans: Nineteenth-Century Black Nationalists and the Civilizing Mission* (Lexington: University Press of Kentucky, 1998), p. 59.

60. Delany, *The Destiny of the Colored People*, p. 208.

61. Ibid.

62. Ibid., pp. 210–211; emphasis added.

63. Tunde Adeleke, *UnAfrican Americans*, p. 59.

64. See George Shepperson, "Notes on American Negro Influences on the Emergence of African Nationalism," p. 303.

65. In chapter 2 of *The Destiny of the Colored People*, Delany insists that his contemporaries needed to be disabused of the notion "among a large body of colored people in this country, that the cause of our oppression and degradation, is the displeasure of God towards us, because of our unfaithfulness to Him, This is not true." He devised his program for expatriation from the material fact, among others, that the religion of blacks represented a quietistic influence on them. For him, "This discloses the secret of the white man's success with all of his wickedness, over the head of the colored man, with all of his religion," p. 40.

66. See George Shepperson, "Notes on American Negro Influences on the Emergence of African Nationalism," p. 302.

67. See Richard Turner, *Islam in the African American Experience*, p. 152.

68. He preferred a fusion of Islam and Christianity in a manner that anticipated Kwame Nkrumah's postcolonial promotion of "consciencism," which sought to syncretize the positive aspects of the major traditions in recovering Africa from colonialism. See Kwame Nkrumah, *Consciencism: Philosophy and Ideology for Decolonization* (New York: Monthly Review, [1964] 1970).

69. See Richard Turner's discussion of the debate between Hollis R. Lynch and Y. V. Mdumbe. The former contended that Blyden never embraced Islam, whereas Mdumbe argues that Blyden's main religious expressions from 1870 to 1910 were Islamic. Turner sides with the latter perspective; see pp. 56–59.

70. Cited in Milfred C. Fierce, *The Pan-African Idea in the United States, 1900–1919: African American Interest in Africa and Interaction in West Africa* (New

York: Garland, 1993), p. 16. Original source is Edwin Redkey (ed.), *Respect Black: The Writings and Speeches of Bishop Henry McNeal Turner* (New York: Arno, 1971).

71. Cited in Tunde Adeleke, *UnAfrican Americans*, p. 74.

72. See Theodore Draper, *The Rediscovery of Black Nationalism*, p. 43.

73. John T. McCartney, *Black Power Ideologies* (Philadelphia: Temple University Press, 1992), p. 22.

74. Gayraud Wilmore, *Black Religion and Black Radicalism*, p. 131.

75. Ibid., p. 126. Emphasis added.

76. Tunde Adeleke, *UnAfrican Americans*, p. 99.

77. Garvey built on this concept, which was articulated previously by Blyden; Garvey's rendition enlisted an explicit pan-Africanist dimension. It was stated at the 1920 New York UNIA meeting.

78. Wilson J. Moses, *Classical Black Nationalism*, pp. 2–3.

79. Pan-Africanist ideology is not synonymous with the pan-African movement of Sylvester Williams and, later, W.E.B. Du Bois and others.

80. The Blair Bill supported federal assistance to public education for African Americans and others. It passed in the Senate rather easily in 1884, 1886, and 1888, but it never went to the House floor. The (Henry Cabot) Lodge Bill promoted federal management of national elections after President Benjamin Harrison asked Congress for a national elections law.

81. See the "Great Commission" in Matthew 28:18–20 and Mark 16:15–16.

82. White sponsors in the religious wing of the ACS, and in William Stewart's Missionary Foundation for Africa at Gammon Theological Seminary, created in Atlanta in 1894, envisioned an opportunity for a sort of "transatlantic enlightenment" for black Americans and indigenous Africans, in which the former would be improved by their role as agents, and the latter as recipients of the Christian message.

83. Milfred Fierce, *The Pan-African Idea in the United States*, p. 101.

84. Ibid., p. 82.

85. It is telling that Adeleke makes no criticism of McAdoo's "revolutionary nationalists," such as David Walker. Consistent with his efforts to prove the "un-Africanness" of African Americans, he can only note that individuals like David Walker and Frederick Douglass employed nationalism instrumentally to achieve their American citizenship objectives.

86. See George Shepperson, "Notes on American Negro Influences on the Emergence of African Nationalism," pp. 304–305.

87. Ibid., p. 302. Between Turner and Garvey's *Negro World*, colonial authorities—whether through paranoia or reality—suspected the hand of African Americans in the major rebellions in Nyasaland, Lagos, and the Congo.

88. Milfred Fierce, *The Pan-African Idea in the United States*, p. 7.

89. Coker (of Baltimore) and his successor in Liberia, Cary (of Richmond, Virginia), were among the earliest groups of blacks sent to Liberia by the ACS (in 1820 and 1821, respectively). Cary, an ordained Baptist who wanted to "labor for my suffering race," was met with a tragic and not at all surprising fate in Liberia, when gunpowder exploded during a confrontation with native groups. See Theodore Draper, *The Rediscovery of Black Nationalism*, p. 10. Adeleke also ignores African American nationalists like Carter G. Woodson, Paul Robeson, John Edward Bruce, Hubert H. Harrison, and Arturo Schomburg and their attempts to recover in African Americans a strong sense of pride in Africa through scholarship, cultural studies, archival research, and politics. See Milfred Fierce, *The Pan-African Idea in the United States*, pp. 48–58; see also George Shepperson, "Notes on American Negro Influences on the Emergence of African Nationalism," p. 309. Bruce and Schomburg created the Negro Society for

Historical Research in 1911. A Garveyite, Bruce was also a major influence on Majola Agbebi, a militant leader of the Native African Church in West Africa. Out of admiration for his race pride as expressed in the inauguration of the "African Church" in 1902, Bruce attempted to establish a "Majola Agbebi" day of observance among African Americans.

90. Ibid., p. 55.

91. Ibid., p. 102.

92. Eddie Glaude Jr., *Exodus! Religion, Race, and Nation in the Early Nineteenth-Century Black America* (Chicago: University of Chicago Press, 2000), p. 14.

6

David Walker and the
Politics of the Black Jeremiad

To be black and conscious in the United States is to be in a constant state
of rage.

—James Baldwin

*I am not sad that black Americans are rebelling; this was not only inevitable
but eminently desirable. Without this magnificent ferment among Negroes,
the old evasions and procrastinations would have continued indefinitely. . . .
[Negroes] were invisible in their misery. But the sullen and silent slave of
110 years ago, an object of scorn at worst or of pity at best, is today's
angry [person].*

—Dr. Martin Luther King Jr., "A Testament of Hope," 1968

Wilson Moses and David Howard-Pitney identify the Afro-American jeremiad
(in relation to the American civil religion thesis, which, for them, is itself a defining principle of Anglo-American nationalism). The black jeremiad provides an
analytical structure for understanding American black nationalism in compatible
terms with emigrationist orientations. In this chapter it is argued that African
American nationalism is best understood as a "stay at home in America" variant, which is epitomized in the work and political thought of David Walker and
his intellectual and movement progeny, including the likes of Maria Stewart,
Frederick Douglass, and other early-nineteenth-century individuals who sought
to substantively democratize the received claims of the American Revolution
and Declaration of Independence. Ultimately, I seek to provide a frame for understanding David Walker as precedent to a specifically American protest heritage that is taken up in the middle and later twentieth century in ways that link
genealogically in black nationalist discourse with the public ministry of Malcolm X and his ideological progeny in Black Power and hip-hop.

The previous chapter focused on the "hard" geographic concerns of emigrationism, separatism, and colonization. This chapter focuses on the "soft"

(but not passive, as the threat of violence is an important component) consciousness or group solidarity efforts. The latter includes those advocated in the *Appeal*, the *Ethiopian Manifesto*, *Productions*,[1] *An Address to the Slaves of the United States*, pan-Africanism, New Negro consciousness, the "don't buy where you can't work" campaign in 1930s Harlem,[2] Black Power, Albert Cleage's black messiah sentiments, cultural nationalist projects, community control nationalism, Afrocentrism, and post–civil rights expressions that culminated in the 1995 Million Man March. Moses rightly traces black nationalism, pan-Africanism, Garveyism, and Afrocentrism in symmetry with (pre-) extant community traditions flourishing in Harlem, which were shaped "in the United States due partially to the persistence of those conditions that originally gave rise to them—the segregation and subordination of the African American population."[3] Further, he notes, "messianic traditions persist because the heritage of oppression persists."[4]

John Bracey and his colleagues identify the periods 1790–1820, the late 1840s and 1850s, the 1880s through the 1920s, and the period since the 1960s as ones of high nationalist salience. From the late 1820s to early 1830s, however, there was a coherent religious-oriented militancy, evident especially in the North, that has been discounted in most accounts of nationalism chiefly because it was devoid of an *explicitly territorial-separatist ethic.*[5] Nation-state black nationalism is one of many racial solidarity formulations that black Americans have strategically employed. In keeping with the "reactionary" and "revolutionary" delineation concerning black nationalism, the ideological component can be described as *black rage dispositionalism*, a phenomenon detected especially in the nineteenth-century Afro-Christian jeremiadic agitation of first or "proto"-nationalist personalities such as David Walker (1785–1830), Maria Stewart (1803–1879), Robert Alexander Young,[6] and Henry Highland Garnet (1815–1882), among the more literate blacks during the American slavery epoch. To be sure, not all of its adherents were necessarily religious or given to a particularly militant psychological orientation. An individual such as Hubert H. Harrison (an atheist) seems to epitomize its US nationality commitments a century later. And, famously, Frederick Douglass understood that there was a concrete difference in *disposition* between his attitude in thanking "God for making me a man simply," and Delany's for thanking "Him for making him a black man."[7] Probably no single individual embodied this orientation more than Muhammad Ali during his Nation of Islam ministry and boxing career, especially in his epic battles with Joe Frazier and George Foreman. It was the most salient aspect of Louis Farrakhan's ministry in the Nation of Islam. When it surfaced in the second Democratic presidential primary contest of the twenty-first century vis-à-vis Chicago's Trinity United Church of Christ pastor Jeremiah Wright Jr., few confused the differences between the "unity" agenda of church member and candidate Barack Obama and Wright's dissident jeremiad damning the nation for its racial heritage. This concept is no more or less ephemeral than the most influential intellectual device employed in African American political thought in the twentieth century to describe the confrontation of black people's hearts and minds in material realities: Du Bois's "double consciousness." The habit is to think of Du Bois's device in terms of a dilemma in black Americans' "identity," longings, and psychological adjustment to white supremacy.

Black Rage Dispositionalism

Black rage dispositionalism conceptually represents a frame of criticism that comports well with David Walker's expression of "revolutionary anger" (identified by Wilson Moses), which constitutes a strand of domestic black nationalism. It elucidates a coherence in black nationalist thought that has been suited to the *American situation* as much as land-based *black* nationalism sought to escape it. The fact that this form of rage is identified as "black" here speaks more to the racialized conditions—material, political, visceral—in which it develops than to any uniquely authentic racial property in and of itself. It is thus a critique of arbitrarily but intentionally constructed social and political realities that have had disproportionate impacts on blacks in the United States. Black rage is also a substantial articulation of disappointment in the African American leadership's inability to deliver life-sustaining critiques, institutions, and opportunity structures in the face of a hostility tempered only by an equally callous societal and governmental indifference.

The neglected individual (among a cohort of neglected nineteenth-century individuals) of this protest tradition is, indeed, David Walker.[8] As a class of leaders and spokespersons, black practitioners of the jeremiad are often recognized analytically with, yet almost always set apart from, the tradition of *black* nationalism.[9] According to North Carolina law, David Walker inherited freedom at his September 28, 1785,[10] birth through his mother's free status; his father, a slave, likely died during Walker's childhood or even before his birth. Conditions for blacks in North Carolina's Black Belt counties nevertheless were sufficiently adversarial to lead V. O. Key to identify the area a "center of consistent resistance."[11] During Walker's childhood in 1795, amid the general slave insurrection on Saint-Domingue (the Haitian Revolution), white North Carolinians in the Cape Fear region were repeatedly under attack by a band of runaways led by a mysterious "General of the Swamps" until the assailants were captured and killed.[12] Walker celebrates the Haitian Revolution in the *Appeal*. Although an inspiration to Walker, the specter of the revolution of 500,000 slaves in Haiti (1791–1803) loomed significantly among African American leaders across their ideological spectrum. France's coveted slave colony was Europe's most important individual market until the rebellion of the blacks resulted in the defeat of the white émigrés, French soldiers, 60,000 British soldiers, a Spanish invasion, 60,000 additional French troops, and the threat of an American naval bombardment. Thomas Jefferson, in turn, refused to recognize the new nation after its focus shifted from revolution to the construction of a polity with diplomatic support from its erstwhile revolutionary inspiration in the United States,[13] Haiti figured prominently in the race-thinking of Thomas Jefferson, the Federalists, and John Adams, who opposed Jefferson on Haiti, as well as certain of his European contemporaries who effected an international embargo against the prospect of a "nigger sovereignty" in the Western Hemisphere less than a hundred miles from the southern slaveocracy of the United States. Three years after Jefferson's purchase of the Louisiana Territory from the exasperated French, his son-in-law John Wayles Eppes "pledge[d] the Treasury of the United States that the Negro government should be destroyed."[14]

Other major events that may have influenced Walker's radicalization as a young man included the aborted insurrection of the black "Gabriel" in Richmond, Virginia, in 1800; general insurrection plots in 1801 and 1802 in Virginia and North Carolina;[15] and the passage of the Missouri Compromise, which partitioned the Union of twenty-two states into half slave and half free in 1820. In 1822, one of the largest slave plots, in neighboring Charleston, South Carolina, led by Denmark Vesey, may have been supported by Walker, who traveled there (and throughout the South) when conditions in North Carolina prompted him to leave on a searching journey that landed him in Boston in the mid-1820s. But this is not certain.[16] Herbert Aptheker agrees that, despite speculation, it is unclear whether Walker had any direct contact with Vesey. Sean Wilentz insists "it is reasonable, however, to suppose that at some point during his time in the small city he met people who were connected with the Charleston A.M.E. Church, and who either knew or had known Vesey and his confederates who were connected."[17] Walker's *Appeal* is the focus of much scholarly discourse and writing. Published in three editions in 1829 and 1830, the *Appeal* consists of a preamble and four successive articles elucidating "Our Wretchedness in Consequence of Slavery" (Article I), "Our Wretchedness in Consequence of Ignorance" (Article II), "Our Wretchedness in Consequence of the Preachers of the Religion of Jesus Christ" (Article III), and "Our Wretchedness in Consequence of the Colonizing Plan" (Article IV). The leitmotif for all of Walker's observations was the institution of racial slavery, what he called "*the principal cause*,"[18] and the moral death it brought to blacks in America and the world. He felt it was anomalous in the history of world slavery, chiefly because of the manner in which black humanity was simultaneously denied and perpetually enslaved. Writing as a lay Christian, Walker, in a manner reminiscent of numerous black Christian elites of a prophetic mode—from Benjamin Mays and Vernon Johns to King and many others— called into question the very idea of racial "white Christianity." Walker's *Appeal*, as an early expression of what would become a traditional mode of prophetic discourse in black protest thought, anticipates a body of criticisms that would span the nineteenth and twentieth centuries. For Henry Garnet, there is no question that his own nationalistic abolitionist commitments were indebted to Walker and the *Appeal* and that his own work shared some genealogical linkages.[19] Moses, too, acknowledges this relationship but methodologically mentions it in relationship to Jefferson: "David Walker's *Appeal* . . . was a jeremiad, inspired by Thomas Jefferson's passing observation in *Notes on the State of Virginia*, 'I tremble for my country when I reflect that God is just.' The messianism of David Walker, and later that of Henry Highland Garnet, was filled with the rhetoric of violence." If Moses is correct, it is worth noting that of all of Walker's citations of Jefferson's *Notes on the State of Virginia*, this most influential passage is *never* mentioned in the *Appeal*.[20] Peter Hinks notes, "In terms of printed sources on which Walker relied, the *Appeal* shows that he used the studies of Josephus, Plutarch, Oliver Goldsmith on the Greeks, Jesse Torrey on the domestic slave trade, and Frederick Butler on America for a significant portion of his knowledge of history. And of course the Bible profoundly colored his understanding of ancient history and his interpretation of history's direction."[21] No single feature of Jefferson so preoccupied Walker as the idea that Africans and black Americans were "not of the human family."[22] For Hinks, Walker merely used Jefferson "as a device for discussing this crisis in a condensed and dramatic form."[23] Jefferson's *Notes on the State of Virginia* (1781) figure prominently in parts of David Walker's *Appeal* (1829), although they were separated by nearly half a century and Jefferson was dead by 1826. The objective conditions of blacks could have been articulated by blacks on their *own terms*, as Walker's journalistic associates Sam Cornish and John Russwurm declared in the publication of the first issue of *Freedom's Journal* in 1827.

It is impossible to deny the omnipresent influence of the revolutionary generation on nineteenth-century struggles for political and social reform, but some scholars have overstated the dependency of blacks on cues from white elites in American protest traditions. Bercovitch conveys the sense of duplicity that characterized the tenets of the Revolution regarding Native Americans and African slaves. The typical American man, he insists, seamlessly coupled the universalism of the Revolution with jingoistic particularity:

> He could denounce servitude, oppression, and inadequate representation while concerning himself least (if at all) with the most enslaved, oppressed and inadequately represented groups in the land. Those groups were part of "the people," but not the chosen people; part of America, but not the America of the Revolution. . . . They used the jeremiad, the leading patriots recast the Declaration to read "all propertied Anglo-Saxon Protestant males are created equal,". . . In short, they used the jeremiad to confine the concept of revolution to American progress, American progress to God's New Israel, and God's New Israel to people of their own kind. Nor is it by accident that under Jefferson's administration the Revolution issued an increasing violation—for blacks and Indians—of life, liberty, and the pursuit of happiness.[24]

McAdoo readily acknowledges the influence of the American Revolution on the generation of David Walker, the main proponent of the "revolutionary" variant in his work.[25] Indeed, the "revolutionary" component of "revolutionary black nationalists" was derived from

> their model . . . the American Revolutionary War of 1776. Their guiding principles were the same as those expounded in the *Declaration of Independence* and the various other documents which reflect the revolutionary character of that conflict. They adapted these principles and precepts to the special history and unique objective existence of the black people in America. They had no illusions about the American Revolutionary War of 1776. They knew that they had been excluded from its benefits. They knew that when the White slaveholding revolutionary leaders of that time said that "all men are created equal," the black man was considered less than an animal and therefore to be excluded.[26]

Walker condemned Thomas Jefferson's validation of racial slavery and notions of black inferiority. Although blacks acquiesced far too much in their oppression and were thus complicit, Jefferson's fourth query in *Notes on Virginia* provided the intellectual justification of white supremacist thought in the early nineteenth century and its attendant colonization plan, on which Walker focuses in the last *Appeal* article. Walker argues that Jefferson (and other whites) did not understand that in blacks' oppressed state "there is an unconquerable disposition in the breasts of the blacks . . . they want us for their slaves, and think nothing of murdering us in order to subject us to that wretched condition—therefore, if there is an attempt made by us, kill or be killed."[27] Kill, he demands, "our natural enemies." This is Walker's explicit statement of the political standpoint attributed to him in this book. Nevertheless, Hinks cautions, "Walker was eager to forgo confrontations so long as the white power structure assented to the essential liberty of African Americans and their entitlement to a spiritual and secular education."[28] For certain, much is made of Walker's reach to whites, urging in the end: "throw away your fears, and prejudices then, and enlighten us and treat us like men, and we will like you more than we do now hate you . . . treat us like men, and there is no danger but we will live in peace and happiness together. . . . What a happy country this would be, if the whites will listen." Here Walker is viewed as operating within the American jeremiad tradition, which typically offers a "way out" of judgment through national repentance. This is plausible. Walker, despite his rage, was no racist or chauvinist lunatic. Indeed, white sailors and individuals, such an Edward Smith, who was jailed for one year and fined a thousand dollars for distributing the document from Boston to Charleston, South Carolina, in March 1830, were a help in disseminating the message of the *Appeal*.[29] For Bercovitch, optimism in the American jeremiad is reflected in "God's frequent threats to 'utterly reject' His people [which] were not meant literally. They were simply metaphors or hyperboles, stylistic devices by which He wished to impress upon those He would *not* reject the importance of reformation."[30] Yet Perry Miller saw the jeremiad as a *grave denunciation* of the fallen city. In Bercovitch's own words, "Miller stressed the dark side of the jeremiad."[31] Repentance among the wayward nation was needed if its faithful penitents might be saved, but certain destruction would still follow the moment of restoration.[32] The sword follows the peace for Miller.[33] If African American leaders participated in the jeremiad, it was with a pitch that had no analogue in Anglo-American versions. From Walker to Garvey[34] to Malcolm X and his ideological progeny, as well as Robert Williams, violence was invoked as a threat not of abstract divine retribution but of *lex talionis* (an eye for an eye).[35] Despite Walker's olive branch, he ends the *Appeal* reminding whites that they must "make a national acknowledgement to us for the wrongs they have inflicted on us," then by highlighting the contradiction in the natural right claims of the Declaration of Independence and the realities of the black predicament. If Walker's olive branch—which stipulated reform among slaveholding and racist whites—summarizes his "real" intentions, where "cries of declension and doom were part of a strategy designed to revitalize the errand," then his black audience was not as sanguine concerning whites' willingness to accept it in peace. The official white *reaction* to the *Appeal* in several southern states that banned it and reading in general among blacks made clear that his gesture was rejected; before his mysterious death, a bounty was placed on his head.[36] Heightened insurrectionary activity, culminating in Nat Turner's uprising in Virginia one year after the *Appeal*'s third edition—whether inspired by the *Appeal* or not—rendered Walker's call for reconciliation moot. As Hinks notes, "The rapid response of Southern authorities of the presence of the *Appeal* was not so much a sign of their tendency to ascribe unwarranted power to some passing antislavery gesture or plot as it was their realistic appraisal of the subversive potential of Walker's plan."[37]

The American Revolution and its democratic appeals, expressed in Thomas Paine's *Common Sense*, in the radical thought of Samuel Adams, and in the Declaration of Independence, for example, comported well with "the notion of the revolutionary overthrow of the oppressor, and the assertion of the rights of what they considered to be an oppressed black nation, in the same fashion that all other oppressed nations had achieved liberation throughout the course of history."[38] Yet Bernard Bailyn nevertheless finds in the ideological origins of the American Revolution a contradiction that inevitably fueled a "contagion of liberty" beyond the control of the Revolution's leaders. Fear of the democratic implications of the American Revolution among the colonial leaders is firmly established; "democracy" is not enumerated in the US Constitution, and it was its potential unleashing that troubled Alexis de Tocqueville and Gustave de Beaumont.[39] And for John Adams, the colonists were slaves of the worst possible kind.[40] The whole of David Walker's commitment in the

Appeal suggested, in all of world historical slavery, that the nature of American slavery was most severe for several reasons, including the longevity of black experience, the notion of inherent inferiority that was sponsored by Jefferson, the racial basis of black slavery, its implications concerning the subhuman status of Africans, and the permanence with which it was passed from generation to generation. It simply did not comport with the Lockean justification that enabled slavery as an alternative to a sentence of death for some justiciable offense.[41] But there were also contemporary opinions represented by the likes of Benjamin Rush and pro-colonizationists such as Levi Hart and Samuel Hopkins who, in their devotion to neo-Puritan covenant theology, castigated the incomplete liberty on the grounds that "the slavery we complain of is lighter than a feather compared to their heavy doom, and may be called liberty and happiness when contrasted with the most abject slavery and intolerable wretchedness to which they are subjected. Our so-called Sons of Liberty: what are they but oppressors of thousands who have as good a claim to liberty as themselves, [and] are shocked with the glaring inconsistence?"[42]

David Walker: Father of the Faith

The scholarly debates concerning David Walker's ideological location and personal associations seem to be critical to the inquiry concerning the genre of black nationalism that had essentially "domestic" commitments to black liberation. I attempt to assess the forms and ideological lineage that bring together, for instance, David Walker and Malcolm X.[43] It should be apparent that Wilson Moses is one of the most important historians of black nationalism, and his tacit acknowledgement that black nationalism can be "literary black nationalism," even when it is attached to no land-grant demands, is a useful revision; but it also becomes apparent that he underwrites a great deal of scholarly confusion. This is not because he enlists Frederick Douglass among the nationalists, where Harold Cruse had previously identified him as the forefather of modern integrationism—juxtaposed to Delany's nationalism—but because in a span of a few years (between 1978 and 1996), Moses states, "no one has yet denied that David Walker was a black nationalist, but he opposed colonization, emigration, racial separatism, and laws prohibiting intermarriage."[44] Moses's subsequent statement is an outright denial of Walker's ties to black nationalism: His *Appeal*'s "ties to black nationalism are problematic" because "Walker was ambivalent with respect to separatism. Although he viewed African Americans as a 'nation in bondage,' he did not advocate a separate national destiny."[45] The problem extends beyond the manner in which Walker ceases to be a nationalist in Moses's thinking. More important, it betrays the narrowing of Moses's definition of black nationalism, from one that initially incorporated Frederick Douglass and Walker to one that problematizes

Walker's nationalism because of his tacit opposition to expatriation programs—most famously the racist colonization program of the American Colonization Society. Moses is noncommittal and reluctant to state plainly how David Walker relates to the black nationalist tradition. His reticence to formulating a black nationalist continuum, linking Walker with Malcolm X (and, by extension, Louis Farrakhan), leaves us with the beginning of a story about what he calls a "revolutionary anger,"[46] which is implicitly nationalistic, with no methodological means to locating it among later generations of elites and individuals. He more readily locates Walker somewhere within the European and Anglo-American jeremiad political sermon traditions that totally ignored African Americans and routinely reinforced the white supremacist status quo. Indeed, Pitney inaccurately argues that Malcolm X participated in a thoroughly "un-American" jeremiad because his religion was black Islam and not black Christianity. Yet the Christian jeremiad is but the Islamic "jihad of words" in the context of US race politics.[47] Both ascribe justice to wayward, fallen, or covenant-breaking nations, and both ultimately offer reconciliation to nations, peoples, and individuals.

There is also little in the criticisms of Malcolm X in the Nation of Islam that is not anteceded in Walker's preamble and initial article. If God is righteous in theodicy, Walker hypothesizes, the degradation of black humanity must and will be avenged. Where the Anglo and Euro-American jeremiads did acknowledge war with Native American tribes as a form of judgment on the white nation, it was just one of many possible plagues. But the black jeremiad as expressed in Walker's thinking imagined blacks would act as God's vicegerents in executing justice because of the impact of slavery on them. Justice here is understood as total liberation. Historian Vincent Harding adds, "For even as he moved with the Great Tradition [of protest], Walker's history, temperament, and commitments urged him toward deeper and more radical levels of struggle. In the fall of 1828 he delivered an address before the General Colored Association of his adopted state, calling on blacks to organize and act on their own behalf." He explains: "In the address Walker first spoke of the need for political and social organization within the black community, identifying such structured, inner cohesion as prerequisite to any effective struggle for freedom."[48] Reflecting Walker's perspective years later at the State Negro Convention of Ohio in 1854, C. H. Langston argued,

> I perfectly agree with the gentleman from Cuyahoga, (Mr. [Ford] Douglass) who presented this resolution, that the United States' Constitution is pro-slavery. It was made to foster and uphold that abominable, vampirish and bloody system of American slavery. . . . It was so understood and so administered all over the country. . . . *I would vote under the Constitution on the same principle, (circumstances being favorable) that I would call on every slave, from Maryland to Texas, to arise and assert their liberties, and cut their masters' throats if they attempt again to reduce them to slavery. . . . Sir, I have long*

since adopted as my God, the freedom of the colored people of the United States, and my religion, to do anything that will effect that object—however much it may differ from the precepts taught in the Bible. . . . Those are the lessons taught us by the religion of our white brethren, when they are free and we are slaves; but when their enslavement is attempted, then "Resistance to Tyranny is obedience to God." This doctrine is equally true in regard to colored men as white men.[49]

As represented in Langston's comments, there is, again, no commitment to emigration in "revolutionary" black nationalist discourses. But it is also inaccurate to view the perspective as one merely of nationalist means to integrationist ends. Harding makes clear that the era produced an alternative tradition rooted in the commitments of David Walker. He notes,

By the 1840s, [integration] was the essential quality of the developing Great tradition of Black Protest, the mainstream line. It began with the same evidence that Delany was gathering in his travels. It presumed the existence of the same God of justice that David Walker had known. But it ended with a non sequitur, a statement of faith in the peaceful working out of the American situation, rather than in the announcement of divine retribution, the clashing of opposing forces, or a call for blacks to emigrate. At the most dangerous level, such an approach encouraged black identification with the goals and interests of an oppressive white society, an identification which had long contributed to the making of American slaves.[50]

As much as the emigrationist variant in the "classical period" assumed that blacks were a nation within a nation, the revolutionary variant equally advocated self-determination, self-reliance, social and political independence, and a willingness to support violence among the slave mass. Reading black nationalism strictly, or even primarily, as an approach to land objectives is not only anachronistically obsolete; it also deprives us of a more complete understanding of the domestic struggles of the American black nation[51] that has crossed generations. It prioritized immediate matters of equality, justice, independence, and solidarity with the end goals being still wholly incompatible with integration, assimilation, and emigration in important ways. Segments of African Americans embrace a resounding sense that race and the practice of racism spring from deep-seated feelings among whites and ethnic immigrant populations that the Americanness of individual blacks lags or is altogether unassimilable.

Joanne Grant notes, in the introduction to *Black Protest*, "the Negro is convinced that his uniquely un-American experience stems from his blackness and that acknowledgement of this . . . concept has operated within the Negro protest movement in two ways and has led it in two directions simultaneously: wanting out and wanting in." Writing of the radical tradition represented (with considerable variation) by the likes of David Walker, Paul Robeson, Claude McKay, Richard Wright, and Martin Luther King Jr., historian Robin Kelley notes that "black self-determination was not simply a matter of guaranteeing democratic rights or removing the barriers to black political and economic power, nor was it a matter of creating a nation wherever black people found themselves to be an oppressed majority. It was about promoting and supporting an independent black radical movement that could lead the way for a revitalized international working-class assault on racial capitalism."[52] Black self-determination here is not inclined to integration or assimilation, and it is not toward "creating a nation." Rather, it is toward a radical, albeit domestic, alternative driven by workers and ordinary people. In the introduction to the *Autobiography of Malcolm X*, for instance, M. S. Handler acknowledges this feature in the politics of Malcolm X (upon leaving the Nation of Islam), urging that he was "a man unreservedly committed to the cause of liberating the black man *in* society rather than integrating the black man *into* that society."[53]

Emigrationism has a more coherent and readily identifiable lineage in African American political thought than the "revolutionary" strand, and in this sense it is more concrete; the latter is more indefinite, especially on the land question. Perhaps this is because scholars have been inclined to identify the black jeremiad as a form of black nationalism without outlining its continuity in African American social, religious, and political thought. For instance, David Howard-Pitney's *Afro-American Jeremiad* associates that black jeremiad with David Walker, suggests its intersection with "Anglo-American nationalism," and concludes, "yet for the Afro American jeremiad also expressed black nationalist faith in the missionary destiny of the black race and was a leading instrument of black social assertion in America."[54] Moreover, even when it does broach the subject of black nationalism (in the introduction), it offers no schema that would provide for an understanding of any lineage between the nationalist individuals he mentions: Garvey and Malcolm X. But he is correct in his insistence that "after its inception in the abolitionist crusade, the black jeremiad *remained a prime form of black social rhetoric and ideology well into the twentieth century.*"[55] Despite this observation and reference to the duality in African American social and political life, the book is not a study of black nationalism per se.[56]

Despite widespread thinking that integrationism was given to wholesale assimilation as an end in itself (and this is certainly true for the likes of Roy Wilkins, Whitney Young, and Bayard Rustin, among others), the indispensability of black solidarity was no less important than in nationalist projects. As president of the Montgomery Improvement Association during the Birmingham boycott, King argued, "I want to say that in all our actions we must stick together. Unity is the great need of the hour, and if we are united we can get many of the things that we not only desire but which we justly deserve."[57] Black solidarity was prerequisite to Martin Luther King's *interracial* "beloved community."[58] In his last book, King insists that blacks must "work passionately for group identity. This does not mean group isolation or group exclusivity. It means the kind of group consciousness that Negroes need in order to participate more meaningfully at all levels of the life of our Nation. . . . This form of group identity can do infinitely more to liberate the Negro than any action of *individuals. We have been oppressed as a group, and we must overcome our oppression as a group.*"[59] Here King moves from the specificity of black Americans' subjugation to ostensibly universal principles of human rights, rather than an "imagined community" of isolated black people. Wilson Moses identifies the same quality in Du Bois's thinking, noting, "If integration was only a means to the end of equality, then [his] racial consciousness was only a means to the goal of the universal uplift of all humanity."[60] Political theorist Wendy Brown applauds King's and Gandhi's invocation of "morality in politics" to the extent that "while [they] did not wholly eschew the phenomenon of identity produced through oppression, neither did they build solidarity on the basis of that production; rather, solidarity was rooted in shared beliefs."[61]

King's use of solidarity was consistent with Paul Sniderman and Thomas Piazza's finding that pride in race or support for racial solidarity—among a sample of black Chicagoans—is not synonymous with antiwhite racial feeling. They conclude, "On the one side, black pride encourages blacks to be more responsive to the needs and interests of fellow blacks, *but* on the other, it does not lead them to be more intolerant or punitive or hostile toward other groups in American society." The authors caution that this dilemma of "distinctiveness and inclusion" at least partly originates from a "sense of distance" and "difference blacks feel from other Americans, especially white Americans; the other underscores their commonality with their fellow Americans, very much including white Americans."[62] But Brown's (and Sniderman and Piazza's) liberal optimism scuttles the King after "I Have a Dream," which gave way to his illiberal thoughts valorizing "temporary segregation" (which is inseparably nationalist) as a precursor to integration. According to Nikhil Singh, "This is also the King who has become part of a mythic nationalist discourse that claims his antiracist imperatives as its own, even as it obscures his significantly more complex, worldly, and radical politics. Indeed, just as King's antiwar stance has been minimized or forgotten, so has the steady incorporation of currents of democratic socialism and black nationalism into his thinking."[63]

King does not clarify the duration of his tentative "temporary" remedy or what it might look like. There is more than a hint of this tendency in Du Bois's advocacy of "separate development" in 1935 and King's statement—ten days before his assassination in 1968—acknowledging, "there are points at which I see the necessity for temporary segregation in order to get to the integrated society. . . . There are some situations where separation may serve as a temporary way-station to the ultimate goal which we seek, which I think is the only answer in the final analysis to the problem of a truly integrated society."[64] Still, what King grappled with here may seem counterintuitive to his reputation as the quintessential American integrationist, but he expresses what is less a tactic or social philosophy than an acknowledgement of the quotidian realities that he observed in travels among black communities in the North, South, and West prior to—and after—the passage of the major civil rights legislation. King's experiences in the South, Harlem, and Chicago led him to accept that blacks had "a separate existence in and a tortured relationship to the U.S. as a nation."[65]

Most black Americans were separated existentially and residentially in fact by the realities of "social isolation," and King's acknowledgement of these realities was a recognition of the obvious. But in saying so, King had to understand the countervailing nationalist implications toward his "ultimate goal" of integration. Nevertheless, doctrinaire nationalists would require that those means be articulated as nationalism, even when it is so otherwise. One of the least articulated aspects of Martin Luther King Jr.'s interest in Gandhi's *Satyagraha* is the extent to which Gandhi activated it to a *nationalist* end and King an integrationist one, especially between 1955 and 1965. King was more interested in the application of Gandhi's moralist approach of nonviolent resistance than the particular relationship of Indians to Britain and the struggle for national independence and self-determination. Even more, Gandhi utilized the ancient ancestral traditions of Indian people, something he learned in Boer-ruled South Africa. Moses notes that Gandhi learned his "pacifist nationalism" in South Africa and his "writings reveal that his political activism was a mere offshoot of his religious beliefs. Nationalism was only a means to spiritual perfection. To Gandhi, British Imperialism meant cultural slavery, the undermining of traditional spiritual values. . . . Gandhi appealed to universal human values to achieve a particularistic goal, *nationalism*. This goal of nationalism, however, was in turn only a means to an end that Gandhi perceived as universalistic."[66]

Gandhi's nationalism was, nevertheless, more congruent with the ethos of the black nationalisms of the 1960s than King's liberal integrationism ideals; the major caveat, of course, is the issue of violence (see below). Several scholars, including James Cone, have interpreted 1965–1968 as the years of King's ideological embrace of a "soft" nationalism. Moses insists, "King consciously utilized the techniques of Gandhi as a revolutionary method, and it hardly seems likely that he could have been unaware of the nationalistic implications of adopting Gandhian methods. This is not to say that King was a black nationalist, but merely to note his ideological immersion in the currents of nationalism that swept over Africa and Asia during his lifetime."[67] Moses insists further, "It would be incorrect, however, to attempt to disassociate him from those traditions of cultural and religious nationalism that have been identified as essential elements of black American consciousness, for the Reverend King shared with the most strident of nationalists a sense of the special mission of black people."[68] King's integrationism, for Moses, was *closer to the nationalist practitioners of the black jeremiad* than to Gandhi. The jeremiad is not treated systematically as black nationalism to the extent that emigrationism is in Moses or in the general literature.

Theologians and other students of religion have been unhesitating in their acceptance of King as quasi-nationalist.[69] Political scientist Robert Smith argues for the employment of nationalist principles to achieve integrationist ends, and it is King with whom he associates this possibility. Smith argues, for instance, "To achieve [integration] or at least to make progress toward its attainment I believe that blacks in America must engage in militant political action and rely on the nationalist principles of self help, self reliance, and group solidarity."[70] Smith identifies in King these and several other nationalist qualities that are frequently attributed to erstwhile black nationalists. However, it is clear that no known political leader (or movement) among African Americans, including Du Bois and King, ever advocated inversely *integrationist* strategies and values to the ultimate *end* of racial separation, independence, or the construction of a nation-state. Such an approach did not comport with the NAACP's litigiousness and Christian integrationism, which dominated the twentieth-century civil rights movement. Harold Cruse recognized the micronationalist (what Anderson refers to as "subnational")[71] character of US social relations. He would likely welcome a continuation of the yet unidyllic urban-centered vibrancy that typified *pre*–civil rights movement residential, leisurely, and cultural realities (e.g., Central Avenue in Los Angeles, the Fillmore in San Francisco, 7th Street in West Oakland, Pennsylvania Avenue in Baltimore, Hastings Street in Detroit, Sugar Hill and Lenox Avenue in Harlem, Bronzeville in Chicago). And this is so regardless of whether it resulted from an overtly integrationist or nationalist ethos and program. In short, integrationism or nationalism should result in a black homologue to the "Chinatown," "Little Italy," "Japan-town," "Irish (South) Boston," and "Koreatown" phenomena found in nearly every major city, suburban, and rural sector of pluralist US society.

For Hubert H. Harrison, nationalist race-consciousness among African Americans manifested in "black churches, newspapers, life insurance companies, banks, fraternities, colleges and political appointees."[72] Harold Cruse points to the Reconstruction-era Blair educational legislation, which had a "separate but equal" provision aimed at appeasing Redeemer Democrats. Although the bill would have targeted the widespread illiteracy among all southerners, for blacks the matter of equal distribution of educational resources far outweighed the matter of separateness that became the focus of *Plessy v. Ferguson* and *Brown v. Board of Education*. He emphasizes that "*many blacks apparently preferred segregated schools. Separate churches and schools became symbols of racial achievement and they provided about the only avenue of opportunity for black professionals. During the 1880's many blacks opposed school integration in the North because it often resulted in the loss of black jobs (just as it happened in the South during the 1950's and 1960's).*"[73] Thus, is it plausible that a self-identified black nationalist (e.g., Richard B. Moore, Hubert H. Harrison, "Harry" Haywood Hall, Cyril Briggs, or the post–Nation of Islam Malcolm X) could employ strategies or principles *associated* with a nationalist approach that may have nothing to do at all with racial separation or the formation of a black nation-state? As noted in Chapter 5, King's organizational base, the SCLC, was a *blacks-only* organization. Despite this, Wendy Brown asserts that King (and Gandhi) be taken to task "precisely for their unreflexive traffic with humanism—their embrace of universal and even essentialized personhood, their inattention to cultural difference, their relative neglect of the historically contingent and the contextual character of political life."[74]

Compared to white Protestantism, African American religion has betrayed qualitatively distinct patterns of belief, worship, cultural expressions, and practice to the extent that they constituted interdependent, but nevertheless separate, developments and conflicting realities. This religious orientation was tacitly devoid of the overt land-grant or geographic separationism that would eventually become predominant among subsequent generations of nationalism among black Americans. The Exodus account provided a way of understanding God's liberationist commitments toward oppressed humanity, generally, and good intentions concerning the plight of the slaves, in particular; those intentions could be carried out, however, within the social and political structures of the United States, but if not, the "American" nation—which did not include blacks—be damned.[75]

There is general agreement that the American jeremiad is the epitome of US white nationalism. A key component of the black jeremiad, as practiced by nationalistic individuals such as David Walker, was the belief that blacks constituted a separate American nation. Eddie Glaude is reluctant to attribute black nationalism to the jeremiad in his critique of Wilson Moses, and for him the jeremiad seems to intersect with nationalism only in nebulous ways. At least to the extent that he neglects to link black rage with the black jeremiad as an expression of black nationalism, Glaude's analysis is more akin to Moses's than he seems aware. And, like Moses, his work focuses strictly on the nineteenth-century origins of the jeremiad and makes no attempt to systematically demonstrate its life after David Walker. He is accurate nevertheless concerning how the black jeremiad emerged out of a unity of opposites: "Out of an ambivalent relation with white evangelical Christianity in the sense that African American uses of the form simultaneously rejected white America and participated in one of the nation's most sacred traditions. The black jeremiad as a rhetorical form ought to be understood as a paradigm of the structure of ambivalence that constitutes African Americans' relation to American culture."[76]

This distinction is critical for delineating the modalities in nationalist thought, particularly in the United States. The dispositional brand, for instance, finds its antecedents in the Christian jeremiadic ethos of antislavery agitation, which seldom expressed an interest in a general return to Africa or emigration elsewhere. For African Americans at every level, biblical Exodus explained the whole of their predicament in America, and collectively it had *greater* explanatory symmetry with their experience than that of the Puritans and any later Euro-American whites. Rather than participating in the construction of the American jeremiads and their property-driven and race biases, on the contrary, for the black *miserable* in America—who, of course, were yet to be considered American citizens—the various jeremiads were used to stall and prevent black liberation and social progress by their moral justifications of the legal, property-commerce, and racial status quos. According to Bercovitch, the practitioners and pioneering influences on the development of the jeremiad constructed them so as to willfully "confine the concept of revolution to American progress, American progress to God's New Israel, and God's New Israel to people of their own kind."[77] This reflects a consciousness of the mostly propertied, Protestant, Anglo- and Euro-American male kind. As the later Euro-American national jeremiads had to do with leaving the European mother continent for America during the middle nineteenth century, when unprecedented waves of Europeans emigrated to the United States, for a small cadre of African American elites, American Pharaohs (in the ACS and federal government) should turn their ships toward Africa, Liberia, South America, or Canada and permit them to quit America. With the help of the American Pharaohs in the ACS, they wanted to leave their Egypt. Moreover, the world that the Puritans and other European Americans imagined was actually neither a nation nor a state; they sought a theocracy, not democracy, which black Americans thought the best form, and it betrayed how one people's social and cultural core is another's marginalization.[78]

According to the American jeremiad tradition, God is on the side of Anglo-American whites who make up the New Israel in exodus toward an American Canaan from imperial Britain. This begs the question, who is Pharaoh in the African American experience in slavery, segregation, and oppression? And to whom should they look for deliverance from the strange predicament of *being slaves to God's chosen (i.e., Anglo-American) people*? Like biblical Israel, they, too, were enslaved for several centuries. Like biblical Israel, they, too, however inversely, crossed great waters from one condition to another, in an inhospitable and strange land. And like biblical Israel, exodus would be the means to their salvation from "national" and racial oppression. Theophus H. Smith argues, for example, that "the most familiar instance of biblical formation in black social history is the Exodus configuration."[79] It had secular relevance as much as it did spiritual. David Howard-Pitney insists, "Similar themes of messianic purpose and identification of a historical Exodus figured prominently in both black and white antebellum culture"[80] and finds that "it is ironic that this earliest expression of messianic black nationalism in America should have sprung up in such close proximity to Anglo-American nationalism."[81] On the point that it is a matter of respective nationalisms that are reflected in the exodus motif, that much is clear. Yet it is not the concurrence of the themes in both Euro-American and black American culture and politics that is so ironic given that the positional meanings these symbols and myths represented in the hearts and minds of individuals among the various populations were starkly different and oppositional. For Glaude, this is explainable on the grounds that "it merely locates the battle on a different terrain: inside the dominant culture, in which new ideas emerge from old ones by way of interpretation and revision."[82]

In their empirical study of contemporary black nationalism, Davis and Brown contend that "it is important to consider nationalism a *psychological disposition* emphasizing a variety of strategies such as the need for self-determination, self-government, separatism (acquisition of land), pride, and social identity."[83] Black Americans are sufficiently domiciled within the American social, political, cultural, and economic systems to render any serious talk of cordoned geographic separation or expatriation obsolete. The black experience in the United States forged a perennial alternative self-understanding in relation to whites, specifically Anglo and more broadly Euro-American, through a prophetic "dispositional" orientation explicit in nearly all epochal moments of black nationalism. It possesses a jeremiadic, tell-truth-to-power (understood and received), moral, and psychic sensibility that has run adjacent to mainstream American civil religion discourse since the eighteenth century. It is where, according to James Cone, normative, ostensibly universal Eurocentric nodes of thought are confronted by the particularistic "value system" rooted in black experience. He writes straight to the point concerning David Walker and the jeremiad: "Instead of studying only Jonathan Edwards, they [white theologians] must also examine the reality of David Walker. Here truth is expanded beyond the limitation of white culture."[84]

Sean Wilentz notes in his introduction to the *Appeal* that "it is difficult to imagine a more thoroughly alienated view of the United States. For Walker, the sins of slavery and racism were so basic to American life that he sometimes sounded as if he were not himself an American—as if whites (about whom he had virtually nothing good to say in the *Appeal*) were Americans, but the sons and daughters of Africa were not."[85] In this perspective, however, expatriations to Africa, Latin America, Canada, or the West Indies were not a first option for African Americans to work out their liberation objectives. This suggests that Walker represents a tradition in black Americans' strategic ideological and emancipationist discourses that was American-born, American-bred, and produced in the black experience in the United States. Walker seems to point to this in asserting "this is [as] much our country as it is [the whites']"[86]—the country, not the codified nation. Contemporaries Robert Alexander Young and Maria Stewart conveyed much the same sentiment, as did Garnet, who, in *that nation*, felt "we Coloured People of these United States, are, the most wretched, degraded and abject set of beings that ever lived since the world began."

There is very little appreciation for the ideological particularities of black Garrisonians generally and black Bostonian antislavery proponents in particular. It is important to note that Garrisonian abolitionism supported colonization (the expatriation of free blacks to Africa or Haiti) *instead* of racial integration as its original programmatic and ideological commitment. And it vehemently condemned the US Constitution as a "covenant with death . . . an agreement with hell," which African Americans viewed as the main guarantor of their rights.[87] Garrison developed his anticolonizationist abolitionism only after caucusing with free black men at the 1831 Negro Convention, which gathered in part to condemn the colonization plan that he and Arthur and Lewis Tappan initially supported. Garrison broke with colonization with the publication of *Thoughts on African Colonization* in 1832.[88] Based on his experience, Martin Delany suggests that antislavery, as a movement development, "took its rise among *colored* men, just at the time they were introducing their greatest projects for their own elevation."[89] He felt this was so essentially because African American leaders' cooperation with whites committed to antislavery was "doomed to disappointment, sad, sad disappointment. Instead of realizing what we had hoped for, we find ourselves occupying the very same position in relation to the pro-slavery part of the community—a mere secondary, underling position, in all our relations to them."

The various antislavery groups that developed among white abolitionists were characterized by their alignment with or opposition to the personality, tactics, and philosophical views of Garrison and the American Anti-slavery Society. Garrison employed a "strict constructionist" view of the US Constitution in the sense that he insisted on interpreting it as a proslavery document. Garrison even refused to engage in political participation and identified with the Republican Party of Lincoln only after the Civil War. The issue of the US Constitution being a "covenant with death" became a contested matter that would divide the New England Garrisonians who insisted on "moral suasion" as the primary policy of abolitionism. Garrison was effective in alienating antislavery religionists—Garrisonians and anti-Garrisonians—even though his movement was indebted to individuals like Charles G. Finney, Theodore Dwight Weld, Lyman Beecher (father of Harriet Beecher Stowe), and the Tappans. Along with mainstream Garrisonians who, for a time, enjoyed the support of Wendell Phillips, there were the anti-Garrisonian political abolitionists, who formed the Liberty and Free Soil Parties, and the religionists, who broke away from Garrison, forming, respectively, the American and Foreign Anti-slavery Society under the leadership of Lewis Tappan, the American Missionary Society, and the pro-Republican Church Anti-slavery Society. Donald Jacobs maintains that "with such strong religious overtones and such deep roots in the religious revivals of the period, abolitionism became a kind of surrogate religion."[90]

The venerated A.M.E. bishop Richard Allen earlier expressed the general feeling among bourgeois black leaders when he suggested that colonization was "anti-Christian in its character, misanthropic in its pretended sympathies."[91] Abolitionism was an initial "liberal" response to a proslavery colonizationist scheme that drew on national support from former president Thomas Jefferson, congressional leader Henry Clay of Kentucky, Supreme Court Justice Bushrod Washington (nephew of the first American president), Francis Scott Key (who wrote the national anthem), several northern congressional leaders, and Abraham Lincoln.[92] In *Black Reconstruction in America*, Du Bois presents "abolition-democracy" as a positive development but seemed to be ambivalent on the abolition-integration question. For example, Du Bois notes that after the Civil War, Garrison rejected the "integrationist implications" of Reconstruction and refused to call for enfranchisement in the *Liberator* in 1864.[93] Yet Du Bois argued that to the abolitionists "slavery was wrong because it reduced human beings to the level of animals. The abolition of slavery meant not simply abolition of legal ownership of the slave; it meant the uplift of slaves and their eventual incorporation into the body civil, political, and social of the United States."[94] Support for integrationism was widespread among noteworthy Negro political elites, such as Frederick Douglass; black abolitionist orator Charles Remond of Salem, Massachusetts; and lesser-known elites like Dr. James McCune Smith and William Nell Cooper—Garrison's steadfast and unabashed black integrationist ally.[95] To the contrary, Garrison argued, "When was it ever known that liberation from bondage was accompanied by a recognition of political equality? Chattels personal may be instantly translated from the auction-block into freemen; but when were they ever taken at the same time to the ballot-box and invested with all political rights and immunities? According to the laws of development, it is not practicable." Garrison and the abolitionists were not alone in their duplicity. Not only did a congressional act banning slavery in Washington, D.C., appropriate $100,000 for voluntary emigration—adding $500,000 at President Lincoln's request; several northern states that abolished slavery erected disfranchisement laws prohibiting African Americans from serving on juries or voting.[96]

Donald Jacobs and his colleagues insist that the relationship between black abolitionists in Boston and William Lloyd Garrison, for instance, was one of reciprocity and mutual dependence. Garrison himself became more dependent on the appeals and legacy of David Walker to access the black community, which was leery of his early support for colonizationism. This was also true for the African American readership—which constituted the overwhelming majority of subscribers—and for financing Garrison's *Liberator* publication. Jacobs locates David Walker's relationship to Boston's militantly nationalistic elements. Within the internal abolitionist politics of Boston, at least in tenor, William Lloyd Garrison co-opted important elements of David Walker's radical criticisms. This provided entry to black Boston, which consisted of all of the ideological elements that could be found in other important cities, such as New York and Philadelphia. But, of these, Boston's black community, 3 percent of the city's population in Walker's five years there, was the most influential black abolitionist activist community in the young country.[97]

For Peter Hinks, David Walker and his *Appeal* were exceptional mainly in pitch, not in substance—aside from the blunt call to violence. Walker articulated common themes in African American thought. Nevertheless, his influence became perennial as "leaders of black America all made clear that they not only endorsed David Walker and his work but also *considered him one of the great inspirational leaders for African Americans.* Henry Highland Garnet, Maria Stewart, Amos G. Beaman, and Frederick Douglass—as well as W.E.B. Du Bois—gave Walker credit for being a central influence on their lives."[98] Walker was to black abolitionism what Malcolm X was to Black Power.

Whether his abolitionist radicalism was nationalistic or integrationist is a matter of debate, especially among historians. Most scholars of Walker have been inclined to uncritically assume the relationship between his abolitionism and the integrationist orientation while altogether ignoring the nationalist qualities of his life and work.[99] Does it follow that African Americans who opposed slavery as a condition thought of or sought integration as the logical extension of abolition in a manner similar to how William Nell Cooper of Boston and other elites of the mid-1800s envisioned it? Should political historians assume that abolitionism was antithetical to the social, political, and economic orientations we now accept as nationalism? Or is it plausible that African American abolitionists simply imagined a "black" coexistential reality free of slavery and racism? Could one be both abolitionist and committed to racial solidarity? If so, then Walker epitomizes this: He regarded black Americans—slave and "free"—as a national entity distinct from Euro-American whites and operating on diametrical and contested understandings of the Christian gospel. Walker's contributions to the African American protest tradition and black nationalism are particularly important to understanding the potentially revolutionary discourses employed in the social criticisms of Malcolm X in the twentieth century, and they have a patently religious structure. Hinks exaggerates Walker's optimism for racial reconciliation with his white contemporaries and reluctance toward *black* nationalism.[100] His interpretation of Walker and the *Appeal* accentuates the deep, personal sense of humanitarianism that pervades the tract. And whereas Walker's hatred of slavery and love of African Americans derive from a Christian sense of egalitarian reform and group affinity, which could be extended to willing Euro-American whites, the *preponderance* of the *Appeal*'s message was not conciliatory toward whites, whom he repeatedly identified as the "natural enemies" of black people in the United States and globally.

If Frederick Douglass was, as Moses rightly argues, a "stay-at-home" black nationalist, it is where he (and Walker) held up the contradiction between the universalism of the Declaration of Independence and the specificity of Native American and black American oppression experiences. Moses, with very different conclusions, is correct in observing that "many black nationalists refused to leave American soil." But we are offered no follow-up, except for an ambiguous note that Frederick Douglass "sought to use nationalistic means for integrationist and assimilationist ends. . . . Although Douglass consistently favored assimilation throughout his life, he was not above pragmatic separatism to suit his personal ends, nor was he totally immune to any sense of racial feeling."[101] Howard-Pitney concurs:

> Douglass endorsed black nationalist themes and social strategies mainly because he deemed appeals to race pride and unity to be most effective for inspiring those efforts for black accomplishment which he thought necessary to help end racism. . . . At the same time, though, Douglass's final social goals were broader and more inclusive than aiding any single group or race, even his own. What he hoped for in America was the eventual birth of a universal democracy in which racial identity would be irrelevant. . . . Although he championed the fight for black liberation and self-development and considered these goals complementary, even prerequisites, to achieving general social justice, Douglass's support for nationalistic racial endeavors occasionally conflicted with his final assimilationist-integrationist goal for his people. Sometimes he criticized racial separatism. . . . Black nationalism to Douglass was a positive but temporary force that he would willingly sacrifice to advance his higher raceless social ideal. When racial loyalty conflicted with his broader social goals and vision, Douglass usually subordinated racial nationalism to transracial Americanism and both these, when necessary, to humanism.[102]

These assessments are stunted by the requirement that nationalism be defined essentially in terms of *land* and expatriation; any other nationalist sentiment must be assigned to the "integrationist-assimilationist" columns. Douglass must be either a duplicitous assimilationist or a duplicitous revolutionary stay-at-home black nationalist who, like most early nationalist-oriented individuals, believed that black Americans existentially constituted a nation within a nation. There is the tendency toward sanitized reading of the extent to which the ostensible "raceless" and "transracial Americanism," which Douglass imagined, existed nowhere in the country—North or South—throughout his life; to achieve such, in the absence of any corroboration, one typically resorted to default "color-blind" universalism, which has never been favorable to African American people. Douglass read the *Appeal*, which was written when he was eleven years old, prior to reading *any* other abolitionist literature.[103] In an 1883 address recalling the early days of abolition, Douglass argued,

> The question is sometimes asked, when, where and by whom the Negro was first suspected of having any rights at all? In answer to this inquiry it has been asserted that William Lloyd Garrison originated the anti-slavery movement, that until his voice was raised against the American slave system, the whole world was silent. With all respect to those who make this claim I am compelled to dissent from it. I love and venerate the memory of William Lloyd Garrison . . . but he was preceded by many other good men whom it

would be a pleasure to remember on occasions like this. Benjamin Lundy, an humble Quaker, though not the originator of the anti-slavery movement, was in advance of Mr. Garrison. *Walker, a colored man, whose appeal against slavery startled the land like a trump of coming judgment, was before either Mr. Garrison or Mr. Lundy.*[104]

Among others, David Walker's *Appeal*, Frederick Douglass's life and speeches—especially his 1852 Fourth of July address—Delany's *Blake*, and Garnet's *Call to Rebellion*, although not perfectly analogous, either warned of or actually called on fire from the heavens in a manner that invokes the biblical "Sons of Thunder," James and John, that is, the sons of Zebedee—not *Jeremiah*.[105] Sometimes, however, the fire was to come from below. For instance, Frederick Douglass's famous Fourth of July speech argued that despite how Euro-American whites viewed and celebrated the achievement of independence, it was duplicitous to Africans in chains in the South and to nominally free and poor blacks in the North. In particular, Douglass's thoughts on American independence highlighted the great asterisk that might be attached to notions such as "the rights of man," "equality," "natural law and natural right," "liberty," and the Lockean "right to revolution" within the African American predicament in the United States: "the contradiction between the ideals professed by the nation's Founders and the practice of denying human rights to black Americans and other minorities."[106] If it is true that the Fourth of July observations epitomized "civil religion," then it is also true that most blacks observed *July 5* as a way of demonstrating the "in but not of" quality of being black in antebellum America; for most blacks, it was "a white holiday, a day of mourning rather than celebration."[107] Douglass channels Walker, especially in the use of the pronouns "you" and "your," to distinguish between the realities of the black nation and the American nation throughout the speech. Indeed, the structure of the entire speech reflects this duality; its first part lauds the founding ideals of the American Revolution, in all its glory, whereas the second half culminates with the rhetorical question, "What, to the American slave, is *your* Fourth of July?" but

a day that reveals to him, more than all other days in the year, the gross injustice and cruelty to which he is the constant victim. To him, *your* celebration is a sham; *your* boasted liberty, an unholy license; *your* national greatness, swelling vanity; *your* sounds of rejoicing are empty and heartless; *your* denunciations of tyrants, brass fronted impudence; *your* shouts of liberty and equality, hollow mockery; *your* prayers and hymns, *your* sermons and thanksgivings, with all *your* religious parade, and solemnity, are to him, mere bombast, fraud, deception, impiety, and hypocrisy—a thin veil to cover up crimes that would disgrace a nation of savages. *There is not a nation on the earth guilty of practices, more shocking and bloody, than are the people of the United States*, at this very hour . . . lay your facts by the side of the everyday practices of this nation, and you will say with me, that for revolting barbarity and hypocrisy, America reigns without rival.[108]

Eddie Glaude's study perceptibly centers David Walker and black rage in an analysis that privileges black agency among active individuals in the first third to half of the nineteenth century. Glaude sees in Walker an inspiration for antebellum African Americans to experience "radical transformation of heart and disposition."[109] Walker's precipitous rage was not wild "kill whitey" anger, but the basis of a

> transvaluation of values. . . . His intent was to shift the center of gravity in our morality to a place where our justification for action emanates not from custom or habit but from conscience or some principle of thought. If African Americans were not rageful about *their conditions*, Walker maintained, then they obviously had failed to analyze and understand the problems of race and its consequences. Expression of rage, then, began the process of purging blacks of the habit of servility (if I can express rage at my tormentor's action, I can rise up against him) and of clarifying the particulars of their miseries and wretchedness. . . . Radical rage served only to jump-start action in light of the moral imperative to respond to the evil of white supremacy—an evil that often shook the foundations of Walker's faith.[110]

Christian insurrectionists "Black Gabriel" Prosser, Denmark Vesey, Peter Poyas, Gullah Jack,[111] and Nat Turner arguably provide its most elemental expression in violence, or the threat of it, for most of the same period, regardless of the (in)frequency of insurrections in the United States. Its chief quality was militantly "speaking truth to power" in a manner that unmistakably warned of a pending retribution with blacks, and their allies, as God's vicegerents in the process. It is also relevant that Wilson Moses's tenuous contention that "it would be incorrect to attribute full-blown nationalistic motives to most North American slave uprisings. . . . slave revolts were frequently no more than opportunistic expressions of resentment. . . . not necessarily indicating concrete plans for an alternative social order" does not altogether discount incipient nationalist motivations in the slave uprisings. Radical abolitionist Thomas Wentworth Higginson's *Black Rebellion: Five Slave Revolts* suggests several dimensions to the uprisings that might be taken as "nationalist." First, "freedom"[112] or "liberty" was as much a new social order as were the Sierra Leone, Liberia, or Haiti settlements of British and American colonizationist or emigrationist schemes on which Vesey and Turner, at least, passed in deference to the immediacy of the slaves' predicament in South Carolina and Virginia, respectively. Freedom would be a new, if imagined, social order devoid of whip, chain, and master. Second, the most notable slave uprisings were often the result of months and years of planning by confidants—Vesey's plan was contrived over four years and executed over six months, and Turner and Prosser's plots were equally as deliberative, not simply opportunistic. In each of these insurrectionist plots, spanning three decades, the goal was to take a city or town, a county, possibly a state, and indeed the nation as the preeminent example. Toussaint and Saint-Domingue pointed to national possibilities even with a numerical disadvantage in most slaveholding states. Richmond was Prosser's object, as it would be for the ultimate "white nationalist" six decades later, Jefferson Davis. A third point concerns the centrality among Christian insurrectionists of the Israel-Exodus mythos, which had overtly nationalist implications and anticipated subsequent generations of black nationalism like those of Moses's "classical" period (1850–1862). A fourth point derives from Moses's own tempered suggestion that "the existence of the slave revolts and conspiracies provides ample evidence of a desire for self-determination."[113] It is shortsighted to think that because slave insurrectionists lacked a coherent position calling for emigration, colonization, or "nationality," they lacked imagination of a better social order.

As such, black rage is not ideologically synonymous with racial violence. Individual African Americans are more inclined to absorb their frustrations, never reaching a point of violence toward others; and if they do reach such a point, it is more likely to be aimed at other African Americans—what some scholars call "double rage"—than toward whites or other groups.[114] It would be fully arbitrary to parse when and under what circumstances an individual with a depraved but clinically paranoid mind, such as Jamaican-born Colin Ferguson of the 1993 Long Island Railroad massacre, is acting in black rage or mere racial violence. The random violence of even a racially frustrated "lone wolf" does not comport well with the actionable sentiments of larger segments of collectives of blacks in a town, a city, or a nation; in fact, the violence of an individual of this sort is the exception that confirms a threshold rule. Colin Ferguson may have taken into account the impact of his premeditated violence on David Dinkins's New York City mayoralty (by waiting until he reached mostly white Garden City in Nassau County), and he may have, in his own mind, been paranoid of whites, but Colin Ferguson is no Robert Charles, an avowed black nationalist who carried out a one-man insurrection amid the pogroms and riots in New Orleans in 1900.[115] Since the mid-1840s, black rage has been employed as an "environmental hardship," diminished-capacity legal defense.[116] A major twentieth-century proponent—attorney Paul Harris—enlists a survey of cases and a long record of its reasonableness in the experiences of ordinary African Americans in his book *Black Rage Confronts the Law* (1999). But he specifically rejects Colin Ferguson's initial consideration of a black rage defense, because he felt Ferguson blamed white society in the abstract and arbitrarily attributed his actions to racism he experienced. To be sure, the massive uprising of April 4, 1968, *made sense* in its madness, at least to a large segment of African Americans, though the majority of blacks may have felt it betrayed "senseless violence" that dishonored King's legacy.

Without regard to specific African American ideology, Joel Kovel has perceptively noted, that insofar as any phenomenon can be raised to the level of a cultural institution [i.e., racism], it must satisfy at least one condition: it must affect and be meaningful to large numbers of people within a social organization. Being meaningful implies congruency with the personalities of the people within society; there must be something within personalities that responds in a mass way to the effect of the institution. The most reliable guide to the psychological importance of any institution is simply its importance as an element in culture. This importance in turn can be measured in one clear way: through its role in history. What is culturally and psychologically negligible will disappear and be forgotten; what is important will endure and matter, will influence other elements of culture and persistently recur in human consciousness.[117]

The range of psychological responses of African American people tends to be consistent with the larger, fluid ideological traditions employed among them. Of this indeterminacy, Myrdal offers some perspective:

Instead of organized popular theories or ideas, the observer finds in the Negro World, for the most part, only a fluid and amorphous mass of all sorts of embryos of thoughts. Negroes seem to be held in a state of eternal preparedness for a great number of contradictory opinions—ready to accept one type or another depending on how they are driven by pressures or where they see an opportunity. Under such circumstances, the masses of American Negroes might, for example, rally around a violently anti-American, anti-Western, anti-White, black chauvinism of the Garvey type, centered around the idea of Africa as the mother country. But they just as likely, if only a slight change of stimulus is provided, join in an all-out effort to fight for their native country . . . for the Western Civilization to which they belong, and for the tenets of democracy in the entire world. . . . Or they might develop a passive cynicism toward it all.[118]

Eric Lincoln describes three broad psychological responses of African Americans to racial oppression that he calls *avoidance, acceptance*, and *aggression*.[119] At the root of each is an operational "*consciousness of kind*," which is defined as "that state of mind in which individuals are vividly aware of themselves as members of a group different from other groups—as a black, a white, an Irish Catholic, an Anglo-Saxon Protestant, a Jew." As a stalwart adherent of black nationalism in the 1930s, Paul Robeson contended that "a *consciousness* of the conditions and attributes which made black people a unique people was required before a nationality or nationhood could be brought into being. Yet he thought far more than consciousness of kind was necessary for the realization of self-determination in any concrete sense."[120] If avoidance and acceptance are alternating possibilities, then the lynchings and race pogroms of the postwar era moved Claude McKay, with "If We Must Die," to call for a new consciousness of self-defense:

If we must die, let it not be like hogs
Hunted and penned in an inglorious spot,
While round us bark the mad and hungry dogs,
Making their mock at our accursed lot.
If we must die, oh, let us nobly die,
So that our precious blood may not be shed
In vain; then even the monsters we defy
Shall be constrained to honor us though dead!
Oh, kinsmen! We must meet the common foe!
Though far outnumbered, let us show us brave,
And for their thousand blows deal one death-blow!
What though before us lies an open grave?
Like men we'll face the murderous, cowardly pack,
Pressed to the wall, dying, but fighting back![121]

McKay's sonnet echoes Garnet's *An Address to the Slaves*, where he urged, "you had far better all die—*die immediately*, than live as slaves. . . . There is not much hope of redemption without the shedding of blood. If you must bleed, let it come at once—*rather die free men than live to be slaves.*"[122] Richard Wright's *Native Son*, with its protagonist Bigger Thomas, on some level betrays the most torturous and "radical effect of racism on the black psyche."[123] Bigger Thomas was "not so much a particular character caught in a specific episode of criminal activity as a crime waiting to happen; all the elements to create Bigger's mentality were historically in place in America, stocked by the criminal racial situation that was America," according to Arnold Rampersad.[124] There were dimensions in Bigger Thomas, like Black Power–inspired violence a quarter-century later that became a marker for collective grievances. From the accusatory pathos of Nina Simone's "Strange Fruit" and "Mississippi Goddamn!" to the unrestrained viscerality of the Last Poets and the final scenes of Spike Lee's *Do the Right Thing*, garrisoning black self-confidence, self-criticism, love, self-hate, and awareness has long emitted from black rage.[125] There is something of it evident in the quality of accusation and condemnation in the comedy of Paul Mooney. Ellis Cose argues that it is as equally present in affluent and accomplished African American individuals as it is in the bugbear "underclass," if not more so. Neither has it been the exclusive property of men. Boston's Maria Stewart—who worked directly with and acknowledged her ideological and personal affinity for David Walker—during the 1820s and Boston's Marita Bonner during the late 1920s Harlem renaissance promoted a "race woman" genre that noted the utility of violence rhetorically and literarily. Bonner's essay "On Being Young—a Woman—and Colored" urged,

in Heaven's name, do not grow bitter. "Be bigger than they are," exhort white friends who have never had to draw breath in a Jim Crow train. Who have never had petty putrid insult dragged over them—like pebbled sand on your body where the skin is the tenderest. You long to explode and hurt everything white; friendly; unfriendly. But you know that you cannot live with a chip on your shoulder. . . . You get hard. So—being a woman—you can wait.[126]

Bonner's 1928 play *Purple Flower* at points reads more like a meeting of the 1950s Nation of Islam listening to Malcolm X, with its main characters being "Sundry White Devils" who "must be artful little things with soft wide eyes such as you would expect to find in an angel. Soft hair that flops around their horns" and the "US's (They can be as white as the White Devils, as brown as the earth, as black as the center of a poppy. They may look as if they were something or nothing)." In this scenario, white and black US's seem to be in a perpetual struggle, with the former daily surveilling the hill where the "purple Flower-of-Life-At-Its Fullest" rests, to prevent the latter from reaching it, which would end the perpetual subjugation of black US's. As the US's find conventional mechanisms insufficient, transformational violence is sought after God provides a "White Devil" ram in the bush.[127] Audre Lorde also outlines black rage as a particular manifestation among black women in the United States.[128]

In an introduction to the *Appeal*, James Turner argues that the pamphlet represented "a magnificent tradition of critical thought *created by Africans in America*."[129] Perhaps no single feature of Walker's *Appeal* stands out more than the call to insurrection. And Turner rejects claims that Walker's politics and *Appeal* were merely an expression of emotional resentment. For him, it was a comprehensive assessment of concrete circumstances begging for protest, organizing, and radical discourse.[130] The psychological enslavement of African Americans could be overcome only by the will of God or at the point of the sword. For, in *that nation*, Walker felt, "we Coloured People of these United States, are, the most wretched, degraded and abject set of beings that ever lived since the world began." True to Walker's form, the sense of immediacy; the need to deconstruct the myths of relative group valuation in the inferiority-superiority complex; the stirring of black self-confidence against seemingly insurmountable odds; and eradicating the psychological devastation of chattel slavery, peonage, lynching, proscription, and unequal resources distribution have all remained a perennial feature of black nationalist discourses.[131] This is not to suggest that erstwhile integrationists, from Douglass and Harriet Tubman to Ella Baker and Robert Williams, were disinclined to self-defensive violence to the extent of King and the civil rights establishment organizations. In an epigraph to this chapter, Martin Luther King Jr. welcomes urban violence; he considered it "desirable," "magnificent," an inversion of the long suffering of slave ancestors. Still, he argued, "rioting and violence provide no solutions for economic problems. Much of the justification for rioting has come from the thesis—originally set forth by Frantz Fanon—that violence has a certain cleansing effect. *Perhaps, in a special psychological sense, he may have had a point . . .* ultimately, one's sense of [person]hood must come from within."[132]

J. A. Rogers felt that African Americans especially suffered inferiority complexes unparalleled by blacks in any other part of the diaspora of African descendants. Of Rogers, it is noted that

> the negative attitudes toward black skin, he discovered, were originally manifestations of Eurocentric mythology and superstitions. Later, many whites would alter these superstitions and apply them stereotypically to blacks, thus affecting the collective mentality of the blacks for centuries. Such mental slavery was achieved by whites as a result of their repeated attempts to destroy several key elements of African self-awareness and traditional life. By the annihilation of a sense of group identity, unity would become impossible, and slavery could be more easily practiced. With African cultural traditions thus destroyed, the slaves' resistance to bondage was severely limited.[133]

Frantz Fanon, like Rogers and, later, Harold Cruse, identifies the inferiority dynamic as extant more among the educated and intellectual classes than among ordinary individuals. Cruse, for instance, viewed Du Bois's "double consciousness" construct as an autobiographical device of the burgeoning black bourgeoisie of the Reconstruction era, not of the recently manumitted slaves or their children, whom Du Bois encountered at Fisk.[134] Fanon's major works, *The Wretched of the Earth* and *Black Skin, White Masks*, both address the psychological impact of slavery and colonization on "the African mind(s)." The latter outlines the ways in which "we must see whether it is possible for the black man to overcome his feelings of insignificance, to rid his life of the compulsive quality that makes it so like the behaviour of the phobic. Affect is exaggerated in the Negro, he is full of rage because he feels small, he suffers from an inadequacy in all human communication, and all these factors chain him with an unbearable insularity."[135]

Wilson Moses looks somewhat askance at the association of violence with black nationalism, and he is right for the most part concerning emigrationism. But for others, "The Reverend Henry Highland Garnet's celebrated address, urging the slaves to revolt against their masters, can be considered a nationalist document in two respects. First, it explicitly expresses the sense of identity and solidarity with the slaves felt by the free people of color. Second, it calls for violent overthrow of the Southern economic system, based implicitly upon united and collective action on the part of the slaves themselves."[136] For Wilson Moses, Delany's *Blake* represented black nationalism not for any of its emigrationist features but—among other reasons—because "it was inspired by the slave revolutionary tradition, which was sometimes nationalistic."[137] Delany links Blake's pan-American schemes of general insurrection to the well-known nineteenth-century plots of Gabriel Prosser, Denmark Vesey, and Nat Turner. Moses concedes, "*Blake* is a typical exhortation to revolt by a free black pamphleteer. It may be compared to Walker's *Appeal*, and the *Ethiopian Manifesto* because of its apocalyptic tone and its promise of a great black messiah." Floyd

Miller insists that *Blake* was a compendium of analysis on "slavery as an institution, Cuba as the prime interest of Southern expansionists, the 'practicality' of militant slaver revolution, and, most importantly, the psychological liberation possible through collective action."[138] Despite Moses's acknowledgment of Blake's black nationalism—which he does not clarify in any detail—he does offer a curious comment suggesting that "the most important promoter of continuity in a literary tradition is neither conscious imitation nor unconscious influences of past authors, but the power of social environments to cause successive generations to repeat certain types of literary behavior."[139] Through *Blake*, Delany focuses less on emigrationism and more on "self-reliance, upon blacks' leading their own rebellions and avoiding undue dependence upon whites and white institutions, while not completely divorced from the thinking of leaders such as Douglass, [who] does, nevertheless, sharply demonstrate the strength of his commitment to nationalism." *Blake* culminates in a nascent revolution in Cuba, which (as in neighboring Haiti three decades earlier) would challenge the very foundation of slavery in the Americas.[140]

Among scholars and intellectuals, bell hooks, Ellis Cose, Cornel West, Jean-Paul Sartre, and Hannah Arendt have taken the concept of collective rage seriously.[141] hooks, who has been a sharp critic of masculinist black nationalist politics of recent decades, is also surprisingly one of the clearest analysts on the subject of black rage and Malcolm X's relationship to it. Malcolm X was not one-dimensional. The many "Malcolms" claimed by adherents of every ideological, intellectual, and programmatic stripe over decades attest to this. He was more than an "angry black man," and his epitomizing black rage should not be lifted from the context of the teeming masses of African Americans who have been most inclined toward raising him as an apparition to speak to their realities in the neoliberal rescission of public and national obligation to black citizens. In the introduction to Malcolm X's autobiography, M. S. Handler insists that "Malcolm articulated the woes and the aspirations of the depressed Negro mass in a way it was unable to do for itself. When he attacked the white man, Malcolm did for the Negroes what they couldn't do for themselves—he attacked with a violence and anger that spoke for the ages of misery."[142]

With the intellectual stigma of Black Power in the academy, its mocking in pop-culture renditions, in politics, and in US society—including among blacks themselves—in this book there is reticence toward invoking black rage as an operational intellectual construct in African American politics and culture.[143] Cedric Johnson is concerned that such a formation is subject to many pitfalls for elites and intellectuals, ranging from King (recall the subtle *warning* of ongoing urban violence before he reached the crescendo of his "March on Washington Speech"), to Stokely Carmichael and Charles Hamilton (in chapter 4 of *Black Power*, "Dynamite and the Ghetto"),[144] to the general repudiation extant in popular-culture films. Whereas Johnson offers a critical assessment of how Black Power, specifically, has been amenable to system validation as it was wed to the War on Poverty agenda, for instance, he is sympathetic to the ways the "prominent trope in U.S. mass media, the 'angry black' invalidates discontent as a legitimate human expression while reducing politicized race consciousness to emotionalism. . . . The bold analysis of the U.S. racial order inherent in much Black Power rhetoric has been reinvented as racial paranoia in contemporary popular discourse. Those who criticize racial domination or white privilege provide comic relief as political misfits—relics of a bygone era."[145] Algernon Austin adds, "Instead of organizing protests to appeal to a general white audience who would then pressure elected officials, Black Power activists built organizations that would achieve black autonomy. While Black Power activists did have angry, aggressive and macho rhetoric, it is clear from the Black Power conferences that they were also concerned with the political and economic structures affecting black life."[146] Robert Self's study of Oakland accounts for the serious campaign of local, elected, religious, and labor leaders to address the "volatile and protracted social and political struggles over land, taxes, jobs, and public policy in the thirty years between 1945 and the late 1970s . . . ultimately giving rise to two of the nation's controversial political ideologies: a black power politics of community defense and empowerment and a neopopulist conservative homeowner politics among whites."[147] Similarly, Daniel Crowe's *Prophets of Rage: The Black Freedom Struggle in San Francisco, 1945–1969*, effectively grounds the activism of Huey Newton and the Black Panther Party in the quotidian realities that the new waves of ordinary African Americans experienced in the region (Berkeley, Oakland, Richmond, San Francisco) since World War II migrations in housing, education, policing, political incorporation, and crime. In short, he notes, "the unsolved problems of the war years would leave a long and bitter legacy for African Americans in the San Francisco Bay Area, and they would be the seeds of the Black Revolution of the 1960s."[148] The epigraphs introducing this chapter—by James Baldwin and Martin Luther King—speak to the vital role that a mind-set of people (or peoples) plays in forging a sustainable politics. James Baldwin, insists that for segments of blacks who live conscious of, and in, adverse conditions in the United States, a state of rage is banal; for King, to the surprise of those who have time-locked him in his "Dream" speech, the modern expression of black rage reversed "old evasions" of the slaves' misery and silence. Karl Marx suggested that consciousness is born of life conditions, not abstractions: "It is not consciousness that determines life, but life that determines consciousness."

In the state of being black daily in a world ruled by European and Euro-American whites, for Fanon, "the Negro is a toy in the white man's hands; so, in order to shatter this hellish cycle, he explodes."[149] Robert C. Smith concurs that various forms of racism have deep psychological implications that "have damaged and continue to damage the material conditions of African Americans in education, employment, housing, health care, and consumer services, as well as their physical well-being and personal safety. Yet, it is frequently said that the most pernicious effects of racism are not material but psychological. They fostered in African peoples, an 'internal inferiorization' rooted in the extant structural apparatuses of the state and society."[150]

Smith's comparative analysis of Fanon and Marx is instructive. His critique focuses on intellectual analogues between Marxian thought and Fanon's reading of the colonial situation of Africans. Marx tended to trivialize the lumpen segments of Europe, whereas Fanon saw the poor (not the co-opted proletariat) of Africa as a revolutionary cohort, which he labels "the wretched of the earth." Alienation in Marx was born of labor relations in "developed" countries, but in Fanon it was born of the dehumanization experienced by their colonial subjects; the psychological effects were not solely individualistic but also social and collective.[151] As Arendt notes, violence is not integral to Marxist thought. And Smith sees political violence as the primary divide between Marx and Fanon. Fanon's subjects must redeem more than society and its economic relations; they must redeem the mental spaces of the colonized subjects. To Smith, Fanon's understanding of the role of violence

> is more than a mere political method or tool to force the removal of the European oppressor; for Fanon, it is a vital *means* of psychic and social liberation. . . . Unlike Marx, Fanon seems to imply that even if the colonialists peacefully withdraw, the decolonization process is somehow aborted, that liberation is incomplete—the native remains an enslaved person in the neo-colonial social system. The native's inner violence remains pent up. . . . The function of violence is only incidentally political; its main function is psycho-social.[152]

Equally tragic, Fanon (as do others) links this black racial resentment not toward its intended subjects; it gives way to "double rage" and the phenomenon that Fanon identified as "Niggers Killing Niggers on Saturday Night." Cornel West notes, "Of all the hidden injuries of blackness in American civilization, black rage is the most deadly, the most lethal. Although black culture is in no way reducible to or identical with black rage, it is inseparable from black rage."[153]

Mad at Master: Hating Oneself

Black rage has been a perennial standpoint among black Americans in *movement politics*. Its cultural deadliness has been mostly black-directed and deeply reflects a psychical form of self-flagellation. Black people, across class lines, hate the racism that has made them hate themselves. J. A. Rogers believed, for instance, "that as a group, African Americans were a sick people, and that those who graduated from college or became 'successful' were perhaps the sicker members of the group."[154] One need look no further than the *self-representations* in ghetto-centric pop culture—film, music, entertainment—to appreciate how bourgeois black filmmakers and producers, rap music moguls, and performers have been resolute in conjuring the madness of being black and poor in contemporary society.[155]

Fanon's work is itself an exhaustive treatment of the psychological resuscitation that exudes from the confrontation between oppressed and oppressor. In true Hegelian frocking, Fanon appropriates native violence, the extreme expression of black rage, as a utility that is not destructive but redemptive. As Sartre saw it, "The rebel's weapon is proof of his humanity. For in the first days of the revolt you must kill: to shoot down a European is to kill two birds with one stone, to destroy an oppressor and the man he oppresses at the same time: there remain a dead man, and a free man; the survivor, for the first time feels a *national* soil under his foot."[156] Such violence is not only redemptive for the oppressed and oppressor; it emits the conscientization of a national awakening.[157] Fanon, like Walker before him, centers religion as he writes, "I speak of the Christian religion, and no one need be astonished. The Church in the colonies is the white people's Church, the foreigner's Church. She does not call the native to God's ways but to the ways of the white man, of the master, of the oppressor."[158]

Violence between the oppressor and the oppressed, between insurrectionist and militia, settler and native, Oakland police and Black Panthers, is a dialogue. This is a discourse that binds "the people" together against power "as a whole, since each individual forms a violent link in the great chain, a part of the great organism of violence which has surged upward in reaction to the settler's violence in the beginning. The groups recognize each other and the future of the nation is already indivisible. . . . In the same way the second phase, that of building up the nation, is helped on by the existence of this cement which has been mixed with blood and anger."[159]

According to Hannah Arendt, people rationally employ this feature of group politics when they believe that government and society can do more to mitigate their predicament. However, Arendt's view of this phenomenon is limited, provincial, and presentist, and her appreciation for its black American variant was retarded by her Burkean-styled antipathy for Frantz Fanon's Jacobinist promotion of discursive violence in the interest of anticolonialist African liberation. Yet her critique of King's strategy of nonviolence, because it sometimes put children on the front line of its civil disobedience tactics, was on the other side of the balance. Arendt strives to debunk the ostensible linkage between revolution and violence; for her, if it is not un-Marxian, it is certainly not of Marx. Arendt seems intellectually, emotionally, and culturally ill-prepared to see any virtue in what she maligns as "clearly silly and outrageous" Negro demands in black militancy, yet she duplicitously celebrates the "the disinterested and usually highly moral claims of white rebels."[160] She plaintively wails, "serious violence entered the scene only with the appearance of the

Black Power movement on the campuses. Negro students, the majority of them admitted without academic qualification. . . . Violence with them was not a matter of theory and rhetoric."[161]

Quitting racist society is, of course, the hallmark of emigrationism and a major impetus for projects seeking racial separation. Smith's assessment of post–civil rights black politics points to a transformation of violent and hostile expressions of white racial attitudes toward black Americans, declining substantially since the 1940s. But this, he contends, is impeached by the organic manner that racial feeling toward blacks as a social group adapts in less obvious ways than previously expressed in specific forms of religious myth, racial attitudes, and stereotypes of black people in general (but especially the poor and less educated), including "scientific" claims concerning African Americans' performance on studies of intelligence and even survey research.[162] The "occasional slips" of racist feeling or attitudes toward blacks coming from public figures and private individuals in the new century, which Smith identifies, persist.[163] They have been particularly fierce since the election of Barack Obama as president.

Post–civil rights black nationalism is theoretically and materially akin to the domestic variant of the tradition, in all of its long-established opposition to Euro-American white domination of social, political, and economic life *in* the United States. Compared to later developments in black politics, the 1960s were significantly more given to a *politics of violence*; there was at least a theory of violence, although it was often disruptive to forging critical and disciplined institutional structures outside the religious sector to any substantial degree.[164] This was the double-edged sword of black rage. On the one hand, it crystallized a largely ill-formed social and political frustration that needed articulation of an antiracist structure of dissent. William Grier and Price Cobbs suggest, for instance, that black rage articulates the ways "individual Black people come 'more and more' to realize that even their inner suffering is due largely to a hostile white majority, and, with this realization [gain] a determination to change that hostile society."[165] This would be an undercurrent of the political hostilities expressed in tangible ways in Los Angeles and New York as recently as the 1980s and 1990s, culminating in the April 1992 disruption in Los Angeles during what Cornel West called a largely multifaceted display of "justifiable social rage" and an impetus for the unprecedented, though poorly executed, MMM/DOA in 1995.[166] On the other hand, it created space for the contradictory and duplicitous co-optation of Malcolm X's cultural and political contributions by Minister Louis Farrakhan, Al Sharpton, Clarence Thomas, and attorney Malik Shabazz.[167]

Pointing to the manner in which Malcolm X's revolutionary criticisms appealed to young people in the 1960s, and beyond (and perhaps despite) his religiosity, Moses enlists the following statements in response to a series of questions from Malcolm in a speech that alluded to a millennial judgment of racist America:

What was this "Divine Destruction" of which he [Malcolm] spoke? Would it be a direct act of God? Would it be a revolt among the masses of black Americans? Would it be a cosmic revolution of the world's darker peoples against Western imperialism? Malcolm's prophecy was similar to David Walker's, 130 years earlier, which had predicted an apocalyptic bloodbath for America in retribution for crimes against the African race. Of course, David Walker, who wrote in 1829, could not have anticipated Malcolm X's optimism at the very real prospects of a decline in Western supremacy. The jeremiadic theme became more pronounced in the next few years.[168]

Contemporary analyses of black nationalism, that is, studies that have emerged since the civil rights movement, have had as their object the lineal relationship of Black Power to the tradition (even though, and this detail is often ignored in the literature, Black Power was uttered by students with integrationist commitments who were increasingly influenced by Malcolm X and the Nation of Islam).[169] Even more interesting analytically is Moses's description of Malcolm's fateful "chickens coming home to roost" comment, which ostensibly led to his expulsion from the Nation of Islam. He notes, "The hour of parting was on the evening of December 4, 1963, less than a week after the assassination of President Kennedy. Malcolm gave a speech in the Manhattan Center called 'God's Judgment on White America.' This was another of his topical *jeremiads, reminiscent of David Walker's Appeal*."[170]

Moses's formulation seemingly requires at least one of three possibilities (and two would be fatal to any unidirectional historiography) of the Euro-American influence on the likes of Walker. A first option might be to offer Malcolm X as a practitioner of the American *Christian* jeremiad.[171] This would vicariously indebt Malcolm X (vis-à-vis David Walker) to Thomas Jefferson. And Malcolm X's rejection of ideological and political liberalism at least with regard to African Americans—he argued that "democracy is hypocrisy," among a long list of charges—complicates such a linkage. A second option would be to root Malcolm X's use of the jeremiad within a formal ideological analysis of Walker, but this undermines Moses's ambivalence in linking Walker with black nationalism, as any comparative analysis of Malcolm X would require. Although Walker rejected racist colonization expatriation and hard emigrationism schemes (promoted by nominally free petit bourgeois elites), he made a last-minute shift in the third edition of his writing to a tempered support for emigration.[172] And a third option would be to systematically link Walker to Malcolm X in terms of the structure of their ideas, personal narratives, and respective political milieus and to treat the black jeremiad, regardless of its particularistic religious sourcing (i.e., Christianity or Islam), as a strand of black nationalism itself.

As noted, the *process* by which black nationalism becomes dominated by Muslims and urban cultic personalities is critical. Here, Walker meets Malcolm X without surrendering time-spatial and ideological integrities. James

Turner asserts, "Modern-day Black radicalism has its roots deep in David Walker's construction of political philosophy." Donald Jacobs goes a step farther in asserting, "there is a direct line between David Walker's *Appeal*, the fiery condemnation of slavery published in 1829 by a Boston free black dealer in clothes, and the rhetoric of such twentieth-century black agitators as El Hajj Malik Shabazz (alias Malcolm Little) and Malcolm X."[173] William Grier and Price Cobbs's black rage thesis is especially instructive to understanding the landless, psychological orientation in black nationalism. In the 1960s, black rage was inextricably wedded to institution-constructing political formations, such as the SNCC, the Lowndes County Freedom Organization, the National Black Political Convention, the Black Power Conferences, and the Black Arts Repertory Theater, however flawed or truncated. During the 1990s, the Nation of Islam remained its clearest and least creative expression, culminating in the 1995 Million Man March.

In the three decades between Black Power and the Million Man March, African Americans have altogether abandoned talk of serious programs of racial separation, but they have not abandoned black nationalism as a social, political, economic, or foreign policy orientation. Malcolm X's self-representation as the "angriest" black man in the United States (conveyed in his widely read autobiography and in popular media) incarnated psychiatrists Grier and Cobbs's black rage thesis. I thus see post–civil rights black nationalism as an iteration of the black rage thesis, which outlines important tenets of domestic black nationalism that first emanated from early *Christian* black nationalists and became the main conduit for Elijah Muhammad, Malcolm X, Louis Farrakhan, and the Nation of Islam to move from remote urban cultic adherents to the fore of radical black criticism for three-quarters of the twentieth century.[174] In the chapter "Malcolm X and Black Rage" in *Race Matters* (and other writings), Cornel West addresses this phenomenon after outlining the ways in which African Americans confronted the material realities of their living situations. He notes,

> They constructed structures of meaning and structures of feeling in the face of the fundamental facts of human existence—death, dread, despair, disease, and disappointment. Yet the specificity of black culture . . . lies in both the African and American character of black people's attempts to sustain their mental sanity and spiritual health, social life and political struggle in the midst of a slaveholding, white supremacist civilization that viewed itself as the most enlightened, free, tolerant, and democratic experiment in human history.[175]

West seems to point to black rage as a nonspecific ideological node that is more readily detected in the worldviews of nationalist individuals, such as Garvey, juxtaposed to the "American optimism" of the likes of Du Bois, more generally. Wracked by this "deeply pessimistic view of American democracy," particularly in "existential, social, political, and economic" realms, black rage tends to emerge not from disappointment in America, but as "bona fide black nationalists, they had no expectations of a white supremacist civilization; they adhered neither to American optimism nor to exceptionalism."[176] Foregrounding Du Bois's decision to quit America was nonetheless a "suppression of black rage," which "reinforced a black obsession with the psychic scars, ontological wounds, and existential bruises that tend to the tragic, to the pathetic. Instead of exercising agency or engaging in action against the odds, one may wallow in self-pity, acknowledging the sheer absurdity of it all." This response is at the cultural and ideological centers of black life in America. West views black rage in terms of a pathological mix of self-hatred, despair, and doubt.[177] West also took up the relationship of Malcolm X to black rage within the context of 1990s black politics. For West, Malcolm X epitomizes black rage in his unequivocal love for blacks: "His love was neither abstract nor ephemeral. Rather, it was a concrete connection with a degraded and devalued people in need of psychic conversion."[178] Much like Walker's, his expression of this sentiment was primarily a discourse emanating among African Americans and secondarily to the larger society. Malcolm X, in turn, "sharply crystallized the relation of black affirmation of self, black desire for freedom, black rage against American society, and the likelihood of early black death."[179]

The black bourgeoisie, more so than the young and ghetto poor, "has always had an ambivalent relation to Malcolm X—an open rejection of his militant strategy of wholesale defiance of American society and a secret embrace of his bold truth-telling about the depths of racism in American society." Indeed, black rage is without the ambiguity of "double consciousness" in its class dimensions.[180] Double rage is the petulant twin of "double consciousness." For Malcolm X, "'double consciousness' is less a description of a necessary black mode of being in America than a particular kind of colonized mind-set of a special group in black America." Malcolm X serves as the critical linkage figure bridging the tradition of David Walker to the immediate and tertiary post–civil rights periods. Nevertheless, the shortcomings of black rage offset its affirmations.

Black rage often refracts black death. In the shibboleth of post–civil rights black nationalist discourses, there is a tendency to leap from critical assessment to self-righteous claims on truth and "things as they are" or, by any means, "ought to be." The psychic conversion of black individuals and groups was, for Malcolm X, affirmation, but his teacher, Elijah Muhammad, reified race chauvinism as a counterpoint to the original idea.[181] This placed black rage in a morally duplicitous position. For King, black rage, if nonviolent, had redemptive capacities, but too often it ceded a lack of discipline in channeling such feeling into constructive mobilization and political organization. For Malcolm X, "The civil rights movement was not militant enough. It failed to speak clearly and directly to and about black rage."[182] Malcolm X, like black nationalists generally, held to a fear that rested upon "the Manichean (black/white or male/female) channels for the direction of black rage—forms characterized by charismatic leaders, patriarchal structures, and dogmatic pronouncements."[183] Thus, West notes, "Malcolm X identified much more with the mind-set of Richard Wright's Bigger Thomas in *Native Son* than with that of Ralph Ellison's protagonist in *Invisible Man.*"[184] But West glosses over the detail that neither Elijah Muhammad, nor Martin Luther King Jr., nor Malcolm X could "channel" the pendular mood of blacks—and not just their native *sons* and invisible *men*—in their varied circumstances as much as *reflect* them; this is the utility of Malcolm X among post-segregation-era blacks.

If Malcolm X anthropomorphizes black rage for the remaining generations of the twentieth century, it cannot be confined to demobilizing and self-pleasuring rhetorical tirades characteristic of Farrakhan rallies in the 1980s and 1990s. Where West chides Malcolm X on his lack of openness to the "hybridity" of black cultural experience in America, evident in the syncretism of jazz, Cheryl Clarke reminds us that "both R&B and bebop, stemming from different roots in the African-American community, broke with previous conventions to create new social, aesthetic, and racial spaces; neither form was particularly hospitable to women."[185] As a critical interval from David Walker's ethos, Malcolm X's representation of black rage must be amenable from the specificity of African American male expressions of dissent to the post–World War II, post-1960s "universal" move on which he was on the verge at the time of his sudden death.

Upon his break with the Nation of Islam, Malcolm X, George Breitman argues, "as a Muslim equated 'black nationalism' and 'separation.' In the press statement proclaiming himself to be a black nationalist, however, he differentiated the two concepts, defining black nationalism in such a way as to include non-separatists too. In the final months of his life he was seeking for a term to describe his philosophy that would be more precise and more complete than black nationalism."[186] Malcolm X's "philosophy" never ceases to be black nationalism; what he seems to have been searching for is an understanding of how his perception of nationalism, while in the Nation of Islam, could *continue to be nationalism without separatism.*

In this view, for example, the Nation of Islam and its leadership represent the dispositional strain, because it never developed a coherent separatist program beyond *claiming* separatism. Its most salient nationalist quality has been its enduring status as the organizational paean of black militancy in the United States as much for those who might be considered "sympathizers" as for those who have held formal membership therein despite its pro-capitalist and otherwise conservative parochial ascriptions. Perhaps the greatest contribution of the Nation of Islam in the United States was its insistence that segregated black America take full advantage of its circumstances and forge a "knowledge of self."

An awareness of one's spiritual and external roots (i.e., Asiatic and/or Bilalian, not slave or African) could fortify embattled black souls in the United

States. C. Eric Lincoln notes, "Black Muslims have made a science of black nationalism. They have made *black* the ideal, the ultimate value. . . . And their extreme doctrine has attracted more than a hundred thousand adherents—a vivid warning of the deep resentment African Americans harbor for their status in our society and the futility they feel about the likelihood of a genuine and peaceful change."[187] The Nation of Islam's foremost capital, indeed its most concrete nationalist essence outside of its black first entrepreneurial projects, is its ability to outline "the deep resentment African Americans harbor for their status" in US society. One of the great (self-)misrepresentations of the Nation of Islam was its seriousness about embracing emigrationist black nationalism.

But do not downplay the Garveyite origins of the Nation of Islam or of Elijah Muhammad; despite the failures of every emigrationist effort, from Paul Cuffee, to James T. Holly, to the founding of Liberia, to Garveyism and Chief Alfred Sam, they at least made the *attempt* to withdraw from the United States. No black nationalist organization in American political history has enjoyed the organizational salience; economic and human resources; leadership stability; sense of millennial religious destiny; and appeal to dissident workers, youth, prison inmates and former convicts, students, and increasingly—as evinced by support for the 1995 Million Man March/Day of Absence—middle-class elements as the Nation of Islam since its founding. Yet two of the most important early students of the Nation of Islam, C. Eric Lincoln and E. U. Essien-Udom, bring into question its emigrationist credentials.

Even though Lincoln acknowledges the Nation of Islam's rhetorical allusion to internal statism, arguing for "a separate nation for ourselves, right here in America," and "some good earth right here in America," or "two or three states," or "four or five states" and also "nine or ten states," he inevitably concludes that "Elijah Muhammad does not really consider the physical separation of the races in this country a viable prospect. He has offered no concrete proposal for effecting such a separation or for a partition of the country."[188] Moreover, Essien-Udom insists, "it is also extraordinary that [the Nation of Islam's] belief in itself as a definite nation of people has produced absolutely no political program for the establishment of a national home."[189] It set no dates for withdrawal (but predicted the end of the white man's rule in the early 1960s), purchased no planes, chartered or bought no ships, and lobbied no American, African, or Arab officials on the plan. This is true of most black nationalist organizations and movements in the United States since the beginning of the twentieth century.[190]

The commitment of the Nation of Islam has been powerfully dispensational in its creation and millennial mythologies, but it acted more as the principal source of revolutionary anger with the emergence of Malcolm X. It is not gainsaying to suggest that Jim Jones, director of the San Francisco Housing Authority (1975–1977) and minister of the Fillmore/Western Addition Disciples of Christ, was a more serious *emigrationist* (not black nationalist) than Elijah

Muhammad. The fateful mass murder-suicides of 913 mostly black residents—a number of them being refugees of the Bay Area's Black Power and integrationist movements—from San Francisco and Oakland in the Guyana settlement are the tragic proof. Clearly the resources of the "Temple People of Islam" (an early name for the Nation of Islam) rivaled those of Jones's Peoples Temple, but emigration remained for the Nation of Islam *a jeremiad*, a "jihad of words,"[191] not a movement program.

For instance, in a 1997 *Meet the Press* interview with journalist Tim Russert—who asked, "Is that your view in 1997, a separate state for Black Americans?"—Louis Farrakhan explained the Nation of Islam's separatist beliefs as follows:

> First, the program starts with number one. That is number four. The first part of that program is that we want freedom, a full and complete freedom. The second is, we want justice. We want equal justice under the law, and we want justice applied equally to all, regardless of race or class or color. And the third is that we want equality. We want equal membership in society with the best in civilized society. *If we can get that within the political, economic, social system of America, there's no need for point number four.* But if we cannot get along in peace after giving America 400 years of our service and sweat and labor, then, of course, separation would be the solution to our race problem.[192]

The underestimation of religion's import among African Americans has contributed to grossly obscurantist historical interpretations of black nationalism. Political scientist Dean Robinson's *Black Nationalism in American Politics and Thought* (2001) best demonstrates the overall tendency to minimize black religion in its conjugated relationship to black nationalism and how such a view leads to a bastardization of American black nationalism. Like the noted studies, Robinson's makes a case against "classical black nationalism" while ignoring its religious structure.[193] It results, in part, from his view that black nationalism is "inherently quasireligious," rather than sourcing the whole of it.[194]

Because black nationalism developed indigenously among African Americans in line with religious articulations, analysis of trajectories highlights political aspects of black religious life in society that have been ignored by most students of black politics and black political ideologies. This becomes clearer with an approach that explains the various periods of high black nationalist salience as mirroring the immediate political and ideological environments ruled by Euro-American whites. Robinson suggests that the various epochs of black nationalism (in the antebellum period, Garveyism, and Black Power) are structurally unrelated to one another *except* that they share in common a mimetic reflex to the "Anglo-Saxon" patterns with which they developed. This is because "from early in the history of the United States, Afro-Americans have been embedded in the same matrices of thought, culture, society, and politics as white Americans."[195] Like Theodore Draper's, this Eurocentric reading of black nationalism—which Benedict Anderson renounces—suggests it primarily has absorptive properties that have no noteworthy organic correspondents. As Wilson Moses first noted, black nationalism "assumes the shape of its container and undergoes transformations in accordance with changing fashions in the white world."[196] Although this overstates the case, it does allow for a longitudinal reading of black nationalism through the post–civil rights era, beginning with Malcolm X in the Nation of Islam and, by extension, Black Power.

Yet Robinson's view can be accomplished only by setting aside Moses's subsequent argument that black nationalism is "one of the earliest expressions of nationalism; while it originated in *unison* with the American and French Revolutions, *it was not an imitation of North American or European nationalism*."[197] Indeed, "such thinking predates the American Declaration of Independence." Kevin Gaines gives in to the same bastardization in his criticisms of Hubert H. Harrison, who he argues "anticipated much of the best and worst of contemporary black nationalism." For Gaines, too, all nationalisms are indiscrete even when one rejects another:

> Although critical of civilizationist ideology, Harrison shared the sentimental association of race progress with Victorian gender roles that nationalists, black and white, subscribed to. In the absence of political struggles, nationalistic objectives often incorporated the rhetoric of domesticity as essential to the imperatives of the nation-state. This has never been more true than recently, illustrated by the frequent references to the family in presidential State of the Union messages under Republican administrations. *Black nationalists were similar with a difference*, echoing the veneration of the patriarchal black family which remains central to black middle class ideology.[198]

Not only is this a torturously anachronistic reading of Harrison (vis-à-vis nineteenth-century civilizationism, Victorianism, and late-twentieth-century Republican family values); more to the point, it misrepresents his commitments to ordinary blacks (as opposed to bourgeois uplift ideology). As noted in Chapter 4, Hubert H. Harrison centered ordinary people in his thinking on racism, capitalism, and imperialism and felt that elite "uniters" failed because "very often the 'intellectuals' assume the air of superior beings."[199] Similar to the "ethnic paradigm," which Robinson employs, for Gaines, black nationalism has etic properties that have no noteworthy emic correspondents.

Wilson Moses's reticence toward sustaining a treatment of the "revolutionary anger," which he locates among pre–Civil War black religionists, as a tenet of black nationalism emanates from his own conceptualization of black nationalism as "an ideology whose goal was the creation of an autonomous black nation-state, with definite geographical boundaries—usually in Africa."[200] Yet he is probably the single best source for understanding aspects of the "jeremiadic" tradition in black religion outlined earlier in this chapter.[201]

The failure to account for the religious basis of black ideological constructions, at least from Walker's *Appeal* to "Black Power," has constrained our understanding of and contributed to a contentious and persistent debate, especially concerning black nationalism's roots, periodization, and patterns of development. Robinson's treatment of David Walker and Malcolm X elucidates how the view of a "quasi"-religiosity in black nationalism undercuts an entire variant of religious expression as he notes, "It is certainly true that both worked out of a jeremiadic framework. However, the similarities do not go further."[202] This is so because the former was a Christian, the latter a convert to Sunni Islam.[203]

The religious dimensions of elites in each epoch from David Walker to Black Power and, say, Louis Farrakhan are not explored beyond this. But the "jeremiadic framework" is a coherent attribute of black nationalism that provides a structure for understanding how it relates to both the emigrationist and "white" variants of nationalism vis-à-vis its *black* religious and oppositional properties, and it elucidates the move from Christian to Islamic hegemony in black nationalist politics. In fact, Robinson actually sought to intervene in the disagreement between Moses and Sterling Stuckey concerning David Walker's relationship to black nationalism.

Moses criticizes Stuckey's position that "David Walker presented a great many more of the ideas which would later become associated with black nationalism." He states: "Indeed it is likely that the *Appeal to the Colored Citizens of the World* contains the most all-embracing black nationalist formulation to appear in America during the nineteenth century. Indeed there is scarcely an important aspect of Afro-American nationalist thought in the twentieth century which is not prefigured in that document."[204] Whether or not religion is the best means to black survival and uplift has been a contested matter, but it does not diminish the fact that revolutionary nationalists had no less of a religious commitment in political history than did the emigrationistic Zionists.[205] Still, Robinson insists that the various black nationalist epochs have in common only *how* they related to their respective Anglo-nationalist analogues.[206] Garveyism, for instance, "was militantly pro-African, in a pro-European or 'Eurocentric' kind of way."[207] This perspective rarely explores European cultural survivals among Euro-American whites and further discounts how, as Joel Williamson argues, that,

> as whites invaded black life with a new intensity in the middle of the nineteenth century, they not only changed blacks; they were changed by blacks. Then and later whites would have been vastly resentful at the suggestion that blacks had educated them, so proudfully intent were they on unilaterally educating blacks. . . . It is probably not too much to say that a significant amount of the African heritage that survived in the slave South survived outside the black world in the white. Southern whites would have passed beyond resentment and into outrage at the idea of themselves being Africanized, but

the idea is not without an element of reality. . . . White people not only adopted and adapted African survivals from Negroes, they also drew more broadly from the well of post-African black culture to fill their own lives. For instance Southern white religion owed something to black religion.[208]

Black Power advocates and analysts should understand that "neither Garvey nor black nationalists who preceded him had any intention of reclaiming African culture. . . . They wanted to be rid of it," according to Robinson.

George S. Schuyler was foremost among the African American intellectuals who denied the existence of black culture as an inherent expression of a black "way of life" in the United States.[209] In criticizing the 1920s Harlem renaissance, Schuyler similarly insisted that, despite their best efforts to the contrary, its poets, writers, and intellectuals should "realize that the Afro American is merely a lamp-blacked Anglo-Saxon."[210] Political scientist Cedric Robinson points to this as "rather bizarre," how "some students of racism have happily reiterated the premise of a sort of mass psychology of chromatic trauma. . . . The root of the methodological and conceptual flaws is the same: the presumption that the social and historical processes which matter, which are determinative, are European. All else, it seems, is derivative."[211] It homogenizes the many ethnic European-derived cultures and ignores their intraracial complexities. Oddly, this formulation ignores the nationalist histories of the various southern and eastern (Catholic) European subgroups that do not share in the Anglo-European paradigm; they have as much difference between them as they do with the African American racial group. But, at best, these nationalisms forged a "unity of opposites" akin to enemies at war, sports, suitors, or people vying to breathe in the same oxygen. It hardly partners them any more than a prosecutor in a criminal trial would be in league with a criminal defendant.

For Dean Robinson, classical black nationalism mirrored what we could loosely call "'white American nationalism' of the time."[212] However, the foregoing was not reflective of the nationalism of ordinary African Americans, which had gone largely ignored until Garveyite black nationalism and Black Power. It is also pertinent that Black Power advocates in the 1960s and in the black arts movement sought to construct pan-Africanist and nationalist programs based on the centrality of anti- and postcolonial Africa as a cultural, political, and economic clearinghouse for black antiracist protest in the tradition promoted by Garveyite black nationalists after World War I. Louis DeCaro Jr. accurately notes that "the black nationalist spirit of [Garvey's] UNIA was a revitalization of the theme of separation and repatriation to Africa that had been argued—with varying characteristics—by nineteenth-century African American leaders such as Martin Delany and Bishop Henry Turner."[213]

The era of Garveyism emerged at an important historical juncture as an eclectic social, cultural, and political philosophy. More consistently than its theoretical predecessors in the emigrationist camp, it promoted a positive view of Africa and Africans, not for the sake of a special class of entrepreneurial individuals but for the emotive and substantive benefits of all people of African descent everywhere and at every socioeconomic level. The national liberation struggles of the third world in Africa, Asia, and Latin America reinforced the post–World War II assessment of Africa and represented, for them, what the poorer oppressed European nations represented to Delany and other early emigrationists: a theater of European imperialism. Had Africa remained in the shackles of unfettered colonialism after World War II without challenge, it is unlikely that this issue would have been as resonant in the rhetoric and social critiques of student activists in the 1960s. Ironically, this positive assessment of things African developed long after the major "back-to-Africa" movements had waned.[214] They thoroughly repudiated the Anglo-American social, cultural, and institutional structures in the rhetoric of Black Power and created the space for cultural nationalist-styled dissent.

The matter of reciprocity within the social or political matrix, or the possibility that both African and European cultures developed in America in tandem with their respective continental dislocations, is set aside in the Eurocentric "Anglo-African" reading of black nationalism. Even during Reconstruction, a period of high integrationist salience and Anglo acculturation among African American elites, particularly in the realms of politics and family, blacks were reluctant mainstreamers in the sphere of religion. The interpretation that American black nationalism is absorptive and parasitical of European and Anglo-American types is sustained by subordinating black cultural life in the relationship, particularly in the area of religion. Cornel West details this phenomenon in *Prophesy Deliverance!* (cited here at length):

In *The Souls of Black Folk* (1903) . . . the dialectic of black self-recognition oscillated between being *in* America but not *of* it, from being black natives to black aliens. Yet Du Bois overlooked the broader dialectic of being American yet feeling European . . . amid uncouth conditions. Black Americans labored rather under the burden of a triple crisis of self-recognition. Their cultural predicament was comprised of African appearance and unconscious cultural mores, involuntary displacement to America without American status, American alienation from the European ethos complicated through domination by incompletely European Americans. This predicament was qualitatively different from that of other Africans in the diaspora, in the Caribbean, Canada, and Central and South America. Africans in the United States confronted a dominant Protestant European population whose own self-identity suffered from an anxiety-ridden provinciality. The black American struggle for self-identity has always contributed constructively to the American struggle for self-identity, though the latter has only exacerbated and complicated it in return. During the colonial provincial stage of American culture, Africans were worse than slaves; they were also denuded proto-Americans in search of identity, systematically stripped of their African heritage and effectively and intentionally excluded from American culture and its roots in European modernity. *Their search for identity focused principally on indigenous African prac-*

tices, rituals, religions, and world views they had somehow retained. The process of cultural syncretism which combined indigenous African practices and provincial American culture generated a unique variant of American life, one far removed from, yet still tied to, European modernity. . . . *Africans valued human life and sustained in their alien environment a religious cosmology* which gave meaning to human existence. *And it was not provincial, because it worshiped neither at the altar of British nor at the altar of American cultural superiority. Black people were relatively uninformed about British culture and not yet fully American.* More pertinently, they had not yet arrived as a synthetic Afro-American identity.[215]

The origin of the "trajectory question" in black nationalism (vis-à-vis Draper, Moses, Painter, Gaines, and Robinson) is largely a matter of interpretive history that is traceable, most coherently, to historian Harold Cruse in 1967.[216] Cruse organizes African American political history in the context of the strivings of political elites who adopt centripetal and/or centrifugal dispositions toward and identification with their competing black and American identities.[217] In "On Explaining 20th Century Negro History," Cruse contends that 1960s Black Power radicals mistook their movement as something "new" (but still traceable to nineteenth-century nationalism) when, in fact, it was a "continuation or repetition of similar trends, issues, slogans, and 'programs' brought to life from 1900 to the 1920s."[218] The Black Power movement, he contends, has very "romantic" and tenuous "historical connections" to nineteenth-century black nationalism.[219] But Cruse puts in abeyance the detail that new structural realities, which may result from war, migrations, economic relations, or shifts in international circumstances, failed to interrupt the broad racial regimes and objective power relations between African Americans and Euro-American whites in the state and economic and social institutions.[220] Yet the concern over nationalist continuities in Cruse's work is less a matter of substantive linkages in the various nationalist epochs than it is a matter of understanding how Black Power fits within the longitude of black politics in the twentieth century schematically.

This illuminates Cruse's own presentist focus, which renders religion and religious political elites, whether or not nationalist—with the exception of Martin Luther King Jr.—irrelevant in his assessment of "Negro intellectuals," even though nineteenth-century black nationalism functioned wholly within the realm of black religion.[221] A foremost theorist on the subject, Cruse had an interest in the lineal development of black nationalism that resulted in interrelated (and mostly unintended) analytical tendencies among subsequent researchers. A second outcome of Cruse's analysis has been contentions over who, for instance, is a nationalist (and how we know nationalism when we see it). It also underestimates the extent to which political elites may not reflect the sentiments of ordinary African Americans. Last, Cruse's approach is useful when comparing black nationalist subhistories, but it confuses more than it elucidates if one seeks to understand the origin points of black political ideologies.

It is widely accepted, as noted in John Bracey et al. (*Black Nationalism in America*, 1970), that "the varieties of black nationalism are often not sharply delineated, nor are they mutually exclusive categories." This fluidity also tends to engender arbitrary categorizations based on characteristics associated with the particularities of individual political elites or organizations. Essein-Udom's work, for instance, gives an account of the linkages among the movements of Timothy "Noble" Drew Ali's Moorish Science Temple, W. D. Fard, Elijah Muhammad and the Nation of Islam, and UNIA's African Orthodox Church, which upholds them as the epitomes of black nationalism. But a more thoroughgoing analysis requires that religion's affectability be analyzed in the longitude of nationalism as an ideological and historical phenomenon. This tendency equates the orbits of the "Negro church," "Negro separatist religious movements," or, say, "religious feeling" with the universe of black religion. It misses the point, as G.J.A. Ojo contends, that "it is not an overstatement to say that *religion is not just one complex of African culture but the catalyst of the other complexes.*"[222]

Religion, with its symbols and substance, has a "shaping" influence in society that points to its import in understanding social-structural processes.[223] In this regard, black religion appears to be the single best measure of black American nationalism.[224] This is to suggest that the decision to attach "separatism" adjectivally to religion, or to speak of a "religious nationalism," for instance, can undermine its explanatory powers, as opposed to it being understood as a parenting source of African American political ideologies, and simultaneously reduces it to the status of being simply a species of nationalism. Not only is black religion inverted as a *product* of ideology in this perspective; it has also contributed to the gross misreading of black nationalism as the child of "white nationalism." Historicizing black nationalism becomes a contested matter between John Bracey and his coauthors. Along with questions of contiguity and its genetic strains, the authors' differing views on the question of the proper alignment of religion in the black American experience are also germane to their disagreement. Although the authors concur that black Americans have displayed a patterned racial solidarity,[225] echoing Cruse, Meier and Rudwick hold the position that "the rise and decline of nationalist sentiment, and of particular varieties of nationalist ideology, must be regarded as caused by the changing conditions which Negroes as a whole . . . faced, and by their changing perceptions of those conditions. Only in this way can we account for such phenomena as the dramatic drop in colonization among the black elite during the Civil War and Reconstruction or among the black masses during the economic depression of the 1930s, or the current [1960s] thrust toward black separatism."[226] Bracey's response suggests that "black nationalism is a variety of the nationalisms of non-Western peoples in general, and of the black peoples of Africa and the West Indies in particular . . . the development of black nationalism has been slow and winding, but persistent and intensifying, from 1787, if not earlier, to the present."[227] Moreover, Meier and Rudwick liken black nationalism in the United States to the experiences of *European Jews* and *American Jews*. And Bracey attaches his perspective to institutional developments among socially marginal, free Negroes (e.g., mutual aid societies, fraternal organizations) and the "enslaved *masses* [who] developed *the 'invisible church'* . . . as their chief nationalist expression. Indeed, Bracey contends, the latter "channeled their nationalistic impulses into their churches and into further development of their folk culture."[228]

As reflected in Bracey's debate with his coauthors, the contesting positions include those analysts who insist black nationalism is a discontinuous, historically compartmentalized hybrid of "white nationalism"[229] versus those who view black nationalism as a historically contiguous and patterned commitment to collective self-determination and group solidarity among African Americans as a product of "black culture," including black religion.[230]

Some recent feminist studies of black nationalism, which build on Robinson's analysis, have equally interpreted black nationalism refractorily as mimetic of white male chauvinism.[231] For them, black nationalism's basic constitution, again, is Eurocentric. Black Power's enigmatic moves from integrationism to nationalism and, later, Marxism pivoted toward an ostensible black nationalist hegemony with all of the rage of previous generations. Black Power represents the intervening period that reaches backward to David Walker and Malcolm X and forward to the hip-hop generation's encounter with modern-day black politics. Malcolm X in the 1950s and 1960s is a segue from the revolutionary anger of the past to that which follows immediately after his death in Black Power. He takes the baton from the past and passes it to Black Power, the focus of the next chapter.

Notes

1. This work of Stewart's was published in 1835.
2. See John Bracey et al., *Black Nationalism in America*, pp. 371, 385–386.
3. Wilson Jeremiah Moses, *Classical Black Nationalism*, p. 35.
4. Moses, *Black Messiahs and Uncle Toms*, p. 8.
5. Although they do concede that this period yielded "an incipient group consciousness," the authors admit that it was the absence of "a detailed argument for group separation" that resulted in the decision to exclude it. They also note that nationalism—that is, advocacy for a nation-state—was itself incipient at the end of the eighteenth century. But no nationalism necessarily inheres all of its recognized tenets over time or at the same time. Moreover, news of the 1820 Missouri Compromise led many blacks, especially the more militant, to believe that they had been set free. Organizationally,

the Negro Convention movement was in full swing, meeting annually, usually with a view toward rebutting the white-led colonization agenda.

6. Young's *Ethiopian Manifesto: Issued in Defense of the Black Man's Rights in the Scale of Universal Freedom* was published in New York in 1829 two months before the appearance of Walker's *Appeal* in September. Gayraud Wilmore affirms that the first of three editions of the *Appeal* appeared in September; the second was seventy-six pages, and the third, published the year of his death (1830), consisted of eighty-eight pages. See *Black Religion and Black Radicalism*, pp. 61–62. There is no known record of his personal origins or biography, although he was apparently one of the 320,000 free Negroes in the United States and a resident of New York at the time of the *Ethiopian Manifesto*'s publication. The mystery concerning Young's personal life and associations is as mystical as the seven-page document that bore his name. The *Ethiopian Manifesto* was written under the pseudonym "Rednaxela" (his middle name in reverse) in New York, a device used by some Negro writers in the antebellum period to avoid the often violent reprisals with which they were met for advocating immediate abolition. During the period in which the *Ethiopian Manifesto* was published, nascent black abolitionism was prevalent among the large and politically important cities of Boston, Philadelphia, and New York. Boston's black community was probably the most well-known because of leading individuals such as Prince Hall, David Walker, Maria Stewart, and, later, Charles Lenox Remond, William Lloyd Garrison, and Frederick Douglass. Boston's brand of black abolitionism had more vitality and activism than those in Philadelphia and New York, as it centered on the Massachusetts General Colored Association, the African Baptist Church, Faneuil Hall, the African Masonic Hall, and Garrison's American Anti-Slavery Society and *Liberator* newspaper in 1831. Philadelphia was significant because Garrison's American Anti-Slavery Society originated there in 1833, after he originally promoted the plan to expatriate free blacks to Africa in the colonization scheme. Opposition to the American Colonization Society was the main rallying point for northeastern black abolitionists. Gayraud Wilmore notes, "Young appealed to blacks of all nations to take stock of the injustices visited upon them by whites and to prepare for the revelation of God's judgment. It was an unmistakable call to a more militant posture, if not revolution." See *Black Religion and Black Radicalism*, p. 59. I do not mean to suggest that Maria Stewart (in Boston) was a nationalist per se, although her close association with David Walker and Alexander Crummell (who performed her eulogy) powerfully shaped her theological and political perspectives. As well, she participated in the city's African Baptist Church, where she articulated much of her jeremiadic preachments. See Marilyn Richardson (ed.), *Maria W. Stewart, America's First Black Woman Political Writer: Essays and Speeches* (Bloomington: Indiana University Press, 1987). See also Wilson Moses, *Black Messiahs and Uncle Toms*. Moses lists her with Young and Walker as constituting a jeremiad tradition. See also Moses, *Classical Black Nationalism*.

7. Theodore Draper, *The Rediscovery of Black Nationalism*, p. 22.

8. It is more accurate, however, that an entire stratum of individuals who reflect Walker's protestations has been neglected. As well as Walker, we can include Robert Alexander Young, Maria Stewart, Henry Highland Garnet, and Hubert Harrison; all are more or less lost to us as critical figures in the tradition.

9. Wilson Moses, *Classical Black Nationalism*, pp. 13–21; Stuckey, *The Ideological Origins of Black Nationalism*, pp. 7–13.

10. Walker's date of birth is in dispute among scholars. James Turner suggests 1785, whereas Sean Wilentz suggests 1796 or 1797. Peter Hinks addresses the problems with locating the date and birthplace of Walker, but he generally trusts the 1785

date in Wilmington, provided by Henry H. Garnet in his reprint of the third edition of the *Appeal*, which he attached to his own work. See Peter P. Hinks, *To Awaken My Afflicted Brethren: David Walker and the Problem of Antebellum Slave Resistance* (University Park: University of Pennsylvania Press, 1997), pp. 10–13.

11. See James Lance Taylor, "The Reverend Benjamin Chavis Muhammad: From Wilmington to Washington, from Chavis to Muhammad," in Jo Renee Formicola and Hubert Morken (eds.), *Religious Leaders and Faith-Based Politics* (Lanham, MD: Rowman and Littlefield, 2001), pp. 117–118. Key does acknowledge a tradition of progressivism in the state he calls a "progressive plutocracy." See V. O. Key, *Southern Politics in State and Nation* (New York: Alfred Knopf, 1949).

12. Sean Wilentz, *David Walker's* Appeal, p. ix. Still later, John Chavis (the paternal great-great-grandfather of Benjamin Chavis, co-convener of the Million Man March and former NAACP executive secretary), whom John Hope Franklin referred to as "the most prominent free Negro in North Carolina," in the early nineteenth century may have distributed and preached the radical message of the *Appeal* contrary to his reputation as an early accommodationist. Michael Myerson, in *Nothing Could Be Finer* (New York: International, 1978), p. 15, links Chavis to Walker. Gayraud S. Wilmore's *Black Religion and Black Radicalism*, at page 4, does not mention Chavis by name but acknowledges a cadre of individuals who secretly distributed the *Appeal*. John Hope Franklin's *The Free Negro in North Carolina, 1790–1860* (Chapel Hill: University of North Carolina Press, 1995), identifies John Chavis as a pre-Washingtonian accommodationist who supported gradual and limited emancipation and spoke strongly against Nat Turner's 1831 insurrection in neighboring Virginia.

13. The greatest fear in Santo Domingo (later Haiti) was the slave peasantry, who embraced the leadership of Jean Jacques Dessalines as they completed the revolution by purging the island of the whites; many of them fled to South Carolina. For further discussion, see C.L.R. James, *The Black Jacobins: Toussaint L'Ouverture and the San Domingo Revolution*, 2nd ed. (New York: Vintage, [1963], 1989).

14. Cited in Paul Finkleman, *Slavery and the Founders: Race and Liberty in the Age of Jefferson*, 2nd ed. (New York: M. E. Sharpe, 2001), p. 152. Bonaparte's and Jefferson's republican colleagues betrayed a strong racial bigotry in response to Toussaint L'Ouverture's initial request for recognition as a loyal French subject in the coveted Banana colony. Whereas John Adams and the Federalists saw Toussaint L'Ouverture as a "black George Washington," Jefferson and Bonaparte treated him with venomous race animus, with the latter arresting him and placing him in a Paris dungeon, where he later died.

15. Peter Hinks, *To Awaken My Afflicted Brethren*, pp. 47–53.

16. Sean Wilentz notes that "events in Charleston around the time that Walker lived there may also have sharpened his thinking about slavery, rebellion, and Christian righteousness." Walker most certainly attended the African Methodist Episcopal (A.M.E.) Church in Charleston beginning in 1821; it was deeply implicated in and razed as a result of the massive Denmark Vesey insurrection plot in 1822—he states as much in the *Appeal*. Yet Wilentz reminds us that "none of the surviving sources on the Vesey affair mention anyone named David Walker. Neither do Walker's writings mention Vesey." See also Vincent Harding, *There Is a River*, ch. 3.

17. Sean Wilentz, *David Walker's* Appeal, pp. x–xi.

18. Ibid., p. 5.

19. This explains why Garnet interviewed Walker's widow and subsequently collated his own militant tract, *Address to the Slaves of the United States of America*, with Walker's *Appeal* in 1848 by the Ayer Company Publishers. See David Walker and Henry Highland Garnet, *Walker's Appeal in Four Articles: Address to the Slaves of the United States of America* (New York: Cosimo, 2005).

20. Peter Hinks, *To Awaken My Afflicted Brethren*, pp. 178–179. Hinks asserts that Jefferson's racial thought had been challenged well before Walker emerged in Boston, and his study, which is among the most extensive treatments of David Walker, apparently found the famous passage unremarkable.

21. Ibid., p. 180.

22. Ibid., pp. 200–201, 205–207. Jefferson's great influence on Walker was that his *Notes* offered a salient validation of burgeoning white supremacist thought, proffering a hypothesis of the ostensible *Homo halibus* or *Homo erectus* stages of African Americans in a world of civilized white *Homo sapiens*.

23. Ibid., p. 206.

24. Sacvan Bercovitch, *The American Jeremiad*, p. 154.

25. A cohort of leading blacks—from Prince Hall, Richard Allen, Absalom Jones, David Walker, and Maria Stewart to Frederick Douglass and insurrectionist individuals such as Gabriel Prosser, Nat Turner, and Denmark Vesey—all took literally the words of the Declaration of Independence. It resounded in King's major speech and was the grounds on which Malcolm X felt "democracy is hypocrisy."

26. Gayraud Wilmore, *Black Religion and Black Radicalism*, p. 9.

27. Sean Wilentz, *David Walker's* Appeal, p. 25.

28. Peter Hinks, *To Awaken My Afflicted Brethren*, p. 108.

29. Wilentz attaches the court confession of Edward Smith to his edition of the *Appeal* in appendix 2. Peter Hinks dedicates a full chapter (ch. 5) to the issue of white and black sailors' roles in distributing the *Appeal* in the South.

30. Sacvan Bercovitch, *The American Jeremiad*, p. 34. Emphasis in original.

31. Ibid., p. xiv.

32. Perry Miller, *Errand into the Wilderness*, pp. 219, 235.

33. Ibid., p. 235. Miller seems to argue that the tendency to restoration among American practitioners of the jeremiad, such as Jonathan Edwards, had less to do with a theology of reconciliation vis-à-vis Jeremiah speaking to a captive nation in declension, and more to do with a loss of heart for destruction engendered by the "apocalyptic physicists" who brought into question the scientific implausibility of a geocentric end of things. In the end, "orthodox Protestants in the early nineteenth century continued to give lip service to the conception of a catastrophic end of the world, but obviously their hearts were no longer behind it."

34. Amy Jacques Garvey is said to have deleted the more strident rhetoric from Garvey's speeches and writings out of fear that it would affect Garvey's mail-fraud trial. It is well-known that Garvey urged black Africans to lynch white men quid pro quo whenever a black American was lynched. This rhetoric initiated J. Edgar Hoover's surveillance of the UNIA. Please see Ula Yvette Taylor, *The Veiled Garvey: The Life and Times of Amy Jacques Garvey* (Chapel Hill: University of North Carolina Press, 2002).

35. As noted, minister Jeremiah Wright Jr. of Chicago Trinity United Church of Christ (and 2008 Democratic presidential candidate Barack Obama's pastor) unleashed a jeremiad damning America for its legacies of violence domestically and in foreign policy. It was a tone that is characteristic of this orientation and that largely alienated the unprecedented support from Euro-American whites that Obama experienced during the Democratic primaries. I will return to the Farrakhan-Wright-Obama connection in Chapter 7, as it provides a clear and recent opportunity to analyze its implications in black political development. For better or worse, the fact of black rage powerfully inserted itself into the conventional politics of the 2008 Democratic campaign, as it had twenty years earlier with Louis Farrakhan in the Jackson campaigns.

36. Peter P. Hinks, *To Awaken My Afflicted Brethren*, pp. xv, 245.

37. Ibid., p. 245.

38. McAdoo, *Pre–Civil War Black Nationalism*, p. 35.

39. Alexis de Tocqueville, *Democracy in America*, edited by J. P. Mayer (New York: Harper and Row, 1966).

40. Bernard Bailyn, *The Ideological Origins of the American Revolution*, p. 233.

41. Ibid., pp. 235, 242.

42. Ibid., p. 244.

43. For an early but superficial attempt at comparison, see William Seraile, "David Walker and Malcolm X: Brothers in Radical Thought," *Black World* (October 1973), p. 68

44. Ibid., p. 39.

45. Wilson J. Moses, *Classical Black Nationalism*, p. 15.

46. Ibid.

47. Richard B. Turner, *Islam in the African American Experience*.

48. Vincent Harding, *There Is a River*, p. 84.

49. McAdoo, *Pre–Civil War Black Nationalism*, pp. 74–75. Emphases added.

50. Vincent Harding, *There Is a River*, p. 132.

51. I use the terms "American black nationalism," "American black nation," and "black nation of America" interchangeably to describe the strand of black nationalist thought and practice that I understand to be distinct from its more widely recognized land-seeking analogue. For a clarification, see Michael C. Dawson, *Black Visions*, pp. 5–6; also Cruse, *Crisis of the Negro Intellectual*, pp. 115–146.

52. Robin Kelley, "Reds, Whites, and Blues People," in Greg Tate (ed.), *Everything but the Burden* (New York: Broadway, 2003), p. 58.

53. Alex Haley, *The Autobiography of Malcolm X* (New York: Random House/Ballantine [1964] 1992), pp. ix–x. Emphases added.

54. David Howard-Pitney, *The Afro-American Jeremiad*, p. 13.

55. Ibid., p. 15.

56. Its subjects are the writings and speeches of Frederick Douglass, Booker T. Washington, Ida B. Wells, W.E.B. Du Bois, Mary McLeod Bethune, and Martin Luther King Jr., individuals who, for the most part, are only tertiarily associated with black nationalism and mainly in the context of scholarly discourse, not general opinion.

57. Clayborne Carson (ed.), *The Autobiography of Martin Luther King, Jr.* (New York: Warner, 1998), p. 60.

58. With the exception of individual elites (Walter White and Roy Wilkins in the NAACP and Whitney Young in the Urban League) who led organizations founded by white liberal allies, one is hard-pressed to identify black political leaders who have not prioritized forms of group solidarity to some extent; this is no less true of leftist, black feminist, or gay-rights projects.

59. Cited in Rodnell P. Collins, *Seventh Child*, p. 190; King, *Where Do We Go from Here: Chaos or Community?* (New York: Bantam, 1968), pp. 146–147. Emphases in original and added.

60. Wilson Moses, *Black Messiahs and Uncle Toms*, p. 174.

61. Wendy Brown, *Politics out of History* (Princeton: Princeton University Press, 2001), pp. 25–26.

62. Paul Sniderman and Thomas Piazza, *Black Pride and Black Prejudice*, p. 8. Unfortunately, these authors further suggest that black pride is a fulfillment of liberal coalition optimism, whereas its counterpoint, "black prejudice" (read: anti-Semitism), is the stuff of Louis Farrakhan, Afrocentrism, and black nationalism generally. Emphasis in original.

63. Ibid.

64. See excerpt in Clayborne Carson (ed.), *The Autobiography of Martin Luther King, Jr.*, p. 325; see also Michael C. Dawson, *Black Visions*, pp. 271–272.

65. Nikhil p. Singh, *Black Is a Country*, p. 3.

66. Wilson Moses, *Black Messiahs and Uncle Toms*, p. 177. Emphasis added.

67. Ibid., p. 178.

68. Ibid.

69. Mary R. Sawyer, *Black Ecumenism*; James Cone, *Martin, Malcolm, and America*; Michael Eric Dyson, *Making Malcolm*.

70. Robert C. Smith, *We Have No Leaders*, p. xvii.

71. Benedict Anderson, *Imagined Communities*, p. 3.

72. Jeffrey B. Perry, *A Hubert Harrison Reader*, p. 17.

73. Harold Cruse, *Plural but Equal: Blacks and Minorities in America's Plural Society* (New York: Quill, 1987), p. 15. Emphasis in original.

74. Wendy Brown, *Politics out of History*, p. 26.

75. See Eddie Glaude Jr., *Exodus!*, p. 3. He iterates how "the story's account of bondage, the trials of the wilderness, and the final entrance into the promised land resonated with those who experienced the hardships of slavery and racial discrimination. Indeed, the story demonstrated God active in history and [the] willingness to intervene on behalf of [the] chosen people." Eugene Genovese points to the functional role that the sense of national destiny played in African American social thought, noting, "Without a sense of being God's Chosen People—that is, to bring His Kingdom, not merely to be delivered by Him—the slaves could not easily develop that sense of national mission which has been so efficacious in the formation of revolutionary ideology." See Eugene Genovese, *Roll, Jordan, Roll: The World the Slaves Made* (New York: Vintage, 1996), p. 279; Peter Hinks, *To Awaken My Afflicted Brethren: David Walker and the Problem of the Antebellum Slave Resistance* (University Park: University of Pennsylvania Press, 1997), p. 242.

76. Eddie Glaude, *Exodus!*, p. 35.

77. Sacvan Bercovitch, *The American Jeremiad*, p. 154.

78. This is a paraphrase of Jon F. Sensbach's in *A Separate Canaan*, p. 297.

79. Theophus H. Smith, *Conjuring Culture: Biblical Formations of Black America* (New York: Oxford University Press, 1994), p. 17.

80. David Howard-Pitney, *The Afro-American Jeremiad*, p. 12.

81. Ibid., p. 13.

82. Eddie Glaude, *Exodus!*, p. 7.

83. Darren Davis and Ronald Brown, "The Antipathy of Black Nationalism," p. 240. Emphasis added.

84. James Cone, *God of the Oppressed*, pp. 48–49.

85. Sean Wilentz, *David Walker's Appeal*, p. xvii.

86. Ibid., p. 70.

87. The abolitionist leaders were also committed to the creation of free segregated schools and colleges for African Americans, as well as reparations for slaveholders in exchange for their loss in slave laborers. See Donald M. Jacobs (ed.), *Courage and Conscience: Black and White Abolitionists in Boston* (Bloomington: Indiana University Press, 1993).

88. John T. McCartney, *Black Power Ideologies: An Essay in African American Political Thought* (Philadelphia: Temple University Press, 1992), p. 35.

89. See pp. 26–27. Emphasis in original.

90. Donald Jacobs, *Courage and Conscience*, p. 33.

91. See Martin R. Delaney, *Destiny of the Colored People*, p. 32.

92. Bill McAdoo, *Pre–Civil War Black Nationalism*, p. 15.

93. W.E.B. Du Bois, *Black Reconstruction: An Essay Toward a History of the Part Which Black Folk Played in the Attempt to Reconstruct Democracy in America, 1860–1880*, with an introduction by David Levering Lewis (New York: Free Press, 1995), p. 200. Whereas Garrison did have a young Negro apprentice named Elijah Smith at his *Liberator* newspaper office and periodically sponsored "mixed" meetings, he was personally no integrationist. The Massachusetts Anti-Slavery Society refused free blacks as late as 1836, four years after Garrison emerged as the chief white proponent of abolitionism with the publication of the *Liberator*.

94. In the end, Du Bois seemed to be more impressed with Radical Republican congressional leaders, such as Thaddeus Stevens and Charles Sumner, for their disappointed but valiant attempts to carry abolition-democracy to its full logic of economic and political incorporation of African Americans into the American political and economic systems.

95. Donald Jacobs, *Courage and Conscience*, esp. ch. 10.

96. At each major juncture—from abolitionism to the creation of the NAACP to the modern civil rights movement—religious and ideological alliances with self-consciously and self-interested white liberal and radical activists have, at times, both aided and undermined black political development among proponents of the integrationist mode. Frederick Douglass and black Bostonian abolitionists who broke with Garrisonian moral suasion experienced strong opposition in the clientage arrangements that characterized biracial coalitions. Frances Willard, the militant leader of the Woman's Christian Temperance Union (WCTU), is noted for assigning responsibility for lynching to the "plague" of African Americans who placed an undue burden on the shoulders of white southerners. This became the source of significant tension between her and Ida B. Wells. See Michael C. Dawson, *Black Visions*. William Monroe Trotter's refusal to join the white-led interracial NAACP in 1910 is also pertinent to understanding how some African American integrationist elites resented entanglements with white liberalism. In this regard, Trotter anticipated the breaks by the Student Nonviolent Coordinating Committee (SNCC) and the Congress of Racial Equality (CORE) with their white liberal supporters in the 1960s. Harold Cruse has pointed to some ways in which white liberal race managers (of the NAACP) have at times co-opted black integrationist elites. The Democratic Party's treatment of Fannie Lou Hamer and the Mississippi Freedom Democratic Party in 1964, Harold Washington's 1983 grassroots campaign in Chicago, and Jessie Jackson's first presidential campaign in 1984 demonstrate continuity in this form of perfidy. See Du Bois's *Black Reconstruction*. Du Bois does note that by 1863 most African Americans had abandoned the emigration proposal; Lincoln repealed the laws relating to colonization on July, 2, 1864. See esp. pp. 147–150.

97. Reformist integrationism developed most coherently in the North, particularly among black Bostonians, who aligned more with Garrison's abolitionism in the 1840s and 1850s as Garrison emerged as the central figure in abolitionism.

98. Ibid., p. 113.

99. McAdoo seems especially irritated by Herbert Aptheker's agnosticism on Walker's nationalist bent. The same can be noted concerning Peter Hinks's *To Awaken My Afflicted Brethren*.

100. Peter Hinks, *To Awaken My Afflicted Brethren*, pp. 249–251.

101. Wilson Moses, *The Golden Age of Black Nationalism*, pp. 33, 41.

102. David Howard-Pitney, "Frederick Douglass: Abolitionist and Political Leader," in Norm R. Allen Jr. (ed.), *African-American Humanism: An Anthology* (Amherst, NY: Prometheus), pp. 20–21.

103. Sean Wilentz, *David Walker's* Appeal, p. xxii.

104. Cited in Peter Hinks, *To Awaken My Afflicted Brethren*, pp. 114–115. Emphasis added. For an extensive treatment of the militancy and organizing among northern blacks, especially in New York, Philadelphia, and Boston, see Donald M. Jacobs, *Courage and Conscience.*

105. The Gospel According to Luke 9:51–56.

106. James A. Colaiaco, *Frederick Douglass and the Fourth of July* (New York: Palgrave/Macmillan, 2007), pp. 1–2.

107. Ibid., p. 8.

108. Ibid., pp. 57–58.

109. Eddie Glaude, *Black Exodus!*, p. 40.

110. Ibid., p. 40.

111. These men were leaders in the Denmark Vesey insurrection plot. Gullah Jack was from Angola and was believed to possess supernatural power. Once the plot was betrayed and the conspirators caught, Poyas is reported to have told the condemned men, "Do not open your lips; die silent as you shall see me do" (cited in Wilmore, *Black Religion and Black Radicalism*, p. 86). This plot was carried out mainly from the local A.M.E. Church in Charleston, a church that David Walker attended (and where he may have come into contact with the conspirators and Vesey himself). See Peter Hinks, *To Awaken My Afflicted Brethren.*

112. See Lincoln and Mamiya, *The Black Church in the African American Experience.* The authors point to the transduction of "freedom" in the distinct contexts of black oppression. Freedom, as a relativist expression, had certain meaning in the specific regime of subordination, although it was always "communal" rather than individualistic in nature. Finally, it includes an emotional worship or religious expressions in dance, song, music, and the call-and-response preaching style.

113. Evelyn Higginbotham, *Righteous Discontent*, p. 7.

114. For an account of its impact on black women's relationship with one another, see Audre Lorde, *Sister Outsider* (Freedom, CA: Crossing Press, 1984). See especially the essays titled "The Uses of Anger: Women Responding to Racism," and "Eye to Eye: Black Women, Hatred, and Anger." Also see Barack Obama, *Dreams from My Father: A Story of Race and Inheritance* (New York: Three Rivers, [1995] 2004), pp. 199–200, where this phenomenon is discussed in detail.

115. See William Ivy Hair, *Carnival of Fury: Robert Charles and the New Orleans Race Riot of 1900* (Baton Rouge: Louisiana State University Press, 1976). Robert Charles was inspired by nationalist A.M.E. bishop Henry McNeal Turner and acted as an agent of his *Voice of Missions* tract. He fully embraced emigrationism and in May 1896 joined the International Migration Society. Charles, like all of his contemporaries in Copiah, Mississippi, experienced personal racism and intimidation, especially in the "redemption phase" of the immediate post-Reconstruction period. He was born in 1865 or 1866. Amid racial violence in New Orleans in 1900; a series of saliently racist events from the violent intimidation of pro-ultraconservative Democrats in Louisiana; a new high of twenty-one lynchings in Louisiana; the highly publicized lynching of Sam Hose in Newton, Georgia; and incendiary antiblack news editorials by local papers, Charles engaged in a fight to the death with local law enforcement, having shot twenty-seven white New Orleanians (including seven police officers) from July 25 to 27, 1900. On his person was found a list of grievances concerning the predicament of blacks in post-Reconstruction America.

116. Paul Harris, *Black Rage Confronts the Law* (New York: New York University Press, 1999), pp. 9–13.

117. Joel Kovel, *White Racism: A Psychohistory* (New York: Vintage), pp. 44–45.

118. Gunnar Myrdal, *An American Dilemma* (New York: Harper and Brothers, 1944), p. 782, cited in John Bracey et al., *Black Nationalism in America*, p. lv.

119. C. Eric Lincoln, *Black Muslims in America*, pp. 33–38. These "subnationalist" responses are particularly resonant, respectively, in the various emigrationist-Zionist, accommodationist, Afrocentric, and militant (cultural and revolutionary) forms of black nationalism.

120. African Americans would have to know and to rely upon themselves, open themselves to African influences, and create self-propelled movements in part of their African heritage. Emphasis in original. See Sterling Stuckey, *Going Through the Storm*, p. 196.

121. Claude McKay, *Harlem Shadows* (New York: Harcourt, Brace, 1922), cited in Herbert Hill (ed.), *Anger and Beyond: The Negro Writer in the United States* (New York: Harper and Row, 1966), p. 13.

122. Henry Highland Garnet, "An Address to the Slaves of the United States," National Negro Convention, in Buffalo, New York, 1843. Speech available at http://www.blackpast.org/?q=1843-henry-highland-garnet-address-slaves-united-states.

123. Arnold Rampersad, introduction in Richard Wright, *Native Son* (New York: HarperPerennial, 2005), p. xvi.

124. Ibid., p. xv.

125. The works of scholars and individuals, from Du Bois and Anna Julia Cooper to Carter G. Woodson, J. A. Rogers, and Hubert Harrison, and later to Richard Wright, Howard Thurman, and Fanon, grappled with the tortured self-consciousness of American blacks, Africans, and West Indians. Having formed on May 19, 1968—on Malcolm X's birthday at Marcus Garvey Park in New York City just weeks after King's assassination and national rioting—the Last Poets are widely considered forerunners of hip-hop; the original members were David Nelson, Gylan Kain, and Abiodun Oyewole (Charles Davis). The group expanded from three poets and a drummer to seven young black and Puerto Rican artists, adding Felipe Lucciano, Umar Bin Hassan, Jalal Nurridin (Alafia Pudim), and Suliamn El Hadi. The group's name is taken from a South African poet, Keorapetse W. Kgositsile, who thought poetry might be put in abeyance in deference to picking up the gun in pending anti-apartheid bloodshed. Their most famous poems, inspired, like the full body of their work, by Malcolm X, were "Niggers Are Scared of Revolution," "This Is Madness," and "When the Revolution Comes." They were released on two albums: the inaugural *Last Poets* (1970) and *This Is Madness* (1971).

126. Joyce Flynn and Joyce Occomy Stricklin (eds.), *Frye Street and Environs: Collected Works of Marita Bonner* (Boston: Beacon), 1987.

127. The US's debate among themselves the value of "work" as "the Leader (read Booker T. Washington) told us to do." An old lady US retorts, "As if two hundred years of slavery had not shown them!" After much dialogue between the old work-minded US's and the frustrated younger US's criticizing the perpetual talk of the US leaders, "A drum begins to beat in the distance. All the US stand up and shake off their sleep. The drummer, a short, black determined looking US (read Marcus Garvey?), appears around the bushes beating the drum with strong, vigorous jabs that make the whole valley echo and re-echo with rhythm. Some of US begin to dance in time to the music." As the US's converse about God, books, and money—all which, as introduced by a series of US characters, fail to change the predicament of the black US's—a White Devil is seen spying in the bushes. Nevertheless, an old man US puts a concoction, mingled with dust in a pot as God—an inner voice—instructs him to do. The most important, missing ingredient—the old and young US's now believe the concoction can bring forth a messianic "New Man" who can get them from Nowhere to Somewhere—is

blood. In short, as a young man US volunteers his own blood for the mixture, the old man retorts, incredulously, "Yours!" The young US, named Finest Blood, in turn asks, "where else could you get it? The New Man must be born. The night is already dark. We cannot stay here forever. Where else could blood come from?" The old man responds, "think child. When God asked a faithful servant once to do sacrifice, even his only child, where did God put the real meat for sacrifice when the servant had the knife upon the son's throat?" The old US's begin singing, "In the bushes, Lord! In the Bushes, Lord! Jehovah put the ram in the bushes!" The White Devil was waiting in the bushes. Curtain.

128. See her essay, "The Uses of Anger," in *Sister Outsider* (Freedom, CA: Crossing Press, 1984).

129. *David Walker's* Appeal, p. 11. Emphasis added.

130. Ibid., p. 10.

131. I have previously clarified that an individual does not necessarily have to advocate an ideological standpoint in order to operate in it from time to time. An individual can engage in nationalist discourse without embracing the broader ideological framework; the same is true of integrationism and socialism.

132. Martin Luther King Jr., "A Testament of Hope," posthumously published essay in James M. Washington (ed.), *A Testament of Hope*, pp. 322–323. Emphasis added.

133. Mike McBryde, "Joel Augustus Rogers: A Leading Scholar, Thinker, and Motivator," in Norm R. Allen, Jr. (ed.), *African American Humanism* (Amherst, NY: Prometheus), pp. 54–55. Integrationists scuttled the potential psychological harm effected with wholesale assimilation.

134. William Jelani Cobb, *The Essential Harold Cruse—A Reader* (New York: Palgrave, 2002).

135. Frantz Fanon, *Black Skin, White Masks* (New York: Grove Press, 1967), p. 50.

136. John Bracey et al., *Black Nationalism in America*, p. 67. Garnet fluctuated between emigrationism and revolutionary black nationalism. He may be the only major nationalist figure who took emigrationism seriously and also called for insurrectionary violence.

137. Wilson Moses, *The Golden Age of Black Nationalism*, p. 149.

138. Floyd Miller (ed.), *Blake*, p. xii.

139. Ibid., p. 154.

140. Ibid., p. xxv.

141. See Hannah Arendt, *On Violence* (San Diego: Harcourt, Brace, 1970), p. 63.

142. Alex Haley, *The Autobiography of Malcolm X*, p. xiii.

143. Like Black Power or Malcolm X's "By Any Means Necessary" admonition, black rage—the perennial sacred qua secular nationalist jeremiad—is likely to engender dismissive critiques and analyses, especially because it connotes the perception of racial violence.

144. See also Cedric Johnson, *Revolutionaries to Race Leaders: Black Power and the Making of African American Politics* (Minneapolis: University of Minnesota Press, 2007), p. 234, n. 19.

145. Ibid., p. xxxii.

146. Algernon Austin, *Achieving Blackness*, p. 87.

147. Robert O. Self, *American Babylon: Race and the Struggle for Postwar Oakland* (Princeton: Princeton University Press, 2003), p. 1.

148. See Daniel L. Crowe, *Prophets of Rage: The Black Freedom Struggles in San Francisco, 1945–1969* (New York: Garland, 2000).

149. Fanon, *Black Skin, White Masks*, p. 140.

150. Robert C. Smith, *Racism in the Post–Civil Rights Era: Now You See It, Now You Don't* (Albany: State University of New York Press, 1995), p. 77.

151. Frantz Fanon, *The Wretched of the Earth* (New York: Grove Press, 1963), p. 26.

152. Robert C. Smith, *Racism in the Post–Civil Rights Era*, pp. 30–31.

153. Cornel West, *The Cornel West Reader* (New York: Basic Civitas, 1999), pp. 108–109.

154. Chancellor Williams, in *The Destruction of Black Civilization*, concurs.

155. The slew of African American Academy Award, Golden Globe, and Sundance Film Festival winners in the twenty-first century, including *Monster's Ball* (2001), *Training Days* (2001), *CRASH* (2004), *Hustle and Flow* (2005), *Precious* (2010), and the Tyler Perry genre, reflect the tortured parallel realities of living within the racial matrix and behind the cultural veil.

156. Fanon, *Wretched of the Earth*, p. 22. Emphasis in original.

157. Ibid., pp. 35, 60. From the very first sentence of the book, violence is a nationalistic phenomenon of the masses, not the nationalist bourgeois parties, which use the violence of the former to engage in brokerage bargaining with white settlers.

158. Fanon, *Wretched of the Earth*, p. 42.

159. Ibid., p. 93.

160. Hannah Arendt, *On Violence*, p. 19.

161. Ibid., p. 19.

162. Robert C. Smith, *Racism in the Post–Civil Rights Era*, pp. 10–19.

163. The seemingly ubiquitous nooses at Ivy League institutions and other public places since the controversial Jena Six protest and criminal trials in 2007 prompted thousands to demonstrate—by circling seven times, in keeping with biblical symbolism, around the US Justice Department—and demand such instances be treated as federal hate crimes. The plight of black former New Orleans residents during and since the 2005 Hurricane Katrina disaster sent a shock to black Americans not witnessed since, perhaps, the civil rights–era assassinations.

164. In addition to studying and attempting to operationalize selective aspects of Malcolm X's ideas—"by any means necessary" and the "ballot or the bullet"—student activists and individuals from the black community looked to Frantz Fanon for a political philosophy of violence and redemption.

165. William H. Grier and Price M. Cobbs, *Black Rage* (New York: Basic Books, 1968), p. 4.

166. Cornel West, *Race Matters*.

167. Khallid Muhammad was the New Black Panther Party's major leader. Malik Zulu Shabazz (née Paris Lewis) is its current leader. The NBPP is Islamic. Khallid Muhammad (now deceased) attached himself to the organization after his break with the Nation of Islam in 1998. There is nothing new about Shabazz's efforts or agenda, and the original Black Panther Party condemns them. Another shyster is former R&B artist Dr. Malachi York, leader of the United Nuwaubian Nation of Moors, based in central Georgia.

168. Wilson Moses, *Black Messiahs and Uncle Toms*, p. 214.

169. It became identified with black nationalism when it took on some of nationalism's core tenets, including the rhetoric of violence, which was extant first in the "revolutionary" strain, exemplified by David Walker and the Reverend Henry Highland Garnet. See Algernon Austin, *Achieving Blackness*.

170. Wilson Moses, *Black Messiahs and Uncle Toms*, p. 215. Emphasis in original.

171. Whereas Louis DeCaro carefully points to the Christian Garveyite and Billy Graham Crusade influences in Malcolm X's public ministry, Malcolm X rejected Christianity on many levels, not the least in the way he interpreted its race heritage.

172. Ibid., p. 229.

173. Donald Jacobs, *Courage and Conscience*, p. 76.

174. Price Cobbs and William Grier's second book, *The Jesus Bag* (New York: McGraw-Hill, 1971), builds on the initial work and makes my attempt to link it with the African American jeremiadic tradition more plausible. The development of collective black rage demonstrates how this nationalistic tendency represents recurrent sentiments in the plights, strategies, ideals, and especially psychic responses of black Americans in a context of high nationalist salience, such as in the atmosphere of racial retrenchment that produced Reaganism in the 1980s and 1990s.

175. Henry Louis Gates Jr. and Cornel West, *The Future of the Race* (New York: Vintage, 1996), p. 79.

176. Ibid., p. 73.

177. Ibid., pp. 94–102.

178. Cornel West, *Race Matters*, p. 95.

179. Ibid., p. 96.

180. Ibid., p. 97.

181. Ibid., p. 100.

182. Ibid., p. 101.

183. Ibid., p. 101.

184. Ibid., p. 102.

185. Cheryl Clarke, *"After Mecca": Women Poets and the Black Arts Movement* (New Brunswick, NJ: Rutgers University Press), p. 15.

186. George Breitman (ed.), *Malcolm X Speaks: Selected Speeches and Statements* (New York: Grove, 1965), p. 19.

187. C. Eric Lincoln, *The Black Muslims in America*, p. 33. Emphasis in original.

188. Ibid., pp. 90–93.

189. E. U. Essien-Udom, *Black Nationalism*, p. 7.

190. Harold Cruse, in *Crisis* (see esp. ch. 2), makes clear some of the differences among African American, Caribbean, and African brands of black nationalism.

191. See Richard Turner, *Islam in the African American Experience*, esp. pages 184–189.

192. See excerpt of interview, "Farrakhan Meets the Press,"April 13, 1997, available at http://www.finalcall.com/national/mlf-mtp5-13-97.html (FCN/NBC, 1997).

193. This would encompass the missionary matter of early emigrationists previously discussed—such as Paul Cuffee, James T. Holly, Henry Highland Garnet, Martin Alexander Crummell, Edward W. Blyden, and Bishop Henry McNeal Turner—in terms of the missionary theological commitments that often motivated the contradictory support for the "civilization" of traditional and "benighted" Africa. The particularities of these individuals, as well as their ideological foci, organizational bases, and religious orientations, have been detailed in the scholarly literature.

194. Despite acknowledging an indebtedness to Wilson Moses's interpretation of black nationalism, Robinson rejects what he calls the "Messianic" qualities of Moses. For a detailed explanation of Moses's perspective, see *Classical Black Nationalism*. See Dean E. Robinson, *Black Nationalism in American Politics and Thought*, p. 1.

195. See Dean E. Robinson, *Black Nationalism in American Politics and Thought*, p. 88. Contrary to the implicit dependency that scholars (including Moses, Draper, and Dean Robinson) attribute to any black initiative in their liberation struggle, an emergent literature on black nationalism recommends important stages in which there has been some reciprocity. Historian Leon Litwack's *Been in the Storm So Long: The Aftermath of Slavery* (New York: Vintage, 1980), p. xi, notes, for instance, "the extent to which blacks and whites shaped each other's lives and destinies and were forced to re-

spond to each other's presence had never been more starkly apparent" than in the period his book covers, indicated in the subtitle.

196. Wilson Moses, *The Golden Age of Black Nationalism*, p. 10.

197. Wilson Moses, *Classical Black Nationalism*, p. 6. Emphases added.

198. Kevin Gaines, *Uplifting the Race*, p. 243. Emphasis added.

199. Jeffrey Perry (ed.), *A Hubert Harrison Reader*, p. 403.

200. Moses, *Classical Black Nationalism*, p. 1.

201. See Moses, *Black Messiahs and Uncle Toms*.

202. See Dean Robinson, *Black Nationalism in American Politics and Thought*, pp. 79–80.

203. The problem here is that Malcolm X had not converted to "orthodox" Sunni Islam until he left the Nation of Islam in 1964. It was not Malcolm X's Sunni commitments but his Nation of Islam ministry that were at the center of Moses's and Stuckey's discussions. The Nation of Islam has only recently moved more in that direction under the leadership of Louis Farrakhan. Arthur J. Magida, *Prophet of Rage: A Life of Louis Farrakhan and His Nation* (New York: Basic Books, 1996); and Louis DeCaro Jr., *On the Side of My People: A Religious Life of Malcolm X* (New York: New York University Press, 1997).

204. Sterling Stuckey, *The Ideological Origins of Black Nationalism*, p. 9.

205. Nationalism is traditionally defined with an emphasis on a people's ambitions with regard to land and government. By "thought" tradition, I mean to convey the strain of African American nationalism that makes no land demands or appeals for geographic separation of races or groups. It is a nationalism of means and is decidedly uninterested in the land question with which nationalism is frequently associated.

206. For instance, Robinson contends that "the ethnic paradigm was to [the] wave of 1960s and early 1970s black nationalism what the civilizationist paradigm was to classical black nationalism."

207. Dean Robinson, *Black Nationalism in American Politics and Thought*, p. 8.

208. Joel Williamson, *A Rage for Order: Black-White Relations in the American South Since Emancipation* (New York: Oxford University Press, 1986), pp. 31–32.

209. Ronald Walters, *White Nationalism*.

210. David Levering Lewis (ed.), *The Portable Harlem Renaissance Reader* (New York: Penguin, 1994), pp. 655–666.

211. See Cedric Robinson, *Black Marxism*, p. 84.

212. Dean Robinson, *Black Nationalism in American Politics and Thought*, p. 9. It is more accurate to say that they wanted to possess the land, and other lands, for the sake of promoting a Christian "black nationality," which would demonstrate the potential for African and black American self-rule and self-determination in concert with the Victorian-Romantic-idealistic cultural matrix and republicanism with which they were inescapably socialized.

213. Louis DeCaro Jr., *On the Side of My People*, pp. 13–14.

214. Up to and beyond Delany's time, the greater the call for a return to Africa vis-à-vis the activities of the ACS, the more African Americans began to disassociate with Africa in name use and in the self-identification of individual blacks, out of widespread fear of forced emigration.

215. Cornel West, *Prophesy Deliverance!*, pp. 30–31. Emphasis added.

216. Theodore Draper's *The Rediscovery of Black Nationalism* (1970) is also related to this development. Wilson Moses's *The Golden Age of Black Nationalism* (1978) sets out as a more sympathetic treatment, although it, too, is somewhat presentist in its attempt to clarify the 1960s relationship to the tradition of black nationalism.

217. For Cruse, this phenomenon is traceable to the debates between Frederick Douglass's commitment to abolitionist-integrationism and Harvard-trained physician Martin

R. Delany, who first spoke of "Africa for the Africans" in the 1840s and 1850s, and extended to the civil rights orientation of Martin Luther King Jr. and Malcolm X. See Cruse, *Crisis*, pp. 6, 564.

218. See William Cobb, *The Essential Harold Cruse*, p. 94.

219. Cruse maintains that events such as the Civil War and Spanish American War fundamentally transformed the social order in which African American political elites sought to make claims against the state and society and thus rendered the objectives of each subsequent generation of nationalists in terms of their proximity to the emergent new realities.

220. Edward G. Carmines and James A. Stimson, *Issue Evolution* (Princeton: Princeton University Press, 1989). It underestimates, for instance, the potential linking capacities of religion and culture and that issues such as race/racism can experience ongoing "evolutions" in heterogeneous societies. In this sense, the "new racism" thesis of the "Second Reconstruction" era was anticipated by the "color-line" that Du Bois hypothesized just after the first Reconstruction period. The more things change, the more they stay the same.

221. Similarly, Dawson suggests that Black Power had more of an affinity with Garveyism than with Malcolm X—its most immediate inspiration—primarily because Malcolm rejected aspects of black nationalist discourse in his last year. This interpretation largely disconnects Malcolm X and the Nation of Islam from the New Negro–Garveyism milieu of the post–World War I period. And it also gives too much to Malcolm X's break with black nationalism philosophically.

222. Ojo, cited in Eugene Genovese, *Roll, Jordan, Roll*, pp. 210–211.

223. This paraphrases Sacvan Bercovitch's *The American Jeremiad*, p. xii, and Clifford Geertz's "Religion as a Cultural System," in *The Interpretation of Culture* (New York: Basic Books, 1973), pp. 122, 125.

224. Tommie Shelby, *We Who Are Dark: The Philosophical Foundations of Black Solidarity* (Cambridge: Belknap Press of Harvard University Press, 2005).

225. In addition to "religious nationalism," the authors describe "racial solidarity," the foundation of all forms of black nationalism; "cultural nationalism," which asserts an essential "lifestyle and worldview" of African Americans in relation to European and Western aesthetic and cultural productions; and "economic nationalism," which concerns preferred economic and social organization in concert with Marxian, socialist, or bourgeois liberalist prescriptions. Political black nationalism has two components: "bourgeois reformism," which is committed to pluralist programs such as slating black candidates or all-black political parties; the "revolutionary" component requires the eradication of all preexisting social, political, and economic relations between African Americans and white society. And "emigrationism" was committed to a separate homeland for blacks in diaspora, whether African, Haitian, or in the Americas, whereas "territorial separatism," a more American manifestation, advocates secession, on the one hand, or land grants of a territory, state, or region of states within the United States, on the other. "Pan-Negroism" focuses on the desired role of an African American advance guard that would spearhead an international movement of black unity; "pan-Africanism" concerns the role of newly independent African nations of the post–World War II era in providing the same leadership toward black unity.

226. John Bracey et al., *Black Nationalism in America*, p. lvi.

227. Ibid., pp. lvi–lvii.

228. Ibid., p. lviii.

229. Theodore Draper, *The Rediscovery of Black Nationalism*, 1970; Tunde Adeleke, *UnAfrican Americans*, 1998; Wilson Moses, *Classical Black Nationalism*, 1996; Dean Robinson, *Black Nationalism in American Politics and Thought*, 2001.

230. Bracey et al., *Black Nationalism in America*, 1970; Sterling Stuckey, *The Origins of Black Nationalism*, 1972; Rodney Carlisle, *The Roots of Black Nationalism*, 1975; Gayraud Wilmore, *Black Religion and Black Radicalism*, 1998; Cedric Robinson, *Black Marxism*, 1983; Michael Dawson, *Behind the Mule*, 1994, and *Black Vision*, 2001.

231. Charise Cheney, *Brothers Gonna Work It Out: Sexual Politics in the Golden Age of Rap Nationalism* (New York: New York University Press, 2005); Nikol Alexander-Floyd, *Gender, Race, and Nationalism in Contemporary Black Politics* (New York: Palgrave Macmillan, 2007).

PART 3
Transformations

7

Black Power and the Problem of Black Nationalism

The most formidable evil threatening the future of the United States is the Presence of the blacks on their soil . . . one is almost always brought up against this fact.
—Alexis de Tocqueville, *Democracy in America*

Of late, the jungle has been creeping in again a little closer to our boundaries.
—California governor Ronald Reagan, 1967

Up to this point I have tried to articulate how a black counterdiscourse, rooted in black religious orientations, permeated black politics to the extent that the jeremiad constitutes an alternative way of reading black nationalism in the United States. Linking the black jeremiad to Black Power is complicated by the latter's ostensible secular character. If contemporary black politics is a "secular" theater, it is not because of a general secularization in African American life per se, or the result of a diminution of religion's importance among black people. The black church *is* synonymous with black religion, but the opposite is not true.

Black religion is integral to understanding black politics, even though black politics has undergone a fundamental process where the leadership, organizational, and institutional protest fulcrums have extended beyond the churches, commencing at the turn of the twentieth century and culminating in the 1960s Black Power era of the African American liberation struggle. In this way, Black Power democratized black politics, both formally and informally. Most would concede the rage of Black Power and even its late-stage nationalism. But Black Power is identified more with Stokely Carmichael than with the Reverend Adam Clayton Powell Jr., even though Carmichael was in the audience when Powell used the term "black power" during a speech at Howard University in 1966.[1]

Black Power was a resounding protest ritual literally in its pitch and also in the fact of its existence. Whereas the traditional Euro-American white jeremiad included the mere threat of violence, Black Power, as an extension of the black jeremiad, was precipitated by the ministry of Malcolm X and events in Watts (Los Angeles) in 1965. Black Power was akin to the "grave denunciation" that Perry Miller attached to the "American" version of centuries past. Black Power became a strident declaration of determined opposition to the "white-over-black" social order, economic structure, and institutional arrangements that prevailed into the late 1960s and 1970s. With Malcolm X dead, it would be left to the students, leaders, scholars, and white-dominated structures of power to define what Black Power meant in all of this. Stokely had his say; Eldridge had his; King, too, had his; Elaine Brown had hers; and black rage mediated the whole discourse, even after all the men here were gone. A sure way to discourage serious inquiry into the genealogy of a political orientation is for critics to telegraph the criticism that a treatment is ahistorical. The analysis offered here attempts to build on *existing contentions* concerning the parallels or ideological linkages between Walker and Malcolm X (including the generations of individuals and cadres that emerge in response to both men's short public ministries) and black nationalism. If it is ahistorical to make such linkages, then all of the scholarship discussed in earlier chapters provided its foregrounding. Karen Orren and Stephen Skowronek frame their understanding of political history in a sharp departure from "chronological history."[2] Their perspective highlights patterns that

> are as likely to overlap one another in irregular fashion as to neatly align within a period, and the patterns of interest often range across broad swaths of time. These might be patterns of the present that extend all the way back to the origins of the Republic and before—like religious "awakening"—or patterns of the past, which, though seeming to fall away, leave traces that affect the operation of the new ones set in motion. . . . APD research indicates political movement *through* time rather than a polity bounded in time and highlights connections *between* politics in the past and politics in the present rather than the separateness and foreignness of past politics.[3]

Thus, patterns or persons can be organic, emerging, adapting, and resurfacing. Building on Moses, Jacobs, McAdoo, and Robinson, all of whom look back in descending order from Malcolm X to David Walker, I have attempted to carry the implications of the black jeremiad protest tradition from Walker to Malcolm X and beyond. If these individuals provide a way of understanding landless forms of black nationalism in the United States—the domestic "stay-at-home" form—I want to suggest, with or without its religious frocking, that it becomes the dominant articulation of black nationalism from Black Power to the MMM/DOA, which for a time was of major interest to millions of ordinary people.

Black Power first emerged out of the organic struggles of black southerners surrounded by a sadistic racial Protestantism. The drives waged by students in the Lowndes County Freedom Organization and Student Nonviolent Coordinating Committee (SNCC) were as much about spirituality as they were about voter registration. King set out in the SCLC movement to save the "soul of America." The murders and lynchings of men, women, and children like Emmett Till brought anguishing questions of theodicy to bear on the seemingly endless violence that terrorized black southerners for decades. Aspects of Black Power's counterdiscourse were focused as much on racial Christianity as on racism in general. Peniel Joseph's description of the many antecedent intellectual, leadership, and organizational influences on Black Power radicalism acknowledges that "King's celebrity coexisted with historic acceptance of black preachers as community leaders and the black church as the headquarters for African American social respectability. Local black militancy in the South existed alongside King's nonviolence, revealing a contested social landscape in which deep-seated traditions of self-defense found as much resonance with Malcolm X's blistering judgment as with King's eloquent pleas."[4] Black religion, black nationalism, and Black Power were all born in the South, where John Hope Franklin traced a bellicose spirit among "the Scots and Scotch-Irish in the back country," where "the habit of war was imagined in the Scots."[5] From the American Revolutionary War to the Civil War, southern Protestantism railed against the North with an intensity superseded only by a totalitarian thirst for Negro blood identified by Franklin as having at its center "race, and outside the white race there was to be found no favor from God, no honor or respect from man. Indeed, those beyond the pale were the objects of scorn from the multitudes of the elect."[6]

Even though Black Power took many forms and permutations, it was initially inspired by Christian liberal integrationists in the South, Richard Wright and Adam Clayton Powell in the North, the Christian integrationism of King, and the Islamic nationalism of Elijah Muhammad and, especially, Malcolm X.[7] In this sense, *Black Power, too, can be understood as a function of black religious discourse.* Dwight Hopkins is clear that King and Malcolm X inspired Black Power's religious dimensions, and he insists that at its inception "Christianity was not alien to black power. Indeed, black power was in itself the contemporary manifestation of Jesus Christ."[8] Altogether, Black Power, both rhetorically and as a movement, is open to an interpretation that its origins lay in a black jeremiad against unreconstructed southern Protestantism. It refracted Harold Cruse's post-Cuba call for "revolutionary nationalism," which, resonating with Moses's "stay-at-home" version, "suggested that black activists in America were in need of an *indigenous political orientation*, similar to what was occurring in Cuba, yet unique to black American history and culture."[9]

Key Black Powerites, like Carmichael, Huey P. Newton, and Amiri Baraka, wanted Malcolm X without his religion—even as they relished in its critiques of nonviolent Christian integrationism and violent white supremacist Christianity. We often think of Black Power as if King were not standing next to Carmichael and Willie Ricks when the salvo was spoken into the Meredith March against fear. What David Walker was to the *Appeal*, Malcolm X was to Black Power, that is, the source and inspiration of an expression of black consciousness that troubled the existing racial order. Both individuals inspired small cadres of men and women who subsequently took up the implications of their warnings against US racism, and both prompted reactionary forces into action against them.

Collective black violence, from Black Gabriel's 1800 insurrection plot in Richmond to David Walker's 1829 *Appeal* in Boston to 1960s Black Power in Mississippi, has powerfully shaped a social paranoia in American society. Many radical integrationists—Frederick Douglass, Harriet Tubman, Ida Wells, Charles Remond of Boston, Cyril Briggs's and Richard B. Moore's African Black Brotherhood (ABB),[10] the Deacons of Defense of Louisiana, the NAACP's Robert Williams in Monroe, North Carolina, SNCC activists, and individuals such as Gloria Richardson[11] in Cambridge, Maryland—advocated and supported the threat of violence as a political instrument. However, since J. Edgar Hoover's pursuit of Marcus Garvey and the UNIA after World War I,[12] primarily black nationalism has been feared and associated with widespread militancy and violence, treasonous disloyalty to the United States, and "black supremacy."

To Prevent the Rise of a "Messiah"

At least since the increasingly militant groundswell after World War I, which became known as the working-class-driven "New Negro" mood, federal and local surveillance targeted Marcus Garvey and his nationalistic UNIA between 1919 and 1925 and surrounded him with infiltrators and "confidential employees."[13] The full weight of federal, state, and military surveillance of Garvey and his movement, which first came to the world's attention as a result of his standout corner preaching performances along Lenox Avenue (now Malcolm X Boulevard) in 1918 and 1919 and the publication of his *Negro World* paper, intensified when Hoover and other Federal Bureau of Investigation (FBI) bureaucrats learned of a speech calling for the lynching of white men in Africa whenever blacks were lynched below the Mason-Dixon Line.[14] As was the case of the early, more militant stages of Garveyism, once Black Power became associated with black nationalism it garnered the rapacious suppression of J. Edgar Hoover's FBI in a manner never experienced by Garvey and the Garveyites.

Standing on the rubble of its own protracted and arrested development in the United States, left-critical discourse tends to diminish the impact of the state's counterintelligence distortions concerning Black Power and its influence on the radicalization of all forms of black political and intellectual activities. This analysis takes into account Professor Adolph Reed's caution that "repression and cooptation can never fully explain the failure of opposition, and an exclusive focus on such external factors diverts attention from possible sources of failure within the opposition."[15] Clearly, the opposite must also be given consideration, as the internal failures of the black struggle were inextricably bound to official repression. Professor Ronald Walters attributes part of the international Counterintelligence Program (COINTELPRO) surveillance during the Black Power era to the state's desire for a more acceptable, more moderate black leadership element than that offered by militant students; Marxist-oriented and black nationalist radicals; and people such as Stokely Carmichael, H. Rap Brown, Amiri Baraka, Angela Davis, Huey Newton, Elaine Brown, Eldridge and Kathleen Cleaver, Ella Baker, and, between 1965 and 1967, an increasingly critical, if not race-radical, Martin Luther King Jr.[16]

The entire governmental apparatus of the United States—executive, legislative, judicial—vis-á-vis the COINTELPRO and its 3,000 black comprador informants and agent-provocateurs—feared black nationalism's ineluctable and transformational potential to fashion a better economic and social order.[17] The state has functioned as a fulcrum of bias and domination in the interest of subordinating the psychological, political, and economic spheres of African American life and those of other populations.[18] The failures and successes of movements, especially those touted as "revolutionary," tend to intersect in many aspects of the host society's political and economic relations, cultures, sociology, and social psychology. One is hard-pressed to find in the critical treatments of black nationalism equally effacing accounts of the pseudomorphous "nationalist" organizations and individuals whose assignment it was, even after the period between 1967 and 1970, to "expose, disrupt, misdirect, discredit, or otherwise neutralize the activities of black nationalist, hate-type organizations and groupings, their leadership, spokesmen, membership, and supporters, and to counter their propensity for violence and civil disorder." Indeed, "no opportunity should be missed to exploit through counterintelligence techniques the organizational and personal conflicts of the leadership of the groups and where possible to capitalize upon existing conflicts between competing black nationalist organizations," and to "prevent the coalition of militant black nationalist groups . . . and leaders from gaining respectability," to "prevent the rise of a 'messiah' who could unify, and electrify, the militant black nationalist movement."[19] The fact that Hoover couched this missive on black nationalism in messianic terms (as had David Walker in the *Appeal*) reiterates the jeremiadic nature of Black Power and how key reactionaries understood its insurrectionary potentials, even before James Cone and his colleagues took it up in black liberation theology.

The tatters of official repression of left-oriented mobilizations best toll the predicament of African Americans' systems-challenging and oppositional political forces in the United States. Although New Left radicals, the Socialist Worker's Party, the NAACP, and individuals such as Martin Luther King Jr. were also targeted, it was especially the nationalist leaders, their organizations, and their sympathizers who were subjected to a comprehensive and protracted campaign that even went to the extent of creating ostensibly "nationalist" organizations in communities where there were none for the purpose of "outing" or shaking the trees to identify any aspiring nationalists. For instance, after University of North Carolina student activist Benjamin Chavis created the nationalist-oriented Black Panther Organization (BPO) in Charlotte in the late 1960s, federal, state, and local police agencies set up a branch of a Los Angeles–based rival US organization headed by a known criminal element in order to justify surveillance, arrests, and violent confrontations with committed student activists in the area.[20] During the first administration of Richard Nixon, the Bureau of Alcohol, Tobacco and Firearms (ATF) and the Department of Justice's Internal Security Division (ISD) and the Intelligence Evaluation Committee focused efforts on what was deemed "The Inter-Relationship of Black Power Organizations in the Western Hemisphere."

These agencies were headed by many of the Watergate principals (first discovered by Frank Wills) in the administration, including Assistant Attorney General Robert Mardian, John Mitchell, H. R. Alderman, John Ehrlichman, and John McCord Jr. When it was then aimed toward whites in the national Democratic Party, this abuse of federal power against enemies was regarded as an impeachable offense. But when the *same* federal surreptitious and surveillance powers were directed at the social justice activism of black organizations and individuals, it was conventionally accepted by both national political parties in terms of "law-and-order" ideology.[21] As early as 1967, the US Army created Operation Garden Plot to coordinate management of domestic rebellions. Concerning its use against California militants, as the epigraph to this chapter indicates, Governor Ronald Reagan stated with less than coded race innuendo: "Garden Plot is in line with the 6,000-year history of man pushing the jungle back, creating a clearing where men can live in peace and go about their business with some measure of safety. Of late, *the jungle has been creeping in again a little closer to our boundaries.*"[22] If one associates "man," "men," and "our boundaries" with "white" here, and "the jungle" with black, Chicano, and Asian student activists, then the real intent of Reagan's speech (to a gathering of military and corporate elites) instructs the racial sentiments of contemporary conservatism and American politics at the time.[23]

Much of what passed as black nationalism in the Black Power era is difficult to delineate from state-initiated internecine rivalries, the general atmosphere of provocateurism, assassinations, and official misconduct. This is so especially in California, from which the Black Panther Party for Self-Defense emerged in the same year that Reagan was elected governor.[24] Legal scholar Randall Kennedy notes the various "racial episodes in which, for racial reasons, officials targeted for surveillance and 'dirty tricks,' or prosecution [the] black activists whom they perceived as threats to national security."[25] The year 1971 was reported by the International Association of Chiefs of Police as the single "worst year in American history of incidents of domestic bombing. More than 2,500 explosives and fire bombs injured 207 persons and killed eighteen others." This pattern of individual-level and organized political violence continued into the 1970s. Accordingly, J. Edgar Hoover

> played an important, often decisive, role in monitoring, hounding, and jailing several of the most important black leaders of the century. This was revolution on the Right and its chief concern and conceptualization of social justice at the state and national level of politics was conceived in terms of social order; the focus tends to be primarily on authority more than on political equality and social justice. A crude racism prompted Hoover to view protest against white domination as itself a danger tending toward treason.[26]

It becomes apparent, regardless of ideology, that federal power was unleashed against black protest activity. This reflects a consistent pattern of selective enforcement among several generations of federal authorities who failed to function as referees between rivaling racial groups in the South, and the use of federal power routinely abetted the operatives of white supremacist power and antiblack racial terrorism.[27] Scholars have demonstrated that King, especially, stirred the ire of Hoover, the police, and the military establishment. King was subsequently the only individual who was not openly committed to "black nationalism" listed in the noted COINTELPRO missive from Hoover as a potential "leader who might unify and electrify these violence-prone elements, prevent these militants from gaining respectability and prevent the growth of these groups among America's youth."

It was these same 1960s youth whom the informants, courts, police, military, propaganda, and surveillance establishments targeted in order to destabilize and thereby impede the maturation of the black-consciousness movement. In 1970, for instance, Hoover ordered that all college and university black student union groups be investigated.[28] This point is not to diminish the thoroughly documented and stultifying internecine conflicts among student activists in the Black Power era, or even the self-defeating ties with "underworld" criminal elements that made it possible for establishment forces to justify their actions against legitimate social and political dissent.[29] The conflicts between Maulana Karenga's US organization and the Black Panther Party, between Black Panthers and the Nation of Islam, and so on sapped much of the dissident energy from the thrust of Black Power. Komozi Woodard suggests, for instance, that "while the ideological interchange between the cultural nationalists and revolutionary nationalists was legitimate, the violent warfare between those two factions amounted to a level of irresponsibility bordering upon *treason*. It turned the black liberation movement into a plaything in the hands of the police."[30]

The reflexive state reconnaissance against black militancy has impaired our understanding of Black Power ideology, as well as its impetus, ramifications, and implications for postsegregation black politics. The complicity of federal authorities with local police in harassment campaigns throughout the nation effectively purged the burgeoning movement's leadership, organizational structures, and ideological foundations. Despite a vast literature (plus films and television broadcasts) that frequently caricatures black militancy as a fetish of hyperbolic and grossly exaggerated opportunism,[31] the modern Black Convention movement and other groundswell efforts reflected serious commitments and critiques of white supremacist domination over public policy and the economic exploitation of black labor. Robert Self argues,

> African American activists in Oakland, San Francisco, and Los Angeles fought to secure a place for black communities within the shifting patterns of metropolitan geography and economy that accompanied the vast spatial transformation of midcentury urban America. They engaged the processes and institutions responsible for the second ghetto and the urban crisis as no other group in California. Industrial restructuring, redevelopment and urban renewal, highway and rapid transit construction, and suburban city building together became the pivots around which black politics turned. These issues were not merely the backdrop to the black liberation struggle. Through them the movement itself was constituted. In Oakland in particular, the political discourse and strategies of the long postwar African American rights movement stressed the failure of urban and metropolitan political economy to secure the promise of democracy and opportunity—they stressed the failure of the postwar metropolis and modernism itself. In this sense, the movement, including liberal, radical, and nationalist variants, was not primarily a response to southern mobilization, but a parallel development that sought to redistribute economic and political power within the increasingly divided metropolis.[32]

The intensification of radicalism, and the centrality of black nationalist thought to it, suggest that at least *state authorities* perceived such radicalism to represent a credible challenge to blatantly uneven resource attainment and a threat to the extant social, political, and economic order. Daniel Patrick Moynihan conceded that "in retrospect, the domestic turbulence of the United States in the late 1960s may come to appear as something less than cataclysmic. . . . *This was not the view of the men then in office.*"[33] In reaction, what emerged from the state and its official and popular constituent bases was in effect a political movement—from above—fueled by the law-and-order ideology and fear of a largely dissident black counterpublic, particularly among those who sought radical reform or eradication of social and political relations. Militant protest demands and traditional black political activity were conveniently conflated into muddy "social-order" issues related to welfare, "pathological" matriarchal family structures, the decimation of urban working spaces, unskilled manufacturing (what some scholars call a "spatial mismatch"),[34] and issues related to urban migration patterns. Most of the order issues could be addressed through bureaucratic impediments with regard to goods and service delivery (e.g., welfare benefits), or even, more draconically, bartering a young woman's reproductive rights for welfare and state medical benefits.[35]

The social-control "law" aspect of the ideology mobilizes images of massive anarchic violence carried out by marauding black males, enraged for no apparent reason except for being crazed by drugs or for the sake of violence itself. Talk of "internal colonization," or of being an oppressed "nation within a nation," and third-world liberation disturbed several consecutive US administrations, from Dwight Eisenhower to Gerald Ford. The clear and simple remedy was reflexive and retaliatory violence, preventive detentions, and propaganda. Political scientist Reginald Gilliam Jr. highlights the extent to which the state and local antisedition laws and features of legislative acts, such as the anticommunist Internal Security Act (1950, especially its emergency detention component), targeted black militancy. Under the detention program, which Congress repealed during the first Nixon administration, broad police powers were extended to provide for the arrest and detention of any would-be black rioters, even though the law was intended for *geopolitical* security threats.[36]

Black Nationalism in a Postnationalist World Milieu

The timing of the 1960s student black nationalism was exacerbated by developments not only within the domestic racial politics and protests of their time but also in the international repudiation of racial nationalism beginning in the 1940s and 1950s. The logic of racial nationalism experienced its apogee and its declension in modern German intellectual developments, with the sentiment that race provided the basis for forging and justifying political attachments and national identity. The systematic Jewish-outing and Jewish-purging Nuremberg Laws, which would equate bloodline heredity with Aryanness and German citizenship, were followed by the Beer Hall Putsch anniversary pogroms in 1938. The rest is tragic race history. Here, race, the people, and the state converged in a national political unit set on ruling continental Europe. Political theorist Andrew Vincent makes the point that German citizenship, for instance, was and remains today tied to an individual's racial bloodline, that is, on the basis of *jus sanguinis* (right of blood), and romanticist notions of "ethnocultural ideas," such as "conceptions of uniqueness, inwardness, feeling over reason and organic growth over conscious artifice." Between 1871 and 1913, anti-immigrant policy led to the construction of national identity in Auslandsdeutsche.[37] The general reticence concerning nationalism (of any sort) since the major wars is captured pointedly by Theodore Vincent, who argues that left and liberal critiques of nationalism after World War II saw it as "recidivist tribalism," "potentially totalitarian, theoretically specious and politically bellicose." Moreover, much of the debate over nationalism in the period from 1930 to the 1950s must be understood in the context of what might be termed the "Weimar debates." Most of the liberal-minded writers, such as Hans Kohn or Karl Deutsch, and many others, who generated the academic debate over nationalism, were European émigrés to America in the 1930s. They had either experienced first-hand, or second-hand through teachers, or through reflections on the World War Two experience, the rise of national socialism in Germany. There was a deep sensitivity about the role of nationalism. However, one could hardly say that nationalism, in itself, was a pressing problem in the 1920 to 1950s period, comparative to, say, Germany. Thus a large contingent of German-speaking writers took their anguished debates with them into the USA. Some retained a profound antipathy to anything nationalist.[38]

Social theorist Hannah Arendt rejects the idea that German provincialism was necessarily nationalist or anomalously racialist in its self-understanding when compared to other European polities. She notes, for instance, "the historical truth of the matter is that race-thinking, with its roots deep in the eighteenth century, emerged simultaneously in all Western countries during the nineteenth century. Racism has been a powerful ideology of imperialistic policies since the turn of our [20th] century."[39] Nowhere is this clearer in her view (and in the view of Du Bois as expressed in the color-line thesis) than in the "scramble for Africa." It was this scramble that moved race-thinking from the margins to the center. Thus, Arendt insists,

> race-thinking entered the scene of active politics the moment the European peoples had prepared, and to a certain extent realized, the new body politic of the nation. From the beginning racism deliberately cut across all national boundaries, whether defined by geographical, linguistic, traditional, or any other standards, and denied national-political existence as such. Race-thinking, rather than class-thinking, was the ever-present shadow accompanying the development of the comity of European nations, until it finally grew to be the powerful weapon for the destruction of those nations.[40]

Michael Banton demonstrates the extent to which race itself interspersed European self-understanding and thinking on questions of lineage, types, subspecies, status, and class.[41] W.E.B. Du Bois's color-line thesis, which declares "the problem of the twentieth century will be the problem of the color-line— the relation of the darker to the lighter races of men in Asia and Africa, in America and the islands of the sea,"[42] was reflective of the race-nation feelings of the period among pan-Africanist and nationalist-oriented Negro elites; it also impacted West and East European thought.

Theodor Herzl's *Der Judenstaat* (appropriately translated *State of Jews* or *Jews' State*, but not, according to Kornberg, *Jewish State*) was published in 1896, the same year that *Plessy v. Ferguson* legally cordoned African Americans into the rural enclaves that post–Civil War redemptionists and Booker T. Washington had already claimed for southern American Negroes. It was also the year that Herzl formed a close association with a Christian leader named William Hechler (1845–1931), who predicted the divinely appointed "restoration of the Jews to Palestine" in 1882. At the very moment in time when the communal base for African American life was being structured in segregation, a crisis in European Jewry (born not of its continued ghettoization but its assimilation, or "deghettoization") precipitated the crisis that led to Herzl's rejection of his Austro-German nationalism (which necessitated Jewish assimilation and cultural annihilation) and his embrace of Zionism.

Whereas Jews in Herzl's Austria enjoyed widespread acceptance in the 1880s, a new cultural anti-Semitism mixed with anticapitalism (as opposed to pogroms or violence) in the 1890s traumatized them. Arendt, citing Jewish historian Jacob Katz, promotes the idea that in the burgeoning modern era,

> Jewish-Gentile relations were at an all time low, Jewish "indifference to conditions and events in the outside world" were at an all time high, and Judaism became "more than ever a closed system of thought." It was at this time that Jews, without any outside interference, began to think "that the difference between Jewry and the nations was fundamentally not one of creed and faith, but one of inner nature" and that the ancient dichotomy between Jews and Gentiles was "more likely to be racial in origin rather than a matter of doctrinal dissension."[43]

In the tradition of nationalists everywhere, Herzl was instrumental in forging the modern Zionist movement with a presentation of Jewish history in which the biblical Exodus story and the conquering armies of Joshua represented heroic, masculine, or Jewish "manliness," which Herzl understood to be critical to overcoming the political realities and general psychological disposition of Jewish inefficacy in Europe. Jacques Kornberg notes, "Herzl reinvented the Jewish past and used Judaic traditions to legitimate modern political nationalism. He linked modern political goals to a reconceived Jewish heritage, a futuristic program to the notion of a revived archaic community. Such linkages between past, present and future gave his nationalist worldview its pedigree, its authority, and its ability to reshape personal identity."[44] Yet Herzl's Austro-German cultural nationalism was the *same* nationalism that Nazism would later embrace. This important father of the modern Zionist movement was, at first, a self-conscious anti-Semite.[45] As Kornberg notes further, "Herzl's starting point was a negative view of Jewry; his solution was radical assimilation."

Herzl, like many Austro-Hungarians, was disturbed by unification under the multinational Hapsburg Empire; their nationalist inclinations superseded union with Germany. Still, Jews in Austria-Hungary craved German culture to the extent that they shunned Judaism or, at the least, the ghetto. Trotsky later conveyed to C.L.R. James how "the Jewish in Germany and Austria wanted nothing more than to be the best German chauvinists . . . but now, with the turn of events, Hitler does not permit them to be German chauvinists. Now many of them have become Zionists and are Palestinian nationalists and anti-German."[46]

At the time of Du Bois's writing, Gilbert Murray contended that "there is in the world a hierarchy of races. . . . Those nations which eat more, claim more, and get higher wages, will direct and rule others, and the lower work of the world will tend in the long-run to be done by the lower breeds of men. This much we of the ruling colour will no doubt accept as obvious."[47] The self-evident fact of white rule over nonwhite peoples and nations—as Du Bois elucidates in the *World and Africa*, pointing to the pact among a small number of key European powers in 1884–1885 at the Berlin (or "Congo") Conference of Otto von Bismarck—fostered presumptive notions in which, according to Banton, "nations, as political units, are equated with races, as biological units. The position of white people at the top of the hierarchy is attributed to their racial character and the future division of labour throughout the world is represented as an expression of this hierarchy."[48] Racism developed across continents and had a local, *national* character as well, and, thus, it was locally activated in any given European or African society. The ambitions of the Nazis exceeded fascism in one state; they were not simple nationalists, as *all* European Jews were held responsible for the Weimar Republic; for association with Godless communism; for capitalism, liberalism, and the nation-state. It should be emphasized that Jews made up less than .08 percent of the total population of Germany prior to World War II.[49] After several Zionist conferences held between 1897 and 1901, Herzl was able to broker a sufficient network of Jewish elites and European powers, who had originally debated settlement in Argentina and Uganda, to forge a map for a modern Jewish sovereignty in Palestine, where it would run headlong against the resident nationalism of Arab Palestinians after World War II. While rejecting the Jewish origins of the nation-state idea, Arendt, a self-proclaimed "pariah" (that is, "social outcast"),[50] contends that "Herzl's Jewish state did not solve 'the Jewish problem': . . . With sovereignty, the pariah people has not ceased to be a pariah—it has created a pariah state."[51]

The progeny of poststructuralist discourses, which tend to dismiss race as a mere socially constructed apparition, also tend to reiterate the extent to which nations have defined themselves in racial terms much as the National Socialists under Hitler vulgarized in the clear grounds of race hatred and racial anti-Semitism. The main point is not to chronicle the genealogy, racial nationalism, or ethnogenesis of nations, especially since most scholars trace this development more to postrevolutionary France than to the Second and Third Reichs; it is to suggest that anyone heralding unabashed race-specific nationalism as a political or normative *end* in politics, as some Black Power advocates had, was treading in Hitler's waters.[52]

The Crisis of Black Nationalism as Anti-Semitism

Late-nineteenth- and early-twentieth-century black nationalist and pan-Africanist leaders, such as Marcus Garvey and W.E.B. Du Bois, *endorsed* pan-Jewish nationalism and the idea of a Jewish state as a model for the potentials of "back to Africa" and pan-Africanism. Garvey saw parallels in the predicament of European Jews and American blacks in terms of its antiblack racialism, and Wilson Moses, although he left the American scene well before Hitler's rise to power in Europe, notes Garvey taught his followers that "what had happened to one minority could happen to another."[53] Even earlier, the nineteenth-century Liberian pan-Africanist and black nationalist Edward Wilmot Blyden was also impacted by Herzl's Zionism.[54] Wilson Moses points out the detail that Blyden linked his version of pan-Africanism to Jewish "Zionism and invited the Jewish people to come to Africa and help with the uplift of the continent."[55] This, of course, was in reaction to the original claim, as noted, that the British powers and European Zionists placed on Uganda, rather than Palestine, as the place of settlement. Moses also points to the contentious cross-fertilization among pan-Africanism, pan-Islamism, and Jewish Zionism and focuses on the messianic religiosity that conjoins them among their black derivatives in the American context (respectively corresponding to black Christian nationalism, black Muslims, and black Israelite Hebrew groups). Despite Garvey's efforts to highlight parallels between pre-Nazi European Jewry and blacks in diaspora, Garvey scholar David Cronon argues, "Garvey sought to raise high the walls of racial nationalism at a time when most thoughtful men were seeking to tear down those barriers." Theodore Vincent retorts, "[Cronon] believed that the American 'melting pot' would solve the race problem, whose only models for racial nationalism were nazism and fascism."[56]

The priorities of the nation-state, as an extension of dominant group political interest and *particularity*, conflict with the universal priorities of international political organization and arrangements, even as the nation-state served as the main source of their political legitimacy (i.e., the United *Nations*). For Harold Cruse, emphases placed on "the 'national question' in theory and International Law of Western States, must deal with nationalism insofar as international relations involve nations, nation-states, national minorities within them." For the United States, Cruse insisted on a bourgeois sponsorship of black American cultural nationalism (which is inseparable from economics and politics); it was essentially the "crisis" of which he wrote.[57] His gripe with African American elites of this era had to do with two interrelated dimensions of nationalism, one having to do with the failure of midcentury intellectuals and elites to convey to the "younger generation" (presumably Black Power advocates) the ideological exigencies between communists and black nationalists historically. To Cruse, the younger individuals "have been kept in the dark about the entire history of destructive Communist duplicity, opprobrium, negligence, and ignorance on questions of Afro-American nationalism." Cruse felt that the contested ideological issues that fulminated in the Garvey era among the contending forces (e.g., African nationalists, West Indian nationalists, and African American nationalists) and in many controversies between nationalists and communists, if brought to bear, might instruct student activists as they attempted to negotiate the cacophonous ideological terrain of the 1960s Black Power era. One of the charges (which Jewish intellectual Theodore Draper viewed as absurd)[58] had to do with the matter of the supposed role of Jewish communists in stirring the Communist Party into an anti-Hitler movement in the 1930s. This is related to a second dimension that Cruse addresses, pertaining to the relationship of American Jews and African Americans in the Communist Party and the implications for black nationalism and Black Power politics.

The Clash of US Nationalisms

The relationship between African Americans and racial nationalism during the Black Power period is captured in the disputed charges, claims, and actual racial resentment among ordinary black Harlemites (and other black communities), organic elites such as Malcolm X (and other Nation of Islam leaders), and Black Power advocates. Without regard to its ideological foil, black anti-Semitism charges reach back at least as early as the Leo Frank lynching in 1915. Its greatest influence came against black nationalist elites such as Amiri Baraka and Louis Farrakhan, who was known in the 1980s and 1990s as the "Black Hitler" and a "fascist" with his own "skinhead *Jungvolk*" whose Million Man March should remind us of "what happened to the German Left."[59] Nigerian political scientist E. U. Essien-Udom took issue with the long-standing tendency among the Nation of Islam's critics to associate its leaders with fascism and Hitler: "It has also been said that he [Elijah Muhammad] is another Hitler in religious disguise. This analogy ignores several important considerations, Where is his army? Where are his arms? Where is the personnel fomenting political intrigue? Why do the Muslims abhor bearing arms of any sort? Why do they surrender this opportunity for training in the use of arms or even for infiltrating the military installations?"[60]

As these are not probing intellectual questions and focus mostly on tactical matters, the point is that the Nation of Islam was no more committed to a serious and systematic program of anti-Semitism than it ever was to leaving the United States. It is interesting to note that in the history of black nationalism the biblical Hebrews (who, of course, the Nation of Islam believes were an originally "Asiatic" black people and not European) provided the model of religiously inspired nationalist separatism to which the Nation of Islam has conformed. We lack a comprehensive study extrapolating the "theological" claims and religious tensions between American Jewish militants (mainly in the Jewish Defense League) and members of the Nation of Islam and whether they are a reflection of Jewish-Muslim relations in the Arabian Peninsula. The extent to which the biting rhetoric of Nation of Islam ministers concerns Judaism may, in fact, reflect religious anti-Jewish feeling that may or may not inhere in racial anti-Semitism, in Arendt's terms.

The race-nation implications of modern Zionism were the object of criticism from African American nationalists in the civil rights and Black Power periods. Black Power nationalists supported the Palestinian position in criticizing US foreign policy in the Middle East. The state of Israel, in Cruse's estimation, complicated the pro-subaltern "Third-World" orientation of 1960s cultural nationalist activists such as Baraka. Israel openly sided with exploitative imperial and neocolonial forces against the interests of black Africans in South Africa, Rhodesia, and the Congo, against which cultural nationalist activists felt obligated to write and speak. Writing within the tumult of Black Power, Cruse captured the positional tension that the postwar establishment of the state of Israel posed for the previously amicable ideological pragmatism that brought the interracial civil rights establishment to the fore of post-Garvey black politics.

> These relations now become colored by the incipient clash of two ideologies—Black Nationalism and Zionism. These nationalists, totally dissimilar in most respects, share one essential motivation: a yearning for national redemption through regaining a "homeland" that was lost. Both Zionism and Black Nationalism have undergone historical conditioning peculiar to themselves, and have never, to my knowledge, confronted each other on any domestic or international issue. But today things are different, and Black Nationalism, Zionism, African affairs, and Negro civil rights organizations are intimately interlocked on the political, cultural, economic, and international fronts, whether Negro intellectuals care to acknowledge it or not. Today it is no longer possible for Negro intellectuals to deal with the Jewish question in America purely on a basis of brotherhood, compassion, morality, and other subjective responses which rule out objective criticism and positive appraisals. Taking a critical approach to the Jewish question does not preface a call to arms against Jews, so much as ensure a critical examination of how the national group question is handled in the United States.[61]

Robert C. Smith contends that Jesse Jackson's inability to garner support from American Jews in his 1984 campaign was an extension of a long-standing conflict over the "black position on the Middle East conflict, specifically support of the Palestinian quest for self-determination . . . a consensus view in black America, shared by its intelligentsia and leadership establishment. This third world approach is anchored in black identification with all oppressed peoples, especially the world's oppressed colored peoples. This identification with the oppressed is rooted in a shared historical experience and perhaps in the Afro-American religious tradition."[62] The fracture of this relationship has been laid at the feet of black nationalists, even where, as in the Jackson case, the nationalists were chiefly marginalized in interracial coalition politics. Smith explains the transition when

> in 1948 most elements of the black leadership community supported the United Nations partitions of Palestine that resulted in the creation of the Jewish state. But by the late 1960s as a result of the growing influence of Pan-Africanism with its emphasis on third-world solidarity, the radical and nationalist elements of the leadership community had adopted an antizionist, pro-Palestinian position. At the convention the District of Columbia delegation proposed a resolution that labeled the Jewish state "fascist" and "imperialistic" and called for the end of all United States military and economic assistance and the return of the historical land of the Palestinian and Arab people to them.[63]

Despite the apparent contradiction in advocating for black American nationality while condemning the existence of a state for Jews as oppressed, albeit mostly bourgeois, European nationalities, the Arab-Israeli conflict loomed significantly in the "Black Agenda" of the 1972 National Black Political Convention (NBPC). Black Power advocates were influenced directly and indirectly by Garveyism, especially if we consider the (originally Garveyite) Nation of Islam's theocratic social and political orientations—which Black Power's patron figure, Malcolm X, embraced for a decade. Harold Cruse was also a towering intellectual influence as a propagandist of cultural nationalism who recognized Jewish bourgeois leadership in Zionism but otherwise saw no substantive linkage, as did Blyden, Garvey, or Du Bois.[64] Cruse actually recommends that would-be African American leaders and intellectuals of the nationalist strand take into account the cultural and programmatic *achievements* of Herzlian Zionism, which, unlike post–World War II black nationalist projects, enjoyed widespread elite sponsorship (epitomized in the cultural work of Theodor Herzl and of financier Edmond de Rothschild).[65] He insists that younger African American activists follow the cultural nationalist route that was the ideological glue of European Zionism.

Cruse's withering critiques of Jewish (communist and integrationist) participation in American politics and culture—especially with regard to the black freedom struggle—influenced many young activists, such as Amiri Baraka, to underscore the tensions in the interest-driven sponsorship of the civil rights movement. Cruse alludes to the formulation of a nationalist triangle (consisting of Anglo-Saxon, African American, and Jewish nationalism) that intersects pro-Zionist sponsorship with the black integrationists (against black nationalists) out of fear that serious black radical agitation would turn white nationalists against both collectivities in the United States. Cruse's "Jewish problem" relies on the manner in which, as he saw it, Jewish elites and

intellectuals dominated nineteenth- and twentieth-century black American social movements (integrationist, communist, and both in opposition to nationalists such as Garvey) even as they operated politically and locally in neutral,
albeit nationalistic, religious and political fulcrums, such as the Kehillah community forums.[66] The African American intellectual's role in this troika was
patently subordinate.

The special nationality and "national group" quagmire confronting African
Americans, reflecting their "twoness," should have been settled between white
Anglo and African American nationalist forces in the governmental, political,
and intellectual sectors. But it remained frustrated by Jewish intellectuals' dominance of the discourse. For Cruse, Jewish communists especially played "the
role of political surrogates for the 'white' working class, and thereby gained
the political whip of intellectual and theoretical domination of the Negro question." For him, this emerged in relation to "an intense undercurrent of jealousy,
enmity and competition over the prizes of group political power and intellectual prestige."[67] And though it is likely that the problem of anti-Semitism is
raised when any nationalist black intellectual, such as Cruse, seeks to flesh out
the complex layers of interracial group relations around twentieth-century
black politics, he nevertheless sought to disentangle the role of the Communist Party in its unabashed anti-Garveyism and misreading (he might say, mis-
leading) of the "Negro question." For Cruse, nation, nationality, "nation within
a nation," and even "minority" were intentionally muddled by the communists
in order to avoid dealing with African Americans' group-specific predicament.
He notes,

> Unable or unwilling to accept the reality that America is a group society, that
> next to the Anglo-Saxon Protestant group, the American Negro is the largest
> national minority in America, the Communists clung to the "oppressed nation
> in the Black Belt" concept of Moscow theoreticians, a concept that separated
> the entire Negro group into two artificial sections—North and South. It was
> meant to leave the non-Southern Negro the option of assimilation (in theory)—
> which logically ruled out nationalistic movements as utopian, reactionary, and
> anti-unity etc. This approach ruled out (again, in theory) all pure cultural group
> expressions such as economic cooperatives, special publications, literary and
> artistic groups. . . . In 1921, when the white leaders were courting the reality
> of organized Black nationalism, the Negroes in the ABB [African Blood
> Brotherhood] were trying to subordinate nationalism to communism. Later,
> when the Communists turned their backs on Black nationalism, the same
> Negro leaders followed suit.[68]

Cruse was no anti-Semite. Anyone who has read his opus *Crisis* can ascertain that he was bitterly critical (perhaps hypercritically so) of *all* forces,
whether well-meaning or hostile: black African, West Indian, Jewish, black
nationalist, the famous, communist, integrationist, Negro, artistic and creative,
activist, bourgeois, or student if they stood in the way of effective strategies

designed to strengthen the group position of African Americans as a national collective. Cruse's argument about the divergent situations of African Americans and Jews in the American context provides reason to look skeptically at the elite-driven ideological jumble wherein committed Jewish nationalists formed coalitions with committed African American integrationists yet remained hostile to all forms of black nationalism from Garveyism to Louis Farrakhan and the Nation of Islam. As with Eldridge Cleaver's treatise on black homosexuality, Cruse was reacting chiefly to James Baldwin's procrustean reading and confusion of the genocidal fate of European Jews, as well as the affluent bourgeois positionality of American Jewish elites; in Cruse's blunt phrasing, "*Jews have not suffered in the United States.*"[69]

In this vein, historian David Levering Lewis notes that Jewish and African American elites, although operating from positions of privilege, attempted to stave off external and internal threats to their movement entrepreneurialism—which was assimilationist in its end yet quasi-communitarian as a means to domestic group politics. They "decided to concert many of their undertakings in the belief that group assimilation could be accelerated through strategies of overt and covert mutual assistance."[70] As the Frank lynching in 1915 prompted American Jews from the periphery of early civil rights to act in concert with Booker T. Washington's accommodationist orientation, Lewis argues there was then a "virtual management of Afro-American civil rights organizations,"[71] which by extension would constitute a "fight against anti-Semitism by remote control."[72] Considering the anarchic race pogroms that characterized the social interaction of African Americans with whites after World War I in American society, any gesture from any group of whites or ethnics was welcomed. Cruse insists, "*Thus, pro-Zionist influences within Negro civil rights organizations are strategically aiding and abetting Negro integration (assimilation), albeit Zionists, themselves, do not believe in integration (assimilation) for Jews.*"[73] Moreover, "the fact remains that pro-Zionist policies in civil rights organizations are prointegrationist for Negroes and anti-assimilationist for Jews."[74] No single figure epitomized this more than Bayard Rustin, who frequently promoted an "uncritical support of Israel. Detractors pointed out while he opposed black nationalism, he had no problem with nationalism when it came to the state of Israel."[75] Lewis writes that "by assisting in the crusade to prove that Afro-Americans could be decent, conformist, cultured human beings, the civil rights Jews were, in a sense, spared some of the necessity of directly rebutting anti-Semitic stereotypes; for if blacks could make good citizens, clearly, most white Americans believed, all other groups could make better ones."[76]

Clearly, Black Power tensions emerged between the SNCC wing among African American student activists and what they perceived as white co-optation years before the catchphrase crystallized into a form of black nationalist politics. That is to say, in accordance with Julius Lester, it was *not* the black nationalists per se who jettisoned white and Jewish liberal alliances—though they would not resist such a purging of liberal participation in the movement. Months before Black Power caught the attention of the nation, SNCC's 1966 "Position Paper on Black Power" promoted a "Third-World" alliance among a diversity of groups, including "the masses of Black people," that is, colonized groups in Asia and Latin America. With regard to the expulsion of whites, "if we are to proceed toward true liberation, we must cut ourselves off from white people. We must form our own institutions. . . . Too long have we allowed white people to interpret the importance and meaning of the cultural aspects of our society."[77] Given the historical tensions especially between liberal integrationists (Negro, white, Jewish) and black nationalists—which are what Cruse defines as "black politics"—it would be more surprising if Black Power advocates did not aim at liberal integrationist alliances between black leadership establishment and American Jewish elites.

As with other "new convert" Black Power nationalists, Amiri Baraka's anti-Jewish tantrums had much to do with a break in interracial coalition politics, with the exigencies of Bohemian counterculture in Greenwich Village, his marriage to Hettie Cohen, a woman Jewish writer, and the necessity to authenticate his embrace of black nationalism. This tragically led to some vitriolic expressions, as in the following poem:

> Smile jew. Dance, jew. Tell me you love me, jew. I got something for you now though. I got something for you, like you dig, I got it. I got this thing, goes pulsating through black everything universal meaning. I got extermination blues, jewboys. I got hitler syndrome figured. . . . So come for the rent, jewboys, or come ask for a book, or sit in the courts handing down your judgments, still I got something for you, gonna give it to my brothers.[78]

This rendition prompted one of Baraka's biographers to suggest that Jones's anti-Semitism, rather than crediting these sentiments to black nationalism per se, "was also a result of the right-wing chauvinism that often inhabits modernism and bohemianism."[79] Indeed it is also plausible that

> Jones may have been entangled in a psychological deference to Jews, and perhaps to whites in general, that must have bordered on a crass desire to be Jewish and/or white. At some point he discovered his complicity in his self-erasure, felt ashamed, and transferred his anger to Jews. Jews were culpable because they disproportionately comprised his closest friends and thus were complicit in accepting and validating his unreal, self-hating, black self. His rage toward them was a testimony to his reliance in their recognition. Irrational and ultimately ineffective, this anger led him to the absurdity of invoking Hitler, absurd not only because of the unimaginable crimes that Jones trivialized but absurd because Hitler also wanted to rid the world of blacks. To attach himself metaphorically to Hitler's final solution was to commit suicide.[80]

If Baraka had been merely a run-of-the-mill student militant (like many of his rank-and-file juniors), his expressions of anti-Semitism might have been dismissed on the grounds of youthful naiveté. But writing in his early to mid-thirties, between 1965, when he left Greenwich Village, and 1972, when he convened the bourgeois protest and political establishment at the NBPC in Gary, Indiana, Baraka so dominated postsegregationist politics to the extent that Lloyd Brown overstates the impact: "Baraka's career as black nationalist is comparable with the black nationalist movement itself."[81] As much as political scientist Adolph Reed deplores the messianic race-leader clientage style of representation as demagoguery, he argues that "there's no such thing as *black* anti-Semitism."[82] Reed is careful to note that there *are* black individuals, including well-known nationalist leaders, such as Baraka and Farrakhan, who may betray anti-Semitic animus, but as a widespread phenomenon it is of

> a species of the same genus as "Africanized" killer bees, crack babies, and now the rising generation of hardened ten-year-olds soon to be career criminals. It is racialized fantasy, a projection of white anxieties about dark horrors lurking just beyond the horizon. . . . Black anti-Semitism's specific resonance stems from its man-bites-dog quality. Black Americans are associated in the public realm with opposition to race prejudice, so the appearance of bigotry among them seems newsworthy. . . . Any black anti-Semite is seen not as an individual but as a barometer of the black collective mind; belief in black anti-Semitism, therefore, is itself a form of racialist thinking.[83]

The claims of black anti-Semitism served to morally discredit legitimate critiques and tensions between (and among) black nationalists, white liberals, and left-oriented intellectuals and activists. For Reed, the logic of the claims follows along these lines: "First, posit the single racial mind, so that whatever any black person does speaks for—and reflects on—all others. Then comes the syllogism: Blacks deserve equal rights to the extent that they are morally exemplary. Black antisemitism shows that blacks aren't morally exemplary. Therefore, black demands for equal citizenship are tainted, and need not be taken seriously."[84]

Black Nationalism as Intellectual Thesis of Black Power

Disappointed with the yields of integration in 1966, young SNCC and CORE *integrationists* hollered, "Black Power!" Black became cool, and cool was black, and then, within two years, Black Power turned "nationalist." This is noted because Black Power has been sloppily, and too often uncritically, linked to black nationalism in scholarly works, in journalism, and in the legal and political establishments even though there is *not a single* reference to "black nationalism" in the book *Black Power* by the late activist Stokely Carmichael and political scientist Charles V. Hamilton. They sought to offer a framework for its operationalization and the meaning of the fulmination.[85]

It is equally pertinent that *Black Power* neglects to mention Malcolm X's influence on the radicalism of the period; instead, true to its reformist integrationism, it pays homage to the famous words of the militantly eclectic Frederick Douglass, who at various stages embraced proto-integrationism, protonationalism, emigration (to Haiti), and assimilationism.[86] One of the striking facets of Black Power activism and discourse is that they relied heavily on a range of incestuous ideological influences, to the point of having few other distinct features, except, perhaps, in the administration of local community programs. Some scholarly studies of black nationalism have gone so far as to treat it as Black Power's sole ideology, even when its most noted proponents (e.g., the Black Panther Party and Amiri Baraka) renounced black nationalism in favor of other, more internationalist and socialistic orientations.

For instance, Eldridge Cleaver's highly touted autobiographical *Soul on Ice* is lionized as a Black Power/black nationalist treatise in Robert Carr's 2002 *Black Nationalism in the New World*, even where Cleaver explicitly attributes his prurient, homoerotic, masculinist, burgeoning political consciousness to the objective conditions of the life of a black man in California's San Quentin prison—following a rape conviction that goes against the stolid Victorian and religious moral codes of traditional black nationalism—and to his reading of Marx, Lenin, Machiavelli, and Nechayev.[87] John Bracey, Augustus Meier, and Elliot Rudwick included an article in their book, written by Cleaver, titled "Black Is Coming Back!" despite the detail that it was written several years before Black Power was declared formally as black nationalism and before Cleaver joined the Black Panthers. Though Cleaver was then an incarcerated member of the Nation of Islam, the article says nothing about black nationalism; neither does it comport well with what Wilson Moses refers to as "literary" black nationalism.

Cleaver's preoccupation with white women, as expressed in the first chapter of *Soul on Ice*, turns early "revolutionary" black nationalist David Walker on his head. And in 1954, when he wrote it, Cleaver was not and never became—despite his Nation of Islam religious affiliation—a politically committed black nationalist. But little of this mattered in the maelstrom of criticism from left-, liberal-, and right-leaning intellectuals, commentators, and propagandists of what was widely read as a break from the program of integration-assimilation and the confrontational strategy of nonviolent resistance promoted by the civil rights leadership establishment and organizations.

A rejection of black nationalist ideas, elites, and projects also stems from the fact that the intellectual terrain on the subject has been dominated not by nationalist intellectuals but by individuals opposed to race-conscious notions of social organization and many veterans of the 1960s and 1970s ideological turf conflicts. Andrew Vincent insists, for instance, that "nationalist myths, fantasies and aspirations—lovingly embodied in academic lexicography, academic historical writing, painting, poetry, literature and monuments during the nineteenth century—arose once again, phoenix-like from the flames, in the closing decades of the twentieth century. Old agendas were still very much the present realities of the 1990s, being re-fought with re-kindled hatreds. Those who service these agendas and hatreds are more often than not the scholarly literati."[88] Robin Kelley also notes that "we have to recognize that the backlash against so-called identity politics is also deeply personal, reflecting a tragic sense of loss or irrelevance experienced by some of their critics."[89]

Algernon Austin's study takes to task the tendency among scholars to dismiss race as simple social invention. For him, there is little consensus across disciplines concerning what "socially constructed" means. From a sociological perspective, "It is ultimately the shared meanings and definitions that create race—not biology. . . . social definitions have social consequences."[90] Adolph Reed Jr. contends that the subsequent turf claims of the various identity interests "emerged as a rhetorical and programmatic vehicle for incorporating an appropriate notion of black interests into this arrangement, in response to popular mobilization associated with civil rights and black power activism. Feminist, other nonwhite minority group, and gay political interests were subsequently incorporated on the same model."[91] Significantly influenced by French intellectuals, the smorgasbord of poststructuralist identity formations strove to transform their marginality in the struggles for liberation.[92] Many of these formations were indebted to black nationalist discourses to the extent that the rebellions and the assemblies in which Black Power discourse was centered formed the "matrix for the political culture that led to the brief hegemony of the politics of black cultural nationalism."[93] This brief hegemony in black political discourse occurred at the precise time when the identity formations were emergent, and thus it became simultaneously the source and object of sustained critical analyses. Reed insists these formations could trace their "ancest[ry] in black power–era racial politics."[94] For him, a major weakness in these perspectives is the "premise that a shared identity confers a special interpretive authority [and] reinforces, more or less subtly, a propriety advantage for practitioners and interpretations able to claim authority."[95]

Perhaps this is what is meant in Reed's contention concerning how black nationalism has singly distorted intellectual constructions of "left-egalitarian" politics. Still, the likes of Du Bois, Paul Robeson, Hubert H. Harrison, Harold Cruse, and Cornel West seem to have understood the dynamics that aggregate these principal categories in heterogeneous contexts. During the era of segregation, African Americans operated largely on a "homogenous unit" principle, which has been activated in the anomalous predicament wherein the once (or still) oppressed classes in society organize themselves politically, specifically around the common feature of their oppressions (whether gender, language, race, religion, ethnicity, or sexuality). The concept is defined as "simply a section of society in which all the members have some characteristic in common."[96] David Harvey lends to this narrative a way of understanding how peoples and societies develop core political values, whether the individuation of neoliberalism or the collectivist assumptions of tribes, clans, or other political forms against which it competes. In his view, "For any way of thought to become dominant, a conceptual apparatus has to be advanced that appeals to our intuitions and instincts, to our values and our desires, as well as to the possibilities inherent in the social world we inhabit. If successful, this conceptual apparatus becomes so embedded in common sense as to be taken for granted and not open to question."[97] If the slippery category of blackness is the "palm of a hand," then other multiple, intersectional, and mutually constituted categories of being might be its multiple phalanges and metacarpals, no less than the hand.

The late documentarian Marlon Riggs likened the diversities among black people to gumbo, insisting that its roux base held all other ingredients together.[98] The notion that people embedded in a matrix of racism would, in turn, mobilize on that most salient basis, rather than some other, is self-evident. This takes seriously the problematic consequences of "consensus issues," which Cathy Cohen underscores on the way to emphasizing equally legitimating "cross-cutting" issues of subunits or subgroups within communities. Indeed, they refer to issues that "*disproportionately and directly affect* only certain segments of a marginal group."[99] Especially challenging essentialist artifacts of the earliest epochs of African American political history, in which racism disproportionately impacted nearly *all* members of "the group," "cross-cutting issues represent the distinct, racialized, experiences of different segments of black communities, the fragmentation that threatens a perceived unified black group identity and interest, and the corresponding reduction in the probability and effectiveness of political mobilization of blacks as a group."[100] Yet both of these ways of being in the world stand in peril of being naturalized.

The problem of competitive issue evolution, or prioritizing, the salience and supremacy of one or some over others is as much dependent upon a given political context as is the mobilization of certain biases. The layers of identity that an individual or collective may make salient in relation to dominant but still competitive issues would necessarily be transient (as unfixed as blackness) in order to avoid the same aggregating tendency that they frown upon. This is to suggest that as scholars disaggregate possible categories of belonging, dichotomizing, or conversely intersecting multiple potentialities, the marginalization of the most marginalized must extend to an infinite point of absurdity. If "blackness" was socially manufactured in the tentacles of white supremacy as an overarching category that absconded with "the often hidden differences, cleavages, or fault lines of marginal communities,"[101] is it not incumbent that we unpack the "subhierarchies" that exist among them? Should not all possible classifications (class, gender, "intersectionality," sexuality) be subject to the same level of scrutiny as, say, blackness in order to safeguard against displacing one form of oppressed hegemony with others? To think that there are not also marginalized individuals who significantly contribute to mobilizations of consensus flies in the face of the supreme efforts of too many perspectives. Powerful women and others whose feminist commitments or sexuality may never be known participated in the epochal movements of African Americans, often shaping agendas.[102]

The homogenous unit principle focuses on endogenous processes in which individual group members agree to attempt or to actually mobilize culturally or politically en masse to some desired end. The homogenous unit principle relates to the collectivist, multi-individual calculus involved in decisionmaking. Elites have no special place in the activation of a group's centripetal or centrifugal tendencies; instead, highly individualized decisions—whether concerning baptism or voting—are obviated.[103] Multi-individualism carries with it the meaning "that many people participate in the act."[104] Consonant with multi-individuality is "mutual interdependence," in which "all those taking the decision are intimately known to each other and *take the step in view of what the other is going to do.*"[105] Its exogenous features refract the broad racial, cultural, or political milieu that powerfully influences the deliberations.

Robin Kelley takes issue with scholars who attribute the decline of the left to "identity" or "oppression" politics and studies in intellectual circles. He believes that Black Power and its post-1960s identity derivatives have been charged with jumping progressive class-centered politics on the way to everybody's liberation, which was, apparently, on the horizon just before the term "Black Power" was uttered. Since then, class—with its ostensibly common-denominator appeal to students, gays, women, white heterosexual males, Latinos, African Americans, Native Americans, and various Asian populations—is thought to have been lost in the fray of identity particularism and parochialism.

There was also the waning sense among Students for a Democratic Society who came to feel a "little tired of the morally satisfying but ultimately vicarious job of 'supporting our black brothers.'"[106] The children of the McCarthy-era left learned from their parents' defeats (and retreats into the nation's establishment business, professional, labor, and academic sectors) and largely had no real ideological commitments toward civil rights, Black Power, or much of anything else until the draft for Vietnam. If the verbal militancy of black activists repelled white radicals, then conditional support of white militants reinforced the feeling among the black community that it was on its own when contending with hostile forces in government and society. To this end, Kelley contends, "the labor movement must make antiracism, antisexism, and antihomophobia foundational. This absurd argument that minority aggressiveness was responsible for white male backlash at the tail end of the 1960s masks the fact that the tragedy of most progressive movements in the United States has been white racism."[107]

In this context, "the traditional revolutionary groups and those seeking a solution in the field of organized labor, found themselves more at a loss than ever as reaction to black demands became more severe. It has finally become clear to the militants that the bitterest resistance to the Negro's struggle comes from the white working class."[108] Despite the race chauvinism of large segments of white workers in social relations, and the general misfit links between European radicalism and the black American predicament, class has been viewed as the "one universal category that unites us all and can lift us out of the dismal swamp of identity politics."[109]

Ira Katznelson's investigation clarifies the functional separation between the communal lives of workers and their assembly-line militancy that, at times, reflected interracial solidarity but were still routinely undermined by the "national histories of working classes" in the United States. In essence, American workers more or less accept their common social class identities in the workplace, but not in residential communities. White workers, especially, separated work from home, and thus racial and ethnic identities have tended to trump social class at home and in communal living.[110] To make the point, Katznelson explains how South Side millworkers in Chicago saw "themselves as labor . . . and as labor they are quite militant. The ordinary idiom of plant life is that of class. There, clear majorities vote for radical insurgencies within their union. Yet as soon as these workers pack up and go home, they cease to see themselves primarily as workers." Adolph Reed rejects identity standpoints only to, in turn, promote the form he prefers: "It is not that class is in some way more real or authentic than other identities, though it is certainly possible to argue that in this society class—as functional location in the system of social reproduction—is the social relation through which other identities are constituted and experienced within political economy." He insists that "there is a pragmatic justification that is sufficient for taking class as the identity around which to organize."[111]

Analysts critical of nationalism and/or nationalists now perfunctorily cite the homophobia of Eldridge Cleaver's defamation of James Baldwin in the 1960s, the reputed inamoratas of white women among the Black Panther Party's male leadership, and the lack of moral agency among male elites in Elijah Muhammad's Nation of Islam, including the relative subordinate status of the group's Muslim Girls in Training, or the mostly male-attended MMM/DOA.[112] Cleaver writes, for instance, that "there is in James Baldwin's work the most grueling, agonizing, total hatred of the blacks, particularly of himself, and the most shameful, fanatical, fawning, sycophantic love of the whites that one can find in the writings of any black American writer of note in our time."[113] Rooted in racial self-hatred, Cleaver contends, black male "homosexuality is a sickness, just as are baby-rape or wanting to become head of General Motors."[114] For whatever it is worth, Cleaver concludes his analysis on the note that considers "cruel" the "ubiquitous phenomenon" of "punk-hunting" (what today we call gay-bashing) and as psychologically related to "the ritualistic lynchings and castrations inflicted on Southern [heterosexual] black men by Southern whites." Add to this Baraka's highly influential call to arms in the posthumous tribute to Malcolm X, "A Poem for Black Hearts," which includes the lines: "for Great Malcolm a prince of the earth. Let nothing in us rest until we avenge ourselves for his death, stupid animals that killed him, let us never breathe a pure breath if we fail, and white men call us faggots till the end of the earth."[115] The reputed homophobic orientation of black nationalist masculinism is thrown into sharper relief. Similarly, the sexual proclivities of intellectuals and political elites, such as Langston Hughes, Countee Cullen, James Baldwin, and Bayard Rustin, were used as political leverage against their heterosexual associates. This was a favorite tactic of Harlem congressman Adam Clayton Powell; he used it against Martin Luther King Jr. on the occasion when King (in concert with A. Philip Randolph) threatened to organize a 5,000-person march against the 1960 Democratic National Convention in order to extend the momentum of the movement; Powell in turn threatened to fabricate a sexual liaison between Rustin and King.[116]

After providing a very useful definition of black nationalism as "black American common sense," Wahneema Lubiano immediately succumbs to the worn-out, nauseating charge that "its most hegemonic appearances and manifestations have been masculinist and homophobic." More troubling is the extent to which Kevin Gaines's study of late-nineteenth- and early-twentieth-century "uplift ideology" morphs into a single-minded emphasis on African American male bourgeois elites and how they imbibed the pervasive and perennial Victorian cultural and familial strictures that muted and mocked women's participation in political discourse. Gaines properly locates the oppositional dimensions in male nationalisms within a coterie of women's marginality, "Black nationalism, like dominant Anglo-American nationalism, was intensely concerned with gender issues and illustrates the affinity between black and white anxieties surrounding racial purity, intermarriage, paternity, and the reproductive sexuality of black and white women."[117] Moreover, "such preoccupation with the race's manhood not only inhibited social analysis and political strategy, but also could lead to attacks on other blacks whose perceived weakness—or lack of manliness—betrayed racial ideals. Within this scheme of manliness as black militancy, black women's racial credentials were already rendered suspect."[118] Thus, "such leading black women intellectuals as Anna Julia Cooper and Ida B. Wells found themselves marginalized within black bourgeois and nationalist ideologies that equated race progress with male dominance and Victorian ideals of sexual difference in both political and domestic life." As an afterthought in this critique, Gaines notes,

> It is difficult in the last analysis, to see the preoccupation with race "conservation" and endogamous marriage entirely in isolation from the southern, and increasingly national, *policing of black male sexuality*. By the "sexual revolution" of the 1960s, black nationalist media celebrities such as Eldridge

Cleaver and Melvin Van Peebles would abandon such decorous, chaste self-restraint and resort to phallo-centric self assertion, inverting the stereotypical terms that had trivialized blacks' political rights with the insinuation of "social equality." . . . In his hyper-masculinist view black women existed not as exalted exemplars of female chastity but as sex objects, and in Cleaver's case, as targets of a vengeful misogyny.[119]

Yet, like many others, Gaines succumbs to the post–Black Power intellectual obligation to isolate black nationalism in this discourse. In his discussion of Anna Julia Cooper and Ida B. Wells (women committed programmatically to integrationism, not nationalism as such) he ignores how Wells was given token recognition in the integrationist NAACP, or how a noteworthy person such as Maria Stewart of Boston had been universally neglected as a literary and activist figure, whom Paula Giddings lists among the "thrown away" black female activists of the nineteenth century.[120] Rather, he attributes Cooper's and Wells's marginalization to *unnamed* male black nationalists.[121] In other words, the bait in Gaines's critique is the marginalization of women historically in uplift ideological discourses, generally. But the switch comes, perfunctorily, when only nationalism is mentioned specifically, which, in turn, reinforces the black nationalist militant's burden of taking on all the transideological baggage of patriarchal abuse. Gaines fails to distinguish between uplift ideology, which is presumably an elite, class-driven tendency that attaches itself to the larger predicament of poor, peasant, and oppressed African Americans, and the continuum of ideological orientations that have informed black politics throughout several centuries of articulated protest thought. His conceptualization of uplift ideology becomes a screen for black nationalism.[122]

Currently, uplift ideology is the ideological tool of its critics, and it is intellectually valorized by them more readily than by any identifiable segment of black leadership (the "moral" uplift of black religion—whether Islamic, Christian, or other—may be the exception). Although the criticisms are pro forma in regard to nationalist adherents, among whom they have their greatest viscidity since Black Power, they would be appropriate across and even internally among the various identity formations.[123] William Jelani Cobb notes that

the caliber of nationalist thought has most certainly declined since Malcolm X issued his "Ballot or the Bullet" ultimatum. And save the intellectual pot liquor of Afrocentrism, Black nationalism is out of vogue—denigrated for its patriarchal and homophobic excesses (problems that, it should be noted, were far from absent within Black liberal and integrationist quarters). Intellectually soldered to the onerous concept of racial "essentialism," Black nationalist thought has fallen into disfavor in an era where race is routinely dismissed as a "social construct." But for most black people in the United States, society is a *racial construct.* . . . That is to say, irrespective of its specious biological origins, race remains a central axis of black—and thereby white—life in America in a way that no amount of deconstruction has altered.[124]

With regard to patriarchy, Patricia Hill Collins maintains that none of the major orientations is devoid of employing myopic "manly" nodes of social criticism and political organization:

> Black women's activism is also distinctive in challenging some fundamental gendered assumptions that underlie both Black nationalism and racial integration. Within U.S. Black politics, both ideologies advance beliefs concerning what constitutes gender-appropriate political behavior for African-American women and men. Within Black nationalist organizations espousing Black nationalist ideologies, women are often associated with the private sphere of family and community—conceptualized as a Black nation within a nation— with men expected to defend this Black community within the public sphere of U.S. social institution. . . . Similarly until recently Black women participants in civil rights organizations routinely did not serve as leaders and spokespersons. In both cases, gender-specific norms associate Black men's political activism with *public* sphere actions outside the organization itself and Black women's activism with *private* sphere activities within the organization. . . . They also limit organizational efficacy on confronting social justice.[125]

Robin Kelley insists the tensions between communists and Garveyites on race and nationalism following World War I "shared in the gendered language which defined the act of resistance as a masculine rite of passage. Indeed, the different organizations' artists and propagandists found common ground on the terrain of gender. Proletarian realism consciously evinced masculine images and defined class *struggle* as a male preserve." Proletarian culture was masculine; the culture of the nationalists was frocked in "manhood" discourses and male-on-male confrontation. In the end, Kelley concludes that during this period, one in which the Communist Party USA and the Socialist Worker's Party finally agreed to promote national self-determination among blacks, it "not only took precedence over women's struggles, but it essentially precluded a serious theoretical framework that might combine the 'Negro' and 'woman' questions."[126] Black socialist Asa Philip Randolph, leader of the Brotherhood of Sleeping Car Porters in its struggle against the Pullman Company, and a leader of the 1941 and 1963 Marches on Washington, stood firmly and singly against the widespread homophobia concerning Bayard Rustin's leadership in the movement in the 1960s. But decades earlier Randolph organized the "Brotherhood" in terms of masculine confrontation despite the union membership of black maids in the group. In fact, it was originally the Brotherhood of Sleeping Car Porters and *Maids* until 1930. Clarence Taylor notes that Randolph's decision to remove "Maids" from the name, not the union, "was clearly a strategic move to genderize the union. Employing Maids in the union's name would have put severe limitations on Randolph's use of gender as a unifying force." The removal of "Maids," coupled with a masculine discourse, strongly suggests that Randolph and union officials would not have tolerated what today some might call the "feminization of their organization."[127] Also, women were not to exercise leadership in the Brotherhood, and their ascribed roles were to be auxiliary and in the domestic realm, leaving work in the public spaces to men.

Many scholars have understated the extent to which community-level and neighborhood violence—overwhelmingly male against male—has impacted the lives of *women* of color as participants, witnesses, mothers, family members, and victims. Aida Hartudo adds, "Drugs, prison, discrimination, poverty, and racism continue to deprive women of Color of their children at alarming rates in contemporary U.S. society."[128] Black women's intersections include the cold, blunt reality of mothering male and female children who are disproportionately impacted. Focusing on the persistent social, educational, penal, and economic problems of, especially, poorer African American boys and men is uniquely within the purview of African American women's public policy concerns. For this reason, Hartudo adds that "white women had similar tensions around gender issues in the political movements of the New Left. But, unlike many white feminists who opted, eventually, for splitting off from the men, most Chicana and Black women, with a few individual exceptions, never contemplated leaving their group, regardless of their dissatisfaction with the men's behavior. Instead, most have stayed and have continued to struggle through the gender issues that persist in the most progressive groups."[129] Yet Hartudo's argument appropriately reiterates how "the masculinist underpinnings of nationalism prevented men activists in the movements from addressing gender issues, and, ultimately, the movements were unable to develop and grow into a more sophisticated analysis. Women of Color, however, did not leave their respective movements but instead, built pockets of mobilizations around gender issues and continued to struggle with men on behalf of their communities."

Carr notes

> this confusion on the question of women and the feminine reemerges in the ideology of Black Power. Black Power sought to transform the operative political paradigm of the black social body from a "woman" into a "revolutionary man," a transformation necessitating arms, which is synonymous with justice, revolt, pride, balls, true blackness, power, the new black body, the new black nation, men, and theoretically women, in the process, punks or faggots—and even more certainly, on the rare occasion the subspecies is mentioned, lesbians—must be weeded out as a disease infesting *the nation*. Sexuality, gender, is thus a central political concept.[130]

All of the talk (and writing) of sex, sexuality, power, gender, and race was not endemic to black nationalism in a vacuum; indeed, this was a salient period during which sex and sexuality loomed in the public consciousness in the throes of postwar and antiestablishment social struggles; the world of Ward and June Cleaver was disrupted by the likes of Eldridge Cleaver.

Black women and others, such as Queen Mother Audley Moore, Grace Lee Boggs, and Yuri Kochiyama, powerfully shaped the politics of Black

Power. Any objective analysis of the audio and video footage of the James Meredith "March Against Fear" will observe a decidedly female chorus in the call-response to Carmichael and Willie Rick's chant for "Black Power!" John Bracey and Sharon Harley argue, for instance, that the key revolutionary nationalist figure Max Stanford (Muhammad Ahmad), leader of Revolutionary Action Movement (RAM), "fused the thought of Robert F. Williams on armed self defense with the philosophy of Malcolm X on black self-determination. To these tenets, Stanford added a sophisticated Marxian revolutionary philosophy, which he derived from a close personal association with the legendary Queen Mother Audley Moore" (an unrepentant Garveyite).[131] Indeed, if Garvey can be viewed as a "father" of Black Power, then women such as Ella Baker, Fannie Lou Hamer, Unita Blackwell,[132] Ruby Davis Robinson,[133] and Queen Mother Moore were, more or less, its mothers. The masculinist afterbirth of Black Power was exigent and more a generational artifact than a theoretical principle of unreconstructable black nationalism.

The ideological framing to which black nationalism has and continues to be subjected is accomplished through a number of selective readings that make the masculine capital it fed no less indefensible. Some African American political scientists and feminist intellectuals rightly credit Kimberlé Crenshaw with coining "intersectional" terminology,[134] and they attribute its practice to the short public career of the nineteenth-century figure Maria (Miller) Stewart. What is instructive is the extent to which some tamp the agency of African American women nationalists, "Despite her [Stewart's] burgeoning feminist views, she continued to reinforce patriarchal norms by daring black men to fulfill their 'manly' duties."[135] Political philosopher Tommie Shelby argues, in turn,

> Delany valued and sought to encourage the moral virtue, if one might call it that, of *manhood*. Despite the unfortunate term, *manhood*, as Delany understood it, is a quality of character that is not peculiar to men, as women also value and fully embody it. No doubt, Delany was not using the term manhood in a purely gender-neutral way. . . . Delany certainly did have patriarchal beliefs and sentiments, as of course did most people at the time. . . . Despite these typical but inexcusable sexist prejudices, Delany clearly wanted women to cultivate "manly" character, though perhaps not to the same extent or in quite the same ways as men. *Vigor* would perhaps have been a more appropriate and less masculinist term to describe the relevant ensemble of traits.[136]

Delany, as Nikol Alexander-Floyd notes, thought contemporaneously with the gendered Victorian assumptions of the day, seeing "in the black man the hope for the future of the race and, in the black woman, the helpmate of the man, minding the home and children," and spoke in the vernacular manliness and metonymic claims: "*Africa for the African race, and black men to rule them.*"[137] It is equally true that Delany's most neglected work, *Blake, or the*

Huts of America (1859–1861 [1971]), presents the protagonist Blake, whose longing for his sold and enslaved wife, Maggie, looms over the book, as does his longing for freedom for her family and all enslaved black people. Blake's love for Maggie causes him to risk death in confronting their master with the detail that his own enslavement was voluntary; he expresses that both "I and my wife have been robbed of our liberty." As if to anticipate black women's multiple struggles, first in slavery, Delany throughout the book highlights the role of white women in Maggie's enslavement, sale, and detainment in Cuba. If African womanist Tolagbe Ogunleye lacks a critical edge in her reading of Delany as a "male-womanist scholar and practitioner who dedicated his life to a gender-inclusive formation and/or restoration of African nations,"[138] her study strains no less than those, such as Paul Gilroy's, that depict Delany as "the progenitor of black Atlantic patriarchy."[139]

What is collateralized by Charise Cheney and others is the extent to which Stewart's "burgeoning feminism" comported with the "protonationalist" and nationalist men who strongly—and singly—supported her unprecedented emergence on the scene of Boston's abolitionist black community; they were not a priori irreconcilable; neither was black nationalism a priori one-dimensionally a masculinist project. From the birth of her public career through her marriage by the Reverend Thomas Paul, pastor of Boston's African Baptist Church, to her late fight for her widow's pension, to writing the introduction to her *Meditations* (1879), and to being eulogized by Alexander Crummell,[140] this harbinger of intersectional praxis (according to Crummell) enjoyed unfettered public support from male nationalists *when it was patently impolitic for women to show interest outside of the domestic sphere.* Namely, Stewart was supported by Walker, Garnet, Thomas Sydney, and Crummell, who claims to have known her over a forty-year period.[141] She is noted as "a forerunner to generations of the best known and most influential champions of black activism, both male and female, including Frederick Douglass, Sojourner Truth, and Frances Harper.[142] According to Joy James, "Radical women embraced and shaped the political ideologies espoused by black male intellectuals such as Malcolm X" and Paul Robeson.[143] In order to sustain a feminist critique of phallic black nationalism, some analysts have necessarily tamped down the legacies of "proto-womanist" black nationalist men and black women nationalists. Conversely, Evelyn Simeon has insisted that African American men have yielded higher levels of support for some measures of *black feminism than black women* generally.[144]

According to Joy James, for instance, Paul Robeson demanded, in *Here I Stand,* that "we need more of our women in the higher ranks, too, and who should know better . . . than the children of Harriet Tubman, Sojourner Truth, and Mary Church Terrell that our womenfolk have often led the way. Negro womanhood today is giving us many inspiring examples of steadfast devotion, cool courage under fire, and brilliant generalship in our people's struggles: and here is the major source for new strength and militancy in Negro leadership in every level."[145] In Harlem, Lorraine Hansberry was a protégé of Robeson's whose advocacy on behalf of "women fighting against racism in the United States, and the struggles of female peace activists in Asia, Africa, South America, and the Caribbean," led John Killens to refer to her as "a black nationalist with a socialist perspective."[146] James, like Collins's *From Black Power to Hip-Hop*, despite the admittedly indefensible vulgarization of black nationalism by some baby-boomer nationalists finds a mutually rein-forcing symbiosis in some male nationalists, and "radical women [who] em-braced and shaped the political ideologies espoused by black male intellectu-als such as Malcolm X."[147]

Community Feminism: Mimicking Men or Broadening Black Nationalist Discourse

Some otherwise useful feminist criticisms of black nationalist excesses have been disinclined to note the manner in which the narratives of "community feminists" militate against one-dimensional characterizations of black nation-alism as solely or a priori a masculinist project. Community feminists include women black nationalists, according to Ula Yvette Taylor, such as Maria Stew-art; Bessie Delany (sister of Martin Delany); Sojourner Truth (though not a committed nationalist, she promoted emigration in the Reconstruction era when it was least popular); Amy Ashwood Garvey; Amy Jacques Garvey; Au-dley "Queen" Mother Moore; the actress Henrietta Vinton Davis (Garvey's second in command in international organizing during UNIA's formative years);[148] Bibi Amina Baraka and the women of the Black Women's United Front (BWUF); Dara Abubakari (who served for a time as copresident of the Republic of New Afrika, RNA, with Imari Obadele); and Dr. Betty Shabazz, who maintained close ties with nationalist efforts in the modern Black Con-vention movement. Indeed, although most of these women's interests in na-tionalism should be viewed in light of their husbands' commitments, these ac-tivists and organizers are too important to be relegated to subsidiary positionality in black nationalist historiographies. And it may also be true that women nationalists like Betty "Bahiyah" Shabazz, Amy Ashwood Garvey, and Amy Jacques Garvey were ideologically predisposed and held analogous ide-ological tendencies akin to their husbands' before marriage.

Other important black nationalist women fought battles from within the black arts component of Black Power. Cheryl Clarke's *"After Mecca": Women Poets and the Black Arts Movement* provides a critical analysis of the manner in which the black arts movement privileged men's compensatory equation of black liberation with black male standing in society and within the movement. For a time, a number of black women nationalists and poets, such as Sonia

Sanchez and Gwendolyn Brooks, employed language, rhetoric, and confrontational style typical of black men in the environment. Clarke notes, for instance,

> Despite its nationalist/separatist gestures, the Black Arts Movement changed the reception of black culture worldwide. However, its theory of redemptive/ compensatory manhood absorbed the "race" as a whole in the United States. The New World social castration collectively experienced by black people feminized the "race." Given this circumstance, the "race" must become "men" and move violently past this historic and collective emasculation.[149]

Carolyn Rodgers, Audre Lorde, June Jordan, Alice Walker, Nikki Giovanni, Toni Morrison, and Ntozake Shange, among many others, developed their feminist-womanist critiques of the black male prerogative from within the black liberation movement and developed their subsequent bodies of work from both negative and affirming experiences within the black arts movement. As some black men would react later to the film rendition of Walker's *Color Purple* for its largely unflattering depiction of the abusive male protagonist, "Mister," and its other men, many black intellectuals, male and female, reacted negatively to Michele Wallace's 1979 book, *Black Macho and the Myth of the Superwoman.* June Jordan's review of the book exposes it as an unbalanced form of feminist chauvinism against African American male activists, black women activists, and white women—little more than an exercise of academic reportage wracked with inaccuracies on critical facts.[150] In the book, the author applies a "sexual analysis" to civil rights and Black Power during the black liberation struggle and reduces them to the matter of interracial dating and love.[151] An intemperate response from one cultural nationalist scholar, Askia M. Toure, likened the work and Shange's *For Colored Girls Who Have Considered Suicide When the Rainbow Is Enuf* to a withering critique associating the works with COINTELPRO and the attempt of white feminists to garrison black women against black men.[152] But even Cheryl Clarke's study fails to address the black nationalism of the black women poets as a product of their own agency. Rather, her work tends to treat the black nationalist commitments of black women as something that inhibited a more mature, multifaceted criticism of race and gender oppression in a question begging promotion of feminist and womanist poststructuralism. So when the lines from Giovanni's famous 1968 poem "The True Import of the Present Dialogue, Black vs. Negro," urges, "Can we learn to kill WHITE for Black Learn to kill niggers Learn to be Black men," it is an appropriation of the "rhetoric often attributed in the main to their male comrades and counterparts . . . while subscribing, through lyric expression, to the dictates of womanhood within the circle. "They, like black men, would use 'culture as a weapon' of construction and destruction."[153]

In essence, black women's nationalism was not their own. According to Ula Yvette Taylor, "community feminists" like Amy Jacques Garvey opted to reconcile their mutually constituted and multilayered commitments as women, workers, the poor, mothers, wives (for those who were married), and racially oppressed with the related extrinsic matters of social and political discourse. For her, these women are those "who may or may not live in a coverture relationship; either way, their activism is focused on assisting *both* the men and women in their lives—whether husbands or sisters, fathers or mothers, sons or daughters—along with initiating and participating in activities to 'uplift' their communities." They are, in fact, "undeniably *feminists* in that their activism discerns the configuration of oppressive power relations, shatters masculinist claims of women as intellectually inferior, and seeks to empower women by expanding their roles and options. . . . [C]ommunity feminism counters a macropolitical model that implies that there is something inherently 'pure' or 'essential' of feminist theory. By decentering feminist epistemologies, the multiple identities of black women, along with communitarian ideas (the rejection of self-interest and the autonomous individual in recognition of the self as collective, interdependent, and relational), take center stage."[154]

As much as their liberation *from* white men would leave them in the throes of sexism and patriarchy, their liberation as women would not mitigate the impact of race in their lives and in the lives of their families and children. Political scientist Michael C. Dawson adds that this focus has led many black feminist women to believe that "the quest to eliminate patriarchy and white supremacy must be connected to the liberation of the entire black community."[155] This approach has led some to reject the term "black feminism" in favor of a term with roots inside the black community: "womanism." Those adopting the term "black feminist" and those who prefer "womanist" believe that this concern "with eliminating all oppressions, and the emphasis on community, necessitate a more communal approach that rejects the liberal individualism of the dominant society."[156]

In addition to the traditions of community feminists and womanists, which have been obfuscated in the post–civil rights ideological conflicts and academic provincialism, large segments of African American women and men participate daily in shaping and refining community-level discourses and share some political and ideological consonance. "Gender suicide" and perfidy have rarely prevented African American women from participating fully in all forms of black American race politics. For Collins, black nationalism has been a two-edged sword. On the one hand, it is not to be regarded as "irrational— it has been essential for Black progress." That is, "Black women's path to a 'feminist' consciousness often occurs within the context of antiracist social justice projects, many of them influenced by Black nationalist ideologies."[157] On the other hand, it inheres in a "norm of solidarity based on Black women's unquestioned support of Black men to Black women"[158] and results in "equat[ing] racial progress with the acquisition of an ill-defined manhood [which] has left much U.S. Black thought with a prominent masculinist bias."[159] If it is true that "all the Blacks are men, all the women are whites"—

a phrase that leaves black women and white men in an irreducible coalitional arrangement (considering that the various subaltern populations in the United States and abroad are positioned in relation to the latter)—then the foregoing analysis suggests that despite the excesses of whole generations of African American male nationalists, *all the womanists are not feminists, all the black nationalists are not men.* If it is true also that gender should be conceptualized as socialized power relations between the sexes, rather than as a binary biological category, it becomes incumbent that this deconstruction take into account the extent to which, in concrete aspects of the long history of race oppression (in the forms of lynching, convict leasing, disproportionate rates of incarceration, unemployment patterns, and so forth), African American men or Chicano men, for example, have been *gender oppressed* as *men*.[160] Otherwise, gender becomes essentialized in inverse only in the service of certain discourses.[161]

As black women feminists and womanists (as well as Chicanas and others) critically allow for an understanding of their relational positionality *within* a feminist, class, race, or language matrix vis-à-vis white bourgeois feminism, it must also be recognized that much of the manly and manhood nodes of engagement that characterized such political discourse, however it has delimited the extent and the rapidity with which hegemonic structures have been or can be toppled, illuminates the gender oppression of black and other nonwhite men. Thus, Ossie Davis's eulogy of Malcolm X stated: as "our manhood, our living Black manhood, this was his meaning to his people." For better and for worse, this was placed in a rubric of male specificity, reflecting the oppression of black men as males. And thus Dwight Hopkins's reading of black theology consequently led him to call for "a new Black heterosexual male" who renounces "the normative definition of the male gender that is established and defined by the larger white male culture."[162]

The struggles of women with Ella Baker's skill within the civil rights movement compounded the general atmosphere of presumptive male leadership, and only very recently have scholars had the temerity to address the sexual utility of women in it vis-à-vis Martin Luther King Jr. and his ministerial colleagues.[163] Baker and the SCLC executive committee member Septima Clark were frustrated by the chauvinism of the ministers and how, as Clark describes, "those men didn't have any faith in women, none whatsoever. They just thought women were sex symbols and had no contribution to make." She adds, "Like other black ministers, Dr. King didn't think too much of the way women could contribute. But working in the movement, he changed so many lives of so many people that it was getting to the place where he would have to see that women were more than sex symbols." Patricia Hill Collins poses the argument that African American women contributed two features of political development that are relevant. The first has to do with the diversity of black women's oppression and how the particularity of those experiences fed a broader vision of institutional transformation. Rather than black nationalism and black specificity being ends in themselves, to her thinking "many women begin their political activism as advocates for African-Americans, the poor, or, less frequently, women. But over time black women activists come to see oppressions as interconnected and the need for broad-based political action. Rather than joining a range of organizations, each devoted to single-purpose issues, many black women activists either start new organizations or work to transform the institutions in which they are situated."[164] Second, she highlights how, even in disrespected spaces while working in the mainstream of civil rights, Septima Clark, Ella Baker, and other women "carried distinctive notions of leadership and empowerment into the black civil rights struggle." "Black women's style of activism also reflects a belief that teaching people to be self-reliant fosters more empowerment than teaching them to follow. . . . The models of leadership offered by both Septima Clark and Ella Baker speak to a distinctively Black female mode of political activism"; they encouraged models of intensely engaged participatory democracy, relational community empowerment, and horizontal principles of mobilization.

Few post–civil rights treatments of black nationalism, especially studies by men, fail to acknowledge the strident heterosexist patriarchal nodes of baby-boomer black nationalisms or those of the hip-hop nation. Failure to acknowledge this implies that contemporary black nationalisms do not "get" what the women of the Cohambee River Collective and its intellectual and activist progeny have forcefully argued for more than three decades. Contemporary studies by African American male scholars have seriously incorporated the critical readings of feminist scholarship without engaging in vindicatory, despiteous, or phallic renditions. Joseph's analysis of Eldridge Cleaver's emergence among Black Panther activists, and his book *Soul on Ice*, led him to conclude, "[If] Cleaver's analysis of race, sex, and power staked a claim for an oppressive type of black masculinity, it also, perhaps unwittingly, spurred intraparty debates about women's role in the Panthers. More a polemical creed than a conventional intellectual analysis, *Soul on Ice* would haunt the Black Power movement long after Cleaver's public change of heart, as well as the party's, would come to adopt progressive ideas about black women's equality."[165] Carmichael's infamous and sophomoric quip concerning the "prone" position of women in the *integrationist* SNCC in 1964, especially in light of white activist women's position paper on sex and caste in the activist realm, exacerbated the position of African American women activists, people whom Joseph identifies as "Black Power feminists."[166] And this comment by Carmichael was a bit of a sarcastic observation after his rant that there was too much sex among student activists, when the focus was supposed to be on mobilizing communities.

Charise Cheney's critique highlights how scholarship dominated by womanist and black feminist intellectuals has effectively critiqued black nationalism's excesses, missteps, and very existence; in fact, feminist scholarship has produced *more* work on black nationalism than any other ideological orientation. The tendency is to elucidate the phallic or, as bell hooks notes, "it's-a-dick-thing" nationalism. Nikol Alexander-Floyd's book theorizes on the intersecting and shared spaces of the rights and rites of interracial male privilege in the seemingly gender-innocent tropes of "the" community, which accompany disdain for pathological ghetto-dwelling black women (welfare queens) and their offspring (e.g., the endangered black male), forging a virtual nationalist "Gentlemen's Agreement" between Euro-American white and African American men concerning the Black Cultural Pathology Paradigm (BCPP), which centers black women as causes célèbres and black feminists as race traitors. Her study launches a veritable call to arms against black nationalism, resuscitating debates around Moynihan's *The Negro Family: A Case for National Action* (1965) and Michele Wallace's *Black Macho and the Myth of the Superwoman* (1979). Wallace's book is celebrated as a widely misunderstood and prescient black feminist analysis that launched a salvo linking ostensibly warring black and white male nationalists, who Alexander-Floyd insists forge a "wounded masculinity" alliance around single black female sourcing of underclass cultural and moral depravities.

Last, intra feminist critiques of US black feminists make similar charges concerning masculinist nationalism and the metonymic ways in which "black" in feminist discourse resounds with a provincial "American" accent, marginalizing diasporic black feminist or womanist voices.[167] The charges of sexism and chauvinism, deservedly aimed at many leading black male nationalists historically, is a charge that heterofeminist discourses have themselves been subjected to of late. Debates concerning sexuality mortgage feminist scholarship until "the emergence of queer theory [in turn] begins to express ambivalence about feminism both for its understanding of gender and for its exclusion of certain concerns." Feminism can be read dialectically to comport with masculinist nationalism; feminism can analogously take on its own terms as "gendered nationalism," policing the boundaries of gender and sexuality. bell hooks's move from charges of "it's-a-dick-thing" masculinity in black nationalism seamlessly to a black feminist discourse heralding "Power to the Pussy" is exemplary.[168] The irony is that both intellectual black nationalism and feminism are patently marginal discourses in the lives of ordinary people outside of what Todd Boyd calls "academic esoterica."[169]

None of the foregoing is intended to trivialize the deservedly critical observations of masculinist excesses of the nationalist activists in early-nineteenth-century black Zionism, in Garveyism and the Nation of Islam, or in Black Power. But it is to suggest that despite the very real and obstructionist effects of patriarchy, chauvinism, and homophobia among civil rights elites, generally, they are cast as problems inherent in black nationalism. As a form of African American political thought and organizing, black nationalism suffered from the several major self-made and external inflictions covered in this chapter that undermined the development of a mature, holistic approach toward racial solidarity.

Notes

1. However, Cedric Johnson reports that the SNCC used the phrase "Black Power for black people" in Alabama in 1965. See *Revolutionaries to Race Leaders: Black Power and the Making of African American Politics* (Minneapolis: University of Minnesota Press, 2007), p. xxi. In a discussion with Willie Ricks in March 2010 at the National Conference of Black Political Scientists annual meeting, he denied any knowledge of Powell's usage. He insists that students tested a number of phrases aimed at moving the consciousness of the movement beyond the "Freedom Now" appeal, which had been the main rallying call before "Black Power" was adopted and publicized.

2. Karen Orren and Stephen Skowronek, *Search for American Political Development*.

3. Ibid., p. 9.

4. Peniel E. Joseph, *Waiting 'Til the Midnight Hour: A Narrative History of Black Power in America* (New York: Owl, 2006), p. 12.

5. John Hope Franklin, *The Militant South, 1800–1861* (Urbana: University of Illinois Press, 1956 [2002]), p. 4.

6. Ibid., p. 84.

7. Peniel Joseph, *Waiting 'Til the Midnight Hour*, p. 53.

8. Dwight Hopkins, *Heart and Head*, p. 15.

9. Peniel Joseph, *Waiting 'Til the Midnight Hour*, p. 31.

10. The ABB was a nationalist organization that embraced Marxism under Briggs. And, of course, Frederick Douglass's placement is the subject of considerable debate in the literature.

11. Gloria Richardson defied many assumptions and conventions concerning expected, proper conduct of an older (she was in her forties when she emerged as a leader in Cambridge), more affluent (she came from a middle-class family background), educated woman (she attended Howard University from 1938 to 1942). Malcolm X valorized her in his 1963 "Message to the Grassroots" speech as an uncompromised local who reflected the kind of leadership that illustrated the spirit and thrust of what he called "The Black Revolution" (the break away from the civil rights leadership establishment and the King-inspired civil rights movement). See Anita K. Foeman, "Gloria Richardson: Breaking the Mold," *Journal of Black Studies* 26, no. 5 (May 1996): 604–615. See also Sandra Y. Milnner, "Recasting Civil Rights Leadership: Gloria Richardson and the Cambridge Movement," *Journal of Black Studies* 26, no. 6 (July 1996): 668–687.

12. Garvey was targeted for violation of the "white slavery" Mann Act for traveling abroad with his future wife (but then secretary), Amy Jacques Garvey (although she was clearly "Negro"); tax evasion through the foundering but highly influential Black Star Line; and finally federal mail-fraud violations.

13. The bureau was active during World War I, but it especially took form in 1919 with the creation of the General Intelligence Division. Between November 1919 and January 1920, the brutal Palmer Raids were exacted against more than 10,000 citizens and suppressed all political dissent and organizing. For a brief article on its suppression of Negro groups, organizations, media, and individuals, see Richard O. Boyer, "Gestapo, U.S.A.," in Samuel Sillen (ed.), *Masses and Mainstream* 4, no. 1 (1951): 15–22; Emory J. Tolbert, "Federal Surveillance of Marcus Garvey and the UNIA," *Journal of Ethnic Studies* 14, no. 4 (Winter 1987): 25–42; Edmond David Cronon, *Black Moses: The Story of Marcus Garvey and the Universal Negro Improvement Association* (Madison: University of Wisconsin Press, 1955); Amy Jacques Garvey, *Garvey and Garveyism* (New York: Macmillan, 1970); Theodore G. Vincent, *Black Power*

and the Garvey Movement (New York: Rampart, 1971); Tony Martin, *Race First: The Ideological and Organizational Struggles of Marcus Garvey and the Universal Negro Improvement Association* (New York: Greenwood, 1976); and Randall Kennedy, *Race, Crime, and the Law* (New York: Vintage, 1997), p. 108.

14. Emory Tolbert, "Federal Surveillance of Marcus Garvey and the U.N.I.A.," pp. 29–30.

15. Adolph Reed Jr. (ed.), *Race, Politics, and Culture: Critical Essays on the Radicalism of the 1960s* (New York: Greenwood, 1986), p. 61.

16. Ronald W. Walters, *White Nationalism*, pp. 224–225.

17. See Komozi Woodard, *A Nation Within a Nation*, p. 9. This is not to set aside the strong procapitalist tendencies among black nationalists, ranging from Paul Cuffee to Martin R. Delany and the Nation of Islam, but it is to suggest that the radical apparatus with which nationalists made their antiracist claims was amenable to anticapitalist protest, as seen, for instance, in the ABB (post–World War I), the Black Panther Party, and the rivaling cultural nationalists who later embraced so-called third-world Marxism.

18. Ronald Walters, *White Nationalism*.

19. George Breitman, Herman Porter, and Baxter Smith, *The Assassination of Malcolm X* (New York: Pathfinder, [1976] 1991), p. 11.

20. Michael Myerson, *Nothing Could Be Finer* (New York: International, 1978), p. 30. Myerson also lists, as sources to this claim, the testimony of a police informant named Louis Tackwood. Louis E. Tackwood and Citizens Research and Investigative Committee, *The Glass House Tapes: The Story of an Agent Provocateur and the New Police Intelligence Complex* (New York: Avon Books, 1973). A January 5, 1976, *New York Post* article suggested the FBI and Criminal Conspiracy Section of the Los Angeles Police Department created the organization for this purpose.

21. For some discussion on the subject of blacks and Watergate abuses, see Reginald Earl Gilliam Jr., *Black Political Development: An Advocacy Analysis* (Port Washington, NY: Kennikat, 1975), pp. 291–292.

22. The contemporary roots of militarized efforts to suppress domestic rebellion lie in the US Army's Garden Plot master plan (Department of Defense Civil Disturbance Plan 55-2). Since at least 1968, the military has expended billions of dollars in this effort. The plan was even activated during and after the Los Angeles uprisings of 1992. A view of details of this plan is possible by examining US Air Force Civil Disturbance Plan 55-2, Garden Plot, which is the "implementing" and "supporting plan for the Department of the Army (DA) Civil Disturbance Plan—GARDEN PLOT dated 1 March 1984 (which) provides for the employment of USAF forces in civil disturbances." It is specifically drawn up "to support the Secretary of the Army, as DOD Executive Agent for civil disturbance control operations (nicknamed GARDEN PLOT), with airlift and logistical support, in assisting civil authorities in the restoration of law and order through appropriate military commanders in the 50 States, District of Columbia, the Commonwealth of Puerto Rico and US possessions and territories, or any political subdivision thereof." The long title is United States Air Force Civil Disturbance Plan 55-2, Employment of USAF Forces in Civil Disturbances. The short title is USAF Civil Disturbance Plan 55-2. It's dated July 11, 1984.

23. Reginald Gilliam, *Black Political Development*, pp. 87–88.

24. With the exception of David Hilliard and Fredricka Newton's Black Panther Party Legacy Tour, the occasional campus speeches by Bobby Seale, who recently relocated there; an inconsequential 2004 voter registration drive in West Oakland (headed by Hilliard and Seale); and Hilliard and Seale's production, sales, and distribution of barbecue products, the Black Panther Party has been officially written out of Oakland's history and erased from the consciousness of all but its most indefatigable community-conscious

citizens. However, it is true that a student center at Merritt College in Oakland—where Newton and Seale were students when they formed the organization—was recently dedicated in honor of its founders. Moreover, on the fortieth anniversary (2006) of the founding of the Black Panther Party, the San Francisco Yerba Buena Center for the Arts presented an exhibit, "Black Panther Rank and File," which featured documents, recordings, film clips, archival photos, as well as the works of artists from the Black Power–Black Panther era.

25. See Randall Kennedy, *Race, Crime, and the Law* (New York: Vintage, 1997), p. 108.

26. Kennedy outlines the FBI's surveillance and harassment of individuals who were as ideologically irreconcilable as William Monroe Trotter, Marcus Garvey, W.E.B. Du Bois, Angela Davis, Martin Luther King Jr., and the Black Panther cadre.

27. Mary Frances Berry, *Black Resistance, White Law: A History of Constitutional Racism in America* (New York: Penguin, 1994).

28. Ibid., p. 111.

29. To get a sense of the thin line between student activism and street elements, see Elaine Brown, *A Taste of Power: A Black Woman's Story* (New York: Anchor, 1994).

30. Komozi Woodard, *A Nation Within a Nation*, p. 267. Hannah Arendt makes a very similar argument in her criticism of the student sit-ins. Not only does Arendt sharply criticize the use of children in the sit-in confrontations; she soundly condemns black rage as a misguided outpouring of emotion that legitimized the brutality of police and other racist forces. See Hannah Arendt, *On Violence*.

31. See Wahneema Lubiano, *The House That Race Built*, and her treatment of the film *Deep Cover*, where she presents an unconvincing analysis of its "black nationalist" cop protagonist, played by Bill Duke. Clarence Williams III's character in Keenon Ivory Wayans's *I'm Gonna Git You Sucka* is most instructive.

32. Robert O. Self, *New Day in Babylon: Race and the Struggle for Postwar Oakland* (Princeton: Princeton University Press, 2003), p. 13.

33. Cited in Ira Katznelson, *City Trenches: Urban Politics and the Patterning of Class in the United States* (New York: Pantheon, 1981), p. 3. Emphasis added.

34. See Stephan Thernstrom and Abigail Thernstrom, *America in Black and White: One Nation, Indivisible* (New York: Touchstone, 1997), pp. 247–250.

35. On these scores, Reginald Earl Gilliam Jr. cites the examples of Montgomery, Alabama, and Aiken, South Carolina, where, respectively, welfare recipients were forced to decide between sterilization and eligibility for welfare eligibility, and between sterilization and Medicaid prenatal care. His work also briefly addresses welfare policy with regard to late-night raids when a recipient was thought in violation of the no-man-in-the-house rules (which were outlawed by the 1968 *King v. Smith* Supreme Court decision). See Reginald Gilliam, *Black Political Development*, pp. 146–149.

36. Ibid., pp. 143–146.

37. Andrew Vincent, *Nationalism and Particularity*, p. 80. For an elaboration on the manner in which immigration policy and case law have shaped the racial character of the United States, please see David Theo Goldberg's *The Racial State* (Malden, MA: Blackwell Publishers, 2002).

38. Andrew Vincent, *Nationalism and Particularity*, p. 91. "The post-1945 generation of theorists—which was also the immediate post-war generation involved in setting up the United Nations and formulating the United Nations International Declaration of Human Rights (1948)—had a powerful effect on social and political thought in the English-speaking world, certainly up to the 1980s," p. 5.

39. See Hannah Arendt, *The Origins of Totalitarianism* (San Diego: Harcourt, Brace, 1973), p. 158.

40. Ibid., p. 161.

41. Michael Banton, *Racial Theories* (Cambridge, UK: Cambridge University Press, 1987).

42. W.E.B. Du Bois, *The Souls of Black Folk* (New York: Bantam Books, [1903] 1989). See chapter 2, "Of the Dawn of Freedom," p. 10.

43. Ibid., p. xii.

44. Jacques Kornberg, *Theodor Herzl: From Assimilation to Zionism* (Bloomington: Indiana University Press, 1993), p. 176.

45. Ibid., p. 35. Note, for instance, that Herzl belonged to two fraternities at the University of Vienna known as *akademische Leschalle* and *Albia*; both required that Jewish individuals substitute their ethnoreligious identity with German cultural values. His fraternity name, Tancred, was taken in honor of a Christian conqueror of Jerusalem and hero of the first Christian Crusade. Cruse lists many other contenders in the chapter "Negroes and Jews" in *Crisis of the Negro Intellectual*.

46. George Breitman, *Leon Trotsky on Black Nationalism*, p. 51.

47. Cited in Michael Banton, *Racial Theories*, p. vii.

48. Ibid.

49. Jewish estimates put the German Jewish population at 500,000–600,000, whereas the Nazis estimated 900,000 out of a total population of about 67 million in Germany. Germany had a Jewish population of just 37,000 after World War II.

50. See Hannah Arendt, *The Jew as Pariah: Jewish Identity and Politics in the Modern Age* (New York: Grove, 1978). During World War II she was a Zionist in Paris who had earlier served in the Youth Aliyah, preparing and relocating youths for emigration. She would later be interned in France before emigrating to the United States after World War II. She identified as a Bernard Lazare "homeland" Zionist born in Germany.

51. Ibid., pp. 35–40.

52. See ibid., pp. 44–46, for a review of scholarly opinion on the ethnic quality of national identities. Hitler is more accurately considered a product of this vulgar phase of European history as well as its instigator.

53. See, for example, Wilson Moses, *Black Messiahs and Uncle Toms*, p. 170.

54. Ibid., p. 101.

55. Ibid., p. 194.

56. Theodore Vincent, *Nationalism and Particularity*, p. 5.

57. Harold Cruse, *Crisis of the Negro Intellectual*, p. 341.

58. Theodore Draper, *The Rediscovery of Black Nationalism*, p. 131.

59. Adolph Reed, *Class Notes*, pp. 61–63.

60. E.U. Essien-Udom, *Black Nationalism*, p. 289.

61. William Cobb, *The Essential Harold Cruse*, p. 83.

62. Robert C. Smith, *We Have No Leaders*, pp. 245–346. Of course, Jackson's campaign was chiefly impaired by his unfortunate "Hymietown" slur concerning New York Jews and association with then–PLO leader Yasser Arafat.

63. Ibid., p. 51.

64. For example, in *Future of the Race*, coauthor Henry Louis Gates Jr. lists *The Crisis of the Negro Intellectual* (and Du Bois's "Talented Tenth") as "two signal works in the black tradition meant to help us find our way through the abyss of integration." Gates also noted that *Crisis* influenced the "first-generation Ivy" and other first-generation college students, many of whom graduated in the late 1960s and early 1970s. See pp. x–xi.

65. Harold Cruse, *Crisis*, p. 84.

66. Robert C. Smith, *We Have No Leaders*.

67. Ibid., p. 169.

68. Greg Tate, *Everything but the Burden*, p. 66.

69. Ibid., p. 76. Emphasis in original.

70. David Levering Lewis, "Parallels and Divergences: Assimilationist Strategies of Afro-American and Jewish Elites, 1910 to the Early Thirties," *Journal of American History* 71 (December 1984): 543–544.

71. Ibid., p. 547. Please also see David Levering Lewis, *W.E.B. Du Bois: Biography of a Race, 1868–1919* (New York: Henry Holt, 1993), pp. 488–492.

72. Ibid., p. 555. Marcus Garvey rejected the white liberal influence of the NAACP in 1917, and the NAACP during the 1920s grew increasingly dependent on the leadership and support of some Jewish elites, such as Joel and Arthur Spingarn, Herbert Lehman, Arthur Sachs, Herbert Seligman, and Martha Gruening. The National Urban League was created in 1911 largely with the support of pro–civil rights Jews. Other Jewish elites, such as Louis Brandeis (who shifted his position from assimilation to soft Zionism), Franz Boas, Felix Frankfurter, and Melville Herskowitz, opposed Zionism politically, culturally, and intellectually.

73. See chapter 9 of William Cobb, *The Essential Harold Cruse*, esp. p. 78. Emphases in original.

74. Ibid., p. 89.

75. Devon W. Carbado and Donald Weise (eds.), *Time on Two Crosses: The Collected Writings of Bayard Rustin* (San Francisco: Cleis, 2003), p. xxxvi.

76. David Levering Lewis, "Parallels and Divergences," p. 564.

77. Cited in Cheryl Clarke, "*After Mecca*," pp. 18–19.

78. Jerry Watts, *Amiri Baraka: The Politics and Art of a Black Intellectual* (New York: New York University Press, 2001), p. 148.

79. Ibid., p. 149.

80. Ibid.

81. Lloyd Brown, *Amiri Baraka* (New York: Twayne, 1980), p. 25.

82. Adolph Reed, *Class Notes*, p. 33.

83. Ibid., p. 35.

84. Ibid.

85. The book clearly criticizes the middle-class bias in integrationism, and it promotes elements associated with the tradition of black nationalism, such as racial solidarity, self-determination, a Manichean notion of "us" (blacks) and "them" (whites), and a sense of "peoplehood," fueled with "black consciousness." It also proffers an analogy likening African Americans to an "internal colony," but the authors avoid the use of the language of black nationalism and neglect to link the concept with the history of the tradition. Moreover, in the 1992 Vintage edition of *Black Power*, the authors do not attempt to explain this relationship in hindsight. See the preface to the 1992 edition of Kwame Ture (formerly Stokely Carmichael) and Charles V. Hamilton, *Black Power: The Politics of Liberation* (New York: Vintage, 1992).

86. Ibid., p. xviii.

87. Eldridge Cleaver, *Soul on Ice* (New York: Dell, 1968). See, for instance, his comment that "I took the *Catechism* [of Nechayev] for my bible and, standing on a one-man platform that had nothing to do with the reconstruction of society, I began consciously incorporating these principles into my daily life, to employ tactics of ruthlessness in my dealings with everyone. . . . And I began to look at white America through new eyes." And, of course, there was Norman Mailer's influence on him.

88. Andrew Vincent, *Nationalism and Particularity* (New York: Cambridge University Press, 2002), p. 45.

89. Robin D.G. Kelley, *Yo' Mama's Dysfunktional! Fighting the Cultural Wars in Urban America* (Boston: Beacon, 1998), p. 105.

90. Algernon Austin, *Achieving Blackness*, p. 3.

91. Adolph Reed, *Class Notes*, p. xxi. Emphasis added.

92. These influences include Jacques Derrida, Jean-Paul Sartre, and Albert Camus.

93. Komozi Woodard, *A Nation Within a Nation*, p. 5.

94. Adolph Reed, *Class Notes*, p. xxv.

95. Ibid., p. xvi.

96. Donald A. McGavran and C. Peter Wagner, *Understanding Church Growth*, 3rd ed. (Grand Rapids, MI: William B. Eerdman's, [1970] 1990), p. 81. The concept is missiological as it relates to promulgating the Christian gospel to the "unreached," in the United States and abroad, but the concept is not based on theology and thus lends itself to an understanding of black politics.

97. David Harvey, *A Brief History of Neoliberalism* (Oxford, UK: Oxford University Press, 2005), p. 5.

98. Marlon Riggs, *Black Is . . . Black Ain't* (San Francisco: California Newsreel, 1995). See also www.newsreel.org.

99. Cathy Cohen, *The Boundaries of Blackness: AIDS and the Breakdown of Black Politics* (Chicago: University of Chicago Press, 1999), p. 13. Emphasis in original.

100. Ibid., p. 16.

101. Ibid., p. 9.

102. Kevin Gaines, *Uplifting the Race*; Devon Carbado and Donald Weise, *Time on Two Crosses*. Even amid great personal and public turmoil related to his sexuality, Bayard Rustin's influence dominated the civil rights movement (and the immediate period that followed), even introducing King to Gandhi's thinking on nonviolence; he chiefly organized the 1963 March on Washington. James Baldwin was also very important to most black Americans who read his works. Bruce Perry, *Malcolm: The Life of a Man Who Changed Black America* (Barrytown, NY: Station Hill, 1991), along with Joe Wood, *Malcolm X: In Our Own Image* (New York: St. Martin's, 1992), even implicates Malcolm X as a bisexual prostitute in his pre-Islamic hustling life in Boston and New York.

103. Donald McGavran and C. Peter Wagner, *Understanding Church Growth*, p. 221.

104. Ibid., p. 227.

105. Ibid. Emphasis in original.

106. Barbara Ehrenreich and John Ehrenreich, *Long March, Short Spring: The Student Uprising at Home and Abroad* (New York: Monthly Review, 1969), p. 157.

107. Ibid., p. 119.

108. Debbie Louis, *And We Are Not Saved: A History of the Movement as People* (Garden City, NY: Doubleday, 1970), pp. 344–345.

109. Robin D.G. Kelley, *Yo' Mama's Disfunktional!*, p. 104.

110. Ira Katznelson, *City Trenches*, esp. pp. 17–19.

111. Adolph Reed, *Class Notes*, p. xxvii.

112. Eldridge Cleaver, *Soul on Ice*. See especially the chapter "Notes on a Native Son." Writing from prison, Cleaver conducts a textual criticism of the major characters in Baldwin's *Another Country* and *Nobody Knows My Name*. Along with Richard Wright, Cleaver is also critical of Baldwin's treatment of Norman Mailer's *The White Negro*. In Cleaver's attempt to intervene in the political and literary criticism of Richard Wright's *Native Son*, where Baldwin insists, among other things, that Wright's work was too long on politics (vis-à-vis Bigger Thomas's black rage in *Native Son*) and too short on sex-love (vis-à-vis the character Rufus Scott in *Another Country*), Cleaver in turn interpreted some of Baldwin's writings as an expression of self-hatred.

113. Cleaver, *Soul on Ice*, pp. 97–98. Cleaver adds, "The case of James Baldwin aside for a moment, it seems that many Negro homosexuals, acquiescing in this racial death-wish, are outraged and frustrated because in their sickness they are unable to have a baby

by a white man. The cross they have to bear is that, already bending over and touching their toes for the white man, the fruit of their miscegenation is not the little half-white offspring of their dreams but an increase in the unwinding of their nerves—though they redouble their efforts and intake of the white man's sperm," p. 100.

114. Ibid., p. 106.

115. Jerry Watts, *Amiri Baraka*, p. 112.

116. King, against the advice of Randolph, accepted Rustin's resignation from the SCLC and severed ties with him until supporting Rustin in the subsequent debates over whether Rustin should be permitted to be the principal organizer of the 1963 March on Washington. Rustin had previously scandalized himself with three embarrassing and humiliating sexual incidents—while a student at Fisk University, in prison, and in Pasadena while raising funds for a trip to India, which led to his arrest. See the introduction in Devon Carbado and Donald Weise, *Time on Two Crosses*, p. xxvi.

117. Ibid., p. xvii.

118. Kevin Gaines, *Uplifting the Race*, p. 102.

119. Ibid., p. 126.

120. Patricia Hill Collins, *Black Feminist Thought: Knowledge, Consciousness, and the Politics of Empowerment*, 2nd ed. (New York: Routledge, 2000), p. 2.

121. This is tantamount to arguing that women in the Black Power movement, such as Kathleen Cleaver, were alienated from the civil rights movement's liberal integrationist commitments, even though they had previously, by their organizational and political alignments and ideological commitments, actively considered those commitments of no consequence to them as women.

122. This again becomes apparent as he raises the case of William Ferris, a Yale- and Harvard-educated divinity student who, after exhausting relationships with Booker T. Washington, W.E.B. Du Bois, and William Monroe Trotter, eventually aligned himself with Marcus Garvey's UNIA program, becoming the editor of its *Negro World* newspaper from 1919 to 1923. He also published *The African Abroad, or, His Evolution in Western Civilization, Tracing His Development Under Caucasian Milieu* (New Haven, CT: Tuttle, Morehouse, and Taylor Press, 1913). He was also a participant at the American Negro Academy in 1897, where Du Bois and Alexander Crummell presented the "Conservation of Races" defense against his criticism that Du Bois had inverted the importance of the race as a group over individual initiative, which might contribute to the group's uplift. See David Lewis, *W.E.B. Du Bois*, p. 170.

123. Patricia Hill Collins, *Black Feminist Thought*, p. 88. Here, Collins enlists several books by black feminist scholars and activists who have demonstrated the problematic manner in which male black nationalists have conceived the roles, "place," and function of black women that reinforce the heterosexist notions of manhood and perpetuated black women's marginalization within the black freedom struggle.

124. William Cobb, *The Essential Harold Cruse*, pp. xvii–xviii.

125. Ibid., p. 208.

126. Robin D.G. Kelley, *Race Rebels*, pp. 112–114.

127. Clarence Taylor, *Black Religious Intellectuals*, pp. 19–22.

128. Ibid., p. 21.

129. Ibid., p. 106.

130. Robert Carr, *Black Nationalism in the New World*, p. 189.

131. Please see John H. Bracey Jr. and Sharon Harley, LexisNexis Primary Sources in U.S. History, Primary Sources in African American History. Black Power manuscripts selected from the UPA microfilm research collections, Part 3: Papers of the Revolutionary Action Movement, 1964–1975 (55 documents). This source notes, "Max

Stanford, the leader of RAM, fused the thought of Robert F. Williams on armed self defense with the philosophy of Malcolm X on black self-determination. To these tenets, Stanford added a sophisticated Marxian revolutionary philosophy. As an underground movement dedicated to building a revolutionary cadre among dispossessed urban ghetto dwellers and the infiltration of mainstream civil rights organizations, RAM guided SNCC, CORE, and the 'Black Arts Movement' leaders towards Revolutionary Black Nationalism." Available at http://cisweb.lexisnexis.com/images/histuniv/img/PrimarySourcesUS.pdf.

132. See Unita Blackwell and JoAnne Pritchard Morris, *Barefootin': Life Lessons from the Road to Freedom* (New York: Crown, 2006). See also Patricia Reid-Merritt, *Sister Power: How Phenomenal Black Women Are Rising to the Top* (New York: John Wiley, 1996).

133. In a conversation with Willie Ricks in March 2010 at the National Conference of Black Political Scientists in Atlanta, he stated that Smith-Robinson "ran SNCC." She succeeded James Forman as SNCC's executive secretary, the only woman to hold the post. A student at Spelman, Smith-Robinson orchestrated the committee's "jail, no bail" campaign and simply refused to accept blacks' second-class position in the United States. From 1960 until her untimely death at age twenty-five in 1967, she was every bit the militant that would characterize Stokely Carmichael, Black Power, and the larger struggle. See Cynthia Fleming, *Soon We Will Not Cry: The Liberation of Ruby Doris Smith Robinson* (Lanham, MD: Rowman & Littlefield, 1998).

134. Kimberlé Crenshaw, "Demarginalizing the Intersection of Sex and Race: A Black Feminist Critique of Antidiscrimination Doctrine, Feminist Theory, and Antiracist Politics" (University of Chicago Legal Forum, 1989), in Joy James and T. Denean Sharpley-Whiting (eds.), *The Black Feminist Reader* (Oxford, UK: Blackwell, 2000); and Crenshaw, "Mapping the Margins: Intersectionality, Identity Politics, and Violence Against Women of Color," *Stanford Law Review* 43 (1991): 1241–1299.

135. Charise L. Cheney, *Brothers Gonna Work It Out*, p. 41.

136. Tommie Shelby, *We Who Are Dark*, pp. 34–35. Emphases in original.

137. Nikol Alexander-Floyd, *Gender, Race, and Nationalism*, p. 117.

138. Tolagbe Ogunleye, "Dr. Martin Robison Delany, 19th-Century African American Womanist: Reflections on His Avant-Garde Politics Concerning Gender, Colorism, and Nation Building," *Journal of Black Studies* 28, no. 5 (May 1998): 628–649.

139. Paul Gilroy, *The Black Atlantic: Modernity and Double Consciousness* (New York: Verso, 1993), p. 26.

140. Marilyn Richardson, *Maria W. Stewart: America's First Black Woman Political Writer* (Bloomington: Indiana University Press, 1987).

141. Ibid., p. 93.

142. Ibid., p. xiv.

143. Joy James, *Transcending the Talented Tenth: Black Leaders and American Intellectuals* (New York: Routledge, 1997), pp. 117, 120.

144. Evelyn Simeon, *Black Feminist Voices in Politics* (Albany: State University of New York Press, 2006).

145. Joy James, *Transcending the Talented Tenth*, pp. 116–117.

146. Peniel Joseph, *Waiting 'Til the Midnight Hour*, p. 26.

147. Patricia Hill Collins, *From Black Power to Hip-Hop*, p. 120.

148. Theodore Vincent, *Black Power and the Garvey Movement*, p. xix.

149. Cheryl Clarke, "*After Mecca*," p. 53.

150. Such as when the SNCC turned toward black nationalism. She says 1968, when its Black Position Paper was presented two years earlier.

151. June Jordan, *Civil Wars: Observations from the Frontlines of America* (New York: Touchstone, 1981), pp. 163–168; for a more sympathetic reading of Wallace's book, see Nikol Alexander-Floyd, *Gender, Race, and Nationalism*.

152. Cheryl Clarke, *"After Mecca,"* pp. 97–98.

153. Ibid., p. 53.

154. Ula Yvette Taylor, *The Veiled Garvey*, p. 64.

155. Michael Dawson, *Black Visions*, pp. 138.

156. Ibid., pp. 138–139. For an explanation of the "womanist" concept, see Dwight N. Hopkins, *Heart and Head*, pp. 37–47.

157. Ibid., p. 31.

158. Ibid., pp. 234–235.

159. Ibid., p. 7.

160. Athena D. Mutua, *Progressive Black Masculinities* (New York: Routledge, 2006), p. 5.

161. For a critical reading of the reproduction of the 1980s and 1990s "crisis of the black male," please see Nikol Alexander-Floyd, *Gender, Race, and Nationalism*.

162. Dwight Hopkins, *Heart and Head*, p. 94.

163. See Michael Eric Dyson, *I May Not Get There with You: The True Martin Luther King, Jr.* (New York: Touchstone, 2000); Barbara Ransby, *Ella Baker and the Black Freedom Movement*.

164. Patricia Hill Collins, *Black Feminist Thought*, pp. 217–219.

165. Peniel Joseph, *Waiting 'Til the Midnight Hour*, p. 213.

166. Ibid., p. 271.

167. Naomi Pabst, "'Mama: I Am Walking to Canada': Black Geopolitics and Invisible Empires," in Kamari Maxine Clarke and Deborah A. Thomas (eds.), *Globalization and Race: Transformations in the Cultural Production of Blackness* (Durham, NC: Duke University Press, 2006), pp. 112–132.

168. bell hooks, *Teaching to Transgress: Education as the Practice of Freedom* (London: Routledge, 1994).

169. Todd Boyd, *Am I Black Enough for You? Popular Culture from the 'Hood and Beyond* (Bloomington: Indiana University Press, 1997).

8

Malcolm X, Louis Farrakhan, and the Haunting of America

These are the twelve he appointed: Simon (to whom he gave the name Peter); James son of Zebedee and his brother John (to them he gave the name Boanerges, which means Sons of Thunder*).*
—Mark 3:17

And when his disciples James and John saw this, they asked "Lord, wilt thou that we command fire to come down from heaven, and consume them?"
—Luke 9:54

In this chapter I intersect the leadership representations of ministers Malcolm X and Louis Farrakhan in an attempt to relate them to the contested social and political climate that confronted many African Americans in the last quarter of the twentieth century, as well as to the means by which some sought to speak to the particular effects of backlash racial and cultural conservatism against poor and working-class individuals. Like Black Power, the very existence of a Farrakhan and revenant Malcolm X at the fore of black politics was the clearest jeremiad that the hip-hop generation—particularly of the earlier "black consciousness" sort—could offer. As much as rap and other elements of hip-hop culture were viewed as urban street phenomena, during its genesis the most immediate influences were Black Power, Jesse Jackson's 1984 presidential campaign vis-à-vis electoral politics, and Ronald Reagan's war on poor black communities. He had been "beat[ing] back the jungle" in California for more than a decade since Watts exploded and Black Power. Responsively, the youngest cohort of African American baby boomers, born between 1960 and 1964, and the black Generation X cohort born between 1965 and 1978,[1] combined, engaged in a heightened sense of group political consciousness among black American men.[2] With "rapnationalism,"[3] urban youth sought to articulate the pain and grievances of the hip-hop generation: the disappointment with the yield of the civil rights movement in terms of its inability to eradicate poverty in US ghettoes. But I do not focus on hip-hop as a cultural phenomenon here. Studies of the hip-hop generation continue to be carried out in critical, popular, and cultural studies. This is not intended to slight the prosaic value of rap or other expressions of hip-hop cultural production. I concur with M. K. Asante Jr.'s insistence concerning "the inextricable link between Black music and the politics of Black life."[4] Frank Kofsky's *Black Nationalism and the Revolution in Music* (1970) also offers a coherent reading of Malcolm X's appeal to the likes of Max Roach and John Coltrane that is amenable to an analysis of black nationalism as ideology, as well as its relationship to African American music forms.

There is some evidence to suggest that the hip-hop generation has, at times, embraced a different orientation than the civil rights generations concerning the major American political parties. Integral to this potentiality is the political ideology of black nationalism. This is how Malcolm X and quasi-nationalistic adherents, such as William Monroe Trotter and, later, Amiri Baraka and Ronald Walters, in some form, would have it.[5] Malcolm X's criticism of the Democratic Party, especially after its 1964 convention deprived Fannie Lou Hamer and members of the Mississippi Freedom Democratic Party of their right to represent the state's official party delegation—the same and most immediate incident that ultimately led to the formation of the Lowndes County Freedom Organization—led him to equate the Democrats with racist and segregationist Dixiecrats. Aspects of this disentanglement have been undermined, however, by the continued prominence of civil rights elites and intellectuals in contemporary black politics and the racial conservatism of the major parties. Barack Obama's 2008 election likely prevents the renewal of insurgent strategies that would necessarily take on bourgeois African American (Democratic) establishment elites and white power structures in order to achieve substantive policy outcomes aimed at improving conditions that have steadily deteriorated since the 1980s. Increasingly, however, it appears that black nationalist discourse must also speak seriously to the commercial and commodity ethic that pervades contemporary hip-hop cultural politics. This, in fact, points to what Marable identifies, at length, as a dynamic encounter between the experiences of the "We Shall Overcome" and hip-hop generations.[6]

On this note, Bakari Kitwana's book *The Hip-Hop Generation* (2002) claims, somewhat arbitrarily, that the hip-hop generation brackets the 1965–1984 period, and he sets it apart from the progenitors of hip-hop based on a separate set of values and socialization. It assumes that the black homologue to the white Generation X actually forged the hip-hop movement that it inherited. At best the black Generation X is not synonymous with *the* (but rather *a*) hip-hop cohort to the extent that hip-hop was created, promoted, and sustained through the 1980s and 1990s by the "infant" or "baby" baby boomers like Afrika Bambaataa (born Kevin Donovan in April 1960), DJ Kool Herc (born Clive Campbell, April 1955), and Grandmaster Flash (born Joseph

Saddler, January 1958), all of whom are recognized as the progenitors of modern hip-hop. Rap icon Kurtis Blow (born Curtis Walker, August 1959) and DJ Red Alert were also born in the 1950s, and Chuck D was born in 1960, so hip-hop is not a particularly *youth* movement anymore, unless writers and commentators begin to think of these individuals as "proto-" hip-hop practitioners. Kitwana offers at least honorable mention:

> I have established the birth years 1965–1984 as the age group for the hip-hop generation. However, those at the end of the civil rights/Black power generation were essentially the ones who gave birth to the hip-hop movement that came to define the hip-hop generationers. The Africa Bambaataas, Grand Master Flashes, Melle Mels, Kool DJ Hercs, as well as journalists like Nelson George and even hip-hop moguls like Russell Simmons, belong to . . . the "bridge generation." Those folks, who were right at the cusp, were too young to be defined by civil rights/Black power and too old to be deemed hip-hop generationers. Nonetheless, they have played a pivotal role in this generation's development by linking both.[7]

The arbitrariness of this formulation is clear: Someone born on January 1, 1965, necessarily had a different encounter with hip-hop than someone born the day before, on December 31, 1964, and the former has a closer socialization and maturation experience than with someone born at any point in 1984. Moreover, by claiming this cohort as neither Black Powerites nor hip-hop, Kitwana strips the progenitors of hip-hop of any coherent socialization they experienced (as if crack and HIV/AIDS, the Los Angeles riots, Farrakhan, and Ronald Reagan did not shape their political socialization). Further, as Barack and Michelle Obama are of this age segment, the insistence that the hip-hop generation begins with 1965 undermines any attempt to link the Obamas aside from the cohort's political or leadership preferences. Obama is younger than most of the founders of hip-hop, including Chuck D. Thus, if the rapper Nas was premature in suggesting "hip-hop is dead," he was not far off in that hip-hop is old(er). Another option might be to designate what emerges with gangsta rap between Niggas with Attitude and Tupac Shakur—what it has been since the early 1990s—West Coast–inspired hip-*pop* music.

Presumably, Kitwana's claim is plausible if it is analogous to Marx not being Marxist, Darwin not being Darwinian, Jesus not being Christian, and Muhammad not being Muslim. Even though all are more or less true, this minimizes the fact that unlike these men, who preceded the movements of their disciples, early hip-hop was *experienced* by the progenitors for more than a decade (and it lasted longer and with more coherence than its latter-day renditions). Kitwana seems to concede this in his subsequent characterization of hip-hop.

> Furthermore, although I believe that the hip-hop phenomenon has been a defining element for this entire age group (those born between 1965 and 1984), I would argue that there are probably three distinctive subgroups

within this generation. Those at the beginning of the age group have a vastly different interpretation of hip hop music, for example, than those at the end. Each subgroup undoubtedly thinks that they were the first ones who really grew up on hip hop (but that's another story). Older hip hop generationers may find a rapper like KRS-One or LL Cool J to be more representative of their idea of hip hop than someone younger, who may see their hip hop truths in say, the Hot Boys or Lil' Bow Wow. Someone in the middle of the age group may be stuck on Wu Tang Clan.[8]

Although this accounts for the varied experiences of individuals on the bookends of this characterization, it renders hip-hop so willy-nilly a shibboleth *within* a cohort that it becomes useless in delineating where hip-hop begins and ends while redacting its most coherent cohort.

Together the age sets that constituted the largest segment of the 1995 Million Man March/Day of Absence attendees corresponded with the infant babyboomer/early Generation X cohort, and from their ranks emerged the soft, common-sense nationalism of Barack and Michelle Obama (see Chapter 9). Their perspective is neither strongly ideological nor at all doctrinaire. Among younger African Americans in the period after civil rights and Black Power, Malcolm X and Louis Farrakhan emerged to represent an increasingly salient mood of protest and dissent that extended into conventional political venues and electoral politics at the end of the twentieth century. Farrakhan's rhetorical powers and defiant leadership of the Nation of Islam foregrounded his prominence among the "rapnationalist" component of early hip-hop cohorts, such as Public Enemy's Chuck D.

Scholars have widely viewed Farrakhan's emergence as retrograde black politics, especially centering on the MMM/DOA and its organizational and programmatic failures and leadership. I am more intent on analyzing the utility of "Malcolm mania" and Louis Farrakhan's emergence to the fore of black protest politics as a rendition of *no confidence* in contemporary leadership structures, most notably elites and organizations that managed the civil rights movement and the failed "sacred covenant" debacle in the early 1990s, which provided the immediate backdrop of the MMM/DOA.[9] Farrakhan incorrectly and repeatedly contends that the American political establishment "raised Malcolm from the dead." This undermined his (and the Nation of Islam's) popularity among younger African Americans in the late 1980s and 1990s. He informed some and reminded others of his role in Malcolm's murder. Influenced by the burgeoning black glitterati of emergent hip-hop discourses, others raised Malcolm from the dead to speak their "truth to power."

There has been criticism aimed at post–civil rights age groups' attempts to relate black nationalism to their circumstances, to interpret the life and meaning of Malcolm X for themselves, and, of course, to associate with the problematic ascension of Louis Farrakhan in black politics in the 1980s and 1990s. In the late 1960s and early 1970s, internecine conflicts among ideologues, student activists, and their organizations demonstrated that even those who encountered Malcolm X while he lived (the cohort that Julius Lester identified as "the angry children of Malcolm X") fought over his ideological and theoretical remains and appropriated them as much as did the earliest hip-hop elements in the late 1980s and 1990s. Gary T. Marx demonstrates that Malcolm X became more popular among African Americans outside of Harlem, *posthumously*. His status was heightened in the post–civil rights period under the influence of the black popular-culture glitterati and as an extension of the black studies academic movement and Afrocentric scholarly works.[10]

There is on-site survey evidence, for instance, that three of four who attended the Million Man March correspond to the hip-hop generation(s); roughly one-third were born between 1966 and 1977, and more than 40 percent were born on the early end, between 1951 and 1965. The smallest groups to attend were Farrakhan's generation and the civil rights generation more generally.[11] Perhaps they were done with protest marches, or perhaps many Black Power activists felt the popularity of Farrakhan as the "new Malcolm X" among the younger generations to be a strange development.[12] It is clear that these individuals numerically predominated in the MMM/DOA, despite its civil rights organizers. Their emergence in American politics, as predicted by Harold Cruse in *Plural but Equal*, was disappointed. (See Chapter 9.)

A central thesis of this chapter suggests that the ideological linkages between Malcolm X and Louis Farrakhan may have more to do with a fellow black Bostonian emigrant, David Walker, with his *Appeal*, than with the contested organizational and traditionally parochial apoliticism of the Nation of Islam during the civil rights and Black Power periods. As noted previously, David Walker is linked with Malcolm X in several important studies on black nationalism, particularly those that analyze the "stay-at-home" strain. The linkages with Malcolm X and Farrakhan are primarily ideological and organizational and have otherwise been studied comparatively. The real subjects of this chapter, the focus of analyses, are not David Walker, Malcolm X, or even Louis Farrakhan per se, except to the extent that they provide a structure for understanding the ideological appeal of the two latter individuals to the post–civil rights–age segments seeking to materialize a strategy of social and political dissent in what was appreciably an increasingly hostile, conservative social and political environment. Fifteen years after hip-hop emerged as a jovial consortium of music, dance, art, poetry, and dress, it became the harbinger of or witness to a contemporary nadir of black people. The anomic proliferation of crack, violence, and the Reaganesque war on the poor facilitated Louis Farrakhan's and Malcolm X's rise among the hip-hop generation. It constituted a jeremiad against antiblack racial conservatism in US politics and against the inability of black elected officials and black religious leaders to develop appropriate strategies and challenges to the abysmal and widespread social death in the United States.

Implicit in the chapter's thesis is the cross-fertilization in African American ideological and leadership fulcrums, elected and protest-oriented, that constituted black political development (see Chapter 1). Why did young African Americans in hip-hop not resurrect the popular rendition of Martin Luther King Jr. (as it relates to the "Dream," which, of course, overshadowed his late radicalism) to respond to the "white nationalism" that Ronald Walters associates with Ronald Reagan's capture of the US state apparatus? How, in the unprecedented era of big-city black mayors and elected officials in the Congressional Black Caucus, do Malcolm X and Louis Farrakhan emerge as the symbols of black political dissent? Why does black nationalism, in its most sectarian forms, experience a decade-long hegemony among the Harold Washington elections, Jesse Jackson's 1984 campaign, and the 1995 MMM/DOA?

The utility of "Malcolm mania," and Louis Farrakhan's emergence to the fore of black protest politics, served as a rendition of *no confidence* in contemporary electoral and protest leadership structures, most notably elites and organizations that managed the civil rights movement and those who primed, but did not follow through in constructing, the apparatus that Cruse thought essential to twenty-first-century black politics. The continued salience of nonelected political elites in a "post-protest," post–Voting Rights Act, post–Jesse Jackson political milieu betrays the contested, alternating, and sometimes mutually interdependent spaces that African American elites (conventional and unconventional) seek to wrest from ordinary African Americans' ambitions into an illusive and elusive black political agenda. Ultimately, I am interested here in explaining the "why" of Malcolm X's and Louis Farrakhan's appeal to a generation that missed the civil rights and Black Power struggles but reached political maturity at the height of the ascendancy of racial, social, and political conservatism in the United States vis-à-vis the Reagan revolution.

The Recruitment of Malcolm X and Louis Farrakhan

Important scholars have agreed in conceptualizing (or contesting) leadership as "cause."[13] These studies tend to illuminate the role of political elites in influencing a given political context sufficient to transform extant institutional and societal arrangements vis-à-vis constituent group mobilization. Anthony Mughan and Samuel C. Patterson suggest two common patterns evident in most leadership-constituent arrangements. First, leadership is understood as a relationship between "one or more persons who exercise influence over one or more persons who submit to that influence." Second, political leadership is depicted as "a relationship that is best studied within the framework of the dynamics of group interaction."[14] Aaron Wildavsky's *The Nursing Father: Moses as a Political Leader* offers a conceptualization of leaders or leadership representations as *effect*, challenging the notion of leaders as *cause*. Political leadership is "a consequence of regime."[15] Offering a "situation thesis," his study of the biblical Moses's myriad experiences with the Israelites codes four different leadership modalities—or regimes—as they are framed, "to give meaning to the events that take place within each regime."[16] In his view, leadership reflects a given political situation. Each generation of leaders is confronted with its own exigent circumstances, and there is no procrustean one-size-fits-all approach in which monadic ideological nodes are handed to or articulated on behalf of constituencies without reciprocity.

Wildavsky's work proposes a construction of leadership that takes into account that elite-constituent relationships do not emerge passively. Attention should be given instead to the processes whereby context both frames and is framed by leaders. Leadership can then be viewed as "cause" or "effect" depending upon the nature of the political environment. For instance, as it pertains to the hip-hop generation's relationship with Malcolm X and Louis Farrakhan, I argue, in the case of Farrakhan, that it is not so much that he led them during the 1980s and 1990s, as much as it was that they chose him to articulate their protest-demand nationalist sentiments, which were a clear rejection of the liberal integrationist strategies and outcomes of civil rights. C.L.R. James's posthumously published work, *American Civilization*, asserts that "the mass seeking to solve the great social problems which face them in their daily lives" prompt elites to action "only when [leaders] see and feel the new force."[17] Wildavsky adds, "leaders are nothing if they cannot attract followers. . . . Once leadership depends upon an acceptability within a group, group leaders are seen to lead as well as follow."[18]

Among African Americans, the hip-hop generation was integral to the recovery of Malcolm X as a cultural and leadership icon and to the protest impetuses of the 1990s. Malcolm X aimed sharp criticisms at the major parties (and, tertiarily, toward establishment black Democrats) and saw them as mutually reinforcing instruments of white supremacist capitalist interests. Michael Eric Dyson insists, rightly,

> Malcolm's defiant expression of Black rage has won him a new hearing among a generation of black youth whose embattled social status due to brutally resurgent racism makes them sympathetic to his fiery, often angry rhetoric. Malcolm's take-no-prisoners approach to racial crisis appeals to young blacks disaffected from white society and alienated from older black generations whose contained style of revolt owes more to Martin Luther King, Jr.'s nonviolent philosophy than to Malcolm's advocacy of self-defense. . . . Malcolm's pointed denunciations of black liberal protest against white racism hinged on the belief that black people should maintain independence from the very people who had helped oppress them—white people.[19]

Later, Dyson notes, "Given the crisis of black bourgeois political leadership and a greater crisis of black liberal social imagination about the roots of black suffering, black nationalist politics becomes for many blacks the logical means of remedy and resistance."[20]

Dyson's observations underestimate the alienation of those most deeply affected by denuded racism in living previous generations (which was, incidentally, the grounds on which Barack Obama initially sought to explain Jeremiah Wright's Christian nationalist criticisms). They also stereotype older blacks as less radical than younger blacks on scores that are neither mapped nor measured. These views caricature King's protracted confrontational activities (including his pointed criticisms of "white moderates," war, and capitalism) and Malcolm X's words as more or less militant. No aspect of post–civil rights or post–Black Power black politics, intellectually or in terms of mobilization, approached the intensity and protractedness of the second Reconstruction period. Dyson discreetly underestimates the radical Protestant heritage that King later advanced, and he interprets black nationalism as filling a "vacuum" in African American political discourse.

Black nationalist intellectuals never developed black nationalism appropriately in what Harold Cruse identified as a poorly negotiated American political context in light of its multiple micronationalisms. Despite Cornel West's observation that Malcolm X "knew that the *electoral political system* could never address the existential dimension of *Black rage*," such is precisely the case.[21] To reiterate, Malcolm X's "By Any Means Necessary" speech enlisted the possibility of creating a "*black nationalist party* or a black nationalist army." Where too many have read into this expression of Malcolm X's militancy *ominous violence*, he preferred a multidimensional approach to strengthening the position on blacks in the United States and their sense of political efficacy.

Whereas nonacademics came quickly to the hip-hop intellectual scene, there is a dearth of rigor of the sort that is offered in some scholastic studies. Much of this journalistic genre is "autobiographical" (generationally), usually vindicating itself as an identifiable cohort that has experienced a movement of sorts and often struggles to speak with a coherence or universality that can incorporate the diversity of social-class claimers—bourgeois, working-class, gangsta, poorer people, suburbanites (white and black), and the global populations—who champion hip-hop. It is understandable that individuals would seek to interpret and articulate their experiences, but the boundaries and categories of what hip-hop is often come across in pop-culture journalism as so much of everything as to be useless as a unit of analysis.

Scholarly renditions of hip-hop culture and politics conducted in African American studies, sociology, history, ethnic studies, communications, media, gender and sexuality studies, and interdisciplinary critical studies have been richly textured, and the quality of the scholarship has brought credibility to the study and intellectual interrogation of hip-hop culture and politics.[22] Yet there is almost no empirical work among these scholars. Political science, in particular, has produced a slate of recent studies.[23] Of these, researchers more or less couple historical, attitudinal, or ethnographic approaches with some mixed methods to tease out the *ideological* properties of post–civil rights politics and African American public opinion on a set of cues focusing on the intersection of radicalism, nationalism, and integrationism in African American politics. Aside from indicting its "nationalist" qualities—and its provincialism and affinities for masculinist discourse—the content of rap music is largely collateral in social sciences. Todd Boyd argues, for instance, even "though several people make cursory mention of rap music, few explore its possibilities . . . I am not suggesting that rap transcends this political dimension, but rather that it is a product of political circumstances in America; it is a defense of and a response to certain historical and social conditions. It need not be defended, though it is constantly under attack; its presence signifies a defense that can come only from the product itself."[24] There is an important value in analyzing the content of rap music as a dimension of hip-hop culture and politics, as well as antecedent musical expressions of black existential and political life, such as ragtime, blues, bebop, and hard bop jazz. Looking at the content of musical expression is instructive of continuities and recurrent themes, particularly in urban music. Although these antecedent cultural forms make it possible to examine analogous political significance of various developments in the hip-hop cultural expressions of the 1980s and 1990s, it is not my interest here.

Individuals born during the post–civil rights period (beginning in the early 1960s) sustained Farrakhan's emergence and utilized the protest ideology of Malcolm X, according to survey research conducted by journalistic and scholarly sources, to "send a message to white people." Protest activities and attitudinal data confirm the period was one of high nationalist salience, and African Americans showed increasing reluctance toward the Democratic Party and some of its most notable black supporters, including Jesse Jackson and the Congressional Black Caucus. Although this chapter insists that the hip-hop generation recruited Louis Farrakhan and "brought back" Malcolm X, it offers a critique of its naiveté concerning the former's corruption of the legacies of Malcolm X and the attempt to respond to the Reagan revolution in US politics.

Louis Farrakhan's prominence in recent years has been of particular interest to students of black politics seeking to understand and critique his conceptualization and practicum of black nationalism. If there are any genealogical continuities among David Walker, Malcolm X, and Louis Farrakhan, at least a partial explanation is rooted in the imposition of the past on the present (the immediate past, in the case of Malcolm X among subsequent generations of African Americans). Jacques Derrida's approach toward understanding the apparition of historically contingent "specters," "hauntings," and "conjurings" of significant events, histories, or individuals by current generations lends itself to the post–civil rights revenance of Malcolm X. Political theorist Wendy Brown's narrative on politics and history identifies what she calls a "spectral consciousness," the ability to resurrect the *pertinently* dead, "to live actively with—indeed, to activate politically—the spirits of the past and the future, the bearable and unbearable memories of the past and the weight of obligation toward the unborn."[25] Her assessment of the thought of Nietzsche, Foucault, Benjamin, and Derrida, in the abstract to be sure, grapples with time-spatial questions of contemporizing previous experience as oppression narratives and whether reconciliation, recompense, or reparation indicts, elides, or liberates the past in the present, whether the present even has a past in the future.[26] European and US slavery, for instance, as memory and as indictment, is often scuttled in the name of "progress." For many US citizens, 1965 became Year One in race relations. It represents, at least contemporarily, the grinding erasure of slavery as the great contradiction of US democracy.

With the seminal civil rights legislation and the 1960s studies, commissions, and blue ribbon reports on urban violence, residential segregation in urban life, and welfare policy, the mirror that blacks held up to the United States was suddenly turned back upon them. As they were distanced from their slave and Jim Crow heritages, so, too, were contemporary Euro-American whites; after all, they never held anyone as slaves (which was and is the trope). Demand-protest politics calling for national responsibility was met with an equally forceful demand for black "personal responsibility." The year 1965 made it immediately possible for black people, the objects of the most stayed racism in modern human history, to become "racists" and to engage in reverse discrimination, as if the previous centuries had no standing. It was also the year that Malcolm X's unrelenting jeremiad pointing to these contradictions came to an end.

Wendy Brown's concern seems to be with the rapidity with which subsequent generations abdicate historical and political consciousness. She asks, "If there are no such sources of continuity to draw on, then from what wellspring do we affirm our time, engage our dilemmas, define our imperatives?" For our purposes, this presentism hints at the *faute de mieux* (lack of anything better) dissatisfaction with contemporary leadership. Despite the prominence of Jesse Jackson, Louis Farrakhan, and Al Sharpton or, say, the Congressional Black Caucus, in recent black politics, it is not uncommon to hear undergraduate students (and the general public) express frustration with having "no black leaders," when there have *never been more at any time in US political history*. This is generative of a longing for the dead in contemporary political life; it reads as an expression of no confidence in the effectiveness of existing leadership fulcrums, whether intellectual, electoral, bureaucratic, institutional, or insurgent, to meet the precedent of systems-challenging criticisms epitomized in Malcolm X. Wendy Brown's reading of Derrida's *Specters of Marx* is instructive, particularly when she explores his interest in "how the dead live among the living, how the past lives indirectly in the present, inchoately suffusing and shaping rather than determining it."[27]

Derrida is concerned with symbiosis between past and present and how they relate, how they may coexist. His "hauntology" accommodates the asymmetrical, anachronistic presence of dead gods, ghosts, angels, or, say, tombs of unknown soldiers, all poised to account for "the press of history on the present." Of necessity, progressive historiography must be rejected in deference to a more malleable reading of spectral interventions: without the conceits of foundations, origins, and progress, and especially without clear distinctions between the real and the fictive, the ideal and the material, the past and the present.[28] This sponsors justice, which Derrida understands as "*relations between generations. Justice* concerns not only our debt to the past but also the past's legacy in the present; it informs not only our obligation to the future but also our responsibility for our (ghostly) presence in the future."[29] Last, Brown's analysis, while rejecting group solidarity tropes, lends itself to our interest in Malcolm X's haunting of America through the hip-hop generation's invocation of his person to speak to their experiences in the 1980s and 1990s.

> Thus, in a historical dimension, the dead and the not-yet-born intermittently press their constraints or demands with unmistakable but invisible power, a power that also exceeds our conventional formulations of agency. . . . The specter reverses the usual understanding of history as origin . . . by virtue of its always being a revenant, a coming back. The specter begins by coming back, by repeating itself, by recurring in the present. . . . We inherit not "what really happened" to the dead but what lives on from that happening, what is conjured from it, how past generations and events occupy the force fields of the present, how they claim us, and how they haunt, plague, and inspirit our imaginations and visions of the future.[30]

Toni Morrison's spectral device in *Beloved* presents the visitation of Beloved upon Sethe as a theme for conjuring the enduring yield of black slavery. With a double meaning, the presence of Beloved haunts her mother's horrifying act of "infanticide"—itself a product of the haunting powers of slavery and its child, racism. And she had already haunted Schoolteacher, at the moment of her "rescue" from slavery's horror, which he embodied. Who of the two was the true "monster" of 124 Bluestone Road standing over the corpse of the infant? Morrison treats history at times as a conjuring and homologous representation, particularly as Beloved intervenes in the real world of Reconstruction years after her death and on the day of her death.[31] Her haunting reminds us that history does not necessarily culminate teleologically for African Americans, who are still struggling to cite the genealogies of their people and to sustain a fleeting historical consciousness.

This provides considerable relief from what some would call the generational "hating" that typifies criticisms of the hip-hop generation's attempts at black nationalism vis-à-vis conjuring Malcolm X. No part of this attempt was carried out without the imposition of veteran interpretations of how Malcolm X ought to be read and applied to contemporary circumstances, although they were considerably more ambiguous than the state-sponsored white-over-black racism of the segregation era. Malcolm X was largely introduced to younger individuals coming of age amid the twin developments of the first of two Jesse Jackson campaigns and of the Ronald Reagan administrations.[32] The generational sense that "opposition is the property of the image of 'the Sixties,' and it is, therefore, like bell-bottom pants, dashikis, and long hair, no longer appropriate," is an observation that hints at several broad influences that facilitated the revenance of Malcolm X—and criticisms of it—in the remaining decades of the twentieth century.[33]

Amid this storm of criticism, Joe Wood insisted, "Malcolm's spirit blends—it is a vague notion, an idea that can resonate everywhere, toothlessly. Malcolm's spirit has been and will be used and misused for as many purposes as there are people; his spirit will mix with many a community's ethos, good and bad. We can consequently expect . . . many resurrections, too."[34] Wood, who was of an earlier generation of individuals that invoked Malcolm X to speak to its experiences, takes note of the extent to which Malcolm X was commodified—initially by Malcolm himself—to "signify the 'truest' distillation of this Black spirit, and therefore the best product to validate and express 'real' Black anger: anger about the way Black People have been treated everywhere we are Black, anger about the way we are now treated in America."[35] But Wood took his observations of merchandising Malcolm X out of its immediate social and political contexts. Although he does acknowledge the potential oppositional power of "Malcolm couture," his analysis never locates the "why" Malcolm question.[36] For the most part, his analysis views this latest, third wave of Malcolm X thinking among hip-hop cohorts as a bad resurrection essentially because interest in and the outward wearing of Malcolm as a brand have cheapened the Malcolm of the 1960s and 1970s waves.[37]

Beyond the anecdotal trappings of thinking that because a younger person may have thought of Malcolm's "X" as the Roman numeral ten[38]—which provides a vitally important teaching opportunity—there is something of an almost sacral judgmentalism that permeated critical intellectual discourse at the time that felt itself capable of reading the hearts and sincerity of other people based on a rejection of how they may have expressed interest in Malcolm X. Where Wood's and his colleagues' essays—and one or two of them cannot be taken too seriously—set to ferret out the complex relationships between the resurgent interest in Malcolm X among individuals in the last quarter of the twentieth century, the common thread appears to be a scholarly critique of its pop-culture frocking. And scholars who focused on the wearing of T-shirts, caps, and medallions in recognition of whatever value or use Malcolm X's memory served were not nearly as self-critical of their own participation in fetishizing Malcolm X in the selling of their books. Indeed, entire academic careers and tenures have been built on Malcolm X and on the very act of criticizing hip-hop's Malcolm X encounter.[39] The hip-hop generation's postmovement attempt at black nationalism has produced a virtual cottage industry among academics and independent scholars; it is, more often than not, filtered through the "reemergence" of the Malcolm X trope. Here, Dyson is among the few scholars to take note of the bait-and-switch quality of the criticisms of the period, especially the parasitic intellectual class dimensions: "Ironically, talk of black cultural solidarity and racial loyalty has propelled the careers of intellectuals, cultural artists, and politicians as they seek access to institutions of power and ranks of privilege, even within black communities, as esteemed *vox populi*. The trouble is they are often cut off from the very people on whose behalf they ostensibly speak, the perks and rewards of success insulating them from the misery of their constituencies."[40]

The default tendency is to cast developments in terms of the most pedestrian manifestation, a kind of racial fundamentalism manifest in "problack" flags, songs, and symbolism. In a manner similar to Jackie Robinson's #42 hovering over major-league ballparks, it is the relative *meaning(s)* of Malcolm X that transcend(s) in black politics. There was no period of intermittence between the Black Power and hip-hop phases of black politics in relation to the common interest in Malcolm X. With the "Cult of Malcolm" in the late 1970s "battered and aging," Rickford insists that

> there remained an army of ideologues who lived by Malcolm's words. Much of their efforts were invisible to White America. Yet the hardcore SNCC, CORE, and Panthers veterans, the militant clergy and the Marxists, the activist-scholars and the artist-intellectuals, the Afrocentrists and the sidewalk vendors and the neighborhood griots all played. . . . Through the 1970s and early 1980s, ghetto peddlers bootlegged cassettes of Malcolm speeches and hawked Malcolm buttons and posters. Streets, schools, parks, and cultural centers in black neighborhoods took his name. . . . The grassroots kept Malcolm's name alive in the street.[41]

Thus, the ubiquitous "Malcolm X" paraphernalia of the "conscious rap" phase of this politics was *contiguous*, drawn on the received wisdom of the time.

Out of partisan divisions among the major ideological representations—nationalist, liberal-integrationist, conservative, feminist, radical-socialist—come the most unrelenting criticisms that rejected post–civil rights black nationalism and speak more about personalities, such as Leonard Jeffries, the opportunistic Al Sharpton, and the cultural nationalist proponents Amiri Baraka, Maulana Ron Karenga, and the Nation of Islam's Louis Farrakhan. They trivialize the widely held feelings of solidarity and periodic displays of outrage that blacks have employed to confront egregious racial conduct or official misconduct in highly visible cities such as Miami, New York, and Los Angeles (and, more recently, Cincinnati, New Orleans, and Oakland) and an overall pessimism about the state of race relations in the United States among segments of African Americans, irrespective of social status. Contemporary black nationalism was limited neither to these periodic paroxysms nor to attending Farrakhan assemblies.

One concrete marker that I outline in Chapter 9 relates to the respective conservative and centrist pivots in the Republican and Democratic Parties that Reagan effected, as well as an increasingly independent proclivity among African Americans from the hip-hop generation. The criticisms of several generations of nationalists grant misfit elasticity that obfuscates more than it reveals. The tendency was reproduced in many criticisms of the 1995 MMM/DOA, when Farrakhan became the litmus of the yearnings of *millions* of African American individuals who had experienced the racial tumult that came with the conservative Reagan revolution. They were largely from a generation fully sensitized by left, critical, and feminist discourses. Eugene Rivers described developments in the post–civil rights era, when hip-hop cohorts encounter black nationalism as "a nationalism of fools." Adolph Reed Jr. has argued that black radicalism, in the form of nationalism in particular, not only "constrains and distorts" black social criticism; "it is now the single greatest intellectual impediment to constructions of a left-egalitarian black politics."[42] Cedric Robinson, conversely, suggests that "the resoluteness of the Black radical tradition [i.e., black nationalism] advances as each generation assembles the data of its experience to an ideology of liberation."[43] And William W. Sales Jr. provides an equally sympathetic "generational" critique of this development, particularly as it relates to Malcolm X and black nationalism.[44]

Post–civil rights African Americans chose to remember Malcolm X mainly according to his *Autobiography* as told to Alex Haley (which, one source claims, sold more than a million copies in 1992 alone, ten times the number sold in 1965)[45] and also according to their own circumstances within the American political and economic systems. Despite scholarly efforts to confirm and/or impeach Malcolm X's many autobiographical claims, what mattered in the post–civil rights generation's appropriation of Malcolm X is not the late shift in his thought and political perspective as much as their invested but still limited self-understanding of Malcolm X's relevance to them in their objective conditions. According to Arnold Rampersad, Malcolm X has become an ideological symbol to generations since his death, and for each he

> has become his admirers. What these admirers "see" in Malcolm's legacy of his life, insofar as we can gauge the truth about an individual or recover it from history, is more or less *immaterial*. Malcolm has become the desires of his admirers, who have reshaped memory, historical record and the autobiography according to their wishes, which is to say, according to *their needs as they perceive them*. . . . The transformation is understandable because the purpose of history is not to serve the past but above all to serve the present, to help us to understand ourselves and where we are going.[46]

Inevitably, distortions and selective memory emerge in the place of serious self-criticism of the sort that led Malcolm X to grow out of the Nation of Islam's teachings to a wider view of domestic and international affairs. Those who touched and *encountered* Malcolm X selectively appropriated his legacies much as the earliest hip-hop elements in the late 1980s and 1990s, under the influence of black popular culture and as an extension of the black studies academic movement and Afrocentric scholarly works.[47]

Charise Cheney acknowledges transgenerational linkages between iconic nationalist influences, such as David Walker, Malcolm X, Louis Farrakhan, and Black Power, and the hip-hop age sets, represented by Chuck D of Public Enemy—essentially because of a shared "phallic nationalism." Yet she also attributes several important observations that inform this study. Her assessment is pertinent on the point of Malcolm X's centrality to Black Power and hip-hop cadres: "The Malcolm who was deified by the Black Power movement in the 1960s and '70s is the Malcolm who is idolized by the Hip-Hop Nation in the 1980s and '90s—the Nation of Islam Malcolm who also instructed and groomed a young Minister Louis Farrakhan in the middle-to-late 1950s."[48] As noted, as much as Malcolm X groomed Louis Farrakhan then, Malcolm would later haunt the political emergence of Farrakhan at the height of his popularity.

Wahneema Lubiano usefully defines *black nationalism* as "a tradition of registered opposition to the historical and ongoing [prejudice] of the state and its various institutions and apparatuses . . . deployed to articulate strategies of resistance." William Julius Wilson argues that "sentiments for racial separation and racial solidarity tend to emerge when minority race members perceive the struggle against racial inequality as hopeless or when they experience intense disillusionment and frustration immediately following a period of optimism of heightened expectations."[49] It is plausible to think of racial solidarity nodes in consequence of disappointment, but given the omnipresence of blacks' minority group status, powerlessness, and condition following the Black Power era, it begs the question why it is not more readily detectable among the black populace. The "stay-in-America" variant of black nationalism has been utilized in justice and policy demands since the 1970s. Its religiosity is in its "revolutionary anger" and choice of articulators of it, not in confessions per se.

This section provides short biographies of Malcolm X and Louis Farrakhan and analyzes their ideological orientations in light of their popularity among younger African Americans in the late twentieth century. Important aspects of Farrakhan's rise are symptomatic of similar political and racial stimuli that produced Malcolm X's Protestant articulation of black rage from the moment he and the Nation of Islam were introduced in Harlem as "God's Angry Men." Yet Farrakhan and Malcolm X do countenance very different postures with regard to the Nation of Islam's theological and political commitments. And any comparison is complicated by Malcolm's transitioning ideological orientation between late 1963 and 1965, as well as Farrakhan's longevity far beyond his peak with the MMM/DOA. Thus, scholars have largely ignored what post–civil rights age sets understood to be self-evident:

Both men articulated a dissident rage that has spoken to an array of public policy questions, answered largely in the callousness of social isolation, unprecedented incarceration, and a veil of poor and working-class black hopelessness throughout US society.[50]

Moreover, Farrakhan helps us understand that, regardless of the changes or transitions Malcolm X underwent after his break with the Nation of Islam, the contextual exigencies that produced Farrakhan's protestations in the 1980s and 1990s were not starkly different from Malcolm's critical perspective in the 1950s and 1960s. Both men were constantly speaking critically to the older and newer periods of dispossession that have characterized the lived experiences of many segments of African Americans. They spoke to their epochs in no uncertain terms, with a brutal honesty that would be political suicide to campaigning black elected and/or appointed officials in certain settings.

Malcolm X was born Malcolm Little in Omaha, Nebraska, on May 19, 1925. His parents were followers of the economic and political philosophy of Garveyism, named after the Jamaican émigré and leader of the UNIA, Marcus Garvey. *All* of the Little children, each of whom became a member of the Nation of Islam, were first introduced to black nationalism by their father Earl Little's itinerant Christian ministry in Omaha, not through the Nation of Islam.[51] William Sales is careful to remind us of what many analysts gloss over in the biography of Malcolm X concerning the trajectory of black nationalism in his life: black nationalism is a legitimate protest tradition indigenous to the African American community. The tradition was handed down to Malcolm both as a youth and as an adult. He was immersed in black nationalism for his entire life. The form and content of that nationalism, however, changed at crucial points in Malcolm's life.[52] Bill Strickland and Cheryl Greene add that "he is unimaginable apart from the Garveyism to which his parents were committed and the Garveyism out of which the Nation of Islam sprang."[53]

Malcolm Little dropped out of high school at fifteen and would be incarcerated in the Massachusetts state prison system[54] before his twenty-first birthday after years of street hustling in Harlem and Boston. His encounter with the mystical teachings of Elijah Muhammad and the Nation of Islam occurred while in prison, the result of his siblings' insistence that he embrace knowledge of "Master W.D. Fard, [who] in 1931, posing as a seller of silks, met, in Detroit, Michigan, Elijah Muhammad. Master W.D. Fard gave to Elijah Muhammad Allah's message, and Allah's divine guidance, to save the Lost-Found Nation of Islam, the so-called Negroes, here in 'this wilderness of North America.'"[55]

Leaving prison at twenty-seven, where he converted to Islam and changed his name, Malcolm X committed most of the rest of his life to espousing the teachings of the Nation of Islam until his abrupt break in 1964. He soon created the Muslim Mosque Incorporated, which was based on the religious and social teachings of Sunni Islam, and established his Organization of Afro-American Unity (OAAU). He followed a commitment to debating the merits of forming a black nationalist fulcrum and shifted increasingly toward a revolutionary pan-African critique of Western imperialism and monopoly capitalism. He also traveled to Africa, the Middle East, and Europe, establishing contacts and expanding his influence with African and Muslim leaders.

He was murdered (shot sixteen times) by at least one member of the Nation of Islam—Talmadge Hayer (now Mujahid Halim)[56]—on February 21, 1965, in front of his wife and four young daughters and an audience gathered at the Audubon Ballroom in Harlem. On that day, Louis X (Farrakhan) was at Mosque No. 25 in Newark, New Jersey. Betty Shabazz would later insist that she found the names of five conspirators on a bloodied sheet of paper in possession of Malcolm X when he was shot; Malcolm X knew none of them, but they were allegedly from the Newark mosque.[57]

Malcolm's Black Nationalisms

Between 1954 and 1964, Malcolm X publicly functioned within the sectarian contours of the nationalist tradition of the Nation of Islam and later allied with militant nationalists like Albert Cleage Jr. Malcolm X's late break with black nationalism has been exaggerated. Domestic black nationalism and diasporic pan-Africanism, at least since Garveyism, are not antithetical political orientations. They have intersected in African American political history among important individuals and their attendant movements and organizations across two centuries. Cedric Robinson's treatment of black Marxism argues that petit bourgeois radicals, such as C.L.R. James, W.E.B. Du Bois, George Padmore, Eric Williams, and Oliver Cox, resorted to the perennial black radical tradition (i.e., black nationalism) after experiencing disappointment with Western Marxism. Through their individual experiences, each came to insist, as did the black novelist Richard Wright, that "a theory of life could not take the place of real life."[58]

Conversely, Malcolm X, who, like Richard Wright, had poor or working-class origins, failed to appreciate, as the pan-African petit bourgeois intellectuals and activists learned, that black nationalism at home is amenable to international and foreign policy criticisms. Harold Cruse finds irony in elite African Americans—including his contemporaries, such as playwright Lorraine Hansberry, Shirley Graham Du Bois, the scholar John Henrik Clark, and the actor Ossie Davis—and their tendency to support nationalism in Africa but not at home in the United States. This is similarly evident in Malcolm X during the "international" phase of his thought (1964–1965), when he frequently pointed to the positive role of nationalist movements of the Mau Mau in Kenya, Kwame Nkrumah in Ghana, and Patrice Lumumba in the Congo while failing to root his own (post–Nation of Islam) understanding of black nationalism in the tradition as carried out by the likes of Walker and Garvey. Malcolm X's "philosophy" thus never ceases to be black nationalism. What he seems to have been searching for was an understanding of how his perception of nationalism could continue to be so without separatism. Indeed, there was no philosophical reason why Malcolm's "Algerian moment"[59] required that he renounce the tradition, especially if he countenanced the place of David Walker in it.

Malcolm X and Louis Farrakhan had little appreciation for the history of pre-Garveyite (and, to a lesser extent, Garveyite) black nationalism with which they have come to be identified.[60] William Seraile argued, for instance, that "Malcolm X appears to have been Walker reincarnated (there is no evidence that the *Appeal* was known to him)."[61] This is not to suggest that these individuals were functioning in a theoretical vacuum as much as it points to the parochial commitments of the Nation of Islam and the preeminence of Elijah Muhammad above all others therein. Still, it is true that in founding the Organization of Afro-American Unity, Malcolm X stated that he intended to return and "try and follow [Garvey's] books." And George Breitman is correct in pointing to the detail that "Malcolm had been grappling with the problem of black nationalism—not in the sense of *rejecting it, but of reappraising it,* in order to discover how it fit into his overall philosophy and strategy."[62] Upon his break with the Nation of Islam, Malcolm X, Breitman argues, "as a Muslim equated 'black nationalism' and 'separation.' In the press statement proclaiming himself to be a black nationalist, however, he differentiated the two concepts, *defining black nationalism in such a way as to include non-separatists too.* In the final months of his life he was seeking for a term to describe his philosophy that would be more precise and more complete than black nationalism."[63]

What is often lost in the "By Any Means Necessary" caricature of Malcolm X is that it was rendered several months *after* his March 1964 break with the Nation of Islam. Citing "By Any Means Necessary" as the Organization of Afro-American Unity motto, Malcolm X proceeded to reiterate a jeremiad consistent with "stay-at-home" nationalism: "We want freedom by any means necessary. We want justice by any means necessary. We want equality by any means necessary. We don't feel that in 1964, living in a country that is supposedly based on freedom and supposedly the leader of the free world. . . . No we want it now or we don't think anybody should have it."[64] At the June 28, 1964, inaugural meeting of the Organization of Afro-American Unity, while outlining the organization's charter (in which he mentions Nat Turner, Toussaint L'Ouverture, and Hannibal about whom black children should be taught), he insists, "We don't care how backward it may sound. In essence it only means we want one thing. We declare our right on this earth to be a man, to be a human being, to be respected as a human being *in this society*, on this earth, in this day, which we intend to bring into existence by any means necessary."[65] Most pertinent, in the "Politics and Economics" section of the group charter, Malcolm X notes,

The [Organization of Afro-American Unity] will organize the Afro-American community block by block to make the community aware of its power and its potential; *"we will start immediately a voter registration drive to make every unregistered voter in the Afro-American community an independent voter." We won't organize any black [person] to be a Democrat or a Republican because both of them have sold us out. Both of them have sold us out; both parties have sold us out. Both parties are racist, and the Democratic Party is more racist than the Republican Party. . . . "We propose to support and organize political clubs, to run independent candidates for office, and to support any Afro-American already in office who answers to and is responsible to the Afro-American community."* We don't support any black [person] who is controlled by the white power structure.[66]

In his post–Nation of Islam transition, Malcolm X's political thinking emphasized independence from the major parties as one of multiple nationalist-oriented means to improve the black condition *within* the United States. In this sense, he is unwittingly closer to David Walker's idea system.[67]

Patricia Hill Collins outlines the transconditional malleability of black nationalism to meet the "political challenges raised by slavery, Jim Crow segregation, industrialization, and urbanization" through the post–civil rights era of color blind "new" or "post-"racialism. For her, the psychic, existential, organizing, and institutional functions of black nationalism extended to the 1980s and 1990s through the Afrocentric intellectual and cultural movements, as well as support for the MMM/DOA event of the Nation of Islam and its antecedents.[68] She asks, "How does Black nationalism 'assume the character of religion to address the oppression and suffering' caused by the new racism?" Extracting Afrocentrism from its academic limitations, Collins views it as a variant of American civil religion discourses in its construction of symbols, rituals, saints and sinners, and a black value system.[69] The mutually constitutive dimensions of the sacred and secular tropes in "American" and "black" civil religion discourses facilitate the pivot to hip-hop discourse in its present-day formations (intellectual, cultural, chauvinist, feminist, and corporate).

Charise Cheney emphasizes the prevalent ideological discourse inherent in Black Power–type black nationalism's most proximate offspring: the earliest formulation of rap music. Her book troubles the chauvinistic lineage of black nationalism transhistorically and sees its main property as paralleling "white nationalism." Although Cheney's overarching assessment of black nationalist political history is persuasive, it exaggerates the "manly glue" that holds black nationalist discourse constitutionally: "The preoccupation with manhood demonstrated in the oral and literary works of black nationalists, from David Walker to Ice Cube, signifies that there has been a 'conceptual and political failure of imagination at work in public life. That is, these black men (and many black women) have not even *conceived* a politics of liberation that is not dependent upon a masculinist discourse that incorporates a subordination of the feminine."[70] Most pertinent here is a summation of black nationalism's continuity vis-à-vis its monadic religious sourcing:

> What began in the early twentieth century with the Moorish-American Science Temple and the Temple of Islam, then, continued to shift the parameters of black liberatory theology during the late twentieth century, as Muslim influences from the Nation of Islam and the Five Percent Nation of Islam informed the nationalist perspectives manifest within the lyrics of groups like Public Enemy, Boogie Down Productions, Poor Righteous Teachers, the Roots, and artists like Ice Cube and Paris. Yet despite this adaptation, the ideations of rap nationalists were reminiscent of those expressed in slave spirituals and in black nationalist publications of the nineteenth century, both of which were informed by Christianity.[71]

Here Cheney perceptively links the masculinist inclinations in the longitude of black nationalist projects in the "black religion" dimensions—whether Christian or Islamic. The nationalism of hip-hop stands *in direct lineage with the dispositional nationalist expressions of previous generations.*

For Algernon Austin, black nationalism was the Nation of Islam's cultural and economic frocking, whereas "religiously it is not" as nationalistic as imagined.[72] "Asiatic" religious identity formed the Nation of Islam's core, but Garveyism sourced its nationalist façade. Thus, when early hip-hop practitioners embraced the Nation of Islam's influence vis-à-vis Malcolm X and Louis Farrakhan, it was on the secular nationalist terms that were sifted from Black Power and the opening that the Nation of Islam—and a transitioning Malcolm X—provided. In the end, hip-hop's appropriation of Malcolm X facilitated Louis Farrakhan's Million Man March (and its antecedents); reciprocally, Farrakhan's appropriation of Malcolm X facilitated hip-hop's move from benign ghetto entertainment to the secular jeremiad against the Reagan revolution, its assumptions, and its effects, especially the "War on Drugs," and the continued hostility toward the welfare state.

The social and political effects of the acute racial conservatism of the 1980s and 1990s are indicated, for instance, by an increase in self-identified social conservatives, the rejection of racial liberalism in the major party system, and a general period of racial saliency and politics. Political scientist Carol Swain's *The New White Nationalism* (2002) suggests tautologically that black American support for group-specific policy demands, such as affirmative action, engendered white race consciousness among erstwhile racists and white supremacists. Ronald Walters's *White Nationalism, Black Interests* (2003) goes farther in clarifying the ubiquitous institutionalization of this phenomenon in the social, cultural, residential, and political structures of the American political system. And Lisa Nikol Nealy argues that "white American *consciousness* called by some scholars as *white nationalism* emerged when Ronald Reagan was elected President of the United States in 1980." As a leading white nationalist, she states, "Reagan supported virtually the entire social agenda of the religious-right. For instance, he not only supported prayer in public schools and restriction on abortion, positions common to great numbers of American voters, but tax exemptions for racially segregated schools and the teaching of 'scientific creationism' in public school biology classrooms." She insists, "A white *nationalist* attitude espoused by white Americans is a reflection of this group's consciousness exhibited in their racial religiosity that is showing up in their voting behavior."[73]

This pits the black nationalist response to the Reagan revolution squarely in the narrative of black religiosity. The struggles of blacks during this era were not only political and economic; they were deeply spiritual. The conflating events and contextual factors that became the impetuses for giving Louis Farrakhan influence between 1983 and 1995 were invoked in the intense spiritual and material doldrums that exposed all sorts of crises in the lives of large segments of the African American collective. This, of course, is pertinent if the events leading to the 1992 Los Angeles unrest and the 1995 MMM/DOA are taken as serious moments of nationalist dissent. As Cornel West argues, "What happened in Los Angeles [and across the nation] in April of 1992 was neither a race riot nor a class rebellion. Rather, this monumental upheaval was a multiracial, trans-class, *largely male display of justified social rage*. . . . What we witnessed in Los Angeles was the consequence of a lethal linkage of economic decline, cultural decay, and political lethargy in American life. Race was the visible catalyst, not the underlying cause."[74] Occurring less than four years later, the Million Man March represented this same "largely male display of justified social rage" but in different form. Several political scientists have highlighted the economic/racial corollary that was exacerbated by the events surrounding the Rodney King beating and verdict in Los Angeles in 1991 and 1992.[75] And even though the rebellion was, in West's view, mostly male-specific justifiable "social rage," we can also see a pattern of increased police brutality directed mostly at Latino and black young men that neither began nor ended with the videotaped Rodney King beating.

Despite the devastating social and political impact of the civil unrest during April and May 1992, veterans of the 1960s civil rights and Black Power phases of the black freedom struggle might find developments in African American culture and politics in the subsequent decades to be relatively quiescent when compared to the fierce culture of dissent and proliferation of dissident political organizations that characterized the earlier period. Komozi Woodard attributes some five hundred street-level paroxysms to the period between 1965 and 1970.[76] The vogue of marching songs and freedom cries, the cool pose of radical militancy, and the teeming shouts and calls for "revolution" came and went and left us with the politics of Ronald Reagan. And Reagan's influence has extended far beyond his administrations and into the current political situation. In the post–civil rights period, political conservatism—traditional and neoconservative—in US society has proved to be symptomatic of a larger cultural and ideological shift. This back-lash conservatism has focused on reclaiming the social and political conventions of previous decades, when oppressive social and political structures ordered the social world; one's social place circuitously determined one's political realities, and political realities determined one's social place.

Manning Marable argues that the "Battle of Los Angeles" highlighted the general condition of anomie in urban America that followed an increased class and racial stratification:

> By contrast, since the late 1970s general conditions for most of the African-American community have become worse. For example, the percentage of black high school graduates between the ages of eighteen and twenty-six who go on to college have declined since 1975. The real incomes of younger black workers have fallen sharply during that same period. Standards in health care for millions within the African-American community have fallen, with the black male life expectancy declining to only 64.7 years in 1993. By 1990 about 12 percent of all Black families now live below the federal government's poverty level, and 46 percent of all black families are headed by single women. . . . By 1992 23 percent of all young African-American men between the ages of twenty and twenty-nine were in prison, on probation, parole, or awaiting trial.[77]

In most measures of socioeconomic progress, such as education, economic wealth, occupation, employment/unemployment, income/poverty, housing conditions, health conditions, neighborhood pollution, as well as crime rates, black progress has been dismal despite improvements in many areas during the 1990s. In such a contested space, standing with Farrakhan and invoking Malcolm X was a "protest against real distress," to echo the words of Karl Marx.

The post–civil rights relevance of Malcolm X and Louis Farrakhan here is not so much that they were religious. Rather, through the religious device of the black nationalist jeremiad (the "jihad of words"), they held explicit ideological themes that have been recurrent in the span of African Americans' encounter with the racially constructed social order from the very beginning of slavery. Its major structure included tenets of the black jeremiads' oral and literary traditions.

Malcolm X offered exemplary, sharp, and lucid historical and contemporaneous criticisms of domestic and pertinent foreign policy relations. He was at his best in the last year of his life, when he outlined his "Message to the Grassroots" (Detroit 1963), "The Ballot or the Bullet" (Detroit 1964), and "By Any Means Necessary" (to the Organization of Afro-American Unity, Harlem, July 1964). In these speeches, he called for common-ground racial solidarity, harshly criticized the March on Washington, and assailed the Democratic Party (in the White House and Congress) as Dixiecrat-led, suggesting that the party's neosegregationist wing made it no more attractive than the Republicans. "No I am not a Republican nor a Democrat, nor an American, and got sense enough to know it. I am one of the 22 million Black victims of the Democrats, one of the 22 million victims of the Republicans, and one of the 22 million Black victims of Americanism. . . . I speak as a victim of America's so-called democracy." He supported, instead, Albert Cleage's Freedom Now Party.

Malcolm X defined black nationalism in its broadest construction (which incorporated all nonwhite individuals and, toward the end of his career and life, white radicals). He also described the disposition of the "new generation of black people," who were increasingly gaining political consciousness, especially in regard to the con game of the major capitalist-class Dixiecrat political parties. He also framed the disposition of blacks within a parallel, separate development, and self-help within the United States, without regard to land set-asides or emigrationist projects; he advocated community empowerment and political control of the urban centers where blacks constitute significant population numbers; black self-reliance was an ongoing theme. He defined the domestic colonial predicament of US blacks as colonized, second-class citizens.

And even though Malcolm X does address a number of "grass-roots" rebellions (e.g., Birmingham) that were, in his estimation, part of the broader "black revolution," he does not mention that of Robert F. Williams in Monroe, North Carolina, in 1961. Like David Walker, Malcolm X as late as April 1964 referred to white segregationists, conservatives, and liberals as "the enemy" of blacks at home and abroad. Despite much talk of political violence in rebellion and urban guerrilla tactics, he felt that the United States could experience a nonviolent revolution if it would only give "the Black man . . . everything that's due him" in terms of "freedom, justice, and equality" *in the United States*. Black self-reliance, like other segments of US society, was linked to disciplined consumerism, black business, landownership, and political independence.[78]

The appeal of Malcolm X and Louis Farrakhan, with shortcomings in tow, was as much about the Reaganist shift of the major American political parties, and in society more generally, as it was about any affirmative assertion of unreconstructed nationalism. This is, perhaps, the single greatest betrayal by Louis Farrakhan (aside from playing a key role in plotting and ordering the death of Malcolm X): the failure to fulfill the contemporary black nationalist project of creating an independent political structure, as promised, or even a manifesto. Manning Marable identifies, at length, the encounter between the experiences of the "We Shall Overcome" and hip-hop generations,

> Compounding this sense of social-class and vocational division within the black community is yet another growing schism: a deepening division of culture, values and social relations. To a real extent, the cultural clash is intergenerational, symbolized by the radical differences in discourse, political experiences, and social expectations between those African-Americans *born before 1964* and those after the great legislative victories of the civil rights movement. Simplistically, one might describe this great division as being between the "We Shall Overcome" generation and the "hip-hop" generation.

The former lived through the most dynamic and icon-shattering decade of the twentieth century, the 1960s. . . . Everything seemed possible for a brief, shining moment. . . . Tomorrow would always be better than yesterday. The "hip-hop" generation's primary experience in politics can be characterized in one word: defeat. The generation's most dominating and influential national political figure was President Ronald Reagan. The generation which produced the dynamic cultural expression of rap music came to maturity in a context of rising black-on-black violence, symbolized by the Crips vs. the Bloods in south-central Los Angeles. During the next five years, more black people will be killed in our major cities than the total number of American troops killed during the Vietnam War. Hip-hop emerged in the context of widespread unemployment, homelessness, and the omnipresence of fear and social alienation. For many of our young people there is no sense or expectation that a future is worth living for, or that it even exists. One lives for today, because tomorrow might never come.[79]

The phenomenal social development that brought younger individuals, whose political socialization occurred in the two decades after civil rights and Black Power, into awareness of Malcolm X's political and religious thought featured an emergent clash between the concomitant forces of nationalist conservatism among Euro-American whites and political black nationalism, which peaked together first in the context of Black Power.

Today, as in the past, only a very small minority of African Americans identify themselves as doctrinaire nationalists committed to land-grant separatism, emigration, or even the idea that black Americans should avoid interaction with other groups, especially whites. With the possible exceptions of Marcus Garvey and the United Negro Improvement Association, nationalist political elites have been of marginal symbolic importance in the struggle for substantive equality in the United States. Most African Americans today (outside of academic and intellectual circles) do not know or talk of Paul Cuffee, James T. Holly, Martin R. Delany, Alexander Crummell, Henry Highland Garnet, Bishop Henry McNeal Turner, Benjamin "Pap" Singleton,[80] Chief Alfred Sam, or even Ron Karenga and Amiri Baraka.

Despite the popularity of the Nation of Islam and Malcolm X, Gary T. Marx's 1964 study reminds us that the Nation of Islam leaders Elijah Muhammad and Malcolm X were very unpopular among most African Americans during the civil rights epoch. In the case of Malcolm X, his star burned brighter only after his 1965 assassination and the advent of Black Power in 1966. Three decades later (at his own event in 1995), Louis Farrakhan scored lower than several black liberal-integrationists in terms of leadership preference choices presented to survey respondents at the MMM/DOA.[81] One should not conclude, however, that black nationalism is passé. The land-based emigrationist form *is* a relic at this point, but black nationalism's currency persisted throughout the twentieth century and, shockingly, intervened in the 2008 presidential campaigns through the jeremiad of Jeremiah Wright Jr. For two decades preceding the turn of the twenty-first century, there continued to be evidence of an existential quality to being black in the United States in the many spheres of life—economic, housing, health care, legal and judicial administration, or simply driving an automobile.

Blacks continue to espouse that we have experienced a halcyonic "end" or "postmodern" or "declining significance" of racism and race at a time when we have witnessed its heightened salience in US society and politics. The catastrophic 2005 Hurricane Katrina betrayed the widespread banality of urban and rural black poverty and the continued significance of black social estrangement and isolation in the United States. It stands as a powerful example against the optimism of Barack Obama's election. Persistent expressions of *political* solidarity among African Americans have forced intellectuals of every ideological stripe to address the programmatic strengths and weaknesses of black nationalism in the United States more than four decades after it was inaccurately eulogized as the end of Black Power. In the meantime, scholars, policy analysts, and various commissions pointed out the cultural pathologies of African American life, especially African American women in the ghettoes. For the child in the crib of her single mother's projects unit in any major city or black suburban ghetto, it was impossible to know that she had inherited a condition or become "a problem." But especially affected by these conditions are the young black men (which we view as different but inseparable from impacts of African American women as grandmothers, mothers, sisters, aunts, wives, lovers, nieces, and so forth). For example, Marcus Pohlmann has found that

> although college-educated blacks and younger two-parent black families are now doing nearly as well as or better than comparable whites in terms of the economic indicators discussed herein, *the story is not nearly as encouraging for the large majority of black males who are not fortunate enough to have a college education.* Black women, by contrast, have begun to approach parity with white women, but both are in a clearly inferior economic position vis-à-vis men, especially white men. . . . And as nationwide unemployment stagnated at recession levels after the mid-1970s, African Americans fell even further behind.[82]

Hanes Walton provides a poignant record of events within the larger context of the racial, economic, and presidential politics of the 1990s, in which "the Reagan-Bush method of transforming political context involved the use of race as political currency and capital."[83] He concludes this proposition by returning to a discussion of presidential politics:

> When race becomes political capital and currency as it did during the Reagan and Bush administrations, it also becomes a topic in the public dialogue. With the advent of the riots in Los Angeles, when the Simi Valley verdict redefined the concept of justice/injustice and discounted legitimate grievances confronted by the African-American community, the issue of race was returned

to the forefront of that dialogue. Acting out of their own community's cultural rendering of morality, *African-Americans were compelled to remind the powers-that-be, in forceful terms, that the view and versions of justice adopted and promoted during the Reagan-Bush era*—a justice based on race and a kind of moral relativism—would be contested. Thus we see that when a transformed political context leads to a negative redefinition of the societal concept of justice, subcultural perspectives will find ways to enter this skewed discourse even if they fail to alter it.[84]

In black politics, the liberal-integrationist orientation that drove antiracist commitments in the struggles for civil and political rights was moribund as a cultural and economic critique to address contemporary structural crises in poor, working-class, and global communities thereafter. What was required, in a period characterized by nationalist saliency within black communities during the 1980s and 1990s, was a coherent analysis of the black predicament in the post–civil rights era. Required was a perspective that was *primarily,* but not exclusively, "of, for, and by" black Americans, a perspective that spoke to the social distress evident in the interrelated familial, penal, employment, poverty, and public health indexes without regard to integration as an end.[85]

Malcolm X and the Haunting of Louis Farrakhan

Louis Farrakhan was born Louis Eugene Walcott on May 11, 1933, in the Bronx borough of New York City. His mother, Mae Clark, was from the Caribbean (St. Kitts), as were his biological father (Jamaica) and his stepfather (Barbados); Malcom X's mother was also from the Caribbean.[86] Louis was raised in a "Black Jew(ish)" West Indian enclave of Roxbury, Boston, where the teachings of Marcus Garvey influenced many. He was introduced to music during his adolescence and earned recognition as a violinist with the Boston College Orchestra, eventually landing on national television—one of the first blacks to ever do so—on the *Ted Mack Original Amateur Hour*, which aired on each of the three major television networks (NBC, ABC, and CBS) from 1948 to 1970.[87] According to one biographer, and also like Malcolm X, Farrakhan was introduced to the political philosophy of black nationalism not through the Nation of Islam but through the influence of a *Christian* black nationalist preacher, the Reverend Nathan Wright at Boston's St. Cyprian Episcopal Church, and through the syncretistic Garvey movement.[88] At the age of twenty-four, he embraced the teachings of Elijah Muhammad, Malcolm X, and the Nation of Islam; became "Louis X"; and took his post at Temple No. 7 in Harlem, where Malcolm X was minister until he was replaced by Farrakhan in 1964.

Louis X (Farrakhan) emerged in the ranks of the Nation of Islam's ministers and the Fruit of Islam and was eventually appointed minister of Temple

No. 11 (Boston), which grew tremendously under his leadership and "fishing" activities among Boston's educated segments. As Vibert L. White Jr. explains, "Blacks who attended the Boston mosque were not just the typical pimp, prostitute, and hustler but were high-school educated and college-trained African Americans interested in Islam."[89]

Several sources depict Farrakhan's status in the Nation of Islam prior to the 1960s through 1975 (the period between Malcolm's break and Elijah's death) as one of an opportunistic underling who garnered little respect from either Betty Shabazz or Malcolm's sister and adviser, Ella Collins. According to Karl Evanzz, neither Tynetta Muhammad nor Elijah Muhammad trusted Farrakhan very much, accusing him of plagiarizing her play, financial irregularities at the Harlem mosque, and too hastily betraying Malcolm X.[90] Farrakhan was, at times, hostile toward the bourgeois element of temple members and accused some of being "agents of the FBI, CIA, or IRS," leading to a mass exodus of the temple's more educated individuals. Perhaps his most difficult member was Malcolm X's oldest sister, Ella Collins, who once noted, "I was always wary of him. He had too much of a lean and hungry look for me. More importantly, he was not his own man. His mother made all his important decisions."[91] Collins insisted that there were also "complexional" issues driving conflicts in Farrakhan's restive temple. One of the more unexamined aspects of the Nation of Islam's most prominent leaders and spokespersons—with the noted exception of Khallid Muhammad—from Fard and Elijah to Malcolm and Farrakhan, has been a pattern of light-skinned men.[92] Ella suggested, for instance,

> I knew Malcolm had initially chosen him as his successor at Temple Eleven because of his light-skin. Malcolm was very much aware of the light-skin, dark-skin thing in Boston. At that time it would be hard enough to talk about the Nation of Islam to such people even if a Colin Powell–like person was the spokesperson; with a dark-skinned person, it would have been nearly impossible. Malcolm, still striving to build up the [Nation of Islam], took the position that if anyone could make even a slight dent among people with that attitude, it was Louis X.[93]

Farrakhan gained notoriety within the Nation of Islam for his play *Orgena: A Negro Spelled Backwards*[94] and *The Trial* (in which "the white man is tried and found guilty for every great crime against humanity") and a musical rendition, "The White Man's Heaven Is a Black Man's Hell." Although he was at one time a trusted confidant of Malcolm X (roughly during 1955–1963), Louis X emerged by 1967 to replace Malcolm X as the national representative of Elijah Muhammad. Farrakhan's ascendance to national prominence within the ranks of the Nation of Islam increased through 1974, during Elijah Muhammad's final decade. Indeed, Farrakhan has presented his first ten years in the Nation of Islam as one of tutelage under Malcolm X, and the second ten years as one under the tutelage of Muhammad.

Throughout Farrakhan's public career, his version of black nationalism has been variously described: "fascistic," "revolutionary," "chauvinistic," "cultural," "religiously parochial," "conservative," and "religious authoritarianism." It may be true that parts of each have some validity, particularly where his thinking meandered into self-defeating "Jewish talk." No single feature of Farrakhan's public ministry refracted attention *from* the desperate and lived situations of many African Americans in the late twentieth century more than his anachronistic, conspiratorial charges against American Jews and, to a lesser extent, the state of Israel. This was largely a treasonous generational beef that subverted an inchoate movement that recruited him to articulate legitimate policy demands and grievances. Robert Smith adds,

> The rhetorical focus of Farrakhan (and other of his ministers) on Jews is a recent development that has no basis in the nationalist tradition generally or the teachings of Mr. Muhammad specifically (it is after all the white, not Jewish, "devil" that bears the burden for black racial oppression). Malcolm X did not single out Jews for special disapprobation, nor did Farrakhan until 1984. Farrakhan told *Time* magazine that his recent focus on Jews came about as a result of harassment of Jesse Jackson by Jewish militants during the 1984 presidential campaign, and a successful effort by Jewish distributors to block the manufacture and sale of the Nation's line of [Clean n' Fresh] toiletries, even going so far, he claims, as to pressure Johnson Products. Thus Farrakhan says, "When I saw that, I recognized that the black man will never be free until we address the relationship between blacks and Jews."[95]

Considering these observations, it is worth note that one of several plausible explanations had to do with Farrakhan's need to construct an equivalent bugbear to Malcolm X's early and resoundingly popular criticism of the reified class of "blue eyed, blonde-haired, pale-skinned devils" (albeit from within the same Nation of Islam that nurtured Farrakhan).[96] It was also largely, for misdirected cathartic and therapeutic purposes, bound up in the psychological needs of a besieged postsegregation black collective, and for the exigencies within the theological and organizational hierarchy of the Nation of Islam. Focusing on American Jews was part of Farrakhan's "new Malcolm X" persona, and this became increasingly apparent in November 1993, when Khallid Muhammad's antiwhite and anti-Jewish rant at Keane College in New Jersey was brought to light, enabling Farrakhan to orchestrate his elevation above Malcolm—who, in this latter scenario, Khallid typifies—and to the level of being officially deemed "Honorable," which had previously been strictly reserved for Master Farad Muhammad and Elijah Muhammad, who have since been designated as "the Most Honorable" by the Nation of Islam faithful.

A young person on campus or in a community drawn to Farrakhan or, say, his erstwhile and now deceased lieutenant, Khallid Muhammad, in the 1980s or 1990s could listen to a powerful articulation of the social and political realities that gave way to an unwelcome diatribe on black people's reified "Jewish problem." This great betrayal and mismanagement of the unapprenticed expression of remnant racial solidarity nodes, employed to speak to the Reagan moment in black politics, dashed blacks' long-standing, though still fringe, interest in finding solutions to their outrageous living conditions in the United States. Wilson Moses concurs in a passing reference: "Regardless of how one feels about Louis Farrakhan's sincerity or his foolish ethnic hostilities, he has undeniable appeal to many black social conservatives. Many of the men who attended his 1995 March on Washington did so neither because they endorsed his ethnic antagonisms, nor because they enjoy two-hour discourses on numerology, but *because black nationalism symbolizes the rejection of the scatological values that predominate in media-generated images of black vernacular culture.*"[97] Students of black politics who focus on the Nation of Islam and its ministers' tensions with American Jews nevertheless are inclined to downplay the seemingly inherent (Abrahamic) *theological* tensions among Jews, Christians, and Muslims. Whereas the former are more or less seen as corrupted by the "Great Devil" that is the West, the anti-Semitism is uncritically located in the nationalism of black politics.[98]

Farrakhan's role in the split between Malcolm X and Elijah Muhammad, and in the events leading to the former's assassination, was a millstone that weighed against his leadership in the broader black community during the 1960s and 1970s—that is, until he emerged from Chicago in the early 1980s. The millstone would resurface at the height of Louis Farrakhan's popularity in the early 1990s, but it seemed to matter little to the generation of individuals born in the 1960s and 1970s, those who knew little to nothing of the divergent paths that Malcolm and Farrakhan followed. Indeed, a great irony is the manner in which Farrakhan emerges in the early 1980s as a second coming of Malcolm X. At the height of his notoriety, Farrakhan inadvertently reaped the benefit of being a *type* of Malcolm X; or better still, he reaped the benefit of Malcolm X being understood as a "type" of leadership modality that suborns playing Malcolm's *khalifa* (successor). Richard B. Turner argues, for instance, that Malcolm X "became the primary model for the signification of black Islamic identity in contemporary America. Indeed, in Malcolm's shifting relationships with the Nation of Islam, and with Islam in the Middle East and West Africa, and in his ambivalence between racial separation and multi-racialism in the contexts, we can discern the models for the various significations of Islamic identity in the ever-changing ideologies of Louis Farrakhan and Warith Deen Mohammed."[99]

Based on Farrakhan's own account of his significance in the 1980s and 1990s, Malcolm X's apparition haunted him as much as it did the forces of antiblack racism. The extent to which Malcolm X broke from the religious tradition that Farrakhan continues to sustain is merely a subtext to a broader historical discourse of social and political engagement in which black nationalism has been mostly extant. Malcolm X's suspension and eventual break from the Nation of Islam should remove him no farther from the larger tradition than, say, Cyril Briggs's and Richard B. Moore's splits and conflicts with the Garveyites removed them from scholarly works on black nationalism in the post–World War I period. Ironically, Louis Farrakhan contends that the popularity of Malcolm X among younger black Americans in the 1990s had to do with the US government's attempt to resurrect Malcolm in order to diminish his own popularity among the same cohort. According to Farrakhan, this was an attempt by his "enemies" to connect him with the assassination of Malcolm X in 1965 because Farrakhan openly called for the death of Malcolm X in the Nation of Islam's official newspaper, *Muhammad Speaks*.

Farrakhan was known for calling Malcolm X a "Judas" and "Benedict Arnold" who was "worthy of death." On the anniversary of Malcolm X's break with the Nation of Islam, Farrakhan's withering editorial ("Boston Minister Tells of Malcolm—Muhammad's Biggest Hypocrite") noted, "only those who wish to be led to hell, or to their doom, will follow Malcolm. The die is set, and Malcolm shall not escape." And he didn't. It is apparent that Elijah Muhammad's followers from the Newark, Philadelphia, New York, and Boston mosques (headed by Louis X Farrakhan) were at the center of the murder of Malcolm X and led a series of violent confrontations with other dissident members of the Nation of Islam. They carried out orders from the Chicago mosque, which had itself demanded Malcolm X's tongue in an envelope.[100] These events included firebombing the East Elmhurst (Queens) family home of Malcolm X one week before his murder. Kofi Natambu, like many others, is careful to implicate government complicity in the murder of Malcolm X, noting, "the FBI and CIA, smelling blood, also moved in for the kill with various agents gloating to their supervisors that Malcolm's days were numbered. By the end of 1964, Malcolm's file in the FBI alone was over four thousand pages."[101] In the end, Malcolm X believed that his would-be assassins had power that far exceeded the reach of the Nation of Islam and its followers. One of the last people to breathe air into Malcolm X's dying body, Gene Roberts, was later revealed to be an undercover agent for the New York Police Department Bureau of Special Services (BOSS) and an FBI informant.[102]

In a speech titled "The Assassination of Malcolm X" at Malcolm X College in 1990, Farrakhan details his conversion after listening to Elijah Muhammad and, later, Malcolm X—under whom he studied in Boston. Because this is one of the rare occasions in which Farrakhan addressed publicly the issue and circumstances of Malcolm X's assassination, we quote from the speech at length. Based on their relationship, Farrakhan states that "Malcolm became the father that I never had," "he taught me how to be a man." But the

greatest man in my life, yesterday, today, and tomorrow, has been, and is, the Honorable Elijah Muhammad, and the way Malcolm represented the Honorable Elijah Muhammad . . . there was not another minister, captain, nobody in the Nation that I saw representing the Honorable Elijah Muhammad like Malcolm. . . . So I adored Malcolm. . . . *I am more spiritual, Malcolm was more political.* But there would come a time, when the Brother Malcolm and the Honorable Elijah Muhammad would be at variance and that was the most painful time of my life. When I had to choose between the man I had looked for all my life—the Honorable Elijah Muhammad—and the man who helped to shape me—Malcolm X. . . .

The FBI and the press created a negative environment right inside the Nation around Malcolm X by projecting Malcolm as the leader over his leader. . . . When Malcolm was silenced [by Elijah Muhammad] it was Louis X that was called to speak in New York. . . . Many of us as Muslims disliked Malcolm when he spoke against the Honorable Elijah Muhammad. And I was one of those. I was hurt that he came out against his teacher and being a lover of Elijah Muhammad, I spoke ill of Malcolm X. I was one of those who spoke into the illness that Malcolm himself created when he left the movement and spoke against Elijah Muhammad who had become an institution. So I spoke against Malcolm. Malcolm spoke against Elijah Muhammad . . . creating the atmosphere into which Malcolm could be assassinated. We were all pawns. . . . Being used by a wicked government who wanted Malcolm dead but wanted the blame on Elijah Muhammad so they could kill two birds with one stone. *And now they have sought to bring Malcolm X back alive because they want to diminish me in the eyes of those who love and adore Malcolm X today.* It is the only thing that they can do.[103]

Malcolm's widow, Betty Shabazz, heightened his intellectual legacy and forced it to the center of black politics during the 1990s. In the early 1980s, during the Harlem campaign to name Lenox Avenue after her husband (which included Muhammad Ali and Arthur Ashe, among other participants, along with this author), Betty Shabazz angrily scolded unnamed members of the audience gathered at the Adam Clayton Powell Jr. state building, in a march organized by Harlem's New Afrikan People's Organization and others: "You know who you are, you know what you did to my husband." And she insisted that there could be forgiveness only if they "bring back my husband." Shabazz knew that Malcolm X was never "out of style" for many of Harlem's faithful nationalist elements, but she seemed to suggest that Malcolm X needed to be given wider acknowledgment and placed in prominence with the likes of Douglass, King, Tubman, and others dedicated to black liberation. Her biographer notes, "Whether Betty was at a memorial, conference, forum, or lecture, her mission was to guard Malcolm's legacy and humanize his memory. She wanted to lift him from the 'street corner' she felt the news media had consigned him to [sic]. She wanted the world to see him as a statesman whose murder was injustice rather than as some rabble-rouser who had perished in a Negro blood feud."[104]

During the February 1993 Savior's Day observation at Mosque Maryam, Louis Farrakhan set off a series of events with comments concerning the assassination of Malcolm X. Farrakhan stridently declared, "Yes, I love Elijah Muhammad and if you attack him I will kill you; yesterday, today, and tomorrow. And I am not a killer. . . . But if somebody attacks what you love, each one of you in here would become a killer instantaneously." In the Nation of

Islam, "we don't give a damn about no white man's law, when you attack what we love. And frankly, it ain't none of your business." Unapologetically, he shrieked to the audience: "What do you got to say about it?; did you teach Malcolm?; did you make Malcolm?; did you clean up Malcolm?; did you put Malcolm out before the world?; was Malcolm your traitor or was he ours? *And if we dealt with him like a nation deals with a traitor, what the hell business is it of yours*?! . . . Because in the future we gonna be a nation and the nation better be able to deal with traitors and cutthroats and turncoats." In March 1994, Betty Shabazz witnessed Farrakhan's apologia on a New York Sunday talk show and, in response, expressed belief that he and the Nation of Islam were involved in her husband's death, saying, "Of course, yes. Nobody kept it a secret. It was a badge of honor. Everybody talked about it, yes."[105]

Qubilah, Betty's second daughter with Malcolm, reportedly feared retaliation against her mother for implicating Farrakhan, and she sought to preempt it.[106] Betty's efforts crystallized when Qubilah was arrested for conspiring with a childhood friend, who had turned FBI informant, to assassinate Louis Farrakhan at the height of his popularity in early 1995, during the lead-up to the MMM/DOA. Not only did Betty Shabazz speak at the MMM/DOA; she was able to provide clearance for Farrakhan even as she used the allegations against her daughter to broker a truce with the reconstituted Nation of Islam and its leader. The guests at the truce included a who's-who of cultural nationalists and civil rights–era veterans and allies.[107]

When he spoke, Farrakhan acknowledged publicly that "members of the Nation of Islam were involved in the assassination of Malcolm. . . . The Nation has taken the heat and carried the burden of the murder of Malcolm X. We can't deny whatever our part was." But Farrakhan's acknowledgment shifted seamlessly to a criticism of the "real culprit": "the government of America." *It* had engineered Malcolm's murder, and even now it was attempting to resurrect Malcolm X to discredit him, because, he felt, no living person could. The fact that the informant, Michael Fitzpatrick, was partly Jewish and a former member of the violent Jewish Defense League, which hounded Farrakhan assemblies with bitter vitriol, was not lost in the conspiracy talk.

Former Nation of Islam minister Vibert White Jr. indicates that Farrakhan's habit of blaming the government for the attacks and murders of dissident Muslims was commonplace. He also argues that "the person that provided the greatest stepping stone for Louis Farrakhan was his onetime friend Malcolm X."[108] Even more vicious than the hounding of Malcolm X is Farrakhan's speaking about the 1973 murders of the babies and children of former Nation of Islam minister and Hanafi Muslim leader Abu Abdul Khaalis in Washington, D.C., for blasphemy against W. D. Fard and Elijah Muhammad. Louis Farrakhan sought to shift the focus to a government conspiracy even after he warned "all hypocrites," in a radio speech, that "they will execute you." Upon arrest, one assassin-turned-state's-witness from Philadelphia, James X Price, was found dead, having been sodomized, with his testicles crushed, and hanged with a bedsheet while in a jail cell with two coconspirators and Nation of Islam companions.[109] Eight years *after* speaking about Malcolm's death, Farrakhan's address warned:

> Let this be a warning to those of you who would be used as an instrument of a wicked government against our rise. Be careful, because when the government is tired of you they're going to dump you back into the laps of your people. And though Elijah Muhammad is a merciful man and will say, "Come in," and forgive you, yet in the ranks of the black people today there are younger men and women who have not forgiveness in them for traitors and stool pigeons. And they will execute you, as soon as your identity is known.[110]

Malcolm X's first haunting of Farrakhan came in the person and theological agenda of Elijah Muhammad's youngest "legitimate" son, Wallace D. Muhammad, who, along with his brother Akbar, initially sided with Malcolm X in the split. Beginning with the death of Elijah Muhammad in 1975, Wallace Muhammad (Imam Warith Deen Mohammed) had been mystically deemed his father's *khalifa* (successor) by a 1930s "prophecy" of Fard—a prophecy that likely saved the life of Wallace in the hours and days after the murder of Malcolm X. Wallace Muhammad would lead a reform movement from within the Nation of Islam, scuttling most of his father's teachings—which Farrakhan would continue to promote throughout the late twentieth century.[111] In the meantime, Wallace deprived Farrakhan of the integral role he hoped to play in the post-Elijah Nation of Islam. In February 1976, Wallace named Harlem's Mosque No. 7 in honor of Malcolm X, even forcing Farrakhan to make the public announcement. This period, according to the loyalists of Muhammad, represented the "Fall" of the original Nation of Islam until Farrakhan would revive it beginning in 1978.[112] Farrakhan was relegated to being transferred from the black universe that was Harlem and the Nation of Islam's keystone mosque to the unremarkable role of assistant minister of a West Side Chicago mosque, headed by a former assistant of his. In Wallace Muhammad's determination this was done "to remove Farrakhan from a base in the midst of large militant black nationalist circles."[113] This was Wallace's attempt to "keep his enemy" close—or to drive him from the Nation of Islam. Vibert White notes, "During this period members of the Nation of Islam believed they were at war with Wallace Muhammad and the World Community of Al-Islam. Farrakhan's polemical rhetoric encouraged the idea that Wallace was an evil conspirator who worked with the government to kill Elijah Muhammad and destroy the Nation. His labeling of Wallace Muhammad as a hypocrite, the anti-Christ, and a rebellious son incited many to talk of attacking members of the rival Muslim sect."[114]

Rod Bush goes farther in noting that FBI surveillance revealed a conversation between Farrakhan and Elijah Muhammad in which the latter demanded that Malcolm X be silenced: "When you find a hypocrite, you have to cut their heads off." Furthermore, Bush cites other sources who claim that Yusef Shah (Captain Joseph)—who personally despised Malcolm X for decades after his assassination—admitted before his own death that "Farrakhan was personally involved in planning the assassination of Malcolm X."[115] The murder of Malcolm X, then, served as a kind of ideological coup d'état in which the increasingly progressive nationalism of Malcolm X was supplanted by the conservative nationalists epitomized by Louis Farrakhan and his allies. Bush notes,

> We moved very quickly from the revolutionary political discourse of Malcolm X, discovered by a new generation seeking to address their situation in U.S. society, to the controversial but nonrevolutionary discourse of Louis Farrakhan and Leonard Jeffries. The conservative Black nationalists opposed racial domination and degradation but lacked a structural or systemic critique of U.S. society. *They injected verbal militance and rhetorical bombast into an already superheated public discourse, forming a perfect target for a white racist backlash that had gained the upper hand in the nation's polity since the Reagan counterrevolution of 1980.* . . . The initial manifestations of nationalistic sentiment in the 1990s were strongly influenced by the egalitarian views and revolutionary sentiment of Malcolm X and took a decidedly ghettocentric form. But since the political and ideological tendency that Malcolm X and the radicals of the 1970s represented had been destroyed, the more conservative tradition survived and grew in the academy and in Black communities. . . . The attack on the memory of Malcolm X and the actual removal of Malcolm X from the scene are inextricably related to this phenomenon.[116]

If Malcolm X haunted Farrakhan, then the specter of Ronald Reagan proved too immediate for younger admirers of Malcolm X to revisit this bitter history. Malcolm X was also useful to individuals who, influenced by the burgeoning black glitterati of emergent hip-hop discourses, themselves raised Malcolm from the dead to speak to their "really existing" conditions. Malcolm X did not "come back in style" in the 1980s and 1990s as much as his representation(s) was (were) raised in the urgency of the period. If the younger generations gave Farrakhan audience and prominence in poetic and artistic expression, then it must have had something to do with a yearning for the critical resolve of Malcolm X. Hip-hop artists, for instance, might be drawn to Farrakhan's musical and entertainment background before and within the Nation of Islam. His life in Roxbury while growing up fatherless might also be attractive to some. But there was nothing in the life of Louis Farrakhan comparable to Malcolm X's self-styled autobiographical account of the urban street narrative of foster care, abandonment, underworld hustling, drug abuse, incarceration, and redemption. They feverishly read Malcolm's account, not Farrakhan's, in the 1980s and 1990s. Malcolm X authenticated Louis Farrakhan. It is equally plausible that many younger supporters of Louis Farrakhan enmeshed their political representations in the amorphous rubric of black rage. Their "jihads of words" resembled and were constitutive of a body of black protest thought.[117] In this, however, we are warned by

Adolph Reed of their limits, "As languages of political criticism and legitimation, those narratives pivoted on normative criteria . . . that were so distant from mundane political life that they could not provide clear bases for apprehending the significance of the everyday micropolitical processes around which the new black political order congealed."[118]

Some scholars conclude that 1983 was critical in the "emergent mobilization" among black American voters. Although Jesse Jackson's Rainbow Coalition campaigns represented the core of this research trend, an almost unnoticed parallel was developing. Whereas in 1963 C. Eric Lincoln had characterized the Nation of Islam as a movement in and of itself, it may be more accurately characterized as a fringe black nationalist religiopolitical movement organization that reached its heyday during the 1950s and 1960s, only to be revived by Louis Farrakhan through the 1980s and 1990s as part of a larger mobilization opposing the racial conservatism in US politics and society.[119] The black leadership establishment—which initially rejected Jackson in 1983—viewed Farrakhan as even more of a nuisance.[120]

Despite Farrakhan's appeal to various segments of the black community, his often vitriolic jeremiads, against American and Palestinian Jewry in particular and whites in general, made him anathema to black liberal integrationists.[121] In addition to criticizing the black-Democratic alliance, Farrakhan, who first registered to vote in 1983, supported the fifty-state independent presidential candidacy of the National Alliance Party's Lenora Fulani.[122] Indeed, the Farrakhan-Sharpton-Fulani coalition represented a twin development alongside the "mainstream" liberal-integrationist strategies evident in the Jackson campaigns of the same period: "From the experience of 1984 a new political development had taken place. Where once the radical elements of the Black political community had been fragmented and marginal, harried by the police and mired in sectarian strife, a new coalition of forces dedicated to radical Black political independence emerged. At its core was the . . . presidential candidacy of Lenora Fulani, who had articulated her 'Two Roads Are Better than One' campaign."[123]

Thus, Farrakhan continued to forge alliances with independent black radical Christian preachers and churches, black fraternal organizations, and fringe leaders such as New York's Reverend Al Sharpton and the 1984 and 1988 presidential candidate Lenora Fulani. Locally, the likes of Al Sharpton and Danny Bakewell (in Los Angeles)[124] mobilized community residents against hostile elements in government and authority. This provided Farrakhan with the organizational readiness and elite alliances that would prove invaluable as he remained on the periphery of black leadership in America. And this would also serve him well, for alienation was the common experience of his supporters. Farrakhan's emergence thus highlighted both coalition and generational tensions in many cities during this period. Among this cohort, the old "Malcolm-or-Martin" debate shifted to "Farrakhan or Jesse."

Yet even though Farrakhan was unacceptable to the black liberal-integrationist leadership class, he was acceptable to the young, black, urban-dwelling, nationalist elements—largely across class lines. For many, ironically, he was the "second coming of Malcolm X." Despite modest increases in black nationalism advocacy among African-American voters throughout the 1990s, Farrakhan would subsequently abandon his fringe alliances as certain nationalist elements (e.g., Benjamin Chavis and Kwame Mfume) within integrationist organizations sought to incorporate him into the black racial and economic discourse. But Farrakhan's attempt at moderation came when his primary lieutenant, Khallid Muhammad (Harold X Moore), delivered a bitterly racist, anti-Semitic diatribe at New Jersey's Kean College in late 1993; it was published as a full-page ad by the Anti-Defamation League (ADL) in *The New York Times*, setting off a firestorm of events, including a unanimous (97–0) vote in the US Senate censuring the speech as "false, racist, divisive, repugnant, and a disservice to all Americans." Such an action was unprecedented in the history of the US Congress.[125]

Farrakhan eventually rejected the "spirit" and "manner," but not the "substance," of Khallid Muhammad's speech. Farrakhan, in subsequent speeches to overwhelmingly black audiences, sought to compare his relationship with Khallid Muhammad to that of Malcolm X with Elijah Muhammad on the verge of their split. Muhammad provided Farrakhan with the opportunity to appear as a sage alternative to the rage that Khallid's words represented.[126] Farrakhan's subsequent press conference also highlighted an alleged "secret document put out by the Civil Rights Division of the Anti-Defamation League." Furthermore, "This document reveals their strategy for dealing with Louis Farrakhan and the Nation of Islam. The ADL raises the question, 'does Farrakhan's acceptance by the mainstream, Black community represent a new found tolerance for anti-Semitism, which the ADL must fight with every weapon at our disposal?' What do these weapons include?" One of the weapons identified by the ADL and mentioned in their document is the exploitation of "some of the nation's top Black political and civil rights leaders who have long been envious of Louis Farrakhan's ability to reach large and enthusiastic audiences." But, as White and others note,

> for all of the diatribes of Farrakhan against Presidents Nixon, Ford, Reagan, and Bush, he is a staunch Republican. The problem is that the minister must behave in front of his followers like a Huey Newton or a Malcolm X militant. In contrast to Farrakhan's theatrical pose as a revolutionary, he had attempted to moderate his racial tone for sympathetic whites, blacks, and Jews who supported the Nation's position of family values, self-help programs, education, and an end to Affirmative Action.[127]

Khallid Muhammad's torturous performance of his Malcolm X minstrel went farther than Malcolm X ever went with Elijah Muhammad.[128] Like

Malcolm X, Khallid Muhammad was more popular among the Fruit of Islam rank and file and among the young and the hip-hop cadre of entertainers who discursively sampled Malcolm X, Louis Farrakhan, and Khallid Muhammad in tracks and videos.[129] In White's view,

> The personality that represented the grassroots members, an undisciplined side of the Nation of Islam, was Minister Khallid Muhammad. Since his acceptance into the Muslim fold, Minister Khallid has characterized himself as a warrior for the street brother and sister. As the minister of mosques in Los Angeles, Atlanta, and New York City, Khallid created a cult-like following that embraced gang members like the Crips and Bloods of south central Los Angeles, the Gangsta Disciples of Chicago, and the Zulu Nation of Miami and the Bronx. More than any other Black Muslim, including Farrakhan, Khallid's devotion ran deep into the hip-hop generation of musical rap entertainers. Hard-core artists and groups like Public Enemy, Niggas With Attitude, Ice Cube, and Tupac Shakur . . . viewed the controversial Muslim with admiration and respect as the leader of Generation X.[130]

This is not to favorably compare Khallid Muhammad to Malcolm X as much as it is to highlight the towering apparition of Malcolm X that infiltrated future generations of the Nation of Islam—from Wallace Muhammad's loyalty, to Farrakhan's perfidy, to Khallid's buffoonery.[131]

* * *

The apparition of Malcolm X—and the jeremiad, or "jihad of words," foisted upon black followers and society by Louis Farrakhan—haunted US race relations and politics in the 1980s and 1990s, particularly when it converged with the serendipitous rise of hip-hop cultural forms and the era of "conservative ascendancy" epitomized by the Reagan administrations through to the early twenty-first century. What should not be lost in critiques of the 1995 Million Man March, for instance, is that despite its predominate *numerical* support by individuals who correspond with the hip-hop generation (i.e., those who were too young to have experienced the civil rights movement's major ideological implosions and formations), it was organized, led, and dominated by the civil rights generation's erstwhile leadership class in all of its religious moralisms and discontent. The next chapter focuses on the hip-hop generation's encountaer with black nationalism as epitomized in their recruitment of Malcolm X and Louis Farrakhan in the 1980s and 1990s period.

Notes

1. We have selected the younger baby boomers on several grounds. First, the oldest of this group—those born in 1960—were not eligible to vote for president until

1980, when Ronald Reagan defeated Jimmy Carter, making the whole of their political socialization an effect of racial conservatism in the party system and in society. Because generations are defined by a "common political experience," the political experience of younger baby boomers would presumably be different from that of their older brethren—born from 1945 to 1959—whose political experience included the civil rights movement, the Black Power epoch, and Vietnam. See Edward G. Carmines and James A. Stimson, "Issue Evolution, Population Replacement, and Normal Partisan Change," *American Political Science Review* 75 (1981): 107–118. This group reached middle age by 1995. Second, 1964 is generally considered the end of the baby boom; this cohort's first presidential voting age occurred within the context of a campaign including a racial conservative white candidacy and a black candidacy—Jesse Jackson in 1984 (and a second time in 1988). And third, 1964 is the point at which, Carmines and Stimson contend, the party system became dominated by racial issues; see Edward G. Carmines and James A. Stimson, *Issue Evolution* (Princeton: Princeton University Press, 1989).

Noteworthy is Louis Farrakhan's evaluation of this activity. Using biblical allegory, Farrakhan's Million Man March announcement stated the following, quoted at length: "It is written in the Book of Ezekiel that the dry bones would hear a word that would stimulate them, causing them to move. . . . When the winds began to blow on the bones, the scripture said, the bones stood up an exceedingly great army. What are the winds? Winds represent forces that create movement to over power the inertia of the bones. . . . The forces that are blowing on the black community, and particularly the black male, are the winds of poverty, want, joblessness, and homelessness; the winds of drugs and crime; the winds of political recalcitrance on the part of those in power; the winds of rejection and increased hatred. The winds of the Republican Party which swept into power calling for more harsh punishment for criminals, and the building of more prisons, saying that anyone who has been guilty of a criminal offense three times will be imprisoned for the rest of his or her natural life. Prisons are now private enterprise, which means that it is becoming big business now to build prisons to incarcerate the Black, the weak, the poor, and the ignorant. This new wave of anti-crime legislation is to legitimize a return to slavery in the name of crime-reduction."

2. Lorenzo Morris (ed.), *The Social and Political Implications of the 1984 Jesse Jackson Campaign* (New York: Praeger Publishers, 1990).

3. Critical writing about hip-hop culture and politics has sought to articulate aspects of the "lived" experience of the often valorized hip-hop generation. See Bakari Kitwana, *The Hip Hop Generation; Young Blacks and the Crisis in African-American Culture* (New York: BasicCivitas, 2002); Kevin Powell, *Keepin' It Real: Post-MTV Reflections on Race, Sex, and Politics* (New York: One World/Ballantine, 1997); Tricia Rose, *Rap Music and Black Culture in Contemporary America* (Middletown, CT: Wesleyan University Press, 1994); Todd Boyd, *Am I Black Enough for You? Popular Culture from the 'Hood and Beyond* (Bloomington: University of Indiana Press, 1997).

4. M. K. Asante Jr., *It's Bigger Than Hip Hop: The Rise of the Post–Hip-Hop Generation* (New York: St. Martin's, 2008), p. 4.

5. James Lance Taylor, "Black Politics in Transition: From Protest to Politics to Political Neutrality?" (Unpublished Ph.D. diss., University of Southern California, 1999).

6. Manning Marable, *Beyond Black and White: Transforming African American Politics* (New York: Verso, 1995), pp. 206–207.

7. Bakari Kitwana, *The Hip-Hop Generation: Young Blacks and the Crisis in African-American Culture* (New York: BasicCivitas, 2002).

8. Ibid., p. xiv.

9. There have been many examples of this sentiment in contemporary black politics. The hip-hop movement itself is pertinent. The relative silence of civil rights leaders during the early moments of Hurricane Katrina—this includes Al Sharpton, who was noticeably silent—and the provocative comments by rap artist Kanye West concerning the George W. Bush administration's obtuse response to the catastrophe, which disproportionately devastated poor African Americans, are instructive. But this has something to do with a general feeling among African Americans, due in part to Dr. King's and Malcolm X's accomplishments and the brokerage leadership styles that they represented, that "we have no black leaders" and there is no black "movement."

10. The irony here is that many of the 1960s "children of Malcolm" were, generationally speaking (not ideologically), too old. Indeed, his widow, Betty Shabazz, and would-be intellectual heir, Amiri Baraka, both reached age thirty just three and eight months (respectively) after Malcolm X's assassination.

11. See James Lance Taylor, "Black Politics in Transition." These data are based on selected demographic characteristics of respondents to the 1995 *Washington Post* Million Man March Survey and the 1995 Howard University Million Man March Survey.

12. Michael Eric Dyson, *Making Malcolm: The Myth and Meaning of Malcolm X* (New York: Oxford University Press, 1995).

13. Robert Dahl, *Who Governs? Democracy and Power in an American City* (New Haven: Yale University Press, 1961); C. Wright Mills, *The Power Elite* (New York: Oxford University Press, 1956); Aaron Wildavsky, *The Nursing Father: Moses as a Political Leader* (Tuscaloosa: University of Alabama Press, 1984); Max Weber, *The Protestant Ethic and the Spirit of Capitalism* (Thousand Oaks, CA: NB Publishing, [1905] 2008). For example, Dahl's seminal study conceptualized leadership as consisting of widely dispersed and plural loci of influence in the body politic, whereas Mills's analysis locates in a social, associational, political, and economic stratum of "power elite." Weber, in contrast, identifies those individuals with institution-transforming personal appeal and "charisma" as indicators of leadership.

14. Anthony Mughan and Samuel C. Patterson, *Political Leadership in Democratic Societies* (Chicago: Nelson-Hall, 1992), p. 13.

15. Aaron Wildavsky, *The Nursing Father*, p. 5.

16. Ibid., p. 184.

17. C.L.R. James, *American Civilization*, edited by Anna Grimshaw and Keith Hart (Oxford, UK: Blackwell, 1993), p. 276.

18. Wildavsky, *The Nursing Father*, p. 185.

19. Michael Eric Dyson, *Making Malcolm*, p. 88.

20. Ibid., p. 114.

21. Cornel West, "Malcolm X and Black Rage," in Joe Wood (ed.), *Malcolm X: In Our Image* (New York: St. Martin's, 1992), p. 53 (emphases added).

22. These include the works of Michael Eric Dyson, *Between God and Gangsta Rap: Bearing Witness to Black Culture* (Oxford: Oxford University Press, 1996); Charise Cheney, *Brothers Gonna Work It Out: Sexual Politics in the Golden Age of Rap Nationalism* (New York: New York University Press, 2005); Todd Boyd, *Am I Black Enough for You?*; Tricia Rose, *Black Noise*; Robin D.G. Kelley, *The Vinyl Ain't Final: Hip-Hop and the Globalisation of Black Popular Culture* (New York: Pluto, 2006); and Patricia Hill Collins, *From Black Power to Hip-Hop: Racism, Nationalism, and Feminism* (Philadelphia: Temple University Press, 2006).

23. Melanye Price, *Dreaming Blackness: Black Nationalism and African American Public Opinion* (New York: New York University Press, 2009); Melissa Harris-

Lacewell, *Barbershops, Bibles, and BET: Everyday Talk and Black Political Thought* (Chicago: University of Chicago Press, 2004); Michael C. Dawson, *Black Visions*; Nikol Alexander-Floyd, *Gender, Race, and Black Nationalism*.

24. Todd Boyd, *Am I Black Enough for You?*, p. 9.

25. Wendy Brown, *Politics out of History*, p. 150.

26. Ibid., pp. 139, 143.

27. Ibid., p. 145.

28. Ibid.

29. Ibid., p. 147. Emphasis added.

30. Ibid., p. 150.

31. *Beloved* is loosely based on the true story of Robert and Margaret Garner, a fugitive family from Kentucky. When slave catchers and US marshals surrounded the family, Robert killed at least one marshal and Margaret killed her two-year-old daughter to prevent her from being taken back to Kentucky. A trial ensued, raising matters of federalism, the Fugitive Slave Act, and freedom of religion (i.e., forcing officers to recover slaves against conscience). Their owner, Archibald K. Gaines, hid the Garners and eventually sent them to his brother's plantation in Arkansas. On the way, the boat—which the *Liberator* reported on—crashed, resulting in the drowning of another child. Margaret tried to drown herself.

32. Here I focus on developments in American social, economic, and political relations that contributed to the emergence of conservative stalwart Ronald Reagan. Reagan's emergence is undertaken as part of a larger conservative reaction to emergent black militancy and social unrest that he first confronted as California's governor (1967–1973) and extended to ideological developments among the major American parties. I critically analyze the period in which conflicting demands—"Black Power!" versus "law and order"—conflated to give way to social-control approaches to punishment beginning in the mid-1980s and peaking in the mid-1990s. This was the nadir for ghetto-locked black Americans, who became the primary human capital for the penal-industrial complex that expanded most significantly from the mid-1980s to the late 1990s.

33. Adolph Reed, *The Jesse Jackson Phenomenon*, p. 4. This is interesting, considering Reed's biting criticisms of both the Black Power and hip-hop cohorts' efforts at solidarity, institution-building (including Malcolm X Liberation University in North Carolina and Malcolm X College in Chicago, and the renaming of Harlem's famous Lenox Avenue after Malcolm X), and, of course, Spike Lee's film *Malcolm X*.

34. Joe Wood, *Malcolm X*, p. 15.

35. Ibid., p. 7.

36. The events ranged from the struggle and subsequent release of African National Congress leader Nelson Mandela (1990) and abolishment of Apartheid in South Africa (1994), the 1992 national upheaval beginning in Los Angeles, the 1993 March on Washington, the June 1994 passage of California's anti-immigration Proposition 187, the mass media–driven racial divide surrounding the O.J. Simpson trial coverage and verdicts (1994–1995), the November 1994 conservative congressional electoral mandate, the 1996 passage of California's anti–affirmative action initiative (Proposition 209), to the burning of more than fifty black churches during the summers of 1996 and 1997. Such events signal that the racial conservatism of the 1990s was deeply implicated in the heightened political activism among younger black subpopulations—those who raised Malcolm X as a response.

37. For an analysis of the earlier literature on Malcolm X, see Michael Eric Dyson, *Making Malcolm*. His study serves essentially as an annotated literature review of Malcolm X scholarship.

38. Michael Eric Dyson, *Making Malcolm*, p. 21.

39. What is the difference in sewing an X on a twenty-year–old's hat (or a picture of Malcolm X on a shirt), say, in 1992, and printing a picture of Malcolm X on the cover and interior of books that criticize the former phenomenon? Are we not both complicit in consumption, marketing, and commodifying subjective versions of Malcolm X?

40. Michael Dyson, *Making Malcolm* p. 99.

41. See Russell Rickford, *Betty Shabazz: Her Life with Malcolm X and Fight to Preserve His Legacy* (Naperville, IL: Sourcebooks, 2003), pp. 408–420.

42. Eugene Rivers III, *Beyond the Nationalism of Fools*, pp. 16–18. See also Adolph Reed, *Stirrings in the Jug*, p. 15.

43. Cedric Robinson, *Black Marxism*, p. 451.

44. William Sales Jr., *From Civil Rights to Black Power*.

45. "*Malcolm X*: What's Missing from Spike Lee's Movie," *Spartacist* Pamphlet No. 10, Black History and the Class Struggle, February 1993. Reprinted from *Workers Vanguard* No. 564 (November 27, 1992).

46. Arnold Rampersad, "The Color of His Eyes: Bruce Perry's Malcolm and Malcolm's Malcolm" in Joe Wood (ed.), *Malcolm X*, p. 118. Emphasis added.

47. This was the received consciousness, but it is not as if Martin Luther King, Huey Newton, Angela Davis, or Stokely Carmichael were not equally available for activation as a "device" with which to speak radically to power.

48. Charise Cheney, *Brothers Gonna Work It Out*, p. 81.

49. William Julius Wilson, *The Truly Disadvantaged*, p. 127.

50. For an elaboration, see Cathy J. Cohen and Michael C. Dawson, "Neighborhood Poverty and African American Politics," *American Political Science Review* 87, no. 2 (June 1993): 286–303.

51. This influence was so powerful that Malcolm X discusses it on the first page of his autobiography as told to Alex Haley. The private papers of his sister and mentor, Ella Collins, who also joined the Nation of Islam, emphasize the Garveyite heritage of Malcolm X over the Nation of Islam and highlight how the Garveyism in the Little family led them to the Nation of Islam—as it did with Elijah Muhammad, himself a former Garveyite. Her account, *Seventh Child: A Family Memoir of Malcolm X* (compiled by her son, Rodnell P. Collins), is authoritative and simmers with a negative view of the Nation of Islam, Elijah Muhammad, and Louis X (Farrakhan)—who she antagonized as a sister at Boston's Temple No. 11. Louis X was minister before replacing Malcolm X as national representative of the Elijah Muhammad and minister of Harlem's Temple No. 7. The book states: "I was so happy to see [Malcolm] so involved with our people. . . . That's what our father and his mother had been doing. He was moving to be the leader that we all knew he could be. I personally wasn't interested in hearing about Elijah Muhammad's message, I wanted him to get his message, his parents' message, Marcus Garvey's message, the Little brothers' message to our people," p. 93.

52. William W. Sales, *From Civil Rights to Black Power: Malcolm X and the Organization of Afro-American Unity* (Boston: South End, 1994), outlines three major stages of Malcolm X's public life: in stage one, from 1952 to 1962, Malcolm X is steeped in the teachings and ministry of the Nation of Islam; stage two is characterized by the creation of the OAAU and the MMI; stage three betrays Malcolm's pan-Africanist internationalism.

53. William Strickland and Cheryl Greene, *Malcolm X: Make It Plain* (New York: Viking, 1994).

54. Malcolm was originally ordered to serve concurrent sentences of eight to ten years for burglary; he was at Charlestown State Prison, then transferred to Concord, and Norfolk Prison Colony.

55. Alex Haley, *The Autobiography of Malcolm X*, p. 193.

56. For more details on Hayer and the falsely accused and convicted assassins of Malcolm X, see Mattias Gardell, *In the Name of Elijah Muhammad: Louis Farrakhan and the Nation of Islam* (Durham, NC: Duke University Press, 1996), pp. 76–85.

57. Kofi Natambu, *The Life and Work of Malcolm X* (Indianapolis: Alpha, 2002), p. 315.

58. Cedric Robinson, *Black Marxism*, p. 428.

59. This was the occasion on which Malcolm X encountered the radical Algerian ambassador Taher Kaid during the Ben Bella regime, who questioned where he, as a white revolutionary in the struggle against French colonialism, fit in Malcolm's provincial view of black nationalism in 1964.

60. For instance, of the many literary influences on his own intellectual development while in prison, Malcolm X is careful to mention the likes of Nat Turner, John Brown, Harriet Beecher Stowe (especially *Uncle Tom's Cabin*), as well as "some bound pamphlets of the Abolitionist Anti-Slavery Society of New England." But there is no acknowledged record of Walker's *Appeal* being included in this literature. See *The Autobiography of Malcolm X*, pp. 202–204. This is similar to many present-day professional athletes, who may dominate their sport but know little about forbears, such as Jackie Robinson, Satchel Paige, Curt Flood, Josh Gibson, Wilma Rudolph, Althea Gibson, Paul Robeson, and "Cool Papa" Bell.

61. William Seraile, "David Walker and Malcolm X: Brothers in Radical Thought," *Black World* (October 1973), p. 72.

62. George Breitman, *Malcolm X Speaks*, p. 157.

63. Ibid., p. 19. Emphasis added.

64. George Breitman (ed.), *By Any Means Necessary: Speeches, Interviews, and Letters by Malcolm X* (New York: Pathfinder, 1970), p. 37.

65. Where many have emphasized violence in this statement, it actually encapsulates a multidimensional vision for the organization, including self-definition, self-determination, and its establishment; self-defense; education; politics and economics; and "social revolution" and "cultural revolution." Malcolm X also envisions a broad pan-Africanist component, intent on linking with allies in newly independent nations in Africa, Asia, and Latin America. The phrase also incorporates drug rehabilitation, a newspaper for propaganda, and even a White Friends of the OAAU wing. Please see Breitman, *By Any Means Necessary*, ch. 3.

66. Cited in Breitman, *By Any Means Necessary*, p. 46.

67. Among other linkages, both men represented the tradition of radical black religion, and both men exuded black American rage in protest of the subalternality of blacks in the United States.

68. Patricia Hill Collins, *From Black Power to Hip-Hop*, 2006, p. 83.

69. Ibid., p. 84.

70. Charise Cheney, *Brothers Gonna Work It Out*, p. 169. Emphasis in original.

71. Ibid., p. 122.

72. Ibid., p. 44.

73. Lisa Nikol Nealy, *African American Women Voters: Racializing Religiosity, Political Consciousness, and Progressive Political Action in U.S. Presidential Elections from 1964 Through 2008* (Lanham, MD: University Press of America), pp. 37–38. Emphases in original.

74. Cornel West, *Race Matters*, p. 1. Emphasis added.

75. Paula D. McClain and Joe Stewart, *"Can't We All Just Get Along?" Racial and Ethnic Minorities in American Politics,* 2nd ed. (New York: Westview, 1998), place the events of April 1992 within a larger racial/ethnic narrative reflecting a two-headed

dilemma having to do with racial/ethnic political inequality and voting rights in the American political system. For instance, just months after the Rodney King beating, a Detroit man—Malice Green—accused of refusing to surrender crack cocaine to arresting officers, was beaten to death in Detroit, a case that gained national attention.

76. See Komozi Woodard, *A Nation Within a Nation*, p. xiii.

77. Manning Marable, *Beyond Black and White*, p. 204.

78. In the end, he looked to South Africa and Angola as models for charging the United States with human rights violations and embarrassing it before the United Nations. The national independence movements in many African, Middle East, and Asian countries after World War II inspired his transitioning understanding of black nationalism and pan-African alliances.

79. Manning Marable, *Beyond Black and White*, pp. 206–207. Yet these intergenerational differences did not pan out in actual voting behavior of African Americans in the 2008 presidential campaign; neither did African American women's and men's voting yield statistically significant differences.

80. Nell Irvin Painter, *Exodusters: Black Migration to Kansas After Reconstruction* (New York: W. W. Norton, 1992). See esp. ch. 9.

81. The 1996 National Black Election Study included a leadership preference measure stating: "Now, I'd like to get your feeling toward some of your political leaders and other people, events, and organizations that have been in the news." Respondents chose Jesse Jackson and Kweisi Mfume (69 percent), followed by Colin Powell (67 percent), US Senator Carol Mosley Braun of Illinois (64 percent), Louis Farrakhan (51 percent), and US Supreme Court Justice Clarence Thomas (41 percent). The reported sample size was 1,020.

82. Marcus D. Pohlmann, *Black Politics in Conservative America*, 2nd ed. (New York: Addison Wesley Longman, 1999), p. 52. Emphases added.

83. Hanes Walton Jr., *African American Power and Politics*, p. 93. Conservatism vis-à-vis Reagan-Bush and, later, Gingrich provides continuity in reading the racial context of this period. The inevitable response was a culturally based moral sanctioning that developed out of the contemporary racial protest narrative of black Americans—which invokes the likes of Denmark Vesey, Henry H. Garnet, Nat Turner, Marcus Garvey, and Malcolm X (p. 94). This moral component "in the African American cultural community is shown as having a moral dimension that can generate, activate, and sustain social outrage, political protest, and nonviolence as well as violence, resistance, and rebellion. Indeed, the resistance raised by African-American spokespersons such as King, Malcolm X, and recently Jesse Jackson has included both violent and non-violent approaches as means of advocating and advancing this moral dimension," p. 105.

84. Hanes Walton Jr., *African American Power and Politics*, pp. 106–107.

85. Joseph McCormick II and Sekou Franklin, "Expressions of Racial Consciousness in the African American Community: Data from the Million Man March," in Yvette M. Alex-Assensoh and Lawrence Hanks (eds.), *Black and Multiracial Politics in America* (New York: New York University Press, 2000); also see Michael C. Dawson, *Behind the Mule* and *Black Visions*.

86. See Mattias Gardell, *In the Name of Elijah Muhammad*, ch. 6.

87. This show was the forerunner to many talent-based amateur-hour shows. Other notables who debuted on the show included Frank Sinatra, Gladys Knight, and Diana Ross.

88. He was married to his childhood sweetheart at age twenty by the Reverend Wright. See Mattias Gardell, *In the Name of Elijah Muhammad* (1996), p. 119. Others note that Wright boasted of providing Farrakhan with the first twenty-five members of his temple in Boston. See Vibert L. White Jr., *Inside the Nation of Islam*, p. 39.

89. Ibid.

90. Karl Evanzz, *The Messenger*, p. 423.

91. Minister Louis X had Ella Collins suspended from Temple No. 11 for insubordination; Malcolm was asked to do it. See Rodnell P. Collins, *Seventh Child*, p. 134. In *The Autobiography of Malcolm X*, he describes the tensions: "Then, there was my sister Ella herself. I couldn't get over what she had done. I've said before, this is a strong big, black, Georgia-born woman. Her domineering ways had gotten her put out of the Nation of Islam's Boston Eleven; they took her back, then she left on her own," p. 367.

92. Others include Ishmael Muhammad (the son of Elijah Muhammad with Tynetta Muhammad, the matriarch of the reconstructed Nation of Islam). Ishmael is minister of Mosque Maryam in Chicago and Farrakhan's national assistant minister. There is also the Nation of Islam minister of health, Dr. Abdul Alim Muhammad. Akbar Muhammad, a longtime associate of Farrakhan, like Khallid Muhammad, is also a noteworthy exception. This observation is not meant to be taken in any absolute terms.

93. Rodnell Collins, *Seventh Child*, pp. 134–135.

94. *Orgena* was first performed at the Connelly Memorial Theater on May 19, 1961 (Malcolm X's thirty-sixth birthday).

95. Rodnell Collins, *Seventh Child*, pp. 134–135.

96. Manning Marable, *Black Leadership: Four Great American Leaders and the Struggle for Civil Rights* (New York: Penguin Press, 1999). See esp. ch. 11, "Black Fundamentalism."

97. Wilson J. Moses, *Afrotopia: The Roots of African American Popular History* (New York: Cambridge University Press, 1998), 235.

98. Richard B. Turner, *Islam in the African American Experience*, p. 175. As I argued earlier, quasi-Christian black nationalists, including Blyden, Garvey, and Du Bois, conversely saw an admirable model of nationality organizing in early, prefascistic Zionism that puts black nationalism's ostensible anti-Semitism in relief.

99. Ibid., p. 175.

100. Jack Baxter's documentary *Brother Minister: The Assassination of Malcolm X/ El-Hajj Malik Shabazz* names individuals believed to be Talmadge Hayer's real accomplices. They were Fruit of Islam enforcers from Newark, New Jersey.

101. Kofi Natambu, *The Life and Work of Malcolm X*, p. 310.

102. These and many other details surrounding the murder of Malcolm X are well-known in the literature. Please see Jan R. Carew, *Ghosts in Our Blood: With Malcolm X in Africa, England, and the Caribbean* (New York: Lawrence Hill, 1994); Kofi Natambu, *The Life and Work of Malcolm X*, p. 315; and Karl Evanzz, *The Judas Factor: The Plot to Kill Malcolm X* (New York: Thunder's Mouth, 1993).

103. Farrakhan, "The Murder of Malcolm X," speech delivered at Malcolm X College, Chicago, February 21, 1990, available at www.finalcall/webcast/malcolmx/; emphasis added. For a more extended discussion of the relationship between Malcolm X and Louis Farrakhan, see Eric Michael Dyson's *Making Malcolm*, Arthur J. Magida's *Prophet of Rage*, and Mattias Gardell's *In the Name of Elijah Muhammad*. See also Eugene Wolfenstein's *Victims of Democracy: Malcolm X and the Black Revolution* (Los Angeles: University of California Press, 1981), in which the author draws a psychological profile of Malcolm X and his relationship with Elijah Muhammad: a frustrated child seeking to compensate for his father, Earl Little, who was murdered by Ku Klux Klansmen. There are striking parallels in the life of Louis Farrakhan that can be drawn from Wolfenstein's application that might be useful in explaining Farrakhan's claim of messianic status or of being "a Jesus for our times" "by whose stripes you [blacks] have been healed." Though certain aspects of Wolfenstein's analyses of Malcolm X have been brought into question by Hanes Walton in *Invisible Politics* (1985), I contend that

a similar psychological profile of Farrakhan might be appropriate in tracing the linkages among Farrakhan's early abandonment by his biological father (while just an infant), who was a follower of Garvey in Roxbury, Massachusetts; his attachment to Elijah Muhammad; and his later claims of messianic status immediately following the MMM/DOA, which no doubt increased his sense of personal accomplishment. But this is far beyond the scope of this study.

104. Russell Rickford, *Betty Shabazz*, p. 410.

105. Dr. Shabazz observed the clip of Farrakhan's comments on NBC journalist Gabe Pressman's Sunday *News Forum* program. She seemed stunned by the comments, not realizing that the footage was more recent than she had initially presumed.

106. Russell Rickford, *Betty Shabazz*, p. 499.

107. The May 1995 event was staged at Harlem's Apollo Theater and organized as a fundraiser for Qubilah's legal defense and billed "A New Beginning," before an audience of 1,400 people who paid $50–$100 for tickets. It included veteran journalist Mike Wallace; attorney William Kunstler; family attorney Percy Sutton; CUNY professor Leonard Jeffries; Ben Chavis (then Muhammad); Charles Rangel; the Reverend Calvin Butts of the Abyssinian Baptist Church; Conrad Worrill, chairman of the National Black United Front; Haki Madhubuti of Third World Press; and poet Sonia Sanchez.

108. Vibert White Jr., *Inside the Nation of Islam*, p. 34.

109. See Karl Evanzz, *The Messenger*, pp. 381–392. Altogether seven people were shot; five died, with the oldest being a fellow Hanafi Muslim who unwittingly went to the scene of the murders on an errand. Two adults survived multiple point-blank shots to the head. In the end, a ten-year-old boy, a two-year-old boy, a one-year-old girl, and a nine-day-old girl infant were murdered. The Hanafi massacres of 1973 were "the biggest mass murder case in the history of the nation's capital," p. 390. On March 9, 1977, seven members of Khaalis's group sought revenge, demanding that the convicted murderers be turned over for retribution. They broke into the headquarters of B'nai B'rith, taking approximately 100 hostages. Less than an hour later, three men entered an Islamic Center in Washington, DC, taking eleven hostages. Two other Hanafis entered the District Building, two blocks from the White House, killing one man and injuring several others, including the future mayor, City Councilman Marion Barry.

110. Cited in Vibert White Jr., *Inside the Nation of Islam*, p. 29. White claims that James X Price committed suicide and does not mention the torture, which Evanzz does; see pp. 381–392.

111. Wallace Muhammad implemented widespread reforms and expunged the most heretical teachings of the Nation of Islam concerning the demonization of all whites, its racial exclusivity, and the divinity of W. D. Fard and of Elijah Muhammad, all while preserving his father's undeniably Paulinian role in planting Islam in North America. See Richard B. Turner, *Islam in the African American Experience*, ch. 5.

112. Karl Evanzz, *The Messenger*, pp. 426–427.

113. Arthur Magida, *Prophet of Rage*, p. 122.

114. Vibert White Jr., *Inside the Nation of Islam*, p. 66.

115. Rod Bush, *We Are Not What We Seem: Black Nationalism and Class Struggle in the American Century* (New York: New York University Press, 1999), pp. 231–232.

116. Ibid., p. 233.

117. Richard B. Turner, *Islam in the African American Experience*, p. 184.

118. Adolph Reed, *Stirrings in the Jug*, p. 6.

119. But black nationalists and nationalist organizations are typically subjected to the biases or ideological prejudices of researchers (Katherine Tate, *From Protest to Politics*, 1993), who tend to reject radical/protest or "organic" alternatives in favor of

political incorporation or integrationist strategies (Adolph Reed Jr., *The Jesse Jackson Phenomenon*, 1986). Note, for example, that despite Farrakhan's prominence in Chicago's politics during the Washington campaign and victory in 1983 and Jackson's 1984 Democratic presidential primary campaign, the University of Michigan's 1984 National Black Election Study completely neglects Farrakhan-related questions. See Arthur Magida, *Prophet of Rage*, and Mattias Gardell, *In the Name of Elijah Muhammad*.

120. This is especially because he deliberately alienated white liberals as potential coalition partners while accusing black elected officials, and black leadership in general, of compromising local and national black interests. Indeed, Farrakhan became a kind of litmus for black elected officials, such as the late Tom Bradley of Los Angeles and New York City's David Dinkins, who were torn between their black and white liberal constituents on the issue of repudiating Farrakhan as a racist and anti-Semite. Dinkins and Bradley would subsequently repudiate Farrakhan, but violent riots in New York and Los Angeles would bring both of their historic mayoralties to an end. A restive element of young, black, and mostly male street-level activists—typical Farrakhan supporters—employed violence as a correction against what was perceived as racial injustices in cities governed by black mayors. Farrakhan's popularity gained momentum not only with poor, urban-dwelling blacks, who were experiencing high unemployment, police brutality, and a general decline in life quality, but also with an equally impressive following among the black middle classes and the young. They filled stadiums such as New York's Madison Square Garden and Los Angeles's Memorial Coliseum by the tens of thousands throughout the 1980s and 1990s.

121. This tension was exacerbated when Chavis, the national secretary of the NAACP at the time, sought to incorporate Farrakhan and other fringe nationalists into the mainstream black establishment class. Chavis came to the NAACP helm with his own radical protest/nationalist credentials. In addition to being arrested repeatedly during the 1960s in political demonstrations, he was numbered with the "Wilmington 10" (in North Carolina) and subsequently convicted of arson; see Marcus D. Pohlmann, *Black Politics in Conservative America*, p. 150. Robert C. Smith, in *We Have No Leaders*, chronicles the rise and fall of Chavis; much of his analysis highlights the ideological problem that Chavis's courting of Farrakhan posed for the NAACP's (black and white) liberal integrationist wings. Smith notes: "True to his [radical/nationalist] roots Chavis quickly became embroiled in conflicts with elements of the board and the white liberal establishment by first inviting Minister Farrakhan to participate in an NAACP-sponsored leadership summit and then holding a meeting with prominent black nationalists and radicals. According to Chavis's letter of invitation the purpose of the meeting was to 'provide a context for input and access of Pan Africanists, progressives and nationalists into increased membership and active participation within the NAACP at national and local levels," p. 94. Chavis was subsequently fired from the NAACP in August 1994 amid charges of sexual improprieties with an NAACP employee. As well, Congressional Black Caucus chairman Kweisi Mfume of Maryland urged the formation of a "sacred covenant" between black leaders and organizations, including the Nation of Islam and Louis Farrakhan, in September 1993, sending white liberals (mostly Jews) into a frenzied state of dismay. Mfume's sacred covenant reflected an attempt by black nationalist elements to align more closely with the mainstream of black Americans—which can be aligned somewhere to the left of the mainstream civil rights black leadership class and their white liberal sponsors—that Farrakhan has successfully tapped into since the Reagan-Bush era began. But, more precisely, Mfume's sacred covenant was a direct response to the backlash that developed when Farrakhan was excluded from the thirtieth-anniversary celebration of the 1963 March on Washington. The King-Young Atlanta coalition re-

fused to allow Farrakhan's participation despite the fact that he was allowed to speak at the 1983 twentieth-anniversary march ten years earlier. The slight of Farrakhan and the firing of Chavis, perhaps more than any other factors, prompted Farrakhan to call for a Million Man March shortly thereafter. Chavis's replacement in 1995—ironically—would be Mfume. For a postmortem on Chavis's career with the Nation of Islam and the tensions and jealousies with other ministers, see Vibert L. White Jr., *Inside the Nation of Islam.*

122. Fulani would eventually distance herself from Farrakhan—as would Karenga and Madhubuti after the Million Man March—over Farrakhan's alliance with Lyndon La Rouche after Farrakhan failed to keep his pledge to distance himself from the controversial former presidential candidate. See Arthur Magida, *Prophet of Rage*, p. 157.

123. Gabrielle Kurlander and Jackie Salit (eds.), *Independent Black Leadership in America: Minister Louis Farrakhan, Dr. Lenora Fulani, Reverend Al Sharpton* (New York: Castillo International, 1990), p. 13. Although this may overstate the case considering Farrakhan's apparent lack of enthusiasm for politics, he did endorse and finance some part of Fulani's initial presidential campaign and her 1990 run for New York governor. In the latter campaign, Farrakhan told a captive audience of New Yorkers, "We pledge to work with and for Dr. Lenora Fulani's candidacy because we believe in her, although we may not necessarily support the New Alliance Party and all of the New Alliance Party candidates and positions and whatnot. We support Dr. Lenora Fulani because we see her as the person that is the alternative in this state to the bad governing stance of Governor Mario Cuomo."

124. Danny Bakewell is a prominent businessman in Los Angeles who also heads the Brotherhood Crusade. The Brotherhood Crusade is a local organization dedicated to black civil rights and economic development. Bakewell's organization gained notice in the events surrounding the videotaped slaying of a fifteen-year-old black girl, Natasha Harlins, by Korean grocer Soon Ja Doo. Bakewell's Brotherhood Crusade organization picketed the store out of business. As well, the Brotherhood Crusade led the campaign against the Los Angeles chief of police, Darryl F. Gates—long held to be hostile, even racist, toward black interests in the city—immediately following the Rodney King beating and revelations of a pattern of unchecked racism among the top brass in the LAPD. Along with the prominent minister Cecil "Chip" Murray—interviewed several times for this study—Bakewell was Farrakhan's chief ally in the city. It is worth noting that after the 1992 unrest, it was at Murray's First African Methodist Episcopal (F.A.M.E.) Church where California's Republican governor, Pete Wilson, President George Bush, and Democratic presidential candidate Bill Clinton caucused with Los Angeles's political and clerical elite before touring the ashes and ruin of the city.

125. See Arthur Magida, *Prophet of Rage*, ch. 9. But not lost on black Americans was the widely reported racist comments of Senator Fritz Hollins of South Carolina in December 1993, referring to black leaders as "cannibals."

126. Additionally, during the Million Youth March in 1998, Muhammad reportedly agitated some of the young marchers into violence in Harlem after giving an acerbic speech aimed at Mayor Rudolph Giuliani, Jews, and whites in general.

127. Vibert White Jr., *Inside the Nation of Islam*, p. 154.

128. The best inside account in print is Vibert White Jr., *Inside the Nation of Islam*. esp. ch. 8, "Cain and Abel." It is unlikely that Khallid could have survived engaging in the rank challenge to Farrakhan, in and out of the Nation of Islam, had the specter of Malcolm X's murder not underwritten it. Because Malcolm X died, Khallid's ignorance could live through his insubordination to Farrakhan.

129. Charise Cheney, *Brothers Gonna Work It Out.*

130. Vibert White Jr., *Inside the Nation of Islam*, p. 144.

131. Several violent confrontations between Khallid Muhammad and supporters of Farrakhan soon followed. Muhammad resurfaced in the unrelated New Black Panther Party, surrounding the murder of James Byrd Jr., a black man, during the summer of 1998; he was tied to the back of a truck and torn asunder by several white men in Jasper, Texas. Muhammad led a garrison of armed men dressed in black (unimaginatively invoking the Black Panthers' 1967 confrontation with authorities in Sacramento). For all of his talk of violence, Muhammad died nonviolently on February 17, 2001.

9

The Black Nationalism
of the Hip-Hop Generation

*"The government gives them the drugs, builds bigger prisons, passes a
three-strikes law and then wants us to sing 'God Bless America.' No, no,
no, God damn America, that's in the Bible for killing innocent people."*
And *"God damn America for treating our citizens as less than human. God
damn America for as long as she acts like she is God and she is supreme."*
—Jeremiah Wright Jr., April 2003

Deep down, all blacks were potential nationalists, *The anger was there, bot-
tled up and often turned inward. . . . I wondered whether . . . that anger
[should] be redirected; whether a black politics that suppressed rage
toward whites generally, or one that failed to elevate race loyalty above
all else, was a politics inadequate to the task. . . . If the nationalism could
create a strong and effective insularity, deliver on its promise of self-
respect, then the hurt it might cause well-meaning whites, or the inner
turmoil it caused people like me, would be of little consequence.*
—Barack Obama, *Dreams from My Father*, pp. 199–200

In Chapter 1 of this book I elaborated on black political development as a theoretical framework for understanding the often contested, sometimes comple-
mentary interaction between clerical and electoral black leadership. It surveyed political developments in Chicago, from Martin Luther King Jr.'s
political defeat to Harold Washington's electoral triumphs. Chicago is a critical theater for understanding the political environment that informed and contextualizes the emergence of Jesse Jackson and Louis Farrakhan in national
politics in the early to late 1980s. Mayor Washington's election was a water-
shed in black politics, and it was precipitous of a nationalist usurpation that
saturated the political milieu of both the West Side and the South Side of
Chicago. The fact that a Chicago-based black religious figure with direct ties
to the civil rights movement emerges as the progressive response to Ronald
Reagan's influence in the parties is instructive. And the fact that Louis Far-

rakhan would spend the next few years challenging Jackson's position (and, later, that of black elected officials) highlights the persistence of sacral protest politics in a burgeoning post–protest politics milieu.

Jesse Jackson's initial campaign for US president was deeply influenced by the nationalist thrust in Chicago, particularly activists' resentments over the local and national Democratics' treatment of issues and leadership preferences within the black community. His ministry is often viewed as more one of personal ambition than, say, one of ideology. But some scholars agree that Jackson's first campaign was rooted in the nationalist struggle for an independent party fulcrum traceable to Gary, Indiana, where he and Amiri Baraka hollered "It's Nation Time!" Add to this the local struggles of black Chicagoans to create an alternative to the Democratic machine that routinely left them on the outside looking in.[1]

Washington's Chicago campaign and Jackson's White House campaign were *independent* within, but also against, the Democratic establishment. The complex of forces that conflated in Chicago's tense relations between city leaders, racial and ethnic groups, and neighborhood and ward activism incubated the contours of "mainstream" black responses to ascendant racial provocations locally and nationally. Political scientist Katherine Tate describes these dynamics:

> There was considerable friction between Jackson and Democratic party leaders who formed an organization outside the national party organization called the Democratic Leadership Council (DLC). This organization of 400 or so elected officials has been highly critical of the party's links to organized interests such as labor, Blacks, and feminists, and critical too, of the "traditional Democrats" who continue to maintain close ties to these groups, which they feel has undermined public support for Democrats in national races. In the spring of 1991, the DLC had sponsored a conference, inviting potential candidates in the 1992 race for president to speak. This list included Al Gore, Richard Gephardt, Bill Nunn, Paul Tsongas, and Doug Wilder. *Jesse Jackson and George McGovern* had not been invited. The DLC's [then] president, Al From, explained the snub of Jackson as an attempt to change the party's image, which for the DLC was the root cause of its losses: "Jackson and McGovern represent the ideological approach to government we are trying to change."[2]

Whether or not Jesse Jackson ever had a real chance to become president, most of those born during the early 1960s and 1970s became eligible to vote for a black presidential candidate with experience in both civil rights and Black Power. He won roughly 10 million primary votes in his two campaigns and, briefly, became the front-runner in 1988. Jackson's first campaign (1984) can be understood as a jeremiad against the conservative Reagan revolution in US politics and, equally, against the emergent class of Voting Rights Act–inspired black elected officials and the civil rights establishment that had initially rejected his candidacy (and many did, including Barack Obama, who was born in

1961 and arrived in Chicago just as Jackson was launching his campaign). Speaking to the conservative revolution, Ronald Walters insists that President Reagan directed "an administration that was working to legitimize reactionary positions describable as antiabortion, antiwelfare, anticommunism, anti–secular education, and pro–free market capitalism. Instead, the administration was lending credibility to an atmosphere and attitudes regarded by many as antiblack and distinctly antiliberal."[3] And on the civil rights leadership establishment, Lorn Foster insists that "from its inception, Jesse Jackson's presidential effort was organized more like a movement than an election campaign. Its structure derived more from the black church and the civil rights movement than from electoral politics."[4]

Indeed, Jackson tested the viability of his first campaign by initiating his "Southern Crusade" voter-registration drive. It "harkened back to the old civil rights movement; most black elected officials were skeptical about using marches and demonstrations to effect change." Jackson's 1984 campaign was rooted in the black church and ministers' attempts to influence public policy (as they had with the key civil rights legislation).[5] The 1984–1996 National Black Election Studies (NBES) show that positive responses to "Jackson support" measures steadily declined over the 1990s (after his two presidential runs).[6] Michael Dawson notes that this occurred as Jackson's image became viewed as too integrationist, following his rightward shift toward the Clintons' Democratic center.[7] By the 1990s, it became apparent that electoral politics and political incorporation were not enough to mitigate the material conditions, social misery, and suffering of poorer, ordinary African Americans who did not substantially benefit from the civil rights movement.

Coming full circle, in this chapter I focus first on aspects of the MMM/DOA and its implications for black politics: specifically, attitudes toward the major political parties and political independence from the "lesser evil" dilemma that has characterized black politics since at least the early 1970s. The decade between the 1972 National Black Political Convention (NBPC) in Gary and Harold Washington's first election produced a series of assemblies, at the highest levels of black political leadership, that sought to forge an electoral strategy with regard to the US presidency. Making the black vote and freedom struggle vital to the establishment parties became the focal point of black nationalists in the modern convention movement. Scholars of public opinion research often include measures of black nationalism, specifically concerning an independent political strategy or political party, ever since Jackson refused the advice of people like Ronald Walters to precipitate an independent candidacy against the Democrats. The most salient "gender effect" of the MMM/DOA may have had less to do with phallic nationalism and more to do with Democratic partisanship among African Americans at the time.[8] The two major US political parties have harbored powerful religious constituencies since the civil rights movement. And perhaps the best students of King's tactics and the

SCLC-led movement were not only black liberation theologians but also the Euro-American conservative Christian right movement, which asserted its power between Jimmy Carter's 1976 election and the elections of Ronald Reagan (1980 and 1984). The parties also sought to influence black Americans' electoral support with the carrot of faith-based programs. As Michael L. Owens argues, "Some black clergy, especially those leading activist churches that collaborate with government, are shifting their support from Democrat to Republican candidates, as well as from progressive Democrats to conservative Democrats."[9] This should answer at least some questions as to how black nationalism and black religion could pivot to a discussion of political parties. After the movements waned, the parties were all that remained in terms of conventional politics, upon which unconventional politics could assert itself.

Second, I locate Barack Obama as one who was politically socialized in Chicago's religious and black nationalist and radical circles, leading him to attend the MMM/DOA event. Barack Obama moved to Chicago when the city's nationalist elements had successfully organized and drafted Harold Washington for mayor. Like others in his generational cohort, Obama's disappointment with the MMM/DOA strengthened his ties to the Democratic Party, even as he affiliated locally with progressive and left-critical networks supporting candidates and issues that were *not* part of the Clinton-centrist Democrat orbit. Obama strove to remain mostly independent of the city's machine apparatus; he even associated with the New Party, which was farther left of centrist and even liberal Democrats. The imposition of Jeremiah Wright Jr.'s Christian nationalist jeremiad against the George W. Bush administration's imperial war in Iraq, and against vestigial Reagan-era economic and domestic policies, facilitated the election of Barack Obama even as the latter renounced his associations with Chicago's radical, grassroots, and intellectual circles.

The period between Jesse Jackson's first campaign (1984) and the MMM/DOA (1995) approximates the period between the MMM/DOA and the campaigns and election of Barack Obama as president (2008). In each of these epochal moments in black politics, African American religious elites, emanating from the base of the black community, sought to assert moral, social-justice demands against an increasingly hostile political environment. Like black elected officials throughout the 1980s, candidate Barack Obama had to pass the "Farrakhan litmus" and renounce the jeremiad of Jeremiah Wright Jr. (see the epigraph to this chapter). Performing the former was easy, given Jesse Jackson's example during his two campaigns and Farrakhan's toxicity in politics. But performing the other—renouncing Wright—shook the very foundation of Obama's personal Christian nationalist faith, as well as ties to the black community in Chicago (including those segments of the black community that Wright's jeremiad affirmed inside the shouting auditorium of Trinity United Church of Christ), to antiwar progressives, and to besieged black communities throughout the United States.

Bill Clinton's Million Man March

The MMM/DOA was an impressive show of Louis Farrakhan's ability to steer the restive energy of black Americans besieged by life crises in the late twentieth century. But Jesse Jackson attributed the event more to the effects of the Reagan revolution, the ongoing War on Drugs, and the Newt Gingrich–led "Contract with America." Survey respondents cited "showing support for the Black community" in the hostile political environment and "showing support for Black men" as the primary reasons for attending. The twentieth century ended with a demand-protest nationalist challenge to electoral leadership, as occurred at the end of the nineteenth, when the likes of Booker T. Washington and Bishop Henry McNeal Turner eclipsed the Reconstruction-era Black and Tan Republicans.[10]

In his book *The Audacity of Hope*, Barack Obama outlined his bouts with militancy—taking in images of Huey P. Newton and the anarchic 1968 Democratic National Convention—and opposition to the Reagan "backlash," which, he notes, "continues to drive our political discourse."[11] His initial discussion of Bill Clinton, typical of the grievances of many blacks and intellectuals during the 1980s and 1990s, quips about Clinton's "Sister Souljah" duplicity and a state execution in Arkansas of Ricky Ray Rector on the eve of a Democratic primary in 1992.[12]

It was argued in Chapter 8 that Louis Farrakhan performed the jeremiad protest tradition and indeed *was* a jeremiad of the hip-hop generation. His crowning achievement and failure was the 1995 MMM/DOA, which assembled millions of African Americans in Washington, D.C., and in satellite gatherings throughout the country on October 16, 1995. It is likely that the increase of 1.5 million black male voters since 1992 was attributable to the MMM/DOA.[13] Its principal organizers, included former NAACP executive secretary and Christian black nationalist Ben Chavis, Ron Maulana Karenga, and others, were veterans of the civil rights, Black Power, and modern black convention movements. The MMM/DOA was the largest black gathering in US political history.[14] Only Marcus Garvey and Martin Luther King Jr. likely could have attracted such an audience, and *no living black elected official could have* at the time.

The flaws and shortcomings of the event are too numerous to list—not least its exclusionary framing as an event only for black men. Rosa Parks—who did not speak at the 1963 March on Washington—was one of many women to address the assembly, as was Betty Shabazz. Louis Farrakhan's speech did not live up to the occasion, and it was viewed as the worst of his public career. As fantastical as the Nation of Islam's early claims to racial separation seem in hindsight, Farrakhan likely delivered the reelection of Bill Clinton with nothing tangible in return. In turn, the MMM/DOA comported with Adolph Reed's observation concerning efforts at "community mobilization for [purposes of] political demobilization."[15]

The Million Man March occurred just eleven months after an unprecedented Republican congressional landslide election in 1994, amid the O.J. Simpson trial and verdict, two years after the important 1993 March on Washington (celebrating the thirtieth anniversary of the first March on Washington), and eleven months before the 1996 presidential election.[16] The MMM/DOA likely reversed the cumulative (presidential) election declines—between 1988 and 1996—in black voter turnout.[17] The "lesser of two evils" dilemma reinforced one party's share of the black vote in that presidential election, as it has since the Radical Republicanism of the 1860s. With no recourse—other than the strategic choice of *abstention*—the 14 percent of MMM survey respondents who said they "intended to register and vote," and the 86 percent who were already registered, overwhelmingly supported the Democrats. Clinton's own Million Man March speech (earlier in the campaign) applauded the commitment to "family, reconciliation, and personal responsibility" expressed on the Mall while also urging both black and white Americans to "clean house" of their more extreme elements.[18]

All but absent during the affirmative-action controversies of the campaign, Clinton, once elected, urged "a great national effort" to create "a more perfect union" (incidentally, the title of Farrakhan's MMM/DOA speech and Obama's April 2008 speech on race in Philadelphia). Targeting California's Proposition 209, which sought to ban affirmative action in the state, Clinton's speech continued, "To those of you who oppose affirmative action, I ask you to come up with an alternative."[19] Other noteworthy comments from this speech urged racial understanding among groups:

> If a black American commits a crime, condemn the act—but remember that most African Americans are hard-working, law-abiding citizens. If a Latino gang member deals drugs, condemn the act—but remember the vast majority of Hispanics are responsible citizens who also deplore the scourge of drugs in our life. If white teenagers beat a young African American boy almost to death just because of his race, for God's sake condemn the act—but remember the overwhelming majority of white people will find it just as hateful.[20]

This may partially explain why one poll reported that the number of African Americans calling themselves Democrats *dropped* from 74 percent in 1992 to 58 percent during the 1996 campaign—that is, just two months after the MMM/DOA; 40 percent expressed a willingness to consider a minor-party candidate.[21] Although none of the major candidates (President Clinton [D], Senator Robert Dole [R], and Ross Perot [I-Reform]) was regarded as racially conservative, the larger issues of affirmative action, immigration, crime, and welfare reform loomed large, especially in California. Based on the electorate's 1994 midterm rejection of liberal Democrats, with the election and re-election of Republican conservatives, no candidate in 1996 could expect to be elected while championing liberal policy on such issues, whether Democrat,

Republican, or Independent. The imagery of the First Couple wearing African Kente cloth attire on the cover of *JET* magazine during an official visit to Africa[22] likely mended grievances for some time.

Blacks' support for Clinton in 1996 obfuscates the dilemma that his "symbolic distance" posed for them as constituents. Disturbed by the 1994 midterm elections, liberal Democrats felt compelled to grant Clinton wide latitude in his campaign to champion traditionally moderate-conservative policy issues as a means to reelection. After all, he was seeking to become the first Democrat reelected president since Franklin Delano Roosevelt in 1944. And like Roosevelt's last vice president and successor, Harry S Truman, he would also govern while the opposition party dominated Congress. In one sense, however, black voters had plenty of reason to be disenchanted with the Democratic administration under Clinton.[23] Given the racial politics, southern Democratic centrists felt that its 1992 campaign strategy ("symbolic distance," which made no clear overture toward black policy interests) could be remedied—once and if victory was attained. In 1992, torn among the Democratic Leadership Council (DLC), the Democratic National Committee (DNC), and liberal forces, Bill Clinton sought space in the middle. Clinton's "symbolic distance" racial *electoral* campaign strategy included a symbolic *governing* component that made his pragmatism more palatable to his African American constituency. Symbolic overtures toward black American voters, such as the appointments of black elites to high office, were his stock-in-trade.[24]

Theodore Cross and Robert Bruce Slater characterize black participation in 1996 as "apathetic" and "unenthusiastic." They base their conclusions on facts: black voters in at least five southern states—where they represented key electoral blocs—failed to organize against the segregationist senators Strom Thurmond (D) and Jesse Helms (R) in reelection bids; this cost the Clinton administration a potential 430–108 Electoral College mandate.[25] Finding fault in Farrakhan's inability to capitalize on his "third political force" MMM speech theme, the authors note that "on this front the march was a bust."[26] Although the authors attribute at least 107 of Clinton's 1996 electoral votes—from Florida, Louisiana, Kentucky, Tennessee, and California—to the black vote, they are somewhat dismayed that blacks did not mobilize in favor of the Democrats or at least *against* the Republicans en masse.[27] They note:

> [The] traditional affinity [which Blacks have had for the Democrats] has produced a false perception of the homogeneity in the African-American political opinion. Consequently, when African Americans have become disaffected with the Democrats, it has been perceived that these disillusioned blacks, lacking anywhere else (i.e., any other viable party alternative) to turn, have chosen to withdraw from the political system entirely. . . . However, *there has been a growing African American dissatisfaction with the Democratic party since the mid-1980s.* Analysis of the 1984 and 1988 NBES survey results reveal that fewer African Americans believed in 1988 that Democrats worked

very hard on black issues. Since 1988, *Newsweek* has reported a large increase in the percentage of African Americans who argue that there would be no difference between a Democratic and Republican administration. . . . *This dissatisfaction with the Democratic party has been reflected in the large jump in the number of African Americans who in the Bush years identified themselves as independents.* . . . Can we determine if the shift in black partisanship is a response to the politics of the Reagan-Bush era? . . . [Our] results show that for every quarter that Reagan and Bush were in office—everything else being held constant—black Democratic party identification declined by three percentage points. In the absence of countervailing influences such as the rise in the gap between black and white unemployment and the steadily increasing unpopularity of President Reagan during his tenure and the fluctuating popularity of President Bush, black Democratic identification could be expected to decline rapidly.[28]

For Michael Dawson, black turnout/participation and voting patterns at the presidential level have indeed oscillated not between the major parties but between grudgingly supporting the Democrats and abstaining altogether. He writes: "Many African Americans view their only choices—the same choices they have considered for nearly half a century—as support for the Democratic party, support for a radical third-party or other independent political effort, and abstention. These are viewed as the only choices for advancing African American group interests. With the new emphasis on electoral politics, *the choice for African Americans increasingly has been between supporting the Democrats and abstention.*"[29]

Initially, David A. Bositis found that as overall turnout declined to the lowest participation levels since the 1924 campaign, black male participation *increased* even beyond a relatively moderate decline in 1992. Whereas overall voting was reported to have declined from 104 million in 1992 to 95.8 million in 1996 (6 percent), black voting was reported as *increasing by nearly 1.5 million votes*. Black men were believed to have even bested black women in turnout, according to researchers using exit polls. This development buttressed Clinton's black support even as that of black women declined. In 1992, black women outvoted black men 5.1 million to 3.06 million, but in 1996 they reportedly had equal turnout rates (4.79 million each). Thus, the purported 1.5 million black voter increase was clearly the result of black male turnout. This is somewhat perplexing considering that Clinton's support among *white women increased significantly*. And studies have shown that black women tend to be more supportive of Democrats than black men. Though we can only speculate about black male turnout without the MMM/DOA mobilization, the reported decline in black female turnout might shed light on the ostensible "apathy" of black voters as a whole.

More telling is the impact of regional turnout. The now defunct Voter News Service consortium showed that between 1992 and 1996, *Clinton lost support among blacks in regions where the Million Man March turnout was lowest (West and Midwest), and it increased in support where the Million Man March turnout was highest (East and Southeast).* Clinton's support increased by 6 percent in the East and 5 percent in the South and decreased 7 percent in the Midwest and 6 percent in the West.[30] Based on exit polls, Farrakhan and the MMM/DOA executive council may have become unwitting agents of the Democrat Party in 1996: They may have mobilized millions of black men for the party's quadrennial unrequited use.[31] Whereas preliminary exit poll data showed one picture of black participation in 1996, Ruy Teixeira's study— based on US Census data—offers conflicting evidence.[32] Regardless, the combined data agree on one critical point: *Democratic black female turnout declined.* To this point, Katherine Tate argues,

> Age strongly affect(s) Black partisan support. *Black women are more likely to identify strongly with the Democratic party, while Black men are more likely to be weak or independent Democratic party supporters, political independents*, or Republicans. Surprisingly, young Blacks, those aged 18 to 29, had weaker identifications with the Democratic party, being more likely to identify themselves as weak Democrats or as Republicans than older Blacks. Those 30 to 54 years of age were no different in party membership and identification than those 55 years of age or older. Even though young voters are not generally known for their political loyalties, it may be that many young White Americans will eventually affiliate with the Republican party given the strong popularity of Ronald Reagan. . . . The young, traditionally Democratic in preference, split their votes between the parties in the 1984 presidential election. At the same time, given the uniformly unfavorable evaluations Reagan received within the Black community, it is unlikely that younger Blacks might be more inclined toward the Republican party than past generations of Blacks.[33]

This decline occurred among black women *before* passage of the 1996 Personal Responsibility and Work Opportunity Reconciliation Act, although Clinton's campaign promise to "end welfare as we know it" signaled his intentions in advance. Moreover, we at least know that the declines did not occur among white females. Together, a rather ominous picture emerges concerning black Democratic partisanship. The Voter News Service data suggest that even with the aid of the Million Man March mobilization and a popular Democratic president seeking reelection, blacks overall (including the *most* Democratic) lost enthusiasm.

In the short term, the 2008 election of Barack Obama to the White House is likely to preclude any major black movement away from the Democrats, making his administration, in effect, a tourniquet for a gaping party wound. Despite Republican Party overtures, blacks continue to support conservative centrist Democrats out of political necessity and show antipathy for Republican Party lily-whitism.

Harold Cruse's Faith in the Future

Joe McCormick and Sekou Franklin accurately identify the MMM/DOA supporters as Democratic "liberal reformers"; they correspond to a category of individuals that Edward Carmines and James Stimson refer to as "unrealized partisans."[34] Whereas President Clinton was preferable to Republican challenger Bob Dole, he still received only a 25 percent approval rating among MMM/DOA survey respondents and, like Jesse Jackson, came in second to "none of the above" in terms of leadership preferences. Data show that as the effect of black racial identity *strengthens* black Democratic partisanship, the period beginning around 1984 yielded an increasingly *lower* Democratic inclination even among black respondents experiencing Jesse Jackson's and Louis Farrakhan's emergence in African American politics. In fact, the MMM/DOA surveys show that attendants yielded an atypical black Democratic Party identification, nearly thirty percentage points below most surveys of black Democratic partisanship. At the same time, this group displayed the normal antipathy for racial conservatism that has predominated in the Republican Party *most clearly* in the decades since Barry Goldwater and Ronald Reagan.

Demographically, aside from corresponding mostly with the hip-hop generation age sets, those surveyed were not only a largely middle-class cohort (52 percent) of black Americans; they exceeded average black American men in terms of income—with 65 percent earning $30,000–$75,000.[35] Whereas 94 percent had at least a high school education, when combined, most (72 percent) had some college, graduated from college, or had postgraduate education. The influence of the wrangling Afrocentric academic phenomenon is undeniable.[36] Respondents were largely Baptist Protestant religionists who attended services at least periodically and ignored the advice of the National Baptist Convention and individual critics, such as Los Angeles's West Angeles Church of God in Christ bishop Charles Blake and Crenshaw Christian Center pastor Frederick K.C. Price, to stay away from the gathering. Two of every three were fathers. And only *half* acknowledged Democratic Party identification, 37 percent were independent, and only 3 percent were Republican. Katherine Tate's observation (above) that "young Blacks, those aged 18 to 29, had weaker identifications with the Democratic party, being more likely to identify themselves as weak Democrats or as Republicans than older Blacks," corresponds with the hip-hop generation. At the MMM/DOA, Democratic Party alignment was weakest. As much as this book has chronicled the imposition of the black nationalist jeremiad tradition, it is worth noting that the MMM/DOA's framing as a religious event harbored an independent strain among those surveyed. But aspects of this sensibility were undermined by the continued prominence of civil rights establishment elites and intellectuals in contemporary black politics, racial conservatism in the major US political parties, and, later, the election of Barack Obama.

Louis Farrakhan was integral to the interplay between conventional and unconventional elites during this period. Having been present at Gary, Indiana, in 1972—there refusing to support any political agenda being taken up by the 8,000 delegates in attendance—he now promised to forge a "third force" political apparatus at the 1995 MMM event that failed to develop. But Vibert White Jr. insists that the failed National African American Leadership Summit (NAALS) was a secular fulcrum of the Nation of Islam intended for such a purpose.[37] Following the MMM event, Louis Farrakhan engaged in the first of several celebratory (and congratulatory) "World Friendship Tours"[38] in Africa, Latin America, the Middle East, Asia, and major US cities, referring to himself as "a Jesus" or one who is "*the* Jesus for our time."[39] During the fall of 1996, the Million Man March conveners organized a National Political Convention in St. Louis to "move toward independent political participation" and to address issues "ignored by Republican and Democrats." Anticipating a draw of nearly 12,000 delegates, the NAALS presented its "National Black Agenda" to the party delegates at the Republican, Democratic, and Reform conventions.[40]

In *Plural but Equal*, Harold Cruse suggested the possible emergence of a post–civil rights generation that would embrace particular forms of independence, especially from political structures, while developing independent institutions, such as a party or convention movement. Integral to this inclination is the political ideology of black nationalism. Cruse called for a black American nationalist elite with the ultimate courage to formulate an independent party in coalition with like-minded groups with a view toward broadening the structural limits of US democracy. Cruse predicted that a post–civil rights–era cadre of individuals, out of necessity to forge independent party politics for African Americans, would emerge with no particular loyalties to—indeed, be hostile to—the conventional political arrangements brokered between the New Deal–Great Society interracial elite coalitions in the Democratic Party and, respectively, the core and semiperipheral civil rights entities, such as the Congressional Black Caucus and the NAACP, which have sponsored cultural and political assimilationism since the early twentieth century.[41]

The great political disappointment, for Cruse, of the immediate post–civil rights period was the failure of elected and unconventional African American leadership to carry out its commitment to formulate a broad-based "third force" political fulcrum that could negotiate the terrain of the nation's *plural* (not "pluralist") racial and ethnic theater. This is consistent with Cruse's earlier work, which acknowledged the "American situation" as one of a nation of national minorities,[42] living their respective, plural nationalisms. Cruse took seriously the need to forge such a fulcrum as a means to strengthening the black position *in* American politics, that is, in essence, *nationalist without separatism*. As utopian as such a phenomenon seemed to the hypermajority of black Americans who typically rejected such an idea, so, too, was the idea of a black person becoming president within two generations of the civil rights movement—or even during their lifetimes. Cruse notes, "An independent black political party *should* have been perceived as a *plural* imperative, rather than a separatist proposition."[43] The fact that this institutional effort would need to include the panoply of African American ideologies and perspectives (e.g., gender, sexuality, black ethnicities) is a matter of operational concern that could be sorted out in caucus. But Cruse iterates that a chief failure of African American politics and leadership has been "to master the art of cooperation, or cooperative methods of social organization."[44]

This is not to impose a procrustean bed of homogeneous politics as much as it is to think of how "a *theoretical* Third Party in the United States would have to be a movement of several independent parts, a *coalition* of independent components anchored around an organized base."[45] For Cruse, this is not a unity or uniformity pitch but rather the operational basis on which a new arrangement of black politics could emerge. In the tradition of W.E.B. Du Bois and William Monroe Trotter, the logic of the American social and political scene has warranted the construction of an independent black political party. And it is not to be an intermittent "issues" party in the vein of American independent or third parties traditionally (e.g., the Green Party and the Reform Party).

The 1960s and 1970s black party formations were a serious step on behalf of nationalist forces (and those who later turned nationalist in the SNCC and Congress on Racial Equality [CORE]). Yet given the stillborn economic yield of (vital) civil rights, the collaterality of economics in the liberal integrationist commitment to equality, and the marginal and vituperative role of nationalist elites, Cruse insists: "Crucially, *they would not establish an independent black political party*."[46] Conventional political bodies, such as the Congressional Black Caucus, were limited in reach beyond electoral politics. Jesse Jackson's campaigns, born of the logic of the modern convention movement, were too wedded to protest-brokerage and clientage politics of recognition, with nowhere to go but to the "least racist" party. In summary, Cruse notes,

> the ending of the civil rights cycle, 1954–1980, would render all original black issues a "Lost Priority." But black minority-group issues would remain unresolved, even though partially remedied through the "vertical integration" of a new black middle class. The vast majority of urbanized blacks, for whom the Civil Rights of integration and upward economic mobility were meaningless, still remain separate and unequal. Now that the civil rights cycle has ended, their future lies in the economics and politics of the "equality of plurality," or "plural but equal," as a racially democratic alternative to the "separate-but-equal doctrine." However, this next stage in the possible evolution of the status of the black minority can be achieved only through the development of a *new style of black leadership*—a leadership that can measure up to the organizational demands of the politics of black ethnicity.[47]

A politics of black economics—cooperative *and* competitive—would need articulation. Cruse insists, "Reaganism personified the political vanguard not only against the federal role in defense of civil rights enforcements but also against federal sponsorship of economic-support supplements in civil rights advocacy."[48] But more than that, "The most obvious obligatory work that loomed was more concentrated political organization by blacks, but *not only* for the elevation of more officials to political office. The organization of blacks into an independent political party would belatedly help make up for the abysmal lack of organizational achievements by blacks over the last sixty years in all areas—political, economic, cultural, educational." Moreover,

the situation called for a new black leadership consensus that was capable of redefining the plausible place of the black minority within the societal complex in which blacks *as a group* found themselves by 1980. Such a redefinition of the legitimate place of the black minority within the system had to take into full account the meaning of *plurality*. It meant the systematic *reorganization* of many areas of black life into first a *political bloc*, then cultural blocs, and then into whatever internal economic organizations are possible within the capitalistic, free-market system. In this context an independent black political party becomes the initial step toward a total reorganization of black life over the remainder of the twentieth century.

In 1987 Cruse writes that "without such a *total* political, economic, cultural, educational, and *institutional* reorganization of black life, the American black minority will not be able to survive into whatever system American society becomes by the year 2000 and after."[49] It is left unclear how a new style of black leadership—trained in an almost monolithic mode of protest—would capture the hearts and minds of the masses-class of black people who have come to understand politics mainly in terms of clientage black politics. Cruse warns, "The traditional civil rights leadership that aims at perpetuating this mode of agitation is *detrimental* to future development in the political, economic, educational, and cultural dimensions of the black cause. More than that, *the traditional civil rights leadership will oppose any attempt on the part of an alternate leadership to organize blacks into an independent political bloc*."[50] One longs to know what Cruse would say or write about the fact of Obama's election and the so-called Joshua Generation of black elected officials in African American politics in light of the support that many higher-profile civil rights leadership elites (e.g., John Lewis, James Clyburn, Maxine Waters, Charles Rangel, and nearly half of the Congressional Black Caucus) gave to Hillary Clinton's primary campaign.[51]

Chronicling the long history of black struggle for political independence vis-à-vis independent parties in his earlier studies, Hanes Walton Jr. later argued that a likely scenario for black politics in the twenty-first century is "political isolationism":

The inner cities and near suburbs would become hopelessly impoverished communities, politically powerless and physically isolated from the rest of American society. Residential segregation would continue to prevent all but a few African Americans from escaping the black ghetto. The African American middle class would be increasingly vulnerable as [racially conservative] politicians in the mold of Jesse Helms and David Duke capitalize more and more on white frustration and racism in their efforts to reverse the hard-earned gains garnered as a result of the civil rights and Black Power movements. Radical politics would flourish not only among less affluent African Americans but could spread to their middle-class peers. However, intense debates over agendas, strategy and tactics are also highly likely in the face of this bleak and volatile scenario. . . . *African Americans' participation in third party and other independent political movements is also likely to increase, perhaps leading to the creation of an independent black political party.*[52]

Key scholarly analyses explored and even predicted that an independent party would emerge from the post–civil rights generations before the turn of the twenty-first century. What Cruse predicted amid the Reagan revolution—and what appears to have been the hope among MMM/DOA supporters—was somehow lost thanks to Louis Farrakhan and the Nation of Islam. To this extent, the MMM assembly, with all of its 1972 National Black Political Convention veteran organizers, may have undermined its full potential. One of the MMM/DOA attendees, Barack Obama, will, in fact, concede that the failures of the MMM/DOA event, which he attended just three weeks after announcing his run for the Illinois state senate, reiterated his determination to impact the future of black politics. It is not possible to know the MMM/DOA's potential as an emergent mobilization given Farrakhan's misreading of the era (i.e., initiated by him, rather than growing out of a moribund postsegregation black political agenda and the craving for an articulation of grievances during the Reagan nadir with the clarity and precision of Malcolm X). As M. K. Asante rightly notes, before its pop-culture form, the hip-hop generation was drawn "to Malcolm because it is this connection that represents hip hop's most potent and dominant sense of rebellion. Put another way, the force that created Malcolm was the same force that created hip hop—a visceral energy aimed at transforming (or at least voicing) the conditions of oppressed people."[53]

The hip-hop generation did, at this critical juncture, maintain an atypical political disposition toward the Democratic Party in tandem with Harold Cruse's foresight concerning post–civil rights black politics. Their political socialization developed in cadence with the final stage of civil rights–styled black politics and the continued dominance of civil rights elites. Louis Farrakhan's version of black nationalism ruled the day and, ultimately, served the perfidious function of deflecting from the ongoing critical discourse in black politics. An irony of the MMM/DOA event indicates that Louis Farrakhan's conservative nationalist jeremiad, fueled with the capital of blacks' dissatisfaction with conservative hostility in both parties, failed to deliver what could have been the most profound secular jeremiad of all—the creation of a black political party—as Harold Cruse imagined would emerge among a post–civil rights cohort. Beyond church institutions and denominational conventions, African American clerics and, for the most part, the nationalists among them have a poor record establishing effective formal political structures like King's SCLC. But from Malcolm X's creation of the Organization of Afro-American Unity and his promise to use it, or to create another institution that would be a "black nationalist political party" (since David Walker's involvement in the African Meeting House[54] and Henry Garnet's African Civilization Society a century earlier), practitioners of the black jeremiad tradition went beyond protest preaching. Such a formation might bridge civil rights protest politics with formal politics. Several studies have carefully documented the substantive policy focuses of the militant strain, particularly those inspired by the Black Power ethos and ideology.

The Million Man March and Political Independence

The 1995 Million Man March has been thoroughly critiqued for its conservative masculinist propensities in the tradition of black nationalism. But there is little analysis of the connections among the Million Man March, black electoral politics, and the plausibility of linkages with the independent ethos that emanated from Black Power in the 1960s and the modern black convention movement. Those who supported the MMM/DOA had a relationship to independent politics as conventionally understood. For instance, McCormick and Franklin show (based on the Howard University–Wellington Group on-site survey) that while creating an independent black political party scored lower than most other black nationalist measures (with the exception of a question on reparations at 51.9 percent), respondents registered 51.9 percent in favor. No modern national survey of black Americans comes close to such a yield of black opinion on the question. The 1984 and 1996 National Black Election Studies (NBES), for instance, respectively show 29 percent and 31 percent answering affirmatively. Both surveys oversampled black women 3–5 percent.[55]

Given its relevance to black nationalism, the 1996 NBES does allow for a "best party" strategy index to be constructed. This index directly tests for the affect of the MMM/DOA on preference for an independent black political party, although[56] devoid of measures that directly ascertain whether or not 1996 NBES respondents actually participated in the MMM/DOA. The coupling of these measures only infers the relationship of the MMM/DOA to independent politics. Here is listed a set of attitudinal measures that allow for the construction of an MMM-independence scale: "How important do you think the Million Man March was for the black community? Would that be *very important, somewhat important,* or *not important at all?*" and "Do you think blacks should form their own political party?" A related but distinct set of best strategy questions asked, "Among the three, which strategy is best for increasing the political power of blacks in the United States? (1) continued support for the Democratic Party and its candidates; (2) increased support for the Republican Party and its candidates; or (3) formation of an independent black political party?" Using ordinary least squares (OLS) regression, this model yields three patterns of party strategy preferences that are categorized below as Million Man March Supporters, Million Man March Moderates, and Million Man March Nonsupporters.

The yield is clearly anti-Republican and (to a lesser degree) anti-Democratic, which is evident in the party strategy patterns model set forth here. Figure 9.1 shows a clear and theoretically plausible pattern that is a statistically significant relationship between those who strongly supported the MMM/DOA event and those who supported the best political party strategy. Here the independents are those erstwhile Democrats who advocated an independent black political party strategy.

Among Million Man March Nonsupporters, we find the strongest pro–Republican Party strategy response (19 percent) and the weakest support for political independence (17 percent). The pro–Democratic Party strategy (64 percent) is higher among the MMM Nonsupporters than among MMM Supporters (56 percent). Among MMM Moderates, the pro–Democratic Party

Figure 9.1   Million Man March and Best Party Strategy

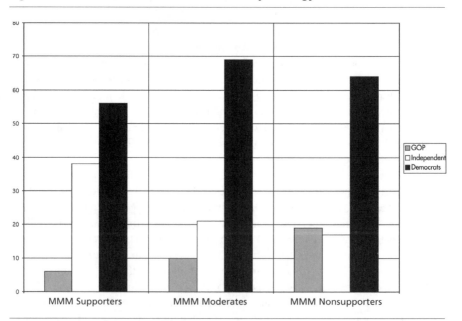

Source: 1996 NBES.

strategy was highest (69 percent); independence (21 percent) was second behind MMM Supporters. MMM Moderates were strongly anti-Republican Party strategy (90 percent against). MMM Supporters yielded the highest support for the independent party strategy (38 percent); they were simultaneously the least favorable of a pro–Democratic Party strategy (56 percent) and Republican Party strategy (6 percent). Black partisanship historically has been affected negatively as much by racial conservatism (lily-white Republican, southern Democrat, Goldwater-Reagan conservatism in both major parties) as by any affirmative alliances with racial liberalism in the party system vis-à-vis the New Deal–Great Society. And it is when racial conservatism seeks to dominate ideological space in politics that alternatives are sought by black American voters. This confirms the preferred party strategy among MMM Supporters, who were theoretically and empirically more inclined toward an independent party strategy in the mode of the 1972 NBPC and the later National Black Independent Political Party, which prompted Jackson's independent campaign insurgency in 1984.

The foregoing illustrates that while all groups were most supportive of a pro–Democratic Party strategy, political independence—in the form of creating a new black political party—was strongest among those who thought that the MMM was very important. When asked "which strategy is best?" 52 percent of NBES respondents preferred creating an independent black political party; 32 percent preferred a Democratic Party strategy; 17 percent supported the Republican Party. This analysis confirms MMM/DOA's positive link with independent politics and is statistically significant ($p < .00$).

Michael Eric Dyson asserted that

> events since the Million Man March prove that those who claimed it was much larger than its leadership were right. . . . One cannot help but grieve at the manner in which Farrakhan has squandered opportunities to extend the arc of his leadership. Having gained a considerable degree of moral authority, political capital, racial influence and spiritual power, Farrakhan has largely disappointed an array of Black communities who hoped his emergence might signal a new direction for him, and renewed imagination in the movement for black equality and justice which had stalled in stale strategies and impotent ideas.[57]

MMM Supporters strongly associated with independent politics on at least two separate measures concerning best party strategy. Had the MMM/DOA political elite in actuality moved beyond certain parochial loyalties, it is plausible that the male attendees might have supported an independent party initiative; despite talk of a "third force," "independent political organizations," and "self-determination" among the MMM/DOA executive council, it failed to extend its nationalist pitch to incorporate one of its central political tenets: insistence on a black independent structure. The incremental movement away from the Democratic Party is not in a Republican direction. This highlights the fact that average black partisanship leveled out in neither major party's direction, even among those blacks who did identify with a major party. This yield is, at bottom, *less pro-Democratic* than previous generations since the civil rights shift toward that party.

Whereas Tate's analysis acknowledges the increasing non-Democratic leanings of both younger blacks and whites—centered on different assessments of the racial conservatism epitomized in the Reagan cultural and political revolution—her study did not address at the time the simple possibility that younger blacks were becoming more inclined toward independence than older generations. But attitudes are not votes: Young people tend not to *vote* with the same enthusiasm with which they *express* support for a given candidate and certain party strategies.[58] This apparent non-Democratic (if not anti-Democratic) yield among younger black American men and women may provide the reserve for those independent forces among the black collective who are less entangled with party allegiances (see the Harold Cruse discussion, above).

Had an appropriate leadership or organizational cue been presented, the conflation of factors that we have outlined here suggest that many black voters may have been willing to adopt independence as an alternative, and the most viable, party strategy; 86 percent of MMM Supporters were registered voters, and *only 11 percent* identified as black nationalists. As part of the larger dissolution in the New Deal–Great Society liberal coalitions, black Americans seemed at least episodically engaged in a softening of their affinities for the Democratic Party. A growing segment of blacks who *do* participate seem to be associated with the party by political necessity and habit—and not with much enthusiasm. The unprecedented support for Barack Obama in 2008 is the exception that affirms the rule. *Candidate-centered* enthusiasm for Obama ought not be interpreted as enthusiasm for the heretofore increasingly centrist party.

The Colin Powell Effect

General Colin Powell (US Army, ret.) appeared to be the preferred black candidate among most black voters when he was considering a White House candidacy in 1995.[59] Although the post–Jesse Jackson moment had already set in, Powell seemed to quench a thirst for a "not Jesse Jackson" (and by extension "not Al Sharpton") type of African American presidential candidacy. Indeed, where Farrakhan represented the favored "organic" approach in black politics, Powell's potential candidacy represented the preferred potential *electoral* strategy. His ties to previous Republican administrations—even conservative—did not diminish his ability to garner a more favorable showing than Jesse Jackson among Million Man Marchers. Jackson (23 percent) placed third behind Colin Powell (37 percent) and "none of the above."[60] Moreover, Powell's political affiliation was unknown until he registered as a Republican in 1995; he had served Republican and Democratic administrations. Powerful black Democrats, like Ron Dellums and Vernon Jordan, attempted to persuade Powell to join Clinton as the vice-presidential candidate in 1992. Republicans equally tried to recruit him for a Dole-Powell ticket. Cary D. Wintz reports that Powell "also expressed interest in a third party as an option."[61]

The media swell surrounding a possible Powell candidacy provided black Americans with some rationale for reconsidering what would have likely been a major disruption of their post–civil rights Democratic alliance. "A consistent theme was that if Powell ran he would alter the American political landscape and he would have a very good chance of winning. The discussions in print and broadcast media focused on Powell as a symbol of change and hope."[62] For his part, Powell had the only strong ratio of favorable to unfavorable ratings among any likely GOP contender. And more important, Powell was the *only* Republican who bested Bill Clinton in a head-to-head contest among the general electorate in New Hampshire, a result that held in early national polls as well.[63] The Voter News Service exit poll suggests that Powell would have defeated Clinton 48 percent to 36 percent. Powell's support among Million Man Marchers may have suffered when he opted neither to attend nor to make a comprehensive statement. Powell's 1996 Republican National Convention speech supporting "a woman's right to choose" abortion, and the admission of being a "strong" advocate of affirmative action, no doubt strengthened Powell's status—though he was booed from the convention floor. And, critically, he did not wrap himself in antiblack public posturing. Future studies of black presidential politics must consider how Colin Powell's flirtation with the White House in the 1990s primed the campaign for a new candidate: Barack Obama.

The campaign of the conservative black Republican Alan Keyes, a former US State Department official, was irrelevant to black Americans throughout the 2004 contest, as was black conservatism in general.[64] Still, some black conservatives saw the Million Man March as an opportunity to increase the GOP's black constituency.[65] However, the 1996 GOP convention's fifty-two black delegates (less than 3 percent of total delegates) were the lowest number in attendance since Ronald Reagan's 1984 reelection campaign.[66] Powell represented considerable relief from the religiopolitical protest tradition's decade-long hegemony in black politics, epitomized by Jackson's campaigns and Farrakhan's MMM/DOA. Powell modeled a path to the US presidency by being an atypical national black political figure, one who certainly supported civil rights and experienced blunt racism in the US Army. But the lasting legacy was the widespread sense that many non–African American voters were warming to the idea of a black person serving as president of the United States. Powell's endorsement of Barack Obama in the weeks before the 2008 general election is yet another legacy of Colin Powell.

The Political Problem of Black Nationalism in the Life, Campaign, and Election of Barack Obama

Commentaries on Barack Obama's ascension to the highest office in US politics range from the celebratory and conspiratorial to factual reports on the 2008 electoral campaigns. Some place the Obama campaign within earlier efforts by African American candidates since the nineteenth century, from Frederick Douglass to Jesse Jackson. Dewey Clayton, in *The Presidential Campaign of Barack Obama*, recounts the overall strategies, coalitions, and "transformational" race politics that delivered victory. Clayton's work trades on the "deracialization" thesis of modern black politics, even when Obama's opponents in the primary and general elections "racialized" him, his campaign, and his constituency. This puts the burden of race on black voters in a manner similar to Martin Luther King's "nonviolent" march strategies. As long as black marchers or voters behave themselves, the racial thing is not "racial," and the violence one sees is "nonviolence." Pragmatic deracialization must be a two-way street if the leadership it produces is to be representative. Deracialization, as applied to black politics, means to de-emphasize blackness, not *race*.

Peniel Joseph attempts to place Obama's election within the legacies of the civil rights and Black Power movements. He notes, for instance, "Barack Obama's audacious presidential candidacy, invigorating campaign, and stunning victory reflect the contours of Black Power's contemporary legacy, relationship with civil rights struggles, and enduring impact on America's racial dialogue."[67] Joseph seems to locate Obama along a rough Black Power continuum, ranging from the more conservative to the more revolutionary wings that emerged in the later 1960s.[68] For Joseph, Malcolm X and Stokely Carmichael should be read fluidly, reflecting the transitions of their public careers. The militant orientations they represented should be understood as paralleling the mainstream Christian liberal integrationist wing that is credited to King and achieving the expansion of democratic institutions in the United States. Critics charge that Barack Obama is not a fulfillment of Black Power but instead its negation. If Obama is to be associated with Black Power, it is with the Nixonian Black Power capitalism wing, not with the phases represented by Malcolm X or Stokely Carmichael.[69] Yet, Joseph is careful to note, "in large measure, Obama has enjoyed the benefits of both the civil rights and Black Power movements while maintaining a safe distance from both."[70] And Joseph insists that Obama mostly interpreted the civil rights and Black Power movements with a warped, static, and romantically caricatured view. Joseph is not attempting to link Obama's *governing* domestic or foreign policy orientations with the major African American ideological orientations that the candidate negotiated along his way *to* the White House. This is also pertinent in relating the left criticisms of Obama as an imperialist, neoliberal, neoconservative, occupationist, Wall Street corporatist executive of the US nation-state. These are different points in Barack Obama's trajectory, and in the end, despite all of his efforts to save capitalism, the major right-wing criticism of Obama has been the charge of "socialism!"

On Burying Moses

David Remnick's account emphasizes Obama as part of a "Joshua Generation," a new breed who is derivative of the civil rights movement but without "the politics of grievance" epitomized in Black Power. Remnick's book is an exhaustive biography that recounts Obama's identity, political, and ideological struggles largely as an appendage to *Dreams from My Father*. Mostly this first generation of Obama studies focuses on the political career of Barack Obama and the meaning of his election for black politics, identity politics, and US politics generally. Its major bias seems to be its "end-of-black-politics" premise, which pits Obama and the latest "new" black leadership class against the very movements that made them possible. Corey Booker, Artur Davis, Adrian Fenty, Jesse Jackson Jr., Kendrick Meeks, Keith Ellison, Deval Patrick, and Obama are the (all-male) Joshuas whose calling it is to bury the Moses Generation, not succeed it. Obama, in turn, is presented as the end of black politics—the politics of black Chicago; Jesse Jackson, Louis Farrakhan, and Jeremiah Wright—as much as he is the beginning of postracial politics.[71] Ignored are the details that Joshua is a religious metaphor for an essentially all-male electoral political class, and that Senator Obama—unlike Senator Ed W. Brooke before him—joined the independent Congressional Black Caucus, which came directly out of the civil rights struggle and Black Power in 1966. It also elides Martin Luther King's Black Power phase beginning that same year. It implies that Barack Obama represents the "good" black politics (of King) and not the "bad" black politics (Wright or Farrakhan) before he "transforms" above both.

The emergence of Barack Obama as Illinois state senator in 1996, junior US senator of Illinois in 2004, and then forty-fourth president of the United States in 2009 is significant to the political developments analyzed throughout this book and its themes: ideology, religion, party politics, leadership, and the hip-hop generation, all of which converged in the election. Barack Obama as an office-seeker adhered to a mundane Christian black nationalism, as conveyed by Jeremiah Wright Jr. in Chicago, for two decades until it was raised during the campaign by his rivals and the national media. The "politics of grievance" that Wright represented is presented as something from the civil rights and Black Power eras, as something that Obama would of necessity "overcome" to launch a political career in Chicago or the state of Illinois or be viable nationally.

Barack Obama's biography in large part reflects all the suspicions, generational successions, and ideological experimentations characteristic of the post–civil rights generation—which he himself identifies in religious terms as the Joshua Generation in black politics—and is tantamount to the hip-hop generation in pop culture. The movement for divestment from Apartheid in South Africa, as well as cultural immersion into the hip-hop encounter with Malcolm X, took the place of nostalgia, of having missed out on the movement action of the civil rights and Black Power generations. As well, hostility toward "the high command of the Reagan administration—an Administration that Obama and his friends saw as the ideological enemy—was at work."[72] Locally, Barack Obama was viewed as naive, "not Chicago enough," noncommittal, opportunistic. He was also viewed as "a callow newcomer from Hawaii and Harvard, too smooth, too willing to dismiss what he called the 'politics of grievance.'"[73] He refused to relinquish his claim to Alice Palmer's former state senate seat in 1995, and dared to challenge incumbent congressman and former Black Panther Party member Bobby Rush five years later.[74]

Running up against the civil rights and Black Power leadership cadres would make his climb locally and in the state difficult. For instance, many of the grassroots organizers, elected officials, and scholars involved in Harold Washington's elections created the Draft Alice Palmer Committee (DAPC) and urged Obama to stand down in deference to Palmer's certain reelection. The likes of Tim Black, Lu Palmer, Bob Starks, Lovana Jones, Donne Trotter, and Adolph Reed Jr. (then of Northwestern University) formed the DAPC group, but Obama refused to step aside and went on to have most of his Democratic challengers, including Palmer, disqualified from the contest.[75] Barack Obama continuously sought openings in the city's or state's electoral seats. Obama was able to stay relatively independent of the city's machine, which has not fully recovered from the Washington insurgency and feared the likes of Obama, that is, should the black political establishment recruit him to challenge it again.[76] Indeed, Obama imagined that he would become the next black mayor of Chicago, but one who "just happened to be black."[77] Obama was either too young or otherwise missed the signal events that grounded the city's black political history: Mayor Richard J. Daley's rule, black Chicago's co-optation and later challenge to it, the police riots at the 1968 Democratic National Convention, the murders of Black Panther Party members Mark Clark and Fred Hampton, and the election of Harold Washington. Barack Obama was "somebody nobody sent."[78] Black Chicagoans had already experienced an Obama-like moment long before the nation did, but it was first in Harold Washington.

Beginning in 1984, Barack Obama immersed himself in Chicago's South Side black communities. In the first of two stints—each for three years—he worked with local residents of various South Side housing projects, including the Ida B. Wells, Roseland, West Pullman, and dilapidated 8,000-resident Altgeld Gardens housing.[79] His work in the community was sponsored by local Catholic ministries, which brought him in to organize the city's black churches and ministers, under the aegis of the Developing Communities Project of Chicago. Its founder, Jerry Kellman, was an organizer trained in the Chicago tradition of Saul Alinsky.[80] As William Julius Wilson has shown, the city's South Side harbors "concentrated poverty [and] magnifies the problems associated with poverty in general: joblessness, crime, delinquency, drug trafficking, broken families, and dysfunctional schools. Neighborhoods of highly concentrated poverty are seen as dangerous, and therefore they become isolated, socially and economically, as people go out of their way to avoid them."[81] Many people do seek to avoid them, but amid the fiercely emergent crack-related violence and War on Drugs during the second Reagan and first Bush terms, Barack Obama did not. Remnick insists "his work on the South Side was bringing him something larger—a deepening connection to an African American community."[82] Yet his work was largely derided by political rivals, still angry with the Palmer episode; by Bobby Rush; and by others who saw it as a form of carpetbagging do-goodism. Barack Obama's connections to Hyde Park, University of Chicago elites, and North Side Jewish communities were whispered about and held forth as evidence of his authenticity problem.[83] Still, the severity of conditions facing the city's poor and working-class communities eventually convinced Obama that he could more effectively address them from within the political structure. When he later announced his candidacy for president in 2007, having attended elite educational institutions from high school to Harvard,[84] he stated, "It was in these neighborhoods that I received the best education I ever had."

Following his exploits at Harvard Law School, Obama returned to Chicago. He and Michelle Robinson were married by the Reverend Jeremiah Wright Jr. in 1992. Michelle Obama's father, Fraser Robinson III, like most black Democrats in the city, was insurgent, disappointed/cynical, or co-opted. This patriarch, a descendant of Georgetown/All Saints Parish (South Carolina) rice-farming slaves, migrated to Chicago as a child and later conveyed his cynicism to his own son and daughter.[85] The Robinson family's self-reliant Gullah lineage was a source of familial pride. And reading her widely critiqued senior thesis from Princeton University ("Princeton-Educated Blacks and the Black Community"), her adviser, Howard Taylor, concluded that young Michelle *"was not an assimilationist, but she wasn't a wide-eyed militant either."*[86] What was portrayed as her seething black rage—epitomized in a subsequently tortured comment concerning her *delayed* pride in US social and political relations— is quotidian in sections of many US black communities. One source cites a fellow black South Side Chicagoan, who insisted: "When you grow up in a black community with a warm black family, you are aware of the fact that you are black, but you do not feel it. . . . After a certain point you do just kind of think you're in your own world, and you become very comfortable in that world, and to this day there are African Americans who feel very uncomfortable when they step out of it. . . . This is a society that never lets you forget you are black."[87] And being black has seldom made them proud of America to the extent it has the majority and some immigrant groups.

Throughout the presidential campaign, Michelle Obama was betrayed as a militant, seethingly resentful, unprincipled, angry, "emasculating"[88] black woman. One writer noted that unlike Barack Obama, "Michelle does fit the public's idea of a black woman (unafraid, confident and blunt). . . . If white women [i.e., Hillary Clinton] are handicapped by a sense of their own vulnerability, black women [i.e., Michelle Obama] are hobbled by their strength and directness."[89] Opponents promised, but never delivered, a supposed bombshell: an anti–Bill Clinton "whitey" rant (concerning his administration's inaction during the Rwanda genocide), allegedly made while attending an event where she took a photo that included Iraq War prisoner of war Shoshana Johnson and Louis Farrakhan's wife, Kadijah Farrakhan.[90] She dared question "how we relate to this democracy" and expressed heightened racial consciousness outside of the black archipelago of Chicago.

Barack Obama had dabbled in anti-apartheid activism as an undergraduate. At Columbia, the Black Student Organization (BSO) formulated the Coalition for Free South Africa, led by Barbara Ransby. In 1998, she would join with a prominent list of mostly socialists, feminists, communists, and other left-critical adherents to create the Black Radical Congress (BRC), largely in reaction to what they perceived to be the troubling presence of Louis Farrakhan, remnant Black Power nationalists, and the absence of "permanent and institutionalized entity." Such had eluded black intellectuals and activists since the 1972 NBPC in Gary failed to produce a clearinghouse, something akin to how the black church served in previous struggles.[91] Political scientist Clarence Lusane writes, for instance,

> Coming at this time, the [Black Radical Congress] is especially significant given the conservative dominance in mainstream U.S. politics, increasing corporate power, the political impotence of liberal black politics, and the spiraling social crisis faced by millions of African Americans and others, both domestically and on a global scale. The Congress should also avoid the temptation to be drawn into putting its energy into massive political carnivals such as the Million Man March, Million Woman March, Million Youth March, and Million Youth Movement, which are long on symbolism, short on sustainability and political efficacy, and led by characters who articulate in Ebonics, Gingrichisms. Although individual BRC members will certainly choose to participate in, and perhaps even lead, some of these events, the organization must use its limited resources judiciously and politically and not be bamboozled down dead-end paths.[92]

Some of those who formed or affiliated with the BRC would also form the leftist Committee of Correspondence and the Democratic Socialists of America, which formulated the New Party.[93] It is suggested that, but difficult to confirm whether, Barack Obama actually joined the New Party. It had strong ties to the Association of Community Organizations Now (ACORN), which was a client of Barack Obama's in 1995. He had previously worked on a successful voter-registration campaign with Project VOTE in 1992. Project VOTE used the popular symbol of the *X* (as in Malcolm X), accompanied by the phrase "It's a Power Thing," on advertisements, seizing on the popularity of the symbol that accompanied promotion of Spike Lee's biographical film, which was released that year. Project VOTE successfully assisted state and national Democrats in the general election, including Carol Moseley Braun and Bill Clinton. Conspiracists are quick to point to Barack Obama's participation in a 2002 University of Illinois conference panel led by Ransby, which included Bill Ayers, Cathy Cohen, Salim Muwakkil, and Doug Casell, as evidence of Obama's ostensible socialist proclivities. As outlined in Chapter 1, Chicago has a longstanding tradition of left-critical and black liberation activism. They existed before Barack Obama arrived—indeed, before he was born. Remnick notes, for instance,

> The South Side was one of the most culturally vibrant black communities in the country. With the ferment of the Harlem Renaissance a memory, the South Side was arguably the capital of black America. . . . Chicago was home to establishment figures like Dawson and Jackson, but also to a range of political radicals, religious leaders, and cultists, including Elijah Poole, who, as Elijah Muhammad, moved the headquarters of the Black Muslims from Detroit to the South Side. Richard Wright . . . insisted that life was so hard on the South Side that no one should be surprised at what political ferment might one day rise there. "Chicago is the city from which the most incisive and radical Negro thought has come," he wrote in his introduction to *Black Metropolis*.[94]

Barack Obama: Retiring His "Politics of Grievance"

Throughout his 1995 book *Dreams from My Father*, Barack Obama conveys thoughts, deliberations, and political searchings akin to most African Americans of his generation. Also like others of his generation, Obama imbibed Farrakhan's mismanagement of the moment and likewise regurgitated it, especially the irredeemable obsession with Judaism and patriarchy.[95] In this, the earlier of his two books, Obama's *political* identity contemplations read as a blueprint of Chuck D's own efforts (in Roosevelt, Long Island) to negotiate the hostile political environment in which they were socialized, which included some of the most disruptive social, legal, and political realities witnessed in nearly a generation. *Dreams from My Father*, set side by side with *The Autobiography of Malcolm X*, Claude Brown's *Manchild in the Promised Land*, or Nathan McCall's *Makes Me Wanna Holler*, tells of a young man's coming-of-age racked with vice, posing, and racial confusion swinging on a pendulum of ideological and personal searching. In fact, in *Dreams*, Obama finds solace in Malcolm X's autobiography, noting that with it "I had tried to untangle the twin strands of black nationalism, arguing that nationalism's affirmative message—of solidarity and self-reliance, discipline and communal responsibility—need not depend on hatred of whites any more than it depended on white munificence. We could tell this country where it was wrong . . . without ceasing to believe in its capacity for change."[96] Obama also discusses his affinities for Malcolm X and black nationalism as antidote to his own multicultural background and tortured racial resentment toward the white heritage of his Irish matrilineal family. Malcolm X's claim to hate the white blood of his "rapist" matrilineal ancestor—with whom his grandmother had multiple children—appealed to Obama viscerally.

Barack Obama epitomizes the soft nationalist politics of his times. Political philosopher Tommie Shelby's assessment of the major ideological and political thought orientations of African Americans (conservatism, conservative black nationalism, liberalism, Marxism, and feminism) lead Shelby to erect a progressive, liberalism-friendly black nationalism that is probably more quotidian in the present era than any historical form (emigration, colonization, separation, cultural, revolutionary). The "pragmatic" nationalist project that Shelby identifies corresponds roughly to the orientation identified with dispositional nodes of black nationalism (see Chapter 6), but it is located more with David Walker and his ideological progeny (and Shelby does more so with Delany). Shelby recommends black nationalism in the post–civil rights era be mobilized around the "politicization of black peoplehood,"[97] forge alliances with sympathetic allies, and be led by a committed leadership cadre that has learned from and built on the failures and successes of previous efforts. To this degree, like his peers, Barack Obama saw virtue in Farrakhan's empowerment talk but also felt "what in the hands of Malcolm had sought to root out: one more feeder fantasy, one more mask for hypocrisy, one more excuse for inaction. Black politicians less gifted than Harold [Washington] discovered what white politicians had known for a very long time: that race-baiting could make up for a host of limitations. . . . *Black rage always found a market.*"[98] What Obama inadvertently confirms is the concreteness of black rage when appended to the realpolitik of American political discourse and the American political system; its reality is as a dimension of domestic black nationalism. Obama attended Farrakhan rallies and speeches—he attended the MMM/DOA during his state senate campaign[99]—and he does admit to purchasing the *Final Call* newspaper while living in Chicago. Characteristically, Obama plays down his affinities by caricaturing the *Final Call*—the most widely distributed national newspaper focusing on African American concerns and interests—as harboring "sensational, tabloid-style headlines (Caucasian Woman Admits:

Whites Are The Devil). Inside the front cover, one found reprints of the minister's speeches."[100]

By Barack Obama's own account, the MMM/DOA was a pivotal event for him—he doesn't mention it in *Dreams from My Father*, which was published the same year. The local *Chicago Reader* newspaper, however, reports that Barack Obama indeed attended the MMM/DOA, and Obama granted it an interview shortly after. Obama left his Illinois State District 13 (South Side) campaign to attend the event.[101] Its failure to forge a coherent agenda beyond Farrakhan's social and political commentary actually reinforced Obama's resolve to seek state-level political office and to align with more left-oriented elements in Chicago thereafter. Concerning the MMM/DOA, he explained, "[W]hat I saw was a powerful demonstration of an impulse and need for African-American men to come together to recognize each other and affirm our rightful place in the society." Moreover, "[T]here was a profound sense that African-American men were ready to make a commitment to bring about change in our communities and lives. . . . But what was lacking among march organizers was a positive agenda, a coherent agenda for change. Without this agenda a lot of this energy is going to dissipate. Just as holding hands and singing 'We shall overcome' is not going to do it, exhorting youth to have pride in their race, give up drugs and crime, is not going to do it if we can't find jobs and futures for the 50 percent of black youth who are unemployed, underemployed, and full of bitterness and rage." As if speaking to Farrakhan and its mostly Chicago-based organizers, Obama continues: "Exhortations are not enough, nor are the notions that *we* can create a black economy within America that is hermetically sealed from the rest of the economy and seriously tackle the major issues confronting *us*." He admonishes further,

> This doesn't suggest that the need to look inward emphasized by the march isn't important, and that these African-American tribal affinities aren't legitimate. These are mean, cruel times, exemplified by a "lock 'em up, take no prisoners" mentality that dominates the Republican-led Congress. Historically, African-Americans have turned inward and towards black nationalism whenever they have a sense, as *we* do now, that the mainstream has rebuffed us, and that white Americans couldn't care less about the profound problems African-Americans are facing. . . . But cursing out white folks is not going to get the job done. Anti-Semitic and anti-Asian statements are not going to lift us up. We've got some hard nuts-and-bolts organizing and planning to do. We've got communities to build.

For him, "elected officials could do much to overcome the political paralysis of the nation's black communities." He thinks they could lead their communities out of the twin cul-de-sac: "*the unrealistic politics of integrationist assimilation—* which helps a few upwardly mobile blacks to 'move up, get rich, and move out'—and *the equally impractical politics of black rage and black nationalism—*

which exhorts but does not organize ordinary folks or create realistic agendas for change." Well before he sought the US Senate or White House, Obama sought to

> create and support progressive programs; he wants to mobilize the people to create their own. He wants to stand politics on its head, empowering citizens by bringing together the churches and businesses and banks, scornful grand-mothers and angry young. Mostly he's running to fill a political and moral vacuum. *He says he's tired of seeing the moral fervor of black folks whipped up—at the speaker's rostrum and from the pulpit—and then allowed to dissipate because there's no agenda, no concrete program for change.*

Barack Obama's participation in the MMM escaped the alarmist journalism of right-wing paranoia, which otherwise tied (and ties) him to a full ideological continuum of black and left radicalism. Obama's reading of black nationalism in practice (as opposed to mere theorizing) was consistent with the common sense of his pursuit of an understanding of urbanized, continental black American life and experience. And like Malcolm X, his understanding of black nationalism was a definite means to some indefinite transgenerational black space or place called "freedom." He writes,

> nationalism provided that history, an ambiguous morality tale that was easily communicated and easily grasped. A steady attack on the white race, the constant recitation of black people's brutal experience in this country, served as the ballast that could prevent the ideas of personal and communal responsibility from tipping into an ocean of despair. Yes, the nationalist would say, whites are responsible for your sorry state, not any inherent flaw in you. In fact, whites are so heartless and devious that we can no longer expect anything from them.

Here, Obama sees himself as a black "we," juxtaposed to a white "them" acknowledging how

> deep down, *all blacks were potential nationalists*. The anger was there, bottled up and often turned inward. . . . I wondered whether . . . that anger [should] be redirected; whether a black politics that suppressed rage toward whites generally, or one that failed to elevate race loyalty above all else, was a politics inadequate to the task. . . . If the nationalism could create a strong and effective insularity, deliver on its promise of self-respect, then the hurt it might cause well-meaning whites, or the inner turmoil it caused people like me, would be of little consequence.[102] (See epigraph to this chapter.)

While teaching law at the University of Chicago, and having studied with Charles Ogletree at Harvard, Barack Obama expressed support for economic reparations in recompense for slavery and segregation in principle, although he viewed such an effort as futile in its impracticality.[103] At face value, the future president does not renounce black rage, at least not here; to the contrary, he seems to argue that (1) its black-to-black "double rage" dimension should shift toward whites; (2) it should elevate race loyalty above other loyalties; (3) it was useful when it created a "strong and effective insularity"; and (4) it should deliver on its self-respect and self-determination claims, its discomfort to the whites and the bourgeoisie notwithstanding. But this all was on the way to explaining away his *strategic* rejection of black nationalism as "tale," reflex, and dissipating attitude lacking "any concrete plan, a collection of grievances and not an organized force, images and sound that crowded the airwaves and conversation but without any corporeal existence."[104] Yet for him, this "dissipating attitude" was *hypothetical*, a notion of deficient concreteness achievable *only* if there was no "concentrating effect of Harold Washington's campaign." And Harold Washington *happened—twice!* And Washington's election and reelection grounded the modern phase of black politics—elected and protest-oriented—for the ensuing three decades. Washington's campaign should be read as *political protest*, rather than as black political development embracing Bayard Rustin's "protest-to-politics" trope as if electoral politics were maturation.

Barack Obama's relationship to Black Power thus is not asymmetrical unless one reads Black Power in the narrowest and most caricatured sense of militancy vis-à-vis violence and self-defense. Black Power certainly emerges with far greater diversity—indeed, it was more democratic organizationally—than the "six headed" civil rights movement (what Malcolm X called "the big six" civil rights leaders in its several leading organizations). Recall that Harold Cruse saw the earliest expression of Black Power within the bounds of reformist, community control commitments, which Malcolm X, too, advocated when he defined black nationalism as blacks selecting and controlling the politicians who represent them. This is best demonstrated—as outlined in Chapter 1—in the grassroots recruitment of Harold Washington by Black Powerite black nationalists, which included the Reverend Jeremiah Wright.[105] Remnick includes another source citing Wright as having a background as "radical . . . as any significant American political figure has ever emerged from, as much Malcolm X as Martin Luther King, Jr."[106] Wright's "background" was anything but radical. His prophetic discourse, however, is consistent with this observation.

Aside from Obama's own references to his interest in and rejection of nationalist orientations, a line of conspiratorial journalistic libels was produced scandalizing Obama as a closet nationalist and socialist with the uncanny ability to unite New Left radicals such as Bernardine Dohrn and William "Bill" Ayers, the Reverend Michael Pfleger and the Reverend Jeremiah Wright, and a host of other "radicals."[107] Harvard University–trained James Corsi dedicated much conspiratorial attention to Obama's "leftist" ideological leanings and commitments, scavenging any impeachable evidence that could deny the Obamas electoral victory in 2008. A primary claim against Barack Obama is his invention of the character "Ray" (childhood friend Keith Kakugawa) who filters much of the "black rage" that otherwise was Obama's own.[108] Obama's "rage," according to this source, is rooted in the thoughts of Frantz Fanon (in *Black Skin, White Masks*), rather than the likes of Stokely Carmichael or Eldridge Cleaver. Indeed, Corsi asserts, "Obama's black rage, by contrast, is anticolonial in nature," whereas Michelle's is akin to what Ellis Cose observed among the privileged black middle classes.[109]

There is no discussion of black nationalism, Malcolm X, Farrakhan, Jeremiah Wright Jr., or much impeachable ideological thought expressed in *The Audacity of Hope*, his second book (the title was lifted from Wright upon Obama's first visit to Trinity's worship services). Instead of overtly discussing political philosophy, the chapter on race tends to outline the broad multicultural themes evident in his presidential campaign strategy. As with Jesse Jackson a generation earlier, who shifted from the "Nation Time!" yelps of the 1972 NBPC to the McGovern camp, then from Rainbow insurgence (1984) to Democratic patronage broker (1988), Barack Obama negotiated a *political* path that went from the specificity of black Chicago to a broader rainbow politics that would lead to his unprecedented election. On the one hand, in *The Audacity of Hope* there is recognition of banal race relations in US society, including the plight of urban-dwelling, unemployed, and unemployable young African American men. Recognition is also given to issues of policing, the benefits of the Earned Income Tax Credit, welfare reform, support for affirmative action, and structural inequalities. He acknowledges, "Black men filling our prisons, black children unable to read or caught in a gangland shooting, the black homeless sleeping on grates and in the parks of our nation's capital." Thus there is the need for a commitment to "completing the unfinished business of the civil rights movement—namely enforcing nondiscrimination laws in such basic areas as employment, housing, and education."[110] At points the plights of the urban unemployed, single-female households, health disparities, black criminality and victimization, as well as blacks' television-viewing patterns give way to a neoliberal critique—but also a resonant black common sense—of "entrenched behavioral patterns" and "personal responsibility"—or the lack thereof. He writes,

> We know that many in the inner city are trapped by their own self-destructive behaviors but that those behaviors are not innate. And because of that knowledge, the black community remains convinced that if America finds its will to do so, then circumstances for those trapped in the inner city can be changed, individual attitudes among the poor will change in kind, and the damage can gradually be undone, if not for this generation then at least for the next.[111]

Jeremiah Wright's Jeremiad and the Farrakhan Litmus

For a time during the campaign, no single force loomed as powerfully over Obama as the black-rage discourse epitomized in the jeremiad of Jeremiah Wright Jr., pastor of Trinity United Church of Christ. Analogous to the emotional furor in reaction among American whites to Walker's *Appeal* and to the call for Black Power, the looping of Wright's call for divine retribution in national cable and local media played a vital role in the election of Barack Obama. Concerning this, T. Denean Sharpley-Whiting wrote, "Wright's homiletics had the effect of coloring Obama in a bit too darkly; his damning of American racism and genocides at home and abroad diminished Obama's averred gift of 'second sight' into both black and white worlds, marred his claim to authenticity and a new politics. . . . *Jeremiah's jeremiads imperiled the currency of the 'O' brand of politics.*"[112]

As Obama won a series of primary victories during February, culminating in the Mississippi caucus (which he won, 60–38 percent), the Democrats' 1984 vice-presidential candidate, Geraldine Ferraro, made comments to a small Southern California newspaper, arguing that "if Obama was a white man, he would not be in this position."[113] Soon, Jeremiah Wright—whom the Clintons commiserated with during the Monica Lewinsky crisis—became a proxy for *liberal* anxiety over Louis Farrakhan and generally persistent black criticism.[114] It prompted the "More Perfect Union" race speech, which was delivered March 18, 2008, at the National Constitution Center in Philadelphia. It sold many American whites on Obama's racial empathy with them, as well as African Americans.

Wright's criticisms in one sermon, "The Day of Jerusalem's Fall," given the Sunday after the September 11, 2001, attacks, inserted Malcolm X's fateful analogy that such violence was begotten by a long history of murderous, imperial ambitions—a case of "chickens coming home to roost." Remnick correctly argues that the black theology tradition, with which Wright identifies, "is rooted in nineteenth-century ideas: in David Walker's abolitionist *Appeal*, published in 1829, which refers to the 'God of the Ethiopians'; in Frederick Douglass's slave narrative that distinguishes between the Christianity of Jesus Christ ('good pure, and holy') and Christianity in America ('bad, corrupt, and wicked'); in Bishop Henry McNeal Turner's newspaper, *Voice of Missions*."[115]

When Wright arrived at Chicago's Trinity United Church of Christ in 1972, most of the black churches there were seeped in the "priestly" functions of sustaining congregants and fulfilling the obligations of what E. Franklin Frazier called the "compensatory" work of the church. Remnick adds,

> Most of the ministers on the South Side at the time were cultural conservatives: wary of the black liberation movement; wary of reform in their services; reluctant to adopt political positions that would put them in opposition

to their patrons in City Hall. As a result, young people, searching for greater black identity as well as a spiritual home, were leaving the church for the Nation of Islam, black nationalism, of small sects like the Black Hebrew Israelites. Trinity promised a Christian home for young people who were politically and socially aware, and wanted that awareness to be part of their church.[116]

Adopting its twelve-point Black Value System, the "unashamedly black and unapologetically Christian" Trinity United Church of Christ reflected the best of the "prophetic" tradition of African American religion.[117] Within heavily Democratic Illinois state politics, the South Side is known as the "blackest electoral district in the United States." There Wright proved to be more of an authenticating mentor than a liability to Obama's early career. The nationalist tradition that Wright represented, and one that Barack and Michelle Obama embraced until the 2008 contest, was indeed the orientation that appealed to many in their generational cohort, shaped as it was by the rightward move in American politics during the Reagan era.

In the 2008 campaign Obama was forced to denounce Louis Farrakhan on national television (and on his campaign's website). He thereby replayed Jesse Jackson's "Farrakhan litmus" in 1984, as well as the black mayors of the "new black politics" era, including Harold Washington (though to a lesser extent, being in Chicago), Tom Bradley (Los Angeles), Willie Wilson Goode (Philadelphia), and (most disastrously) David Dinkins (New York City). Although Louis Farrakhan would in 2008 become the litmus for Barack Obama's "acceptability," to his credit he refrained from speaking on the campaign for fear of influencing white voters to reject Obama's candidacy, which his organization largely supported in its *Final Call* publications and recent Farrakhan speeches.

After two decades of salience in black politics, Farrakhan could have prevented Barack Obama from becoming president of the United States. His offline endorsement of Obama interpreted the campaign's success in messianic terms, much the same as he did for Jesse Jackson and Harold Washington in the early 1980s.[118] Among most African Americans, Louis Farrakhan lost credibility with his confusing "I am a Jesus," giving no account for monies collected at the MMM/DOA, waiting for Elijah in the "mothership" spacecraft, taking world friendship tours, haggling over $5 billion from Muammar Khadafi and Libya with Clinton officials, the Million Family March, the Millions More Movement, a cancer scare, and his curtsey to "orthodox" Arab Islam. In summary, Farrakhan's post–MMM/DOA agenda was totally irrelevant to what moved individuals to tolerate his bungling "leadership" of the previous quarter-century.

Jeremiah Wright Jr. was largely unknown outside of Chicago and religious and cultural nationalist leadership circles. Yet he had garnered academic institutional acclaim—honorary degrees from several prominent US universities—and was named one of *Ebony* magazine's "15 Most Influential Preachers" in

1993. Given the exaggerated caricature of Jeremiah Wright Jr.—a navy man who stood over the bed of President Lyndon Johnson at Bethesda Naval Hospital in November 1966 (during LBJ's second gallbladder operation and the removal of a polyp on his throat) and gave spiritual counsel to Bill and Hillary Clinton during the 1998 Monica Lewinsky impeachment debacle—he may later be absolved. Martin Luther King Jr. previously performed the function of "pariah preacher" *for the last year of his life*, given his opposition to Vietnam and US domestic economic and race relations.

Increasingly, King's April 4, 1967, speech, "Beyond Vietnam: A Time to Break Silence," has been put to use to highlight analogous criticisms appropriate to the Iraq War, which began just three weeks before Wright's April 2003 "Confusing God and Government" jeremiad—otherwise known as the "God damn America" sermon. But King's speech, overshadowed by his 1963 "I Have a Dream" masterpiece, is not widely recognized as the jeremiadic manifesto as it is within the academy, left progressive and antiwar circles, and black liberation theology adherents. The 1967 Vietnam speech severed King's ties to the Johnson administration, divided his lieutenancy, and was met with harsh criticism from national media outlets, including *Time* magazine (which had placed King on three covers and recognized him as "Man of the Year" three years earlier). His basic focus was the "triplets of evil" in the modern world: racism, militarism, and economic exploitation. King directed his comments at "the greatest purveyor of violence in the world today—my own government."

This speech was replete with charges more somber in tone, but substantively it was every bit as devastating as Wright's reading of US foreign and domestic policy immediately following US mobilization against Iraq. For instance, King continued, "If America's soul becomes totally poisoned, part of the autopsy must read Vietnam. It can never be saved so long as it destroys the deepest hopes of men the world over." King spoke of a "deadly Western arrogance that has poisoned the international atmosphere for so long." Thus, "they must see America as strange liberators." American policy in the region, he contended,

> create[s] hell for the poor. Somehow this madness must cease. We must stop now. I speak as a child of God and brother to the suffering poor of Vietnam. I speak for those whose land is being laid waste, whose homes are being destroyed, whose culture is being subverted. I speak for the poor of America who are paying the double price of smashed hopes at home and death and corruption in Vietnam. I speak as a citizen of the world, for the world as it stands aghast at the path we have taken. I speak as an American to the leaders of my own nation. The great initiative in this war is ours. The initiative to stop it must be ours.

Speaking in the tradition of the black jeremiad, King continued: "*Communism is a judgment* against our failure to make democracy real and follow through on the revolutions we initiated. Our only hope today lies in our ability to recapture the revolutionary spirit and go out into a sometimes hostile world declaring eternal hostility to poverty, racism, and militarism." King also counseled conscientious objection and supported Muhammad Ali's refusal of military induction. *There is scarcely a theme in King's dissent that did not portend Jeremiah Wright's critiques.* Again, King anticipated Jeremiah Wright during the last years of his life, a period that shifted increasingly to a more strident form of racial solidarity than the ten years between 1955 and 1965. Wright, in turn, engaged in the best of African American prophetic discourse; it was also the oldest form of American oracular political criticism. Yet it is the civil religion discourse practiced by the Puritan founders of what is, today, the United Church of Christ and Congregationalist tradition.

Barack Obama's crisis management of the Jeremiah Wright moment incorporated and articulated his own acknowledgement in blunt terms: the nation's failures on slavery and race, as well as white guilt, labor, ethnicity, religion, affirmative action, disproportionate minority incarceration, corporate oligarchy, and racial common ground. It is pertinent that in its marginalized, caricatured space, Jeremiah Wright's commitment to "everyday" black people and others reclaimed black nationalism—vis-à-vis its Christian heritage—from (or along with) Louis Farrakhan's Nation of Islam. As much as Obama sought to contain Wright's jeremiads as *anachronistic* black protest discourse, Wright is influenced by the writings of the younger Dwight Hopkins, who represents the progeny of 1960s black theology discourse, as he is a student of James Cone (and his colleagues). Hopkins, like Obama, experienced pedigreed education (Harvard) and chose community organizing in a major black metropolis (Harlem) over more lucrative opportunities. And both embraced critical prophetic discourse.

Although some of the Obamas' critics caricatured them as angry black people, it was the more foreboding and offputting racial resentment and condemnation of American domestic and foreign policy expressed by Wright Jr. that actually *moderated* white fear of a black president. This is analogous to what Malcolm X imagined he was performing on behalf of King following Malcolm X's break with the Nation of Islam: a less palatable, unacceptable alternative. Although critics may dismiss such a device as black rage as abstraction, scholars and nonacademics must contemplate how and whether it was the black rage of black nationalism in Chicago that ultimately delivered the most *integrationist moment since the civil rights movement.* Historian Scott Kurashige notes: "And for this reason, a moment like this was sadly inevitable, for there [was] no Obama path to the presidency that does not require him to rise above charges that he is unpatriotic or that he is a black extremist. Such is the inescapable reality of running for president as a progressive African American whose formative experiences came as an inner-city community organizer on the South Side of Chicago."[119]

Black rage, by way of the theology of Wright, may have delivered the first US president of African descent. It may have acted both as a source of Obama's authentication and empowerment—testing Obama within the bounds of the city's and state's politics—and as an expendable ingredient in pursuit of administering the US state. Obama's ability to maintain composure during an inelegant media blitz—one that made the 1988 William "Willie" Horton campaign of George H.W. Bush seem mild—reinforced voter confidence, especially among black voters and young people: If Obama could manage the ongoing crisis of race in America, then economic crisis was no more intractable. Indeed, as much as there is fatuous talk and writing these days about colorblindness and postracial society, it took the near-total collapse of the US (and global) capitalist financial system during the campaign to collateralize the haunting condemnation of Wright's preachments.

The opportunity that Obama's opponents, the Internet, and media loops of Wright's words afforded him was to articulate a moderating speech that seemed lifted from the pages of *The Audacity of Hope*, not the ideological searching of *Dreams from My Father*. Bruce Glasrud and Cary Wintz concur:

> The controversy probably helped Obama in three ways. First, it gave him a forum to once again discuss race with the entire nation listening. He frankly confronted the dilemma of race in the United States. He was able to talk about segregation, racism, and poverty, while at the same time extolling the progress the nation had made in the last half century. . . . Obama was able to discuss race and the need for change and progress without seeming radical or threatening. The Wright incident provided Obama with yet another forum to denounce "a politics that breeds division, and conflict, and cynicism."[120]

Their assessment insists that his election was achieved *in spite* of black rage, which makes it no less valuable to Obama than Bill Clinton's Sistah Souljah performance was to him. As well, unprecedented African American electoral support and solidarity facilitated the incorporation of African Americans into the highest reaches of the American political system. Political expediency necessitated distancing from African American protest traditions in an electoral environment. However, Wright's words, as projected, were *within* the mainstream of African American political thought even if they were of a minority opinion regarding the American state and society. Whereas Obama views nationalism as both legitimate protest against real distress and dead end, his own tortured "double consciousness" enabled him to sort through and articulate the broadest perspective on race probably since King's "Dream" speech in the 1960s. King's warning gave way to the "Dream" crescendo. Jeremiah Wright's warning gave way to Barack Obama. If Obama had feigned a Tiger Woods–styled "caublanasian" identity, his candidacy may never have attracted black voters. And it was they who made his victory over Hillary Clinton possible in the southern primaries, giving him their electoral support more than any presidential candidate in US history. Without "the politics of grievance" being fought on the mainland in his youth, neither Occidental, nor Columbia, nor Harvard would have been accessible to Barack Obama and the Joshua/hip-hop generation.

Future Black Politics: Beyond Hope

Within two weeks of Obama's taking office, al-Qaeda leader Ayman al-Zawahri, in an apparent attempt to interpret the new president for the larger fundamentalist base, referred to Obama as an "Uncle Tom" "who is the direct opposite of honorable black Americans" like Malcolm X.[121] He also referred to the two preceding US secretaries of state, Condoleezza Rice and Colin Powell, as "house slaves," as video footage played in the background of Malcolm X explaining his use of the term "house slaves," most famously in his "Message to the Grassroots" speech delivered at the King Solomon Baptist Church of Detroit.[122] Within the months between Obama's election and inauguration, Oakland—where the Black Panther Party and Huey P. Newton emerged during Black Power—experienced weeks of political violence and dissent stemming from the beating and murder of a young unarmed African American named Oscar Grant by a white transit officer. The incident prompted Louis Farrakhan to travel to Oakland and deliver a speech at West Oakland's Olivet Missionary Baptist Church.[123]

Contemporary African American politics has never witnessed anything approaching a black president and First Family—of course, it pales in comparison to the advent of abolition and, arguably, the release and eventual election of Nelson Mandela after twenty-seven years in South Africa's gulags. But all of the available data suggest a halcyonic moment experienced only by those who witnessed the major achievements in Olympic and professional sports—from Jack Johnson to Jesse Owens and Wilma Rudolph, Joe Louis, and Jackie Robinson. Obama, being the second "first" black president, is *irrelevant* apart from the experiences of these individuals and the millions of ordinary people who know and knew that his election was about the "River" that historian Vincent Harding chronicled as the full measure of the resilient black spirit and determination in a hostile world, from the Middle Passage forward. Barack Obama, with all of his gifts—which include Michelle—is merely a drop in that river—a fulfillment of its flow and determination that has yet to reach its shore; too many black people are still swimming upstream and drowning in the midst of the storm. As during the 1960s black theology movement, Jeremiah Wright Jr. intercepted the lulling effect of the piggish images of T. D. Jakes standing with George W. Bush after Hurricane Katrina where dead bodies floated, the religious entrepreneurialism of the likes of Bishop Eddie Long and Creflo Dollar, and the feel-good attitude of Juanita Bynum and others. Perhaps it was their intention to close the "prosperity gap" among segments of society that led United for a Fair Economy, in its 2004 "State of the [King] Dream Report," to warn that without public policy intervention it would take 1,664 years to close the racial gap in home ownership in the United States four years *before* the 2008 economic collapse that trivialized Obama's "blackness" for at least 66 million American voters.

The joy and optimism among many upon Obama's election will, in the long run, likely become tragic disappointment in the flow of the African American experience unless the material realities of rank-and-file blacks, like those he encountered on Chicago's South Side, improve substantively and structurally. Black Power, it must be remembered, became prominent *after* the great legislative achievements of the 1960s. The challenge of the Joshua Generation is how to project the perception that the basis of the Moses Generation's grievances are passé to others' satisfaction when conditions on the ground among their base communities suggest otherwise. In the days of national distress in Hebraic biblical lore, Jeremiah spoke *after* Moses's movement *and* Joshua's battles failed to deliver the people. German-born Marxist Ernest Bloch (1885–1977), known for his massive work *The Principle of Hope* (1959), insisted that "Christianity introduced in the world the category of hope, the notion that real change is possible."[124] This was the campaign mantra of Barack Obama—and of Jesse Jackson before him. The quarter-century between their campaigns was a new (or perennial) nadir in African American politics, culture, and life. Today, hope for ordinary people, whether it is presented by elected or protest-oriented African American political elites, must accompany a new Reconstruction of life in the United States for African Americans and other populations. And it must do so in a most inhospitable environment. Two generations of black Americans resurrected Malcolm X since his death to speak to the conditions in which they lived; his relevance, should it carry beyond Barack Obama's brief presence in the White House, should be read as a jeremiad against the incomplete promises of democracy in America and the tragedy of hope.

Conclusion

I have tried in this book to highlight how the black jeremiad articulates a form of US-based black nationalism with inspiration in the continental commitments of the children of the revolutions in America and Haiti, especially in the person of David Walker. He represents this "stay-at-home" orientation in a manner that most scholarship on black nationalism understands Martin R. Delany's relationship to emigrationism. I have also sought to track a three-decade intellectual and academic discourse concerning the structure and lineage of black nationalism in its relationship to European, Jewish, and Anglo-American nationalisms. Even where there may be low ebbs or pendular shifts in its articulation, it is foundational to the black freedom struggle—from abolition to Garveyism, from Malcolm X to the Million Man March and Jeremiah Wright's rendition of black liberation theology. I have also tried to offer a substantial interpretation of why the hip-hop generation "brought back Malcolm X," as Betty Shabazz suggested be done just as Ronald Reagan was planning for his second term. And the hip-hop cohort rode and facilitated Louis Farrakhan's presence in black politics—to their own disappointment.

The fact that Barack and Michelle Obama emerged from this cohort is perhaps the most profound realization of some aspects of Harold Cruse's call for a generational shift to meet the new realities of the post–civil rights period. However, along the way, it seems that it was rendered stillborn by the activities of Louis Farrakhan and his coterie. If this book has been read carefully, then it should be clear that Malcolm X's jeremiad included resolving the problem of African Americans in relation to the major parties. How to replace the black church as an organizational, institutional, ideological, and strategic clearinghouse to the end of realizing total black liberation remains a historical problem.

It may be an opportunity permanently lost, for Barack Obama, and others of the Joshua Generation, are likely to strengthen blacks' unrequited allegiance to the Democratic Party for another generation or two. If black rage is a perennial consciousness among a strand of black nationalists in the United States, then today's white nationalist backlash is full of white rage. And the fact that white nationalist rage is located in a loose amalgam of Tea Party activists and groups is instructive of the argument in Chapter 8 concerning Louis Farrakhan and the disappointments of the Million Man March. The climate of denuded hate, armed marches on Washington, calls for violence against elected officials throughout the country (ominously, for "taking these bastards out"), and other vitriol spilling from talk radio and elsewhere looms over African Americans' relative silence. Today, African Americans are pausing to see, as Michelle Obama said during the campaign, "how we relate to this democracy." Should harm come to Barack Obama or not, it is likely that this rendition of white nationalist rage ("take back our country," "I want my country back," socialism, Black Hitler ad nauseam) will further alienate African Americans from the legitimate economic and cultural populist push-back against the corporatism of the major parties.

Obama understood his succession in the terms of a Judeo-Christian religious analogue, which eerily invokes David Walker's contemporary, Robert Alexander Young, who wrote his *Ethiopian Manifesto: Issued in Defense of the Black Man's Rights in the Scale of Universal Freedom* in 1829. In it, Young's jeremiad predicts that liberation will come through the coming of a biracial Messiah whose mother was white and father black. In several sections of *Ethiopian Manifesto*, Young identifies himself as a mixed-race individual, but it is not clear whether he understood himself to be the Messiah. Young predicted that the Messiah would subsequently emerge from the Caribbean island of Grenada and have webbed toes and long hair. The Messiah would also gather Africans into a "body politic" and "call together the black people as a nation in themselves." I do not know if Obama has webbed toes, and he certainly has no father from Grenada or long hair. Obama categorically rejects that there is a "black America," and he certainly *is no messiah or messianic figure.* But he, like George Washington and Abraham Lincoln and Martin Luther King before him, is likely to be incorporated into the American exceptionalism narrative of civil religion discourse in a manner that reinforces uneven status quo social and political relations by reinforcing the lie that we have reached (postblack) postraciality. And much to the dismay of intellectual communities, Barack Obama's election is deeply implicated in black Americans' quest to resolve the nationality problem of being *in* America but only marginally *of* America, even at this late date.

During most epochal moments in black political development, one of the more predictable responses is a reactionary impulse from some segment of cultural or racial populists among whites. This could be "southern redemption" following abolition; Jim Crow segregation following the short era of Reconstruction, lynch pogroms, reaction to Jack Johnson winning the heavyweight championship of boxing during the enforcement of the "white-slavery" Mann Act, southern resistance to *Brown v. Board of Education* at midcentury, or the coalition of conservatism that converged in the Reagan presidencies against the advances provided by civil rights and Black Power legislation. In this sense, the reaction to the prospect (and now reality) of a black family occupying the White House is a consortium of economic, political, social, pro-gun, cultural conservatives and white-supremacist elements, organized as parallel movements that reinforce the media's appetite for incivility. Barack Obama's "otherness" metonymically harbors the still-pariah status of ordinary African Americans, who are viewed much less favorably than the emergent black political class.

The desperation, displacement, and invisibility of the Hurricane Katrina survivors—indeed, their depiction as noncitizen refugees—signaled the extent to which twentieth-century vestiges extended into the twenty-first. It is likely not lost on the witnesses and survivors of Hurricane Katrina, and many African Americans, that the racist "birther movement" (which questions the president's US citizenship) echoes the alien, "refugee," noncitizen tag that was initially applied to them. Hurricane Katrina disabused the postracial talk that is an inevitable outcome of the multicultural project in academics. Even though all subaltern experiences are valid and must be articulated—and there were thousands of nonblacks across the Gulf region who were devastated by Katrina—all oppression experiences are not equal. Discourse, to the contrary, foregrounded the trivialization of concrete, unreconciled struggles for social and economic justice, as seen in the images of the black bodies floating in the Ninth Ward and elsewhere; many were too poor to evacuate even had they wanted to. Just four years after the September 11 attacks, US citizens have never witnessed such widespread devastation—and such wholesale bureaucratic failure and incompetence.

We still cannot believe what we saw: the floods, the broken levees, the cries of desperation, the disorientation, the bodies—even though so much of ordinary American blacks' daily experiences were captured in Katrina. The election of Barack Obama has been hailed as a new opening in the US racial and social contracts, making it easier to diminish the racial implications of Katrina. The floods of Katrina have been lost in the flood of tears of joy that millions of African Americans and others shed upon Obama's election and inauguration. We have tried already to set aside the horror and facts of Katrina—to use Obama as if Katrina did not happen. Indeed, Obama's election may have unintended consequences that expedite the further immiseration of an already immiserated segment of the African American collective in the United States.

The media-sponsored "leaders" and spokespersons clamor over whether a "black agenda" is necessary or even desirable during the administration of a self-identified African American as president. Deeply implicated is the persistence of unreconstructed fear among American whites that African Americans hold on to some latent racial resentment. Black Americans truly ought to be able to leverage their unprecedented electoral support for Barack Obama. How he governs, how his advisers steer him away from race-specific policy matters (or encourage him to be "deracialized"), is suggestive of a cynicism concerning whether ordinary American whites can weigh the desperation of contemporary life for too many young and older African Americans, especially in the anarchic environs of the cities, against latent or salient anxieties. Sociologist William Julius Wilson's 2009 book, *More Than Just Race: Being Black and Poor in the Inner City*, concedes that his earlier advocacy of class-driven, race-neutral policy responses was ill suited to the crisis evident since the 1970s. He praised Barack Obama's measured and pragmatic twoness on race and the manner in which it spoke to the specificity of black people's general plight in a search for common ground among American whites and other communities.

Wilson notes:

> In my previous writings I called for the framing of issues designed to appeal to broad segments of the population. Key to this framing, I argued, would be an emphasis on policies that would directly benefit all groups, not just people of color. My thinking was that, given American views about poverty and race, a color-blind agenda would be the most realistic way to generate the broad political support necessary to enact the required legislation. I no longer hold to this view. . . . The question is whether the policy is framed to facilitate a frank discussion of the problems that ought to be addressed and to generate broad political support to alleviate them. So now my position has changed: in framing public policy we should not shy away from an explicit discussion of the specific issues of race and poverty; on the contrary, we should highlight them in our attempt to convince the nation that these prob-

lems should be seriously confronted and that there is an urgent need to address them. The issues of race and poverty should be framed in such a way that not only is a sense of fairness and justice to combat inequality generated, but also people are made aware that our country would be better off if these problems were seriously addressed and eradicated.[125]

The proponents of the plurality character of US politics and society, such as Harold Cruse or the young Stokely Carmichael, never vacillated in their understanding of the group basis of the country's social structure. Demographics predict a leveling of population shares among Latinos, American whites, African Americans, Asian populations, and other groups in the middle twenty-first century; the future bodes more, not less, solidarity. The black vote is likely to increase in importance as other groups' share of the electorate increases and decreases. The problem of being taken for granted—that is, by the major parties and ideological political interests—can minimize and moderate hostile and antiblack political operatives and institutions. In the South, the Voting Rights Act expanded the potential vote power among recalcitrant Dixiecrats. Is it not plausible that African Americans, if organized around interest-driven common ground by competent leadership, stand to strengthen their position in US politics?

Barack Obama's election may obviate the critical thinking and organizing to meet the challenges of the unprecedented political and demographic realities of the future. But Obama can be president only for one or two terms, at most. By whatever means, when he is no longer president, and possibly even while he is in office, African Americans must move to strengthen their ability to direct policy focus to the issues that plague segregated, poor, and isolated populations. And it is predictable, given the history from David Walker and his generation, to Malcolm X and Black Power and the hip-hop generation, to Jeremiah Wright's jeremiadic imposition, which may have midwived Barack Obama's election, that some form of critical militant discourse will activate from among their precedence.

Notes

1. Lorn S. Foster, "Avenues for Black Political Mobilization: The Presidential Campaign of Reverend Jesse Jackson," in Lorenzo Morris (ed.), *The Social and Political Implications of the 1984 Jesse Jackson Presidential Campaign* (New York: Praeger, 1990). See also Robert C. Smith, "From Insurgency Toward Inclusion: The Jackson Campaigns of 1984 and 1988," in Morris (ed.), *Social and Political Implications*.

2. Katherine Tate, *From Protest to Politics: The New Black Voters in American Elections* (New York: Russell Sage; and Cambridge: Harvard University Press, 1993), p. 201.

3. Ronald Walters, "The Issue Politics of the Jesse Jackson Campaign for President in 1984," in Morris (ed.), *Social and Political Implications*, p. 15.

4. Lorn Foster, "Avenues for Black Political Mobilization," p. 203.

5. Ibid., pp. 209, 212–213.

6. Katherine Tate, *Protest to Politics*; Patricia Gurin, et al., *Hope and Independence: Blacks' Response to Electoral and Party Politics* (New York: Russell Sage, 1990); and Michal Dawson, *Behind the Mule: The Roots of Contemporary African American Political Ideologies* (Chicago: University of Chicago Press, 2001).

7. Michael Dawson, *Behind the Mule*. Jesse Jackson's relationship with Clinton would be strengthened during Clinton's second term. Appointed as Special Envoy for the President and Secretary of State for the Promotion of Democracy in Africa, Jackson would accompany President Clinton and his family on the historically unprecedented twelve-day, six-nation Journey to Africa. When midway through Clinton's second presidency he was accused and subsequently impeached in the US House of Representatives on four specific articles of impeachment stemming from an extramarital affair, Jackson emerged as one of Clinton's several spiritual counselors/advisers.

8. Please see Joseph P. McCormick II and Sekou Franklin, "Expressions of Racial Consciousness in the African American Community: Data from the Million Man March," in Yvette M. Alex-Assensoh and Lawrence Hanks (eds.), *Black and Multiracial Politics in America* (New York: New York University Press, 2000). The Million Woman March was held in Philadelphia on October 25, 1997. An earlier march of African American women was to be held in Los Angeles (in the area of the Memorial Coliseum) but was scrapped due to poor organization. The Philadelphia event appeared to be headed for the same fate until Farrakhan dispatched Chavis to offer guidance. The Howard University study is based on a sample of 456 voting-age eligible women and notes that "this was the second largest mass based demonstration of African Americans held in the late 1990s."

9. Michael Leo Owens, *God and Government in the Ghetto* (Chicago: University of Chicago Press, 2007), p. 207.

10. I do not view Washington as an advocate of any sort of demand-protest politics. The point is that the tugs and pendular shifts between the various leadership forms has been consistent since the Reconstruction era. Negro elected officials were supplanted by the likes of Booker T. Washington and Bishop Henry McNeal Turner (who, like Adam Clayton Powell Jr., represented both).

11. Barack Obama, *The Audacity of Hope: Thoughts on Reclaiming the American Dream* (New York: Vintage Books, 2006), p. 40.

12. Rector was an African American death-row inmate in Arkansas who shot part of his own brain out after two murders he committed in 1981, rendering him mentally incapacitated.

13. James Lance Taylor, "Black Politics in Transition: From Protest to Politics to Political Neutrality?" Ph.D. diss., University of Southern California, 1999.

14. Only a few events in black history even approach the widespread saturation of individual and organizational responses; exceptions arguably would include abolition itself, Jack Johnson's championship, Joe Louis's Olympics and professional victories, Jesse Owens's performance in Munich, and Jackie Robinson's arrival in the Major Leagues.

15. Adolph Reed, *Stirrings in the Jug*, p. 188.

16. Beyond our interest in the MMM/DOA's association with independent politics, black voter turnout, and participation in 1996, is its derivative effect: inspiring subsequent march mobilizations by the race-conscious Christian men's movement (known as the Promise Keepers) in 1996, the 1997 black Million Woman March in Philadelphia, and the Million Youth March held in several major US cities in 1998. The MMM/DOA representatives have made other claims. In particular, the MMM is credited with in-

creasing black male volunteerism in programs such as Big Brothers mentoring. Also, many of the traditional civil rights organizations, such as the National Urban League, reported increases in membership following the MMM/DOA. After the Federal Bureau of Investigation reported a decrease in violent crime in 1995 (murder down 6 percent, rape down 5 percent, and violent crimes down 5 percent), Farrakhan and Chavis-Muhammad joined the chorus of claimants who took credit. *JET* magazine reports, "The spirit of the Million Man March helped to reduce violent crime across the country, Nation of Islam leader Minister Louis Farrakhan told thousands of participants who gathered in New York to celebrate the March's anniversary. At last year's March of more than one million Black men in Washington, D.C., Farrakhan led a mass pledge to 'never raise my hand with a knife or a gun to beat or cut or shoot any member of my family or any human being,'" "MMM Anniversary Observed with World's Day of Atonement in New York," *JET* 90, no. 25 (November 4, 1996): 6. Others attributed the decline to tougher laws such as three strikes. But no study directly links the causes for crime reduction in that year. A clear political outcome of the Million Man March was the most comprehensive public statement on race ever to be made by an American president; Bill Clinton spoke on several national news shows and at the University of Texas in a nationally televised speech.

17. The Million Man March conveners produced a Declaration and a Mission Statement—authored by cultural nationalist Dr. Maulana Karenga—that was religious in tone, but it encouraged a set of actions that were political in scope. For example, the Mission Statement called for participants to engage in "no work, no school, no sport or play, no entertainment, and nothing profane." Part of the MMM program was to effectuate a Day of Absence that was not unrelated to the many boycotts of the 1960s civil rights movement. Indeed, the intent of the "Black Out," as it was called at the MMM, was to show "white power"—corporate, political, economic—how dependent it had become on black consumerism and black labor. As well, among the long list of themes that emanated from the keynote speech, there was a call to "register to vote" and "become politically and culturally active."

18. During the summer of 1997, President Clinton plainly called for a "National Dialogue" on race at a graduation speech in San Diego. This unprecedented presidential appeal for American racial reconciliation lost out to a series of events that would eventually lead to Clinton's impeachment by the House of Representatives in 1998 and 1999. When Clinton and the John Hope Franklin–led commission submitted their findings, it received very little media coverage because of the more pressing issue of impeachment. All but AWOL on the issue of affirmative action during the campaign, Clinton, once elected, urged "a great national effort" to create "a more perfect union" (incidentally, the title of Farrakhan's MMM/DOA speech). Targeting California's Proposition 209, Clinton's speech continued, "To those of you who oppose affirmative action, I ask you to come up with an alternative."

19. The Clinton administration gave little support to the opposition forces organized to defeat the statewide Proposition 209 in California, where the white majority—no doubt angered by the Los Angeles riots and the O.J. Simpson verdicts there—voted to abolish affirmative action (54–46 percent). Confronted by an increasingly conservative white electorate that mandated the Republican "Contract with America" just two years earlier, and white-majority protest demonstrations throughout California university campuses, Clinton sought to make good on two other major (traditionally conservative) policy pledges: policing and welfare. This equally angered many blacks (and, ironically, Republicans) yet ensured his reelection by women and working-class or white "populist" elements; Ruy Teixeira, "The Real Electorate," *American Prospect* (March–April 1998): 82–85. Propostioin 209, known as the California Civil Rights Initiative and authored by white university professors Glynn Custered (California State

University–Hayward) and Thomas E. Woods, was supported by nearly 80 percent of white Californians. In the California campaign, Republican candidate Bob Dole—the former Senate majority leader from Russell, Kansas, who supported affirmative action earlier in his political career—stated that "such programs are divisive and have outlived their usefulness." Republican Patrick Buchanan pledged that if elected he would "issue an executive order ending all 'preferential treatment' in federal policy"; Clinton continued to weakly promote his vague campaign position: "mend it, don't end it" (Patrick McDonnell, "California Election Puts Focus on Multiculturalism Concerns," *Los Angeles Times*, March 20, 1996, p. A5). The *Los Angeles Times* describes the presidential campaign of 1996: "Voters are already hearing a lot about a broad sweep of 'multicultural' concerns—everything from immigration to affirmative action, to bilingualism and gay and lesbian rights." The initiative passed despite opposition from three in four blacks, seven in ten Latinos, and 55 percent of Asians. *Newsweek* reported that Republican presidential candidates Phil Gramm, Patrick Buchanan, and the ultraconservative California governor Pete Wilson all tied their conservative presidential candidacies to the issue of affirmative action (Howard Fineman and Andrew Murr, "Race and Rage," *Newsweek*, April 3, 1995, p. 22). For example, just before declaring his candidacy, Wilson stated that it was his "duty" to seek the White House in the name of "fundamental fairness" for people who "work hard, pay their taxes, and obey the law." The article continues: "Wilson's decision to move toward a formal presidential candidacy underscores affirmative action's appeal to GOP politicians. They see it as a way to prove their conservative bona fides to the rank and file." The fact that the Democrats lost the white male vote by a margin of 62–36 percent in 1994 was doubtless on the minds of the candidates and their campaign advisers in the pending presidential election.

20. Jonathan Peterson, "Clinton Calls for 'National Effort' to End Racism," *Los Angeles Times*, June 15, 1997, pp. A1, A18.

21. Bob Sipchen, "Republicans Weighing Best Way to Reach Out to Blacks," *Los Angeles Times*, December 23, 1995, p. A20.

22. "President Clinton Journeys to Africa, *JET* 93, no. 21 (April 20, 1998): 5–18, 54–60. The Clintons' trip included Ghana, South Africa, Uganda, Senegal, Botswana, and Rwanda for the purpose of working with Africa: "to nurture democracy," "to increase trade and investment in Africa," "to resolve the war and genocide that still tear at the heart of Africa," and "to preserve the magnificent natural environment that is left." A highlight was Clinton's visit to South African president Nelson Mandela's former prison cell on Robben Island. Jesse Jackson accompanied them as a special envoy, along with other prominent black Democrats.

23. With the political calculations relating to the Sister Souljah incident, the aborted appointment of Lani Guinier to the Attorney General's office, and Clinton's support of the execution of a lobotomized black man named Ricky Ray Rector in Arkansas, black criticisms of Clinton were tempered only by the prospect of the harsher Republican alternative in the 104th Congress. Clinton's New Democrat moderation resembled a brand of Rockefeller Republicanism. Larry Sabato (ed.), *Toward the Millennium: The Elections of 1996* (Boston: Allyn and Bacon, 1997). If nothing else, it was not the Republicanism of Ronald Reagan or even George Bush that many blacks otherwise regarded as racist.

24. President Clinton also removed Surgeon General Jocelyn Elders (an African American) from her post following conservative attacks on several statements she made concerning condom use and masturbation. Clinton replaced her with an African American named Dr. Henry W. Foster Jr. of Tuskegee, Alabama. Other key appointments include Secretary of Commerce Ron Brown, former chair of the Democratic National Committee who spearheaded Clinton's reelection bid; federal judgeships; Secre-

tary of Labor Alexis Herman; and Secretary of Agriculture Mike Espy, a former Mississippi congressman appointed to the USDA during Clinton's first administration. Espy resigned in 1994 amid thirty charges of ethical misconduct in the acceptance of gifts from several large corporations; he would subsequently be acquitted of all charges and honored by Clinton in a high-profile celebration and unveiling of an official portrait of Espy in the USDA headquarters. See "Portrait of Mike Espy, Ex–Agriculture Dept. Secretary, Is Unveiled in Washington, DC," *JET* 95, no. 5 (December 28–January 4, 1999), p. 4. A more recent example would be Clinton's late 1998 advancement of Lieutenant General Benjamin O. Davis Jr. to the rank of four-star general. Davis is noted for his command of the all-black Tuskegee Airmen (332nd Fighter Group) during World War II.

25. The other states include Alabama, Mississippi, and Georgia. The ninety-three-year-old senator Strom Thurmond of South Carolina (a state's rights presidential candidate in 1948) won an eighth term. The authors contend that if an additional 12 percent (100,000) of the 800,000 eligible black voters—in one of Jesse Jackson's home states—had turned out against Thurmond, he would have been defeated. They note also that Helms, challenged for a second time by black former Charlotte mayor Harvey Gantt, also won because of apparent disinterest. Gantt won 90 percent of the black vote and 40 percent of the white vote. Theodore Cross and Robert Bruce Slater, "The 1996 Elections: The Real Victor Was Black Voter Apathy," *Journal of Black Higher Education* (Winter 1996): 120.

26. Ibid.

27. The black voter apathy thesis, however, does not attempt to explain how such a massive turnout of black men did not translate into enthusiastic support for Democrats. They assume the Democratic Party to be blacks' only rational political course. Yet even as blacks failed to oust vulnerable (racist) southern congressional leaders, they granted Republican Party congressional candidates nearly 20 percent of their vote, a 10 percent increase over 1994. Ibid., p. 125.

28. Ibid., p. 149, Emphasis added.

29. Michael C. Dawson, *Black Visions*, p. 131.

30. In January 2003, the Voter News Service was disbanded largely because of failures in 2000 and 2002 elections. It resurfaced as the National Election Pool, using exit polls and official returns, with little more success than the VNS.

31. Indeed, Clinton's meager turnout improvement, from 49 percent in 1992 to 49.2 percent in 1996, allowed him to boast a meager 0.3 percent increase (to 24.1 percent) over his 23.8 percent performance in 1992 among the voting-eligible public. This may be attributed to black men. Based on the VNS, white turnout declined by a full 4 percent. Only the 10 percent increase among Hispanics between 1992 and 1996 bettered blacks. Still, the data do not distinguish between black Hispanics and black non-Hispanics in these years. As well, Hispanics, even more than blacks, do not participate at levels equal to their proportion of the voting-age public (VAP). Thus, the VNS suggests—as Bositis and Slater argue above—that black men vis-à-vis the Million Man March had a major but selective (what they call apathetic) impact.

32. Teixeira's study argues that the VNS exit polls are a poor measure of the voting performance of blacks in 1996 because of a "chronic bias" related to the economic class of respondents; specifically, the poor tend to be underrepresented in exit polling. Moreover, Teixeira's census-based data also suggest that black men actually suffered a decline in 1996 of 4 percent, which actually exceeded the 3 percent decline among black women (p. 83). But Teixeira, no more than those representing the black apathy perspective, attempts to explain the black turnout declines in recent presidential elections. More determinative than the black vote in the 1996 presidential election, Teixeira argues, is that the

Democratic victory should be attributed to white (mostly female) Americans with less than a college education: "Clinton's support increased by about eight percentage points (over 1992) among the noncollege educated, but by only four points among the college educated. And among women, the disparity was even greater: Clinton's support went up more than 11 percentage points among voters without degrees and just five points among college graduates. While Clinton may not have delivered much to them, the voters who have most often lost out in the new economy saw the Republicans as having less to offer. . . . Working mothers without a college education increased their support of Clinton by 20 points, while their college-educated counterparts did so by only two points. The median household income of noncollege-educated women was just $34,000 in 1996. Thus the true swing voter starts to look less like an affluent Volvo driver and more like a Cavalier driver struggling to get by economically and build a better life. . . . So current and future success for the Democrats depends, most plausibly, not on increasing black turnout (now 11 percent of voters, just about their representation in the adult population) or even on increasing Hispanic turnout. . . . Instead it lies with the strugglers: the overwhelming majority of U.S. voters who lack a college degree and, more particularly, the huge pool of non-college-educated white voters (57 percent of the electorate) whose support for the Democrats has improved substantially but remains shaky (just 44 percent for the President and 47 percent for the House in 1996)" (Teixeira, p. 84).

The electoral strategy implications for the Democrats are clear. The US Census data highlight a potentially troublesome prospect for black Democrats. Considering these numbers, and the weak support that nonunion, non-college-educated whites have given Democrats and the party's centrist shift, it is likely that the Democratic Party and future candidates will cater to this largely untapped segment of the electorate. Teixeira's study rightly juxtaposes African American voters with this largely "struggling" or working-class white cohort. Historically—with the Truman exception in 1948—black Democrats have not fared well when these constituent groups have attempted to occupy the same political space. For example, on the one hand, there is the (1948) Thurmond-led Dixiecrats and Wallace's (1968) American Independent party; and on the other, we have Fannie Lou Hamer and the Mississippi Freedom Democratic Party (MFDP) (1964).

33. Katherine Tate, *From Protest to Politics*, pp. 64–65.

34. For an analysis of this cohort, please see Edward G. Carmines, John P. McIver, and James A. Stimson, "Unrealized Partisanship: A Theory of Dealignment," *Journal of Politics* 49, no. 2 (1987): 376–400. "Unrealized partisans" generally are those who developed weak party loyalty compared to preceding generations. The youngest of the Generation X cohorts—those born in 1978—in the study reached voting age with the 1996 presidential election.

35. The Howard University survey reports an estimated median income of $43,000 (compared to $19,333 for all black households nationally); 10 percent earned less than $30,000. This is somewhat surprising, as black nationalist leaders and movements such as those of Garvey and Malcolm X typically find their strongest support among the poor and working classes. The poor and working classes were obviously hindered from attending the Million Man March due to costs related to travel, food, and accommodations. Aside from the immediate District of Columbia (15.1 percent), New Yorkers and Philadelphians predominated in the Million Man March. This middle-class aspect of the MMM/DOA is somewhat unconventional. During the civil rights movement, the typical militant was young, urban, male, and anti-establishment. Respondents in the MMM sample suggest that this fringe ideology had taken center stage in the 1990s. This should explain—at least partially—the popularity of Louis Farrakhan among Million Man Marchers. The *Washington Post*'s Million Man March survey lists the demographic and political orientations of the Million Man Marchers. When millions of black

American men and women gathered in Washington (not including the hundreds of thousands who simultaneously assembled in satellite gatherings in large cities, such as Chicago, Los Angeles, San Francisco, Oakland, and Miami), they represented the broadest spectrum of economic, political, social, religious, and generational classes of blacks assembled to date. Still, the Million Man Marchers were not representative of all black Americans. In many ways, they exceeded average black Americans in terms of economic class and political advocacy; therefore generalization to all black Americans is not possible using the data sets that we employ for this study.

36. It is likely that these attributes would yield considerably different patterns had the poorer and less educated from more distant states who attended the satellite gatherings been included.

37. Vibert White Jr., *Inside the Nation of Islam*, p. 162.

38. Farrakhan's travels took him to Africa (Ghana, Liberia, Nigeria, Tunisia, Libya, Senegal, Gambia, Zaire, South Africa, Nigeria, and Sudan), the Middle East (Saudi Arabia, United Arab Emirates, Iran, Iraq, Syria, and Turkey), Latin America (Guam and Cuba), and Asia (Malaysia).

39. While haranguing the Clinton administration over the propriety of his accepting a US$2 billion loan from Libyan leader Muammar Khadafi, Farrakhan spent much of the 1996 campaign season returning to key cities, such as New York, Los Angeles, Philadelphia, and Chicago, to articulate his elevated status among black American leadership. At the first speech given in Los Angeles following the Million Man March, Farrakhan shocked a largely black Christian audience assembled at F.A.M.E., as he ranted against white Christianity, then Christianity in general, only to end up calling himself a "savior" of black peoples. Farrakhan proceeded to tell of his now well-documented "mother-ship" visit to the late leader and founder of the Nation of Islam, Elijah Muhammad, as F.A.M.E. pastor Cecil "Chip" Murray, Ben Chavis (later Muhammad), Danny Bakewell, and an exhausted audience looked on in astonishment.

40. Before the St. Louis Summit, Chavis repeatedly alluded to the 1972 National Black Political Convention, arguing that the 1996 convention was superior in that there would be a consensus among delegates. However, the National African American Leadership Summit was poorly attended, with less than 10 percent of the projected delegates.

41. And this was several years *before* the emergence of the centrist Democratic Leadership Council's emergence as the party's leadership and propagandistic apparatuses: Al From (founder and CEO), Bill Clinton, Al Gore, Charles "Chuck" Robb (Lyndon B. Johnson's son-in-law), and Senator Joe Lieberman of Connecticut. It is unclear if, as with other segments of the American electorate, these individuals will tend toward their parents' political allegiances as they grow older.

42. Harold Cruse, *Crisis of the Negro Intellectual*.

43. Harold Cruse, *Plural but Equal*, p. 352. Emphases in original.

44. Ibid., p. 342.

45. Ibid., p. 352. Emphasis in original.

46. Ibid., p. 349. Emphasis in original.

47. Ibid., pp. 369–370.

48. Ibid., p. 358.

49. Ibid., p. 378. Emphasis in original.

50. Ibid., p. 379. Emphasis in original.

51. Others, like former SCLC leader Joseph Lowery and Jesse Jackson Sr., supported Obama's campaign from the outset.

52. Hanes Walton Jr., *African American Power and Politics*, p. 53. These sentiments are expressed nearly verbatim by Dawson (*Behind the Mule*, p. 210), except that Dawson's

work acknowledges that the potentialities for such a scenario depend largely on the ability of blacks and Latinos to formulate and maintain common-ground coalitions.

53. M.K. Asante Jr., *It's Bigger Than Hip Hop*, p. 10.

54. According to Robert L. Hall, "Massachusetts Abolitionists Document the Slave Experience," in Donald Jacobs, *Courage and Conscience*, the African Meeting House in Boston was a key institution at which Walker was a leader. It was also referred to by locals as the black Faneuil. It was also known as the Abolitionist Church or African Baptist Church and housed the New England Anti-Slavery Society, p. 80.

55. James Lance Taylor, "Black Politics in Transition," pp. 277, 430–431; Katherine Tate, *From Protest to Politics*, p. 156.

56. Unfortunately, no data exist to directly measure the impact of the MMM/DOA on voting in the 1996 presidential primaries or general election. Although the various MMM/DOA surveys ask respondents if they "intend to vote in the upcoming election," there is no way to determine their actual participation with available data. The 1996 NBES also neglected to gauge whether or not the MMM/DOA factored into the decision to participate in 1996. To this degree, we rely on 1996 exit poll data and US Census reports concerning the participation levels of black Americans. Still, the 1996 NBES does provide several measures to test the linkages between the MMM/DOA and contemporary black political partisanship—independent partisanship.

57. Michael Eric Dyson, *Between God and Gangsta Rap*, p. 103.

58. For instance, even where younger American voters improved their turnout performance between the 2004 and 2008 elections, with 20–22 million voting overwhelmingly for Democratic candidate Barack Obama, their performance was unimpressive when compared to turnout and participation patterns since the 1970s.

59. His late endorsement of Barack Obama against fellow Republican and Vietnam POW John McCain in 2008 certainly endeared him further to many of Obama's supporters.

60. As to blacks' favorable response to a potential Powell presidential or vice-presidential bid—when compared to Jackson—Morris cites Powell's "outsider image," the image of not being beholden to "either political party in the past nor with electoral politics in general," as the most likely reason.

61. Cary D. Wintz, "Colin Powell: The Candidate Who Wasn't," in Bruce Glasrud and Cary Wintz (eds.), *African Americans and the Presidency: The Road to the White House* (New York: Routledge, 2010), p. 199.

62. Ibid., p. 200.

63. Larry Sabato (ed.), *Toward the Millennium*, p. 30.

64. Cross and Slater, "The 1996 Elections: The Real Victor Was Black Voter Apathy."

65. Federal civil rights commissioner Arthur Fletcher also ran as a GOP presidential candidate in 1996. As a black Republican, Fletcher had a short-lived campaign that was largely symbolic. But Fletcher did argue, "After the Million Man March, which was all about economic development, the first thing [the GOP] should have done was call together African Americans and others and say: 'Let's have a summit on depressed neighborhood economic development.' . . . Instead, GOP leaders began pontificating on 'the sociology' of welfare mothers and crime" (Bob Sipchen, "Republican Weighing Best Way to Reach Out to Blacks," *Los Angeles Times*, December 23, 1995, p. A20). Also worthy of note is the decline the relevance of black conservatives during the 1996 campaign. Cross and Slater ("The 1996 Elections: The Real Victor Was Black Voter Apathy," p. 127) report a sharp decline in the number of times the term "black conservative" appeared in major newspapers and magazines between 1988 and 1996. The data show a peak in 1994 (at approximately 1,400) followed by a steady decline (to 1,000) in 1996. Also, high-profile black conservative spokesmen Glenn C. Loury and

Robert Woodson withdrew from the American Enterprise Institute in 1995, a conservative think tank that buttressed black conservatism, after the institute financed Indian-born author Dinesh D'Souza's diatribe *The End of Racism*. In it he claims that blacks suffer from pathological behavior rather than racism and that American slavery was more benign than originally thought. After the campaign, House Speaker Newt Gingrich initiated the conservative New Majority Council, which would recruit Latino, Asian, and black candidates. Whereas the number of congressional black Republicans was reduced to one in 1996, the party did double the number of black Republican congressional candidates between 1992 and 1994 (to twenty-seven). After leading Bush's "Willie Horton" campaign in 1988, the now deceased national party chairman, Lee Atwater, spearheaded the Republicans' 1989 Operation Outreach—which sought to increase black support up to about 20 percent (see Robert Shogan, "GOP Launches Drive to Attract Minority Voters," *Los Angeles Times*, September, 17, 1997, p. A14).

66. See *The Final Call*, August 27, 1996, p. 8. In 1992 the 107 black delegates who attended the GOP convention made up 5 percent. And in 1988, the sixty-one black delegates constituted a meager 2.7 percent of the total.

67. Peniel E. Joseph, *Dark Days, Bright Nights: From Black Power to Barack Obama* (New York: BasicCivitas, 2010), p. 33.

68. Ibid., pp. 200–201.

69. See, for instance, a national radio debate between Joseph and Jared Ball (of Morgan State University) in "Defining Black Power: Drs. Jared Ball and Peniel Joseph Debate." Available at http://www.voxunion.com/?p=2396 (accessed April 16, 2010).

70. Peniel Joseph, *Dark Days*, p. 195.

71. Also see Matt Bai, "Is Obama the End of Black Politics?," *New York Times Magazine*, August 6, 2008. Available at http://www.nytimes.com/2008/08/10/magazine/10politics-t.html (accessed 4/17/2010).

72. David Remnick, *The Bridge: The Life and Rise of Barack Obama*, p. 122.

73. Ibid., pp. 288–289.

74. Defeated in 2000 by a former Black Panther Party member and incumbent South Side Democratic congressman (1st District), Bobby Rush, Obama received 30.36 and Rush received 61.02 percent. The, district, which was about 65 percent black, is considered the blackest electoral district in the United States. Obama won the US Senate seat over black Republican archconservative and carpetbagging political hack Alan Keyes (of Maryland) in 2004.

75. David Remnick, *The Bridge*, pp. 288–289.

76. Ibid., p. 408.

77. Ibid., pp. 175, 425.

78. Ibid., ch. 7.

79. They are the oldest housing projects in the city and are located on an isolated landfill with the highest concentration of toxic waste in the country. More than two of three of its residents are poor, although other tracts in the city are poorer still.

80. Remnick, *The Bridge*, pp. 131–133.

81. William Julius Wilson, *More Than Just Race: Being Black and Poor in the Inner City* (New York: W. W. Norton, 2009), p. 27.

82. David Remnick, *The Bridge*, p. 139.

83. Ibid., p. 328.

84. These are Punahou School in Hawaii, Occidental College, Columbia University, and Harvard School of Law.

85. David Colbert, *Michelle Obama: An American Story* (Boston: Sandpiper/Houghton Mifflin Harcourt, 2009), pp. 11–12.

86. Ibid., p. 83.

87. Liz Mundy, *Michelle: A Biography*, cited in Ta-Nehisi Coates, "American Girl," *Atlantic Online*, January–February 2009, pp. 1–8, available online at www.theatlantic .com/magazine/archive/2009/01/american-girl/7211.

88. Raina Kelley, "A Real Wife, in a Real Marriage, an Outspoken, Smart Black Woman or a Bossy, Emasculating Wife? Michelle Obama Defies Stereotypes, but Cannot Escape Them Either," *Newsweek*, February 25, 2008, p. 35.

89. Ibid., p. 35.

90. During the campaign, supporters of Hillary Clinton fueled the rumor on a now defunct blog at hillbuzz.blogspot.com, claiming that Michelle Obama's "whitey" rant tape was filmed between June 26 and July 1, 2004, in Chicago at the Rainbow/PUSH Coalition Conference at Trinity United Church, specifically the Women's Event. She was joined by women of the Rainbow/PUSH organization, Mrs. Farrakhan, and Shoshana Johnson (the country's first female POW and survivor), who is, once again, ignored in the criticisms of the photos of Mrs. Obama and Mrs. Farrakhan. The photo was published in *JET* magazine, July 26, 2004.

91. There are, however, at least a few current and onetime nationalists who were included in the early deliberations that evolved into the BRC. The list included Abdul Alkalimat and Salim Muwakkil, Angela Davis, Amiri and Amini Baraka, Cornel West, Robin Kelley, Lewis Gordon, Manning Marable, Bill Fletcher, Charlene Mitchell, Sonia Sanchez, Leith Mullings, Julianne Malveaux, and Van Jones of the Socialistic Standing Together to Organize Revolutionary Movement (STORM).

92. Clarence Lusane, "From Crisis to Congress: Assessing the Black Radical Congress," *Social Justice* (Fall 1998). Available at http://findarticles.com/p/articles/mi _hb3427/is_3_25/ai_n28718168/pg_6/?tag=content;col1 (accessed April 3, 2010).

93. New Party members and supporters include Cornel West, Manning Marable, Noam Chomsky, Bill Fletcher, and Quentin Young, a local Chicago Marxist.

94. David Remnick, *The Bridge*, p, 148.

95. Barack Obama, *Dreams from My Father*, pp. 199–201.

96. Ibid., p. 198.

97. Tommy Shelby, *We Who Are Dark*, p. 33.

98. Barack Obama, *Dreams from My Father*, p. 203.

99. See Hank De Zutter, "What Makes Obama Run?" *Chicago Reader*, December 8, 1995. Available at http://www.chicagoreader.com/obama/951208/.

100. See p. 202. Emphasis in original. Obama knew and knows that *Final Call* has been a serious newspaper rarely given to such hyperbole. Yet this characterization is disingenuous on too many levels to elucidate, mainly because *Final Call* is a quality newspaper—created originally as a replacement of *Muhammad Speaks* (edited by Malcolm X)—that covers domestic and international issues and matters not covered by the Associated Press and other sources.

101. See Hank De Zutter, "What Makes Obama Run?" See also David Remnick, *The Bridge*, p. 284.

102. Obama, *Dreams from My Father*, pp. 199–200. Emphasis added.

103. David Remnick, *The Bridge*, p. 265.

104. Obama, *Dreams from My Father*, p. 200.

105. Remnick, *The Bridge*, pp. 169–175.

106. Ibid., p. 468.

107. See, for instance, Jerome R. Corsi, *The Obama Nation: Leftist Politics and the Cult of Personality* (New York: Threshold, 2008); and David Freddoso, *The Case Against Barack Obama: The Unlikely Rise and Unexamined Agenda of the Media's Favorite Candidate* (Washington, DC: Regnery, 2008).

108. Jerome R. Corsi, *The Obama Nation*, pp. 77–82.

109. Ibid., p. 83.

110. Barack Obama, *The Audacity of Hope*, p. 288.

111. Ibid., p. 303.

112. Cited in Remnick, *The Bridge*, p. 520. Emphasis added.

113. She subsequently became a regular commentator of FOX News entertainment for the remainder of the primary.

114. The more Obama advanced as a candidate, the more race seemed to be inserted into the campaign. On January 20, 2008, at Martin Luther King's (former) Ebenezer Baptist Church in conjunction with an observation of King's birthday in front of a large African American audience, Obama spoke out against anti-Semitism *within the African American community*. In February 2008, Obama was forced to "reject and denounce" Louis Farrakhan's endorsement during a presidential primary debate with Hillary Clinton, when moderator and NBC Washington bureau chief Tim Russert repeatedly questioned Barack Obama on his reaction to Louis Farrakhan's endorsement at the Nation of Islam's annual Savior's Day event. Russert cited a *Chicago Tribune* article in which Obama rejected Farrakhan's politics generally and reminded the paper that he was a "consistent denunciator of Louis Farrakhan." Russert began the discussion of Farrakhan by asking Obama, "On Sunday, the headline in your hometown paper, *Chicago Tribune*: 'Louis Farrakhan backs Obama for president at Nation of Islam convention in Chicago.' Do you accept the support of Louis Farrakhan?" But Russert did not note the article's subheading: "Senator has criticized him, says support not sought." Much like the black mayors of a generation before, Obama was required to prove his loyalty—to white liberals—by denouncing Farrakhan. Following Obama's answer, Russert asked, "Do you reject his support?" Obama then replied, "Well, Tim, you know, I can't say to somebody that he can't say that he thinks I'm a good guy," adding: "I have been very clear in my denunciations of him and his past statements, and I think that indicates to the American people what my stance is on those comments." Russert continued: "The problem some voters may have is, as you know, Reverend Farrakhan called Judaism 'gutter religion.'" With Hillary Clinton watching the exchange, Obama replied, "I am very familiar with his record, as are the American people. That's why I have consistently denounced it." Indeed, in his answer to Russert's initial question, the first thing Obama said was, "You know, I have been very clear in my denunciation of Minister Farrakhan's anti-Semitic comments," calling them "unacceptable and reprehensible." Russert persisted: "The title of one of your books, *Audacity of Hope* . . . you acknowledge you got from a sermon from Reverend Jeremiah Wright, the head of the Trinity United Church. He said that Louis Farrakhan 'epitomizes greatness,'" before asking Obama, "What do you do to assure Jewish Americans that, whether it's Farrakhan's support or the activities of Reverend Jeremiah Wright, your pastor, you are consistent with issues regarding Israel and not in any way suggesting that Farrakhan epitomizes greatness?" Further, following Farrakhan's endorsement, Obama gave a speech on February 25 at a Jewish community meeting in Cleveland in which he stated: "It is true that my Pastor, Jeremiah Wright, who will be retiring this month, is somebody who on occasion can say controversial things. . . . He does not have a close relationship with Louis Farrakhan. I have been a consistent, before I go any further, a consistent denunciator of Louis Farrakhan, nobody challenges that. And what is true is that, recently this is probably, I guess last year. An award was given to Farrakhan for his work on behalf of ex-offenders completely unrelated to his controversial statements. And I believe that was a mistake and showed a lack of sensitivity to [the] Jewish community and I said so."

Barack Obama's well-known "A More Perfect Union" speech on race in Philadelphia in March 2008 of necessity—given the media-generated furor over Wright's looped comments—sought to balance his personal biography, in true Du Boisian style, with that of the major racial populations of the United States. And his 2008 "Father's Day" speech at Apostolic Church of God in South Side Chicago echoed Father's Day sermons spoken in African American churches for decades, yet the preacher Jesse Jackson—assuming he was off-mic—expressed a desire to castrate Obama for "talking down to black people." Speaking to the black congregation, Obama reiterated the traditional, conservative message of nuclear family values that would make Louis Farrakhan and FOX TV commentators proud. Please note that these exchanges were observed by this author, but the citation here comes from a February 27, 2008, posting on *Media Matters for America* titled "Russert Persisted in Questioning Obama on Farrakhan—even after his repeated denunciation(s) of Farrakhan's 'unacceptable and reprehensible' comments." Please see the site at http://mediamatters.org/items/200802270006.

115. David Remnick, *The Bridge*, p. 172.

116. Ibid., p. 170.

117. Trinity United Church of Christ adopted the Black Value System in 1981 (amid the challenge to the Jane Byrne administration's hostility to the South Side community and its leadership): "We believe in the following *12 precepts and covenantal statements*. These Black Ethics must be taught and exemplified in homes, churches, nurseries and schools, wherever blacks are gathered. They must reflect on the following concepts: Commitment to God, Commitment to the Black Community, Commitment to the Black Family, Dedication to the Pursuit of Education, Dedication to the Pursuit of Excellence, Adherence to the Black Work Ethic, Commitment to Self-Discipline and Self-Respect, Disavowal of the Pursuit of 'Middleclassness,' Pledge to make the fruits of all developing and acquired skills available to the Black Community, Pledge to Allocate Regularly, a Portion of Personal Resources for Strengthening and Supporting Black Institutions, Pledge allegiance to all Black leadership who espouse and embrace the Black Value System, Personal commitment to embracement of the Black Value System. . . . The Pastor as well as the membership of Trinity United Church of Christ is committed to a *10-point Vision*: A congregation committed to *adoration*; a congregation preaching *salvation*; a congregation actively seeking *reconciliation*; a congregation with a non-negotiable *commitment to Africa*; a congregation committed to *Biblical education*; a congregation committed to *cultural education*; a congregation committed to the *historical education of African people in diaspora*; a congregation committed to *liberation*; a congregation committed to *restoration*; a congregation working towards *economic parity*."

118. Joseph D. Eure and Richard M. Jerome (eds.), *Back Where We Belong: Selected Speeches by Minister Louis Farrakhan* (Philadelphia: PC International, 1989), pp. 74–75.

119. Please see Scott Kurashige, "Obama's Crisis and MLK's Hard Truths," at http://www.huffingtonpost.com/scott-kurashige/obamas-crisis-and-mlks-_b_91807.html#. Accessed March 17, 2008.

120. Bruce Glasrud and Cary Wintz (eds.), *African Americans and the Presidency*, pp. 222–223.

121. In a June 25, 2008, interview with *Rocky Mountain News* reporter M. E. Sprengelmeyer, Lebanese American consumer advocate and perennial presidential candidate Ralph Nader also argued that "there's only one thing different about Barack Obama when it comes to being a Democratic presidential candidate. He's half African-American." Moreover, "whether that will make any difference, I don't know. I haven't heard him have a strong crackdown on economic exploitation in the ghettos. Payday loans, predatory lending, asbestos, lead. What's keeping him from doing that? *Is it because he wants to talk white? He doesn't want to appear like Jesse Jackson?* We'll see all that play out in the next few months and if he gets elected afterwards." On November 4, the

day and night of Obama's election, Nader gave two interviews to FOX-TV (Houston and New York) in which he respectively stated, "to put it very simply, he is our nation's first African American president; or he will be. And we wish him well. But his choice, basically, is whether he is going to be Uncle Sam for the people or Uncle Tom for the giant corporations." In the later FOX interview with anchor Shepherd Smith, Nader reiterated, "It's very simple, he has gone along with corporate power from the moment he entered politics in the State Senate; voted for the Wall Street bailout; supports expanding the military budget that is desired by the military industrial complex; it doesn't really have a tax reform thing for the ordinary fellow in this country; opposes single payer full Medicare for all because the giant HMOs Aetna and CIGNA do; doesn't have a living wage, he is supposed to be respectful of the poor, hardly mentions them in his speech [sic], he only mentions the middle class, doesn't have a comprehensive program." Smith says, "You talk about respect and you utter the words 'Uncle Tom'? Are you kidding me?" To which Nader replies, "Yeah that's the question he has to face. He's the first African American." Smith interrupts: "Is that what you want your legacy to be, the man who on the night that the first African American in the history of this nation was elected, you ask if he is going to be Uncle Sam or Uncle Tom?" To which Nader replied, "Yes, of course, he has turned his back on a hundred million people in this country, African American, and Latinos, and poor whites, and we are going to hold him to a higher standard."

122. George Breitman, *The Last Year of Malcolm X*, p. 61. It was at the Northern Negro Grass Roots Leadership Conference, led by Albert Cleage Jr. The noted Christian black nationalist cleric convinced Malcolm X that "black nationalism is being taught in the Christian church."

123. Several weeks later, African American assailant and California parolee Levell Mixon shot five Oakland police officers, killing four—including three sergeants and SWAT officers, just miles from the Oscar Grant murders in East Oakland. Multiple unsolved murders had occurred in the area, which partially explains the strong department presence before the shooting of the officers.

124. Cited in Herbert Aptheker (ed.), *Marxism and Christianity* (New York: Humanities, 1968), p. 24.

125. William Julius Wilson, *More Than Just Race*, pp. 141–142.

Timeline of Key Events

1701   Society for the Propagation of the Gospel in Foreign Parts begins mission in the US colonies.

1706   The English governor of New York, Lord Cornbury, orders all officers to seize, apprehend, fire upon, kill, or destroy any Africans assembled in Kings County (Brooklyn). It signaled a long-standing concern with black liberation and retaliatory violence in the colonies.

1773   Four slaves in Boston petition the legislature to allow them time off from labor so that they can finance their return to Africa.

1774   A large number of slaves petition the Massachusetts legislature, urging, "we have in common with all other men a natural right to our freedom without Being depriv'd of them by our fellow men as we are a freeborn Pepel and have never forfeited this Blessing by any compact or agreement whatever."

1776   Thomas Jefferson writes an original draft of the Declaration of Independence, which includes an antislavery clause that does not make the final draft.

1781   Thomas Jefferson writes *Notes on the State of Virginia*(through 1784).

1787   Richard Allen creates the Free African Society in Philadelphia during the spring.

        The Constitutional Convention meets in Philadelphia from May 25 through September 17.

        Richard Allen and Absalem Jones withdraw from St. George's Methodist Episcopal Church to establish the African Methodist Episcopal Church in Philadelphia.

        Establishment of Sierra Leone as a colony under the British government.

1791   Revolution in Santo Domingo (Haiti) begins, which lasts through 1804, resulting in the creation of the First Black Republic and expansion of the US boundaries.

1800   "Black Gabriel" and his coconspirators attempt to lead slaves in revolt to take Richmond, Virginia.

1811   Emigrationist leader and seaman Paul Cuffee leads the first of two voyages with African American families (1811 and 1815) to the British colony of Sierra Leone.

1816   The Society for the Colonization of Free People of Color of America (American Colonization Society, or ACS) is established by prominent American whites. The ACS consults with Paul Cuffee, but Cuffee's death in 1817 ends further efforts toward collaboration.

1820   Congress passes the Missouri Compromise, partitioning the country between free and slave at the 36′30 parallel.

1822   Members of the African Church in Charleston, South Carolina, including Morris Brown, "Gullah" Jack Pritchard, and Peter Poyas, are implicated in the insurrection plot of Denmark Vesey, a free Negro.

1827   John B. Russwurm and Samuel Cornish create *Freedom's Journal*, considered the first black newspaper in the United States.

David Walker arrives in Boston from Wilmington, North Carolina. He becomes an agent for *Freedom's Journal* and lectures and organizes among the General Colored Association of Massachusetts.

1829   David Walker publishes the first of three editions of his pamphlet between October 1829 and June 1830: *The Appeal to the Colored Citizens of the World but in Particular and Very Expressly to Those of the United States of America.*

1830   Slavery is abolished in the North and is replaced with segregation.

The first of many National Negro Convention meetings is held in Philadelphia. Delegates were overwhelmingly from the North until 1864.

Congress passes the Indian Removal Bill.

1831   Nat Turner leads an insurrection in Southampton, Virginia, in August. He is captured in October and executed in November.

1833   The American Anti-Slavery Society is founded by William Lloyd Garrison after his break with the ACS agenda.

1838   Escaped slave Frederick Augustus Washington Bailey flees to New York before settling in Boston; he takes the surname Douglass.

1839   The Liberty Party is established and holds its convention. It later nominates Frederick Douglass for New York secretary of state.

1841   Frederick Douglass speaks at Massachusetts Anti-Slavery Society event in New Bedford and begins his association with William Lloyd Garrison.

1843   Henry Highland Garnet issues his *Address to the Slaves of the United States* at the Negro Convention in Buffalo, New York. In five years it will be published along with David Walker's Appeal.

1846   The US war with Mexico begins; it lasts through 1848.

1847   Frederick Douglass publishes the *North Star* newspaper. For a short time, he is joined at the paper by Martin R. Delany.

1850   Congress passes the Compromise of 1850, which includes a fugitive slave clause.

1852   Martin R. Delany writes and publishes an important pamphlet, *The Condition, Elevation, and Destiny of the Colored People of the United States*, and becomes a major promoter of emigration.

        Frederick Douglass delivers his Fourth of July speech on July 5.

        Harriet Beecher Stowe publishes *Uncle Tom's Cabin*.

1853   Frederick Douglass organizes the National Negro Convention in Rochester, New York.

1854   Congress passes the Kansas-Nebraska Act, effectively rescinding the 1820 Missouri Compromise.

        Negro leaders representing a spectrum of opinion and thought meet and debate the implications of the recently passed congressional laws. It features Delany, H. Ford Douglas, John Mercer Langston, and James McCune Smith.

        The Republican Party is founded.

1856   Frederick Douglass is nominated as the vice-presidential candidate of the Political Abolition Party.

1857   The US Supreme Court issues the *Dred Scott v. Sanford* decision.

1858   Delany publishes *Blake, or The Huts of America*.

1859   Frances Watkins Harper publishes the poem "A Slave Mother: A Tale of Ohio," commemorating the lives and trials of Robert and Margaret "Peggy" Garner. The fugitive slave mother killed her daughter and attempted to kill her other children and herself rather than return to slavery. Her husband shot several slave catchers and US marshals; at least one died. A trial ensued, and issues concerning the Fugitive Slave Law arose. Toni Morrison's *Beloved* (1987) depicts the story of Peggy.

        John Brown and his sons, along with free and slave blacks, attempt to take over a US military depot at Harpers Ferry, West Virginia. Harriet Tubman and Frederick Douglass are implicated in the plot.

1860   Abraham Lincoln is elected US president in November; South Carolina secedes in December.

1861   The US Civil War nearly splits the Union in two; the war ends in 1865.

1864   The National Negro Convention meets in Syracuse, New York. Delegates demand perpetual federal protection against slavery, as well as political enfranchisement, full citizenship, and land; the National Equal Rights League is also created.

1865   Thirteenth Amendment—Abolition.

1868   Fourteenth Amendment—Citizenship Conferred.

1870   Fifteenth Amendment—Negro Male Suffrage.

1870   Political Reconstruction (through 1901) in the South leads to the first wave of black elected officials, a total of twenty-two members of Congress, including two US senators from Mississippi. There are no governors or big-city mayors. Congressmen serve twenty-four terms between 1869 and 1879, but only fourteen between 1879 and 1901.

1877   The domestic "Exoduster" movement, led by Benjamin "Pap" Singleton and others, follows the 1877 Hayes-Tilden presidential compromise. Some 50,000 blacks flee the South by 1879.

1891   Ida B. Wells begins her research and campaigns against lynching among black Tennesseans after three of her male friends are murdered by a white lynch mob. She is forced to leave and settles in Chicago.

1895   Frederick Douglass dies at seventy-seven.

Booker T. Washington emerges as a Douglass-type leader, criticizing Reconstruction, elected officials, and Negro preachers. He delivers his "Atlanta Compromise" speech, which is, for a short period, widely celebrated by white and Negro leaders alike.

1896   The US Supreme Court's decision in *Plessy v. Ferguson* establishes the "separate-but-equal" doctrine.

1897   Dr. Albert Thorne, a Barbadian forerunner of Marcus Garvey, attempts to lead a movement for black colonization until 1920.

1900   Robert Charles of Copia, Mississippi, a follower of A.M.E. bishop Henry McNeal Turner, and a salesman of his *Voice of Missions* tract in New Orleans, shoots twenty-seven white New Orleanians (including seven police officers) during white riots from July 25 to 27.

1903   W.E.B. Du Bois publishes his first book, *The Souls of Black Folk*, which is noted for its criticism of Booker T. Washington's "separate development" political accommodationism.

1904   The National Liberty Party nominates George Edwin Taylor, a Negro, for president.

1905   William Monroe Trotter, W.E.B. Du Bois, and other leaders form the Niagara Falls Movement (Canada) to challenge the "Tuskegee Machine" of Booker T. Washington.

1913   Timothy "Noble" Drew Ali establishes the Moorish Science Temple in Newark, New Jersey.

1914   Marcus Garvey creates the United Negro Improvement Association (UNIA) in Jamaica, based on his philosophy of black nationalism.

1915   Booker T. Washington dies at age fifty-nine.

Bishop Henry McNeal Turner dies at age eighty-two.

George Baker (aka Father Divine) establishes the Peace Mission Movement; he settles the first mission in Sayville, Long Island, in 1919. His movement is interracial and flourishes during the lean years of the Great Depression. The Reverend Jim Jones will later model the fateful Peoples' Temple on Divine's Peace Mission model.

1916   Marcus Garvey arrives in the United States; he relocates the UNIA to New York the following year.

After supporting Woodrow Wilson and the Democratic Party in New York City during the 1912 national elections, W.E.B. Du Bois urges blacks to form an all-black independent political party. Over the ensuing decade, several local parties are formed in southern cities opposing lily white Republicans.

1917　The United States enters World War I.

　　　Labor and race riots occur in East St. Louis, Illinois.

　　　Hubert H. Harrison founds the Liberty League and the *Voice* newspaper. He also introduces Marcus Garvey to Harlem's nationalist and pan-Africanist circles.

1919　Widespread rioting leads to this period being designated "Red Summer."

1920　UNIA holds its First International Convention in Harlem.

1921　The UNIA chaplain George Alexander McGuire establishes the African Orthodox Church.

　　　Massive race riots occur in the Greenwood neighborhood of Tulsa, Oklahoma.

1922　Marcus Garvey fatefully meets with the Ku Klux Klan in Atlanta.

1925　Marcus Garvey is sentenced to prison in Atlanta for mail fraud. His sentence is commuted by President Calvin Coolidge, and he is deported.

　　　Alaine Locke publishes *The New Negro: An Interpretation*. The New Negro and Harlem Renaissance movements in the 1920s and 1930s are driven mainly by the influx of many African American and Caribbean blacks to the North and Midwest.

1928　During the Sixth Congress of the Comintern, Stalinist Russia supports the idea of self-determination among American blacks, particularly recognizing them as a nation within a nation in the "Black Belt" states and counties of the South (Virginia, Mississippi, Louisiana, Alabama, Georgia, and Texas). White workers are mostly alienated from the Communist Party USA for its efforts to organize among blacks.

1930　The Nation of Islam is established in Detroit by W. D. Fard Muhammad.

1935　Elijah Muhammad assumes leadership of the Nation of Islam until his death in 1975.

1940　Richard Wright's tome *Native Son* is published and widely critiqued for the rage of its protagonist, Bigger Thomas, in the slums of Chicago.

　　　At age fifty-two, Marcus Garvey dies in England.

1941　Labor leader Asa Phillip Randolph, Bayard Rustin, and A. J. Muste threaten to march on Washington, appealing to the Franklin D. Roosevelt administration to desegregate the US armed forces and to eliminate job discrimination in the war industries. FDR issues an executive order establishing the Fair Employment Practice Commission.

1941　The United States enters World War II, which causes global political and economic chaos before it ends in 1945.

1947　Jackie Robinson enters Major League Baseball.

1952   Malcolm Little is paroled from prison in Massachusetts after his decade of street hustling in Harlem and Boston. He was raised in a devoted Garveyite family but accepted the Nation of Islam's teachings while in prison, where he became Malcolm X.

1954   The landmark US Supreme Court decision *Brown v. Board of Education* desegregates public education in the United States, effectively overturning the "separate-but-equal" doctrine of *Plessy v. Ferguson* (1896).

1955   Martin Luther King earns his Ph.D. from Boston University.

King is elected head of the Montgomery Improvement Association and is the leading figure among thousands who boycott the city of Montgomery's bus system after the arrest of Rosa Parks in December.

At the age of twenty-two, Louis Eugene Walcott hears an address by Elijah Muhammad in Chicago and soon embraces the teachings of the Nation of Islam. He is from a West Indian Garveyite family in Boston and a musician. He is introduced to black nationalism through Garveyism and a Christian minister.

The barbaric lynching of fourteen-year-old Chicago youth Emmett Till in Money, Mississippi, galvanizes Chicago's black community. King eulogizes Till.

1956   Quaker organizer and activist Bayard Rustin promotes the teachings of Mahatma Gandhi to King and other leaders. He helps King create the Southern Christian Leadership Conference the next year.

1957   Kwame Nkrumah hosts King, Richard Nixon, and other dignitaries who visit Ghana, Africa, on the occasion of its independence from England. King goes to Africa before Malcolm X.

1959   The Lost Found Nation of Islam in the Wilderness of America (the Nation of Islam) is introduced to Negroes and whites outside Harlem when Negro journalist Louis Lomax and Jewish American journalist Mike Wallace broadcast "The Hate That Hate Produced" on a New York TV station. It also broadcasts the United African Nationalist Movement in Harlem as another example of "black supremacy." The United African Nationalist Movement is a Graveyite movement.

1963   The March on Washington provides a historic gathering foreshadowing the coming civil rights legislation.

1964   Congress passes the Civil Rights Act.

Malcolm X breaks from the Nation of Islam.

1965   Malcolm X is murdered after Nation of Islam ministers, most notably Louis X (Farrakhan), call for his death.

Congress passes the Voting Rights Act.

Violence erupts for days in the Watts section of Los Angeles.

1966   Willie Ricks and Stokely Carmichael make an appeal for Black Power.

The Black Panther Party of Oakland emerges under the leadership of Huey P. Newton and Bobby Seale.

1967   Urban violence erupts in Cleveland, Detroit, and Newark.

1968   Oakland Black Panther "Little" Bobby Hutton is allegedly murdered by Oakland police. No police officers are convicted of the murder.

Martin Luther King Jr. is assassinated; violence erupts in more than a hundred US cities.

1969   The Congressional Black Caucus is formed.

1972   Some 8,000 delegates from forty-five states converge on Gary, Indiana, for the National Black Political Convention.

The New York congresswoman Shirley Chisholm runs for president.

1973   The former cop and city councilman Tom Bradley is elected as the first black mayor of Los Angeles.

1974   Black feminists and womanists formulate the Combahee River Collection Statement, which is antiracist and antisexist.

1975   At age seventy-seven, Elijah Muhammad, leader of the Nation of Islam, dies.

Wallace Muhammad assumes leadership of the Nation of Islam and oversees a massive reform toward Arab Sunni orthodoxy, giving it a series of new names and integrating it racially.

1977   Alex Haley's televised miniseries *Roots*, depicting the cruelties of US slavery, becomes the most watched modern TV drama.

1978   Louis X Farrakhan emerges as the leader of the Nation of Islam in Chicago.

In the jungles of Guyana, South America, Disciples of Christ and Peoples' Temple leader Jim Jones orders the mass murders and suicides of more than 900 mostly black Bay Area residents, including more than 300 children. Many adults are veterans of the civil rights, Black Power, and New Left movements.

1980   Former California governor Ronald Reagan is elected president of the United States for the first of two terms.

The National Black Independent Political Party is formed.

1982   Congressman Harold Washington is elected mayor of Chicago.

Wilson Goode is elected mayor of Philadelphia.

1983   Jesse Jackson launches his "Southern Crusade" voter-registration drive, setting the stage for his Democratic presidential campaign.

Louis Farrakhan emerges as a national figure during Jackson's campaign, most significantly at the twentieth anniversary of the March on Washington.

1984   Ronald Reagan is reelected.

Barack Obama moves to Chicago to begin organizing among South Side black churches.

1988   Jesse Jackson runs for president a second time.

1992   Violence erupts in Los Angeles in reaction to the acquittal of four LAPD officers who were videotaped beating a black man named Rodney King.

Barack Obama helps organize Project VOTE.

Bill Clinton is elected president.

Carol Moseley Braun is elected to the US Senate from Illinois.

1993   Louis Farrakhan and Benjamin Chavis are rejected by the King-Atlanta organizers of the thirtieth anniversary of the March on Washington.

1994   The Republican Party promotes its "Contract with America" and gains its first congressional majority since the end of World War II.

Tim McVeigh is charged with bombing a federal building in Oklahoma City in April.

1995   The O.J. Simpson murder trial; the verdict is decided on October 3.

The Million Man March/Day of Absence is held in Washington, D.C., on October 16. Louis Farrakhan delivers a poorly executed speech, titled "A More Perfect Union."

1997   Bill Clinton delivers a speech on race and affirmative action in San Diego, also called "A More Perfect Union," following the yearlong National Dialogue on Race headed by historian John Hope Franklin.

2001   The administration of President George W. Bush initiates war in Afghanistan after the September 11 attacks.

2003   The pastor of Trinity United Church of Christ in Chicago, Jeremiah Wright Jr., joins the opposition to the Iraq War and condemns the Bush administration in his speech, "Confusing God and Government," delivered three weeks later.

2004   Barack Obama, an Illinois state senator, is elected to the US Senate. His profile is heightened by his speech delivered at the 2004 Democratic National Convention.

2005   Hurricanes Katrina and Rita devastate major swaths of poor African American communities across five southern states in August and September. Nearly 2,000 perish. Hundreds of thousands of residents, especially in New Orleans, are temporarily or permanently displaced. Government responses are widely criticized. The economic impact approaches US$100 billion.

2007   Barack Obama announces his decision to run for president.

2008   Barack Obama emerges as the front-runner; the Democratic primaries include intense contests against Senator Hillary Rodham Clinton of New York. Jeremiah Wright Jr. becomes a prominent issue in the Obama campaign.

Barack Obama breaks with Wright and Trinity United Church of Christ.

In Philadelphia, Barack Obama delivers his speech "A More Perfect Union," which articulates his pragmatist, common-ground view of race in US politics and society.

Barack Obama wins the 2008 presidential election over John McCain, the Republican senator from Arizona.

2009   The populist grassroots coalition Taxed Enough Already (known as the Tea Party) formulates a backlash against socialism as represented in the person of Barack Obama; threats of violence permeate the dialogue.

Bibliography

Abraham, Kinfe. *Politics of Nationalism: From Harlem to Soweto*. Trenton, NJ: Africa World Press, 1991.

Adeleke, Tunde. *UnAfrican Americans: Nineteenth-Century Black Nationalists and the Civilizing Mission*. Lexington: University Press of Kentucky, 1998.

Alexander-Floyd, Nikol. *Gender, Race, and Nationalism in Contemporary Black Politics*. New York: Palgrave Macmillan, 2007.

Alkalimat, Abdul, and Doug Gills. *Harold Washington and the Crisis of Black Power in Chicago*. Chicago: Twenty-First Century Books, 1989.

Allen, Norm R., Jr., ed. *African-American Humanism: An Anthology*. Amherst, NY: Prometheus Books, 2003.

Anderson, Benedict. *Imagined Communities: Reflections on the Origin and Spread of Nationalism*. London: Verso, [1983] 2006.

Aptheker, Herbert. *Marxism and Christianity: A Symposium*. New York: Humanities Press, 1968.

Aptheker, Herbert, ed. *Prayers of Dark People*. Amherst: University of Massachusetts Press, 1980.

Arendt, Hannah. *On Violence*. San Diego: Harcourt, Brace, 1970.

———. *The Origins of Totalitarianism*. San Diego: Harcourt, Brace, 1973.

———. *The Jew as Pariah: Jewish Identity and Politics in the Modern Age*. New York: Grove, 1978.

Asante, M. K., Jr. *It's Bigger Than Hip Hop: The Rise of the Post–Hip-Hop Generation*. New York: St. Martin's, 2008.

Austin, Algernon. *Achieving Blackness: Race, Black Nationalism, and Afrocentrism in the Twentieth Century*. New York: New York University Press, 2006.

Bailyn, Bernard. *The Ideological Origins of the American Revolution*. Cambridge: Belknap Press of Harvard University Press, [1967] 1992.

Baldwin, Lewis. "Revisiting the 'All-Comprehending Black Institution': Historical Reflections on the Public Roles of Black Churches." In R. Drew Smith, ed., *New Day Begun: African American Churches and Civic Culture in Post–Civil Rights America*. Durham: Duke University Press, 2003.

Ball, Terrance, and Richard Dagger. *Political Ideologies and the Democratic Ideal*, 4th ed. New York: Addison Wesley Educational, 2002.

Banton, Michael. *Racial Theories*. Cambridge, UK: Cambridge University Press, 1987.

Bell, Howard M. "National Negro Conventions of the Middle 1840s: Moral Suasion v. Political Action." *Journal of Negro History* 22: 247–260.

Bellah, Robert N. *The Broken Covenant: American Civil Religion in Time of Trial*, 2nd ed. Chicago: University of Chicago Press, [1975] 1992.

Bercovitch, Sacvan. *The American Jeremiad*. Madison: University of Wisconsin Press, 1978.

Berger, Peter. *The Heretical Imperative: Contemporary Possibilities of Religious Affirmation*. Garden City, NY: Doubleday/Anchor Press, 1979.

Berlin, Edward A. *King of Ragtime: Scott Joplin and His Era*. New York: Oxford University Press, 1994.

Berry, Mary Frances. *Black Resistance, White Law: A History of Constitutional Racism in America*. New York: Penguin, 1994.

Bittle William E., and Gilbert Geis. *The Longest Way Home: Chief Alfred C. Sam's Back to Africa Movement*. Detroit: Wayne State University Press, 1964.

Blackwell, Unita, and JoAnne Pritchard Morris. *Barefootin': Life Lessons from the Road to Freedom*. New York: Crown, 2006.

Blauner, Robert. "Internal Colonialism and Ghetto Revolt." *Social Problems* 16 (Spring 1969): 393–408.

Blyden, Edward Wilmot. *Christianity, Islam, and the Negro Race*. Baltimore: Black Classic, [1888] 1994.

Boeke, Richard. "Black Mystic of San Francisco: A Collection of Photos and Remembrances of Dr. Thurman." *Creation Spirituality Magazine* (March/April 1991): 12–16.

Bositis, David A. "Blacks and the 1996 Elections: A Preliminary Analysis." Unpublished paper. Washington, DC: Joint Center for Political and Economic Studies, 1996.

Boyd, Todd. *Am I Black Enough for You? Popular Culture from the 'Hood and Beyond*. Bloomington: University of Indiana Press, 1997.

Boyer, Richard O. "Gestapo, U.S.A." In Samuel Sillen, ed., *Masses and Mainstream* 4, no. 1 (January 1951): 15–22.

Bracey, John H., Jr. *Primary Sources in U.S. History*, and *Primary Sources in African American History*. Black Power manuscripts selected from the UPA microfilm research collections, part 3: Papers of the Revolutionary Action Movement, 1964–1975 (55 documents). Available at http://cisweb.lexisnexis.com/images/histuniv/img/PrimarySourcesUS.pdf.

Bracey, John H., Jr., August Meier, and Elliott Rudwick, eds. *Black Nationalism in America*. Indianapolis: Bobbs-Merrill, 1970.

Breitman, George, ed. *Malcolm X Speaks: Selected Speeches and Statements*. New York: Grove, 1965.

———. *The Last Year of Malcolm X: The Evolution of a Revolutionary*. New York: Pathfinder, 1967.

———, ed. *By Any Means Necessary: Speeches, Interviews, and Letters by Malcolm X*. New York: Pathfinder, 1970.

———. *Leon Trotsky on Black Nationalism and Self Determination*, 2nd ed. New York: Pathfinder, 1978.

Breitman, George, Herman Porter, and Baxter Smith. *The Assassination of Malcolm X*. New York: Pathfinder, [1976], 1991.

Brossard, Mario A., and Michael A. Fletcher. "Last Year's Gathering Has Lasting Effects, Poll Says." *Washington Post*, October 16, 1996, p. A14.

Brown, Elaine. *A Taste of Power: A Black Woman's Story*. New York: Anchor, 1994.

Brown, Lloyd. *Amiri Baraka*. Boston: Twayne Publishers, 1980.

Brown, Robert A., and Todd C. Shaw. "Separate Nations: Two Attitudinal Dimensions of Black Nationalism." *Journal of Politics* 64, no. 1 (2002): 22–44.

Brown, Wendy, ed. *Politics out of History*. Princeton: Princeton University Press, 2001.

Browning, Rufus P., Dale Rogers Marshall, and David H. Tabb, eds. *Racial Politics in American Cities*, 2nd ed. New York: Longman, 1997.

Burnham, Walter Dean. *Critical Elections and the Mainsprings of American Politics*. New York: W. W. Norton, 1970.

Bush, Rod, ed. *The New Black Vote: Politics and Power in Four American Cities*. San Francisco: Synthesis, 1984.

———. *We Are Not What We Seem: Black Nationalism and Class Struggle in the American Century*. New York: New York University Press, 1999.

Butler, Kim. *Freedoms Given, Freedoms Won: Afro-Brazilians in Post-Abolition São Paulo and Salvador*. New Brunswick, NJ: Rutgers University Press, 1998.

Campbell, Angus, Philip E. Converse, Warren E. Miller, and Donald E. Stokes. *The American Voter*. New York: John Wiley and Sons, 1960.

Carbado, Devon W., and Donald Weise, eds. *Time on Two Crosses: The Collected Writings of Bayard Rustin*. San Francisco: Cleis, 2003.

Carew, Jan R. *Ghosts in Our Blood: With Malcolm X in Africa, England, and the Caribbean*. New York: Lawrence Hill, 1994.

Carlisle, Rodney. *The Roots of Black Nationalism*. Port Washington, NY: Kennikat, 1975.

Carmines, Edward G., John P. Mclever, and James A. Stimson. "Unrealized Partisanship: A Theory of Dealignment." *Journal of Politics* 49, no. 2 (1987): 376–400.

Carmines, Edward G., and James A. Stimson. "Issue Evolution, Population Replacement, and Normal Partisan Change." *American Political Science Review* 75 (1981): 107–118.

———. *Issue Evolution*. Princeton: Princeton University Press, 1989.

Carr, Robert. *Black Nationalism in the New World: Reading the African-American and West Indian Experience*. Durham, NC: Duke University Press, 2002.

Carson, Clayborne, ed. *The Autobiography of Martin Luther King, Jr*. New York: Warner, 1998.

———. *Malcolm X: The FBI File*. New York: Carroll and Graf, 1991.

Chapman, Mark L. *Christianity on Trial: African American Religious Thought Before and After Black Power*. Maryknoll, NY: Orbis Books, 1996.

Cheney, Charise L. *Brothers Gonna Work It Out: Sexual Politics in the Golden Age of Rap Nationalism*. New York: New York University Press, 2005.

Clarke, Cheryl. *"After Mecca": Women Poets and the Black Arts Movement*. New Brunswick, NJ: Rutgers University Press, 2005.

Clarke, Kamari Maxine, and Deborah A. Thomas. *Globalization and Race: Transformation in the Cultural Production of Blackness*. Durham, NC: Duke University Press, 2006.

Clayton, Dewey M. *The Presidential Campaign of Barack Obama: A Critical Analysis of a Racially Transcendent Strategy*. New York: Routledge, 2010.

Cleage, Albert B., Jr. *The Black Messiah*. New York: Sheed and Ward, 1968.

———. *Black Christian Nationalism*. New York: Morrow, 1972.

Cleaver, Eldridge. *Soul on Ice*. New York: Dell, 1968.

Clegg, Claude Andrew, III. *An Original Man: The Life and Times of Elijah Muhammad.* New York: St. Martin's, 1997.

Clubb, Jerome M., William M. Flaningan, and Nancy H. Zingale. *Partisan Realignment: Voters and Government in American History.* Beverly Hills, CA: Sage Library of Social Research, 1980.

Cobb, William Jelani. *The Essential Harold Cruse.* New York: Palgrave, 2002.

Cobbs, Price, and William Grier. *The Jesus Bag.* New York: McGraw-Hill, 1971.

Cohen, Cathy J. *The Boundaries of Blackness: AIDS and the Breakdown of Black Politics.* Chicago: University of Chicago Press, 1999.

Cohen, Cathy J., and Michael C. Dawson. "Neighborhood Poverty and African American Politics." *American Political Science Review* 87, no. 2 (June 1993): 286–303.

Colaiaco, James A. *Frederick Douglass and the Fourth of July.* New York: Palgrave/ Macmillan, 2007.

Colbert, David. *Michelle Obama: An American Story.* Boston: Sandpiper/Houghton Mifflin Harcourt, 2009.

Collins, Patricia Hill. *Black Feminist Thought: Knowledge, Consciousness, and the Politics of Empowerment,* 2nd ed. New York: Routledge, 2000.

———. *From Black Power to Hip Hop: Racism, Nationalism, and Feminism.* Philadelphia: Temple University Press, 2006.

Collins, Rodnell P., with A. Peter Bailey. *Seventh Child: A Family Memoir of Malcolm X.* New York: Kensington, 1998.

Cone, James H. *The Spirituals and the Blues: An Interpretation.* Maryknoll, NY: Orbis Books, [1972] 1991.

———. *Martin and Malcolm and America: A Dream or a Nightmare.* Maryknoll, NY: Orbis Books, 1999.

———. *God of the Oppressed.* Maryknoll, NY: Orbis Books, 1997.

Corsi, Jerome R. *The Obama Nation: Leftist Politics and the Cult of Personality.* New York: Threshold Editions, 2008.

Cose, Ellis. *The Rage of a Privileged Class: Why Are Middle-Class Blacks Angry? Why Should America Care?* New York: HarperPerennial, 1993.

Craig, Robert H. *Religion and Radical Politics: An Alternative Christian Tradition in the United States.* Philadelphia: Temple University Press, 1992.

Crenshaw, Kimberlé. "Demarginalizing the Intersection of Sex and Race: A Black Feminist Critique of Antidiscrimination Doctrine, Feminist Theory, and Antiracist Politics" (University of Chicago Legal Forum, 1989). In Joy James and T. Denean Sharpley-Whiting, eds., *The Black Feminist Reader.* Oxford, UK: Blackwell, 2000.

———. "Mapping the Margins: Intersectionality, Identity Politics, and Violence Against Women of Color." *Stanford Law Review* 43 (1991): 1241–1299.

Cronon, Edmond David. *Black Moses: The Story of Marcus Garvey and the Universal Negro Improvement Association.* Madison: University of Wisconsin Press, 1955.

Cross, Theodore, and Robert Bruce Slater. "The 1996 Elections: The Real Victor Was Black Voter Apathy." *Journal of Blacks in Higher Education* 14 (Winter 1996): 120–127.

Crowe, Daniel L. *Prophets of Rage: The Black Freedom Struggles in San Francisco, 1945–1969.* New York: Garland, 2000.

Cruse, Harold. *The Crisis of the Negro Intellectual.* New York: Quill, [1967] 1984.

———. *Plural but Equal: Blacks and Minorities in America's Plural Society.* New York: Quill, 1987.

———. "New Black Leadership Required." *New Politics* 2 (1990): 39–49.

Cullen, Countee. *The Black Christ and Other Poems.* New York: Harper and Brothers, 1929.

Curtis, Edward E., IV. *Islam in Black America: Identity, Liberation, and Difference in African-American Islamic Thought*. Albany: State University of New York Press, 2002.

———. *Black Muslim Religion in the Nation of Islam, 1960–1975*. Chapel Hill: University of North Carolina Press, 2006.

Dahl, Robert. *Who Governs? Democracy and Power in an American City*. New Haven: Yale University Press, 1961.

Davis, Darren W., and Ronald E. Brown, "The Antipathy of Black Nationalism: Behavioral and Attitudinal Implications of an African American Ideology." *American Journal of Political Science* 46, no. 2 (April 2002): 239–253.

Dawson, Michael C. *Behind the Mule: Race and Class in African-American Politics*. Princeton: Princeton University Press, 1994.

———. *Black Visions: The Roots of Contemporary African-American Political Ideologies*. Chicago: University of Chicago Press, 2001.

DeCaro, Louis A. *On the Side of My People: A Religious Life of Malcolm X*. New York: New York University Press, 1997.

———. *Malcolm and the Cross: The Nation of Islam, Malcolm X, and Christianity*. New York: New York University Press, 1998.

Delany, Martin R. *The Condition, Elevation, Emigration, and Destiny of the Colored People of the United States*. Baltimore: Black Classic, [1852] 1993.

de Tocqueville, Alexis. *Democracy in America*, edited by J. P. Mayer. New York: Harper and Row, 1966.

De Zutter, Hank. "What Makes Obama Run?" *Chicago Reader*, December 8, 1995. Available at http://www.chicagoreader.com/obama/951208/.

Douglass, Kelly. *The Black Christ*. Maryknoll, NY: Orbis, 1994.

Drake, St. Clair, and Horace R. Cayton. *Black Metropolis: A Study of Negro Life in a Northern City*, vol. 2. New York: Harper TorchBooks, 1962.

Draper, Theodore. *The Rediscovery of Black Nationalism*. London: Secker and Warburg, 1970.

Du Bois, W.E.B. *The World and Africa: An Inquiry into the Part Which Africa Has Played in World History*. New York: International Publishers, [1947] 1979.

———. *Dusk of Dawn: An Essay Toward an Autobiography of a Race Concept*. Piscataway, NJ: Transaction, [1940] 1984.

———. *The Souls of Black Folk*. New York: Bantam Books, [1903] 1989.

———, with an Introduction by David Levering Lewis. *Black Reconstruction: An Essay Toward a History of the Part Which Black Folk Played in the Attempt to Reconstruct Democracy in America, 1860–1880*. New York: Free Press, 1995.

Dyson, Eric Michael. *Making Malcolm: The Myth and Meaning of Malcolm X*. New York: Oxford University Press, 1995.

———. *Between God and Gangsta Rap: Bearing Witness to Black Culture*. Oxford, UK: Oxford University Press, 1996.

———. *I May Not Get There with You: The True Martin Luther King, Jr*. New York: Touchstone, 2000.

Ehrenreich, Barbara, and John Ehrenreich. *Long March, Short Spring: The Student Uprising at Home and Abroad*. New York: Monthly Review, 1969.

Essien-Udom, E. U. *Black Nationalism: A Search for an Identity in America*. Chicago: University of Chicago Press, 1962.

Eure, Joseph D., and Richard M. Jerome, eds. *Back Where We Belong: Selected Speeches by Minister Louis Farrakhan*. Philadelphia: PC International Press, 1989.

Evanzz, Karl. *The Judas Factor: The Plot to Kill Malcolm X*. New York: Thunder's Mouth, 1993.

———. *The Messenger: The Rise and Fall of Elijah Muhammad*. New York: Pantheon Books, 1999.

Fanon, Frantz. *The Wretched of the Earth*. New York: Grove, 1963.

———. *Black Skin, White Masks*. New York: Grove, 1967.

Fauset, Arthur Huff. *Black Gods of the Metropolis: Negro Religious Cults of the Urban North*. New York: Octagon Books, 1970.

Ferris, Jeri Chase. *Demanding Justice: A Story About Mary Ann Shadd Cary*. Minneapolis: Carolrhoda Books, 2003.

Fierce, Milfred C. *The Pan-African Idea in the United States, 1900–1919: African American Interest in Africa and Interaction in West Africa*. New York: Garland, 1993.

Fleming, Cynthia. *Soon We Will Not Cry: The Liberation of Ruby Doris Smith Robinson*. Lanham, MD: Rowman and Littlefield, 1998.

Fluker, Walter Earl, and Catherine Tumber, eds. *A Strange Freedom: The Best of Howard Thurman on Religious Experience and Public Life*. Boston: Beacon, 1998.

Flynn, Joyce, and Joyce Occomy Stricklin, eds. *Frye Street and Environs: Collected Works of Marita Bonner*. Boston: Beacon, 1987.

Foeman, Anita K. "Gloria Richardson: Breaking the Mold." *Journal of Black Studies* 26, no. 5 (May 1996): 604–615.

Foner, Philip S. *American Socialism and Black Americans: From the Age of Jackson to World War II*. Westport, CT: Greenwood, 1977.

———, ed. *Black Socialist Preacher: The Teachings of Reverend George Washington Woodbey and His Disciple, Reverend G. W. Slater, Jr.* San Francisco: Synthesis, 1983.

Formicola, Jo Renee, and Hubert Morken, eds. *Religious Leaders and Faith-Based Politics*. Lanham, MD: Rowman and Littlefield, 2001.

Fox, Stephen R. *The Guardian of Boston*. New York: Atheneum, 1970.

Franklin, John Hope. *The Free Negro in North Carolina, 1790–1860*. Chapel Hill: University of North Carolina Press, 1995.

———. *The Militant South, 1800–1861*. Urbana: University of Illinois Press, [1956] 2002.

Frazier, E. Franklin. *The Negro Church in America*. New York: Schocken Books, 1964.

Frazier, E. Franklin, and C. Eric Lincoln. *The Negro Church in America: The Black Church Since Frazier*. New York: Schocken Books, 1974.

Freddoso, David. *The Case Against Barack Obama: The Unlikely Rise and Unexamined Agenda of the Media's Favorite Candidate*. Washington, DC: Regnery, 2008.

Freeden, Michael. "Is Nationalism a Distinct Ideology?" *Political Studies* 46, no. 4 (1998): 748–765.

Gaines, Kevin K. *Uplifting the Race: Black Leadership, Politics, and Culture in the Twentieth Century*. Chapel Hill: University of North Carolina Press, 1996.

Gardell, Mattias. *In the Name of Elijah Muhammad: Louis Farrakhan and the Nation of Islam*. Durham, NC: Duke University Press, 1996.

Garvey, Amy Jacques. *Garvey and Garveyism*. New York: Macmillan, 1970.

Gates, Henry Louis, Jr., and Cornel West. *The Future of the Race*. New York: Vintage, 1996.

Geertz, Clifford. *The Interpretation of Culture*. New York: Basic Books, 1973.

Genovese, Eugene. *Roll, Jordan, Roll: The World the Slaves Made*. New York: Vintage, 1972.

Giddings, Paula. *When and Where I Enter: The Impact of Black Women on Race and Sex in America*. New York: Bantam Books, 1988.

Gilliam, Reginald Earl, Jr. *Black Political Development*. Port Washington, NY: Kennikat, 1975.

Gilroy, Paul. *The Black Atlantic: Modernity and Double Consciousness*. New York: Verso.

Glasrud, Bruce A., and Cary D. Wintz, eds. *African Americans and the Presidency: The Road to the White House*. New York: Routledge, 2010.

Glaude, Eddie S. Jr, *Exodus!: Religion, Race, and Nation in the Early Nineteenth Century in Black America*. Chicago: University of Chicago Press, 2001.

———, ed. *Is It Nation Time? Contemporary Essays on Black Power and Black Nationalism*. Chicago: University of Chicago Press, 2002.

Goldberg, David Theo. *The Racial State*. Malden, MA: Blackwell, 2002.

Green, Adam. *Selling the Race: Culture, Community, and Black Chicago, 1940–1955*. Chicago: University of Chicago Press, 2007.

Greene, Thomas H. *Comparative Revolutionary Movements: Search for Theory and Justice*, 3rd ed. Englewood Cliffs, NJ: Prentice Hall, 1999.

Grier, William H., and Price M. Cobbs. *Black Rage*. New York: Basic Books, 1968.

Grimshaw, William J. *Bitter Fruit: Black Politics and the Chicago Machine, 1931–1991*. Chicago: University of Chicago Press, 1992.

Gurin, Patricia, Shirley Hatchett, and James S. Jackson. *Hope and Independence: Blacks' Response to Electoral and Party Politics*. New York: Russell Sage, 1990.

Gwaltney, John Langston. *Drylongso: A Self-Portrait of Black America*. New York: The New Press, 1993.

Hacker, Andrew. *Two Nations: Black and White, Separate, Hostile, and Unequal*. New York: Ballantine Books, 1992.

Hair, William Ivy. *Carnival of Fury: Robert Charles and the New Orleans Race Riot of 1900*. Baton Rouge: Louisiana State University Press, 1976.

Haley, Alex. *The Autobiography of Malcolm X*. New York: Random House, 1964.

Hamilton, Charles. *The Black Preacher in America*. New York: Morrow, 1972

Harding, Vincent. *There Is a River: The Black Struggle for Freedom in America*. San Diego: Harcourt Brace, 1981.

Harris-Lacewell, Melissa Victoria. *Barbershops, Bibles, and BET: Everyday Talk and Black Political Thought*. Princeton: Princeton University Press, 2004.

Hartudo, Aida. *The Color of Privilege: Three Blasphemies on Race and Feminism*. Ann Arbor: University of Michigan Press, 1996.

Harvey, David. *A Brief History of Neoliberalism*. New York: Oxford University Press, 2005.

Hayes, Carlton J.H. *Nationalism: A Religion*. New York: Macmillan, 1960.

Henry, Charles P. *Culture and African American Politics*. Bloomington: Indiana University Press, 1990.

Higginbotham, Evelyn Brooks. *Righteous Discontent: The Women's Movement in the Black Baptist Church, 1880–1920*. Cambridge: Harvard University Press, 1993.

Higginson, Thomas Wentworth. *Black Rebellion: Five Slave Revolts*. New York: Da Capo, [1969] 1998.

Hill, Herbert, ed. *Anger and Beyond: The Negro Writer in the United States*. New York: Harper and Row, 1966.

Hill, Robert A., ed. *Marcus Garvey and the Universal Negro Improvement Association Papers*, vol. 3. Berkeley: University of California Press, 1987.

Hinks, Peter P. *To Awaken My Afflicted Brethren: David Walker and the Problem of Antebellum Slave Resistance*. University Park: Pennsylvania State University Press, 1997.

Hobsbawm, E. J. *Nations and Nationalism Since 1780: Programme, Myth, Reality*, 2nd ed. New York: Cambridge University Press, 1992.

hooks, bell. *Teaching to Transgress: Education as the Practice of Freedom*. London: Routledge, 1994.

———. *Killing Rage: Ending Racism*. New York: Owl Books, 1995.

Hopkins, Dwight N. *Introduction to Black Theology of Liberation*. Maryknoll, NY: Orbis Books, 1999.

———. *Heart and Head: Black Theology—Past, Present, and Future*. New York: Palgrave, 2002.

Howard-Pitney, David. *The Afro-American Jeremiad: Appeals for Justice in America*. Philadelphia: Temple University Press, 1990.

———. "Frederick Douglass: Abolitionist and Political Leader." *African-American Humanism: An Anthology*, edited by Norm R. Allen Jr. Amherst, NY: Prometheus Books, 1991.

Ignatiev, Noel. *How the Irish Became White*. New York: Routledge, 1995.

Jacobs, Donald M. *Courage and Conscience: Black and White Abolitionist in Boston*. Bloomington: Indiana University Press, 1993.

James, C.L.R. *The Black Jacobins: Toussaint L'Ouverture and the San Domingo Revolution*, 2nd ed. New York: Vintage, [1963] 1989.

James, Joy. *Transcending the Talented Tenth: Black Leaders and American Intellectuals*. New York: Routledge, 1997.

James, Winston. *Holding Aloft the Banner of Ethiopia*. London: Verso, 1998.

Johnson, Cedric. *Revolutionaries to Race Leaders: Black Power and the Making of African American Politics*. Minneapolis: University of Minnesota Press, 2007.

Johnson, Paul E. *African-American Christianity: Essays in History*. Berkeley: University of California Press, 1994.

Jones, William R. *Is God a White Racist? A Preamble to Black Theology*. Garden City, NY: Anchor/Doubleday, 1973.

Jordan, June. *Civil Wars: Observations from the Frontlines of America*. New York: Touchstone, 1981.

Jordan, Winthrop D. *White over Black: American Attitudes Toward the Negro, 1550–1812*. Chapel Hill: University of North Carolina Press, 1968.

Joseph, Peniel E. *Waiting 'Til the Midnight Hour: A Narrative History of Black Power in America*. New York: Owl Books, 2006.

———. *Dark Days, Bright Nights: From Black Power to Barack Obama*. New York: BasicCivitas, 2010.

Joyner, Charles. "Believer I Know: The Emergence of African-American Christianity." In Paul E. Johnson, ed., *African-American Christianity: Essays in History*. Berkeley: University of California Press, 1994.

Karim, Imam Benjamin, ed. *The End of White World Supremacy: Four Speeches of Malcolm X*. New York: Arcade, 1971.

Katznelson, Ira. *City Trenches: Urban Politics and the Patterning of Class in the United States*. New York: Pantheon, 1981.

Keil, Charles. *Urban Blues*. Chicago: University of Chicago Press, 1966.

Kelley, Raina. "A Real Wife, in a Real Marriage: An Outspoken, Smart Black Woman or a Bossy, Emasculating Wife? Michelle Obama Defies Stereotypes, but Cannot Escape Them Either." *Newsweek*, February 25, 2008, p. 35.

Kelley, Robyn D.G. *Race Rebels: Culture, Politics, and the Black Working Class*. New York: The Free Press, 1994.

———. *Yo' Mama's Dysfunktional! Fighting the Cultural Wars in Urban America*. Boston: Beacon, 1998.

———. *The Vinyl Ain't Final: Hip-Hop and the Globalization of Black Popular Culture*. New York: Pluto, 2006.

Kennedy, Randall. *Race, Crime, and the Law*. New York: Vintage Books, 1997.

Key, V. O. *Southern Politics in State and Nation*. New York: Alfred Knopf, 1949.

———. "A Theory of Critical Elections." *Journal of Politics* 17 (1955): 3–18.

Kilson, Martin. "The Interaction of the Black Mainstream Leadership and the Far-rakhan Extremists." In Ishmael Reed, *MultiAmerica* (New York: Penguin Books, 1997), pp. 238–245.

King, Martin Luther Jr. *Where Do We Go from Here: Chaos or Community?* Boston: Beacon Hill Press, 1967.

———. "A Testament of Hope." In James M. Washington, ed., *A Testament of Hope: The Essential Writings and Speeches of Martin Luther King, Jr.* San Francisco: HarperCollins, 1986.

Kitwana, Bakari. *The Hip-Hop Generation: Young Blacks and the Crisis in African-American Culture*. New York: BasicCivitas, 2002.

Knight, Michael Muhammad. *The Five Percenters: Islam, Hip Hop, and the Gods of New York*. Oxford, UK: Oneworld, 2007.

Kofsky, Frank. *Black Nationalism and the Revolution in Music*. New York: Pathfinder, 1970.

Kornberg, Jacques. *Theodor Herzl: From Assimilation to Zionism*. Bloomington: Indiana University Press, 1993.

Kovel, Joel. *White Racism: A Psychohistory*. New York: Vintage Books, 1970.

Kurlander, Gabrielle, and Jackie Salit, eds. *Independent Black Leadership in America: Minister Louis Farrakhan, Dr. Lenora Fulani, Reverend Al Sharpton*. New York: Castillo International, 1990.

Lee, Martha F. *The Nation of Islam: An American Millenarian Movement*. Syracuse: Syracuse University Press, 1996.

Levine, Lawrence. *Black Culture and Black Consciousness: Afro American Folk Thought from Slave to Freedom*. New York: Oxford University Press, 1977.

Lewis, David Levering. "Parallels and Divergences: Assimilationist Strategies of Afro-American and Jewish Elites, 1910 to the Early Thirties." *Journal of American History* 71 (December 1984): 543–567.

———. *W.E.B. Du Bois: Biography of a Race, 1868–1919*. New York: Henry Holt, 1993.

———, ed. *The Portable Harlem Renaissance Reader*. New York: Penguin Books, 1994.

———. *W.E.B. Du Bois, 1919–1963: The Fight for Equality and the American Century*. New York: Henry Holt, 2000.

Lincoln, C. Eric. *The Black Muslims in America*, 3rd ed. Grand Rapids, MI: William B. Eerdmans, and Trenton, NJ: Africa World, [1961] 1994.

———. *Race, Religion, and the Continuing American Dilemma*. New York: Hill and Wang, 1999.

Lincoln, C. Eric, and Lawrence H. Mamiya. *The Black Church in the African American Experience*. Durham, NC: Duke University Press, 1990.

Lipset, Seymour Martin, and Gary Marks. *It Didn't Happen Here: Why Socialism Failed in the United States*. New York: W. W. Norton, 2000.

Litwack, Leon. *Been in the Storm So Long: The Aftermath of Slavery*. New York: Vintage, 1980.

Logan, Rayford W. *The Betrayal of the Negro: From Rutherford B. Hayes to Woodrow Wilson*. New York: Da Capo, 1997.

Louis, Debbie. *And We Are Not Saved: A History of the Movement as People*. Garden City, NY: Doubleday, 1970.

Lorde, Audre. *Sister Outsider: Essays and Speeches*. Freedom, CA: Crossing, 1984.

Lubiano, Wahneema, ed. *The House That Race Built*. New York: Vintage Books, 1998.

Magida, Arthur J. *Prophet of Rage: A Life of Louis Farrakhan and His Nation*. New York: Basic Books, 1996.

Marable, Manning. "Booker T. Washington and African Nationalism." *Phylon: The Atlanta University Review of Race and Culture* 35, no. 4 (March 1974): 398–406.

———. *Beyond Black and White: Transforming African American Politics*. New York: Verso, 1995.

———. *Black Leadership: Four Great American Leaders and the Struggle for Civil Rights*. New York: Penguin Books, 1998.

———. "Black Fundamentalism and Conservative Black Nationalism." *Race and Class* 39, no. 4 (April–June 1998): 1–22.

Marquesee, Mike. *Redemption Song: Muhammad Ali and the Spirit of the Sixties*. London: Verso, 1999.

Marsh, Clifton E. *The Lost-Found Nation in America*. Lanham, MD: Scarecrow, 2000.

Martin, Tony. *Race First: The Ideological and Organizational Struggles of Marcus Garvey and the Universal Negro Improvement Association*. New York: Greenwood, 1976.

Marx, Gary T. *Protest and Prejudice: A Study of Belief in the Black Community*, rev. ed. New York: Harper TorchBooks, 1967.

Mayer, J. P., ed. *Democracy in America,* by Alexis de Tocqueville. New York: Harper and Row, 1966.

Mays, Benjamin. *The Negro's God as Reflected in His Literature*. New York: Simon and Schuster, [1938] 1968.

McAdoo, Bill. *Pre–Civil War Black Nationalism*. New York: David Walker, 1983.

McCartney, John T. *Black Power Ideologies: An Essay in African American Political Thought*. Philadelphia: Temple University Press, 1992.

McClain, Paula D., and Joe Stewart. *"Can't We All Just Get Along?" Racial and Ethnic Minorities in American Politics*, 2nd ed. New York: Westview, 1998.

McCormick, Joseph, II, and Sekou Franklin. "Expressions of Racial Consciousness in the African American Community: Data from the Million Man March." In Yvette M. Alex-Assensoh and Lawrence Hanks, eds., *Black and Multiracial Politics in America*. New York: New York University Press, 2000.

McKoy, Sheila Smith. *When Whites Riot: Writing Race and Violence in American and South African Cultures*. Madison: University of Wisconsin Press, 2001.

McGavran, Donald A., and C. Peter Wagner. *Understanding Church Growth*, 3rd ed. Grand Rapids, MI: William B. Eerdmans, [1970] 1990.

McGraw, Barbara A., and Jo Renee Formicola, eds. *Taking Religious Pluralism Seriously: Spiritual Politics on America's Sacred Ground*. Waco, TX: Baylor University Press, 2005.

Miller, Floyd J., ed. *Blake, or The Huts of America: A Novel by Martin R. Delany*. Boston: Beacon, 1970.

Miller, Perry, ed. *The American Puritans: Their Prose and Poetry*. New York: Columbia University Press, 1956a.

———. *Errand into the Wilderness*. Cambridge: Belknap Press of Harvard University Press, 1956b.

Milnner, Sandra Y. "Recasting Civil Rights Leadership: Gloria Richardson and the Cambridge Movement." *Journal of Black Studies* 26, no. 6 (July 1996): 668–687.

Morris, Lorenzo, ed. *The Social and Political Implications of the 1984 Jesse Jackson Campaign*. New York: Praeger Publishers, 1990.

Moses, Wilson Jeremiah. *The Golden Age of Black Nationalism, 1850–1925*. New York: Oxford University Press, 1978.

——. *Black Messiahs and Uncle Toms: Social and Literary Manipulations of a Religious Myth*. University Park: Pennsylvania State University Press, 1982.

——, ed. *Classical Black Nationalism: From the American Revolution to Marcus Garvey*. New York: New York University Press, 1996.

——. *Afrotopia: The Roots of African American Popular History*. New York: Cambridge University Press, 1998.

Mosse, George L. *Toward the Final Solution: A History of European Racism*. New York: Howard Fertig, 1978.

Mughan, Anthony, and Samuel C. Patterson. *Political Leadership in Democratic Societies*. Chicago: Nelson-Hall Publishing, 1992.

Mundy, Liz. *Michelle: A Biography*. New York: Simon and Schuster, 2008.

Mutua, Athena D. *Progressive Black Masculinities*. New York: Routledge, 2006.

Myerson, Gregory. "Rethinking Black Marxism: Reflections on Cedric Robinson and Others." *Cultural Logic: An Electronic Journal of Marxist Theory and Practice* 3, no. 2 (Spring 2000). Available at http://eserver.org/clogic/31%262/myerson.html.

Myerson, Michael. *Nothing Could Be Finer*. New York: International Publishers, 1978.

Myrdal, Gunnar. *An American Dilemma*. New York: Harper and Brothers, 1944.

Natambu, Kofi. *The Life and Work of Malcolm X*. Indianapolis: Alpha Books, 2002.

Nealy, Lisa Nikol. *African American Women Voters: Racializing Religiosity, Political Consciousness and Progressive Political Action in U.S. Presidential Elections from 1964 Through 2008*. Lanham, MD: University Press of America, 2008.

Nelsen, Hart M., and Anne Kusener Nelsen. *Black Church in the Sixties*. Lexington: University of Kentucky Press, 1975.

Nelson, Michael, ed. *The Elections of 1996*. Washington, DC: Congressional Quarterly, 1997.

Newton, Huey P. *To Die for the People*. New York: Writers and Readers, 1995.

Nkrumah, Kwame. *Consciencism: Philosophy and Ideology for Decolonization*. New York: Monthly Review, [1964] 1970.

Obama, Barack. *Dreams from My Father: A Story of Race and Inheritance*. New York: Three Rivers, [1995] 2004.

——. *The Audacity of Hope: Thoughts on Reclaiming the American Dream*. New York: Vintage Books, 2006.

Ogunleye, Tolagbe. "Dr. Martin Robison Delany, 19th-Century African American Womanist: Reflections on His Avant-Garde Politics Concerning Gender, Colorism, and Nation Building." *Journal of Black Studies* 28, no. 5 {May 1998): 628–649.

Orren, Karen, and Stephen Skowronek. *The Search for American Political Development*. New York: Cambridge University Press, 2004.

Owens, Michael Leo. *God and Government in the Ghetto*. Chicago: University of Chicago Press, 2007.

Painter, Nell Irvin. "Martin R. Delany: Elitism and Black Nationalism." In Leon Litwack and August Meier, eds., *Black Leaders of the Nineteenth Century*. Urbana: University of Illinois Press, 1988.

——. *Exodusters: Black Migration to Kansas After Reconstruction*. New York: W. W. Norton, 1992.

Patterson, Orlando. *The Ordeal of Integration: Progress and Resentment in America's "Racial Crisis."* New York: BasicCivitas, 1997.

——. *Rituals of Blood: Consequences of Slavery in Two American Centuries*. New York: BasicCivitas, 1998.

Perry, Bruce, ed. *Malcolm X: The Last Speeches*. New York Pathfinder, 1989.

——. *Malcolm: The Life of a Man Who Changed Black America*. Barrytown, NY: Station Hill, 1991.

Perry, Jeffrey B., ed. *A Hubert Harrison Reader*. Middletown, CT: Wesleyan University Press, 2001.

Peters, James S., II. *The Spirit of David Walker: The Obscure Hero*. Lanham, MD: University Press of America, 2002.

Pinderhughes, Dianne. "An Examination of Chicago Politics for Evidence of Political Incorporation and Representation." In Rufus Browning, Dale Rogers Marshall, and David H. Tabb, eds., *Racial Politics in American Cities*, 2nd ed. New York: Longman, 1997, pp. 119–122.

Pohlmann, Marcus D. *Black Politics in Conservative America*, 2nd ed. New York: Addison Wesley Longman, 1999.

Powell, Kevin. *Keepin' It Real: Post-MTV Reflections on Race, Sex, and Politics*. New York: One World/Ballantine, 1997.

Quarles, Benjamin. *Black Abolitionists*. New York: Da Capo, 1969.

Rabinowitz, Howard N., ed. *Southern Black Leaders of the Reconstruction Era*. Urbana: University of Illinois Press, 1982.

Raboteau, Albert J. *Slave Religion: The "Invisible Institution" in the Antebellum South*. New York: Oxford University Press, 1978.

Rampersad, Arnold. "The Color of His Eyes: Bruce Perry's Malcolm and Malcolm's Malcolm." In Joe Wood, ed., *Malcolm X: In Our Own Image*. New York: St. Martin's, 1992.

Ransby, Barbara. *Ella Baker and the Black Freedom Movement: A Radical Democratic Vision*. Chapel Hill: University of North Carolina Press, 2003.

Redkey, Edwin S. *Black Exodus: Black Nationalist and Back-to-Africa Movements, 1890–1910*. New Haven: Yale University Press, 1969.

———, ed. *Respect Black: The Writings and Speeches of Bishop Henry McNeal Turner*. New York: Arno, 1971.

Reed, Adolph, Jr. *The Jesse Jackson Phenomenon*. New Haven: Yale University Press, 1986.

———, ed. *Race, Politics, and Culture: Critical Essays on the Radicalism of the 1960s*. New York: Greenwood, 1986.

———. *Stirrings in the Jug: Black Politics in the Post-Segregation Era*. Minneapolis: University of Minnesota Press, 1999.

———. *Class Notes: Posing as Politics and Other Thoughts on the American Scene*. New York: The New Press, 2000.

Reed, Ishmael. *MultiAmerica*. New York: Penguin Books, 1997.

Reid-Merritt, Patricia. *Sister Power: How Phenomenal Black Women Are Rising to the Top*. New York: John Wiley and Sons, 1996.

Remnick, David. *The Bridge: The Life and Rise of Barack Obama*. New York: Borzoi/Alfred Knopf, 2010.

Renard, John. *Responses to 101 Questions on Islam*. New York: Paulist, 1998.

Richardson, Marilyn. *Maria W. Stewart: America's First Black Woman Political Writer*. Bloomington: Indiana University Press, 1987.

Rickford, Russell. *Betty Shabazz: Her Life with Malcolm X and Fight to Preserve His Legacy*. Naperville, IL: Sourcebooks, 2003.

Rivers, Eugene, III. "Beyond the Nationalism of Fools: Toward an Agenda for Black Intellectuals." *Boston Review* 20 (Summer 1995): 16–18.

Roberts, J. Deotis. *A Black Political Theology*. Louisville, KY: Westminster John Knox, 1974.

Robertson, David. *Denmark Vesey: The Buried Story of America's Largest Slave Rebellion and the Man Who Led It*. New York: Vintage Books, 1999.

Robinson, Cedric J. *Black Marxism: The Making of the Black Radical Tradition.* London: Zed, 1983.

Robinson, Deane E. *Black Nationalism in American Politics and Thought.* New York: Cambridge University Press, 2001.

Robinson, Randall. *Quitting America: The Departure of a Black Man from His Native Land.* New York: Penguin Group, 2005.

Rogers, J. A., and John Henrik Clarke. *World's Great Men of Color, Volume I: Asia and Africa, and Historical Figures Before Christ, Including Aesop, Hannibal, Cleopatra, Zenobia, Askia the Great, and Many Others.* New York: Touchstone, [1946] 1996.

Rose, Tricia. *Rap Music and Black Culture in Contemporary America.* Middletown, CT: Wesleyan University Press, 1994.

Russell, Jean. *God's Lost Cause: A Study of the Church and the Racial Problem.* Valley Forge, PA: Judson, 1969.

Rustin, Bayard. "From Protest to Politics: The Future of the Civil Rights Movement." *Commentary* 39, no. 2 (1965): 25–31.

Sabato, Larry, ed. *Toward the Millennium: The Elections of 1996.* Boston: Allyn and Bacon, 1997.

Sales, William W. *From Civil Rights to Black Power: Malcolm X and the Organization of Afro-American Unity.* Boston: South End, 1994.

Salmon, Lester. "Leadership and Modernization: The Emerging Black Political Elite in the American South." *Journal of Politics*, no. 35 (1973): 615–646.

Sartre, Jean-Paul. *Anti-Semite and Jew.* New York: Schocken Books, 1948.

Sawyer, Mary R. *Black Ecumenism: Implementing the Demands of Justice.* Valley Forge, PA: Trinity Press International, 1994.

Segal, Ronald. *Islam's Black Slaves: The Other Black Diaspora.* New York: Farrar, Straus and Giroux, 2001.

Self, Robert O. *American Babylon: Race and the Struggle for Postwar Oakland.* Princeton: Princeton University Press, 2003.

Sensbach, Jon F. *A Separate Canaan: The Making of an Afro-Moravian World in North Carolina, 1763–1840.* Chapel Hill: University of North Carolina Press, 1998.

Seraile, William. "David Walker and Malcolm X: Brothers in Radical Thought." *Black World* (October 1973): 68–73.

Shawki, Ahmed. *Black Liberation and Socialism.* Chicago: Haymarket Books, 2006.

Shelby, Tommie. *We Who Are Dark: The Philosophical Foundations of Black Solidarity.* Cambridge: Belknap Press of Harvard University Press, 2005.

Shepperson, George. "Notes on American Negro Influences on the Emergence of African Nationalism." *Journal of African History* 1, no. 2 (1960): 299–312.

Simeon, Evelyn. *Black Feminist Voices in Politics.* Albany: State University of New York Press, 2006.

Sindquist, Eric J. *To Awake the Nations: Race in the Making of American Literature.* Cambridge: Belknap Press of Harvard University Press, 1993.

Sindquist, James L. *Dynamics of the Party System: Alignment and Realignment of Political Parties in the United States.* Washington, DC: Brookings Institution Press, 1983.

Singh, Nikhil Pal. *Black Is a Country: Race and the Unfinished Struggle for Democracy.* Cambridge: Harvard University Press, 2004.

Smith, John David. *Black Judas: A Story of Racial Self-Hatred in America—William Hannibal Thomas and the American Negro.* Chicago: Ivan R. Dee, 2000.

Smith, R. Drew. *New Day Begun: African American Churches and Civic Culture in Post–Civil Rights America.* Durham, NC: Duke University Press, 2003.

Smith, Robert C. *Racism in the Post–Civil Rights Era: Now You See It, Now You Don't.* Albany: State University of New York Press, 1996a.

———. *We Have No Leaders: African Americans in the Post–Civil Rights Era.* Albany: State University of New York Press, 1996b.

Smith, Theophus H. *Conjuring Culture: Biblical Formations of Black America.* New York: Oxford University Press, 1994.

Smythe, Hugh H., and James A. Moss. "The Negro Church and Black Power." *Journal of Human Relations* 17, no 1 (First Quarter 1969): 119–128.

Sniderman, Paul M., and Thomas Piazza. *Black Pride and Black Prejudice.* Princeton: Princeton University Press, 2002.

Strickland, William, and Cheryl Greene. *Malcolm X: Make It Plain.* New York: Viking, 1994.

Stuckey, Sterling. *The Ideological Origins of Black Nationalism.* Boston: Beacon, 1972.

———. *Going Through the Storm: The Influence of African American Art in History.* New York: Oxford University Press, 1994.

Sundiata, Ibrihim. *Brothers and Strangers: Black Zion, Black Slavery, 1914–1940.* Durham, NC: Duke University Press, 2003.

Tackwood, Louis, and the Citizens Research and Investigative Committee. *The Glass House Tapes: The Story of an Agent Provocateur and the New Police Intelligence Complex.* New York: Avon Books, 1973.

Tamir, Yael. "The Right to National Self-Determination." *Social Research* 58, no. 3 (Fall 1991): 565–590.

Tate, Greg. *Everything but the Burden: What White People Are Taking from Black Culture.* New York: Broadway, 2003.

Tate, Katherine. *From Protest to Politics: The New Black Voters in American Elections.* New York: Russell Sage, and Cambridge: Harvard University Press, 1993.

———. Principal Investigator, 1996 National Black Election Study. Conducted through the Ohio State University and the National Science Foundation, March 1997.

Taylor, Clarence. *Black Religious Intellectuals: The Fight for Equality from Jim Crow to the 21st Century.* New York: Routledge, 2002.

Taylor, James Lance. "Black Politics in Transition: From Protest to Politics to Political Neutrality?" Ph.D. diss., University of Southern California, 1999.

———. "The Reverend Benjamin Chavis Muhammad: From Wilmington to Washington, from Chavis to Muhammad." In Jo Renee Formicola and Hubert Morken, eds., *Religious Leaders and Faith-Based Politics* Lanham, MD: Rowman and Littlefield, 2001.

———. "The Black Church: Sacred Cosmos Meets Sacred Ground." In Barbara McGraw and Jo Renee Formicola, eds., *Taking Religious Pluralism Seriously: Spiritual Politics on America's Sacred Ground.* Waco, TX: Baylor University Press, 2005.

Taylor, Ula Yvette. *The Veiled Garvey: The Life and Times of Amy Jacques Garvey.* Chapel Hill: University of North Carolina Press, 2002.

Thernstrom, Stephan, and Abigail Thernstrom. *America in Black and White: One Nation, Indivisible.* New York: Touchstone Books, 1997.

Thurman, Howard. *Jesus and the Disinherited.* Boston: Beacon, 1976.

Tolbert, Emory J. "Federal Surveillance of Marcus Garvey and the UNIA." *Journal of Ethnic Studies* 14, no. 4 (Winter 1987): 25–43.

Ture, Kwame (né Stokely Carmichael), and Charles V. Hamilton. *Black Power: The Politics of Liberation.* New York: Vintage Books, 1992.

Turner, Richard Brent. *Islam in The African American Experience*. Bloomington: Indiana University Press, 1997.

Tyson, Timothy B. *Radio Free Dixie: Robert Williams and the Roots of Black Power*. Chapel Hill: University of North Carolina Press, 1999.

Van De Burg, William. *Modern Black Nationalism: From Marcus Garvey to Louis Farrakhan*. New York: New York University Press, 1997.

Vincent, Andrew. *Nationalism and Particularity*. New York: Cambridge University Press, 2002.

Vincent, Theodore G. *Black Power and the Garvey Movement*. Baltimore: Black Classic, [1970] 2006.

Wald, Kenneth D., and Allison Calhoun-Brown. *Religion and Politics in the United States*, 5th ed. Lanham, MD: Rowman and Littlefield, 2007.

Walker, David. *Appeal to the Coloured Citizens of the World, but in Particular, and Very Expressly to Those of the United States of America*. Introduction by James Turner. Baltimore: Black Classic, [1830] 1993.

Walker, David, and Henry Highland Garnet. *Walker's Appeal in Four Articles: Address to the Slaves of the United States of America*. New York: Cosimo, 2005.

Wallace, Michele. *Black Macho and the Myth of the Superwoman*. New York: Verso, 1990.

Walters, Ronald W. "African American Nationalism: A Unifying Ideology." *Black World* (October 1973): 9–27.

———. "Black Presidential Politics in 1980: Bargaining or Begging?" *Black Scholar* 11, no. 4 (March/April 1980): 22–31.

———. *Black Presidential Politics in America: A Strategic Approach*. Albany: State University of New York Press, 1988.

———. *White Nationalism, Black Interests: Conservative Public Policy and the Black Community*. Detroit: Wayne State University Press, 2003.

Walters, Ronald W., and Robert C. Smith. *African American Leadership*. Albany: State University of New York Press, 1999.

Walton, Hanes, Jr. *Invisible Politics: Black Political Behavior*. Albany: State University of New York Press, 1985.

———. *African American Power and Politics: The Political Context Variable*. New York: Columbia University Press, 1997.

Washington, James M., ed. *A Testament of Hope: The Essential Writings and Speeches of Martin Luther King, Jr.* New York: HarperCollins, 1986.

Watts, Jerry. *Amiri Baraka: The Politics and Art of a Black Intellectual*. New York: New York University Press, 2001.

West, Cornel. *Prophesy Deliverance! An Afro-American Revolutionary Christianity*. Louisville, KY: Westminster John Knox, 1982.

———. *The American Evasion of Philosophy: A Genealogy of Pragmatism*. Madison: University of Wisconsin Press, 1989.

———. *Race Matters*. Boston: Beacon, 1993.

White, John. *Black Leadership in America: From Booker T. Washington to Jesse Jackson*, 1st ed. New York: Longman Group, 1985.

White, Vibert L., Jr. *Inside the Nation of Islam: A Historical and Personal Testimony by a Black Muslim*. Gainesville: University Press of Florida, 2001.

Wildavsky, Aaron. *The Nursing Father: Moses as a Political Leader*. Tuscaloosa: University of Alabama Press, 1984.

Wilentz, Sean. *David Walker's* Appeal: To the Coloured Citizens of the World, but in Particular, and Very Expressly to Those of the United States of America. New York: Hill and Wang, 1965.

Williams, Chancellor. *The Destruction of Black Civilization: Great Issues of Race from 4500 B.C. to 2000 A.D.* Chicago: Third World, 1987.

Williams, Delores S. *Sisters in the Wilderness: The Challenge of Womanist God-Talk.* Maryknoll, NY: Orbis Books, 1993.

Williamson, Joel. *A Rage for Order: Black-White Relations in the American South Since Emancipation.* New York: Oxford University Press, 1986.

Wilmore, Gayraud S. *Black Religion and Black Radicalism: An Interpretation of the Religious History of African Americans*, 3rd ed. Maryknoll, NY: Orbis Books, 1998.

Wilson, William Julius. *More Than Just Race: Being Black and Poor in the Inner City.* New York: W. W. Norton, 2009.

Wolfenstein, Eugene V. *The Victims of Democracy: Malcolm X and the Black Revolution.* Los Angeles: University of California Press, 1981.

Wood, Joe, ed. *Malcolm X: In Our Own Image.* New York: St. Martin's, 1992.

Woodard, Komozi. *A Nation Within a Nation: Amiri Baraka (LeRoi Jones) and Black Power Politics.* Chapel Hill: University of North Carolina Press, 1999.

Woodford, Maize. "A Chronology of Louis Farrakhan's 'World Friendship Tour' to Africa and the Middle East: January–February 1996." *Black Scholar* 26, nos. 3–4 (Fall–Winter 1996): 35–40.

Wright, Richard. *Native Son.* New York: HarperCollins, [1940] 2005.

———. *Black Power: Three Books from Exile:* Black Power, The Color Curtain, *and* White Man, Listen! New York: HarperPerennial, [1954] 2008.

Young, Josiah Ulysses, III. *No Difference in the Fare: Dietrich Bonhoeffer and the Problem of Racism.* Grand Rapids, MI: William B. Eerdmans, 1998.

Young, Lowell. "Introduction" to *The 1928 and 1930 Comintern Resolutions on the Black National Question in the United States.* Washington, DC: Revolutionary Review Press, 1975. Available at www.marx2mao.com/other/CR75.html.

Zachery, Julia S. Jordan. *Black Women, Cultural Images, and Social Policy.* New York: Routledge, 2009.

Zuckerman, Phil, ed. *Du Bois on Religion.* Walnut Creek, CA: Altamira, 2000.

Index

About the Book

Black nationalism. Is it an outdated political strategy? Or, as James Lance Taylor argues in his rich, sweeping analysis, a logical response to the failure of post–civil rights politics?

Taylor offers a provocative assessment of the contemporary relevance and interpretation of black nationalism as both a school of thought and a mode of mobilization. Fundamental to his analysis is the assertion that black nationalism should be understood not simply as a separatist movement—the traditional conception—but instead as a commonsense psychological orientation with long roots in US political history. Providing entirely new lines of insight and analysis, his work ranges from the religious foundations of black political ideologies to the nationalist sentiments of today's hip-hop generation.

James Lance Taylor is associate professor of politics at the University of San Francisco.

DATE DUE

JUN 1 0 2013	

BRODART, CO.   Cat. No. 23-221